AF696334

LEVITICUS

Other Books by Gary North

Marx's Religion of Revolution (1968, 1989)
An Introduction to Christian Economics (1973)
Puritan Economic Experiments (1974, 1988)
Unconditional Surrender (1981, 1988, 1994)
Successful Investing in an Age of Envy (1981)
The Dominion Covenant: Genesis (1982, 1987)
Government by Emergency (1983)
Backward, Christian Soldiers? (1984)
75 Bible Questions Your Instructors Pray You Won't Ask (1984)
Coined Freedom (1984)
Moses and Pharaoh (1985)
The Sinai Strategy (1986)
Conspiracy: A Biblical View (1986)
Honest Money (1986)
Fighting Chance (1986), with Arthur Robinson
Unholy Spirits (1986, 1994)
Dominion and Common Grace (1987)
Inherit the Earth (1987)
Liberating Planet Earth (1987)
Healer of the Nations (1987)
The Pirate Economy (1987)
Is the World Running Down? (1988)
When Justice Is Aborted (1989)
Political Polytheism (1989)
The Hoax of Higher Criticism (1990)
Tools of Dominion: The Case Laws of Exodus (1990)
Victim's Rights (1990)
Westminster's Confession (1991)
Christian Reconstruction (1991), with Gary DeMar
The Coase Theorem (1992)
Politically Incorrect (1993)
Salvation Through Inflation (1993)
Rapture Fever (1993)
Tithing and the Church (1994)

Leviticus
An Economic Commentary

Gary North

Institute for Christian Economics
Tyler, Texas

copyright, Gary North, 1994

Library of Congress Catalouing-in-Publication Dats

North, Gary.
Leviticus : an economic commentaty / Gary North
p. cm.
Includes index
ISBN 0-930464-72-9
1. Bible. O.T. Leviticus – Criticism, interpretation, etc. 2. Economics in the Bible. 3. Economics–Religious aspects – Christianity. 4. Jewish law. 5. Law (THeology). 6. Dominion theology. I. Institute for Christian Economics. II. Title.
BS1255.2.N67 1994
222'.1306–dc20 94-37832
CIP

Institute for Christian Economics
P. O. Box 8000
Tyler, Texas 75711

This book is dedicated to

R. C. Sproul

who has never been one
to rest on his *a posteriori*.

TABLE OF CONTENTS

Part 4: Covenantal Acts

Part 5: Inheritance

NOTE TO THE READER

You have in your hands a drastically stripped-down version of a far longer book: *Boundaries and Dominion: The Economics of Leviticus*. As of mid-1994, the manuscript was over 2,300 double-spaced pages. The typesetting costs would have been either $11,500 or three days of work for me.[1] To have printed 2,000 stitched hardback copies would have cost about $20,000. Add to this a minimum of 150 hours of my indexing time, a price I preferred not to pay. The price tag for the book would have been at least $50. What reader is going to invest $50 plus, say, 80 hours to read an economic commentary on the Book of Leviticus? What book stores would carry such a book? Few.

The day after I completed the manuscript, after having invested some four years (2,000+ hours) of work, I decided not to publish it in the traditional format, at least not before I published this shorter commentary. I have therefore painfully removed well over half of the text of the 38 chapters of *Boundaries and Dominion*. I have not reprinted its 11 appendixes. Readers who are really serious about Leviticus can and should consult *Boundaries and Dominion*.

But how? Easily! Today, as a result of the ever-multiplying wonders of computer technology, *Boundaries and Dominion* is available on a pair of 3.5-inch plastic disks. Eventually, it will be

1. I typeset all the ICE books with a remarkable semi-automatic macro that Ruben Alvarado wrote for my WordPerfect 5.1 program.

put onto a CD-ROM disk with all of my other books and newsletters. With a lot of work, it will be possible to link all of this material through hyper-text electronic links. Technology is wonderful.

So, how much will this pair of plastic disks cost you? As of 1994, one U.S. dollar. Send a photocopy of this page plus one dollar to the ICE. Write to: Disks, ICE, P. O. Box 8000, Tyler, TX 75711. We will send you *Boundaries and Dominion*.

The conclusions that appear at the end of the chapters in *Leviticus: An Economic Commentary* appear exactly as they appear in *Boundaries and Dominion*. If the reader is not persuaded that my conclusions follow from the text in *Leviticus*, he should consult the full text of the chapter as it appears in *Boundaries and Dominion*.

How do you eat an elephant? One bite at a time. In *Boundaries and Dominion*, I include handy summaries at the end of each chapter: its main points listed in one-sentence bite-sized portions. Consult these summaries.

Another large benefit: when I want to add new material to *Boundaries and Dominion* as I continue to read and think about the theological issues, I can do so easily. I plan to do this with my other books, too: continuing revisions as a result of continuing thought. This is the most cost-effective way for a writer to keep his published works current. It is also cheap for readers to keep abreast of his thought. An electronic search engine makes it easy to check a writer's latest thoughts regarding problems he may have addressed initially many years earlier.

Eventually, I will publish *Boundaries and Dominion* as the fifth volume in *The Dominion Covenant* series: *The Dominion Covenant: Genesis* (1982), *Moses and Pharaoh: Dominion Religion vs. Power Religion* (1985), *The Sinai Strategy: Economics and the Ten Commandments* (1986), and *Tools of Dominion: The Case Laws of Exodus* (1990). But that will have to wait on finances. Until then, this shortened version, plus the electronically indexed computer disks, will be adequate for most readers.

FOREWORD

In the fall of 1991 I began a series of sermons on the first several chapters of Leviticus. My decision to preach on an obscure and difficult book (in the morning service, no less!) runs against the grain of contemporary pastoral theory. . . . Early on in my series, in fact, I spent most of one sermon explaining why a study of Leviticus is valuable for Christians. I am convinced that Leviticus is not only valuable but essential to a proper understanding of the New Testament. But anyone who preaches on Leviticus to an American congregation at the end of the twentieth century owes somebody an explanation.

Peter J. Leithart[1]

The Book of Leviticus, more than any other biblical book, has kept readers from getting to the biblical books that follow it. Leviticus calls to mind the old Negro spiritual: "So high, you can't get over it; so low, you can't get under it; so wide you can't get around it." But we should recall the conclusion: "So, hear the word of the Lord." The problem is, Leviticus has to be taken as a unit. It is a very difficult book. Therefore, lots of people quit reading. Some make it through the five types of sacrifice. Others actually get through the consanguinity laws. But not many people finish the book. Many are called, but few are chosen.

1. Peter J. Leithart, *The Kingdom and the Power: Rediscovering the Centrality of the Church* (Phillipsburg, New Jersey: P&R Publishing, 1993), p. ix.

Why an Economic Commentary?

You may be thinking: "Why should anyone write an economic commentary on the Bible?" My answer: "Because there is no neutrality." This is another way of saying that all knowledge is based on some view of morality, which in turn provides a concept of historical cause and effect. The Bible teaches that God brings positive sanctions in history to those who obey His law (Lev. 26:3-13). Our knowledge advances as we increase both our moral perception of His law and our covenantal obedience to His law. So does our success, long term.

The Bible speaks authoritatively in every area of life. This means that every area of life must be explored and then disciplined in terms of revelation in the Bible. We need specialized commentaries that apply biblical law to specific tasks: our occupations (jobs) and our callings (unique services) before God. As we study the Bible from the perspective of modern academic disciplines, we will increase our knowledge of the Bible and also these academic disciplines. We will gain insights that were unavailable to commentators in earlier eras. That is to say, *there is supposed to be intellectual and moral progress in history*. (Warning: any widely heralded "biblical world-and-life view" that has not been supported by detailed commentaries on applied theology is either a sham or is in the very early development stage: a slogan rather than a reality.)

The church's knowledge of the Bible is not static. Creeds – the universal grammar of Christianity – should be improved over time. So should detailed confessions: the dialects of competing denominations and traditions. So should Bible commentaries. This is why we should expect to see biblical exegesis improve as time moves forward. The church will become progressively more alert to the interaction of biblical texts with specialized knowledge in all fields of study, but especially those dealing with man and his institutions. As history advances, our knowledge regarding our personal and corporate responsibilities will increase. With greater knowledge comes greater responsibility (Luke 12:47-48).

This means that the church's knowledge of the Bible cannot remain static. Only by sealing off culture from biblical ethics could the church's knowledge of the Bible become static. This is an impossible goal, for the ethics of the world surrounding an ethically isolated, culturally defensive church eventually makes inroads into the thinking of its members. It is therefore an illegitimate goal. Nevertheless, a sealed-off church and a sealed-off external culture are the twin cultural goals of pietism.[2] *Pietists seek to place an exegetical boundary around the arena of Christian responsibility*. The smaller this boundary is, the pietist believes, the better.

What this commentary is designed to show is that the church as an institution and Christians as individuals have far more responsibility than Protestant pietistic churches have taught for over four centuries. More to the point, these responsibilities will grow over time. But so will God's grace in history. This is the meaning of progressive sanctification, both personally and corporately.

There are a lot of laws in Leviticus. As in the case of my previous commentaries, I ask two questions of each law that I consider: 1) How was this law applied in ancient Israel? 2) How should it be applied today, if at all? A few commentators ask the first question about a few laws in their selected biblical books. Hardly anyone since the year 1700 has bothered to ask the second, let alone answer it clearly.

This Book Called Leviticus

In a humorous book about psychologically afflicted people who cannot resist buying books, especially used books – I am one of these people – the author provides a brief history of

2. J. Gresham Machen, "Christianity and Culture," *Princeton Theological Review*, XI (1913), pp. 4-5.

what book reviewing might have been like before the invention of the printing press. Here is how he imagines an early book industry report on the sales of Leviticus:

> Highly publicized diet book published under the title *Leviticus*. Sales flop. "Too many rules, too depressing, not enough variety, not enough attention to cholesterol," cry the critics. "And for crying out loud, give it a decent title."[3]

This parody is not too far from the opinion of the average reader who has started but not finished Leviticus. He sees it as a kind of "healthful living" diet book. It isn't.

Then what is Leviticus all about? It is a book about limits: *boundaries*. There are a lot of boundaries laid down in the Book of Leviticus. Some of these limits are liturgical. Others are familial. Some are tribal. Some are dietary. There are also limits that have to do with the status of the Promised Land as God's holy place of residence. Finally, a lot of them establish economic limits. I have discussed these applications at considerable length, especially the economic ones. This is why *Boundaries and Dominion* is longer than *Tools of Dominion*.

I offered several pages of reasons to justify the length of *Tools of Dominion* in its Introduction. I have adopted what I call a "fat book" strategy. A movement that seeks to change the world cannot make its claims believable with only short books. The world is much too large and much too complex to be capable of being restructured in terms of large-print, thin paperback books – the only kind of books that most Christians read these days. The best that any movement can expect to achieve if it publishes only short books is to persuade readers that the world cannot be changed. This is why contemporary dispensationalism is limited to short paperback books. Dispensa-

3. Tom Raabe, *Biblioholism: The Literary Addiction* (Golden, Colorado: Fulcrum, 1991), p. 39.

tional authors do not expect their readers to be around long enough to wear out paperback books, let alone hardback books. Neither do their readers. That they will not wear out their paperback books is a safe assumption, but it has nothing to do with the timing of Christ's Second Coming. It has everything to do with the reading habits and attention spans of most dispensational readers. A movement based on such reading habits and short attention spans is not going to be dominant indefinitely.[4] It will be replaced.

Applying the Bible's Texts Today

I am targeting an audience that is not yet in existence. This nonexistent audience is the future leadership of Christianity. At some point, there will be an unprecedented Christian revival. The Holy Spirit will make His worldwide move.[5] Many will be called, and many will be chosen.[6] One of the results of this worldwide revival will be the revival of the ideal of **Christendom**: *the civilization (kingdom) of God in history*. Christianity will eventually possess sufficient judicial authority, by means of Christian candidates' popular election to political office and their election or appointment to judicial office, to begin to apply God's Bible-revealed laws to civil government. That victorious generation and the generations that will follow it will need a great deal more than a 200-page commentary. Those future generations will need many commentaries like this one: comprehensive within a specialized field of study. I want *Boundaries and Dominion* to become a model for those future commentaries in such fields as education, social theory, and political theory. Until such studies exist, and exist in profusion, Christianity will

4. Gary North, *Rapture Fever: Why Dispensationalism Is Paralyzed* (Tyler, Texas: Institute for Christian Economics, 1993).

5. Kenneth L. Gentry, Jr., *He Shall Have Dominion: A Postmillennial Eschatology* (Tyler, Texas: Institute for Christian Economics, 1992).

6. Few have been chosen so far over the history of mankind's time on earth; this does not prove that few will be chosen in every generation.

not be taken seriously as a religion with answers to the world's problems. Christianity will continue to be dismissed as simply one more experiment in mystical personal escape and well-organized fund-raising.

A short commentary that offers only conclusions is not going to be taken seriously as a book for restructuring economic theory and practice. Two hundred or so pages of brief conclusions can be dismissed as a list of unsubstantiated speculations. I wrote this large book in order to substantiate my opinions. A commentator should include reasons for his exclusions: why he rejected other possible interpretations and applications. He must show what he believes to be true, but he must also show clearly what he is *not* saying, so as to avoid confusion after he is dead and gone. This requires large commentaries. Those who are serious about understanding the Bible and applying it to this world require books as large as this one. Those who are not equally serious are not my targeted audience. Besides, such people will not read a book like this anyway.

This commentary, like *Boundaries and Dominion*, does things that normal Bible commentaries seldom do. First, it applies biblical texts to the modern world – specifically, to economics and law. Second, it cites the opinions of non-Christians who have reached either similar or rival conclusions regarding the judicial issues that Leviticus deals with. Third, it offers examples from history about how societies have enforced or failed to enforce these laws, and what the results were. Fourth, it offers the logic and evidence that led to the conclusions. The reader can evaluate for himself my reasoning process, case law by case law.

The Book of Leviticus is not understood by Christians, not obeyed by Jews, and not taken seriously by anyone else. For example, Christians do not understand the five Levitical sacrifices, Jews do not offer them, and everyone else thinks of them as archaic, barbaric, or both. Then there is the factor of the higher criticism of the Bible, which first began getting a hearing by a handful of New England scholars in the United States in the first half of the 1800's. But interest in higher criticism faded in New England during the Civil War.[7] Then, independent of the moribund New England critical tradition, it revived in the mid-1870's and spread rapidly among German-educated American theologians.[8] Today, most of the very few Bible scholars who pay attention to Leviticus adhere to the interpretive principles of higher criticism. They assume that the Old Testament is the product of several centuries of highly successful forgers.[9] I do not.

But the question remains: How should we interpret this difficult book? Are there principles of interpretation – a hermeneutic – that enable us to understand it correctly and apply it to our social problems?

Five Examples

There is more to the texts of Leviticus than meets the eye on first reading, or even second reading. The size of this book indicates just how much more. Let me offer the five Levitical sacrifices as examples. Here are a few one-sentence conclusions stemming from the five Levitical sacrifices.

Whole Burnt Offering. There are limits on man's sacrifice, yet a perfect sacrifice is required. There is no autonomy of possessions. God imposed an economic loss: a sacrifice. God's mercy requires sacrifice on the part of the recipient. There is a hierarchy of debt in life: I owe

---

7. Jerry Wayne Brown, *The Rise of Biblical Criticism in America, 1800-1870: The New England Scholars* (Middletown, Connecticut: Wesleyan University Press, 1969), p. 8.

8. Thomas H. Olbricht, "Rhetoric in the Higher Criticism Controversy," in Paul H. Boase (ed.), *The Rhetoric of Protest and Reform, 1878-1898* (Athens, Ohio: Ohio University Press, 1980), p. 285; Walter F. Petersen, "American Protestantism and the Higher Criticism," *Wisconsin Academy of Sciences, Arts and Letters*, L (1961), p. 321.

9. See Gary North, *Boundaries and Dominion: The Economics of Leviticus* (computer edition; Tyler, Texas: Institute for Christian Economics, 1994), Appendix J: "Conspiracy, Forgery, and Higher Criticism."

God; someone owes me; therefore, he owes God. These debt laws remain in force in the New Covenant. Economic theory must begin with the Bible if the State is to be restrained.

Meal Offering. Being a priest adds to a man's responsibility. Authority is hierarchical. Leaven was prohibited on the altar: a symbol of completion in history. Salt was mandatory on the altar: a symbol of permanent destruction.

Peace Offering. The peace offering was the premier boundary offering. Leaven was required. Eating fat was a blessing. Leaven, law, and dominion are linked. The peace offering was not the predecessor of the Lord's Supper. The peace offering was voluntary. The New Covenant is more rigorous than the Old Covenant. Offerings above the tithe are peace offerings.

Sin (Purification) Offering. This sacrifice points to corporate responsibility. Priestly sins are the greatest threat to a biblically covenanted society. Biblical authority is through the people. This sacrifice mandated a theocratic republic. Modern political theory dismisses adultery as politically irrelevant. The church is more important than the State.

Guilt (Reparation) Offering. The tithe is the equivalent of sharecropping. God favors private ownership. The free market pressures producers to count costs. God's economic sanctions are proportional to personal wealth.

I consider many other applications in chapters 1-7. Thirty-one chapters follow.[10] This is not the place to summarize all of them, but as in the case of the five Levitical sacrifices, there are many practical applications that follow from these laws. These applications are not intuitive. People who want to understand ancient Israel must be familiar with these laws and their applications. So do people who want to be faithful to God today.

10. In *Boundaries and Dominion*, there are also 11 appendixes.

A Question of Trust

Because I really do expect some parts of Leviticus to be applied to modern life some day, I could not adopt the standard commentator's implicit assurance to his readers: "Trust me." The stakes are too high. A serious reader of a serious subject should not be asked to take the author's word for anything. This rule applies to Bible commentaries. The author should be expected to spell out in detail both his reasoning and his evidence; conclusions alone are not sufficient. Only if a commentator expects nothing in a biblical text to be applicable in the real world should he expect his readers to trust him.

The problem is not simply that the reader has been asked previously to trust the commentators. He has also been told to distrust the Mosaic law. First, dispensational commentators have argued that the Mosaic law is in a kind of suspended animation until Jesus returns in person to establish His earthly millennial kingdom. This exclusion includes even the Ten Commandments.[11] Second, higher critics of the Bible for over two centuries have argued that the Pentateuch is unreliable judicially because Moses did not really write it; instead, lots of anonymous authors wrote it. Third, Protestant theologians for almost five centuries have denied that the Old Covenant provides moral and judicial standards for personal and corporate sanctification. Fourth, Roman Catholic and Eastern Orthodox theologians for a millennium and a half have substituted the legal categories of Greek philosophy, either Platonic (before the eleventh century) or Aristotelian (after the eleventh century in the West), for Old Testament law. Thus, Christians have been told for almost two millennia: "Don't trust the Mosaic law!" So, most Christians do not trust it. Most Christian leaders not only do not trust it; they hate it. They are outraged by it. The Mosaic law is an insult to their sense of justice. They are relieved to

11. S. Lewis Johnson, "The Paralysis of Legalism," *Bibliotheca Sacra*, Vol. 116 (April/June 1963).

learn that Jesus supposedly had nothing to do with it. So, it would be silly for me to say, "Trust me; the theologians are all wrong about the Mosaic law," and then offer a 200-page commentary as evidence. Who would believe me? (Not many of them will believe me even with this commentary plus *Boundaries and Dominion*.)

Short Commentaries and Judicial Relativism

There are at least three reasons why we have short Bible commentaries today: 1) modern Christian readers do not read very much, and certainly not long books filled with detailed arguments, let alone footnotes; 2) modern Christian scholars do not expect their conclusions to be applied to society, so they announce their conclusions rather than defend them in detail; and 3) nobody wants the responsibility of applying biblical texts to the contemporary world.

In a time of widespread apostasy and imminent judgment, silence is the preferred stance of God's people: "And Elijah came unto all the people, and said, How long halt ye between two opinions? if the LORD be God, follow him: but if Baal, then follow him. And the people answered him not a word" (I Ki. 18:21). Why such silence? Because God's covenant people see themselves as outnumbered: "Then said Elijah unto the people, I, even I only, remain a prophet of the LORD; but Baal's prophets are four hundred and fifty men" (I Ki. 18:22). God's people do not like the visible odds, not even prophets. Judicial silence seems safer, though not for prophets. The covenant-keeper asks himself: "Why bring a covenant lawsuit against a majority of voters? It is better to remain silent, even if this means booking passage on a summer cruise to Tarshish."

One result of this outlook is short Bible commentaries. I did not write this commentary to meet the needs of those readers who prefer short commentaries. If Christians are ever to become doers of the word and not hearers only, they need someone to tell them exactly what the word requires them to do, and why. Leviticus tells Christians what they must still be doing.

"That's just your opinion," some critic may respond. Yes, sir, it is indeed my opinion. The far more relevant question readers need to answer is this: *Is it also God's opinion?* If every controversial statement in this commentary is automatically dismissed as "just one person's opinion," then all controversial opinions in this life are judicially irrelevant. How about this controversial opinion? "Think not that I am come to destroy the law, or the prophets: I am not come to destroy, but to fulfil. For verily I say unto you, Till heaven and earth pass, one jot or one tittle shall in no wise pass from the law, till all be fulfilled" (Matt. 5:17-19). Or this one? "He that believeth on the Son hath everlasting life: and he that believeth not the Son shall not see life; but the wrath of God abideth on him" (John 3:36). But, as the Pharisees said in effect to Jesus: "That's just your opinion. Who are you to say?" This persuaded them that God's judgment was not coming. But in A.D. 70, judgment came.[12]

Homosexuality and Hermeneutics

There can be no doubt that the Bible is absolutely hostile to homosexuality. Jewish author Dennis Prager has minced no words: ". . . my religion not only prohibits homosexuality, it unequivocally, unambiguously, and in the strongest language at its disposal, condemns it."[13] He correctly points to the Bible's absolute break with any conception – literal or figurative – of God as a sexual being. "The first thing the Hebrew Bible did was to desexualize God: 'In the beginning God created the heavens and the earth' – by His will, not through any sexual

12. David Chilton, *The Great Tribulation* (Ft. Worth, Texas: Dominion Press, 1987); Chilton, *The Days of Vengeance: An Exposition of the Book of Revelation* (Ft. Worth, Texas: Dominion Press, 1987).

13. Dennis Prager, "Homosexuality, the Bible, and us – a Jewish Perspective," *The Public Interest* (Summer 1993), p. 61.

behavior. This was an utterly radical break with all religion, and it alone changed human history. The gods of virtually all civilizations engaged in sexual activity. The gods of Babylon, Canaan, Egypt, Greece, and Rome were, in fact, extremely promiscuous, both with other gods and with mortals."[14] In the case of Egypt, he says, homosexuality with a god was the mark of a man's lack of fear of that god. One Egyptian coffin text reads: "Atum has no power over me, for I copulate between his buttocks."[15] This attitude of defiance – the professed lack of any fear of God – is basic to all homosexuality.

Gomes vs. Moses

The *New York Times* is the most prestigious newspaper in the United States. It is sometimes referred to as America's newspaper of record. This identification is accurate. It is a thick, politically liberal,[16] rhetorically bland,[17] well-indexed newspaper. Its published index may be its primary strength, even more important than its widespread availability on microfilm. Historians become dependent on indexes, and the *Times* has always provided the best index of any American newspaper. Therefore, historians quote the *Times*. Therefore, it has become the nation's newspaper of record.

On the page opposite the editorial page – the famous Op-Ed page – appear essays by famous and not so famous people, usually liberals. On August 17, 1992, an article by Peter J.

---

14. *Ibid.*, p. 63.

15. David Greenberg, *The Construction of Homosexuality* (University of Chicago Press, 1988), cited in *ibid.*, p. 64.

16. Herman Dinsmore, *All the News That Fits* (New Rochelle, New York: Arlington House, 1969). Dinsmore was the editor of the international edition of the *Times*, 1951-60. His book's title comes from the words on the masthead of the *Times*: "All the News That's Fit to Print." The word "liberal" in the United States has meant "statist" since the late nineteenth century. It meant the opposite prior to the 1890's. The transition can be dated: the 1896 Presidential campaign of Presbyterian fundamentalist and populist William Jennings Bryan.

17. "The good, gray lady."

Gomes appeared: "Homophobic? Re-Read Your Bible." Gomes is an ordained Baptist minister and a professor of Christian morals at Harvard University, the most prestigious university in the Western hemisphere. He is also minister of the university's Memorial Church.

Within a year of the appearance of his Op-Ed essay, the publishing firm of William Morrow/Avon paid Rev. Gomes a $350,000 advance on royalties to write a book on conservative Christianity's distortions of the Bible. Nine of the largest publishers in the U.S. had bid in a competitive auction for the rights to acquire this as-yet unwritten book.[18] Consider the economics of such a payment. If the book sells for $20, and if Gomes received the standard author's contract of 10 percent of the book's retail price, the publisher will have to sell 175,000 copies – an unheard of number of copies for an unheard-of academic theologian – just to get back its advance on royalties, not counting forfeited interest income. To achieve this many sales – best-seller status – the publisher will probably have to spend far more on advertising than the author's advance, and even then the book is unlikely to sell 175,000 copies unless the media deliberately subsidize it by giving the author free television time and laudatory book reviews in prominent journals. Either Morrow/Avon was rewarding Rev. Gomes for his opinions or else, like the other publishing houses, the firm expected substantial support from those inside the media who share Rev. Gomes' view of homosexuality, the Bible, and conservative Christianity.

Professor Gomes refers in his essay to various anti-homosexual initiatives on state ballots in 1992. He says that such initiatives are defended by Christians, who appeal to the supposedly clear texts of the Bible that condemn homosexuality. But these Christians have moral blind spots, he implies. "They do not,

---

18. Don Feder, "Literary limits on the right side," *Washington Times* (Sept. 6, 1993), p. F4.

however, necessarily see quite as clear a meaning in biblical passages on economic conduct, the burdens of wealth and the sin of greed." An intelligent reader knows by now what is coming, and it does.

Gomes says that four biblical passages are customarily cited: Deuteronomy 23:17, I Kings 14:24, I Kings 22:46, and II Kings 23:7. He says that these passages refer to prostitution, not homosexuality. Quite true; this is why these passages are *not* customarily cited, contrary to Professor Gomes. The passages that *are* customarily cited are these: "Thou shalt not lie with mankind, as with womankind: it is abomination" (Lev. 18:22). "If a man also lie with mankind, as he lieth with a woman, both of them have committed an abomination: they shall surely be put to death; their blood shall be upon them" (Lev. 20:13).

Leviticus: Automatically Dismissed

These two passages present a problem for Professor Gomes. He refers to them in his next paragraph. But he has an answer: they are both in Leviticus, and you know what Ph.D.-holding Harvard theologians think about Leviticus! These two passages "are part of what biblical scholars call the Holiness Code. The code explicitly bans homosexual acts. But it also prohibits eating raw meat, planting two different kinds of seed in the same field and wearing garments with two different kinds of yarn. Tattoos, adultery and sexual intercourse during a woman's menstrual period are similarly outlawed." End of argument. He then goes to the New Testament. Such is the state of theological scholarship today in America's most honored university, founded in 1636 by Calvinist Puritans.

The holiness code is not taken seriously by Professor Gomes as a guide to modern behavior. I think it is safe to say that it is not taken seriously by Harvard University. What is very likely true is that it is not taken seriously by well over nine-tenths of the evangelical Christian community. This is the problem that this commentary seeks to overcome.

Chapters 18 to 20 of Leviticus present the most detailed list of laws in the book. This section forbids sexual contacts between close relatives (18:6-20). Are these laws annulled today? Leviticus prohibits child sacrifice: passing through Molech's fire (18:21). Has this law been annulled because Molech is no longer worshipped? Leviticus prohibits theft and lying (19:11), defrauding a neighbor (19:13), and rendering unjust judgment (19:15). Are these laws also annulled? It prohibits making a prostitute of one's daughter (19:29). It prohibits the mistreatment of resident aliens (19:33-34). It prohibits false weights and measures (19:35-36). It prohibits children from cursing parents (20:9). It prohibits bestiality (20:15-16). Are these, too, merely "holiness code" artifacts?

On what biblical basis can a Christian speak of legitimate civil sanctions against homosexuality if the Book of Leviticus is automatically dismissed? Natural law? But the ancient Greeks accepted the legitimacy of homosexuality with only a few restrictions,[19] yet they (the Hellenistic-era Stoics) invented natural

---

19. Socrates, in the *Symposium*, praised the love between adult males and adolescent boys as the highest form of love, i.e., the love extended not toward very young boys "but intelligent beings whose reason is beginning to be developed, much about the time at which their beards begin to grow." This true love is demonstrated by older men's faithfulness to their adolescent lovers as the young men mature into adulthood. Socrates insisted that "the love of young boys should be forbidden by law, because their future is uncertain; they may turn out good or bad, either in body or soul, and much noble enthusiasm may be thrown away upon them; . . ." That is, adult male lovers may waste their emotions on such youths; this should be prohibited by law. Nevertheless, there should be no laws against pederasty between older men and adolescents, "for surely nothing that is decorously and lawfully done can justly be censured." He praised the laws of Elis and Boetia that governed relations among post-pubescent males, where "the law is simply in favour of these connexions, and no one, whether young or old, has anything to say to their discredit; . . ." He disparaged the laws in Ionia "and other places, and generally in countries which are subject to the barbarians, [where] the custom is held to be dishonourable. . . ." Hostility to man-adolescent homosexuality is regarded in such barbarous societies – Israel was one such society – as threatening to political tyranny. Pederasty fosters attachments, Socrates said, that are inimical to tyranny. "And, therefore, the ill-repute into which these attachments have fallen is to be ascribed to the evil condition of those who make them to be ill-reputed; that is to say, to the self-seeking of the governors and

law theory. So, the Christian world has a problem. The average evangelical suspects – though he is really not quite sure – that the Bible authorizes civil sanctions against homosexuality. The sanction required by Leviticus is public execution. Already, the evangelical is growing nervous. But if he repudiates the civil sanction established by Leviticus, on what biblical basis can he assert that some other civil penalty should be imposed? *By what other standard?*[20] If he can lawfully play "pick and choose" from the texts of Leviticus, not to mention the whole of the Mosaic law, then why should he be upset with Professor Gomes? But he is.

Antinomianism: Liberal and Pietist

The evangelical knows there is something wrong with Gomes' arguments. He recognizes Gomes' rhetoric as theologically liberal: "To recover a liberating and inclusive Christ is to be freed from the semantic bondage that makes us curators of a dead culture rather than creatures of a new creation." He knows that he and his beliefs are Gomes' target: "Religious fundamentalism is dangerous because it cannot accept ambiguity and diversity and is therefore inherently intolerant." Such intolerance is "dangerous" and "anti-democratic." Anti-democratic? This begins to sound bad. The evangelical begins to shift in his chair nervously. His discomfort increases when he reads: "The same Bible that the advocates of slavery used to protect their wicked self-interests is the Bible that inspired slaves to

---

the cowardice of the governed; . . ." Plato, *Symposium*, sections 181-82, in *The Dialogues of Plato*, translated by Benjamin Jowett, 2 vols. (New York: Random House, [1892] 1937), I, pp. 309-10. Aristotle was somewhat less tolerant: he objected to homosexuality between older and younger men, though not between adult males generally so long as they were not related by kinship ties. These limited objections, Barker argues, depended on "contemporary Greek notions and practices. . . ." Ernest Barker (ed.), *The Politics of Aristotle* (New York: Oxford University Press, [1946] 1958), p. 46n. Comment on 1262a.

20. Greg L. Bahnsen, *No Other Standard: Theonomy and Its Critics* (Tyler, Texas: Institute for Christian Economics, 1991).

revolt and their liberators to action." This is a true statement regarding the history of slavery. How can a Bible-believing Christian explain what seems to be the Mosaic law's moral blind spot on the question of slavery (Lev. 25:44-46)? Yet he knows there is something wrong with this statement:

> And the same Bible that on the basis of an archaic social code of ancient Israel and a tortured reading of Paul is used to condemn all homosexuals and homosexual behavior includes metaphors of redemption, renewal, inclusion and love – principles that invite homosexuals to accept their freedom and responsibility in Christ and demands that their fellow Christians accept them as well.

What can the typical evangelical say in response? He, too, believes that Leviticus promoted "an archaic social code." It also established laws that seem to have been annulled, such as the laws of separating seeds in the same field or avoiding clothing made of both wool and linen. Is the social code of Leviticus inextricably tied to such laws of separation? If so, how can this social code be honored today? If not, how can we separate the still-valid social code from the annulled laws? Gomes puts it well: "The questions are, By what principle of interpretation do we proceed, and by what means do we reconcile 'what it meant then' to 'what it means now?'" Here he is on target. These are the two absolutely fundamental questions of biblical interpretation (hermeneutics) that I have sought to answer in this commentary and in my previous commentaries. These are the two questions that deliberately have been left unanswered by Protestant commentators on the Old Testament ever since the Reformation. It is time to begin answering both of them.

Let me remind my Bible-affirming readers that these two questions are not intellectual curiosities proposed by academic theologians. If Christians cannot find answers to both of them, then they had better learn to live with (and perhaps die with)

AIDS and the new killer strains of drug-resistant tuberculosis that AIDS-carriers also carry.

Michener vs. Moses

On March 30, 1993, best-selling American novelist James Michener followed up on Gomes' essay with a similar one: "God Is Not a Homophobe," which also appeared on the Op-Ed page. This article was published two months after newly inaugurated President Bill Clinton announced his intention, as Commander-in-Chief of the armed forces, to remove all restrictions against homosexuals serving in the military.[21] Michener, like Gomes, cited Leviticus 20:13. He, too, dismissed this law as no longer relevant. He invoked the same line of reasoning: changing times. The Hebrews "lived in a rude, brutal, almost uncivilized place where abominations abounded. To read the list of the things the Jews were enjoined to stop doing is to realize that God had to be unusually strict with such an undisciplined mob." Their society was in "deplorable disarray." He continued: "As order was installed, the extreme penalties advocated in Leviticus were relaxed in the civilized nations that followed. . . . Western society, reacting in its own way, has advanced far beyond the primitive days of Leviticus." Pity the primitive Israelites!

It was the residents of the city-states of Canaan who practiced such abominations, just as the Athenian Greeks would in Plato's era over a millennium later. It was not because Israel was "primitive" that God declared His law and its morally appropriate civil sanction; Israel was not primitive. Israel was God's agent to establish a new civilization in Canaan. God announced this law because He despises homosexuality and ho-

21. Clinton backed down when he met a firestorm of national outrage. He then recommended a policy of silence and secrecy: military recruiters must not ask about a volunteer's sexual preference, and the homosexual recruit must not indulge these preferences on a military base.

mosexuals. He hates the sin and the unrepentant sinner. He does not hate the sin and love the sinner. He hates the sin and hates the sinner. This is why there is a hell: God hates unrepentant sinners. God is indeed a homophobe. He hates the practice and those who practice it, which is why He destroyed Sodom. God warned Israel: practice such an abomination, and the land will vomit you out, just as it vomited out its former inhabitants (Lev. 18:24-29). But modern God-haters pay no attention to the written text of God's revelation, except to ridicule it or reinterpret it to confirm their immoral ways. God's revealed law is irrelevant in modern times, they insist. But they have an escalating problem: AIDS is not irrelevant.

Michener goes on: "So when zealots remind us that the Bible says male homosexuals should be put to death rather than be admitted to the armed forces, it is proper to reply: 'You are correct that Leviticus says that. But it also has an enormous number of edicts, which have had to be modified as we became civilized.'" Here we see cultural relativism applied to ethics: a form of social evolutionism. But is Michener's line of reasoning different in principle from the arguments of Christian antinomians who dismiss the laws of Leviticus with an almost equally intense hatred? Is his hermeneutic fundamentally different from theirs? More to the point, is his hermeneutic fundamentally different from yours?

Dispensationalism's Dilemma: Bahnsen or Gomes?

Dispensational scholars John and Paul Feinberg have issued a hermeneutical challenge: "The evangelical must decide which rules as stated in Scripture apply to our own day, and he must know how to decide which apply."[22] They are correct; the evangelical is morally bound to do this. He will resist doing this as long as he can, however. Evangelicals sense where such

22. John S. Feinberg and Paul D. Feinberg, *Ethics for a Brave New World* (Westchester, Illinois: Crossway, 1993), p. 33.

questions lead: toward self-conscious antinomianism, or self-conscious compromise with humanism, or self-conscious theonomy. The more socially relevant they want to be, the more the first choice is closed to them. They do not want to join dispensational author Dave Hunt in a spiritual and intellectual campground for Protestant pietists and mystics.[23]

As dispensationalists, the Feinbergs deny any mandatory judicial continuity between the Old Testament's civil law and today, since New Testament life "is not life under a theocracy."[24] This is the most important statement for social ethics that any anti-theonomic Christian can assert. But until it is proven exegetically, it remains only an assertion. I ask: Would any Christian assert the same anti-theocratic[25] thesis with respect to the family covenant under God and the church covenant under God? If not, then on what judicial basis is such a statement correct regarding the civil covenant under God? An appeal to Western history since, say, 1788 (U.S.) or 1789 (France), begs the judicial question. What must be proven is their assertion that the New Testament "assumes that believers will be under the political rule of non-believing rulers. . . ."[26] That the New Testament *makes provision* for such a calamity there can be no doubt; but what is the evidence that Jesus and the New Testament authors assumed that this is an eschatologically permanent condition throughout history? Where is it implied in Scripture that Nero's Rome – or Julian the Apostate's – is inevitable eschatologically and therefore binding judicially (or vice versa), whereas Constantine's Rome – or Theodosius' – is a departure from New Testament judicial standards? Why should Calvin's Geneva be dismissed as a covenantal deviation in civil government? Is Stalin's Russia to be

---

23. On Hunt's pietism, see Gary DeMar and Peter Leithart, *The Reduction of Christianity: A Biblical Response to Dave Hunt* (Ft. Worth, Texas: Dominion Press, 1988).

24. Feinbergs, *Ethics*, p. 36.

25. *Theocracy* is defined as "God rules."

26. *Ibid.*, p. 37.

accepted on principle as having conformed far closer than Calvin's Geneva to the covenantally binding New Testament standard with respect to its official source of civil law? These are not merely rhetorical questions. They deserve straightforward answers, but I do not think I will see such answers in the books and journals of Christian political pluralists.[27]

The Feinbergs argue: "It is inconsistent to say the Church is governed by the New Covenant when it comes to salvation, but by the Mosaic Code (and Covenant) when it comes to law."[28] This is quite true – as true as it is irrelevant to the theological point they are trying to make. I ask: What Christian theologian, theonomist or otherwise, has ever argued that the Old Covenant had a way of salvation different from the New Covenant? Paul cites Habakkuk 2:4: "The just shall live by faith" (Gal. 3:11b). Lutheran scholar and theologian Robert G. Hoerber has put the issue well: ". . . there is no evidence in the Old Testament or in Judaism that Jews believed that good works merit salvation. . . . The Jews observed the ceremonial laws of the Old Testament in order to belong to God's people, not to earn salvation."[29] The Feinbergs do not acknowledge this view of Old Covenant Judaism. They continue: "A discontinuity position avoids this problem" – a non-existent, utterly bizarre theological problem of their own invention – "by claiming that the Church is governed by the New Covenant as to salvation and by the Law of Christ as to law."[30]

Judicial Content

The three-fold ethical problem that a "discontinuity theologian" has to answer (and steadfastly refuses to) is this: 1) show

---

27. Gary North, *Political Polytheism: The Myth of Pluralism* (Tyler, Texas: Institute for Christian Economics, 1989).

28. Feinbergs, *Ethics*, p. 37.

29. Robert G. Hoerber, "Minors and Majors," *Christian News* (Oct. 4, 1993), p. 19.

30. Feinbergs, *Ethics*, p. 37.

exegetically why, where, and how "the Law of Christ" is different in content from the law of Moses; 2) discuss the biblically binding judicial content of this new law-order; 3) do this without abandoning the very concept of a unique biblical ethics, i.e., without surrendering civil law to covenant-breakers. The Christian world has been waiting patiently since 1830 for a dispensational theologian to write a book on New Testament social ethics – a book based exclusively on "the Law of Christ." This is a long time to wait. Frankly, I do not think the book is ever going to appear. There is a reason for this: *dispensationalism's hermeneutic implicitly denies the possibility of developing an explicitly biblical social theory prior to Jesus' earthly millennial kingdom.* Dispensational theologians implicitly recognize that without Mosaic law, there can be no explicitly biblical social ethic. But they view Mosaic law as defunct until Jesus returns to set up His earthly kingdom during the future millennium.

The Feinbergs understand their problem: identifying the biblical source of judicial content. Is it in the Old Testament, the New Testament, or both? They assert: "Where the content of the Mosaic Law, for example, and the Law of Christ overlap, appeal to the OT is proper."[31] This appeal to overlapping content is judicially and theologically irrelevant on dispensational terms. There is no reason, given their view of the law, to appeal to Moses if Christ has affirmed a particular law. The Mosaic law is superfluous, dispensationally speaking. It is either annulled or else merely supplemental and non-binding. I ask: Exactly where are these New Testament principles of civil law affirmed and developed in detail comparable to the Mosaic case laws? The Feinbergs know: nowhere.

They repeatedly try to escape this embarrassing problem. For example, they try to identify a New Testament passage that forthrightly affirms capital punishment. They appeal to Romans 13:1-7 (which does not mention capital punishment) and also

---

31. *Ibid.*, p. 39.

appeal back to Noah (Gen. 9:5-6).[32] But what, on their presupposition, has Moses got to do with either? Dispensational theologians House and Ice have rejected all appeals to the Mosaic law in search of capital crimes; they appeal solely to the Noachic Covenant. The nations are (they use the present tense) under the Noachic Covenant, not the Mosaic.[33] But the only crime mentioned to Noah was the shedding of human blood. Try to build a civilization on just one civil law. It cannot be done.

Hermeneutics and Abortion

In their desire to become socially relevant dispensationalists – a self-conscious break with American dispensationalism, 1925 to 1975 – the Feinbergs cannot let the matter rest here. They want to say something biblically relevant against abortion. They have therefore broken with Dallas Seminary and Talbot Seminary, both of which have remained deathly silent on this topic. They turn to a case law of Exodus to affirm their commitment to the anti-abortion movement. They have a problem: the only place in all the Bible that clearly sets forth a law against abortion is Exodus 21:22-25. So, rather than declare their hostility to abortion based on an unswerving commitment to a Mosaic law, they declare their willingness to accept a Mosaic law because of their hostility to abortion. "For example, nowhere in the NT does one find the specific regulations of Exod 21:22-25 that protect pregnant women and their unborn children. Those ordinances are part of the Mosaic Code but are not part of the NT Law of Christ. On the other hand, as we shall argue when discussing abortion, proper understanding of that passage shows it to be one of the strongest passages of Scripture defending the rights of pregnant women and unborn children. Given

32. *Idem.*

33. H. Wayne House and Thomas D. Ice, *Dominion Theology: Blessing or Curse?* (Portland, Oregon: Multnomah Press, 1988), p. 130.

that fact, it seems proper to appeal to it as indicating God's attitude toward any kind of harm to the unborn, including abortion. Since nothing in the NT suggests that God's attitude toward the unborn has changed, the OT passage is relevant for determining God's attitude toward the unborn and for demanding protection of them."[34]

They know not what they say. They began this section of their book by rejecting Bahnsen's statement of the theonomic position, namely, "that unless Scripture shows change with respect to OT law, NT era believers should assume it is still in force."[35] Bahnsen does indeed teach this; this is his theonomic hermeneutic: the presumption of judicial continuity. Yet they defend their appeal to a Mosaic case law on this same basis: "Since nothing in the NT suggests that God's attitude toward the unborn has changed, the OT passage is relevant for determining God's attitude toward the unborn and for demanding protection of them." That is to say, *they adopt Bahnsen's hermeneutic as the only one that can deliver them, in the name of the Bible, into the camp of the pro-life movement.*

In July, 1970, over two years before the U.S. Supreme Court handed down the *Roe v. Wade* decision, which legalized abortions on demand, Rushdoony challenged Christians to return to Exodus 21:22-25 as the judicial basis of their opposition to abortion. Anything less, he warned, has led in the past to compromises with paganism on this question. He wrote:

> Among the earliest battle-lines between the early Christians and the Roman Empire was the matter of *abortion*. Greek and Roman laws had at times forbidden abortion, even as they had also permitted it. The matter was regarded by these pagan cultures as a question of state policy: if the state wanted births, abortion was a crime against the state; if the state had no desire for the birth of certain children, abortion was either permissible or even required. Because the state represented

34. Feinbergs, *Ethics*, p. 39.

35. *Ibid.*, p. 34.

ultimate order, morality was what the state decreed. To abort or not to abort was thus a question of politics, not of God's law. Plato, for example, held that the state could compel abortion where unapproved parents proceeded without the approval of the state.

Very early, the Christians accused the heathen of murder, holding that abortion is a violation of God's law, "Thou shalt not murder." It was also a violation of the law of Exodus 21:22-25, which held that even accidental abortion was a criminal offense. If a woman with child were accidentally aborted, but no harm followed to either mother or child, even then a fine was mandatory. If the foetus died, then the death penalty was mandatory.

Because the law of the Roman Empire did not regard abortion as a crime, the early church imposed a life sentence as a substitute: penance for life, to indicate that it was a capital offence. The Council of Ancrya, 314 A.D., while making note of this earlier practice, limited the penance to ten years. There were often reversions to the earlier severity, and for a time, in later years, the administration of any draught for purposes of causing an abortion were punishable by death. The Greek and Roman influence tended to weaken the Christian stand by sophisticating the question, by trying to establish when the child or foetus could be considered a living soul. The Biblical law does not raise such questions: at any point, abortion requires the death penalty.[36]

The leaders of conservative Protestant churches in the United States remained prophetically silent when *Roe v. Wade* was handed down on January 22, 1973. Conservative theological seminaries also remained silent. (Most of them still remain silent.)[37] When, in the late 1970's, a few fundamentalist leaders very tentatively began to get involved in the pro-life movement, they sought a biblical justification for this move into

---

36. *Chalcedon Report* (July 1, 1970). Reprinted in Rousas John Rushdoony, *The Roots of Reconstruction* (Vallecito, California: Ross House, 1991), p. 710.

37. In an undated flyer, presumably released in the summer of 1994, over 21 years after *Roe v. Wade*, Westminster Seminary's California campus did make a mild anti-abortion statement. It announced that abortion "as practiced today is a scandal and a grievous sin." *A Testimony To Our Time*, p. 4. The question arises: What about abortion as practiced in some other day, in some other way? Why the qualifying language?

political activism.[38] This raised a major theological problem, one which none of them is ever forthright enough to admit in public. By acknowledging that Exodus 21:22-25 is the only biblical law prohibiting abortion, they would have had to admit that Rushdoony had already pre-empted this judicial position because of his view of the continuity of the Mosaic law. *They understood that to appeal to Exodus 21:22-25 is to invoke the theonomic hermeneutic*. They have generally feared to do this. The Feinbergs are an exception, and the results are intellectually embarrassing: "We are not theonomists, but. . . ."

Today, many Christian anti-abortionists blithely assert that "abortion is murder." We theonomists ask them a question: *What is the biblically mandatory civil penalty for murder?* They see a terrifying chasm opening up before them. They refuse to combine their pro-capital punishment stance with respect to murder – a biblically correct connection – with their rhetoric about abortion's being murder. If they did, they would have to call for legislation demanding the future execution of physicians, nurses, and former mothers who have been lawfully convicted of having participated in an abortion. So, they either remain silent or judicially schizophrenic on this issue. They do not take the Bible's mandated sanctions seriously. They do not even take their own rhetoric seriously. Not surprisingly, the politicians see no need to take them seriously. Abortion continues to be legal.

The self-contradictory hermeneutic of the two Feinbergs is a visible result of the fundamentalists' long-term judicial dilemma. They want judicial continuity when convenient (e.g., anti-abortion), while rejecting judicial continuity when inconvenient (e.g., anti-Bahnsen). They cannot have it both ways. Step by

38. Social activism in fundamentalist circles has always meant opposing something, especially the "big four" temptations of life: alcohol, tobacco, social dancing, and (in the twentieth century) the movies. Occasionally, fundamentalists band together to call on the State to do the repression: political activism. This is why the anti-abortion movement does contain some fundamentalists. But on the whole, except for publicly supporting anti-alcohol laws, fundamentalist churches have avoided politics.

step, fundamentalists and evangelicals are being forced to choose between Bahnsen's hermeneutic and Gomes' hermeneutic. They are willing to do almost anything, such as write theologically befuddled books, to defer this decision.

Conclusion

In 1993, Simon & Schuster, a major publishing firm, released an updated version of Ernest Sutherland Bates' 1936 expurgated version of the King James Bible. The text is 1,248 pages long. Approximately two and a quarter pages comprise Leviticus. It is the shortest book in Bates' text until he reaches the minor prophets.

Boundaries and Dominion is longer than Bates' text for the entire Bible. Why should anyone struggle through a book as large as this one, let alone *Boundaries and Dominion*? Neither book is easy reading. They were surely not easy writing. What possible benefits are likely to offset the large investment cost of forfeited time: mine (past) and the reader's (future)?

For most readers, the costs are far higher than the prospective gains. Such readers will not even begin. Few people are sufficiently interested in the Bible to read it cover to cover. Of those who are this interested in the Bible, few are interested in the Old Testament. Of those interested in the Old Testament, few (including pastors) are interested in theology.[39] Of those who are interested in theology, few are interested in biblical law. Of those who are interested in biblical law, few are interested in Mosaic laws that are no longer in force. In this commentary, I show why most of the economic laws in Leviticus are no longer in force. Professional advertisers would call mine a product-driven campaign, in contrast to a market-driven campaign. Product-driven campaigns almost always lose money.

---

39. David F. Wells, *No Place for Truth; or Whatever Happened to Evangelical Theology?* (Grand Rapids, Michigan: Eerdmans, 1993).

Why spend so much time, space, and money to prove my thesis in a period of history in which hardly any Christian assumes that any of these laws are still in force? Answer: because Christians need a principle of biblical interpretation to sift through the case laws of the Bible. Without such a sifting principle – a hermeneutic – Christians risk falling into one of two disastrous errors: legalism-Phariseeism or antinomianism. A careful study of no other biblical book is better calculated to force Christian interpreters to discover and then apply a principle of biblical judicial interpretation. Leviticus is the hard case, judicially speaking. Get through Leviticus intact, and the other 65 books of the Bible become comparatively smooth sailing.

There is another issue to consider. Some of the laws of Leviticus are still binding. Which ones? This is a difficult question to answer, but Christians need to find the correct answer. This, too, requires a hermeneutic: a consistent, coherent principle of biblical judicial interpretation that enables us to study other books of the Bible and their case laws. A serious Bible commentary on the Mosaic law should instruct the reader on how to do this work of interpretation. Very few commentaries on the Old Testament do this.

There is an old saying: "Give a man a fish, and you have fed him for a day. Teach him to fish, and you have fed him for a lifetime." This principle of feeding always holds true, at least until the fish give out. In biblical interpretation, the fish will never give out. Finite minds will never succeed in exhausting the potential of infinite projects. The work of interpretation and application must go on. It is therefore not sufficient for me to present a series of conclusions. The reader deserves to know how a commentator reached his or her conclusions.

Let me state the obvious: this is a Bible commentary. It is not a treatise on economics. It was written one chapter at a time; it should be read the same way. A commentary is supposed to throw light on specific verses or passages. Because the Book of Leviticus is structured in terms of a unifying concept –

boundaries – this commentary can be read cover to cover, but most readers will probably confine themselves to specific chapters.

This commentary is aimed at economists, who in my day are unlikely to pay any attention. It is aimed at pastors, who rarely read long books, especially on economics. Most of all, it is aimed at intellectually serious Bible students who have not yet decided what their callings in life should be.[40] I hope this book will give them a larger picture of what full-time Christian service really is. They, too, can devote their lives to discovering what God requires from His people, and then try to persuade Christians to believe a word of it – a seemingly foolish task, indeed, *if there were not covenantal sanctions in history*. But there are: positive and negative. The positive sanctions are wonderful, but seeking to avoid the negative sanctions is imperative.

I know, I know: that's just *my* opinion.

---

40. They may have occupations. These jobs are rarely their callings. I define a person's calling as follows: "The most important lifetime service that he can render to God in which he would be most difficult to replace."

PREFACE

And further, by these, my son, be admonished: of making many books there is no end; and much study is a weariness of the flesh (Eccl. 12:12).

When I began writing my economic commentary on the Bible in the spring of 1973,[1] I did not imagine that it would take me over two decades just to begin Numbers. When I escalated my time commitment to the project in the fall of 1977 to 10 hours per week, 50 weeks per year, I also did not imagine that it would take this long. I did not imagine that I would write such lengthy appendixes as *Dominion and Common Grace*, *Is the World Running Down?* and *Political Polytheism*. But most remarkable of all, I did not imagine that what now appears to be a 30-year task to complete the Pentateuch will, if completed, turn out to be the world's longest footnote to another man's thesis: Ray Sutton's 1985 discovery of the Bible's five-point covenant structure.[2] Not four, not six, not seven: five. I also want to make it unambiguously clear that I am talking only about a *covenant* model. I am not saying, nor have I ever implied, that this five-point model is the only model or structure in Scripture. The seven-day week model, the three-fold Trinitarian model, and other numeric and non-numeric models are

1. The first installment was published in the *Chalcedon Report* in May, 1973.

2. Ray R. Sutton, *That You May Prosper: Dominion By Covenant* (2nd ed.; Tyler, Texas: Institute for Christian Economics, 1992).

valid and have their place in a comprehensive, integrated biblical hermeneutic. What I am saying is this: the five-point covenant model is the model for covenants, i.e., judicial bonds that are lawfully established by a self-maledictory oath under God. There are four – and *only* four – such covenants: personal, ecclesiastical, family, and civil. The five points of the biblical covenant model are:

1. **T**ranscendence/immanence/sovereignty
2. **H**ierarchy/representation/authority
3. **E**thics/boundaries/dominion
4. **O**ath/judgment/sanctions
5. **S**uccession/inheritance/continuity

The acronym in English is THEOS, the Greek word for God.

I am not alone in my surprise. When I hired David Chilton to write a commentary on the Book of Revelation, neither of us imagined that his *Days of Vengeance* (1987) would also wind up as an eloquent footnote to Sutton's *That You May Prosper* (1987), but it did.[3] Prior to Sutton's discovery, Chilton had been totally bogged down for over a year, unable to complete the book's manuscript. After he heard Sutton present his discovery at a Wednesday evening Bible study that he and I attended, Chilton re-structured the manuscript, added some new material, and completed it within a few months. Seven years after its publication, critics have not yet attempted to refute Chilton's book, let alone Sutton's. (Note: a brief negative book review is not a refutation. Rather, it is a public notice of the need for one.)

While I have never been bogged down with any volume in this set of economic commentaries, there is no doubt that *Tools of Dominion* and especially *Boundaries and Dominion* would have looked very different if Sutton had not made his discovery, and

---

3. David Chilton, *The Days of Vengeance: An Exposition of the Book of Revelation* (Ft. Worth, Texas: Dominion Press, 1987).

I had not grasped its importance for my work. The five points of the biblical covenant are crucial for understanding Leviticus.

The Pentateuch's Five-Point Covenant Structure

As far as I am aware, what no one had seen – or at least no one had published – when I began this commentary project is this: the Pentateuch is structured in terms of the Bible's five-point covenant model. I recognized this structure of the five books of Moses only after I had finished reading (as I recall) the third draft of Sutton's manuscript. My discovery forced me to think through my strategy for the entire commentary. I wrote a Preface at the last minute for *The Sinai Strategy* (1986), introducing the five-point model. Then I wrote a General Introduction to the entire economic commentary series in the second edition of *The Dominion Covenant: Genesis* (1987).

So far, I have completed commentaries on only three of the five books of the Pentateuch. I can say with considerable confidence that the first three books of the Pentateuch conform to the model. I can see that the last two also conform, although I have not worked through them in detail yet. Honest critics who reject Sutton's thesis will eventually have to take into account my commentaries and the support volumes I have published. (Dishonest critics will, as usual, murmur in private to their students that nothing has been proven, that this model is all smoke and mirrors. But I am confident that they will not go into print on this, also as usual.)[4] Here is the five-point outline of the Pentateuch.

Genesis

Genesis clearly is a book dealing with God's transcendence. Transcendence is point one of the biblical covenant model. The

---

4. See Gary North, *Boundaries and Dominion: The Economics of Leviticus* (computer edition; Tyler, Texas: Institute for Christian Economics, 1994), Appendix K: "Critics of the Five-Point Covenant Model."

opening words of Genesis affirm God as Creator, testifying to God's absolute *transcendence*, the foundation of the Creator-creature distinction: "In the beginning God created the heaven and the earth" (Gen. 1:1). God established a *hierarchy* through His covenant: mankind over nature (Gen. 1:26-28), each man ruling over his wife (Gen. 2:18). He gave them a *law*: no eating from the prohibited tree (Gen. 2:17a). He promised to bring *judgment* against them if they disobeyed (Gen. 2:17b). They violated His law, but out of His grace, God promised them an *heir* (Gen. 3:15). Here are the five points of the biblical covenant model.

What is the story of Abraham all about? It is the story of a promise that was sealed by a covenant act and sign (circumcision). Tribal Israel's story is one of covenant-breaking, God's negative sanctions, and the renewal of Abraham's covenant. Genesis ends with Jacob's verbal blessings and cursings on his sons. Jacob transferred the inheritance, tribe by tribe. Then he died. But above all, Genesis is the story of God the absolutely sovereign Creator and providential Sustainer of history, the transcendent God who has revealed Himself to His people.

Exodus

Exodus is clearly the book of the covenant itself. "And he took the book of the covenant, and read in the audience of the people: and they said, All that the LORD hath said will we do, and be obedient" (Ex. 24:7). "And the king commanded all the people, saying, Keep the passover unto the LORD your God, as it is written in the book of this covenant" (II Ki. 23:21). God established His authority over the Israelites by delivering them out of Egypt. This is what Kline calls historical prologue: point two of the covenant.[5] But what did the historical prologue of

5. Meredith G. Kline, *Treaty of the Great King: The Covenant Structure of Deuteronomy: Studies and Commentary* (Grand Rapids, Michigan: Eerdmans, 1963), pp. 52-61: "Historical Prologue: Covenant History, 1:6-4:49."

an ancient covenant treaty affirm? Hierarchy: the power of the king over all of his rivals. Exodus was written to prove that God was above Pharaoh in history. Hierarchy, not historical prologue, is the heart of point two of the biblical covenant model.

God brought visible historical sanctions against Egypt. This was evidence of His covenantal authority in history. Deny God's predictable covenantal corporate sanctions in New Covenant history, and you necessarily deny the historical prologue aspect of the New Covenant. You reduce the rule of the God of the New Testament to the status of a supreme ruler of a priestly hierarchy. You deny His kingly authority.[6] This leaves Christians at the mercy of a divine State – the divine rule of politics. It leaves them without any possibility of constructing either a systematically biblical political theory or a broader Christian social theory.[7]

One important implication of point two is that God has established the hierarchical principle of *judicial representation*. The principle of representation began with God's call to Moses out of the burning bush, telling him to go before Pharaoh as His representative. God delivered the Israelites from Egypt,

---

6. This is what Kline does with his theory of the Mosaic Covenant as an intrusion – an ethical discontinuity – that pointed to God's final judgment, therefore (???) having no judicial relevance in the New Covenant era. Specifically, it is the covenant's negative sanctions, revealed in the imprecatory psalms, that led to Kline's neo-dispensational ethical theory. See Kline, *The Structure of Biblical Authority* (2nd ed.; Grand Rapids, Michigan: Eerdmans, 1972), pp. 161-67. Kline argues that God's sanctions in history today are covenantally unpredictable. Kline, "Comments on an Old-New Error," *Westminster Theological Journal*, XLI (Fall 1978), p. 184.

7. This is why pietists and dispensationalists of all kinds, including Kline's followers, are so hostile to theonomy. It is not just because of theonomy's theology of the covenant but also because of its necessary application: the construction a revelational social theory based on God's corporate sanctions in history and theonomy's demand that the State impose the Mosaic civil sanctions. This is an affront to the modern State and modern politics, and Protestant pietists have had an operational alliance with modern politics for over three centuries based on Roger Williams' theory of pluralism and the secular State. On this alliance, see Gary North, *Political Polytheism: The Myth of Pluralism* (Tyler, Texas: Institute for Christian Economics, 1989).

and then He met with Moses, their representative, at Sinai. In Exodus 18, Moses established a hierarchical civil appeals court system, whereupon God met with Moses as Israel's representative and delivered His covenant law. The Book of Exodus is a book about rival kings and rival kingdoms, God vs. Pharaoh.[8] Men must subordinate themselves either to God or Satan through their covenantal representatives.

The Book of Exodus is easily divided into five sections: 1) the intervention of God into history to deliver His people; 2) the establishment of Israel's judicial hierarchy; 3) the giving of the law; 4) the judgment of Israel after the golden calf incident; and 5) the building of the tabernacle, which they would carry with them into Canaan. Also, the Ten Commandments are divided into two sets of five points – one set is priestly; the other set is kingly – with each set paralleling Sutton's five-point model.[9] The first commandment, honoring God, is paralleled by the sixth commandment, the prohibition against murdering man. Man is made in God's image. The fifth commandment, honoring father and mother (household priests), has to do with succession: that we may live long lives in God's land. The tenth commandment, the prohibition against covetousness, also has to do with succession: not desiring to appropriate another person's inheritance.

Leviticus

Leviticus is the book that established Israel's ritual and moral boundaries. It is therefore about dominion, for boundaries in the Bible are always associated with dominion. The third point of the biblical covenant deals with boundaries. The third commandment deals with the prohibition of obscenity and false

---

8. Gary North, *Moses and Pharaoh: Dominion Religion vs. Power Religion* (Tyler, Texas: Institute for Christian Economics, 1985).

9. Gary North, *The Sinai Strategy: Economics and the Ten Commandments* (Tyler, Texas: Institute for Christian Economics, 1986), Preface.

oaths and incantations (magical power), thereby affirming a boundary surrounding God's name and implying dominion through ethics rather than magical invocation,[10] and the eighth commandment parallels the third, for it is law three in the second list of five.[11] "Thou shalt not steal" is a command regarding legal boundaries.[12] The eighth commandment indicates that the concept of boundaries is basic to economic ethics, the third point of the covenant.[13]

Gordon Wenham comments on Leviticus' place in the Old Testament's covenant-treaty structure: "(3) The centerpiece of every treaty was the stipulations section. In collections of law, such as Hammurabi's, the laws formed the central section. The same holds for the biblical collections of law. In the treaties a basic stipulation of total fidelity to the suzerain may be distinguished from the more detailed stipulations covering specific problems. In this terminology 'Be holy' could be described as the basic stipulation of Leviticus. The other laws explain what this means in different situations."[14] Leviticus is literally the center of the Pentateuch: two books precede it; two books follow it.

God *sets apart* His people and their worship. He makes them *holy* – set apart. He places ritual boundaries around them. "Leviticus centers around the concept of the holiness of God, and how an unholy people can acceptably approach Him and then remain in continued fellowship. The way to God is only through blood sacrifice, and the walk with God is only through

---

10. *Ibid.*, ch. 3.

11. I conclude that the Lutherans' structuring of the Ten Commandments is incorrect. The fifth commandment is "Honour thy father and thy mother: that thy says may be long upon the land which the LORD thy God giveth thee." This is a law of inheritance: point five.

12. *Ibid.*, ch. 8.

13. Gary North, *Inherit the Earth: Biblical Blueprints for Economics* (Ft. Worth, Texas: Dominion Press, 1987), ch. 3.

14. Gordon J. Wenham, *The Book of Leviticus* (Grand Rapids, Michigan: Eerdmans, 1979), p. 30.

obedience to His laws."[15] The issue is sanctification, and this requires boundaries: "The Israelites serve a holy God who requires them to be holy as well. To be holy means to be 'set apart' or 'separated.' They are to be separated *from* other nations *unto* God. In Leviticus the idea of holiness appears eighty-seven times, sometimes indicating ceremonial holiness (ritual requirements), and at other times moral holiness (purity of life)."[16] R. K. Harrison writes that the first 15 chapters deal with sacrificial principles and procedures relating to the removal of sin. "The last eleven chapters emphasize ethics, morality and holiness. The unifying theme of the book is the insistent emphasis upon God's holiness, coupled with the demand that the Israelites shall exemplify this spiritual attribute in their own lives."[17] Holiness means *separation* from the heathen.[18] It means *boundaries*.

Numbers

I have not begun my commentary on Numbers, so I will be brief. Numbers is the book of God's judgment against Israel in the wilderness. Judgment is point four of the biblical covenant model: God's response to oath-keeping or oath-breaking. God judged them when they refused to accept the testimony of Joshua and Caleb regarding the vulnerability of Canaan to invasion (Num. 14). They rebelled against Him, and He punished the nation by delaying their entry into Canaan until they were all dead, except Joshua and Caleb. "Numbers records the failure of Israel to believe in the promise of God and the result-

15. *The Open Bible: Expanded Edition* (Nashville, Tennessee: Thomas Nelson, 1983), p. 95.

16. *Ibid.*, p. 96.

17. R. K. Harrison, *Leviticus: An Introduction and Commentary* (Downers Grove, Illinois: Inter-Varsity Press, 1980), p. 14.

18. Jacob Milgrom, "The Biblical Diet Laws as an Ethical System: Food and Faith," *Interpretation*, XVII (1963), p. 295.

ing judgment of wandering in the wilderness for forty years."[19] Furthermore, "Israel as a nation is in its infancy at the outset of this book, only thirteen months after the exodus from Egypt. In Numbers, the book of divine discipline, it becomes necessary for the nation to go through the painful process of testing and maturation. God must teach His people the consequences of irresponsible decisions. The forty years of wilderness experience transforms them from a rabble of ex-slaves into a nation ready to take the Promised Land. Numbers begins with the old generation (1:1-10:10), moves through a tragic transitional period (10:11-25:18), and ends with the new generation (26-36) at the doorway to the land of Canaan."[20]

Deuteronomy

Deuteronomy is the book of Israel's inheritance, point five of the biblical covenant model. "It is addressed to the new generation destined to possess the land of promise – those who survived the forty years of wilderness wandering."[21] The children of the generation of the exodus renewed their covenant with God and inherited Canaan on this basis. Moses blessed the tribes (Deut. 33), a traditional sign of inheritance in the Old Testament (Gen. 27; 49). Moses died outside the land, but before he died, God allowed him to look from Mt. Nebo into the promised land (Deut. 34:4). He saw the inheritance. The book closes with the elevation of Joshua to leadership, the transitional event of inheritance or succession (Deut. 34:9-12).

Those who reject Sutton's thesis need to present an alternative model of the Pentateuch, one which fits it better, and one which also fits the Ten Commandments better, since they are also structured in terms of the five-point model: 1-5 and 6-10. Critics need to pay attention that old political aphorism: "You

---

19. *Open Bible*, p. 127.

20. *Ibid.*, p. 128.

21. *Ibid.*, p. 171.

can't beat something with nothing." It is not enough to mumble that "Sutton's book tries to prove too much," or "There are lots of different models in the Bible." There are indeed lots of proposed biblical models, among them the Trinity, the seven-day week, and the biblical covenant model.[22] But when we come to the question of *God's formal judicial relationships with men*, we always come to the covenant. It is a five-point structure. Accept no substitutes!

The Five Levitical Sacrifices

Most Christians have trouble remembering the required sacrifices of Leviticus. When people have difficulty remembering something, it is usually because they have no handle, no model by which to classify what appear to be unconnected facts.[23] This has been the problem with the five Levitical sacrifices.

Five sacrifices. "Oh, no," moan the critics. "Here it comes. He's going to argue that they conform to Sutton's five-point covenant model." Exactly!

---

22. In my Publisher's Preface to Sutton's 1987 first edition, I wrote: ". . . the author has discovered the key above all other keys to interpreting the Bible, from Genesis to Revelation. . ." (xi). But what about the doctrine of God? It is included in the first point of the biblical covenant model. The covenant model is more comprehensive than the doctrine of God. It includes hierarchy – God> man> creation – law, sanctions, and eschatology. What about the doctrine of the Trinity? What about creation? The Trinity and the doctrine of the Creator-creature distinction (creation) are guiding presuppositions of orthodoxy, as reflected in the creeds. Nevertheless, the Trinitarian doctrine of God, like the doctrine of creation, appears in very few texts in the Bible. The Trinity is a doctrine derived from a comparative handful of texts in the New Testament. In contrast, the covenant structure is found in hundreds of texts and even whole books of the Bible, including Leviticus. If you are trying to interpret a large number of texts in the Bible, the texts that are explicitly structured by the covenant vastly outnumber the texts explicitly structured by the Trinity or the creation. The traditional Christian exegetical exercise called "find the implied but camouflaged Trinity in the Old Tesatament," is far more difficult and far less persuasive than "find the implied or explicit covenant model in the Old Testament."

23. This is why military history is so demanding, and why so few academic historians work in the field.

1. The Whole Burnt Offering (Lev. 1)

This offering had to be completely consumed on God's altar, except for the hide, which belonged to the officiating priest (Lev. 7:8). None of the food portion could be retained, either by the priest or the donor. The animal had to be perfect: without blemish. The Hebrew word *olaw*, "burning," means "going up," as in smoke. It was a holocaust. Hartley calls this the main sacrifice under the Mosaic sacrificial system.[24] "As an atoning sacrifice the whole offering was offered not so much for specific sins but for the basic sinfulness of each person and the society as a whole."[25] The entire offering went to God, a symbol of the total sacrifice required by God of every man.[26]

There was a strict law for the priests: "And the fire upon the altar shall be burning in it; it shall not be put out: and the priest shall burn wood on it every morning, and lay the burnt offering in order upon it; and he shall burn thereon the fat of the peace offerings. The fire shall ever be burning upon the altar; it shall never go out" (Lev. 6:12-13). Why so strict? Because this fire testified to the nature of God. The Book of Hebrews calls God a consuming fire (Heb. 12:29). This is the God who must be feared above all other gods, all other fears. This is the God who consumes sacrifices on His altar.

This transcendent God is an immanent God. He meets men at His altar. If men fail to offer an appropriate sacrifice, God will consume them with fire. *This is the presence of God in fiery judgment*. "Whither shall I go from thy spirit? or whither shall I flee from thy presence? If I ascend up into heaven, thou art there: if I make my bed in hell, behold, thou art there" (Ps. 139:7-8). This is a sovereign God: transcendent and immanent.

---

24. John E. Hartley, *Leviticus*, vol. 4 of the *Word Bible Commentary* (Dallas, Texas: Word Books, 1992), p. 17.

25. *Ibid.*, p. 18.

26. *Ibid.*, p. 24.

2. The Grain Offering (Lev. 2)

The King James Version has this as a *meat offering*. This is incorrect. It was a grain offering. There are two keys to understanding this offering. First, it had to be of unleavened grain (Lev. 2:4, 11). Second, it was required when Aaron was anointed high priest (Lev. 6:20). Commentators presume that this sacrifice was required also at the anointings of subsequent high priests.

First, the requirement of unleavened grain points back to the exodus. The Passover mandated unleavened bread, too. This was God's memorial of His deliverance of His people out of bondage. They were to bring none of Egypt's leaven out of Egypt or into the Promised Land. This sacrifice pointed back to what Kline identifies as the historical prologue of the exodus: God's sovereign acts in history to deliver His people.[27] This means that this grain sacrifice is linked to point two of the covenant: historical prologue.

Second, the requirement that the sons of Aaron offer this sacrifice at the anointing of the high priest points to ecclesiastical hierarchy. The high priest was the most important officer in Israel. He met God in the holy of holies once a year. He was the primary mediator between God and Israel. This also points to point two: hierarchy/representation.

3. The Peace Offering (Lev. 3)

This offering was voluntary. It was not part of the system of atonement. Hartley translates it the offering of *well-being*. So does Milgrom.[28] There were three types of peace offerings: praise offering (Lev. 2:15), vow (votive) offering (Lev. 7:16), and freewill offering (Lev. 7:16). Hartley writes: "A primary aim of this sacrifice is for the offerer and his family or class, includ-

27. Kline, *Structure of Biblical Authority*, p. 53.

28. Jacob Milgrom, *Leviticus 1-16*, vol. 3 of *The Anchor Bible* (New York: Doubleday, 1991), p. 217.

ing invited guests, to eat the meat returned to them in a festive meal."[29]

The significant judicial fact of this offering was its openness. The offerer joined in a meal with God and his family. This indicates that the judicial barriers that always exist between God and sinful man were reduced. The participants' sins had already been dealt with judicially by another sacrifice. The sacrifice of well-being was a communion meal. The meal's participants were visibly identified as holy before God, set apart to praise Him and rejoice in His grace. The boundaries separating the offerer and this sacrifice were minimal compared to the boundaries around the other offerings. The offerer received back most of the offering. This points to point three of the covenant: ethics/boundaries.

4. The Purification Offering (Lev. 4-5:13)

This is called the *sin offering* in the King James Version. This was the sacrifice governing unintentional sins committed by the high priest, the civil ruler, the congregation as a whole, or individuals. "It describes behavior that violates the community's standards."[30] Without the purification offering, the whole community was endangered. These sacrifices were required to avoid God's negative sanctions in history. They were offered to escape "a religious judgment on deviant behavior."[31] Hartley cites a 1989 article by A. Marx, who argued that this sacrifice was required on three formal occasions: the investiture of Levites (Num. 8:1-36); the ordination of Aaron (Lev. 8:1-36; Ex. 29:1-37), and the consecration of the altar (Lev. 8:11, 15; Ex. 29:36-37). The Nazarite had to make a purification offering at the termination of his vow (Num. 6:13-20).[32]

---

29. Hartley, *Leviticus*, p. 38.

30. *Ibid.*, p. 55.

31. *Idem.*

32. *Ibid.*, p. 56.

David's concern is illustrative: "Who can understand his errors? cleanse thou me from secret faults. Keep back thy servant also from presumptuous sins; let them not have dominion over me: then shall I be upright, and I shall be innocent from the great transgression" (Ps. 19:12-13). In other words, if we are careful about the small sins, we will not fall into the great ones. If the high priest, the civil ruler, the whole congregation, and the individual all take such precautions, then God's wrath will not fall on Israel.

One sin that had to be dealt with by means of the purification offering was the false oath. "And if a soul sin, and hear the voice of swearing, and is a witness, whether he hath seen or known of it; if he do not utter it, then he shall bear his iniquity" (Lev. 5:1). Also, "if a soul swear, pronouncing with his lips to do evil, or to do good, whatsoever it be that a man shall pronounce with an oath, and it be hid from him; when he knoweth of it, then he shall be guilty in one of these" (Lev. 5:4). Here is the penalty: "And he shall bring his trespass offering unto the LORD for his sin which he hath sinned, a female from the flock, a lamb or a kid of the goats, for a sin offering; and the priest shall make an atonement for him concerning his sin" (Lev. 5:6). This is a trespass offering, or reparation offering (point five), but in the case of false oaths heard in secret or pronounced in ignorance, it is the judicial equivalent of the purification offering: "a sin offering." Point four of the biblical covenant model deals with oaths: the formal invoking of God's negative sanctions, the self-maledictory oath. Such an oath calls down upon the oath-taker God's curses, should the oath-taker break the law of the covenant.

The law of purification stated that the vessels in which the animal's remains were cooked had to be broken (clay pots) or thoroughly scourged (metal utensils) (Lev. 6:28). Again, the ritual concern is judgment. The concern, therefore, is sanctions: point four of the biblical covenant model.

5. The Reparation Offering (Lev. 5:14-6:7)[33]

This is called the *trespass offering* in the King James Version. This sacrifice was required in cases of theft: an illegal appropriation of another man's inheritance, a violation of the tenth commandment (point five). A man uses deception to gain ownership of another man's goods. Then he lies to the victim and the civil authorities. To restore the legal relationship after the criminal voluntarily confesses the crime and the two false oaths, he must pay the victim the value of the item stolen plus a 20 percent penalty (Lev. 6:5).[34] He also has to offer a ram as a trespass offering to make atonement (Lev. 6:6-7).

There should be no confusion about what is involved in the sacrifice. First, the lost inheritance is restored to the victim, plus an extra one-fifth. The judicial relationship between the victim and the criminal is thereby restored, making it possible to gain the advantages of social cooperation. Second, God is repaid because of the criminal's false oath in civil court. The criminal avoids being cut off by God: disinheritance. The goal is continuity: survival and covenantal prosperity in history. This is point five of the biblical covenant model: succession.

Conclusion

The requirement that God's people be holy is still in force. There will never be an escape from this requirement. It is eternal. To understand at least some of the implications of this ethical requirement – point three of the biblical covenant model – Christians need to understand the Book of Leviticus. They need to understand that it is a very practical book, many of whose laws still have valid applications in modern society. We ignore this book at our peril.

33. *Ibid.*, pp. 72-86.

34. Had he not confessed, and had he been convicted, the penalty was at least two-fold restitution.

The Pentateuch is itself revelatory of the five-point structure of God's covenant. My economic commentary on the Pentateuch is therefore a commentary on a covenant. I call it the dominion covenant, for it is the God-given, God-required assignment to mankind to exercise dominion and subdue the earth that defines mankind's task as the only creature who images God the Creator (Gen. 1:26-28).

INTRODUCTION

And the LORD spake unto Moses, saying, Speak unto all the congregation of the children of Israel, and say unto them, Ye shall be holy: for I the LORD your God am holy. Ye shall fear every man his mother, and his father, and keep my sabbaths: I am the LORD your God. Turn ye not unto idols, nor make to yourselves molten gods: I am the LORD your God (Lev. 19:1-4).

The book of Leviticus is the Bible's premier book of holiness. The biblical meaning of "holy" is "set apart by God." It is related conceptually to "sanctify," "sanction," and "saint." It refers to any person, place, or thing with a God-ordained covenantal boundary around it. Everything inside such a boundary is sacrosanct. For example, we correctly speak of marriage as holy. This does not mean that every marriage is Christian. It means that God has placed a special judicial boundary around every marriage.

The book of Leviticus is the Bible's premier book of boundaries. There is an element of separation in every boundary, just as there is in holiness: *separation by sanctions*.[1] The Book of Numbers is the Pentateuchal book of sanctions, but the civil sanctions of Leviticus have alienated Christians and have outraged pagans. That certain sexual acts are forbidden in Leviti-

---

1. See "Holiness," *A Dictionary of the Bible*, edited by James Hastings, 5 vols. (Edinburgh: T. & T. Clark, 1900), II, p. 395.

cus is generally acceptable to most Christians, but the specified civil sanctions are a terrible mental burden for them. They will do almost anything, including dismissing the continuing validity of almost all the laws in Leviticus, in order to escape any personal or corporate responsibility for pressuring civil rulers to enforce the Levitical civil sanctions. Christians are tempted to deny all of the Levitical separations rather than affirm any of the Levitical civil sanctions. In short, they would rather deny the ethical terms of the Levitical system of holiness than affirm the judicial terms of Levitical civil justice.

Escaping Cultural Relevance

Here is a major dilemma for the modern church. Christians confidently affirm that "the Bible has answers for all questions." But one question is this: What relevance should Christianity have in culture? Modern antinomian Christians emphatically deny the judicial foundation of Christianity's cultural relevance in history: biblical law and its biblically mandated sanctions. Most Christians prefer pietism to cultural relevance, since civil responsibility accompanies cultural relevance. They seek holiness through withdrawal from the prevailing general culture.

This withdrawal has forced them to create alternative cultures – ghetto cultures – since there can be no existence for man without culture of some kind. Mennonites have achieved a remarkable separation from the general culture, though not so radical as tourists in Amish country like to imagine, by abandoning such modern benefits as electricity in their homes and the automobile. But they travel in their buggies on paved highways, and they use electricity in their barns. They are always dependent on the peace-keeping forces of the nation. Pietistic Christians have longed for a similar separation, but without the degree of commitment shown by the Amish. They send their children into the public schools, and they still watch television. The result has been catastrophic: the widespread erosion of pietism's intellectual standards by the surrounding humanist culture, and the creation of woefully third-rate Christian alternatives. I offer as evidence the quality of American Christian radio broadcasting, especially contemporary Christian popular music. It is better than hard rock "music" and rap "music," no doubt, but compare it to classical music. Compare it to Bach, Mozart, or Beethoven. Compare hymns written after 1920 to those written by Isaac Watts and Charles Wesley.

The ultimate form of personal Christian withdrawal from culture is mysticism: placing an emotional and epistemological boundary between the Christian and the world around him. But there is a major theological risk with all forms of theistic mysticism. The proponents of theistic mysticism again and again in history have defined mysticism as union with God. But their primary motive is to escape social responsibility and social ethics. By defining mysticism as metaphysical rather than ethical, mystics have frequently come to a terribly heretical conclusion: their hoped-for union with God is defined as metaphysical rather than ethical. They seek a union of their *being* with God. Meister Eckhart, the heretic of the early fourteenth century, concluded in his 28th Sermon that "God and I are One."[2] This is a representative expression of the pantheism found in most forms of mysticism.[3] The mystic's quest for unity with God denies the Bible's ultimate definition of holiness: the separation of God from the creation.

The Creator/Creature Distinction

The ultimate boundary is the one separating God from man: the Creator/creature distinction. While man is made in God's

2. *Meister Eckhart: A Modern Translation*, trans. Raymond Bernard Blakney (New York: Harper Torchbooks, 1941), p. 232.

3. Richard Maurice Bucke provides extracts of dozens of passages to this effect in the teachings and writings of numerous religious thinkers, from Buddha to Plotinus to the homosexual, nineteenth-century American poet, Walt Whitman. R. M. Bucke, *Cosmic Consciousness: A Study in the Evolution of the Human Mind* (New York: Dutton, [1901] 1969), Part 4.

image (Gen. 1:26), he is not God, nor does he participate in God's being. Man is commanded to be holy, for God is holy (Lev. 11:44-45; 19:2), but man is also warned not to seek divinity for himself (Gen. 11:6; Deut. 29:29; Job 38-41). Man is commanded to seek ethical unity with the perfect humanity of Jesus Christ, God incarnate, but man cannot attain ontological unity with God. A permanent boundary is placed between God's being and man's being. *The unity between God and man is to be ethical, never ontological or metaphysical.*

The doctrine of the Creator/creature distinction has enormous consequences for social theory and practice. A contemporary Jewish political scientist has correctly observed: "The boundary between God and man is His supreme safeguard against social chaos. For what would men not do to one another if they were to claim ultimate authority?"[4] When covenant-breaking men have sought to erase this divine-human boundary, they have reaped their appropriate reward: social chaos followed by tyranny. Twentieth-century Europe is a monument to this reality: World War I, Communism, Nazism, Italian Fascism, World War II, the Cold War, and the break-up of Yugoslavia in civil war after 1990. In addition to the politics of despair have come existentialism, nihilism, the self-conscious meaninglessness of modern art, pornography, the drug culture, and the mindlessness of hard rock music. The laws of Leviticus were designed to remind men not to erase the divine-human boundary. The Mosaic law was designed to avoid social chaos and tyranny. It established laws – boundaries – governing the relationships between men in order to remind men of the ultimate boundary between God and man.

This leads me to a very important point: any attempt to define Christian "relationships" apart from God's Bible-revealed

---

4. Aaron Wildavsky, *The Nursing Father: Moses as a Political Leader* (University, Alabama: University of Alabama, 1984), p. 97. Professor Wildavsky died before I completed this manuscript. I had hoped to send him a copy of the book. He was one of the great conservative academic scholars in this century.

law is a form of rebellion. *Relationships apart from God's revealed law and its mandated judicial sanctions are inherently antinomian.* It is common for modern Protestant evangelicals to blather on and on about "relationships" while denying the continuing validity of biblical law. This way lies tyranny. And adultery.

The fundamental boundary in history is the one between God and His creation. A subordinate boundary in history is the one between the State and the individual. Modern conservatism ignores the first boundary and therefore finds itself incapable of maintaining the second, either theoretically or institutionally. Rushdoony has described the importance of biblical boundaries for biblical political theory: "Man's realm is on earth, and, since every man's heart is alien ground to every other man, he must rule by force in order to gain total dominion. God's realm and sovereignty is [*sic*] universal as Creator. He is on home ground everywhere in the universe, as much in command in the heart of every man as in heaven. For God, there is no alien ground, and hence no compulsion: He simply exercises His will over His own domain and creation in every crevice of the universe, and in every man's heart. Wherever the state moves beyond its God-appointed grounds, it is on alien ground, as indeed all men and institutions are wherever and whenever they transgress their appointed bounds."[5]

Israel's Boundaries

As we shall see in this commentary, most of Israel's economic boundaries were based on geography (land laws), tribal membership (seed laws), and ritual requirements (laws of sacrifice). These economic rules constituted a covenantal unity. As Americans say, they were a "package deal." These rules were temporary boundaries designed to shape the nation of Israel in very special ways. These judicial boundaries maintained the land

5. R. J. Rushdoony, *Politics of Guilt and Pity* (Fairfax, Virginia: Thoburn Press, [1970] 1978), p. 42.

and the people as a special province of God. The land of Israel became like the garden of Eden: a temporary residence uniquely under God's revealed law and uniquely under His historical sanctions. The land of Israel, like the garden of Eden, was to serve as a training area for covenant-keeping men. It was also to serve as an example for covenant-breaking men (Deut. 4:4-8). It was to serve both as God's boot camp and as His general headquarters for worldwide evangelism and cultural conquest.

The laws of Leviticus were designed to keep the leaven of evil outside of the land of Israel, but they were also designed to push the leaven of righteousness into the world around Israel. Levitical law was both defensive and offensive. One problem with virtually all commentaries on Leviticus is that they emphasize the defensive aspects of the Levitical laws: separation and exclusion. In this book, I do my best to point out the inclusive aspects of some of these laws. There were laws of inclusion, at least to the extent of placing the gentile world under the Ten Commandments and therefore inside the zone of predictable external blessings: positive sanctions in history. This was Jonah's message to Nineveh: God's covenant lawsuit. Had all of God's revealed laws been solely exclusionary, Jonah would not have been sent by God on his missionary journey. As I argue in this commentary, some of the Mosaic laws were cross-boundary laws that governed other nations, and are still valid today.

The Book of Priestly Holiness

Behind Jonah's prophetic ministry was a nation of priests. As Jacob Milgrom points out in the introduction to the first volume of his extraordinarily learned, extraordinarily large, and extraordinarily unreadable commentary on Leviticus, Leviticus is not about the tribe of Levi. It is about the priesthood. The Book of Numbers rather than Leviticus deals in detail with the laws governing the Levites. The reason why the book is called Leviticus is because in Hellenic times, when the Greek version of the Hebrew Old Testament appeared (the Septuagint), the term "Levites" meant priests.[6]

Milgrom writes: "Theology is what Leviticus is all about. It pervades every chapter and almost every verse. It is not expressed in pronouncements but embedded in rituals."[7] But what is the focus of the book's theology? *Holiness*. Leviticus is pre-eminently the Old Covenant's book of holiness. To be holy is to be *set apart* by God: judicially, ethically, culturally, and in the case of the Old Covenant people of God, geographically. God establishes boundaries. Leviticus is the Pentateuch's book of boundaries.

Leviticus also is the book of life. "Because impurity and holiness are antonyms," Milgrom writes, "the identification of impurity with death must mean that holiness stands for life."[8] The book's rituals and ethical injunctions point to *separation from evil*, which is the sole basis of life in God's world. Adam's wilful violation of a verbally identified boundary in the garden brought universal death into history. Man's continuing imperfections also point to death. But the perfect honoring God's boundaries therefore brings life. Thus, the ritual and judicial rigors of Leviticus point to man's need of redemption by means of a perfect substitute whose death brings life to the boundary violator. *God's law kills those who are already under the sentence of death; on the other hand, it provides a better life for those who are alive*. The pre-eminent example of this truth is Jesus Christ, who contrasted His own ministry with that of a thief: "The thief cometh not, but for to steal, and to kill, and to destroy: I am come that they might have life, and that they might have it more abundantly" (John 10:10).

---

6. Jacob Milgrom, *Leviticus 1-16*, vol. 3 of *The Anchor Bible* (New York: Doubleday, 1991), p. 1.

7. *Ibid.*, p. 42.

8. *Ibid.*, p. 46.

Israel's boundaries were established in terms of God's unique presence among His people: "And I will set my tabernacle among you: and my soul shall not abhor you. And I will walk among you, and will be your God, and ye shall be my people" (Lev. 26:11-12). The Book of Leviticus rests on the assumption that God's unique covenantal presence among His set-apart people had geographical implications. *The Mosaic Covenant was a geographical covenant.* God's covenant with Abram (renamed Abraham: "father of nations") involved *land* because it involved *seed*: "In the same day the LORD made a covenant with Abram, saying, Unto thy seed have I given this land, from the river of Egypt unto the great river, the river Euphrates" (Gen. 15:18).

God's goal in all of His laws is to place men under certain moral and judicial boundaries. Men are to acknowledge God's absolute sovereignty over them by accepting the authority of His covenant's hierarchy. The stipulations enforced by His hierarchical institutions serve as the legal boundaries of covenant-keeping man's existence. Men are to learn to live within these boundaries. *There is both inclusion and exclusion in establishing and enforcing all boundaries.* God in effect puts a "No Trespassing" sign around something, and man is required to honor the stipulations of that sign. If he refuses, God threatens to impose negative sanctions on him in history and perhaps even eternity. God is not mocked at zero cost.

The Book of the Kingdom

Leviticus is also the book of the kingdom. God delivered His people from bondage in Egypt, a false kingdom. In doing so, He gave them an opportunity to gain land for a new kingdom. The next generation did inherit this land. The generation of the exodus did not. They died in the wilderness. Because of their rebellion and lack of faith, their boundary was the wilderness. They could not return to Egypt, nor could they enter the Promised Land. The kingdom grant of land could be claimed only by their children, and only after their covenant renewal at Gilgal (Josh. 5).

Leviticus presents the rules governing this kingdom grant from God. This land grant preceded the giving of these rules. *Grace precedes law in God's dealings with His subordinates*. We are in debt to God even before He speaks to us. The land grant was based on the original promise given to Abraham. That promise came prior to the giving of the Mosaic law.[9] This is why James Jordan says that the laws of Leviticus are more than legislation; the focus of the laws is not simply obedience to God, but rather on *maintaining the grant*.[10] The basis of maintaining the grant was *ethics*, not the sacrifices. Man cannot maintain the kingdom in sin.[11] The fundamental issue was sin, not sacrifice; ethics, not ritual. God told them this repeatedly through His prophets:

> For I spake not unto your fathers, nor commanded them in the day that I brought them out of the land of Egypt, concerning burnt offerings or sacrifices: But this thing commanded I them, saying, Obey my voice, and I will be your God, and ye shall be my people: and walk ye in all the ways that I have commanded you, that it may be well unto you. But they hearkened not, nor inclined their ear, but walked in the counsels and in the imagination of their evil heart, and went backward, and not forward (Jer. 7:22-24).

> To what purpose is the multitude of your sacrifices unto me? saith the LORD: I am full of the burnt offerings of rams, and the fat of fed beasts; and I delight not in the blood of bullocks, or of lambs, or of he goats. When ye come to appear before me, who hath required this at your hand, to tread my courts? Bring no more vain oblations; incense is an abomination unto me; the new moons and sabbaths, the calling of assemblies, I cannot away with; it is iniquity, even the solemn meeting. Your new moons and your appointed feasts my soul hateth: they are a

---

9. James B. Jordan, *Covenant Sequence in Leviticus and Deuteronomy* (Tyler, Texas: Institute for Christian Economics, 1989), p. 8.

10. *Ibid.*, p. 9.

11. *Ibid.*, p. 11.

trouble unto me; I am weary to bear them. And when ye spread forth your hands, I will hide mine eyes from you: yea, when ye make many prayers, I will not hear: your hands are full of blood. Wash you, make you clean; put away the evil of your doings from before mine eyes; cease to do evil; Learn to do well; seek judgment, relieve the oppressed, judge the fatherless, plead for the widow (Isa. 1:11-17).

The Book of Property

The Book of Leviticus is also the book of property in the Pentateuch. The grant of the kingdom was in the form of a land grant. The land itself was the visible manifestation of the historical reality of the kingdom. So was the promised economic prosperity. *Leviticus is the book that presents the ethical foundations of prosperity* (Lev. 26:3-10). It also presents the legal foundations of *judicial peace with God*, the only long-term basis of prosperity. God begins with a gift to His people, and then He sets forth the ritual and legal foundations of maintaining this gift. He promises to uphold this grant if they obey Him. God's promise cannot be separated from their requirement of obedience. Jordan writes:

> God's covenant Word is always first and foremost promise, and then command based on promise. Point three has to do with God's grant of the Kingdom, His gift and promise, and then our duties consequent thereto. God's Word is always both promise and command, and in Reformed theology, promise comes first. (In Lutheran law/gospel theology, law comes first to drive us to Christ; but in Reformed theology, grace comes first to put us in the Kingdom, and then the law is given as guidance for our Kingdom duties.)[12]

Respect for the property of others clearly connects largely with the third zone of the five-fold covenant structure, because the third area is that of the distributed grant. We have to respect what God has granted to others. Also, disobedience to any part of God's law is regarded as a

12. *Ibid.*, p. 8.

trespass or more literally a "debt," as we see it in the Lord's Prayer. Thus, any lawbreaking is a form of theft, creating indebtedness, which must be covered by a Trespass or Compensation Sacrifice. Theft has to do with boundaries, which is why it is equivalent to trespass. Leviticus is the book of boundaries, of who is allowed to go where, and of how to become cleansed once you have trespassed.[13]

The Book of Leviticus is book three of the Pentateuch. It is the book of property. The eighth commandment, "Thou shalt not steal," is the third law of the so-called second table of the law, i.e., the third law in the second group of five covenantally structured laws. The third commandment, "Thou shalt not take the name of the LORD thy God in vain," establishes a boundary around God's name. God's name is His property, and He in effect licenses the use of His name only for specific uses. The parallels should be obvious. Point three of the biblical covenant model establishes boundaries. Leviticus is the book of property because it is the book of boundaries.

A Holy Walk Before the Lord

We now come to a topic that is never discussed by the commentators. I have never seen any commentator devote as much as one page to it, yet it is more important for understanding the unique nature of the economic life of ancient Israel than any other topic. I am not trying to exaggerate; I really mean this. Here is the question that demands an answer: **How did they have time to earn a living?** The mandatory sacrifices ate up time as well as crops. Whatever answers to this question that Israel came up with were fundamental to the life of the nation for almost 14 centuries, yet we honestly do not know how Israel answered it. As far as I know, nobody has discussed in detail the economics of the festival journeys. The rabbis who compiled the Mishna and Talmud in the four centuries after the fall of

---

13. *Ibid.*, pp. 12-13.

Jerusalem forgot their ancestors' answers, and the Christians have never thought to ask the question.

In Exodus 23, we read: "Three times thou shalt keep a feast unto me in the year. Thou shalt keep the feast of unleavened bread: (thou shalt eat unleavened bread seven days, as I commanded thee, in the time appointed of the month Abib; for in it thou camest out from Egypt: and none shall appear before me empty:) And the feast of harvest, the firstfruits of thy labours, which thou hast sown in the field: and the feast of ingathering, which is in the end of the year, when thou hast gathered in thy labours out of the field. Three times in the year all thy males shall appear before the Lord GOD" (Ex. 23:14-17). Passover, Pentecost, and Tabernacles: three feasts a year were required of every adult circumcised male if he was inside the land's boundaries. Every adult male had to journey to a central location and participate in a festival (ritual feast) three times a year. A parallel passage promised that during their absence from their homes, no invaders would disturb them: "Thrice in the year shall all your men children [males] appear before the Lord GOD, the God of Israel. For I will cast out the nations before thee, and enlarge thy borders: neither shall any man desire thy land, when thou shalt go up to appear before the LORD thy God thrice in the year" (Ex. 34:23-24). God promised to bless the land when they honored these requirements. The nation's circumcised adults were on the march three times each year.

Centralization

This geographically centralized system of ritual sacrifice was what motivated Jeroboam to create a pair of false worship centers at Bethel and Dan in his newly created northern kingdom (I Ki. 12:25-29). He did not want the people of Israel journeying to Judah to worship, for fear that this would divide their loyalty politically (v. 27). He set up a rival altar and a rival Passover celebration at Bethel (v. 32).

We need to understand just how central, and how centralizing, these mandatory sacrifices were. We need to remember this: *there was only one lawful altar in Israel.* Unless there was a way for local religious and civil leaders in a community to represent the entire community at these feasts, which the Bible's texts do not indicate there was, this meant that the entire adult male population – or at least those eligible for numbering for military service – came to Jerusalem a minimum of three times a year, not including their participation in any of the five special sacrifices discussed in Leviticus 1-7.

Most of them had to walk. A few might have had horses, but not many. Horses cost too much feed and do too little work for small farms to support. There are few references to horses in Israel. They are always spoken of in a military context: the possession of foreign armies. Perhaps some people had donkeys, but riding two hundred miles on a donkey is no picnic. Think about it. Despite rain, mud, dust, and bad weather, three times each year every adult male had to walk or ride a donkey to the tabernacle-temple. In David's day, this meant Jerusalem. Some sections of the nation were located over a hundred miles from Jerusalem "as the crow flies." Winding highways would have added to this estimate. At an average speed of three miles per hour, this would have required up to four or five eight-hour days of walking, each way, plus whatever time was spent in Jerusalem, three times a year. Not every Israelite had to spend this much time on the road, but members of some tribes did.

The Walk: Physical and Spiritual

When God spoke of a holy walk before Him, He really meant it. It was a judicial walk, but it was also a literal walk. *The difficulty of the physical walk was to reflect the difficulty of the spiritual walk.* Life in Israel was to be a kind of boot camp experience – a temporary period of preliminary training for worldwide dominion. In Eden, Adam had been told to *keep away* from a tree:

a physically easy task. In Israel, they were told to *journey to* a central location: a physically difficult task. If they walked faithfully, He promised, the land of Israel would make them rich.

> If ye walk in my statutes, and keep my commandments, and do them; Then I will give you rain in due season, and the land shall yield her increase, and the trees of the field shall yield their fruit. And your threshing shall reach unto the vintage, and the vintage shall reach unto the sowing time: and ye shall eat your bread to the full, and dwell in your land safely. And I will give peace in the land, and ye shall lie down, and none shall make you afraid: and I will rid evil beasts out of the land, neither shall the sword go through your land (Lev. 26:3-6; see Deut. 28:8-13).

God promised to intervene in the operations of nature in order to make good on His promise. The heavens would deliver rain in due season. But to obtain these blessings, Israelites had to sacrifice – not just offer sacrifices, but sacrifice a large portion of their lives to the boredom of walking. This nation, more than any other non-nomadic nation in history, was to be on the move. Like a literal army, they were to march a minimum of three times a year. Marching was to keep them in good shape, both physical and spiritual, as God's holy army.

At Passover, entire families journeyed to the tabernacle city and later to Jerusalem. Families were required to celebrate the Passover (Ex. 12). They could not celebrate the feast at home, for they were required to slay the Passover lamb on the night Passover began (Ex. 12:6). This had to be done at the appointed national place of worship after they entered the Promised Land (Deut. 16:2-6). There were about 625,000 adult males when they entered the Promised Land (Num. 26:51, 62). This means that about two million people would have arrived in one city at the same time, to spend a week.[14] Imagine four million

---

14. The average Israelite family had approximately two children at this stage in the nation's history. The number of adult males had been almost the same when they

people arriving. Or perhaps 10 million if the population grew. This did not happen, for God withheld the blessing of population growth, but until the sacrificial system changed, this long walk was required. Then they all walked home.

Mothers today complain about the trouble involved in planning a day's drive or a plane ride plus a week's visit in a motel. Think about organizing a family for a week's walk, a week's stay, probably camping out in a tent. Bear in mind, there was no running water, no indoor plumbing, no toilet paper, no disposable diapers, and no fast food restaurants. This was no picnic. Then, after a week of jammed masses of humanity and assembly-line sacrifices, they walked home. Less than two months after arriving home, all the men walked back to celebrate another feast, which we call Pentecost: the firstfruits offering. This was Israel's celebration the anniversary of God's giving of the Ten Commandments.[15]

During Pentecost ("weeks") and Tabernacles ("booths" – the feast of ingathering), those eligible to serve in God's holy army arrived in the central place of sacrifice in order to offer their individual sacrifices. The feasts' celebrations were family-centered, with each family inviting in Levites and strangers to share in the festivities (Deut. 16:13-17). During Tabernacles, the altar was used the whole week during the daytime for mandatory national sacrifices (Num. 29:13-34). Pentecost[16] was different; the festival's formal sacrifices were completed on one day – day 50 after Passover (Lev. 23:16). So, the special five sacrifices of Leviticus 1-7 could have been conducted after

---

left Egypt (Num. 1:46; 3:43), which meant they had experienced zero population growth. Stable population growth requires a little over two children per family: 2.1 children – one male, one female on average (in monogamous societies). This means that Israel had a national population of about 2.4 million people at the time of the conquest. See Gary North, *Moses and Pharaoh: Dominion Religion vs. Power Religion* (Tyler, Texas: Institute for Christian Economics, 1985), pp. 22-25.

15. Alfred Edersheim, *The Temple: Its Ministry and Services As They Were in the Time of Jesus Christ* (Grand Rapids, Michigan: Eerdmans, [1874] 1983), p. 261.

16. *Pentekoste* is Greek for *fiftieth*.

Pentecost ended. The costs of making the journey were high; the time in Jerusalem was brief; perhaps many people stayed behind to offer these special sacrifices. But Pentecost was a summer festival, when agricultural time is most valuable. For as long as Israel remained predominately agricultural, there would have been economic pressure to return home immediately after Pentecost. Also, the pressure of so many visitors at any festival would have raised food and housing costs. Less busy periods were less expensive, but to take advantage of this, the sacrificer would have been required to make another journey to the temple. In short, the costs of sacrifice were very high. Conclusion: faithful people would have been very careful to obey the details of God's law, just to avoid an extra journey to the tabernacle-temple to make a sacrifice for having violated some detail. In the phrase of modern political theory regarding men's exodus from tyranny, Israelites voted with their feet. The marched for liberty. In their case, however, they voted *for* God's covenant order with their feet, not against it.

The Challenge to Tribalism

There is another aspect of the three marches, but especially Passover, that must be considered: the mitigating effects on tribalism. The three feasts were national celebrations. Clans and tribes from across the nation were required to meet together in one city: the earthly dwelling place of God where the sacrifices had to be conducted. Loyalty is ultimately to God and His law. This cross-tribal loyalty was to be demonstrated at the national feasts.[17]

When all the families of Israel journeyed to Jerusalem, young adults of marriageable age could meet each other: those of the opposite sex who were members of different tribes.[18]

---

17. The feast still promotes unity across judicial boundaries, acknowledged or not: at the communion table.

18. The denominational college or Bible college has long served a similar

Marriage was not limited to members of the same tribe; it was limited only confessionally. The one judicial pressure to marry inside a tribe was the unique case law that applied only to a family of daughters. They could inherit their father's land, but only if they married within the tribe. This was for the sake of the preservation of land ownership within the tribe, not for theological or spiritual reasons (Num. 36:7). (The existence of the bride price/dowry system was another factor loosening the power of the tribe and the clan. Daughters did not carry title to land with them when they left their fathers' households; instead, they carried transportable capital: gold, silver, jewels, etc. Because this capital was transportable, marriage could cut across clan and tribal boundaries.)[19]

In a tribally based society, the power of the clan is very great. Ethics tends to be associated with the tribe. "My brother and I against our cousin; my cousin and I against the world." The tribal outlook is "brotherhood over otherhood," insiders over outsiders. Justice is owed only to insiders. The universalism of fixed moral law is denied by such tribal brotherhoods. This is why Mosaic Israel was not primarily tribal; it was confessional-judicial. It was a society based on the historical acts and the revealed laws of a universal God. The tribes had a temporary role to play because of the tribal identification (Judah) of the prophesied Seed-Messiah, Shiloh (Gen. 49:10).[20] The structure of landed inheritance kept citizenship loosely associated with the tribes inside the Promised Land, as we shall see,[21] but the absence of judicial restrictions on marriage outside the

---

function: a place for people of the same accent (in the broadest sense: confession and culture) to send their children to meet and marry others who are outside the local church community.

19. The Mosaic law did not specify who would inherit the wife's dowry upon her death. It is easy to imagine that such funds would go to unmarried sons (bride price assets), daughters (dowries), or unmarried grandchildren.

20. Chapter 17.

21. Chapters 15, 17, 25, 30.

tribe, the bride price/dowry system, and the central feasts mitigated the effects of tribalism-clannism.

Who Paid? Who Benefitted?

The costs of travel, lodging, food, and forfeited time required to participate in the three festivals were very high. We can only guess at the rents charged in Jerusalem when the city experienced a massive influx of participants. Even upper rooms would have come at a premium price. The farther away from Jerusalem a man lived, the higher these festival expenses were. The festivals took place in the months of agricultural labor, not in the dead of winter. That is, they occurred during periods of very valuable time for agricultural laborers. The value of the alternative uses of a farmer's time was high; thus, the costs of the festivals were high. As we shall see, it is reasonable to estimate that the total costs associated with making sacrifice in Israel were five percent (near Jerusalem) to 15 percent (distant) of a family's annual income. To this must be added the costs of the sacrifices themselves, plus tithing, gleaning, and giving to the poor. This does not count morally mandatory, zero-interest charitable loans (Deut. 15:7-11).

Edersheim said that the rabbis of the post-Old Covenant era estimated the expenses associated with the required sacrifices and payments, not counting forfeited travel time and personal expenses, at one-quarter of gross income.[22] This does not count the farmer's reduced income when the land rested during the sabbatical year. While this estimate of 25 percent may be too high, there is no doubt that 15 percent is a reasonable estimate, not counting travel and lodging costs, and not counting forfeited labor time. All of this was required before civil taxes, and not counting the sabbatical year. It is likely that the combined costs of the sacrificial system, plus the system of morally compulsory charity, plus civil taxes at 10 percent (I

22. Edersheim, *Temple*, p. 379.

Sam. 8:15, 17) would have been in the range of one-third to one-half of an agricultural family's income. This is comparable to the middle-class member's tax burden in the twentieth century – a very high-tax era. In the modern world, most of this money goes to various levels of the State. In ancient Israel, most of it went to the priestly tribe and the poor. Theirs was a far better system, but it was expensive. I know of no society in the ancient world with anything like these external costs on the average farmer-citizen.

An Israelite could have chosen to live in a city located closer to Jerusalem, but this would have led to higher real estate prices in those cities. What a man saved in travel costs he paid for in housing costs. The costs of sacrifice had to be borne. There should be no question about it: Old Covenant Israel was an expensive place to live, especially for Israelites.

The Farming Subsidy to Resident Aliens

This brings us to a controversial but inescapable conclusion: non-Israelites, who did not have to pay these temple-based costs, had a tremendous economic advantage as farmers in Israel. Except for one year in seven (Deut. 31:10-12), they were not required to attend the feasts. They could invest their time and money into farming while the Israelites were on the march. They were allowed to lease agricultural property from Israelites for up to 49 years (Lev. 25:47-52). This means that there was an indirect economic subsidy in ancient Israel for foreigners and covenant-breakers to occupy the agricultural areas, with the Israelites occupying the cities. Covenant-breakers would have paid rent for rural land to the Israelites who moved to the cities.

The larger the Israelite families became, the smaller and less economically efficient each generation's share of the original family plot. If the jubilee laws were enforced, this must have led to the creation of professionally managed farms along the lines of modern corporate farming. It is likely that non-Israelites eventually would have managed most of these farms, especially in regions remote from Jerusalem, where the implicit subsidy to aliens was greatest, i.e., relief from the costs of the most expensive journeys.

Consider the Jew who lived on one of Israel's distant borders. If he leased his land to a foreigner across the border, he might have been able to afford to move to a city closer to Jerusalem. As a city dweller, he could become a craftsman or trader. His thrice-yearly trips to Jerusalem could have become business-related. He could seek out new goods, new markets, and new business contacts. The division of labor would have been extended. So would the transfer of information. For an urban producer, the festivals could have become economically productive. Economically speaking, there is little doubt that the sacrificial system and the gleaning system (which was strictly agricultural)[23] subsidized the transfer of land stewardship to covenant-breakers, especially near the borders of the nation.

I am not arguing that foreigners actually did occupy most of the rural land in pre-Jeroboam Israel. I do not think they did. I am arguing that if this did not happen, it was because the Israelites ignored biblical laws, especially the jubilee land law. We know they did not obey the sabbatical-year law to rest the land (II Chron. 36:21). Perhaps they did not pay all of the temple fees, or perhaps they paid corporate representatives to attend some of the festivals. Maybe they did not pay their tithes, or else refused to participate in any of the five Levitical sacrifices.

Whatever the case, *the ceremonial laws were designed to move Israelites off the land and into cities*. If the Israelites as a nation remained on the land, it was because they broke some of these laws, or else they were willing to suffer very high worship-related costs – a very doubtful proposition, given their subsequent behavior.

---

23. Chapter 11.

As far as I know, I am the first commentator to discuss the land ownership aspect of Israel's sacrificial system, and I discovered it only after I had completed two-thirds of the manuscript pages of *Boundaries and Dominion*. Having spent almost two decades writing an economic commentary on the first three books of the Bible, at age 51, I finally noticed what should have been obvious all along to any thoughtful investigator: *the festival system subsidized gentiles in the nation*. I say this, not in a self-congratulatory tone, but in shocked humility. What else haven't I figured out? How much don't we know about the actual operations of biblical law in Old Covenant Israel? A very great deal, I suspect. I ask myself: Why don't Bible commentators think economically? Why did it take two thousand years for someone to observe what should have been obvious? Am I completely off the mark about the costs of sacrifice and its economic implications? If so, what am I overlooking? If not, why did it take two thousand years for someone to write about it? If someone else has written about it, why haven't his observations found their way into any standard Bible commentary or history of Israel?

The Import-Export Business

For a farmer in a tribe on the fringes of the nation, the festivals brought immediate costs rather than immediate economic benefits. Only if he became a part-time specialist could he have made these journeys pay at least part of their cost. If he set up a cottage industry and produced something of value for those families living along the highways to the tabernacle-temple, he might make the trips pay. Or perhaps he could become a middleman for goods produced across Israel's borders. He could sell imported goods to wives, daughters, younger sons, and resident aliens who lived close to the highways and who had been left behind during Pentecost and Tabernacles. But he probably would not have been able to sell his agricultural products to nearby foreign nations. Those nations close to Israel's borders would have been "free riders" on the good weather God promised to bring on the land when the nation obeyed Him. The very high ecclesiastical costs of living in Israel would have placed the Israelites at a competitive disadvantage in relation to those foreign farms located close to Israel's border. If anything, Israelites living on the borders of the nation would have had to become manufacturers, trading their goods for imported food and other manufactured goods. Conclusion: inside Israel, journeying Israelites would have been forced to exchange manufactured goods or services for other manufactured goods. This would have made Jerusalem a center of trade and information: goods and information brought from the edges of the nation's borders.

The required feasts would have created economic incentives for residents located close to foreign borders to import goods from abroad in exchange for goods produced in Israel, and then use these imports to pay for their mandatory journeys. But they would not have exported any crop that was not unique to Israel. What is called the law of comparative advantage operated in agriculture. Israel must have imported food from abroad in cases where transportation costs were low, especially in cities close to the Mediterranean or close to foreign borders. Why? Because there is no question that foreigners who did not bear the high agricultural production costs borne by Israelites could serve as exporters of food to Israel. Foreign farmers who lived close to roads into Israel or the sea had a decisive economic advantage in those years in which famine did not strike their land – a curse God promised to keep away from Israel if His people obeyed Him. It should be clear that God's law was designed to move His people from the farms to cities. From the cities, they were to move out across the entire globe.

Those living near highways probably did not farm crops that were immediately consumable, such as corn, fruit, olives, etc. The law allowed neighbors to pick a handful of the crop free of charge (Deut. 23:25). This would have included Jews on a journey in Israel.[24] To keep from getting their fields stripped at Pentecost and harvest time (Passover took place early in the growing season), they would have had to plant root crops or other hard-to-pick or hard-to-process crops. Also, there would have been an economic incentive for those living near highways to go into the tavern and lodging business. They would therefore have been in the barter business, selling prepared food and lodging for whatever goods the travellers had to offer in exchange. These highway businessmen would have become the local region's middlemen for imported goods.

Those who know anything about late-nineteenth century U.S. history think of the early immigrant Jews as peddlers, which some were. Jews in medieval Europe were also traders and peddlers. But given the costs of sacrifice in Israel, a lot of them must have become at least part-time peddlers in ancient Israel. Men try to decrease the net loss from mandatory tasks. Trade would have been one way to achieve this.

The International Division of Labor

If a majority of Israelites were not supposed to remain strictly agricultural producers and rural residents, then what were they to do for a living? Where would they live? As population grew, they would have become urban manufacturers, international traders, and specialists in finance: exactly what Jews became when the second diaspora began in A.D. 135, after Bar Kochba's failed rebellion. Rome forced the Jews to move out of Palestine. But from the beginning, Israelites were supposed to become involved in international commerce, both as a national center of trade for visitors and as men sailing across oceans. The economics of centralized sacrifice made this economically likely: cross-border importing and exporting. The laws of Pass-

24. Jesus relied on this conclusion in His parable of the good Samaritan on a journey through Israel (Luke 10:30-35), which He offered in response to the lawyer's question: "Who is my neighbor?" (Luke 10:29).

over allowed those on journeys to celebrate Passover a month later (Num. 9:10-11). This would have been during the harvest season but after winter storms on the Mediterranean. This exception to Passover's laws was a sign of what God wanted for them. They were to take the message of Jehovah's sovereignty and grace to every land, just as Jonah took it to Nineveh. They were to trade and preach. They were to do well while doing good.

Passover alone among the three mandatory festivals had a second date so that travellers could attend. Someone returning to Israel might have been caught in a winter storm. The Mosaic law acknowledged this possibility. This indicates that the other two festivals were not mandatory for Israelites who were outside the nation's geographical boundaries. For those who lived far from the central place of worship but inside the land, and for those living close to the Mediterranean, there was a lawful way to avoid the economic burden of these two festivals' time and travel expenses: become involved in international commerce. The traveller could arrange his affairs to be on a business trip when the two festival dates occurred. The festivals were held in the spring and the fall, when the Mediterranean was suitable for travel.

The extension of God's message of salvation to the rest of the world was inherent in the original covenant. Foreign nations were supposed to learn of God's grace in granting Israel His law (Deut. 4:4-8)? Foreign commerce of one kind or other would have facilitated the spread of the word of God. This was God's conditional promise to them: "[T]hou shalt lend unto many nations, and thou shalt not borrow" (Deut. 28:12b) – a blessing better understood by modern Japan than modern America.

Did God really expect the Jews to evangelize the whole world? Yes. But how? What about the Americas? Hadn't God condemned the Western hemisphere to spiritual darkness merely by placing its residents across the Pacific Ocean? No.

Here I must break with the textbook accounts of exploration. On this point, we have been misled.

World Trade Before Jerusalem Fell

Rome was a trading nation in the era of the fall of Jerusalem. An important trade existed between Rome and China, based on the exchange of silk for raw materials. Frederick Teggart's extraordinary book, *Rome and China* (1939), discussed this international trade connection,[25] but the topic still receives scant or no attention whatever in the textbooks. In any case, this trade is presumed to have been exclusively overland trade. What the textbooks never discuss is cross-Atlantic trade prior to Columbus. This is a mistake that has only begun to be rectified, most notably by Barry Fell and the diligent members of his Epigraphic Society.

Jews were probably trading in North America as early as Jesus' time, and perhaps centuries earlier. There were traders from Europe in North America in the early second millennium B.C., so this should not be surprising.[26] There is evidence – automatically dismissed as fraudulent ("forgeries") by establishment scholars[27] – that someone brought the message of God's Ten Commandments to the American southwest before the time of Jesus, possibly centuries before. I refer to the inscription, written in a Hebrew "stick" script,[28] which records the decalogue. It was written on a boulder weighing 80 tons, located 30 miles southwest of Albuquerque, New Mexico, near the

---

25. Frederick J. Teggart, *Rome and China: A Study of Correlations in Historical Events* (Westport, Connecticut: Greenwood, [1939] 1983). Teggart traced the tight correlation between barbarian invasions in Northern Europe, 58 B.C. to 107 A.D., and 1) Rome's wars on its eastern frontiers and 2) China's wars on its western frontiers. When wars disrupted the silk trade, barbarian invasions soon followed.

26. Barry Fell, *Bronze Age America* (Boston: Little, Brown, 1982).

27. See "Los Lunas Attracts Epigraphers," *Epigraphic Society Occasional Papers*, XII (Aug. 1985), p. 34.

28. Donald Cline, "The Los Lunas Stone," *ibid.*, X:1 (Oct. 1982), p. 69.

town of Los Lunas.[29] The script (alphabet) dates from the twelfth century B.C.[30] Professor Robert Pfeiffer of Harvard University's Semitic Museum first translated the inscription in 1948.[31] A more recent translation than Pfeiffer's reads:

> I [am] Yahve your God who brought you out of the land of the two Egypts out of the house of bondages. You shall not have other [foreign] gods in place of [me]. You shall not make for yourself molded or carved idols. You shall not lift up your voice to connect the name of Yahve in hate. Remember you [the] day Sabbath to make it holy. Honor your father and your mother to make long your existence upon the land which Yahve your God gave to you. You shall not murder. You shall not commit adultery or idolatry. You shall not steal or deceive. You shall not bear witness against your neighbor testimony for a bribe. You shall not covet [the] wife of your neighbor and all which belongs to your neighbor.[32]

It mentions two Egypts, an obvious reference to the two regions of Egypt, upper (close to the head of the Nile) and lower (close to the Mediterranean).[33] As to when the inscription was made, George Morehouse, a mining engineer, has estimated that this could have taken place as recently as 500 years ago and as far back as two millennia.[34] A "revisionist" who has studied the inscription in detail believes that the text may be from the era of the Septuagint, i.e., over a century before the birth of Jesus – surely no comfort for conventional

---

29. David Allen Deal, *Discovery of Ancient America* (Irvine, California: Kherem La Yah, 1984), ch. 1.

30. Barry Fell, "Ancient Punctuation and the Los Lunas Text," *Epigraphic Society Occasional Papers*, XIII (Aug. 1985), p. 35.

31. A photocopy of Pfeiffer's translation appears in Deal, *Discovery*, p. 10.

32. L. Lyle Underwood, "The Los Lunas Inscription," *Epigraphic Society Occasional Papers*, X:1 (Oct. 1982), p. 58.

33. *New Bible Dictionary* (2nd ed.; Wheaton, Illinois: Tyndale House, 1982), p. 302.

34. George E. Morehouse, "The Los Lunas Inscriptions[:] A Geological Study," *Epigraphic Society Occasional Papers*, XIII (Aug. 1985), p. 49.

textbook authors. The stone's tenth commandment prohibiting covetousness mentions the wife before property, a feature of the Septuagint text.[35]

Evidence of the ancient world's advanced tools, maps,[36] international trade, and highly sophisticated astronomical and observational science[37] never gets into college-level world history textbooks. The evidence is automatically rejected or downplayed by conventional – and woefully uninformed – historians because it breaks with the familiar tenets of cultural evolution. Time is supposed to bring science, technology, and cultural advance. Cultural evolution, not cultural devolution, is supposed to be mankind's legacy to future generations. The thought that international trade across the oceans existed five centuries before Columbus, let alone five centuries before David,[38] is an affront to cultural evolutionists. This is probably why a book like Patrick Huyghe's *Columbus was Last* (1992) had to be published by an obscure New York company, Hyperion. It also explains why there is so little awareness regarding amateur archeologist Emilio Estrada's 1957 discovery of buried Japanese pottery on the coast of Ecuador: Japan's Jomon-era stone-age pottery.[39] Scholars do not want to face the obvious question: How did it get there? And why are there artistic similarities between the China's Shang dynasty and the Mesoamerica Olmec culture – large cats (sometimes without their

35. Michael Skupin, "The Los Lunas Errata," *ibid.*, XVIII (1989), p. 251.

36. Charles Hapgood, *Maps of the Ancient Sea Kings* (Philadelphia: Chilton, 1966).

37. O. Neugebauer and A. Sachs (eds.), *Mathematical Cuneiform Texts* (New Haven, Connecticut: American Oriental Society, 1945); Neugebauer and Richard A. Parker, *Egyptian Astronomical Texts*, 3 vols. (Providence, Rhode Island: Brown University Press, 1960); Neugebauer, *The Exact Sciences in Antiquity* (2nd ed.; Providence, Rhode Island: Brown University Press, 1957); Livio C. Stecchini, "Astronomical Theory and Historical Data," in *The Velikovsky Affair: The Warfare of Science and Scientism*, edited by Alfred de Grazia (New Hyde Park, New York: University Books, 1966), pp. 127-70. See also Giorgio de Santillana and Hertha von Dechend, *Hamlet's Mill: An essay on myth and the frame of time* (Boston: Gambit, 1969).

38. Fell, *Bronze Age America*.

39. Patrick Huyghe *Columbus was Last* (New York: Hyperion, 1992), ch. 2.

lower jaws), the dragon, and the use of jade – which overlapped each other from the fifteenth to the twelfth centuries, B.C.?[40] Why were the implements and techniques used by the Mayans to make bark paper five centuries before Christ so similar to the implements and techniques used by the Chou dynasty in the same era? Of 121 individual traits, the two systems shared 91, half of which were non-essential, and the other half, while essential, had alternative approaches available.[41] Why didn't the Mesoamerican techniques match papermaking techniques used by cultures in other parts of America?[42] Why do Mayan stone art works after 500 B.C. shift from earlier forms to match Asian art forms of the same era?[43]

Meanwhile, at the other end of the hemisphere, slate technologies have been discovered in burial sites of the ancient Red Paint (red ochre) People in Maine and Labrador. These artifacts match slate technologies in Scandinavia. The era of conjunction was some 4,000 years ago.[44] Huyghe writes: "The principal deterrent to the notion of historical contact is the widespread belief that ancient man was incapable of making ocean voyages in primitive boats. But there is certainly no doubt that Europeans had oceangoing watercraft quite early. Bronze Age rock carvings in Europe show plank-built ships were sailing Atlantic coastal waters more than 4,000 years ago."[45]

How many people know that the Carthaginians were sending trading ships to North America in the late fourth century B.C.? Throughout the eastern United States, Carthaginian coins

40. *Ibid.*, p. 84.

41. *Ibid.*, pp. 86-87. See Paul Tolstoy, "Paper Route," *Natural History* (June 1991).

42. *Ibid.*, p. 87.

43. *Ibid.*, pp. 87-91. See Gunnar Thompson, *Nu Sun* (Fresno, California: Pioneer, 1989). Thompson is director of the American Discovery Project at California State University, Fresno.

44. *Ibid.*, pp. 52-54.

45. *Ibid.*, p. 54.

from the 325 B.C. era have been discovered near navigable rivers and off the Atlantic coast.[46] Beginning in the late eighteenth century, farmers in New England started digging up hoards of Roman coins.[47]

Few people know that numerous commercial bronze replicas of Assyrian deities have been discovered in Cuenca, Ecuador. The Phoenicians were producing these replicas on Cyprus as early as 600 B.C. Carthage, an offshoot of Phoenecia, exported them to barbarian peoples.[48] We know that after 300 B.C., Carthage began to mint electrum coins: mostly gold, but with some silver. Where did Carthage get the gold? These fake deities in South America are evidence that Carthage imported gold from South America through the sale of these replicas.[49] These trips would also explain where Carthage got the pine lumber for building huge warships[50] until the end of the First Punic War with Rome in 241 B.C.[51] (In that war, 264-41 B.C., Carthage lost 334 of these giant ships.)[52] Barry Fell speculates that before the defeat, they had brought trees as ballast from North America, which is why we discover bronze coins there. They bought lumber from the Indians.[53] After 241 B.C., Carthage concentrated on building her army, not her navy. Carthaginian trade with the Americas ceased.

Roman trade replaced it.[54] Paintings of Roman-Iberian coins appear on cave walls in Arkansas and as far west as Castle Gardens, near Moneta ("money"), Wyoming.[55] There were

---

46. Barry Fell, *Saga America* (New York: Times Books, 1980), pp. 25-26, 62, 64.

47. *Ibid.*, p. 27. Cf. Huyghe, *Columbus Was Last*, pp. 97-98.

48. *Ibid.*, p. 82.

49. *Ibid.*, p. 85.

50. Quinquiremes: five rowers per oar, 250 rowers, 120 marines plus officers: 400 men per ship. *Ibid.*, p. 75.

51. *Ibid.*, p. 76.

52. *Ibid.*, p. 75.

53. *Ibid.*, p. 86.

54. *Ibid.*, chaps. 6, 7.

55. *Ibid.*, pp. 134-35, 144, 148-49, 159-60.

Iberian-based banks all across North America in the time of Jesus. These contacts continued, and they left traces. "In 1933, an astonished Mexican archeologist excavated a terra-cotta head of a Roman figurine of the third century A.D. from an undisturbed ancient grave sealed under the Calixtlahuaca pyramid, thirty-five miles southwest of Mexico City."[56]

The Carthaginians and Romans were late-comers. The Scandinavians were trading in North America during the Bronze Age, possibly as early as 1700 B.C.[57] – the era of Joseph in Egypt. A visiting Norwegian sailor-king left an account of one of these visits in what is now called Petroglyph Park in Peterborough, Ontario, in Canada. He had an inscription chiseled into rock, written in a nearly universal alphabet of the ancient world, *ogam consaine*,[58] and another alphabet, equally universal, *Tifinag*, an alphabet still employed by the Tuaregs, a Berber tribe in North Africa. The Norse inscription was accompanied by a comment written by an Algonquin Indian scribe in a script common among the pre-Roman Basques, but using a form of the Algonquin language still understood.[59] The inscription was discovered in 1954.[60]

This same Basque script was also employed by the Cree Indians well into the nineteenth century. It was not known to be related to Basque until Fell transliterated into Latin consonants a document written in this "Indian" script. The document had been sent to him by a Basque etymologist who had been unable to decipher it. When it was transliterated, the Basque scholar recognized it as a pre-Roman dialect of the Basque

56. Huyghe, *Columbus Was Last*, p. 98.

57. Fell, *Bronze Age America*, ch. 1. The dating is calculated by the zodiac data in the inscription: ch. 5, especially pp. 127, 130.

58. A gift to man from the Gaulish god Ogimos, god of the occult sciences. *Ibid.*, p. 165.

59. *Ibid.*, p. 36. For additional information, see Huyghe, *Columbus Was Last*, ch. 5.

60. *Ibid.*, p. 39.

tongue, one which was still in use in the medieval period.[61] Some of the words are virtually the same in both the Algonquin and ancient Basque tongues.[62] (Fell also reads Greek, Latin, German, French, Danish, and Gaelic; he has a working knowledge of Sanskrit, Kufic Arabic, and several Asian and African languages.)[63]

A thousand years before the birth of Jesus, Celtic traders[64] were serving as missionaries in North America, bringing the stories of their gods across the continent: central and Western Canada, and as far south as Nevada and California. The petroglyphs of this era reproduce Norse gods whose names are in ogam.[65] Needless to say, none of this information has moved into college history textbooks. Textbooks include only certain kinds of texts. Textbook authors dismiss all such petroglyph evidence as "forgeries" – the same way they dismiss the texts of the Bible that challenge their concept of chronology. But this is beginning to change. A few academic specialists are beginning to admit that there is something of value in Fell's work.[66] We can therefore predict the traditional three stages of academic surrender: 1) "It isn't true." 2) "It's true, but so what?" 3) "We always knew it was true." As of the final decade of the twentieth century, we are still in stage one.

If Celtic traders were able bring their gods to North America, so were Jewish traders. God expected them to do this. To some extent, they did, as the Los Lunas stone indicates. But they did not do it on a scale that matched the Celts. The requirement that they return for Passover each year must have

61. *Ibid.*, p. 146. Comparisons of the North American Indian script and the ancient Basque script appear on pages 148-49.

62. *Ibid.*, p. 151.

63. Huyghe, *Columbus Was Last*, p. 59.

64. Fell, *Bronze Age America*, ch. 14.

65. *Ibid.*, chaps. 7-13.

66. Cf. David H. Kelley, "Proto-Tifinagh and Proto-Ogham in the Americas," *Review of Archeology*, XI (Spring 1990).

inhibited their journeys. This was a barrier to world evangelism. It was a temporary barrier. Israel's old wineskins would inevitably be broken because the geographical boundaries of the Mosaic law would eventually be broken if God's law was obeyed. Population growth would have seen to that. So would the cost of journeying to Jerusalem, especially for international Jewish traders. But even if the Mosaic law was disobeyed, those wineskins would be broken. This is what took place definitively with Jesus' ministry, progressively with the establishment of the church, and finally in A.D. 70.[67] The fire on God's earthly altar was extinguished forever.

When, sixty years later, Bar Kochba revolted, the Romans crushed the revolt in 135. There is a continuing stream of archeological discoveries indicating that some of the survivors fled to Tennessee and Kentucky. An early find in Bat Creek, Tennessee by Smithsonian field assistant John Emmert in 1889 is a five-inch stone inscribed with eight Hebrew characters. The significance of this was denied by the Smithsonian's curator, who claimed this was Cherokee syllabic script. As the saying goes, "Nice try, but no cigar" – he had read it upside-down. Over half a century later, Hebrew scholars turned it right-side up and discovered these consonants: LYHWD. In the early 1970's, Brandeis University's Hebraicist Cyrus H. Gordon identified the era of the style of these letters: Bar Kochba's. He translated the phrase: "A comet for the Jews," which was a standard phrase during the revolt. Similar coin finds from this era had been made in Kentucky, which Gordon believed had not been faked.[68]

Needless to say, none of this is in the textbooks. Neither will you find a reference to the massive 1,375-page two-volume bibliography *Pre-Columbian Contacts with the Americas Across the*

---

67. David Chilton, *The Great Tribulation* (Ft. Worth, Texas: Dominion Press, 1987).

68. Huyghe, *Columbus Came Last*, pp. 98-99. See Cyrus H. Gordon, *Before Columbus: Links Between the Old World and Ancient America* (New York: Crown, 1971).

Oceans, which contains over 5,500 entries.[69] For those of you who want to spend a lifetime following the trails into and out of America, here is the place to start.

Jesus' Liberation Theology: More Net Income

Commentators should not ignore the economic burdens for Israelite covenant-keepers prior to Jesus Christ's liberation of His people. When Jesus substituted the mandatory tithe and voluntary offerings for all of the economic burdens of Israel's sacrificial system, He liberated His people. That the vast majority of Christians have always resented paying the tithe shows that they are rebellious at heart. They regard the liberation of the tithe as a threat to their economic autonomy. Their hoped-for economic autonomy is an extension of their hoped-for moral autonomy. The theology undergirding the familiar slogan, "we're under grace, not law," has delivered them into the hands of the tax collectors. The rapacity of today's tax collectors is on a scale undreamed of by the tyrants of the ancient world. Yet Christians continue to re-elect their masters. They cannot discern the difference between tyranny and liberty. They have rejected the authoritative standard by which to judge the difference: God's revealed law.

I have never seen these economic aspects of Israel's sacrificial system and tithe system discussed by any Bible scholar. This may be because I have not read enough commentaries and academic journals written by higher critics and liberals. I suspect it is because Bible commentators are not trained to think economically.

Contrary to the great Edersheim, who wrote that "the Law seems to regard Israel as intended to be only an agricultural people,"[70] the Mosaic law pressured Israelite families off their

---

69. Provo, Utah: Research Press, 1989. Compiled by John L. Sorenson and Martin H. Raish.

70. Edersheim, *Temple*, p. 379.

farms and into the cities. The eschatological task of filling of the earth is to bring all of nature under man's dominion (Gen. 1:27-28). So was the economic pressure of Mosaic Israel. There should be little doubt that Mosaic laws that dealt with the land, the tribes, and the sacrifices were designed to be temporary. As the population of Israel grew as a result of God's covenantal blessings,[71] the Israelites would have had to move out of the land into the cities, and then out of Israel into the world: away from Jerusalem. The centralized structure of temple sacrifice and worship would have become impossible to maintain. The Mosaic laws governing worship and sacrifice pointed to their annulment: the sooner, the better for a growing, prospering, urbanized population.

Conclusion

The Book of Leviticus is above all the book of holiness. It is the book of boundaries: ethical, familial, tribal, liturgical, cultural, and geographical. It is the book of ownership, property, and sacrifice. It probably is the most difficult book in the Bible to explain, verse by verse. That a commentary devoted only to the economics of Leviticus should be this large testifies to the problem. That mine is the first one ever written on this aspect of Leviticus also testifies to the problem. The commentators have ignored Leviticus for too long. Their prudence has come at a very high price.

Israel was to be a nation of priests (Ex. 19:6). The priests lived and worked in the holy city, just as the Levites lived in walled cities (Lev. 25:32-33). The earth is to be filled by city-dwellers. Nature is to be subdued by the nearby presence of myriads of men: the domestication of nature. To reverse a

71. North, *Moses and Pharaoh*, ch. 1: "Population Growth: Tool of Dominion"; Appendix B: "The Demographics of Decline"; North, *Tools of Dominion: The Case Laws of Exodus* (Tyler, Texas: Institute for Christian Economics, 1990), ch. 29: "The Curse of Zero Growth."

popular slogan of the ecology movement: "In wildness is the damnation of the world." The people of God are to dwell in the city of God. This does not mean that there should be no gardens in cities. The tree of life is in the midst of the perfect city (Rev. 22:2). But it does mean that the city is fundamental; the garden is supplemental.[72]

The economic pressure on Jews to move from the farm to the city was basic to Levitical law. The closer a man lived to Israel's holy city, the less time he had to spend on the road. If he had to spend time on the road, he might as well become a traveling salesman. The Israelites were pressured economically by the laws of the festivals and the sacrifices to become a nation of traders. The economic laws of Leviticus also pressured the farmers of Israel to move into the cities. The residents of cities were in turn pressured to become international traders. This does not mean that there were to be no Israelite farmers in Israel, but there can be no doubt that the general thrust of the economic incentives under the Mosaic law's system of costs and benefits was to move God's covenant people off the farms and into the cities. They were to become a nation of manufacturers, shopkeepers, traders, and bankers – an early version of what England became in the nineteenth century. They were also to become a nation of missionaries. If there is a unique thesis found in this commentary, this is it.

* * * * * * * * * *

In this book, I refer to laws, case laws, and statutes. Following Rushdoony's lead in *Institutes of Biblical Law*, I define a

72. Christianity is at war with paganism. "Pagan" means "rustic, villager." Christianity triumphed in the cities of Rome; rural villages resisted. "Pagan," *Oxford English Dictionary* (Oxford University Press, 1971). Rural people clung to belief in animistic local gods. The public resurrection of occultism in the West after 1965 has been accompanied by the resurrection of earth worship, animism, and a self-consciously pagan environmentalist movement.

biblical case law as a Bible-revealed statute that reveals a general principle of biblical law in a specific case. Rushdoony writes that "the law, *first,* lays down broad and basic principles," but there is also "a *second* characteristic of Biblical law, namely, that the major portion of the law is *case law,* i.e., the illustration of the basic principle in terms of specific cases. These specific cases are often illustrations of the extent of the application of the law; that is, by citing a minimal type of case, the necessary jurisdictions of the law are revealed."[73] God has provided us with *case laws in advance* in the form of *legally binding statutes*. A case law illustrates a general legal principle, making this principle clearer by making it specific. God, as the sovereign Legislator, is also the sovereign Judge. Thus, biblical laws are simultaneously statute laws and case laws.

This usage does not conform to legal terminology in the United States. The modern humanist legal theorist defines a case law as a judge-made law that serves as a legal precedent. He regards case laws as the products of specific legal disputes, in contrast to statute laws enacted by legislatures. The modern dichotomy between case laws and statute law reflects the dichotomy between humanistic English common law, which floats on legal precedents announced by self-proclaimed autonomous judges, and Continental Europe's humanistic Napoleonic code, which floats on legal enactments announced by self-proclaimed autonomous legislatures.[74] Ultimately, this dichotomy reflects the autonomy in all humanist thought between historical flux and fixed principles of logic: Heraclitus ("all is in flux") vs. Parmenides ("logic is constant"). Neither approach solves the problem of discovering binding fixed principles of law that can be applied to a changing world. The Bible provides this; humanistic law schools do not.

---

73. R. J. Rushdoony, *The Institutes of Biblical Law* (Nutley, New Jersey: Craig Press, 1973), p. 11.

74. Cf. A. V. Dicey, *Introduction to the Study of the Law of the Constitution* (8th ed.; Indianapolis, Indiana: Liberty/*Classics*, [1915] 1982), esp. Chapter 12.

Note: As in previous volumes of this commentary, I capitalize the word *State* when I refer to the civil government in general. I do not capitalize it when I refer to the intermediate American legal jurisdiction known as the state (e.g., California, Texas, Kansas).

Part 1

SACRIFICES
(Lev. 1-7)

INTRODUCTION TO PART 1

And they shall no more offer their sacrifices unto devils, after whom they have gone a whoring. This shall be a statute for ever unto them throughout their generations. And thou shalt say unto them, Whatsoever man there be of the house of Israel, or of the strangers which sojourn among you, that offereth a burnt offering of sacrifice, And bringeth it not unto the door of the tabernacle of the congregation, to offer it unto the LORD*; even that man shall be cut off from among his people. And whatsoever man there be of the house of Israel, or of the strangers that sojourn among you, that eateth any manner of blood; I will even set my face against that soul that eateth blood, and will cut him off from among his people. For the life of the flesh is in the blood: and I have given it to you upon the altar to make an atonement for your souls: for it is the blood that maketh an atonement for the soul. Therefore I said unto the children of Israel, No soul of you shall eat blood, neither shall any stranger that sojourneth among you eat blood (Lev. 17:7-12).*

Sacrifice is an inescapable concept. It is never a question of "sacrifice vs. no sacrifice." It is always this question: Sacrifice to whom? And also this subordinate question: Which kind of sacrifice?

The Bible makes it clear that fallen man owes his sacrifices to the God of creation. This is the absolutely sovereign God who rules in heaven and on earth, in eternity and time. The five sacrifices of Leviticus 1-7 were required because of the absolute holiness of an absolutely sovereign God. Men have broken God's law; as unholy covenant-breakers, they are in need of means of covenant renewal. The first point of the biblical covenant model, *transcendence/immanence*, appears in Leviticus in the section that presents laws establishing the five types of common sacrifice. These five sacrifices were not the mandatory corporate sacrifices associated with the national covenant renewal festivals of Passover, Pentecost (firstfruits), and Tabernacles, but rather the sacrifices of personal and familial covenant renewal that were available to the faithful on a year-round basis.

Because the judicial foundation of covenant renewal between God and man is ethics rather than ritual precision, the prophets made it clear that God would pay no attention to the sacrifices of covenant-breakers who persisted in their rebellion. "Behold, ye trust in lying words, that cannot profit. Will ye steal, murder, and commit adultery, and swear falsely, and burn incense unto Baal, and walk after other gods whom ye know not; And come and stand before me in this house, which is called by my name, and say, We are delivered to do all these abominations?" (Jer. 7:8-10). "Wherewith shall I come before the LORD, and bow myself before the high God? shall I come before him with burnt offerings, with calves of a year old? Will the LORD be pleased with thousands of rams, or with ten thousands of rivers of oil? shall I give my firstborn for my transgression, the fruit of my body for the sin of my soul? He hath shewed thee, O man, what is good; and what doth the LORD require of thee, but to do justly, and to love mercy, and to walk humbly with thy God?" (Mic. 6:6-8). Ethics is primary; this is why the laws governing the sacrifices are found in Book Three of the Pentateuch: Leviticus, the book of holiness. Sacrifice and ethics are closely linked in the Mosaic law, but the prophets made it clear that ethics is more important than sacrifice.

Holiness and Sacrifice

Before we begin an analysis of the meaning of the five sacrifices of Leviticus 1-7, we must have an understanding of the role of the family of Levi in Mosaic Israel. The Levites were the guardians of the sacramental boundaries (Num. 18). The family of Aaron within the tribe of Levi served as the priests, i.e., those who actually performed the sacrifices. They had legal access to the inner area of the temple that was closed even to the Levites. The high priest once a year had access to the holy of holies (Ex. 30:10). Thus, the ultimate boundaries in Mosaic Israel were judicial-spatial.[1] The temple, the place where the Ark of the Covenant resided – the royal residence of the God on earth – was supremely holy, geographically speaking.[2] Inside the Ark were the two tables of the law: the Ten Commandments (Deut. 31:9, 26). The holiest place on earth was where the original records of God's covenantal law rested. The *judicial links* among God's revealed law, Israel's national and cultural boundaries, holiness, sacrifices, and the priestly family of Levi constitute the central message of the Book of Leviticus.

What about the economics of Leviticus? We begin with this observation: based on God's ownership both of the land (Lev. 25:23) and the Israelites (Lev. 20:26), He established a unique set of property rights over Israel and inside Israel. As is true in all cases of property rights, these rights were marked by a series of legal boundaries. Leviticus, the third book in the Pentateuch, is most closely associated with these boundaries.[3]

The Five Year-Round Sacrifices

There are five year-round sacrifices in Leviticus. As with the three mandated festival-feasts (Lev. 23), all five sacrifices had to be offered to God at a central location. To get to this central location, most of the Israelites had to walk.

---

1. These ended forever with the fall of Jerusalem in A.D. 70.

2. Meredith G. Kline, *Images of the Spirit* (Grand Rapids, Michigan: Baker, 1980), pp. 39-42.

3. The third commandment establishes a boundary around God's name: "Thou shalt not take the name of the LORD thy God in vain" (Ex. 20:7a). The eighth commandment (the third in the second table of the law) establishes property rights: "Thou shalt not steal" (Ex. 20:15).

All five of these Levitical sacrifices had to be cut into pieces or divided before they were placed on the altar. Only the Passover lamb was placed on the altar whole. Its flesh was first penetrated, allowing the blood to flow out (Ex. 12:7), but there is no mention that it was to be cut into pieces before roasting.[4] This is consistent with the New Testament's identification of Jesus Christ as the Passover lamb (I Cor. 5:7): His body was not broken by the Roman guards, although one of them pierced His flesh with a spear (John 19:32-37).

The first section of Leviticus, chapters 1-7, deals with ritual offerings and the labor of the priests. James Jordan has divided Leviticus into five sections: 1) the sacrifices, five in number[5] (Lev. 1-7); 2) the cleansing of God's house (Lev. 8-16); 3) holy living before the Lord (Lev. 17-22); 4) holy times or feasts (Lev. 23); and 5) the historical perspective (Lev. 24-27).[6] I divide Leviticus differently:

1. The five sacrifices (Lev. 1-7)
2. The priestly, hierarchical cleansing of God's house and man's house, including the land – a means of deliverance (Lev. 8-16)
3. Laws of separation (Lev. 17-22)

---

4. "And they roasted the passover with fire according to the ordinance: but the other holy offerings sod they in pots, and in caldrons, and in pans, and divided them speedily among all the people" (II Chron. 35:13).

5. Burnt offerings (Lev. 1), cereal offerings (Lev. 2), peace offerings (Lev. 3), purification offerings (Lev. 4:1), and compensation offerings (Lev. 5:14, 6:1).

6. James B. Jordan, *Covenant Sequence in Leviticus and Deuteronomy* (Tyler, Texas: Institute for Christian Economics, 1989), pp. 15-17. It is interesting that John E. Hartley has found a five-part message in Leviticus: God's holiness, presence, covenant, sacrifice, and continuity with the New Testament. Hartley, *Leviticus*, vol. 4 of *Word Bible Commentary* (Dallas, Texas: Word Books, 1992), pp. lvi-lxiii. Using Sutton's five-point covenant model, I would rearrange the list: God's presence (as in transcendence/presence), covenant (which Hartley identifies with God's deliverance of Israel from bondage, i.e., historical prologue), holiness (boundaries), sacrifice (sanctions), and continuity with the New Testament. Hartley sees a six-part division in Leviticus: *ibid.*, p. xxxiv. He also refers to rival theories: two sections, four sections, and nine sections. *Ibid.*, p. xxxii. He does not mention five sections.

4. Covenant-renewal festivals and covenant-breaking acts (Lev. 23-24)
5. Inheritance (Lev. 25-27)

The five-fold system of sacrifices parallels the five-point covenant model that Ray Sutton has elaborated.[7] Writes Jordan: "The sacrifices that occupy the first seven chapters are themselves arranged by this pattern. The first section, chapters 1-3, concerns the relationship between God and man directly: The Burnt Offering affirmed God's transcendence, the Cereal or Tribute Offering affirmed the Israelite's fealty to God, and the Peace Offering affirmed God's fellowship with man. The Purification Offering had to do not with cleansing the individual sinner, but with cleansing God's house, society at large, which was symbolically defiled by the presence of sinners. The house of God was the place of *mediation*, so appropriately the Purification Offering is discussed next. The Compensation Offering had two purposes: to deal with theft (point three) and with perjury (point four). Finally, the last point of the covenant/re-creation sequence has to do with succession, the appointment of servants to continue the work begun by the master."[8]

Covenant Structure in the Sacrifices

By structuring the five offerings in terms of the five points of the biblical covenant, God reminded the Israelites of their covenantal obligations. Let us review this structure. First, except for the hide, which was retained by the priest (Lev. 7:8), the whole burnt offering was completely consumed; none of the edible portion remained in the possession of men, either the priests or the offerer. This pointed to God's complete *transcen-*

---

7. Ray R. Sutton, *That You May Prosper: Dominion By Covenant* (Tyler, Texas: Institute for Christian Economics, 1987). Revised edition: 1992.

8. Jordan, *Covenant Sequence*, p. 22.

dence. The hide, like the hides in which God wrapped Adam and Eve (Gen. 3:21), testified to God's *presence* with them in history.

Second, the grain offering represented point two of the covenant. This offering pointed back to the *historical prologue* (associated with point two)[9] of the nation: the exodus events. As with the Passover meal of the exodus, this offering could not be leaven (Lev. 2:4). Point two is also associated with the *covenant* itself, just as Exodus, the second book of the Pentateuch, is called the book of the covenant (Ex. 24:7). The grain offering was the unique offering of the covenant, for it was associated with salt, a mineral used to flavor or preserve something or else destroy it, e.g., salting the land (Jud. 9:45): *the salt of the covenant*. Salt was specifically associated with the grain offering. "And every oblation of thy meat [meal] offering shalt thou season with salt; neither shalt thou suffer the salt of the covenant of thy God to be lacking from thy meat [meal] offering: with all thine offerings thou shalt offer salt" (Lev. 2:13).

Third, the peace (well-being) offering, dealt with *boundaries*: how covenant-keeping man can lawfully cross the boundaries and come into God's presence in a shared meal. The priests – guardians of the boundaries of holy places and things – ate part of it (Lev. 7:14-15, 32-34). The offerer ate part of it, so long as he or she was ritually clean (Lev. 7:19). To violate this rule was to create a new judicial boundary: "But the soul that eateth of the flesh of the sacrifice of peace offerings, that pertain unto the LORD, having his uncleanness upon him, even that soul shall be cut off from his people" (Lev. 7:20).

Fourth was the sin (purification) offering. It was offered in order to avoid God's *sanctions*. The vessel in which it was prepared was either smashed or scoured afterward (Lev. 6:28).

---

9. Meredith G. Kline, *Treaty of the Great King: The Covenant Structure of Deuteronomy: Studies and Commentary* (Grand Rapids, Michigan: Eerdmans, 1963), pp. 52-61. See also Kline, *The Structure of Biblical Authority* (rev. ed.; Grand Rapids, Michigan: Eerdmans, 1972), pp. 53-57.

Fifth, there was the trespass or guilt offering. The priest kept the skin of the animal (Lev. 7:9). Animal skins were also God's gift to Adam and Eve just before they were cast out of the garden (Gen. 3:21). These skins were the coverings that would preserve them: a testimony to God's grace to them by providing a *future*.

Atonement for Sin, Not Food for God

Milgrom points out that all the food sacrifices were to be performed where laymen could view them: on the outer altar in the open courtyard.[10] This courtyard was open to all Israelites.[11] These sacrifices were public acts. Speaking of the altar of incense, which was inside the tent or tabernacle, God said: "Ye shall offer no strange incense thereon, nor burnt sacrifice, nor meat offering; neither shall ye pour drink offering thereon" (Ex. 30:9). The sacrifices were for the benefit of the nation. They were not for "the care and feeding of God" – a fundamental error of Mesopotamian religion generally.[12]

The sacrifices atoned for men's sins. This also meant cleansing. "For on that day shall the priest make an atonement for you, to cleanse you, that ye may be clean from all your sins before the LORD" (Lev. 16:30). By appeasing God through sacrifice, the nation was enabled to escape God's wrath in history. But the fundamental sacrifice is always ethical: avoiding sin after payment to God has been made. That is to say, the essence of acceptable sacrifice is ethical holiness, just as the judicial foundation of holiness is sacrifice.

The Book of Leviticus is the book of holiness, the book of sacrifices, and the book of property. That is to say, Leviticus is

---

10. Jacob Milgrom, *Leviticus 1-16*, vol. 3 of *The Anchor Bible* (New York: Doubleday, 1991), p. 59.

11. *Ibid.*, p. 148. He provides a suggested sketch of the outer court, which was separate from, but contiguous to, the tent and the inner court: p. 135.

12. *Idem.*

the book of boundaries. It begins with the sacrifices, for man in Adam has crossed a holy boundary and has become profane. He is fit for the everlasting fire. To avoid that fire, he would have to place various substitutes on the flaming altar. These five sacrifices forced covenant-keeping Israelites to confront the consequences of sin.

1

SACRIFICE, STEWARDSHIP, AND DEBT

And the LORD called unto Moses, and spake unto him out of the tabernacle of the congregation, saying, Speak unto the children of Israel, and say unto them, If any man of you bring an offering unto the LORD, ye shall bring your offering of the cattle, even of the herd, and of the flock. If his offering be a burnt sacrifice of the herd, let him offer a male without blemish: he shall offer it of his own voluntary will at the door of the tabernacle of the congregation before the LORD. And he shall put his hand upon the head of the burnt offering; and it shall be accepted for him to make atonement for him (Lev. 1:1-4).

To understand any biblical law, we should first seek to discover its theocentric meaning. What does a law have to do with God and His relation to man? James Jordan argues that the whole burnt sacrifice symbolized *the death of the sacrificer*. This death was imputed judicially to the animal. The animal became covenantally dead. The sinner's liability to death was transferred to the animal. Death must be dealt with before sin is. Jordan writes: "What the sacrifice removes is not sin but death, the judgment for sin. Death having been removed, it is now possible to live a righteous life."[1] The effect of this transfer of

1. James Jordan, "The Whole Burnt Sacrifice: Its Liturgy and Meaning," *Biblical Horizons Occasional Paper*, No. 11, p. 4. For a more extensive extract from Jordan's

covenantal death to the animal was the removal of sin and guilt of the sacrificer, but the cause was the sacrifice's removal of the sinner's liability to death.

Leviticus begins with the law governing the burnt offering. "A male without blemish" was required, which was also the requirement for the Passover lamb: "Your lamb shall be without blemish, a male of the first year: ye shall take it out from the sheep, or from the goats" (Ex. 12:5). The phrase, "without blemish," is repeated throughout Leviticus.[2] The blemish-free sacrificial animal symbolized God's requirement of a final sacrifice that alone serves as a legal ransom payment (atonement)[3] to God for man's sin. This pointed to the substitutionary death of a perfect man, Jesus Christ (I Pet. 1:18-21).

The requirement of a blemish-free sacrifice meant that the individual who was seeking a legal eradication of the legal effects of sin could not expect to attain it at a discount. He had to forfeit something of obvious value. He could not offer an imperfect, less valuable animal and still expect to please God. The offering had to cost him something: an animal with higher market value than a blemished animal. David later declared: "Nay; but I will surely buy it of thee at a price: neither will I offer burnt offerings unto the LORD my God of that which doth cost me nothing. So David bought the threshingfloor and the oxen for fifty shekels of silver" (II Sam. 24:24).[4] A later genera-

---

essay, see Gary North, *Boundaries and Dominion: The Economics of Leviticus* (computer edition; Tyler, Texas: Institute for Christian Economics, 1994), ch. 1.

2. Leviticus 1:10; 3:1,6; 4:23,28,32; 5:11,18; 6:6; 9:2-3; 14:10; 22:19; 23:12,18. It also appears repeatedly in Numbers.

3. Wenham says that the Hebrew word *kippur*, "to make atonement," may be derived from one of two words. One means "ransom price," and the other means "to wipe away." The ransom price was the money a legally condemned man could pay to escape the death penalty (Ex. 21:30; Prov. 6:35). In some passages, the former seems more appropriate (Ex. 30:15; Num. 31:50). The latter seems more appropriate in passages that deal with the altar (Lev. 15:33). Gordon J. Wenham, *The Book of Leviticus* (Grand Rapids, Michigan: Eerdmans, 1979), p. 28.

4. David paid 600 shekels of gold for the land (I Chron. 21:25). The 50 shekels were the price of the oxen.

tion of Israelites broke this law by offering blind, lame, and sick animals (Mal. 1:8).

The same principle of costly sacrifice applied to the grain offerings: "And when any will offer a meat [meal] offering unto the LORD, his offering shall be of fine flour; and he shall pour oil upon it, and put frankincense thereon" (Lev. 2:1). (This rule did not apply to sacrifices involving birds, presumably for the sake of the poor.)[5]

A Blemish-Free Sacrifice

I begin with the question: In what way does this law reflect the character of God? Second, in what way does this law reflect God's relationship with man, especially fallen man?

The whole burnt offering was the first of five Levitical sacrifices. This sacrifice established two legal principles. First, God deserves the best we have to offer: a blemish-free male sacrifice. Second, God places limits on our mandated sacrifices: men owed God only one animal. So, while the blemish-free male sacrifice testified to the Israelites' *total indebtedness to God*, the requirement of only one animal placed *limits on the sense of guilt and obligation*. We are not supposed to become paralyzed by the thought of our total depravity. We are not asked by God to burn up everything we own in a hopeless quest to placate Him with acts of personal sacrifice. We owe Him far too much for such futile acts of self-sacrifice to repay our massive debts.

When we offer a blemish-free male sacrifice to God, God acknowledges this as a *representative act of our total submission* to Him as absolutely sovereign. A blemish-free male sacrifice publicly symbolizes our acknowledgment of our total dependence on His absolutely sovereign mercy. In Leviticus 1, this blemish-free male sacrifice was a bull. In the New Covenant, this sacrifice was Jesus Christ (Heb. 9).

---

5. Jacob Milgrom, *Leviticus 1-16*, vol. 3 of *The Anchor Bible* (New York: Doubleday, 1991), p. 167.

As we shall see in this chapter, any attempt to offer a blemished sacrifice is a judicially representative assertion of man's own partial autonomy: a denial of man's total depravity and also God's absolute sovereignty. It asserts that man's sin is really not so bad. On the other hand, any attempt to offer more than what is required is also an assertion of man's partial autonomy: a declaration that men are capable of paying God everything they owe Him out of their own assets. To argue either way – less than an unblemished animal or more than one unblemished animal – is to argue for the autonomy of man: man's ability to buy his own salvation. God does not allow man to substitute sacrifices.[6]

Stewardship and Ownership

The whole burnt offering symbolized God's primary ownership (point one of the biblical covenant model) and man's stewardship under God (point two). Whatever man owns has been granted to him by God. Both wings of the Enlightenment have denied this fact emphatically. The Enlightenment's right wing has attempted to substitute the market for the State as the primary sovereign. This is the basis of the doctrine known as consumer's sovereignty. In reaction, the Enlightenment's left wing has transferred it to the State, which is an easier concept for most men to grasp: sovereignty as power.[7] *Whenever the doctrine of sovereignty is transferred from God to the State, so is the concept of primary ownership*. The State is then regarded as the absolute owner. Individuals become stewards of the State. They own only what the State allows them to retain. A grant of tax exemption by the State is regarded as revocable at any time. *This is why a successful defense of freedom must begin with the doctrine of God's sovereignty and permanent restraints on those covenantal agencies that represent God in history*. The permanent economic

6. See North, *Boundaries and Dominion*, ch. 1, section on "Substitute Sacrifices."

7. *Ibid.*, ch. 1, section on "Public Sacrifices and Implicit Sovereignty."

limit on the church is the tithe: 10 percent of a person's net output (= income). The permanent economic restraint on civil government is also the tithe: all combined levels of the State may not lawfully claim so much as a tithe (I Sam. 8:15-17).

Whenever men deny God's absolute sovereignty, they also deny His right to place economic and judicial limits on those institutions that represent Him judicially. This leads inevitably to an attempt by men to transfer final sovereignty in history: from God to some human agency, usually the State. The State then seeks to place boundaries around God's revealed word, the Bible. The alternative is to admit that God's revealed word has placed boundaries around the State. *Boundaries are an inescapable concept*. The questions are: Who creates them? Who lawfully announces them? What are they? How are they enforced? How are they modified over time? The one who successfully commands sacrifice is the god of the society, the lawgiver.

Substantial Losses

The ultimate sovereign is God, the one to whom we, as His stewards, are indebted. It is He who cancels our debts. We do not have sufficient assets to repay Him, for He gave us all that we own. When He commands sacrifice, He reminds us that we are in debt to him.[8]

Why was there a Levitical requirement of blemish-free sacrifices? Because man is made in the image of God, and his acts are supposed to reflect God's acts. This raises the question of God's acts. God has offered a sacrifice to Himself: a high-value, blemish-free sacrifice. To meet His own judicial standards, God forfeited in history the most valuable Lamb of His flock, His own Son. It is not what fallen man pays to God that repays God for sin (a trespass or boundary violation); it is *what God pays to*

8. *Ibid.*, ch. 1, section on "Debt Relief."

Himself. The blemish-free animal in the Mosaic sacrificial system symbolized (i.e., judicially represented) this perfectionist aspect of lawful atonement. Even closer symbolically than slain animals was God's announcement to Abraham that he would have to sacrifice Isaac, a payment for which God later mandated a substitute: the ram (Gen. 22:13). The faithful Israelite of the Old Covenant acknowledged ritually and economically that such a sacrifice by God would be substituted by God in the future; until then, he would have to bear earthly economic losses in order to regain lawful standing before God. Isaiah made it clear that the coming Messiah would be the one to pay God's full price (Isa. 53:2-12).

There can be no mercy without sacrifice. God's mercy to mankind as a whole is demonstrated in his willingness to sacrifice His Son, a perfect man.[9] Men's mercy to the animal kingdom as a whole under the Mosaic system was demonstrated by the Israelites' willingness to sacrifice their own blemish-free animals. The fact that God was willing to sacrifice His Son testifies to His protection of mankind. Similarly, covenant-keeping men's willingness to sacrifice their most valuable animals testified to their hierarchical obligation to protect the creation. God's required sacrifices are testimonies to His mercy. When men refuse to offer God's mandatory sacrifices, they become progressively merciless.[10] In the New Covenant, the blood sacrifices are no more. There is only one sacrifice: the death of

---

9. Jesus did not die to save all men from hell, but His death provided the legal basis of the gift of life in history: common grace. Gary North, *Dominion and Common Grace: The Biblical Basis of Progress* (Tyler, Texas: Institute for Christian Economics, 1987), ch. 1.

10. The animism and the pantheism of the modern ecology movement are denials of the God of the Bible and His required system of sacrifice. If this movement's stipulations are enforced by international civil law, we can expect tyranny on an international scale. Men will seek to overturn the Bible's hierarchical system: God> man> nature. Mankind will be sacrificed to nature. For a defense of just this sort of sacrifice, see Bill McKibben, *The End of Nature* (New York: Random House, 1989).

Jesus Christ (Heb. 9:12). But all men are required by God to acknowledge this sacrifice: verbally, ritually, ethically, and financially, i.e., the tithe.

Man's debt to God was not forgiven under the Old Covenant economy; its repayment was only deferred. In a sense, the sacrifices could at most meet the required "interest payments" to God; they did not repay the principal. Analogously, whenever Israel quit paying because of her rebellion, these missed payments were added to the principal owed. Israel's debt to God grew ever-larger.[11] Finally, in A.D. 70, God called in the debt.[12] Israel went bankrupt publicly. "Forgive us our debts" (Matt. 6:12) is no idle phrase. The presence of the required sacrifices in the Mosaic economy testified to the continuing presence of the debt in God's account books, and also to each man's need to repay God in the future. The cosmic Creditor will eventually demand repayment of everything owed to Him. On that final day of reckoning, every person will have to produce one of two things: sufficient funds to repay his debt (impossible) or evidence that he had already accepted the generosity of the Kinsman-Redeemer who had repaid his debt. At the final judgment, the books are forever closed. So is the exit from the ultimate debtor's prison.

By forgiving a sin against us, we symbolically and legally forgive *a debt owed to God* through us. This is why one version of the Lord's prayer says "forgive us our sins" (Luke 11:4), while the parallel in Matthew says "forgive us our debts" (Matt. 6:12).[13] By extending forgiveness as God's representative

11. In real estate contracts, this is called a *backward-walking mortgage*: the missed monthly mortgage payment is added to the principal owed, so the subsequent payments must be larger. The national debt of the United States by 1994 is well advanced into a backward-walking phase.

12. David Chilton, *The Great Tribulation* (Ft. Worth, Texas: Dominion Press, 1987).

13. Protestant churches that place heavy emphasis on liturgy (i.e., sacrifice-oriented) often pray "forgive us our trespasses." This is closest to the covenantal focus of Leviticus: boundaries and their violation.

agents, we are showing God's mercy to God's debtors in God's name. Offering up a scarce economic resource to God as a *sacrificial offering* is economically the same as *forgiving a debt* legally owed to us.

The loss of the value of a sacrifice made to God symbolizes two things: 1) God's payment of His own Son, the Messiah, and 2) the patience that we have shown to those who had sinned against us. We are stewards, not owners. When we forgive others, we offer up a sacrifice to God: extending grace to sinners by forfeiting whatever they legally owed to us.[14] Of course, we are gaining heavenly resources by doing this. "Lay not up for yourselves treasures upon earth, where moth and rust doth corrupt, and where thieves break through and steal: But lay up for yourselves treasures in heaven, where neither moth nor rust doth corrupt, and where thieves do not break through nor steal" (Matt. 6:19-20).

God will not collect what we owe to Him if we acknowledge publicly that Jesus has paid our gigantic debt.[15] But we must also acknowledge that those who owe us ultimately owe God through us. There is a hierarchy of debt.[16] The kinsman-redeemer lawfully redeemed the debtor in the Mosaic economy. This pointed to a future Kinsman-Redeemer, Jesus Christ, who has redeemed His people in history. He redeems us; we are to show mercy to those under our authority.[17] If men fail to acknowledge in history that He has paid their debt to God, God will collect it from them for all eternity.[18]

---

14. We can still lawfully ask for economic restitution, but we can also forgive this payment or any penalty payment.

15. "For with the heart man believeth unto righteousness; and with the mouth confession is made unto salvation" (Rom. 10:10).

16. North, *Boundaries and Dominion*, ch. 1, subsection on "The Hierarchy of Debt."

17. *Ibid.*, ch. 1, subsection on "Representative Forgiveness."

18. *Ibid.*, ch. 1, subsection on "New Covenant Burdens."

Because of the shift in covenants, people no longer are required by God to spend money for, or forfeit income from, animals or grains offered as sacrifices. We nonetheless are required to suffer losses when God extends financial mercy through us to impoverished debtors: the legal right of a poor man to declare bankruptcy, thereby escaping his obligation to repay beyond the market value of his assets, which he forfeits. *This is why bankruptcy laws are a legitimate aspect of a Christian society*. That a person in the United States is allowed this God-granted privilege once every seven years is a dim reflection of the Mosaic Covenant's law of sabbatical release (Deut. 15:1-7). Since the late nineteenth century, there have been no debtors' prisons in the West. In the United States, if a debtor is willing to forfeit all his assets except the clothes on his back and the tools of his trade, he has identified himself as an impoverished person. He therefore is allowed to escape the demands of his creditors by declaring bankruptcy. If he is wise, however, he will later repay his creditors if he can; because he owes so much to God, he should not seek to profit from the sacrifices borne by those who willingly extended credit to him.[19]

Mandatory Sacrifices and Free Markets

Covenant-breaking man instinctively looks to the works of his own hands as the basis of his redemption. He believes that

---

19. I am not speaking here of civil governments. Anyone so unwise as to extend civil governments credit should not complain when these debtors declare bankruptcy, either directly or through mass inflation. Also, any Bible-affirming new administration in a civil government should feel no moral compunction against declaring the government's bankruptcy if previous administrations unwisely pledged the government's obligation to repay. Defaults on loans made to governments by foreign governments or foreign commercial banks are especially productive in this regard. Periodic bond defaults by civil governments are healthy for capital markets: they remind creditors not to loan money to institutions that are as wasteful and corrupt as modern civil governments. Investors should loan their money to productive enterprises, not governments, except in emergency situations such as wartime (maybe). The only other justification for lending to civil governments is in cases where private debtors are even less reliable.

the work of his hands will placate God. He exhibits this faith in two ways. First, he seeks to offer a public sacrifices of reduced value. Cain's offer of agricultural produce rather than a slain animal is representative of man's search for an alternate sacrifice. He proclaimed ritually that he believed that his blood (life)[20] was not on the line. Second, man repeatedly places himself under the covenantal jurisdiction of false divinities that time and again claim total sacrifice. This is why *the quest for autonomy from the God of the Bible has led politically to the divinization of the State*, no matter how strong the technical case against the omnicompetent State may be. Autonomous man returns to the theology of the messianic State like a dog to its vomit. That which can command unlimited sacrifice is seen as the savior of man and society.

Covenant-breaking man is schizophrenic. He seeks a divinity in history powerful enough to bless the works of his hands, yet not so powerful as to constitute a threat to his autonomy. This is why, whenever and wherever God's required public sacrifices[21] are either ignored or denied by society, we can expect to see increasingly successful attacks on the legitimacy of private property. Put differently, whenever and wherever the limits (boundaries) placed by God on man's required sacrifices are ignored, we can expect to see the State substitute itself as a new god which in principle requires unlimited sacrifice. Whatever property that the State allows men to retain under their personal control will be understood as due to the present grace of the State, or due to the State's present political inability to confiscate everything, or due to the State's present perception

---

20. Blood and life are linked biblically: "For the life of the flesh is in the blood: and I have given it to you upon the altar to make an atonement for your souls: for it is the blood that maketh an atonement for the soul" (Lev. 17:11). "For it is the life of all flesh; the blood of it is for the life thereof: therefore I said unto the children of Israel, Ye shall eat the blood of no manner of flesh: for the life of all flesh is the blood thereof: whosoever eateth it shall be cut off" (Lev. 17:14).

21. The Lord's Supper is public. It is not mandated by the State; it is mandated by God.

that individuals acting as taxpaying stewards can more efficiently expand the State's capital base. What God has delegated to the family in history, the Moloch State will eventually attempt to confiscate.[22] We must defend the free market from the Moloch State, but we must appeal to the Bible; it is the moral high ground. Technical, "value-free" economics is not.[23]

What must become central to economic analysis is the underlying theology of the five-point covenant that preceded God's imposition of negative sanctions against the creation:

1. The integrated doctrines of the special creation, the sovereignty of God as Creator, and therefore His absolute ownership of the creation (Gen. 1:1);

2. The doctrine of God's delegation of secondary ownership of the creation to man (Gen. 1:26-28);[24]

3. The doctrine of the law of God, which appears in the form of an exclusive (and therefore exclusionary) property boundary (Gen. 2:17a);

4. The doctrine of God's negative sanctions against the person who violates His law and His property (Gen. 2:17b);

5. The doctrine of the promised negative historical sanctions against Satan through God's promised Seed (Gen. 3:15).

The acknowledgment of the reality of God-cursed economic scarcity is necessary but not sufficient for the reconstruction of economic analysis. We must also discover in God's word *and apply covenantally* the judicial foundations of economic recon-

---

22. Gary North, *The Sinai Strategy: Economics and the Ten Commandments* (Tyler, Texas: Institute for Christian Economics, 1986), ch. 5: "Familistic Capital."

23. North, *Boundaries and Dominion*, ch. 1, subsection on "The Moral High Ground."

24. That is, the dominion covenant.

struction: the progressive removal in history of the effects of God's curse.[25]

Conclusion

By sacrificing to something sovereign over him (point 1), man acknowledges his debt to this higher authority (point 2). He seeks to draw a boundary of safety or immunity around himself, his works, and his property (point 3). He believes that his sacrifice will enable him to avert the wrath and/or gain the blessings of this higher authority (point 4), enabling him to leave a valuable legacy to his heirs (point 5). Offering sacrifice is a ritual acknowledgment of someone else's sovereignty and one's own economic subordination: stewardship.

Covenant-keeping man in the Mosaic Covenant era was told by God to sacrifice animals from his flock. The animal had to be the best of his flock: *blemish-free*. This pointed symbolically (representatively), as had Abraham's sacrifice of the ram in place of Isaac, to the ultimate sacrifice: God's ethically blemish-free Son. At the same time, God did not require total sacrifice from His holy people. That which would constitute total sacrifice from fallen man is insufficient to pay the required bill to God. Thus, the person who presented the sacrifice to the priest was proclaiming ritually and publicly that he in principle owed everything to God (i.e., the best of his flock), but at the same time, all that he owned would not suffice to repay God (i.e., one animal only). The individual sacrifice was to be of high value but not total.

God placed specific limits – boundaries – on the required sacrifices.[26] These sacrificial boundaries put man in his proper place. They also allowed him to retain the majority portion of the wealth under his jurisdiction. In order to keep what he

---

25. Gary North, *Is the World Running Down? Crisis in the Christian Worldview* (Tyler, Texas: Institute for Christian Economics, 1988), chaps. 8, 9.

26. North, *Tools of Dominion*, ch. 30: "God's Limits on Sacrifice."

owned, he had to acknowledge ritually that it was all a gift from God. He acknowledged that his property was a *residual*: things left over for his use after God had taken His fair share. This same theology of residual ownership undergirds the tithe.

Mosaic sacrifices were representative. They represented the death of man and the death of nature. Both man and nature are under the curse of death because of Adam's rebellion. When God extended grace to man through Jesus Christ, He also extended grace to nature. No longer does God require animal sacrifices. Men may lawfully keep their blemish-free animals, and the blemish-free animals now keep their lives. Because God the Father has definitively extended grace to man and nature in history through the perfect sacrifice of Jesus Christ, there is no further need for man to shed blood in order to placate God.

Economically, bankruptcy laws acknowledge the Bible's view of debt forgiveness. When a man declares bankruptcy, he hands over all his assets to his creditors, including all debts owed to him. He can no longer demand payment of debts owed to him, for they are no longer owed to him. Whatever had been owed is now paid to his creditors. This acknowledges the hierarchical nature of stewardship and forgiveness.

The Bible's definitive limitation on blood sacrifice has placed a definitive limit on mandatory economic sacrifice. Neither the State nor the church possesses an unlimited claim to our wealth. The tithe sets the maximum limits of both institutions in New Covenant times. This is a great blessing from God; under the Mosaic law, the combined burden was far greater – at least twice as great.[27] But when men refuse to sacrifice to God, they eventually wind up sacrificing far more to the State. God graciously limits His economic demands on us. The State, representing the collective god, *autonomous man*, is not equally gracious. This is why widespread moral rebellion always brings

---

27. See the Introduction, above, pp. 18-19.

high taxes and inflation. The State demands to be placated. It claims the moral high ground by proclaiming the economics of confiscation. It robs the productive and gives to the unproductive. This is Satan's political economy: the disinheritance of the righteous. To thwart this satanic system of wealth redistribution, men must place God's boundaries around the State, but this means that they must pay their tithes to their local institutional churches.

2

PRIESTLY REPRESENTATION

And when any will offer a meat [meal] offering unto the L*ORD*, *his offering shall be of fine flour; and he shall pour oil upon it, and put frankincense thereon: And he shall bring it to Aaron's sons the priests: and he shall take thereout his handful of the flour thereof, and of the oil thereof, with all the frankincense thereof; and the priest shall burn the memorial of it upon the altar, to be an offering made by fire, of a sweet savour unto the* L*ORD*: *And the remnant of the meat [meal] offering shall be Aaron's and his sons': it is a thing most holy of the offerings of the* L*ORD* *made by fire (Lev. 2:1-3).*

The theocentric principle governing the interpretation of this passage is that fallen man does not have direct access to God. He must have an ecclesiastical mediator: a priest. This priest represents God before man and man before God. In the New Covenant, the ultimate and final high priest is revealed: Jesus Christ, the Messiah.[1]

This sacrifice was the second of the five Levitical sacrifices, and was associated with point two of the biblical covenant model: *hierarchical authority*. This sacrifice is called the *allegiance gift*

1. The Epistle to the Hebrews is the central book for the development of the New Covenant priesthood.

by the rabbis.[2] As we shall see, it was uniquely associated with the doctrine of the covenant, for it was the hierarchical (*hieros*: Greek for priest) sacrifice.

Of the five Levitical sacrifices, this one had the least to do with economics. Yet in other contexts, the actual Hebrew word had much to do with economics. The Hebrew word translated as *meat offering* by the King James translators, *minkhaw* (Lev. 2:4-11), is the word for *tribute offering*. This is what Jacob gave to Esau when he passed through Esau's territory (Gen. 32:13, 18); it was the "present" that Ehud promised to deliver to the tyrant Eglon (Jud. 3:15); it was what the Moabites brought to David (II Sam. 8:2) and the Syrians brought to David (II Sam. 8:6). This tribute payment was used by those under another's authority to purchase the favor of those ruling over them.

The Priesthood

Significantly, it was this *minkhaw* or tribute offering which was brought to a priest by a husband in cases where the husband accused his wife of adultery: the offering of jealousy (Num. 5:15). When the wife had falsely sworn that she was innocent, her eating of this offering would cause her thigh to rot and her belly to swell (v. 22). More than any other Mosaic priestly ritual, this one produced a predictable, immediate, judicially binding result: a physiologically revealed falsehood – the closest thing to traditional magic in the Mosaic law. The priest could gain access to knowledge that was normally closed to judges. God responded immediately to this jealousy offering, intervening in history to identify a guilty wife, but only in cases of adultery: the supreme representative act of spiritual rebellion

2. See the comments of S. R. Hirsch, the mid-nineteenth-century founder of what is today called Orthodox Judaism. He refers to this sacrifice as "a gift by which the giver recognises the receiver as the arbiter of his fate, and by the gift acknowledges and expresses his dependence on, and bondage and subjection to, the receiver of the gift." Samson Raphael Hirsch, *The Pentateuch*, 5 vols. (Gateshead, London: Judaica Press, [1962] 1989), III:1, p. 51.

(Hos. 2). God's refusal to intervene visibly was legal evidence of the wife's innocence (Num. 5:28).

In Leviticus, the meal or tribute offering was closely associated with the priesthood, although common Israelites could bring this offering. This offering accompanied the inauguration of the Aaronic priesthood. The day Aaron was anointed, he and his sons had to offer a meal offering (Lev. 6:20). This had to be done with every anointing of a new priest, for it was a permanent statute (Lev. 6:22). At these Aaronic anointings, the meal offering could not be eaten; it had to be burned on the altar (Lev. 6:23). This fully consumed sacrifice represented the death of the priest for whom it was offered. As the administrator of the consuming fire of the altar, he had to be reminded that he, too, was under the threat of God's eternal fire.

The meal offering established the principle of priestly sacrifice at the time of each priest's anointing. When the authority of the priestly office was transferred to any male heir of Aaron, he and his sons had to offer this sacrifice. This sacrifice reminded them of their unique position of representation. They represented the nation before God. Those under them were at risk. The priests' moral conduct had to be exemplary because of their representative function. Also, their official conduct in offering the various sacrifices had to conform to the requirements of the covenant. Both moral purity and ritual precision were required of them, but the greater requirement was moral purity. One sign of this greater priestly responsibility was the law's requirement that a priest's daughter who became a prostitute had to be burned alive (Lev. 21:9). This sanction did not apply to any other prostitute. The daughter of a priest represented her father's household; she was therefore under greater condemnation. Whoredom was representative (symbolic) of false worship: whoring after other gods.

When an Israelite brought a meal offering to the priest, the major part of this offering belonged to the priests: "And the remnant of the meat [meal] offering shall be Aaron's and his sons': it is a thing most holy of the offerings of the LORD made by fire" (Lev. 2:3). The priests burned a handful of the meal on the altar as their portion of the offering and then ate the remainder (Lev. 6:15-16). This had to be eaten in the court of the tabernacle of the congregation (v. 16). No females could participate in this common meal (v. 18). This is because priestly activities are uniquely representative of God, and God is exclusively male.

Leaven and Fire

This offering could not include leaven (Lev. 2:4-5). The reason for this is that part of it had to go on the altar. Leaven was not allowed on the altar (Lev. 2:11). Unleavened bread was required during Passover (Ex. 12:15). Unleavened bread symbolized Israel's radical break with Egypt, the symbol of pagan religion and tyranny. It was not that unleavened meal represented righteousness as such; rather, it represented Israel's discontinuous break in history from evil. Unleaven represented *historical discontinuity* – the transition from wrath to grace – prior to the oath-bound establishment of a covenantal nation.

The meal offering served as the priests' acknowledgment of their subordination to God and their break with the religion of Egypt. Thus, "It shall not be baken with leaven. I have given it unto them for their portion of my offerings made by fire; it is most holy, as is the sin offering, and as the trespass offering" (Lev. 6:17). Leaven was not allowed on the altar, but not because it somehow represented evil as such. It represented a fully risen or completed product, as did honey, so it could not be burned on the altar. Leaven symbolized *historical continuity*. But men are still in history; their work is not yet completed. Thus, leaven was not symbolically proper on the fiery altar. Nevertheless, part of this offering had to be burned on the altar:

And thou shalt bring the meat [meal] offering that is made of these things unto the LORD: and when it is presented unto the priest, he shall bring it unto the altar. And the priest shall take from the meat offering a memorial thereof, and shall burn it upon the altar: it is an offering made by fire, of a sweet savour unto the LORD. And that which is left of the meat offering shall be Aaron's and his sons': it is a thing most holy of the offerings of the LORD made by fire (Lev. 2:8-10).

The fire on the altar was God's permanent, day-and-night testimony of His wrath. The animal and agricultural sacrifices placed on this fire produced a sweet savor for God (Lev. 1:9; 2:2; 3:5; 4:31). God delighted in the ritual burning of representative animals and meal. This symbolized (represented) God's delight in the eternal burning of His enemies, angelic and human (Rev. 20:14-15). This particular delight of God ought to be the terror of man. The smoke ascending day and night from God's altar was to serve as a reminder to man of what awaits covenant-breakers in eternity. This was God's testimony in history to the wrath that awaits covenant-breakers beyond history.

The Salt of the Covenant

The meal offering, more than the other sacrifices, was the sacrifice of the covenant. It was the one sacrifice in which salt was specifically mentioned: "And every oblation of thy meat [meal] offering shalt thou season with salt; neither shalt thou suffer the salt of the covenant of thy God to be lacking from thy meat offering: with all thine offerings thou shalt offer salt" (Lev. 2:13). This phrase, *the salt of the covenant*, ties this sacrifice to the Bible's system of covenantal subordination.

Why salt? First, it is an agency of incorruption, keeping things from spoiling.[3] Second, salt imparts flavor. Third, and

3. Alfred Edersheim, *The Temple: Its Ministry and Services As They Were in the Time of Jesus Christ* (Grand Rapids, Michigan: Eerdmans, [1874] 1983), p. 109.

most important with respect to sacrifices, it is an agent of permanent destruction. It was used by armies to destroy permanently the fertility of their defeated enemies' land (Jud. 9:45). Salt is therefore associated with God's wrath in eternity: "And if thine eye offend thee, pluck it out: it is better for thee to enter into the kingdom of God with one eye, than having two eyes to be cast into hell fire: Where their worm dieth not, and the fire is not quenched. For every one shall be salted with fire, and every sacrifice shall be salted with salt" (Mark 9:47-49).[4] It is also associated with God's covenantal wrath in history. God warned Israel at the time of the nation's act of covenant renewal, just before they entered the promised land, regarding Sodom's burning and Sodom's salt. Sodom had so thoroughly broken the terms of God's covenant that it was doomed to be salted over: final judgment.

> So that the generation to come of your children that shall rise up after you, and the stranger that shall come from a far land, shall say, when they see the plagues of that land, and the sicknesses which the LORD hath laid upon it; And that the whole land thereof is brimstone, *and salt*, and burning, that it is not sown, nor beareth, nor any grass groweth therein, like the overthrow of Sodom, and Gomorrah, Admah, and Zeboim, which the LORD overthrew in his anger, and in his wrath: Even all nations shall say, Wherefore hath the LORD done thus unto this land? what meaneth the heat of this great anger? Then men shall say, Because they have *forsaken the covenant* of the LORD God of their fathers, which he made with them when he brought them forth out of the land of Egypt: For they went and served other gods, and worshipped them, gods whom they knew not, and whom he had not given unto them: And the anger of the LORD was kindled against this land, to bring upon it all the curses that are written in this book (Deut. 29:22-27; emphasis added).

4. For a discussion of this passage in the light of the New Testament's doctrine of eternal punishment, and the background of the Old Testament's sacrifices, see Gary North, "Publisher's Epilogue," in David Chilton, *The Great Tribulation* (Ft. Worth, Texas: Dominion Press, 1987), pp. 171-95.

The conclusion: "Keep therefore the words of this covenant, and do them, that ye may prosper in all that ye do" (Deut. 29:9).

The threat of God's covenant sanctions was not limited to the nation; it also included the individual. God warned what would happen to the covenant-breaking individual. Notice the language of smoke, which accompanies burning. "And it come to pass, when he heareth the words of this curse, that he bless himself in his heart, saying, I shall have peace, though I walk in the imagination of mine heart, to add drunkenness to thirst: The LORD will not spare him, but then the anger of the LORD and his jealousy shall smoke against that man, and all the curses that are written in this book shall lie upon him, and the LORD shall blot out his name from under heaven. And the LORD shall separate him unto evil out of all the tribes of Israel, according to all the curses of the covenant that are written in this book of the law" (Deut. 29:19-21).

Firstfruits (Pentecost)

The meal offering is associated in the text with the firstfruits offering, another meal offering (Lev. 2:12, 14). Firstfruits was a mandatory annual offering (Ex. 23:16, 19). This offering was a man's public acknowledgment that God must be paid "off the top." That is, the farmer owed God the best of his field and the first portion of his crop. He was not to pay God last; he was required to pay God first. Firstfruits was one rare case in the Bible where God taxed capital rather than the net increase. The farmer did not deduct the replacement seed before offering the firstfruits; whatever came up was God's. But it was a small offering – a token offering.

The firstfruits payment was mandatory. This was his public acknowledgment of his subordination to God through the Aaronic priesthood. When the blessings of God's bounty appeared in his field, the owner was required to acknowledge the source of this bounty by bringing a meal offering to God.

According to rabbinic tradition, the tithe was paid on what remained after the firstfruits offerings and after gleaning had taken place.[5] This interpretation of the tithe is consistent with the idea that the tithe is paid only on that which is at the lawful disposal of the owner. We do not owe the church a tithe on that which has been lawfully appropriated by others. Counting all the required tithes (including the tithe of celebration: Deuteronomy 14:23), the sacrifices, and the gleaning laws, the rabbis estimated that about one-quarter of the agricultural productivity of the land would have been transferred to others, not including civil taxes.[6] Many of these offerings beyond the tithe did not burden non-agricultural occupations.[7] This is additional evidence that biblical law indirectly subsidized urban employment by penalizing farming. Contrary to Edersheim, who wrote that "the Law seems to regard Israel as intended to be only an agricultural people,"[8] the Mosaic law did a great deal to move Israelite families off the farm and into the city, as I explained in this book's Introduction.

Exodus 23:17 indicates that the public offering of the firstfruits, like the feast of ingathering (Tabernacles), was mandatory for all the men of Israel: "Three times in the year all thy males shall appear before the Lord GOD." Because the firstfruits offerings were explicitly agricultural, the products of other occupations were exempt. Still, in a predominantly agricultural society, the crowds entering Jerusalem would have been immense. Edersheim says that the later rabbinical estimate of the size of the original temple indicated that 210,000 people could worship there.[9] We ask ourselves: How did the priests handle the immense flow of individual sacrifices? Where did the people

---

5. Edersheim, *Temple*, p. 379.

6. *Idem*. The rabbis assumed that the third-year and sixth-year festival tithes of Deuteronomy 14:26-29 were additional tithes.

7. *Idem*.

8. *Idem*.

9. *Ibid*., p. 138.

stay? How long did these round-trip journeys take? What expenses along the road did the travelers incur? This traveling expense would have been considerable, in contrast to the value of the firstfruits' representative grain offering.

These festivals were acts of covenant renewal. They were expensive and time-consuming. They would have required a great deal of patience, such as standing in long lines for many hours. God required the men of the nation to go through these ceremonies, despite the costs involved. Why? Because they were a nation of priests (Ex. 19:6).

Of all the festivals, firstfruits was the one least likely to have been attended by women. It was held fifty days after Passover (Lev. 23:15). Passover was a family celebration (Ex. 12). Women who had just walked home from the central location would have been tired of travelling with children. The men were required to attend; the women were not. Firstfruits would have tended to be a more male-oriented festival, analogous to the meal offering, which was exclusively masculine (Lev. 2:18).

Conclusion

This sacrifice was an aspect of point two of the biblical covenant model. Bear in mind that Exodus is the second book in the Pentateuch. First, the phrase "salt of the covenant" (Lev. 2:13) parallels the Book of Exodus' identification as the book of the covenant (Ex. 24:7). Second, the prohibition of leaven points back to the exodus: the definitive break in Israelite history from bondage to false gods. All of Egypt's leaven had to be left behind. None could be brought into the Promised Land. This sharp break with the evil of Egypt was celebrated at the Passover meal, which also excluded leaven (Ex. 12:15). Third, the meal sacrifice was the second of the five sacrifices of Leviticus. Fourth, this sacrifice had to do with the priesthood: hierarchy.

The meal offering pointed to Israel as a nation under a covenant. It was under hierarchical authority, both civil and ecclesiastical. The meal offering more than the other four pointed to this hierarchical system of representation. The priests were required to make a meal offering at the time of their anointing. The common Israelite, when he had committed an unnamed infraction, brought a meal offering to the priest for sacrifice.

What was the nature of this transgression? We are not told, but we can deduce the answer. The transgression had no victim, or else the fifth sacrifice would have been appropriate: the trespass or reparation offering. It was not an unintentional sin, since the fourth sacrifice was not involved: the sin offering or purification offering. It was not a peace offering, which was voluntary and was not part of the atoning sacrifices. The whole burnt offering was associated with man's total submission to God. Thus, I conclude that the meal offering had something to do with a known infraction of a priestly law – what we call today ceremonial law.

The Israelite was a member of a nation of priests. As a household priest, he was under rigorous requirements regarding washing, bodily discharges, bodily contact, and so forth. To maintain his purity, he had to follow certain rules. A violation of these priestly rules brought him under the threat of sanctions. The meal offerings pointed to his position as a subordinate officer in a national priesthood.

For a man outside the temple's priesthood, the cost of bringing this sacrifice to Jerusalem was far greater than the value of the food sacrificed. This was true of all of the national festivals. These transportation and participation costs testified to God's sovereignty over Israel. They also imposed special economic burdens on agricultural production. This is evidence that God intended the Israelites to be urban people, with most farms in the land being managed in the name of original owners by specialists. The management of agriculture would have been representative, much as modern agriculture is.

The meal offering was priestly. It was associated with Israel's status as priest of the nations. The common Israelite was held responsible by God for honoring the priestly laws of separation from the nations. This sacrifice probably atoned for violations of the laws of separation.

3

LEAVEN AND PROGRESSIVE SANCTIFICATION

And if his oblation be a sacrifice of peace offering, if he offer it of the herd; whether it be a male or female, he shall offer it without blemish before the LORD. . . . *It shall be a perpetual statute for your generations throughout all your dwellings, that ye eat neither fat nor blood (Lev. 3:1, 17).*

And this is the law of the sacrifice of peace offerings, which he shall offer unto the LORD. *If he offer it for a thanksgiving, then he shall offer with the sacrifice of thanksgiving unleavened cakes mingled with oil, and unleavened wafers anointed with oil, and cakes mingled with oil, of fine flour, fried. Besides the cakes, he shall offer for his offering leavened bread with the sacrifice of thanksgiving of his peace offerings. And of it he shall offer one out of the whole oblation for an heave offering unto the* LORD, *and it shall be the priest's that sprinkleth the blood of the peace offerings. And the flesh of the sacrifice of his peace offerings for thanksgiving shall be eaten the same day that it is offered; he shall not leave any of it until the morning (Lev. 7:11-15).*

The theocentric focus of these judicially unified passages is the presence of a state of war between God and fallen man. Man must seek peace on God's terms. God does not seek peace on man's terms. There are the terms of peace: unconditional surrender.[1] The question is: Must man surrender unconditionally to God, or must God surrender unconditionally to man? The irreconcilable conflicting answers to this question constitute the essence of the war between Christianity and humanism.

The Mosaic sacrificial system testified to the possibility of peace. The peace offering was the third of the five Levitical sacrifices. It corresponded to point three of the biblical covenant model because it dealt with boundaries: the boundary separating God from man. In Mosaic Israel, this boundary principle applied above all to the temple-tabernacle.

The goal of this sacrifice was peace with God: a goal for all seasons. When an Israelite sought to establish special peace with God, he brought a sacrificial animal to the priest. This offering had to be blemish-free, as was the case in the other offerings. The blemish-free animal was the mark of the best a man could offer God. As we shall see, this is also why leaven had to accompany the peace offering. But the offering had to include unleavened bread as well. This mixture of leaven and unleaven creates a problem for the commentator. What did each of these offerings symbolize? They seem contradictory, yet both were required in the same offering. Why? To answer, we need to understand the special nature of this sacrifice.

The Peace Offering

The peace offering was not tied to a vow or an oath. We know this because the Israelite was not allowed to eat this sacrifice over a period of two days (Lev. 7:15), unlike a votive (vow) offering, which could lawfully be eaten the second day (Lev. 7:16). An unclean person who ate the peace offering had to be excommunicated: cut off from the people (Lev. 7:20). This sacrifice, more than the other four, involved boundaries (point three): lawful and unlawful crossing into God's presence.

---

1. Gary North, *Unconditional Surrender: God's Program for Victory* (3rd ed.; Tyler, Texas: Institute for Christian Economics, 1988).

This sacrifice is designated by the Hebrew word transliterated *zehbakh*. Milgrom says that this word always means "slain offering whose meat is eaten by the worshipper." He cites as particularly revealing Jeremiah 7:21: "Thus saith the LORD of hosts, the God of Israel; Put your burnt offerings unto your sacrifices [*zehbakh*], and eat flesh."[2] I conclude that the common person could eat part of this offering because of the laws governing uncleanness. The law stated that an unclean person could not lawfully eat this sacrifice (Lev. 7:20-21). But this law of uncleanness always applied to priests. If this law applied only to priests, there was no need to mention this requirement. By singling out the possibility that a clean person could enter the sacrifice (priestly) area, this law identified this sacrifice as a shared meal in which the common offerer could participate. This sacrifice was unique among the five in that it allowed a common Israelite or circumcised resident alien to eat a ritual meal in the presence of God. The priest collected part of this offering for his own use (Lev. 7:14). This indicates, though does not prove, that the priest ate the meal with the sacrificer and his family and friends.

Where was it eaten? Milgrom argues that it was eaten inside the sanctuary's boundaries. He refers to the sacrifice of the Shilonite sanctuary (II Sam. 2:13-14): a *zehbakh*, a shared meal. The offerer's sacrifice was boiled on the sanctuary premises. There were probably special halls for eating the sacrificial meal, he concludes (I Sam. 9:22; Jer. 35:2). This is why there were rules governing the offerer's uncleanness, he says.[3]

The Israelite was not allowed to eat fat or blood when making this sacrifice. Normally, fat was regarded as a blessing; blood was always prohibited. So, in this case, God reserved to Himself both the fat and the blood.[4]

---

2. Jacob Milgrom, *Leviticus 1-16*, vol. 3 of *The Anchor Bible* (New York: Doubleday, 1991), p. 218.

3. *Ibid.*, p. 223.

4. See Gary North, *Boundaries and Dominion: The Economics of Leviticus* (computer

Offerings from the Field

The Israelite brought more than an animal to the priest for the peace offering; he brought the fruit of the field, too. He brought baked cakes, both leavened and unleavened. The peace offering testified publicly that God had blessed him in his fields and his barns; he was bringing to God representative samples of the best of his produce. This is why leaven had to be part of the sacrifice of the peace offering. Leaven is the symbol of expansion in history: God's blessings compounded over time. Leaven was the best that an Israelite was able to offer God from his field.

We discover here a very important theological principle: *the close association between law and dominion.* Leaven is a physical agent of expansion. The issue of boundaries, of holiness, in Leviticus is associated with the leaven of the peace offering, the third sacrifice. The message conveyed by this symbol is that God's leaven progressively replaces Satan's leaven in history. This cultural replacement process – the dominion covenant's process – is associated more closely with holiness (moral set-apartness) than it is with transcendence, hierarchy, sanctions, or inheritance. Point three of the biblical covenant model is law.[5] Leaven, dominion, and biblical law were linked.

The Meaning of Leaven

Leaven is not a principle of evil; rather, it is the principle of *compound growth in history*. It is associated with progressive sanctification, both personal and corporate. Then what of unleaven? It always symbolizes a discontinuity. In the context of the Passover meal, unleavened bread was mandatory. Unleavened bread marked the historical discontinuity between Egypt and

---

edition; Tyler, Texas: Institute for Christian Economics, 1994), ch. 3, section on "Neither Blood Nor Fat."

5. Ray R. Sutton, *That You May Prosper: Dominion By Covenant* (2nd ed.; Tyler, Texas: Institute for Christian Economics, 1992), ch. 3.

the Promised Land. None of Egypt's leaven was to be carried out of Egypt. This discontinuity was specifically religious and cultural: the break with Egypt's religion and civilization. The Passover meal was to symbolize a covenantal break with Egyptian thought and culture, not a break from the establishment of culture as an outworking of God's covenant. This is why the peace offering required leaven. It reminded the Israelites of their kingdom requirements. So, there were two rival leavens, Egypt's and Israel's, just as there are two kingdoms in history, God's and Satan's.[6] They could not eat leaven during Passover, since leaven in this context symbolized Egypt. But they were required to offer leaven as the firstfruits of the Lord, meaning the *best* of a family's productivity: "Ye shall bring out of your habitations two wave loaves of two tenth deals: they shall be of fine flour; they shall be baked with leaven; they are the firstfruits unto the LORD" (Lev. 23:17). It is man's offering to God. (The festival of firstfruits in the New Testament is associated with Pentecost: Acts 2.)

This has not been a common interpretation. A far more familiar interpretation teaches that leaven represents man's corruption. The rabbinical tradition has long associated leaven with man's evil propensities.[7] Also, the high priest in Rome in Plutarch's day was forbidden to touch leaven.[8] Milgrom refers to "an older and universal regard of leaven as the arch-symbol of fermentation, deterioration, and death and, hence, taboo on the altar of blessing and life."[9]

This traditional interpretation is incorrect. The reason why leaven was prohibited is that it would have been a mature burnt offering, like honey, which was also prohibited (Lev. 2:11). *Leaven symbolizes progressive sanctification through history*. It does

6. North, *Unconditional Surrender*, pp. 316-19; 325-29.

7. Milgrom, *Leviticus 1-16*, p. 189.

8. *Idem.*

9. *Idem.*

not symbolize definitive sanctification at a point in time, i.e., historical discontinuity. Leaven also does not symbolize final sanctification at the end of time, i.e., history's completion. As a symbol of growth through time with continuity, leaven was kept from the fiery altar because God will not bring His all-consuming fire until the end of time. Leaven was not burned on the altar because it was a symbol of *growth moving toward completion.* Leaven has no ethical connotation; it does not represent any taboo.

The unleavened bread at Passover symbolized God's overnight deliverance, since it was not the best of what man can offer God under the best of circumstances. Leaven was. God broke into the daily affairs of His people and delivered them from Egypt's bitter herbs. God delivered them out of bondage overnight. He led them to a land flowing with milk and honey, a land in which men have the wealth and time to bake and eat leavened bread. Once in the promised land, they were to offer this bread to God in thankfulness. Unleavened bread was a symbol of discontinuity: from wrath to grace. Leaven was a symbol of continual growth through time: dominion.

Once they entered the land of Canaan as conquerors, they were required to eat leavened bread and offer it as a peace offering to God. This was the reason for the leavened bread of the peace offering (Lev. 7:13) and the Firstfruits offering (Lev. 23:7). This is also why Christians are supposed to eat leavened bread when they celebrate Holy Communion. It is a symbol of conquest. *We are now on the offensive, carrying the leaven of holiness back into Egypt, back into Babylon.* We are the leaven of the world, not corrupting the unleavened dough, but "incorrupting" it – bringing the message of salvation to Satan's troops, tearing down the idols in men's hearts. God's holy leaven is to replace Satan's unholy leaven in the dough of history.

Leaven is therefore not a symbol of sin and corruption, but a symbol of growth and dominion. It is not a question of an "unleavened" kingdom vs. a "leavened" kingdom; it is a question of *which* (whose) leaven. It is not a question of "dominion vs. no dominion"; it is a question of *whose* dominion. The dough (history) is here. Whose leaven will complete it, God's or Satan's? This is why Jesus described His kingdom as one of righteous leaven.[10]

Leaven takes time to produce its positive effect. *Leaven requires historical continuity.* Men can wait for their leavened bread, for God gives them time sufficient for the working of His spiritual leaven. They may not understand how it works, how its spiritual effects spread through their culture and make it a delight, any more than they understand how yeast works to produce leavened bread, but they can see the bread rising, and they can see the progressive effects of the leaven of the kingdom. They can look into the oven and see risen bread.

Free-Will Offering and Covenant Renewal

The peace offering in Leviticus 7 was what in modern English phraseology would be called a free-will offering.[11] This language is found in Psalm 119:108: "Accept, I beseech thee, the freewill offerings of my mouth, O LORD, and teach me thy judgments." The peace offering was brought by the individual of his own free will; that is, he was not required by law to do this because of a particular sin. It was not a legal payment for sin. *It was a token of his appreciation for the grace that God had shown to him*. It was this Mosaic Covenant sacrifice that Paul had in mind when he wrote this injunction to Christians: "I beseech you therefore, brethren, by the mercies of God, that ye present your bodies a living sacrifice, holy, acceptable unto God, which is your reasonable service. And be not conformed to this world:

---

10. For a more detailed exegesis, see Gary North, *Moses and Pharaoh: Dominion Religion vs. Power Religion* (Tyler, Texas: Institute for Christian Economics, 1985), pp. 158-72.

11. Andrew A. Bonar, *A Commentary on Leviticus* (London: Banner of Truth Trust, [1846] 1966), p. 131.

but be ye transformed by the renewing of your mind, that ye may prove what is that good, and acceptable, and perfect, will of God" (Rom. 12:1-2). Paul was not calling men to offer their lives as payments for their sins. This had been done by Jesus Christ at Calvary once and forever (Heb. 9). He was instead calling men to a life of peace with God through sacrificial service.

The peace offering was a public act. It renewed the special friendship between God and a particular individual. It was an acknowledgment on the part of the sacrificer that he was completely dependent on God for everything he had been given. It was *a ritual confession* that God is the sustainer of the covenant. As the covenant sovereign, God deserves tokens of subordination beyond the tithe and ransom payments for sin, yet He does not demand them. He places men under the terms of the covenant, and these requirements are light (Matt. 11:30). He lawfully could demand much more. He could demand more than everything a man possesses. "For what shall it profit a man, if he shall gain the whole world, and lose his own soul?" (Mark 8:36). In His grace, however, He restricts His demands. God possesses the authority to compel men; therefore, we are warned, we should go the extra mile voluntarily. "And whosoever shall compel thee to go a mile, go with him twain" (Matt. 5:41). The person who "goes the extra mile" with God is publicly announcing his acceptance of God as the sovereign Lord of the covenant and himself as a *covenant vassal*.

The Lord's Supper

Because the peace offering was a covenant act requiring the services of a priest, we need to ask this question: Is there a connection between this sacrifice and the sacrament of the Lord's Supper? The Lord's Supper involves participants in a formal act of covenant renewal. It cannot be an offering for sin, since the taking of communion must be preceded by inner confession of personal sins of omission and commission, and also by formal acts of restitution for crimes involving a victim.[12] The emphasis is on self-examination (I Cor. 11:28-29).

The peace offering was a meal eaten by the donor, the only shared meal in the Levitical system's five sacrifices.[13] The Lord's Supper is also a shared meal. But is the Lord's Supper an act of covenant renewal analogous to the freewill offering of Leviticus 7? I think not. The Lord's Supper is judicial. It is an aspect of the covenant oath (point four).[14] Regular participation in the Lord's Supper is required from God's covenant vassals, just as the Passover feast was. It is not optional. It is a regularly scheduled public event. Any church member who refuses to take this sacrament, or who has been excluded from the table by the church, receives a formal declaration from God: "Guilty!" This public declaration takes place every time the Lord's Supper is served by the church. This is one reason why it should be offered weekly: to bring under God's judicial condemnation all those who are not participating, whether inside the church or outside. Calvin believed that the Lord's Supper should be offered *at least* weekly.[15]

In contrast to the sacrament of the Lord's Supper, which is analogous to the Mosaic Covenant's sacrament of Passover, the peace offering was optional. It was a self-conscious additional act of sacrifice, "beyond the call of duty." One manifestation of our personal quest for peace with God is the presentation of gifts and offerings above the mandatory tithe. These constitute the New Covenant's version of the animal sacrifice of the peace offering. When the pastor calls publicly for "tithes and offerings," meaning money for the church, he is calling for the

---

12. Gary North, *Tools of Dominion: The Case Laws of Exodus* (Tyler, Texas: Institute for Christian Economics, 1990), ch. 7; see also Gary North, *Victim's Rights: The Biblical View of Civil Justice* (Tyler, Texas: Institute for Christian Economics, 1990).

13. R. K. Harrison, *Leviticus: An Introduction and Commentary* (Downers Grove, Illinois: Inter-Varsity Press, 1980), p. 79.

14. Sutton, *That You May Prosper*, ch. 4.

15. John Calvin, *Institutes of the Christian Religion* (1559), IV:XVII:43.

peace of God. Tithes are obligatory payments to the owner of the universe as our acknowledgment of our position as share-croppers in His field, the world (Matt. 13:38).[16] Offerings in this context are peace offerings that are analogous to the sacrificial peace offering of Leviticus 7.[17]

The Lord's Supper is both individual and corporate. So is progressive sanctification. The kingdom of God on earth is revealed progressively through redeemed mankind's renewal and re-structuring of all of man's institutions, including the State. It is this vision of the kingdom's corporate expansion which modern pietistic fundamentalism and almost equally pietistic amillennialism reject. They proclaim "souls-only redemption."[18] The New Testament offers a more profound concept of the Great Commission.[19] There can and must be social progress in history, not as a product of humanism but of Christianity.[20] Modern Christian social theory, pluralistic to the core, rejects this possibility.[21] It rejects the idea that there will be an cultural expansion of Christianity in history, as with rising leaven, culminating in the cosmic fire of the Second Coming.[22]

Boundaries After Calvary

Who owns this world? God does (Ps. 24:1). But because of Adam's fall, Adam subordinated himself covenantally to Satan, who claimed Adam's legacy for himself. But Adam could main-

---

16. Gary North, *Tithing and the Church* (Tyler, Texas: Institute for Christian Economics, 1994), Part 1.

17. See North, *Boundaries and Dominion*, ch. 3, section on "Living Sacrifices."

18. *Ibid.*, ch. 3, section on "Progressive Corporate Sanctification."

19. Kenneth L. Gentry, Jr., *The Greatness of the Great Commission: The Christian Enterprise in a Fallen World* (Tyler, Texas: Institute for Christian Economics, 1990).

20. North, *Boundaries and Dominion*, ch. 3, section on "Covenant Sanctions and Social Progress."

21. *Ibid.*, ch. 3, subsection on "Pluralism."

22. *Ibid.*, ch. 3, section on "Total Victory: Final Judgment."

tain his inheritance only by God's common grace; so, therefore, does Satan. Satan exercises ownership only as a rebellious, cheating leaseholder under God. From Joshua to Jesus, Satan controlled all parts of the earth that were not controlled by the Israelites. Ever since the defeat of Satan at Calvary, however, the legal boundaries of God's kingdom have been the boundaries of the whole earth. The second Adam, Jesus Christ (I Cor. 15:45), has regained for His people the inheritance which the first Adam had forfeited. Christ has delegated management responsibilities over this kingdom to His redeemed people. Their historical task is to buy back – i.e., *redeem* – the whole world. They are not to take it by physical force, except in historically unique cases (e.g., settling a nearly empty land when local tribes resist by force). Extending these legal boundaries in history is a task that cannot legitimately be avoided. We cannot legitimately point to whole portions of the unleavened cultural dough and say: "Well, that's not the responsibility of Christians. The dominion covenant doesn't cover that zone. The law of God doesn't apply there. Neither do his sanctions. Satan owns that section: lock, stock, and barrel. His disciples will have to leaven it."

What does Satan own? Nothing. The very gates of hell cannot prevail against the church (Matt. 16:18). Satan does not hold legal title to anything. He occupies portions of the earth through his covenanted earthly followers. God the Father has publicly transferred legal title to the whole earth to Jesus Christ (Matt. 28:18). At Pentecost, Christ publicly transferred title to the church. Jesus announced in the vision given to John: "I am he that liveth, and was dead; and, behold, I am alive for evermore, Amen; and have the keys of hell and of death" (Rev. 1:18). *Satan is a lawless squatter.* The world belongs to God, and He has designated it as the inheritance of Christians. But Christians are told to subdue it, *to lease it back from God*, by demonstrating our commitment to the judicial terms of His peace treaty with us. We are to conquer the world progressively by the preaching of the gospel of salvation and either the purchase of the world from our opponents or their conversion to God's kingdom as fellow heirs. Our sword is the *sword of the gospel.* (Surely the sword coming out of Christ's mouth is not literal: Rev. 19:15.) It is still our assignment to subdue the earth, and by the sword of the gospel we can and will conquer in history. Christianity is a religion that rests on continuity in history: a continuity of cultural victory, not just psychological victory, for the kingdom of God is like leaven (Matt. 13:33).[23]

Conclusion

The peace offering involved the lawful crossing of a boundary. Man and God could eat a meal together. *This meal required the eating of leaven.* Leaven is the biblical symbol of growth. It represents the expansion of a kingdom in history. God calls His people to extent His kingdom, thereby replacing Satan's.

How is this to be done? First, by preaching the gospel. Second, by conforming ourselves to God's ethical standards: biblical law. The close association among biblical law, cultural dominion, and holiness is visible in the peace offering's requirement of leaven. Third, by imposing the civil law's required negative sanctions on law-breakers before God imposes negative sanctions on society.

God progressively brings His kingdom to fruition over time in terms of His covenant's standards. He makes His kingdom visible in history as surely as He makes His people visible in history: through 1) their public professions of faith and subsequent actions and 2) His visible responses to them. The visible boundaries of Christ's earthly kingdom are progressively extended in history by means of the preaching of the gospel, by men's responses to this preaching, and by their subsequent external and internal obedience to the ethical boundaries of

23. *Ibid.*, ch. 3, section on "The Question of Continuity."

God's Bible-revealed law. This is all grace: "For by grace are ye saved through faith; and that not of yourselves: it is the gift of God: Not of works, lest any man should boast. For we are his workmanship, created in Christ Jesus unto good works, which God hath before ordained that we should walk in them" (Eph. 2:8-10).

The leaven of the Mosaic Testament sacrifices symbolized this process of progressive sanctification in history. Men brought the best of their fields to God in leavened form. This leavened offering symbolized the full development in history of the best gifts they had received from God. Today, we do the same with our lives. Representationally, this process of moral sanctification in history has an ecclesiastical manifestation in men's *gifts and offerings above the ecclesiastically mandatory tithe*. We no longer bring an animal to be sacrificed; we bring the fruits of our labor, embodied in the form of money. We bring our voluntary offerings.

God rewards this faithfulness in history. He brings positive sanctions to His covenant people in history. This is the basis of the expansion of His kingdom progressively over time. Any attempt to deny the covenantal relationship between faithfulness and blessing in history is necessarily an attack on the idea that God's kingdom steadily replaces Satan's in history. It does not deny the leavening process in history; it asserts instead that Satan's leaven triumphs in history. Any denial of the success of the leaven of the gospel in history is necessarily and inescapably also an assertion of the success of the leaven of satanic rebellion in history. There is no neutrality. Beware the leaven of the Pharisees and Sadducees, but beware also the hypothetical unleaven of pessimillennial eschatologies.[24]

---

24. Gary North, *Millennialism and Social Theory* (Tyler, Texas: Institute for Christian Economics, 1990), chaps. 4, 7.

4

CORPORATE RESPONSIBILITY

And the L*ORD spake unto Moses, saying, Speak unto the children of Israel, saying, If a soul shall sin through ignorance against any of the commandments of the* L*ORD concerning things which ought not to be done, and shall do against any of them: If the priest that is anointed do sin according to the sin of the people; then let him bring for his sin, which he hath sinned, a young bullock without blemish unto the* L*ORD for a sin offering (Lev. 4:1-3).*

When a ruler hath sinned, and done somewhat through ignorance against any of the commandments of the L*ORD his God concerning things which should not be done, and is guilty; Or if his sin, wherein he hath sinned, come to his knowledge; he shall bring his offering, a kid of the goats, a male without blemish: And he shall lay his hand upon the head of the goat, and kill it in the place where they kill the burnt offering before the* L*ORD: it is a sin offering (Lev. 4:22-24).*

The theocentric message of these judicially unified passages is that God must be placated for sin. When He is not placated by sinners under His authority, He threatens negative corporate sanctions against them. Those people who are innocent of open rebellion will nevertheless suffer the consequences merely by assenting to the transgression through inaction. To avoid negative corporate sanctions, societies must conform to God's mandatory means of placating Him publicly through formal repentance.

In the Mosaic Covenant, the sin offerings were the mandatory means.[1] They are also known as the *purification* offerings. These offerings, more than any other offering in Leviticus – and perhaps more than any other passage in Scripture – established the judicial principle of corporate responsibility. They raised the issue of hierarchical representation (point two), but in the context of corporate sanctions (point four). The judicial issue is *oath-breaking*.

The purpose of the purification offerings ("sin offerings": KJV), the fourth sacrifice, was the restoration of sinful people to the presence of God after a covenantal oath had been broken through sin. Without these offerings, the Israelites could not lawfully cross the boundaries associated with God's sanctuary: local (tabernacle) and regional (nation). The people needed double protection: from their own sins and from the sins of their covenantal representatives, the priests and princes. Rulers had to offer sacrifices for their own sins in order purify the boundaries in which God resided: the temple-tabernacle and the nation.

The sins in question were unintentional. "And if the whole congregation of Israel sin through ignorance, and the thing be hid from the eyes of the assembly, and they have done somewhat against any of the commandments of the LORD concerning things which should not be done, and are guilty" (Lev. 4:13). The context of these verses is *the legal relationship between the people and a ruler*. To speak of going astray within a context of judicial hierarchy has the implication that someone in authority has taken the lead: the biblical shepherd and sheep relationship. It is never said anywhere in the text precisely what these sins were. Presumably, they were not major, self-conscious sins

1. In the case of Nineveh, fasting and sackcloth were the required means (Jonah 3:5).

on the part of the congregation, since the atoning rituals listed in this passage applied to unintentional sins. Yet even a minor sin committed by a priest threatened the whole community.

The required offerings in Leviticus 4:1-3 were called purification offerings.[2] They had to do with the tabernacle and temple, God's dwelling place, the geographical location around which He had drawn a boundary. Writes Wenham: "Under the Levitical laws the blood of the purification offering was used to cleanse the tabernacle from the pollution of sin. . . . [T]he primary purpose of this purification was to make possible the continuing presence of God among his people."[3] Sin, if it was not judicially dealt with according to God's holy standards, would drive God away from His place of residence among His covenant people. This in turn would open the nation to invaders, for God would no longer defend the nation's boundaries. Israel would be invaded and oppressed by foreigners dwelling in the land, or worse, invaded and then dragged into captivity. This was the threat that made mandatory a series of acts of ritual cleansing.

Broken Oaths

Leviticus 4 is entirely devoted to the various atoning rituals for unintentional sins: by priest, congregation, civil ruler, and common citizen. It begins, significantly, with the sin of the priest. The New American Standard Version translates the introductory clause of verse three as follows: "if the anointed priest sins so as to bring guilt on the people. . . ." The New English Bible translates it exactly the same way. The Revised Standard Version reads: "if it is the anointed priest who sins, thus bringing guilt on the people. . . ." There is no doubt that the priest could commit a sin which in some way brought into

---

2. Gordon J. Wenham, *The Book of Leviticus* (Grand Rapids, Michigan: Eerdmans, 1979), p. 84.

3. *Ibid.*, p. 101.

jeopardy all those who were under his authority. It was not just that he sinned on his own behalf; he sinned *representatively*. In contrast, this high degree of corporate responsibility for unintentional sins did not rest upon the civil ruler, as we shall see.[4]

How could the priest's unintentional sin bring the people under visible judgment? Because of the structure of the biblical covenant. Responsibility is covenantal, which means that it is imposed *hierarchically*. Human accountability is simultaneously upward and downward. God is at the top of the hierarchy; nature is at the bottom. In between, God gives men and women varying degrees of accountability, depending on their ordained offices, their economic positions, and their social roles.

Because of the existence of God's covenant sanctions in history, the doctrine of covenantal hierarchy leads us to conclude that responsibility is both upward and downward. Those who are under the legal authority of a covenantal officer are under the historical sanctions of God, both positive and negative, which God applies to them through this ordained agent and also sometimes because of him. *Authority is always hierarchical. It is therefore necessarily representative.*[5] No one can legitimately claim judicial innocence based merely on his claim of autonomy. Participation in any covenantal institution is inevitably a form of assent to representative authority, though always limited by God's law in the degree of required obedience.[6] This assent is made in history; the sanctions are applied in history. This includes God's sanctions.[7] This was true in

---

4. I am not speaking here of intentional sins of a civil ruler, such as in the case of David, who intentionally numbered the people in peacetime, against the advice of Joab (II Sam. 24).

5. Ray R. Sutton, *That You May Prosper: Dominion By Covenant* (2nd ed.; Tyler, Texas: Institute for Christian Economics, 1992), ch. 2.

6. Gary North, *When Justice Is Aborted: Biblical Standards for Non-Violent Resistance* (Ft. Worth, Texas: Dominion Press, 1989); cf. *Christianity and Civilization*, Nos. 2 and 3 (1983).

7. Gary North, *Boundaries and Dominion: The Economics of Leviticus* (computer edition; Tyler, Texas: Institute for Christian Economics, 1994), ch. 4, subsection on

Adam's case; it is true of us. As God's curse on nature, which was subordinate to Adam, informs us, responsibility is hierarchical: upward and downward.[8] This is why we are required to sware allegiance to church, State, and family. This allegiance is definitive and progressive.[9] Our covenantal responsibility is both corporate and hierarchical. When a nation's senior military commander wins or loses a war, so do all those under his protection.[10]

Ritual Cleansings

The atoning ritual requirements for the priest were specific: a bullock (young bull)[11] had to be slain and its blood used to wipe away the sin (Lev. 4:4-8). The atoning ritual requirements of the congregation were similar, and the sacrificial animal was the same (Lev. 4:13-21).

The question arises: What was the "whole congregation," and what was "the assembly"? Wenham argues that the congregation was a smaller body within the worshipping assembly. This smaller group possessed representational and legal functions. Thus, when the congregation had committed an unintentional sin, and the assembly later learned of this, the assembly brought the bullock as an offering.[12] If this thesis is correct, then there was an added degree of hierarchy in the relationship: priest, congregation, assembly. The assembly, the larger body, brought the offering for the sake of its representative body. Jordan sees it the other way around: the congregation

---

"God's Sanctions in History."

8. *Ibid.*, ch. 4, section on "Corporate Sin and Covenantal Hierarchy."

9. *Ibid.*, ch. 4, section on "Covenantal Allegiance."

10. *Ibid.*, ch. 4, section on "Responsibility: Collective and Hierarchical."

11. A young bull is not a vicious animal. Its temperament is still sweet. Its character changes when it becomes mature. See Jordan, *The Law of the Covenant: An Exposition of Exodus 21-23* (Tyler, Texas: Institute for Christian Economics, 1984), p. 122.

12. Wenham, *Leviticus*, pp. 98-99.

[*'edah*] was the nation as such; the assembly [*qahal*] was the formal gathering.[13] He sees this gathering as primarily sabbatical.[14] I think he makes the stronger case.[15] On this point, he has followed Rushdoony's lead: "*Congregation* has reference to the whole nation in its governmental function as God's covenant people. G. Ernest Wright defined it as 'the whole organized commonwealth as it assembled officially for various purposes, particularly worship.'"[16]

In either case, *there was a unique covenantal link between the priest and the people*, a link identified by the identical nature of the appropriate atoning sacrifices: a bullock. This covenantal link was judicially grounded in the designation of Israel as a kingdom of priests (Ex. 19:6). The high priest was a priest to the other priests; they in turn were priests to the priestly nation of Israel; and the nation of Israel served as priests for the entire pagan world.[17] Thus, as Milgrom says, "The high priest assumes responsibility for all Israel."[18]

Civil and Ecclesiastical Representation

In contrast to the priest, the tribal leader[19] who sinned unintentionally had to bring a male goat without defect for his

---

13. James B. Jordan, *The Sociology of the Church* (Tyler, Texas: Geneva Ministries, 1986), Appendix A: "Biblical Terminology for the Church."

14. *Ibid.*, p. 298.

15. The silver donated by the congregation to build the tabernacle was a hundred talents (Ex. 38:25). This was an enormous sum. A large collective must have contributed it. Also, God said all the congregation would die in the wilderness, a reference to the entire nation (Num. 14:35).

16. R. J. Rushdoony, *The Institutes of Biblical Law* (Nutley, New Jersey: Craig Press, 1973), p. 85. Wright's statement appears in *The Interpreter's Bible*, II, p. 468.

17. This is why 70 bullocks had to be sacrificed each year at the feast of ingathering (booths or tabernacles) during the first eight days (Num. 29:13-36). These were representative atoning sacrifices for the whole gentile world, symbolized by the 70 nations. Jordan, *Law of the Covenant*, p. 190.

18. Jacob Milgrom, *Leviticus 1-16*, vol. 3 of *The Anchor Bible* (New York: Doubleday, 1991), p. 54.

19. Wenham, *Leviticus*, p. 99.

offering (Lev. 4:23). The common man who sinned unintentionally had to bring a female goat without defect (Lev. 4:28). He could also bring a female lamb without defect (Lev. 4:32). The symbolism is obvious: *masculinity under the Mosaic Covenant was associated in the civil covenant with rule, femininity with subordination.*[20] In neither case – civil ruler or citizen – was a bullock an appropriate sacrificial animal, for the bullock was associated with priestly authority.

We have seen that the sin of the priest and the sin of the whole congregation were of similar consequence in God's eyes. Likewise, the sins of the ruler and the lone individual were comparable. The sacrificial link between priest and people indicates that the priest had sufficient representative authority for his unintentional sin to bring the people under God's negative sanctions. The civil ruler did not possess comparable representative authority.

What is indicated in Leviticus 4:1-3 is that *there was a much closer judicial link between the priesthood and the covenanted society than there was between the civil ruler and the covenanted society*. This is why we must conclude that the church was covenantally more important in Israel than the State was. The unintentional sin of the priest was treated by God as comparable to the unintentional sin of the whole congregation, while the unintentional sin of the ruler was treated on a par with the unintentional sin of the average citizen.[21] Conclusion: the laxity of the priesthood regarding their personal sins threatened greater direct negative

20. The abolition of all required ritual sacrifices in the New Covenant (Heb. 9) has removed the male-female distinction in the civil covenant. Without civil sacrifices, there is no legitimate judicial restriction on women participating in civil rulership. The male-female distinction is maintained in matters of the church's ordained elders only because a male must represent a male God in the administration of the sacraments and the covenantally authoritative declaration of God's word (I Cor. 14:34-35). Prohibiting female elders has nothing to do with sacrifices.

21. Economically speaking, the king's sacrifice was less burdensome than the commoner's, for a female goat can produce offspring and milk. The male animal was symbolically more important in the ancient world, but not economically.

consequences for the citizens of Old Covenant Israel than the moral or judicial laxity of the civil authorities.[22]

Corporate Sanctions and Authority: The People

This raises the question of the locus of authority for the initiation of corporate sins. Temporally and functionally, this infraction was initiated by the priests, who were in repeated contact with the holy implements of the tabernacle-temple. But the corporate nature of God's negative sanctions indicates that primary institutional responsibility lay elsewhere. The priests were legal representatives placed by God between Himself and His people. As representatives, they did in fact *represent*. A representative, judicially speaking, is legally the initiating agent, but this act must be sanctioned by those represented. His actions are to reflect the wishes of those whom he represents.[23] *Their continuing consent is the basis of his authority*. Thus, the priest was required by God to offer a sacrifice because of this representative infraction that he unknowingly had initiated.

The representative represents both God and society. If society does not bring negative sanctions against evil representatives, then God will. *God delegates authority to the people to serve as His covenantally sovereign agents, meaning those who bring lawful sanctions in His name*. If the people refuse to act as God's representatives, then He acts on His own behalf against both the rulers and the people. This covenantal threat is to serve as their motivation for imposing positive and negative sanctions against their rulers. Even revolution is lawful, when led by faithful lower civil magistrates against lawless higher civil magistrates. This is the traditional Calvinist doctrine of interposition: *Institutes*, Book IV, Chapter 20, Section 31.[24]

---

22. Cf. Jordan, *Judges*, on Judges 17-21.

23. This is not true, short-term, in tyrannies, but tyrannies do not indefinitely survive a change in heart in their subjects.

24. North, *Boundaries and Dominion*, ch. 24, subsection on "The Doctrine of

The Priestly Office

It is clear from Leviticus 4 and from many other texts in the Bible that those who are at greatest risk in relation to the imposition of God's covenantal sanctions in history are those who are the primary sanctioning agents of the specific covenant: the people rather than their covenantal representatives. We discover in this principle a fundamental rule of all biblical social authority: *those who are threatened as the primary recipients of God's national covenantal sanctions are the society's primary sovereign agents*. From him to whom much is given, much is expected (Luke 12:48). Again and again in the Old Testament, God's capital sanctions fell on the people rather than the kings and the priests.[25] This indicates that *it was the people who possessed primary institutional authority, not their representatives*. This is why Israel was a theocratic republic. The Bible's holy commonwealth ideal necessarily involves the establishment of an oath-bound civil covenant. In this civil covenant, the corporate people possess primary responsibility and therefore primary authority. In this sense, the republican ideal is biblical. Authority extends downward from God to the people and upward from them to their representatives. God validates rulers in the name of the people.

Modern democratic theory (popular sovereignty) is a secularization of this biblical holy covenant ideal (delegated sovereignty), in which the people exercised judicial authority under God because of the covenant they had made with God. The evils of democracy, familiar from Aristotle's era to today, are no worse than the evils of any other political system. The evils stem from an attempted divinization of the State, not from democracy as a political arrangement. Whenever the political order is viewed as beyond earthly appeal – the divine right of politics – politics

---

Interposition."

25. The Levites killed 3,000 after the golden calf incident (Ex. 32:28). Aaron was not executed. Numbers 25:8 records the death of 24,000 by plague. In II Samuel 24:15, we read of 70,000 who died in a plague.

will become progressively tyrannical, no matter which authority structure the State adopts: oligarchic, democratic, republican, bureaucratic, or monarchical (today a defunct ideal).

The Door of the Tabernacle

The priest had to sacrifice a young bullock in order to turn back the negative sanctions of God against those who were under the priest's authority. These sanctions threatened not only the priest; they threatened that segment of the covenanted community under his lawful jurisdiction. The atoning sacrifice had to take place at the door of the tabernacle of the congregation. "And he shall bring the bullock unto the door of the tabernacle of the congregation before the LORD; and shall lay his hand upon the bullock's head, and kill the bullock before the LORD" (Lev. 4:4). The very place of sacrifice is designated by God as the *congregation's tabernacle*, i.e., a dwelling place. This was the place where God met the congregation. "This shall be a continual burnt offering throughout your generations at the door of the tabernacle of the congregation before the LORD: where I will meet you, to speak there unto thee" (Ex. 29:42). This was the dwelling place of God, but it was also the dwelling place of the congregation. Although the people were not allowed bodily into the presence of God, the furniture of the tabernacle symbolically represented them. *The tabernacle was the place where the dual citizenship – heaven and earth*[26] *– of both man and God was publicly revealed.* Covenant-keepers in history are not citizens merely of earth (Phil. 3:20), and God in history is King not merely in heaven. The whole creation is His kingdom, and to prove this, He brings His sanctions in history, both directly and representatively.

---

26. This was fulfilled in Christ: "That in the dispensation of the fulness of times he might gather together in one all things in Christ, both which are in heaven, and which are on earth; even in him" (Eph. 1:10).

Sacrilege is the theft of God's property. This was Adam's sin, the primary sin in history.[27] This sin was essentially priestly: a sacramental boundary violation. Adam's priestly sin extended downward to his heirs, bringing death. In a similar sense judicially, a priest under the Mosaic Covenant possessed delegated authority, thereby enabling him to place the covenanted community under God's condemnation. An unintentional sin committed by the priest was a greater threat than an unintentional sin committed by the king. Conclusion: *the judicial link between the priest and the people was more binding covenantally in Israel than the link between the king and the people.*

This is evidence that the church is more fundamental than the State in the political economy of the Bible. The church is central to society: not the State and not the family.[28] The family and the State have been more universal in time and place; neither has been central in history. It is the ancient error of natural law theory that has led pagan and Christian social theorists to assume that the geographical universality of family and State implies the social centrality of one or the other. On the contrary, the formal preaching of the gospel and the administration of the sacraments – inclusion and exclusion – are central in history because they are central in eternity. (Note: the word *sacrament* is derived from the Latin word *sacramentum*, a military oath of enlistment.[29] Sacraments are an aspect of point four of the biblical covenant model: oath-sanctions.[30]) This does not

---

27. North, *Boundaries and Dominion*, Appendix A: "Sacrilege and Sanctions."

28. The church perseveres institutionally in the resurrected world beyond the final judgment (Rev. 21, 22). The family surely does not: "For in the resurrection they neither marry, nor are given in marriage, but are as the angels of God in heaven" (Matt. 22:30). The State apparently does not, since its judicial function is to bring negative sanctions against public evil. Public evil will end at the final judgment.

29. "Sacrament," in *Cyclopaedia of Biblical, Theological, and Ecclesiastical Literature*, edited by John M'Clintock and James Strong, 12 vols. (New York: Harper & Bros., 1894), IX, p. 212.

30. Sutton, *That You May Prosper*, ch. 4.

imply that the institutional church is at the top of a single institutional hierarchy in society; no such single hierarchy exists. It *does* imply the institutional church is the most important institution in history, for the Bible calls it called the Bride of Christ. The Christian family and the Christian State are not so designated. Only the Old Covenant priests, best represented by Melchizedek, possessed control over the public signs of eternal life: the sacraments. Only church officers do today. This is why the church alone possesses a lawful claim over all of a person's tithe.[31] While the State and certain life-saving occupations possess a quasi-priestly function, allowing some civil restrictions on the free market principle of "high bid wins," this is not the same as a lawful claim on the tithe.[32]

The Authority of the People

The people as a collective unit exercised greater judicial authority in Mosaic Israel than the priesthood, who merely represented the people before God. It was the people who were derivatively sovereign under God, in both church and State, not their representatives. This should be obvious: *the judicial function of representatives is, after all, to represent.* The representative's judicial authority is based solely on his occupying a mid-way position between God and the covenanted assembly that he represents. *God therefore held the people of Israel corporately responsible for the official actions of the priests.*

This leads to an important covenantal conclusion: *it is the moral character of the people that determines the public character and historical fate of society.* The collective nation is represented in church and State by ordained individuals whose acts necessarily have covenantal consequences in history because of God's sanc-

31. North, *Boundaries and Dominion*, ch. 4, section on "The Priestly Function." See also Gary North, *Tithing and the Church* (Tyler, Texas: Institute for Christian Economics, 1994).

32. *Ibid.*, ch. 4, section on "The Quasi-Priestly Function."

tions; nevertheless, it is the people who will receive the brunt of God's judgment, for it is they who possess greater authority under God.

If my thesis on the primary connection between priest and people is correct, then the fundamental political thrust of Old Testament covenant theology was toward *theocratic republicanism*: the political authority of formally covenanted citizens. In both church and State, *the locus of institutional authority in Old Covenant Israel flowed upward*: from the people to their legal representatives. The moral integrity of the ecclesiastical hierarchy was of greater importance for the survival of a biblically covenanted society than the political hierarchy's integrity was.

In church and State, those people who possess initiatory earthly authority – church members and citizens – are those who are under the formal jurisdiction of superiors who possess *derivative* authority: officers. The officers' authority is derived from above – God – but also from below, i.e., those who are under their oath-bound authority. Those who are under the visible sanctions of these two covenantal institutions are those who are required by God to exercise institutional sanctions: positive and negative. Formal acts of covenant renewal periodically manifest this God-derived sanctioning authority of the people.[33] This is why there are no acts of covenant renewal for the family: there are no formal sanctioning powers held by those who are under the authority of the head of the household.[34] Authority is delegated downward by God to the head of the household, not upward from his wife or children.

---

33. The negative sanction may be imposed by leaving the jurisdiction of the particular institutional authority. This is called "voting with your feet."

34. Minor children are not legally allowed to flee the jurisdiction of the head of the household. Civil governments are required to return runaway children to their parents unless the civil authorities can prove in civil court that the parents have broken the family covenant by child abuse, either moral or physical. On the other hand, adult children cannot legally be compelled to return to their parents' household. This is why the parent-authorized, forcible "de-programming" of adult cult members is biblically illegal; it is a form of kidnapping.

The Authority of the Priest

The priest who committed an unintentional sin brought the covenanted nation of Israel under the threat of God's negative sanctions. He had to sacrifice a bullock to atone judicially for this sin. Similarly, if the people *as a covenanted nation* committed an unintentional sin, the priest had to sacrifice a bullock to atone for their sin. Because the people could not know of a priest's sin, he had to guard himself carefully. Their ignorance was no automatic safeguard to them, any more than the ignorance of the 36 victims of the first battle of Ai regarding Achan's sin safeguarded them (Josh. 7:5).

The atoning sacrifice was killed at the door of the tabernacle of the congregation. This ritual barrier was a two-way barrier: keeping the polluting effects of the priest's sins contained inside the tabernacle until he could offer a sacrifice, and containing the pollution of the people's sin outside the tabernacle, so that God would not depart from the holy of holies. *The doorway was the place of judgment, just as it had been on the night of the first Passover*. It was the barrier against God's sanctions, just as it had been on the night of the first Passover.[35] This threat of God's departure accentuated the importance of boundaries. These boundaries could not be violated with impunity.

The Mosaic Covenant's sacrificial system announced that the integrity of the priests and the people regarding unintentional sins was of greater consequence in relation to God's negative covenant sanctions than was the integrity of the civil authorities. It is incumbent upon theologians, whether liberal or fundamentalist, who assert that there is no comparable relationship in the New Covenant era, to prove their case from Scripture. The fundamentalist tends to adopt the atomism of right-wing Enlightenment thought.[36] He allies himself with free market con-

---

35. Jordan, *Law of the Covenant*, Appendix F: "Proleptic Passover (Exodus 4:22-26)."

36. North, *Boundaries and Dominion*, ch. 4, sections on "The Social Atomism of

servatives and libertarians. The liberal adopts the statism of left-wing Enlightenment thought.[37] He allies himself with Keynesian economists and secular liberals. Meanwhile, the secular conservatives, libertarians, and liberals disregard the corporate implications of adultery in high places.[38] The secularist affirms the necessity of exclusively earth-bound "transmission belts" for historical cause and effect; God's omniscience and sanctions are dismissed as historically irrelevant.[39] The vast majority of humanist-trained and university-certified Christian social theorists agree with this view. They adopt humanism's pluralism, so they are unable to identify the primary locus of civil responsibility in society: the church and the sacraments.[40]

Priesthood and People

The required sacrifices of Leviticus 4 reveal a tighter judicial link between priest and people than between king and people. The priest sacrificed a bullock for his sin. A bullock also atoned for the sin of the congregation (vv. 14-15). Civil rulers and private citizens brought lesser sacrifices. The civil ruler brought a male goat (vv. 22-26). The individual brought a female goat or lamb (vv. 27-35). This indicates that the congregation was sacrificially closer to the priesthood than it was to the civil ruler. *The congregation possessed primary authority in civil government because the threat against them was great; hence, the more holy the required sacrificial animal.* The king operated by the authority delegated to him by the congregation (I Sam. 8). His required sacrificial animal was less holy – less associated with priestly sacrifice.

Christian Individualism" and "The Moral Atomism of the Enlightenment."

37. *Ibid.*, ch. 4, subsections on "The Enlightenment's Two Wings" and "Enlightenment Thought and Corporate Responsibility."

38. *Ibid.*, ch. 4, section on "Adultery in High Places." I study the effects of the behavior of Martin Luther King, John F. Kennedy, and King Edward VII.

39. *Ibid.*, ch. 4, section on "Transmission Belts."

40. *Ibid.*, ch. 4, section on "Sacramental Priesthood and Civil Congregation."

This tight covenantal relationship between sacramental priesthood and congregation still exists. God expects men to honor it. Nothing in the New Covenant has changed it. Without specific New Testament revelation to the contrary, there is judicial continuity from the Mosaic covenant to the New covenant: the Ten Commandments, the statutes, and their required civil sanctions. This is both the testimony and the offense of Christian Reconstruction. The New Testament's standard for civil government has to be the same as in Old Covenant law: *a theocratic republic*. The biblical concept of civil authority mandates republicanism: public consent by representatives of the nation to certain laws and forms of rulership (Ex. 19). A theocratic republic preceded kingship in Israel. Theocracy – i.e., rule by God – is established today through a biblically mandatory Trinitarian civil oath. The alternative is either another god's theocracy (e.g., Islamic nations and the State of Israel) or political polytheism, i.e., religious pluralism.[41] All liberals and most fundamentalists agree: political polytheism is morally mandatory for every nation except the State of Israel.[42] This worldview is a denial of the ideal of Christendom.

The theocratic status of a civil government is also manifested by the presence of a priesthood. The congregation is a nation of priests (Ex. 19:6); so is the New Covenant church (I Pet. 2:9). This broad priesthood is represented before God in the church by a sacramental priesthood, one which is responsible for administering baptism and the Lord's Supper. The covenantal faithfulness of this sacramental priesthood is more important for the preservation of continuity and peace in society than the

41. North, *Political Polytheism*, ch. 7.

42. Jacob Neusner (b. 1932) is a Jewish conservative and the author, translator, or editor of about 500 books. His bibliography fills over 23 single-spaced pages. He reminds his readers: "We cannot build a decent society on secular foundations. Islam knows that; Judaism knows that; why should Christians say any less?" Jacob Neusner, "Who's Afraid of the Religious Right?" *National Review* (Dec. 27, 1993), p. 37. Yet he, too, calls for a political alliance among Christians, Jews, and Moslems: political pluralism.

faithfulness of the politicians. (If God's blessings on society hinged primarily on the covenantal faithfulness of politicians, all would have been lost by Nimrod's day.)

The Centrality of the Church[43]

Christians are required by God to affirm the social centrality of the church. This presupposition must govern Christian social theory. The New Covenant church is the fulfillment of the promise of God to establish a kingdom of priests. "But ye are a chosen generation, a royal priesthood, an holy nation, a peculiar people; that ye should shew forth the praises of him who hath called you out of darkness into his marvellous light" (I Pet. 2:9). In this sense, God regards the church as a nation. Jesus prophesied to the leaders of Israel: "Therefore say I unto you, The kingdom of God shall be taken from you, and given to a nation bringing forth the fruits thereof" (Matt. 21:43). Like the priests of Israel, the ordained priests of the new temple must protect the assembled saints by not committing unintentional sins. Similarly, the assembled saints must not commit unintentional sins, in order to protect the society around them.

I conclude: *what is central to biblical social order is the preservation of Bible-based judicial sanctions inside the church*. The church is more important than the State. A society's creeds are more important than its civil constitution.[44] The sacraments are more important than the franchise. The tithe is more important than taxes. This is why combined taxes should not equal the tithe (I Sam. 8:15, 17). Until the twentieth century, with its messianic humanistic State and its endless, power-centralizing wars,[45] taxes in the West were below 10 percent of net capital

43. Peter J. Leithart, *The Kingdom and the Power: Rediscovering the Centrality of the Church* (Phillipsburg, New Jersey: P&R Publishing, 1993).

44. R. J. Rushdoony, *Foundations of Social Order: Studies in the Creeds and Councils of the Early Church* (Fairfax, Virginia: Thoburn Press, [1968] 1978).

45. Robert Higgs, *Crisis and Leviathan: Critical Episodes in the Growth of American Government* (New York: Oxford University Press, 1991); Robert Nisbet, *The Present*

increases plus income. The evidence of God's civil judgments on the once-Trinitarian West is the historically unprecedented escalation of wars and taxes in the twentieth century. There are predictable sanctions in history. (You have a choice: believe Meredith Kline[46] or believe your tax bills.)

What goes on inside the church sets the standard for the world. If the church refuses to enforce biblical law, then the State will surely also refuse. If moral corruption is the standard in the church, then moral corruption will be the standard in the State. Why is there this sociological pre-eminence of the church? Because the *priest-people relationship* is far more vital for social order than the *civil ruler-people relationship*. God has established His institutional church as the primary ethical model, not the family or the State. Neither the family nor the State – the bringer of exclusively negative sanctions – enters the post-resurrection New Heaven and New Earth; the church does (Rev. 21). But whenever the church refuses to preach and enforce God's revealed law on its own members, the ethical and judicial standards of the political realm will become dominant in the church and family. This is the underlying motivation behind humanism's war against the authority of the church. This is why the State insists that the church does not possess an equal jurisdiction and therefore equal immunity from lawsuits. This is why the enemies of the church promote lawsuits against churches that excommunicate members for such public sins as adultery. (Another reason is income for lawyers.)[47] The humanists have a better grasp of the sociological implications of biblical covenantalism than the Christians do.[48]

Age: Progress and Anarchy in Modern America (New York: Harper & Row, 1988), ch. 1; Jonathan Kwitny, *Endless Enemies: The Making of an Unfriendly World* (New York: Congdon & Weed, 1984).

46. Meredith G. Kline, "Comments on an Old-New Error," *Westminster Theological Journal*, XLI (Fall 1978), p. 184.

47. J. Shelby Sharpe, "The Nuclear Attack on Christianity in America Has Begun in Earnest," *Chalcedon Report* (Nov. 1990), pp. 2-9.

48. The leaders in Jerusalem felt compelled to set up a guard in front of Jesus'

Conclusion

The purification offerings linked ordained rulers to God's covenant people. The representatives of the people in both church and State were bound to the people through the details of God's law. There are no unacknowledged private sins on the part of ordained rulers that do not threaten the safety of the holy commonwealth. The corporate implications of private sins were the reason why rulers had to offer public sacrifice for their unintentional private transgressions of God's law.

The institutional church in the Mosaic social order was basic to the survival of that order. The church was also crucial for the successful defense of liberty. The State possesses concentrated power; without the church's unique power of the gospel, the sacraments, and the threat of excommunication from the Lord's Supper, neither the family nor the institutional church can successfully resist the concentrated power of the modern State. Men's only reasonable hope in such a sanctions-free ecclesiastical world is in the collapse of the existing civil order because of its own incompetence – again, a kind of self-inflicted (autonomous) judgment: the bureaucratic suicide of the existing State.[49] But the problem still remains for reconstruction during the post-collapse era: *By what standard?* Whose sanctions will be enforced, God's or self-proclaimed autonomous man's?

The political theorists of the Enlightenment's right wing, most notably John Locke, lodged ultimate sovereignty in the

tomb in order to keep the disciples from stealing His body and claiming that He had risen from the dead (Matt. 27:62-66). Meanwhile, the disciples had scattered. The covenant-breakers understood the specifics of Jesus' prophecy; the disciples did not. This has been a continuing curse on the church from the beginning.

49. In Eastern (now Central) Europe in the final quarter of 1989, the collapse of Communist rule was in part an act of either treachery against Communism on the part of the ruler or else a highly risky deception of the West – Gorbachev, for whatever reasons, refused to send in the tanks – and in part the prayerful work of the national churches. In this revolt, the churches were recognized as the friends of the people, not the allies of the rulers and the targets of the revolution's rulers, as had been the case in the French and Russian revolutions.

individual. The right wing of the Enlightenment was therefore morally atomistic. This is the legacy of the Whig tradition. This philosophical individualism has greatly influenced Protestantism, especially Anglo-American Protestantism. Protestants do not feel comfortable with doctrines of corporate responsibility. The biblical doctrine of the covenant, especially the civil covenant, disturbs them. But without comprehensive biblical covenantalism, the State is freed from the restraints of biblical law and biblical sanctions. The church is then left to create a tenuous alliance with the family against the State. But the State, with its promise of endless money for education, health, and retirement, eventually lures away the support of families until the State finally goes bankrupt. In nations where the churches are funded by taxation, the allegiance of the churches to God is also compromised. This is why we need a doctrine of the covenant, with God's law at the center, and the with church as the primary counsellor and therefore the primary institution. But this does not alter the primary locus of authority in both church and State: the people, who are at greatest risk of God's historical sanctions. The purification offerings testified to this fact.

5

PROPORTIONAL PAYMENTS TO GOD

And he shall bring his trespass offering unto the Lord *for his sin which he hath sinned, a female from the flock, a lamb or a kid of the goats, for a sin offering; and the priest shall make an atonement for him concerning his sin. And if he be not able to bring a lamb, then he shall bring for his trespass, which he hath committed, two turtledoves, or two young pigeons, unto the* Lord*; one for a sin offering, and the other for a burnt offering (Lev. 5:6-7).*

But if he be not able to bring two turtledoves, or two young pigeons, then he that sinned shall bring for his offering the tenth part of an ephah of fine flour for a sin offering; he shall put no oil upon it, neither shall he put any frankincense thereon: for it is a sin offering. Then shall he bring it to the priest, and the priest shall take his handful of it, even a memorial thereof, and burn it on the altar, according to the offerings made by fire unto the Lord*: it is a sin offering (Lev. 5:11-12).*

This passage extends the law of purification offerings: point four. This was a special form of purification offering that applied to a specific kind of sin: a *sin of omission* (vv. 2-4).[1] A purification offering was required to purify the tabernacle or the

1. The sins were hidden sins. Gordon J. Wenham, *The Book of Leviticus* (Grand Rapids, Michigan: Eerdmans, 1979), p. 100.

temple, so that the worshipper could enter into the presence of God. A burnt offering was the means of reconciling God and man through the sinner's re-dedication.[2] In the case of the turtledoves, one was for the purification offering, while the other was for the burnt offering.[3] Both the sinner and God's sanctified environment had to be cleansed.

Why was a female animal required? James Jordan argues that this was because "The animals represented Israelites in terms of their social or symbolic order." Laymen were regarded as the social brides of God, so their representative sacrifices had to be female.[4] This was a sign of their subordination.

The law granted to the one bringing a sacrifice the right to make a substitution: a less expensive animal for a more expensive animal, or meal for the less expensive animal. The word of the individual regarding his ability to pay was acceptable to the priest unless there was evidence to the contrary. This means that *self-government under God* was the operational assumption of the laws of sacrifice. God delegated considerable authority to the individual to decide how much he could afford to pay, even in the case of a violation of God's law by the individual, although a minor violation.

The Taxation of Capital

What is important for purposes of economic analysis is the fact that this sacrifice to God was proportional to the wealth of the transgressor. Milgrom calls this a graduated purification offering.[5] Because of the deliberately non-proportional nature of the modern income tax – those in higher income brackets

---

2. *Ibid.*, p. 101.

3. *Ibid.*, p. 100. Birds were not used as guilt (reparation) offerings; the second passage therefore must be dealing with purification: *ibid.*, p. 104.

4. James Jordan, "The Whole Burnt Sacrifice: Its Liturgy and Meaning," *Biblical Horizons Occasional Paper*, No. 11, p. 2.

5. Jacob Milgrom, *Leviticus 1-16*, vol. 3 of *The Anchor Bible* (New York: Doubleday, 1991), p. 312.

pay a higher percentage of their income than those in lower brackets – the use of the term "graduated" is misleading. The required payment was proportional. This element of proportionality was analogous to God's required system of ecclesiastical financing: the tithe. The tithe to God is a fixed percentage – 10 percent – of a person's net income from his labor or his net increase from investing. This percentage payment to the local church – and *only* to the local church[5] – is made on the basis of the increase that God gives to a person: "Thou shalt truly tithe all the increase of thy seed, that the field bringeth forth year by year" (Deut. 14:22).

There were cases in which God did require payment on the gross, irrespective of costs of production. One case was the firstfruits offering. Firstfruits was a tiny representative payment, small enough to be carried by a man who walked to Jerusalem. The cost of delivering this payment to the temple was vastly higher than the value of the firstfruits offering itself. Second, the poor were paid out of gross production when they gleaned. Third, a payment was required for the firstborn (Num. 18:15-17). Fourth, when the nation was numbered, all men over age 20 who were eligible to serve in the armed forces paid half a shekel to the priests (Ex. 30:12).[6] But these were either very small payments or infrequent. The major ecclesiastical tax, the tithe, was paid out of net income. In the New Covenant, only the tithe remains as a mandatory payment, so God no longer taxes capital, except in the sense that the sabbath principle must still be honored: forfeited income one day in seven.

---

5. The institutional church is a monopoly institution which alone can lawfully offer the sacraments and which alone collects the tithe on the basis of this sacramental monopoly. See Gary North, *Tools of Dominion: The Case Laws of Exodus* (Tyler, Texas: Institute for Christian Economics, 1990), ch. 32. Cf. Gary North, *Tithing and the Church* (Tyler, Texas: Institute for Christian Economics, 1994), ch. 3.

6. For a summary of these payments, see Alfred Edersheim, *The Temple: Its Ministry and Services As They Were in the Time of Jesus Christ* (Grand Rapids, Michigan: Eerdmans, [1874] 1983), p. 379.

Let us consider the case of a modern farmer. When a farmer begins his career, he has a stock of "after-tithe" seed corn. From this point on, when he saves the *same quantity* of seed corn from a harvest and plants his next crop with it, there is no tithe required on the land's fruitful replacement of that original capital investment. Whatever quantity of seed and other inputs that it took to plant this season's crop is not subject to the tithe. So, if a farmer had to pay wages to his workers through the year, the tithe begins only after he has replaced the equivalent of the wages paid. God taxes only the increase on capital invested. Except for the previously listed payments, there was to be no taxation of gross income in Israel's economy; there should be none today.

This is true for the church's tithe; it is also true for the State.[7] Both church and State must be supported by proportional levies based on income rather than property. A farmer who makes no income in a bad year, but is instead forced to consume capital and borrow, is not to face the threat of the confiscation of his inheritance by either church officers or tax collectors merely because he holds legal title to land and equipment. The same objection applies to a head tax or a poll (voting) tax.[8] God's monopolistic ministries of church and State are to prosper economically only to the extent that their members do. God authorizes both church and State to tax success at a low, common, fixed rate, with the combined taxes of all branches of the State at less than the tithe (I Sam. 8:15, 17). Neither institution is authorized to tax the capital that makes success possible.

---

7. R. J. Rushdoony, *The Institutes of Biblical Law* (Nutley, New Jersey: Craig Press, 1973), p. 283.

8. God does not impose a head tax. North, *Tools of Dominion*, ch. 32. In the fall of 1990, Prime Minister Margaret Thatcher of England was forced to resign from her position by her own political party. The Conservative Party had suffered a serious decline in popularity as a result of decision to add a kind of head tax to the existing property tax. (Had she not strongly opposed England's entry into the European Community, she might have retained her office.)

Off the Top

God is entitled a tithe on our net productivity. His share comes "off the top." But the modern State in many cases demands this initial payment, leaving the church with a tithe on whatever remains. This is wicked but common. In the United States, the taxpayer is allowed to deduct payments to charitable organizations before the U.S. government assesses an income tax on whatever remains. But this is not the case with the Social Security (old age pension) payroll tax, which is euphemistically called a contribution. The U.S. government collects its tax on total wage income – no deductions allowed. This is standard practice in most nations with respect to the taxation of all income.

The question arises: Does the Christian owe God a tithe on his pre-tax net income? He does if the State does not collect the tax first. But if the State collects the money "off the top" and does not allow the taxpayer to deduct his tithe payments from his gross income before estimating his income tax obligation, the answer is clear: the tithe is 10 percent of whatever remains after the tax collector has collected the State's immorally extracted tax. The State has stolen from God: sacrilege. This is not the tithe-payer's responsibility. He is a victim. If the tithe-payer had to pay a tithe on his pre-tax income, God would be taxing what the tithe-payer never received. This would constitute a tax on capital.

Put another way, God does not tax us on that portion of our net crop that the locusts eat. Tax collectors are the economic equivalent of locusts, except that we can lawfully eat locusts.

On the other hand, if the State allows us to deduct our tithe payments before it computes our taxable income, we owe the tithe on our pre-tax income. God should always get paid first. If a man takes in a hundred ounces of gold a year, net, and he pays his tithe, the State should tax him on the remaining 90 ounces. If it collects a tax equal to the tithe – immoral (I Sam. 8:17) – it receives 9 ounces. An even more immoral State will collect 10 ounces, leaving the tithe-payer with 90 ounces of gold after taxes. He then pays 9 ounces to the church. In both examples, he retains 81 ounces. In the first example, the church collects 10 ounces and the State collects 9; in the second example, it is the reverse. The first example is closer to God's standards than the second.

Sharecropping

We can understand this better if we think of the pre-twentieth-century agricultural practice of sharecropping. Land owners owned land and capital. (Capital is the product of land and labor over time).[9] After slavery was abolished, they no longer owned people. Instead, they hired people.[10] Rather than paying them wages, land owners leased to sharecroppers tools and land. Owners concluded that it was less expensive to monitor economic results – a local crop – than it was to monitor the productivity of their employees' labor inputs to the production process, requiring them to specify a wage for these labor inputs.[10] What mattered to land owners was results, not labor inputs. ("Activity is no substitute for production.")

Hourly wages are based on the average productivity of a particular class of workers. An above-average producer in any given class is usually much better off to become a sharecropper, a piece-rate worker, or a commissioned salesman. He is paid in terms of his measurable net productivity, not in terms of his

9. Murray N. Rothbard, *Man, Economy, and State: A Treatise on Economic Principles* (Auburn, Alabama: Mises Institute, [1962] 1993), pp. 285-88.

10. In the American South, 1865-80, sharecropping became a way of life for ex-slaves and ex-slave owners. It was a cost-effective system for a defeated post-war society with minimal financial capital. Roger Ransom and Richard Sutch, *One Kind of Freedom: The economic consequences of emancipation* (New York: Cambridge University Press, 1977).

10. The cost of monitoring people's behavior is fundamental in the evolution of economic and political institutions. Thomas Sowell, *Knowledge and Decisions* (New York: Basic Books, 1980), pp. 55-56, 65-66, 111-12, 215-26. See Sowell's index for more entries: "Monitoring."

membership in a class of laborers. The lower the percentage of the crop owed contractually to the owner, the better this arrangement is for the efficient producer. To gain the services of such workers, owners are willing to take a lower percentage of the crop: a smaller percentage of a much larger pie.

God is the owner; we are His sharecroppers. He does not tax capital today for the same reason that the land owner does not tax his own land and tools. They are being used by the sharecroppers to produce a crop. The land owner collects a fixed percentage of the crop after the replacement of seed and tools. So does God. God demands a low percentage of our net output – 10 percent to the church; less that 10 percent to the State – in order to encourage us to work efficiently. He does not have to monitor our inputs except for prohibiting our labor one day a week. He authorizes His agents, meaning ordained ministers (church and State), to monitor our net output and collect God's mandated share.

This system of taxation is appropriate to a decentralized economic order. It is consistent with God's system of representative government. God's kingdom, unlike Satan's, is not a top-down commonwealth. God delegates tremendous authority and responsibility to the individual. He treats us as sharecroppers: people who are responsible for final results, not bureaucratic wage-earners. This structure of ownership and taxation is why a Christian social order rewards economic growth rather than time-serving. God as the owner is paid in terms of our net productivity, not a fixed tax. We sharecroppers keep the lion's share of our crop: above 80 percent in a society that honors God's law. The twentieth century has not honored it. It has suffered wars, taxation, inflation, regulation, and socialist impoverization as its appropriate reward. God is not mocked.

God assigns the costs of ownership to owners because he allows them to reap the dual harvest of rent and profit. The owner's task is to add value to whatever has been placed under his authority. Only through private ownership can both the costs and rewards of production be rationally calculated by society.[11]

The Ability to Pay

All sin is an affront to God. The rich man's sin as well as the poor man's sin enrages God. But there is this distinction: the rich man has sinned in the face of greater blessings from God. He therefore owes more to God than the poor man does in absolute terms. Making restitution to God is supposed to hurt, but one man's economic pain is another man's economic destruction. Thus, sinners are to make restitution to God in terms of the proportional benefits they expected to gain from their sin.

A fundamental biblical principle is invoked at this point: *from him to whom much is given, much is expected*. The context of this rule is the imposition of God's eternal sanctions (Luke 12:42-48). If this system of proportional sanctions is true throughout eternity, then it surely must be true in terms of the restitution payments in history owed to God by men. Marx's principle of expectation and economic remuneration is therefore wrong: "From each according to his ability, to each according to his needs!"[12] The first half of the statement is correct; the second half is true only in the case of the physically or mentally incompetent, or those who in the West were for centuries referred to as "the deserving poor"[13] The general rule is this: "To each according to market value of his *actual production*." We know this from the parable: "And the Lord said, Who then is that

---

11. Gary North, *Boundaries and Dominion: The Economics of Leviticus* (computer edition; Tyler, Texas: Institute for Christian Economics, 1994), ch. 5, section on "Costs of Ownership."

12. Karl Marx, *The Critique of the Gotha Program* (1875); in Karl Marx and Frederick Engels, *Selected Works*, 3 vols. (Moscow: Progress Publishers, 1969), III, p. 19. Marx stole this phrase from Morelly's *Code de la Nature* (1755-60).

13. Peter Mathias, *The First Industrial Nation: An Economic History of Britain, 1700-1914* (New York: Scribner's, 1969), p. 26.

faithful and wise steward, whom his lord shall make ruler over his household, to give them their portion of meat in due season? Blessed is that servant, whom his lord when he cometh shall find so doing. Of a truth I say unto you, that he will make him ruler over all that he hath" (Luke 12:42-44).

Discontinuities of Sacrifice

When men were required by God to sacrifice animals as substitutes, the priests faced a problem: How were the required restitution payments to correspond with the sinner's ability to pay? When the tithe was owed, this payment could be estimated easily: so many pieces of silver or so many units of grain. It could also be done in terms of so many animals. "And concerning the tithe of the herd, or of the flock, even of whatsoever passeth under the rod, the tenth shall be holy unto the LORD. He shall not search whether it be good or bad, neither shall he change it and if he change it at all, then both it and the change thereof shall be holy; it shall not be redeemed" (Lev. 27:32-33). The animals would be lined up randomly and passed under a rod; every tenth animal was culled out of the flock to be given to the Lord. If a man saw that a favorite animal was lost to this procedure, he could redeem it by paying its market value plus 20 percent (Lev. 27:31). If he in any way tampered with the lining-up process, he could not subsequently redeem the animal. Thus, God created risks for tampering with the flock; if the herdsman miscalculated in his prohibited calculations, he could lose a cherished animal.[14]

The animal sacrifice system created a problem that did not exist to the same degree in the case of the tithe. A tithe was proportional to net increase. A net increase could be measured or at least estimated fairly well. But offering an animal sacrifice was not the same as paying God a fixed proportion of net income. A specific kind of sin required a specific sacrifice. The

14. Chapter 38, below.

nature of the sin determined the nature of the sacrifice. Then how could God maintain the principle of *proportional pain?* Had the sacrifice been a specified amount of money, either the rich man would have paid too little proportional to his economic benefits in life or the poor man would have paid too much. The penalty would not have been proportional.

There is no way to sacrifice one-third of an animal without killing it. This is the problem of *sacrificial discontinuity*. Thus, proportional restitution to God is not possible in a world that requires a single type of animal sacrifice. If killing a lamb or goat is the only legitimate way to placate God, then both the rich man and the poor man have to pay it. But this would violate the biblical principle of greater responsibility on the part of those possessing greater wealth.

The problem of sacrificial discontinuity is reflected in the specified sacrificial animals in Leviticus 5: lambs or goats, a pair of birds,[15] or fine flour and oil. The payment for sin to God (as distinguished from an earthly victim) was not to be made in terms of money, except by someone who was willing to pay an extra 20 percent to buy back (redeem) the animal. The wealth (capital) of the sinner was to determine which animal he was to sacrifice, or even if he was to sacrifice an animal. The poor man could legitimately sacrifice fine flour and still meet the judicial requirement, but the sacrifice had to impose pain on the sinner. The sacrifice was to reflect or represent the intensity of the negative sanction he was avoiding, on earth and in eternity.

Rich Man, Average Man, Poor Man

The tripartite division that we commonly make in class analysis – upper, middle, and lower – is reflected in this passage. The idea that each wealth group was bound by differing ritual obligations pointed to the biblical principle of *present obligations*

---

15. One for a purification offering and the other for a burnt offering: Wenham, *Leviticus*, p. 100.

in terms of *prior benefits*. If the rich man imagined that he could escape God's condemnation by the payment of a trifle, he did not understand God's analysis of the nature of the specific infraction. The earthly restitution payment to God was to be a token of the required eternal payment, what Paul called an *earnest* (Eph. 1:14), meaning a down payment. God promises to inflict great pain for sin in eternity; the pain endured by sinners in history is to reflect this coming pain. The sanctions of Israel's sacrificial system were designed to teach this lesson before it was too late for repentance.

On the other hand, had the poor man been expected to pay a rich man's obligation, he would have lost sight of the reality of differing sins: any sin would bankrupt him. Such a restitution system would economically subsidize the worst sins by poor people. Why not commit really serious infractions if the end result in history is the same for great and minor infractions, i.e., bankruptcy and enslavement? To impose an impossibly high penalty on all crimes or sins is to make it equally expensive to commit all crimes or all sins. Man being what he is – totally depraved apart from God's grace – this system of sanctions would be a subsidy to his depraved nature. It would be comparable to imposing the death penalty for murdering a policeman and also for stealing a bicycle. It would result in extreme danger for any policeman attempting to arrest a bicycle thief. The thief would know that killing the policeman would not result in any greater earthly penalty. This assessment of comparative risk would eventually lead to very high expenses for the arrest of suspected bicycle thieves. Squads of police would have to be allocated to the arrest every suspected bicycle thief. Meanwhile, someone calling the police department's emergency phone number in order to stop a murder might find that there were very few police left to respond; too many of them would be assigned to arresting some armed and dangerous bicycle thief.

Conclusion

The Bible teaches the principle of proportional tithing and proportional restitution to God. The problem with animal sacrifices in the Old Covenant was that they could not be precisely proportional: men cannot slay just half an animal. Thus, God imposed a system of different sacrifices for people of varying wealth.

The priests collected the sacrifices, and they could lawfully use them personally: "And the priest shall make an atonement for him as touching his sin that he hath sinned in one of these, and it shall be forgiven him: and the remnant shall be the priest's, as a meat offering" (Lev. 5:13). But these sacrifices were not part of a predictable stream of income. These payments were the result of specific sins. These penalties were not based on income but on the sinner's total wealth; they were specific restitution payments. They were the economic equivalent of sin taxes – *literal* sin taxes to God through His church. This system enabled men to reduce these sin taxes by sinning less frequently.

The market value of these sacrifices was limited by the wealth of the sinner. This was to make certain that every sinner felt the appropriate pain of economic loss; it would remind him of the eternal loss to come. There were "different strokes for different folks" only to make sure that *all the folks felt an appropriate degree of economic pain.* Had the sacrificial system been strictly a system of fines, the proportionality of the sanctions would have been easy to maintain. Because a living animal is not divisible on the same basis as monetary fines, God established a system of differing sacrifices for the same transgression, so that all transgressors were to feel a similar psychological burden for their transgressions irrespective of their net worth.

6

SACRED, PROFANE, AND COMMON

And the LORD *spake unto Moses, saying, If a soul commit a trespass, and sin through ignorance, in the holy things of the* LORD*; then he shall bring for his trespass unto the* LORD *a ram without blemish out of the flocks, with thy estimation by shekels of silver, after the shekel of the sanctuary, for a trespass offering: And he shall make amends for the harm that he hath done in the holy thing, and shall add the fifth part thereto, and give it unto the priest: and the priest shall make an atonement for him with the ram of the trespass offering, and it shall be forgiven him. And if a soul sin, and commit any of these things which are forbidden to be done by the commandments of the* LORD*; though he wist it not [unaware], yet is he guilty, and shall bear his iniquity. And he shall bring a ram without blemish out of the flock, with thy estimation, for a trespass offering, unto the priest: and the priest shall make an atonement for him concerning his ignorance wherein he erred and wist it not, and it shall be forgiven him. It is a trespass offering: he hath certainly trespassed against the* LORD *(Lev. 5:14-19).*

The theocentric meaning of this passage is that there are degrees of sin in trespass. Some sins are committed in ignorance. The two greatest sins in history were committed by some of the participants in ignorance: the fall of man – Eve was ignorant (I Tim. 2:13b) – and the crucifixion of Christ: the Roman soldiers were ignorant (Luke 23:34). Nevertheless, ignorance is no defense. Reparation for transgression is still necessary.

This is the fifth sacrifice: a guilt (reparation) offering.[1] As the fifth offering, it was associated with point five of the biblical covenant model: succession or inheritance. It had to do with *continuity*. To be restored to the legal status he had enjoyed before the transgression, the trespasser had to offer a sacrifice. The transgression had been individual. The judicial implication of the passage is this: the sanctions God would apply to the transgressor would be personal, not corporate. His sin was not representational. He had transgressed a holy thing or a holy commandment. Thus, the appropriate institutional sanction was ecclesiastical: excommunication. This would cause him to lose his inheritance in Israel: his land, but more important, his citizenship.[2] To continue as a free man in Israel – to leave an inheritance to his children – he had to offer a sacrifice.

A Trespass Offering

A 20 percent penalty was applied to the transgression of a holy thing. Not so with a transgression of one of God's commandments. Here is the theological question: Why the difference?

The King James translators translated the Hebrew word *'asham* as *trespass*. The English word "trespass" is readily associated with a boundary violation, as in "No Trespassing." The New American Standard Bible translates *'asham* as *guilt*. So did the medieval Jewish commentator Nachmanides.[3] Grammatically, this is the more precise translation. What is described here is a *guilt offering*. A person in ignorance commits a trans-

---

1. Jacob Milgrom, *Leviticus 1-16*, vol. 3 of *The Anchor Bible* (New York: Doubleday, 1991), p. 319.

2. See Chapter 31, below: "Slaves and Freemen."

3. Ramban [Rabbi Moshe ben Nachman], *Commentary on the Torah: Leviticus* (New York: Shilo, [1267?] 1974), p. 55.

gression of God's law, later recognizes this infraction, and then offers sacrifice to pay for his transgression. He recognizes his own guilt, and he then offers a sacrifice as his acknowledgment. Nevertheless, the King James Version comes closer to the theological meaning of the type of transgression involved: a *trespass* – a boundary violation – in the same sense that Adam's sin involved a transgression of the judicial boundary which God had placed around the forbidden fruit. Adam and Eve were indeed guilty, but their guilt was based on a literal trespass.

Holy Things and Holy Commandments

This passage rests on a distinction between holy things of the Lord and holy commandments. A transgression of holy things in ignorance required a 20 percent penalty plus the offering of a ram (vv. 15-16). In contrast, a transgression of God's commandment in ignorance required only the sacrifice of the animal (v. 18). This seemingly minor distinction becomes the basis of the analysis of the present chapter – specifically, acknowledging the biblical distinction between the sacred and the common, but denying the legitimacy of a far more widely accepted distinction: *sacred vs. profane*. The latter distinction undergirded ancient and modern religion.[4] This false distinction has become an important aspect of modern sociology and anthropology, especially as a result of the work of Émile Durkheim.[5] One of the most serious errors that has resulted from a misunderstanding of the biblical categories of sacred, common, and profane is the false distinction between what is sometimes called full-time Christian service and secular employment. Full-time Christian service is regarded as sacred; secular employment is

4. Gary North, *Boundaries and Dominion: The Economics of Leviticus* (computer edition; Tyler, Texas: Institute for Christian Economics, 1994), ch. 6, section on "False Distinctions Within Ancient and Modern Religion."

5. See my detailed treatment of Durkheim's error in this regard: *ibid.*, ch. 6, section on "False Distinctions Within Modern Academia."

seen as common when not actually profane. This theological confusion has led to the retreat of Christians from leadership in the arts, industry, and most other fields.[6]

Under the Mosaic Covenant, an inadvertent violation of God's commands was settled by paying the victim whatever he had lost as a result of the transgression. The ethical transgression covered by this law must have been a transgression of one of God's verbal boundaries; no human victim is identified here. God did not impose a 20 percent payment in addition to the sacrifice of a ram for the violation of a commandment (Lev. 5:17-18). But when someone violated a sacred space or sacred object, he violated God's word (the law) as well as the actual thing or space (Lev. 5:15-16). *The transgression was a double boundary violation: word and place.* The penalty was therefore greater.

Sacred Boundaries

There is so much confusion over the relationship between the sacred and the common that interpreters have tended to misrepresent the relationship. *They have confused the common with the profane.* This false interpretation has undermined Christian social and ethical theory whenever it has appeared. It makes the common appear as if it were a realm "naturally" opposed to grace and ultimately beyond grace – legitimately so in history. *This places a boundary around grace.* The interpreters have not understood that every created thing begins as common and remains common unless judicially sanctified: actively set apart by God or His law. Nothing begins as profane; it must become profane, just as something becomes sanctified. This may seem like a minor point, but it is not, as we shall see.

The sacred here refers to the sacramental, i.e., having to do with the twin covenantal signs of ecclesiastical subordination: in

6. *Ibid.*, ch. 6, section on "Full-Time Christian Service."

the Mosaic Covenant, circumcision and Passover; in the New Covenant, baptism and the Lord's Supper. The word *sacrament* comes from the Latin word *sacramentum*, a military oath of enlistment.[7]

Anything that violates these holy things of the Lord is considered profane. In contrast, anything that violates a non-holy thing is not considered profane. Such a violation is illegal, but it is not profane. This is the heart of my thesis in this chapter: the association of the biblical concept of *profane* with *unique acts of violation*, namely, violations of a boundary surrounding a judicially holy place or holy object. Profanity in the broadest sense is a breach of a judicial wall of separation between the holy and the common.

Leviticus 5:14-19 offers evidence of a judicial distinction between the sacred and the common, but this difference is minimal in the case of unintentional transgressions: a 20 percent penalty for violating either a sacred object or sacred space (vv. 15-16). What kind of boundary had been transgressed? Was it geographical? This seems unlikely. We know that the common Israelite was not permitted to enter the inner core of the temple, on threat of death (Ex. 28:43). He would never have been in a position to commit a tabernacle or temple trespass in ignorance. Furthermore, no common priest in his right mind would have tried to enter the holy of holies. He could not have committed such a transgression ignorantly. So, the element of the sacred here must refer to something broader in scope than the performance of temple rituals.

If we are properly to understand the nature of each type of transgression in Leviticus 5:14-19 – each type of boundary violation – we must first understand what the idea of the sacred meant under the Old Covenant. Then, and only then, can we

7. "Sacrament," in *Cyclopaedia of Biblical, Theological, and Ecclesiastical Literature*, edited by John M'Clintock and James Strong, 12 vols. (New York: Harper & Bros., 1894), IX, p. 212.

begin to understand the meaning of the Bible's concept of the profane.

Profane Violations of the Sacred

What "the sacred" refers to is something pertaining to *the ecclesiastical activity of the priesthood in its broadest sense*. Something that belongs to God must not be misused or appropriated unlawfully. Something delegated for exclusive use by God's priesthood must not be used by an unauthorized agent, or used in an unauthorized way by an authorized agent. To understand what this improper (profane) usage might have been, we need first to consider what it could not have been. To do this, we must consider false interpretations – some ancient, some modern – of the biblical distinction between sacred and common.

In the Bible, the contrast between sacred and profane is never a contrast between a sacred object or place and a geographically separate object or place. The biblical contrast of sacred vs. profane is between a sacramental object or place and something common, i.e., something non-sacramental, that is *unlawfully inside* a sacred boundary. This distinction is ultimately a contrast between *something* lawfully inside a boundary and *someone* unlawfully inside.

Both realms on each side of the boundary are judicially legitimate: the sacred realm and the common realm. The contrast in Leviticus 5:14-16 is not between the sacred and the common; it is the contrast between sacred and profane. The biblical contrast between sacred and profane is not a contrast between moral opposites; it is instead *a distinction between judicially authorized forms of worship*: sacramental vs. non-sacramental. As I argue throughout this chapter, there is a biblical distinction between sacred and profane, but this distinction is not the equally biblical distinction between sacred and common. These two completely separate sets of distinctions have been repeatedly intermingled by commentators. This confusion of categories has led to some disastrous false distinctions, as we shall see.

Christians can better understand the biblical distinctions between "sacred vs. common" and "sacred vs. profane" by considering the difference between a communion meal held during a worship service in church and a family meal eaten at home by a Christian family. Both meals are equally religious. Both meals are legitimately introduced by prayer. But only one meal is sacramental: the church's communion meal. What must be understood from the beginning of our discussion is this: *the family meal is not profane*. It is common, but it is not profane. Also, it is religious despite its legal status as common.

It is incorrect to contrast an inherently sacred place with an inherently profane place. A sacred place has been made sacred by the *judicial declaration* of God or by a priest acting in God's name. It has been sanctified: set apart judicially. It is neither naturally nor metaphysically sacred. Similarly, there can be no naturally or metaphysically profane place in the way that there can be a naturally common place. A profane place is a *violated sacred place*. It has been the victim of an illegal trespass. The Hebrew word translated most frequently as "profane" (*khawlawl*) is usually translated as "slain."[8] It is sometimes translated as "wounded" (I Sam. 17:52). This Hebrew word means *pierced*. It conveys the sense of someone's having violated a boundary. The word is not used in the sense of a common place that just sits there being common. A common place cannot become profane, for it possesses no sacred boundary to trespass; only a sacred place can become profane.

The Sacred as Priestly

What is "the sacred," biblically speaking? It is not merely the religious sensibility in man, a need analogous to the need for food or sex, as modern academic usage would have it. Rather, it has to do with the church's sacraments. In its narrowest

---

8. Num. 19:16; 19:18; 23:24; and dozens of other verses.

sense, the sacred refers to *formal ecclesiastical acts of covenantal subordination*: applying the covenant mark[9] and partaking of the covenant meal.[10] That which pertains to the sacred is formally under the authority of an ordained church officer. This officer's task is to restrict certain people's access beyond certain specified judicial boundaries. These boundaries are always legal and are sometimes spatial.

There is a biblical distinction between the sacred and the profane, yet they are always linked. A sacred act involves the lawful crossing of a sacred boundary, meaning *a boundary guarded by ordained priests*. A profane act is the unlawful crossing of a priestly boundary, meaning a *judicially segregated* area of atonement. The transgressor has either invaded sacred space or has misused a sacred object that has been set aside by God for a particular use. The essence of the distinction between sacred and profane, biblically speaking, is judicial rather than metaphysical. The profane act is *ritually unauthorized*, either because of the legal status of the transgressor (a non-priest) or because of restrictions placed by God against specific acts by even a priest. It is the *crossing of the boundary* that constitutes the profane act.

When Adam sinned, he violated a legal boundary. It was not that he ate of a magical tree (realism). It was not that he ate of a symbolic tree that transformed his consciousness or self-awareness only (nominalism). He ate of a judicially prohibited tree (covenantalism).[11] He violated sacred space.[12] In the New Covenant, permanent sacred space no longer exists: the special dwelling place of God. It exists only during formal worship services. Sacred objects do exist: the sacraments during worship.[13]

---

9. In the Old Covenant, circumcision; in the New Covenant, baptism.

10. In the Mosaic Covenant, Passover; in the New Covenant, the Lord's Supper.

11. North, *Boundaries and Dominion*, ch. 6, section on "Adam's Transgression."

12. *Ibid.*, ch. 6, section on "Sacred Objects, Sacred Space."

13. *Ibid.*, ch. 6, section on "Sacred Space in the New Covenant Era."

Nature and Grace

The removal of sacred boundaries in the New Covenant does not imply that nature (the common) is somehow swallowing up grace (the sacred). It is not that nature is pushing grace into ever-smaller corners of man's existence. The Bible teaches that all of nature is sustained by God's grace, i.e., God's unearned gifts to men, beasts, and even demons. He gives us life, time, knowledge, and power, none of which is in any way autonomously deserved by the recipients. Ours is a providentially sustained world. In the New Covenant, as in the Old, nature does not swallow up grace. *Both the sacred and the common are under grace*.

God's special grace to His people – and only to His people – is the foundation, judicially (justification) and ethically (sanctification), of comprehensive transformation, both personal and cultural. Special grace is *marked publicly* by the presence of church sacraments. Grace is *empowered spiritually* by the sacraments, but it is not restricted to (bounded by) the sacraments. Special grace also operates in the realm outside the institutional church: in family and State covenants, and in all the other social institutions that are under the lawful jurisdictions (plural) of family and State.

Not only does nature not swallow up grace in history, the realm of common grace is steadily transformed by special grace, either through widespread conversions or by example and imitation by the unconverted for the sake of the external positive sanctions associated with external covenant-keeping.[14] To deny that common grace is affected by what takes place in the realm of special grace is necessarily to deny the covenantal basis of New Covenant history: progress or decline in terms of covenant-keeping. The directionality of history then loses its character as biblically progressive; its events becomes random, cov-

14. Gary North, *Dominion and Common Grace: The Biblical Basis of Progress* (Tyler, Texas: Institute for Christian Economics, 1987).

enantally speaking. History is then seen as linear but not progressive.[15]

The biblically valid distinction between the sacred and the non-sacramental reminds us that *all of nature is under grace*, either special or common. Without the unearned gifts (grace) of life, law, time, and knowledge, and power, there could be no history.[16] The processes of nature have been definitively redeemed by Jesus Christ by His death, resurrection, and ascension.[17] This is equally true of culture. The Bible is clear: nature is sustained by God's common grace and is progressively sanctified in history in response to His extension of special grace to the church. *Grace progressively redeems nature in history because Jesus Christ definitively redeemed nature at Calvary*. Nature is therefore sanctified: definitively, progressively, and finally.

What Constituted "Ignorant Profanity"?

A profane act involves the misuse of God's name. It is primarily a priestly misrepresentation of God. Profanity is worse when committed by an ordained special priest (guardian of the sacraments) than by a non-ordained special priest (guardian of the kingdom), i.e., a redeemed person. It can also be committed by a general priest, i.e., an unredeemed person under Adam's original priestly status.[18] These profane acts are public acts.

Leviticus 5:14-19 referred to a profane act committed in ignorance. A profane act under the Old Covenant necessarily involved the church, for it involved some aspect of the sacraments, i.e., the priesthood. To violate the office of priest, either

15. This is Meredith G. Kline's view of New Covenant history: Kline, "Comments on an Old-New Error," *Westminster Theological Journal*, XLI (Fall 1978), p. 184.

16. North, *Dominion and Common Grace*.

17. North, *Is the World Running Down?*

18. North, *Boundaries and Dominion*, ch. 6, sections on "Profanity, Priesthoods, and Pagans" and "New Covenant Sanctions."

as a priest or as a layman, was considered profane. If done in ignorance, there was an added penalty of one-fifth.

There was an ownership principle involved. God had established legal boundaries around the sacraments: spatial boundaries and liturgical boundaries. These were ultimately *ownership boundaries*, analogous to the boundary He placed around the tree of the knowledge of good and evil. *That which belongs exclusively to God is specially protected by law*. Jesus' distinction between God and Caesar would apply here: render to each what is lawfully claimed by each (Matt. 22:21).[19] God is sacred; Caesar is common. (It was this confession that later became the legal basis of the Roman Empire's persecution of Christians.) Jesus' distinction between God and Mammon would not apply here: no one should ever serve Mammon. No one should ever be profane (Mammon: false worship). What was established in Leviticus 5:14-19 was a legal distinction between sacred and common, not between sacred and profane. *That which is common cannot be profaned*.

What did the church in the Mosaic Covenant require? The sacrifice of unblemished animals, for one thing. What if a man had ignorantly offered an animal with a defect – a disease, for example? He had mistakenly brought the wrong animal to the altar. He owed another animal, plus a penalty payment of one-fifth. Since he could not kill one-fifth of an animal, a monetary equivalent according to the shekels of the temple was allowed. To offer a blemished animal was the equivalent of stealing from God – profaning His table-altar (Mal. 1:8-12). God's warning was clear: "But ye have profaned it, in that ye say, The table of the LORD is polluted; and the fruit thereof, even his meat, is contemptible" (Mal. 1:12).

19. Because God brings Caesars to the throne who unlawfully claim far more than a tithe, we are usually to obey even the unlawful claims. God brings such men to power in order to judge us. However, God allowed Jeroboan to revolt against Rehoboam in protest against Rehoboam's taxes (I Ki. 12).

What else would have come under the law against profanity? Tithes. The tithes were to be set aside to God. They were His property, collected and administered solely by the priesthood. To refuse to pay a tithe to the local Levite was the legal equivalent of stealing from God (Mal. 3:8-9). If a person discovered in retrospect that he had earned more net income than he had originally calculated, he owed more to God. This would have been an unintentional transgression. He now owed the tithe, plus an animal sacrifice, plus an extra 20 percent on that portion of the tithe that he had neglected to pay. If he had earned an additional ten ounces of silver, he owed, first, an additional ounce to the Levite. He would also have been required to offer an animal sacrifice, plus pay an additional one-fifth of an ounce to the Levite.

A person might also have made a complicated vow to God. If he neglected to fulfill all of its terms, he would have owed the extra payment.

The civil government of every nation should impose sanctions against public verbal profanity. It is a form of assault. The third commandment is binding on all nations. No one is allowed by God to transgress the boundary placed around His name. No civil government ought to tolerate such transgressions. The inherited general status of priest to which all men are born as sons of Adam brings all men under God's civil laws regarding profanity. It is on this legal basis, among others, that the civil government of a formally covenanted Christian nation could and should bring sanctions against certain practices of cults and rival religions: their public transgression of God's sacramental boundaries. *Sacrilege is a civil offense*.

Unintentional sacrilege seems far less likely in a modern nation that is not formally covenanted to God. That it could take place in Old Covenant Israel is clear. It is far less clear how laws against unintentional violations of priestly boundaries would apply today.

Conclusion

A non-deliberate trespass of a holy thing required a 20 percent penalty payment plus a slain ram. A non-deliberate trespass of God's commandment required only a slain ram. The trespass of a holy thing was the greater (i.e., worse) trespass.

The importance today of these two Levitical laws governing these two guilt offerings lies in their distinctions and varying penalties. The Levitical distinctions between "the holy things of the Lord" and "the commandments of the Lord" enable us to discern a fundamental distinction between the sacred and the non-sacramental (i.e., the common or conventional). The common is obviously not profane, for this realm includes God's commandments. There is surely nothing inherently profane about "the commandments of the Lord" or the comprehensive realms of life governed by them. What *is* profane is any transgression of "the holy things of the Lord." These Levitical laws therefore reveal the error of the standard textbook distinctions drawn between "sacred and profane" and "religious and secular."

There is remarkably little discussion of the ascension of Christ in modern orthodox theology.[20] This topic inevitably raises fundamental historical, cosmological, and cultural implications that modern premillennial and especially amillennial theologians find difficult to accept, such as the progressive manifestation of Christ's rule in history through His representatives: Christians.[21] In a world in which grace is believed to be progressively devoured by nature, there is little room for historical applications of the doctrine of the historical ascension.

---

20. Gary North, *Millennialism and Social Theory* (Tyler, Texas: Institute for Christian Economics, 1990), pp. 227-29.

21. No theological or eschatological school denies that there can be prolonged set-backs in this manifestation of Christ's rule. Conversely, none would totally deny progress. I know of no one who would argue, for example, that the creeds of the church prior to the fourth century were more rigorous or more accurate theologically than those that came later.

Covenantal postmillennialism alone can confidently discuss the doctrine of Christ's ascension, for postmillennialism does not seek to confine the effects of Christ's ascension to the realms of the internal and the trans-historical.[22] That is to say, postmillennialism does not assert the existence of supposedly inevitable boundaries around the effects of grace in history. On the contrary, it asserts that all such boundaries will be progressively overcome in history, until on judgment day the very gates (boundaries) of hell will not be able to stand against the church (Matt. 16:18).[23]

It is now the task of Christians to work out progressively in history the implications of what these definitive transformations have already accomplished judicially. *Whatever God has declared judicially, He requires to be manifested progressively*. This dominion assignment to His people involves extensive personal responsibility, which is why dominion theology is resisted so adamantly by pietists. But the church has been given a written Bible, the Holy Spirit, and the division of labor (I Cor. 12) to enable Christians to extend God's dominion covenant. This historical task is huge, but our tools are more than adequate.

Sadly, most Christians in my generation prefer intellectual slumber and life in a cultural ghetto, living on "hand-me-downs" from the world of humanism. They, too, have adopted the false dualisms of humanism: sacred vs. profane, religious vs. secular, nature vs. grace. They, too, have adopted the view that

---

22. This is why amillennialism drifts so easily into Barthianism: the history of mankind for the amillennialist has no visible connection with the ascension of Jesus Christ. Progressive sanctification in this view is limited to the personal and ecclesiastical; it is never cultural or civic. The ascension of Christ has no transforming implications for society in amillennial theology. The ascension was both historical and publicly visible; its implications supposedly are not. The Barthian is simply more consistent than the amillennialist: he denies the historicity of both Jesus' ascension and His subsequent grace to society. Christ's ascension, like His grace, is relegated to the trans-historical. North, *Millennialism and Social Theory*, pp. 111-13.

23. Kenneth L. Gentry, Jr., *He Shall Have Dominion: A Postmillennial Eschatology* (Tyler, Texas: Institute for Christian Economics, 1992), chaps. 12, 13.

without Jesus' bodily presence in history, nature swallows up grace.

Nature should not be contrasted with grace, for it is part of God's common grace and can be renewed (healed) over time through comprehensive covenantal faithfulness. *Nature should be contrasted with the sacramental: a judicially segregated realm. Both realms are equally under grace*. Therefore, nature (the common) – families, businesses, civil government, etc. – can be healed progressively in history by special grace. This is one application of the doctrine of the bodily ascension of Christ: overcoming death in history.

In contrast to the biblical view of nature and grace stand all forms of anti-Christianity. *In all non-Christian systems, nature swallows up grace in history*. Tragically for the history of the church, both amillennialism and premillennialism necessarily adopt this non-Christian view of nature and grace in history (i.e., the period prior to Jesus Christ's bodily return). The world supposedly remains under the accelerating curses of God, deteriorating both ethically and physically (the entropy process). The common blessings of God in history are progressively overwhelmed by the common curses.[24]

Nature does not swallow up grace. Nature is not separate from grace; nature is under grace. For example, all Christian service is under God's special grace. All Christian service is in this sense redemptive. When a Christian engages in any honest labor, he is engaged in full-time Christian service. But he is not engaged in full-time sacred service. Sacred service is limited to the performance of the formal duties of an ecclesiastical ministry: preaching the gospel in worship services, serving the sacraments, anointing the sick with oil (James 5:14), etc. Formal church worship involves an added layer of holiness, i.e., judicial separation. This is why it can be profaned.

---

24. North, *Millennialism and Social Theory*, ch. 4.

7

GUARDIAN OF THE CIVIL OATH

And the L*ORD spake unto Moses, saying, If a soul sin, and commit a trespass against the* L*ORD, and lie unto his neighbour in that which was delivered him to keep, or in fellowship, or in a thing taken away by violence, or hath deceived his neighbour; Or have found that which was lost, and lieth concerning it, and sweareth falsely; in any of all these that a man doeth, sinning therein: Then it shall be, because he hath sinned, and is guilty, that he shall restore that which he took violently away, or the thing which he hath deceitfully gotten, or that which was delivered him to keep, or the lost thing which he found, Or all that about which he hath sworn falsely; he shall even restore it in the principal, and shall add the fifth part more thereto, and give it unto him to whom it appertaineth, in the day of his trespass offering. And he shall bring his trespass offering unto the* L*ORD, a ram without blemish out of the flock, with thy estimation, for a trespass offering, unto the priest: And the priest shall make an atonement for him before the* L*ORD: and it shall be forgiven him for any thing of all that he hath done in trespassing therein (Lev. 6:1-7).*

The theocentric meaning of this passage is that theft is a transgression against God. God is here identified as the primary victim of crime: "If a soul sin, and commit a trespass against the LORD. . . ." This principle is fundamental to biblical law. It is therefore not sufficient for a thief to make restitution to his earthly victim; he must also make restitution to God.

This passage continues the laws governing trespasses and guilt (reparations) offerings. The sin in this instance is high-handed, unlike the sin of Leviticus 5:15.[1] It is said to be a sin against the Lord, yet what is described is a sin against a neighbor. God mandated a 20 percent penalty plus the sacrifice of a blemish-free animal.

The text identifies the presence of a false oath in conjunction with crimes against property. The question is: Was the false oath the basis of the 20 percent penalty payment? I argue in this chapter that it was not. The false oath made mandatory the animal sacrifice, but the theft itself, confessed prior to the trial, was what invoked the 20 percent penalty. My line of reasoning rests on what I have previously identified as God's economic subsidy for early confession of crime, i.e., reduced restitution penalties.[2]

Deception is here singled out as a sin against the Lord. This includes deception regarding: 1) keeping an item entrusted for safekeeping or keeping a pledged item (collateral for a loan), 2) robbery, 3) extortion, and 4) keeping someone's lost item.[3] Theologically speaking, every sin is a sin against the Lord, to be judged in God's final court. The victim of every crime becomes *God's legal representative*, for he is an earthly target of man's rebellion against God's standards.[4] He is the victim, therefore, of a *boundary violation*. But this passage specifically identifies four transgressions as trespasses against God, whereas other trespasses listed in the Bible are not specifically identified as such. Why not? No ram offering was required for those other

---

1. "If a soul commit a trespass, and sin through ignorance, in the holy things of the LORD; then he shall bring for his trespass unto the LORD a ram without blemish out of the flocks, with thy estimation by shekels of silver, after the shekel of the sanctuary, for a trespass offering" (Lev. 5:15).

2. Gary North, *Tools of Dominion: The Case Laws of Exodus* (Tyler, Texas: Institute for Christian Economics, 1990), pp. 513-14.

3. The New American Standard Version makes these crimes clearer than the King James Version does.

4. North, *Tools of Dominion*, pp. 278-80.

sins. Why not, if every sin is judicially a trespass against God? Why single out deception?

The Presence of a False Oath

The answer lies elsewhere than in the enumerated sins themselves. It is the transgressor's *false verbal testimony to the victim* regarding these *crimes against property* that serves as the differentiating factor: either lying to the neighbor directly or swearing falsely to a civil court. Writes Wenham: "By abusing the oath, a person took God's holy name in vain, and trespassed against his holiness. Therefore a reparation offering was required to make amends."[5] The sin is two-fold: a violation of a neighbor's property rights (point three of the covenant: boundaries), coupled with a violation of either personal verbal assurances to the victim or the violation of a formal judicial oath (point four: oath).

Because a crime against property is involved, *the lie or deception becomes a judicial oath*. The victim becomes God's covenant agent, the one who initiates a lawsuit against the thief.[6] The oath violation takes a specific form: the implicit (though not legally explicit)[7] misuse of God's name. This is a boundary violation: the third commandment (Ex. 20:7). This oath implicitly and inescapably invokes God's negative sanctions, as all lawful oaths must.[8]

In a court, there must be interrogation of the suspects. God in the garden publicly interrogated Adam and Eve regarding

---

5. Gordon J. Wenham, *The Book of Leviticus* (Grand Rapids, Michigan: Eerdmans, 1979), p. 108.

6. North, *Tools of Dominion*, pp. 278-80, 289.

7. Jesus warned men not to make oaths to each other: "But let your communication be, Yea, yea; Nay, nay: for whatsoever is more than these cometh of evil" (Matt. 5:37). He was not speaking of civil or ecclesiastical trials, in which an oath was legitimate because both State and church have been entrusted with the authority to bring God's negative sanctions in history.

8. Ray R. Sutton, *That You May Prosper: Dominion By Covenant* (2nd ed.; Tyler, Texas: Institute for Christian Economics, 1992), ch. 4.

the facts of the case. It is a crime to testify falsely in God's court or in man's. False testimony is intended to deflect God's justice. Offering it implies that God can be deceived, or at the very least, He can be deterred from bringing His negative sanctions in history. False testimony rests on a man's self-confidence in his ability to deceive God's representative agents in history. He believes that he can deflect or delay God's judgment in history by means of misleading information. This faith in false testimony rests on a theology that assumes that God is non-existent, or not omniscient, or not omnipotent, or does not bring significant negative sanctions in history. It assumes that heaven's court is non-existent, or that God is forgetful, or that time, apart from restitution, pays for all sins (universal salvation), i.e., that God does not bring negative sanctions in eternity. It assumes, at the very least, that God's negative sanctions outside the earthly court (in history and eternity) are minimal compared to the negative sanctions that can be imposed by the court, i.e., double restitution to the victim (Ex. 22:4). This law denies all of these assumptions.

Restitution and Atonement

Two separate sins were involved: one formal-covenantal (false oath), one conventional-economic (theft or fraud). Therefore, there had to be two separate acts of restitution. The first form of restitution – sacrificing a ram – was paid to God to compensate Him for the oath-taker's attempt to thwart God's civil court. This was necessary to satisfy God in His capacity as both High Priest and King of the heavenly court. The second – the return of the stolen item plus a 20 percent payment – was required by God's law to satisfy the earthly victim in his legal capacity as a victim. Both the victim and the priest served as *covenantal agents of God*: the first civil, the second ecclesiastical.

The penalty for unconfessed theft is double restitution (Ex. 22:4). This is reduced to the restoration of the stolen property plus a 20 percent penalty if the thief confesses his crime before either its discovery or his conviction, as we shall see. *The 20 percent penalty payment constituted a double tithe.*[9]

Why impose a 20 percent penalty, the equivalent of a double tithe? What did the tithe have to do with restitution to the victim? James Jordan suggests that it was because guardianship is associated with Levitical office, and so is the tithe. Numbers 18 established the Levites as the guardians of sacred space and sacred things. "And thy brethren also of the tribe of Levi, the tribe of thy father, bring thou with thee, that they may be joined unto thee, and minister unto thee: but thou and thy sons with thee shall minister before the tabernacle of witness. And they shall keep thy charge, and the charge of all the tabernacle: only they shall not come nigh the vessels of the sanctuary and the altar, that neither they, nor ye also, die" (Num. 18:2-3). They were required to keep the common Israelites away from the sacred spaces of the tabernacle. This entitled them to a tithe as their lawful inheritance (Num. 18:21-24). Conclusion: the tithe and the Levitical protection of sacred space were linked judicially.

Death was the civil penalty for invading the temple's sacred space, which was protected by the Levites (Num. 18:7), just as an invasion of the priests' sacred space by the Levites would bring God's death sentence against both priest and Levite (Num. 18:3). The penalty for other invasions of sacred areas was the 20 percent penalty: a double tithe. A vow to a priest was redeemed by paying a 20 percent penalty (Lev. 27:19). Refusal to pay this redemption price resulted in the permanent loss of the property, even rural land (Lev. 27:20-21).[10] Unintentional boundary violations of sacred things also required a double tithe penalty: "And if a man eat of the holy thing unwittingly, then he shall put the fifth part thereof unto it, and shall

---

9. Andrew A. Bonar, *A Commentary on Leviticus* (London: Banner of Truth Trust, [1846] 1966), p. 109.

10. See Chapter 37, below.

give it unto the priest with the holy thing" (Lev. 22:14). "Speak unto the children of Israel, When a man or woman shall commit any sin that men commit, to do a trespass against the LORD, and that person be guilty; Then they shall confess their sin which they have done: and he shall recompense his trespass with the principal thereof, and add unto it the fifth part thereof, and give it unto him against whom he hath trespassed" (Num. 5:6-7).

In the same sense that every man is a priest through Adam, every man is a Levite through Adam. He is a designated guardian of God's property: a Levitical function. The property owner is inescapably God's steward because God owns everything: "For every beast of the forest is mine, and the cattle upon a thousand hills" (Ps. 50:10). All subordinate ownership is necessarily representative. It is therefore stewardship. This judicially bounded sphere of economic responsibility is not to be invaded unlawfully: the eighth commandment (Ex. 20:15). Adam is the archetype. He was established as a guardian of God's property – a Levitical function – even before he acted as a priest. He was told to serve as a guardian on the day of his creation (Gen. 2:15). His profane, sacrilegious act of priestly defiance – eating a prohibited communion meal in the presence of an invading serpent – took place later (Gen. 3:6).

Thwarting Civil Justice

The criminal had lied to the victim in order to escape civil justice. This was an affront to God's kingly justice. The victim, as God's judicial agent, becomes the civil court's judicial agent. He has a direct economic incentive to pursue justice.[11]

The court should establish a system in which both parties, accuser and accused, are treated equally. All court expenses

---

11. Gary North, *Boundaries and Dominion: The Economics of Leviticus* (computer edition; Tyler, Texas: Institute for Christian Economics, 1994), ch. 7, section on "Thwarting Civil Justice."

should be borne by the civil government. There should also be some way to insure that both parties are represented equally in the court. The general principle is that the loser should pay for the legal fees of the winner. If a poor man is too fearful to prosecute on this basis, fearing bankruptcy, the State may do so in his name if he approves, granting him post-trial immunity. But then the State must provide the equivalent of vouchers for both sides' legal costs. It covers the legal fees for both sides, but only to a limit. The model here is Christ's intercession for His people before the throne of justice (Rom. 8:34).[12]

Priestly Agents of God's Heavenly Court

When the plaintiff brings a lawsuit in his own name, he inevitably also brings it in God's name, for God is the primary victim of crime. If he was a victim, he is acting as God's agent. The civil court is required to examine the evidence and announce judgment, but this judgment is made in the name of the two victims: God and the earthly victim, either the plaintiff or the defendant. The civil court is an agent of the victim in a way that the ecclesiastical court is not. The civil court acts to defend the victim's rights, whereas the priest acts to defend the civil court's authority in the case of a false oath.

The required animal sacrifice served as an atonement for a crime against God's civil court. This sacrifice wiped away the sin ritually. It was a public acknowledgment of a transgression against God's civil court. What is significant here is that *an ecclesiastical act was required to atone for a civil transgression*. The verbal cover-up (false witness) required a ritual payment.

This raises a key question: Why was there a ritual connection between a civil court and the priesthood? Because of the twofold character of God's judgment. The civil court always represents God's heavenly court in a subordinate fashion, analogous to the victim, who in his legal capacity as a victim also repre-

12. *Ibid.*, ch. 7, section on "Allocating the Costs of Civil Justice."

sents God subordinately. The civil court acts on behalf of the victim, but only in its judicial capacity as the minister of kingly justice (Rom. 13:4), as the institution that lawfully bears the monopolistic sword of vengeance. But God requires more than civil sanctions to placate His wrath against the criminal. He sits on His throne as both High Priest and King; on earth, these offices are divided except in two unique cases: Melchizedek (Gen. 14:18) and Jesus Christ. *God must be placated in both of His offices*. This is why no single earthly court can lawfully offer twofold atonement to a criminal. God therefore requires a priestly sacrifice.

New Testament Sacrifice

In the New Testament, this priestly sacrifice was made by Jesus Christ at Calvary. The various animal sacrifices in the Old Testament representationally prefigured this ultimate sacrifice (Heb. 9). A question legitimately can be raised: Is any post-Calvary public mark of contrition lawfully imposed by the church on the perjurer? If so, on what legal basis?

If the perjurer is a church member, he has partaken of the Lord's Supper throughout the period following his false testimony to the court. This placed him in jeopardy of God's negative sanctions (I Cor. 11:30). He ignored this threat, thereby implicitly adopting the same false theology of God's minimal sanctions, previously described. The church's officers deserve to know of the transgression, and can lawfully assign a penalty. This penalty should not exceed the value of a ram in the Mosaic economy.

If the perjurer is not a church member, he is still dependent on continuing judgments by the church to preserve God's common grace in history. The State can lawfully function in non-Christian environments, but only because of the common grace of God mediated through His called-out church to the world. In the Mosaic covenant, the church served as a mediating agency for the entire world. This is why the priests had to offer 70 bullocks annually (Num. 29:12-32) as sacrifices for the symbolic 70 pagan nations of the world (Jud. 1:7), plus a single bullock for Israel on the eighth day (Num. 29:36).[13]

The Church: Guardian of the Civil Oath

What this means is that the church is the guardian of the covenantal civil oath. This is an inescapable conclusion from the fact that only the church has the authority to accept the perjurer's sacrifice in atonement for the false oath. The State cannot offer this release from guilt. The oath involves the formal calling down of God's negative covenant sanctions on the oath-taker. He who uses God's name in vain in a formal judicial conflict must then seek judicial cleansing from the church. The reason why the oath is guarded by the church is that the church alone can lawfully invoke the eternal negative sanctions of God against an individual.[14] *Thus, by invoking the oath in a civil court, the criminal necessarily brings himself under the judicial authority of the church.*

The modern practice of allowing atheists to "affirm" to tell the truth in court, but not to swear on the Bible or in God's name, is a direct affront against God and against the church as the guardian of the oath. It is also inevitably an act of divinizing the State by default. The State becomes the sole enforcer of the public affirmation. In such a worldview, there is no appeal in history beyond the State and its sanctions. *The atheist's affirmation is therefore a judicial act demanding the removal of God from the courtroom.* Thus, it requires the creation of a new oath system, with the State as the sole guardian of the oath. The State acts not in God's name but in its own. Rushdoony's comments are

13. When Israel fell in A.D. 70, she had become like all the other pagan nations. She could no longer offer efficacious sacrifices for them or for herself. From that point on, only the sacrifice of Jesus Christ at Calvary could serve as any nation's atonement – covering or ransom – before God.

14. Gary North, *The Sinai Strategy: Economics and the Ten Commandments* (Tyler, Texas: Institute for Christian Economics, 1986), pp. 52-56.

on target: "If a witness is asked to swear to tell the whole truth and nothing but the truth without any reference to God, truth then can be and is commonly redefined in terms of himself. The oath in God's name is the 'legal recognition of God'[15] as the source of all things and the only true ground of all being. It establishes the state under God and under His law. The removal of God from oaths, and the light and dishonest use of oaths, is a declaration of independence from Him, and it is warfare against God in the name of the new gods, apostate man and his totalitarian state."[16]

The biblical State can lawfully impose negative sanctions against a perjurer, but only on behalf of the victim. The State cannot lawfully pronounce the permanent negative sanctions of the oath against anyone. The State can lawfully require an oath, but it is not the institutional enforcer of this oath. The presence of the oath to God is a public acknowledgment of the non-autonomy of the State. God is above the State, and the church stands next to it as the guardian of the oath.[17]

This means that theocracy is required by God's civil law. Without the God-given authority to require an oath, the State would lose its covenantal status as a lawful monopolistic institution with the authority to enforce physical sanctions against evil-doers. It would lose its status as a covenantal institution. Yet by imposing an oath, it inevitably places itself under the protection of the church, for the church is the defender of the oath. As the great seventeenth-century jurist Sir Edward Coke put it, "protection draws allegiance, and allegiance draws protection."[18]

---

15. T. Robert Ingram, *The World Under God's Law* (Houston, Texas: St. Thomas Press, 1962), p. 46.

16. R. J. Rushdoony, *The Institutes of Biblical Law* (Nutley, New Jersey: Craig Press, 1973), p. 115.

17. The State, in turn, is responsible for the preservation of the legal environment that protects the church. The church is not institutionally autonomous, either.

18. Cited by Rebecca West, *The New Meaning of Treason* (New York: Viking Press, 1964), p. 12; in Rushdoony, *Institutes*, p. 118.

Civil Identification of a True Church

This law requires that the local civil government identify the local ecclesiastical guardians of the oath. It must identify those congregations that are confessionally orthodox and therefore eligible to receive the trespass offering. This authority to identify confessionally orthodox churches implies that members of associations not so identified as orthodox cannot legally be granted the legal status of citizens. In short, the State is a confessional, oath-bound, covenantal institution. It is required to establish what constitutes a valid civil oath, but only after consultation with churches. Churches are confessional, covenantal institutions, separate from the State. They may lawfully impose added confessional requirements beyond the civil oath for their members and officers, but if they do not confess the Trinity, they are not to be recognized as guardians of the civil oath.

Conclusion

We see in this law the application of the Bible's fundamental principle of civil justice: victim's rights. The twin issues in this case involve the defense of a pair of judicial boundaries: private property and the civil oath. The ecclesiastical issue is this: What is the meaning of the trespass offering? I argue that the trespass offering is tied judicially to the defense of the civil oath against the criminal who falsely declares his innocence. That is, *there is more to a legitimate defense of the civil oath than the imposition of civil sanctions.*

The primary victim of the theft is God, against whose majesty the theft is committed. The secondary victim is the earthly victim. He then becomes the primary agent of God in this legal dispute between God and the criminal. God brings a lawsuit against the criminal in His heavenly court; He authorizes the victim to bring a lawsuit in a civil court. This is the biblical principle of victim's rights.

An important goal of the criminal justice system is to gain a confession from the criminal before a trial is held or a verdict is handed down. This reflects the desire of God to gain a public confession from the sinner before his death, and therefore before his heavenly trial begins.[19] To gain early confessions, God's law imposes escalating penalties for each formal judicial stage transgressed by the criminal's deceptive activities. Put another way, each time the criminal transgresses one of these legal barriers – these judicial opportunities for public confession – the penalties increase. Early confession reduces the costs of prosecution. It lowers the cost of justice. The double restitution penalty (Ex. 21:4) is imposed only after the person is convicted by a court. This is analogous to God's reduced penalty on sinners when they confess in history, before final judgment.[20] But early confession does not remove the requirement to make a trespass offering.[21] Jesus Christ's office in history as both King and High Priest must be upheld.

The court defends the rights of the victim. The church defends the integrity of the court, i.e., its right to be told the truth by the criminal. The criminal's transgression of ownership boundaries sanctified – set apart judicially – the stolen property: set it apart judicially. The lying criminal owes the victim double restitution because of the theft if the court convicts him. He owes him full restoration if he admits his guilt before the court tries him. He also owes the victim a double tithe (20 percent) because the act of theft sanctified the stolen goods. Finally, he owes God a sacrifice through the mediating institution of the priesthood because of his false oath in civil court.

The 20 percent penalty payment to the victim is still in force in New Testament times. It was not tied uniquely to the Prom-

---

19. "That if thou shalt confess with thy mouth the Lord Jesus, and shalt believe in thine heart that God hath raised him from the dead, thou shalt be saved. For with the heart man believeth unto righteousness; and with the mouth confession is made unto salvation" (Rom. 10:9-10).

20. North, *Boundaries and Dominion*, ch. 7, sections on "A Subsidy for Early Confession," "Calculating the Required Restitution," and "After the Accusation, But Before the Trial."

21. *Ibid.*, ch. 7, section on "Restitution Plus a Trespass Offering."

ised Land or the Mosaic Covenant priesthood. There has to be a double-tithe (priestly) penalty payment in order to de-sanctify the stolen property. He pays this penalty to the victim, not to the church.

If the criminal confesses his sin to the victim before the trial begins, he escapes the threat of double restitution. A 20 percent penalty payment to the victim is sufficient, plus the return of the asset or its present market value. In Mosaic Israel, if he had also lied to the court regarding his theft, he had to offer the sacrifice of a ram. Today, he would confess to church authorities and make whatever sacrifice they impose on him, not to exceed the comparable value of a ram in the Mosaic economy.

Part 2

CLEANSING
(Lev. 8-16)

INTRODUCTION TO PART 2

For I am the Lord *your God: ye shall therefore sanctify yourselves, and ye shall be holy; for I am holy: neither shall ye defile yourselves with any manner of creeping thing that creepeth upon the earth. For I am the* Lord *that bringeth you up out of the land of Egypt, to be your God: ye shall therefore be holy, for I am holy (Lev. 11:44-45).*

God here identifies Himself as a holy God. He also identifies Himself as the God who had delivered the Israelites from the bondage of Egypt. This self-identification as the God who delivered His people in history is the identifying aspect of point two of the Mosaic Covenant: historical prologue.[1] In Leviticus 11:45, God identifies Himself as possessing lawful authority over His people: hierarchy.

Leviticus 8-16 is concerned with the priesthood in general,[2] but with cleansing in particular. The priesthood was in charge of identifying and attending to the marks of ritual and physical uncleanness in society: food laws, childbirth laws, leprosy, discharges of the flesh, and the day of atonement.[3] This section begins with the ritual washing of the priests: Aaron and his sons (Lev. 8:6). It ends with the day of atonement, which is specific-

---

1. Meredith G. Kline, *The Structure of Biblical Authority* (rev. ed.; Grand Rapids, Michigan: Eerdmans, 1972), pp. 53-57.

2. The Greek word for priest is *hierus*, as in hierarchy.

3. James B. Jordan, *Covenant Sequence in Leviticus and Deuteronomy* (Tyler, Texas: Institute for Christian Economics, 1989), p. 16.

ally identified as a means of cleansing: "For on that day shall the priest make an atonement for you, to cleanse you, that ye may be clean from all your sins before the LORD" (Lev. 16:30).

Ritual cleanliness was mandatory for a nation of priests (Ex. 19:6) that had been set apart (sanctified, made holy) by God as His special people. This national separation was the heart of the Mosaic Covenant. Cleanliness laws were temporal boundary devices that had a covenantal function for as long as the Mosaic Covenant was valid. To enforce them, there had to be a priesthood for the nation of priests. Like the nation of priests, these ordained priests had boundaries placed around them as a separate family (Aaron) in a separate tribe (Levi). It was their task to identify holiness and unholiness, cleanliness and uncleanliness (Lev. 10:10). As we find in the laws governing leprosy, their very physical presence inside the boundary of a house made unclean a house infected with the disease. It was not legally unclean until a priest crossed its boundary. This was analogous to the moral uncleanliness of Canaan, which became judicially unclean – and subject to God's corporate negative sanctions – only after the Israelites had crossed the Jordan river and entered the land.

8

WINE AS A BOUNDARY MARKER

And the Lord *spake unto Aaron, saying, Do not drink wine nor strong drink, thou, nor thy sons with thee, when ye go into the tabernacle of the congregation, lest ye die: it shall be a statute for ever throughout your generations: And that ye may put difference between holy and unholy, and between unclean and clean; And that ye may teach the children of Israel all the statutes which the* Lord *hath spoken unto them by the hand of Moses (Lev. 10:8-11).*

The theocentric meaning of this passage is that God has the authority to establish boundaries that temporarily separate a holy person from a blessing. The wine in this passage is analogous to the tree of the knowledge of good and evil.

This prohibition applied to the priests only while they were inside the tabernacle or temple. There is no reference to the Levites. For a priest to drink wine inside the tabernacle constituted a boundary violation. The tabernacle-temple was God's place of residence in Israel. It was there that He manifested His judicial presence. This law had something to do with the special presence of God and the holiness of God. It also had something to do with the office of priest. It had nothing to do with a general prohibition against wine.

There can be no doubt that the average Israelite was allowed to drink wine. He was specifically authorized by God to drink it at the third-year feast. "And thou shalt bestow that money for whatsoever thy soul lusteth after, for oxen, or for sheep, or for wine, or for strong drink,[1] or for whatsoever thy soul desireth: and thou shalt eat there before the LORD thy God, and thou shalt rejoice, thou, and thine household" (Deut. 14:26). Wine is described in the Bible as a blessing from God (Deut. 7:13; 11:14; II Chron. 31:5). God even goes so far as to say that the *absence of wine* is a sign of His *covenantal curse* against a covenanted nation: "And he shall eat the fruit of thy cattle, and the fruit of thy land, until thou be destroyed: which also shall not leave thee either corn, wine, or oil, or the increase of thy kine, or flocks of thy sheep, until he have destroyed thee" (Deut. 28:51). Why, then, this unique Mosaic Covenant prohibition for the priests? Wenham understands that there is a problem here. "The commands given to Aaron, however, are strange. Why should a ban on drinking alcohol be introduced here, and then be coupled with instructions about teaching the Israelites?"[2] He correctly identifies both aspects of the prohibition: 1) clear-headed officiating over the administration of the sacrifices, and 2) the teaching function of the priests. But he avoids discussing a very difficult and all-too-obvious problem: teaching by the priests that took place outside the boundaries of the tabernacle and the temple. Why did the prohibition against wine cease when the priest left the tabernacle? Wasn't clear instruction in the word of God just as important outside the temple's boundaries as inside?

The ban did not apply to the Levites, yet they also had a teaching function. Their office was lower than the priestly office. They did not speak with comparable authority. Was this additional authority of the priesthood an aspect of the ban?

---

1. This did not refer to Coca Cola Classic. Fundamentalist Christians and other anti-alcohol legalists have great exegetical problems with this passage.

2. Gordon J. Wenham, *The Book of Leviticus* (Grand Rapids, Michigan: Eerdmans, 1979), p. 158.

Boundaries: God's Ownership and Priestly Sobriety

The boundary of the tabernacle involved a prohibition regarding their personal use of wine. Wine was required in the sacrifices. The wine of Mosaic sacrifice was to be poured out exclusively to God and never consumed by the priest. It was not burned on the altar because, like leaven, it was a fermented product.[3] Wine accompanied the offerings (Num. 15:5; 28:7). Like the tree of the knowledge of good and evil, wine was specially reserved for God in the Mosaic sacrifices. *The wine of sacrifice was exclusively His property*. Also like the boundary in the garden, this was not intended to be a permanent boundary, but it was a requirement of that dispensation. Contrary to the anti-alcohol heresy,[4] it was not that God despised wine; it was that He regarded it as exclusively His possession in formal worship ceremonies. He saved the best for Himself.

Sobriety and Sanctuary

The priest was the person who offered sacrifices, but he was also the person who authoritatively interpreted and applied the law of God in formal judgment. This authority to pronounce judgment was also a possession of the king, who was also prohibited from drinking wine. "It is not for kings, O Lemuel, it is not for kings to drink wine; nor for princes strong drink: Lest they drink, and forget the law, and pervert the judgment of any of the afflicted" (Prov. 31:4-5). This advice – it was not a Mosaic law – governed the highest civil magistrates: kings and princes. The identifying issue for the king was the enforcement of justice. The king was the high civil court of appeal. Was this high court status also the issue for the priests within the tabernacle? In some cases it was, when the priest declared the law

---

3. Jacob Milgrom, *Leviticus 1-16*, vol. 3 of *The Anchor Bible* (New York: Doubleday, 1991), p. 189.

4. For a critique, see Kenneth L. Gentry, Jr., *The Christian and Alcoholic Beverages* (Grand Rapids, Michigan: Baker, 1986).

and then imposed sanctions on someone who had come to bring a sacrifice or during one of the required feasts. Some legal counseling may have gone on. But the imposition of sanctions was not what the text refers to. The two stated reasons for this priestly prohibition were related to two priestly tasks: distinguishing clean from unclean and teaching the people God's law.

The priest knew the details of the sacrificial system. He acted as a representative agent: a *boundary* (mediator) between God and the people of Israel, but also between Israel and the world. Wine might disorient him. Such self-inflicted disorientation was not permitted. Therefore, if the priests failed to officiate correctly at the sacrifices, God would bring sanctions against both priesthood and people. These boundaries had to be respected. This required sobriety, but it also required the priests to respect God as the sole owner of the drink offerings. More was involved here than the mere sobriety of the priests. This law rested on the distinction between holy and unholy. In this case, the priest, as a fallen man and fallen mankind's agent, was unholy or unclean. He could not touch wine within the confines of the tabernacle. God is holy; wine was His exclusive property inside the tabernacle. This did not change during the period of the Mosaic Covenant. Only in the New Covenant era, after the resurrection and ascension of Christ, did wine again become lawful for laymen in worship, as it had been for Abram (Gen. 14:18).

Within the tabernacle, there could be discussion and study, just as there was later in the temple (Luke 2:46). When discussing God's law, men are to be alert. It is their proper service before God, their calling. But the prohibition applied only to the tabernacle. Why not outside? Because the focus of concern was not the teaching of the law as such; it was *the teaching of the law in a holy place*. A holy place is a sanctuary: a place sanctified by God. The declaration of the law from within the tabernacle had far greater authority than the declaration of God's law outside the tabernacle. God dwelt with Israel inside the tabernacle. His presence was judicial: throne-related (the mercy seat: Ex. 25:17-22). Any declaration of His law from within His own house had the force of supreme law. The law declared here was not mere advice. It could not be appealed. This was Israel's highest ecclesiastical court of appeal. *The priest was acting as a boundary guard on holy ground*. This was the boundary. It was not simply that his office was holy; his environment was holy. Jesus did not apply a whip to the backsides of the moneychangers outside the temple, but only inside. It was here that God was most offended. The temple was a house of prayer, the place where men brought their cases before God and sought God's authoritative pronouncements.

The Third Book of the Pentateuch

This interpretation is consistent with the structure and role of the Book of Leviticus: boundaries. The priest within the tabernacle was a student of the law as a *boundary guard* for the people in their role as God's dominion agents. As God's dwelling place, the tabernacle was the place of God's judgment. The tabernacle was therefore *sanctified* – set apart judicially by God. When in the geographical-judgmental presence of God in the Mosaic Covenant era, the priest had to avoid anything that would make him lightheaded, meaning artificially lighthearted. The priest was also the one who offered sacrifices as a boundary guard whose efforts placated the wrath of God. Offering sacrifices was the crucial official activity within the tabernacle. If the priest was not alert to the ritual requirements of the sacrifices, he risked bringing under judgment both himself and those represented by him.

There was a secondary consideration. If the priesthood as a whole failed to declare and observe God's law correctly, this would undermine all lawful judgment: self-judgment, family judgment, civil judgment, and ecclesiastical judgment. This would in turn undermine the dominion activities of the family, the primary agent of dominion in history (Gen. 1:26-28). The priest was therefore to listen to God's word carefully, for it is a word of judgment. This word included His liturgical word. He was required to adhere to it precisely, just as men are to adhere to His written word precisely. The priest's actions in the tabernacle were therefore representative, which is why Jesus was so outraged by what was going on in the temple (Matt. 21:13).

The king was analogous to God. The king brought negative sanctions in history. He was required to study the law daily (Deut. 17:18-20), but he also had to execute judgment. His task was more closely associated with point four of the biblical covenant: sanctions. Thus, the king was under a sort of double prohibition. He was unwise ever to drink wine, whereas the priests could lawfully drink wine outside the boundaries of the tabernacle.[5]

Permanent Prohibitions?

The question arises: Are these prohibitions still in force? The fundamentalist insists that every redeemed person is now a priest. Because of the annulment of Israel's feasts, Christians supposedly are no longer authorized to drink strong drink. The prohibition against drinking wine inside the temple has now been extended to the whole world, the fundamentalist insists. The New Testament is therefore seen as far more hostile to wine than the Old Testament was.

The problem with this viewpoint is that wine was legitimate for the priest outside of tabernacle services, unless he had taken a Nazarite's vow (Num. 6:20; Jud. 13:7), which also prohibited grape juice and even raisins – an aged grape product not on

---

5. R. K. Harrison does not discuss the "inside-outside" aspect of the prohibition. He relates the prohibition to the teaching function of the priesthood, as well as the ritual function, ignoring the obvious: most of this priestly public teaching would have been conducted outside the tabernacle. But there the absolute prohibition did not apply. R. K. Harrison, *Leviticus: An Introduction and Commentary* (Downers Grove, Illinois: InterVarsity Press, 1980), pp. 114-18.

the fundamentalists' list of innately evil products. Why should the extension of the priesthood to every Christian require the removal of wine from the tables of the land? It is the essence of Christianity's doctrine of the priesthood of all believers that all believers are allowed to enter the temple and partake of the communion feast of God. God's full table is now open to us. He now shares with us by His grace the wine that had been ritually poured out exclusively to Him under the Mosaic Covenant. The entire priesthood can now lawfully partake of this wine inside the temple.

The Roman Catholic Church has reversed the Mosaic Covenant's prohibition in formal worship: only the priest may drink communion wine, since it supposedly becomes Christ's literal blood.[6] The Catholic layman is denied access to the full table. Outside of worship, the Catholic Church teaches, wine is as legitimate today as it was in the Mosaic economy.

In contrast to both positions, the Reformed or Lutheran Christian says that this Mosaic restriction on the priest was annulled by the establishment of the Lord's Supper, which commands all followers of Christ to take wine. Presumably, the New Covenant king is also allowed to drink wine, since the King of kings made wine at the wedding at Cana. Jesus made wine, not grape juice. The reason why it was customary to serve the less expensive wine later in a feast (John 2:10) was that people's sense of taste would have been impaired by the previous consumption of wine. A declining sense of discriminating taste is not a problem with the consumption of grape juice. (I have never heard of "discriminating taste" regarding grape juice. International grape juice competitions are quite rare. The product is seldom advertised.)

One physical boundary between man and God in the Mosaic Covenant was wine.[7] The priest could not drink it during wor-

---

6. On what legal basis are Catholic layman allowed to eat Christ's body? What is so special about the blood?

7. On the removal of the Old Covenant's physical boundaries between God and

ship. It was a ritual barrier. Wine in worship visibly represented a judicial boundary between God and man, just as the tree of knowledge did in the garden. Wine still does, but in a totally different way. The sacraments physically mark the boundary between God and man. This is the reason for the ritual use of wine in New Covenant times. Those who do not have legal access to this wine are warned by the very existence of the ceremony that they are judicially separated from God. The *wine boundary* keeps covenant-breakers outside the special protection of God – His positive sanctions – but God requires covenant-keepers to partake of it.[8] This includes covenant-keeping kings.[9]

Breaking Cultural Boundaries

Grape juice cannot expand until it begins to ferment. It then loses its character as grape juice. The kingdom of God broke the boundaries of the Old Covenant, just as new wine breaks old wineskins (Matt. 9:17). The imagery of broken wineskins testifies to a new, expanding kingdom that is no longer confined by old geographical and cultural boundaries. The new kingdom means a new mentality: dominion-oriented, expansionist, and comprehensive in its scope. This imagery was present in Old Covenant Israel, as the use of wine indicates: wine was not universally prohibited, and prior to the Mosaic economy, it was even allowed to the priesthood. "And Melchizedek king of Salem brought forth bread and wine: and he was the priest of the most high God" (Gen. 14:18). Isaac's blessing of Jacob demonstrates the link between wine and dominion: "Therefore God give thee of the dew of heaven, and the fatness

---

redeemed men, see Gary North, *Boundaries and Dominion: The Economics of Leviticus* (computer edition; Tyler, Texas: Institute for Christian Economics, 1994), ch. 8, section on "Boundaries of the Heart."

8. An exception is valid for former alcoholics: weaker brethren (I Cor. 8:9).

9. For a more detailed discussion of wine and civil servants, see North, *Boundaries and Dominion*, ch. 8, section on "The Supreme Civil Ruler."

of the earth, and plenty of corn and wine: Let people serve thee, and nations bow down to thee: be lord over thy brethren, and let thy mother's sons bow down to thee: cursed be every one that curseth thee, and blessed be he that blesseth thee" (Gen. 27:28-29). The boundary of wine for the priests testified that Israel was under temporary constraints geographically; the element of worldwide dominion was not present to the same extent that it is in the New Covenant.

Denying Expansion

The worldview of fundamentalism denies the reality of an expanding kingdom in history, meaning before Christ returns in person to set up an earthly kingdom. The kingdom of God is said to be limited to the family and the church. In some extreme formulations, the kingdom of God is equated only with the church; even the family is understood to be outside it. According to this view of history, a millennium of medieval society was either at bottom religiously neutral or else it was not really a society. This is the history of Western civilization according to Voltaire, Diderot, the Enlightenment generally, and the standard American high school world history textbook. It is fundamentalism's worldview, too, which is why there is a continuing operational alliance between pietism and humanism.[10]

Grape juice is the pietist's preference: a sweet, red liquid that looks like wine but has no bite, bubble, or joy to it. Fundamentalists do not use wine in any form because wine can be misused by undisciplined people. (They are not equally wary about their diets and their weight. It is fermented sugar that arouses their wrath, not unfermented.)[11] The imagery of bro-

---

10. Gary North, *Millennialism and Social Theory* (Tyler, Texas: Institute for Christian Economics, 1990), pp. 43-44, 135-36, 144, 147, 151, 179-80, 258, 277-78.

11. Typical of the fundamentalist mindset is the concordance at the back of the *Scofield Reference Bible* (Oxford University Press, 1909). If you are trying to locate Deuteronomy 21:20, "And they shall say unto the elders of his city, This our son is stubborn and rebellious, he will not obey our voice; he is a glutton, and a drunkard,"

ken wineskins also does not appeal to pietistic fundamentalists. They want to keep those old wineskins intact. The thought of cultural wine that breaks the institutional structures of society is foreign to their thinking. Like wine, cultural and political power can be abused, so they reject it as a matter of morality. Thus, Christians are supposed to shun power, influence, and culture in the same way that they are to shun wine. Culture means dirty movies and perversion; people who even study cultural affairs are risking being engulfed by a morally polluting worldliness.

Pietistic fundamentalists do not have confidence in those fellow Christians who would exercise public authority in the name of Christ and in terms of His law. They prefer to be ruled by pagans. Similarly, they have no faith in culture.

Rendering Good Judgment

It is clear why liquor and justice do not mix. The ruler is required by God to render judgment in His name. This judgment must apply the general principles of biblical justice to specific infractions. This work takes considerable skill. A person who is under the influence of alcohol in this task is to that degree not under the influence of God's law. But why should this not be true in every other instance? Why is the decision-making of civil law so crucial? The answer is this: because the civil magistrate renders judgment in God's name.

Whenever good judgment is required for the safety of others, equally rigorous standards are required. Pilots of airplanes are not allowed to drink liquor for hours prior to flights. Were it not so common for automobile drivers to drink before driving, thereby making it difficult for prosecutors to get juries to

---

you can find it by looking up the word "drunkard," but not "glutton." Similarly with Proverbs 23:21: "For the drunkard and the glutton shall come to poverty: and drowsiness shall clothe a man with rags." There is no reference at all to "glutton" in the concordance.

convict drunk drivers, harsh economic sanctions would be applied to those driving while intoxicated. Other people are at risk; thus, the person under the influence of alcohol or drugs is a threat to society.

But what about after work? Why should alcohol be prohibited, if the person does not subsequently drive? What about relaxation? There is no biblical prohibition. The enjoyment of conviviality is sometimes enhanced by the loosening of inhibitions that alcohol produces. This is the "merry heart" phenomenon: the reduction of worldly cares that interfere with interpersonal relationships. The merry heart is a legitimate goal when one's work is completed. "Go thy way, eat thy bread with joy, and drink thy wine with a merry heart; for God now accepteth thy works" (Eccl. 9:7). Anyone who would translate the Hebrew word for wine as "grape juice" in this passage is personally unfamiliar with the merrying effects of wine – and proud of it!

Modern fundamentalism views the God of the Old Testament as horribly harsh. For example, God's law requires witnesses to stone those convicted of a capital crime. "The hands of the witnesses shall be first upon him to put him to death, and afterward the hands of all the people. So thou shalt put the evil away from among you" (Deut. 17:7). Such judicial barbarism is not required today, they tell us. "We're under grace, not law." (In fact, Christians are today universally under covenant-breakers and their laws.) Yet at the same time, they view the God of Israel as far too morally lax, allowing people to drink alcohol. In both cases, Mosaic law is a great embarrassment to them. They do not consider an alternative viewpoint, namely, that pietistic fundamentalism is a great embarrassment to God.[12]

---

12. Reformed pietism is only half embarrassed by the Old Testament. Its defenders are repulsed by the thought of the capital sanction of stoning, but some of them do enjoy drinking. On the fundamentalists' hostility to the cultural dominion that is symbolized by wine, see North, *Boundaries and Dominion*, ch. 8, section on "Breaking

Conclusion

Is the prohibition against wine judicially relevant in New Testament times? No. The offices to which the prohibition applied – priest and king – no longer exist. The average citizen has legal access to the offices of minister and senior civil ruler, if he meets certain specified judicial criteria. Neither office is attained through inheritance in modern society. The Mosaic priesthood has not been inherited since its demise at the fall of Jerusalem.

The prohibition against wine for priests was limited by the boundary of formal worship before God's throne. The issue here was the *ritual monopoly over wine* possessed by God. He refused to share this wine with the people or their representatives. Holy Communion changed this: ministers and members can and must partake of God's blessing. The prohibition applied to kings because of the unique judicial boundary of their own persons. The issue here was the proper rendering of judgment, not ritual exclusion.

The warning to the king is still with us: when rendering formal judgment or performing actions that place others under risk, wine and strong drink are still prohibited. Wine is for celebration after daily work is over. A mild alteration of the senses in this case is legitimate, for the responsibility of rendering daily judgment is past. This points to a view of life that renounces the stress of perpetual, inherited responsibility – the kind of responsibility appropriate only to Old Covenant kings. The pressures of New Covenant responsibility ebb and flow; they are not to become continual. The internally stressful lives of modern men point to their violation of the biblical rhythm of responsibility and celebration. Instead of hard work followed by relaxation, men today adopt killing stress and worry alternating with mindless, addictive escapism: distilled liquor, drugs, and television.

Cultural Boundaries."

We are not to become either alcoholics or workaholics. We are also not to become either abstainers or slothful. Alcoholism is a denial of personal responsibility. Abstaining from all liquor is also a denial of personal responsibility: "If I take one drink, I'll become an alcoholic."[13] Both are wrong. Workaholism is a denial of God's sovereignty. It is the attitude of autonomy: "My power and the might of mine hand hath gotten me this wealth" (Deut. 8:17b). Slothfulness is a denial of man's responsibility.

The New Testament prohibition against drunkenness is a boundary against alcoholism (Eph. 5:17-18). But God also mandates fermented wine for His Supper, a judicial rejection of the mentality of the absolute prohibition against liquor, which in turn leads to the withdrawal from culture and its responsibilities. Similarly, the law of the sabbath is an affront to workaholics: a judicial barrier. It is also an affront to the slothful: six days we are to work.

Responsibility involves the recognition *and honoring* of the boundary between hard work and addiction to work. It also involves recognizing *and honoring* the boundary between feasting and gluttony, between making merry and getting drunk. Jesus' enemies accused Him of having transgressed both of these boundaries: "The Son of man came eating and drinking, and they say, Behold a man gluttonous, and a winebibber, a friend of publicans and sinners. But wisdom is justified of her children" (Matt. 11:19).

Modern man thinks of himself as wise, but he is foolish. He refuses to recognize God's boundaries. He ignores them and then risks falling into personal addiction, or else he creates absolute but artificial boundaries where none exist in God's word, and he then falls into a cramped personal legalism that frequently produces cultural irrelevance. Man finds many ways to deny God's boundaries. These ways are all illegitimate.

---

13. This may be true for recovered alcoholics. They are under a God's physiological curse because of their former rebellion.

9

BIBLICAL QUARANTINE

And the leper in whom the plague is, his clothes shall be rent, and his head bare, and he shall put a covering upon his upper lip, and shall cry, Unclean, unclean. All the days wherein the plague shall be in him he shall be defiled; he is unclean: he shall dwell alone; without the camp shall his habitation be (Lev. 13:45-46).

We come now to the longest passage in the Bible that deals with a specific law. This is the law of plague or leprosy. It fills two very long chapters in the Bible, Leviticus 13 and 14. Leviticus 13 presents the law as it applied to the priest: examining whether or not a person had been afflicted with plague or leprosy. Leviticus 14 deals with the specified sacrifices that enabled a person who had been healed from the plague or leprosy to be cleansed judicially and then re-enter the congregation of the Lord. Leviticus 14 also deals with the extremely peculiar phenomenon, namely, plague of garments and houses.

The theocentric meaning of this law is that Mosaic-era leprosy was a sign of God's curses in history and eternity. God's curses separate some men from others. Mosaic-era leprosy testified to the ultimate separation of heaven from hell, of the New Heaven and New Earth from the lake of fire (Rev. 20:14-15). Community is therefore evidence of God's grace. Autonomy, as a theory of separation, is a demonic social theory. God's final curse against self-professed autonomous man is eternal separation.

This law was given by God directly to Moses and Aaron (v. 1). The priesthood enforced this law, not the Levites (v. 2). This means, first of all, that there was a civil function for the priesthood. The civil magistrate had to enforce the declaration of the priest. Second, while the text does not say so, this law indicates that a priest had to reside in every city. He did not offer sacrifice there. Jerusalem was the exclusive place of official sacrifice. The priesthood performed a civil function: declaring people and things unclean within the boundaries of a city.

I argue in this chapter that the leprosy of Leviticus was not a communicable biological disease but rather a judicial affliction. It was not what is known today as Hansen's disease. The quarantine law governing this affliction applied only within the camp or a city; it did not apply in a man's house in the country. Thus, it was a very peculiar disease.

The Plague on a House

Instead of going into great detail about the nature of either plague or leprosy as it affected the individual human being, I want to discuss the plague on a house. The plague was not simply inside the confines of the house; it was literally on it. By beginning here, I focus on what I believe is the crucial point: *this plague was judicial in its frame of reference, not biological.*[1] We can recognize this more clearly in the case of inanimate objects.

1. The rabbis interpreted this law as applying only to Israelites and proselytes, not to resident aliens. Jacob Milgrom, *Leviticus 1-16*, vol. 3 of *The Anchor Bible* (New York: Doubleday, 1991), p. 772. This view is called into question because Naaman, a Syrian military leader, contracted the disease (II Ki. 5). He was not an Israelite or a proselyte. The Syrians had invaded Israel (v. 2); this boundary violation may have been the basis of his leprosy, despite his honor before God (v. 1). Naaman's cure was to dip himself seven times in the Jordan River, the boundary that separated Israel from the world (v. 14).

The house law, which was given in the wilderness period, specified that when the people came into the land of Canaan, and built or inherited houses, those houses would sometimes be subjected to the curse of plague. It began: "When ye be come into the land of Canaan, which I give to you for a possession, and I put the plague of leprosy in a house of the land of your possession. . ." (Lev. 14:34). This law was restricted to Canaan, as we shall see.

God said that He would put the plague of leprosy on a house. When the owner of the house discovered an outbreak of mold in the house's walls, he was required to go to the priest and inform him of the fact (Lev. 14:35-38).

The Sanctity of the Priest

Before entering the house, the priest saw to it that everything inside the house was first removed. It is specifically said that this would keep everything inside the house from becoming unclean. "Then the priest shall command that they empty the house, before the priest go into it to see the plague, that all that is in the house be not made unclean: and afterward the priest shall go in to see the house" (Lev. 14:35). After the house was emptied, the priest would go into the house. This indicates very clearly that the problem was not the spread of disease inside the house, but rather *the judicial sanctity of the priest*. If this sanctified agent were to enter the house when the house was under suspicion, this would make all of the implements and furniture of the house unclean if the house was found to be unclean. *The boundary here was primarily judicial rather than biological*. The house was not judicially unclean until the priest crossed its doorway boundary. He himself would not become unclean. When he did cross it, if he then corroborated the symptoms, everything inside the house at the time of his entrance would become unclean.

Note carefully that the text does not say that the things inside the house would become unclean after the priest entered the house only if the house itself was biologically unclean. The text says that everything in the house would become legally unclean merely by the priest's entering into the house in order to inspect it. This indicates that it was the priest's legal status, as an agent of God, that produced the unclean judicial status of the things inside the house. The house itself was only under suspicion. Everything in the house therefore came under suspicion. It was the entrance of the priest into the house that transformed suspicion into the actual legal status of being unclean. When the priest crossed the boundary of the house – that is to say, when he crossed the door or threshold – his legal status as a holy agent of God created the unclean status of everything inside. Conclusion: *these two chapters are primarily concerned with legal status rather than biological condition*. If this was not the case, then why wasn't it mandatory to burn the furniture that had been moved outside the house?[2]

It was the priest's declaration of a suspected house that would make ritually unclean everything inside the house at the time that he entered it. It was not the biological organism itself that would make everything inside the house unclean. Individuals who entered the house would become ritually unclean, which is why they had to wash their clothes. It was *legal status* that was in question, not biological status. The proof of this is the requirement that a house that had been pronounced unclean and re-plastered, when found to be healed, had to have a ritual cleansing. The priest cleansed the house with two birds, cedar wood, scarlet, and hyssop (Lev 14:49-53). He killed one of the birds in an earthen vessel over running water. He took the cedar wood and the hyssop and the scarlet and the living bird and dipped them into the blood of the slain bird and in the running water then he would sprinkle the house seven

---

2. On stones with plague, see Gary North, *Boundaries and Dominion: The Economics of Leviticus* (computer edition; Tyler, Texas: Institute for Christian Economics, 1994), ch. 9, section on "The Plague on a House," subsection on "A Week of Testing."

times. The text actually says that the house was cleansed with the blood of the dead bird, the running water, the living bird, the cedar wood, the hyssop, and the scarlet (Lev. 14:52). The legal status of *unclean* went from the house to the dead bird, and from there to the live bird. The priest then was to let the living bird out of the city into the open fields, thereby making an atonement for the house, in order to make it clean (Lev. 14:53). An unclean thing could not legally remain inside the city. The bird flew away, carrying the unclean legal status of the house. Conclusion: the threat was judicial; so was the cure.

Total Infection: Covenantal Inclusion

One of the most remarkable aspects of this plague was the law governing the degree of affliction. "Then the priest shall consider: and, behold, if the leprosy have covered all his flesh, he shall pronounce him clean that hath the plague: it is all turned white: he is clean" (Lev. 13:13). What this says is that if an individual was *completely covered with leprosy*, turning his flesh entirely white, he was then pronounced *clean*. This means that he had legal access to the tabernacle or to any other element of corporate worship in Israel. He posed no threat to his neighbors, either ritually or biologically. He was not contagious.[3] We would normally think of the leprosy as being an affliction that required him to be totally separate, permanently. This is not the case. A *partial affliction* of leprosy did require his separation. So did all of the other sores and discolorations of the flesh that are described in Leviticus 13. Nevertheless, *the individual who was completely afflicted became legally clean*.

When an individual was so completely afflicted by the whitening of his skin, *he became like God*: pure white (Dan. 7:9; Rev. 1:14). This is why God discusses man's sins as scarlet, and promises that they will be white as snow: "Come now, and let us

3. Gordon J. Wenham, *The Book of Leviticus* (Grand Rapids, Michigan: Eerdmans, 1979), p. 203.

reason together, saith the LORD: though your sins be as scarlet, they shall be as white as snow; though they be red like crimson, they shall be as wool" (Isa. 1:18). The red splotchy marks on the body made the individual legally unclean. If the white leprosy replaced those marks, he became legally clean.

This means that the individual could be restored to his status as clean in one of two ways: either by becoming totally afflicted by the leprosy or by becoming totally unafflicted by any of the diseases of the skin. *What would otherwise have been regarded as total affliction became a means of judicial liberation.*

In my opinion, this points directly to Christ's suffering on the cross. He became totally afflicted, yet this led to his death, resurrection, and ascension, and it also led to the liberation of His people. Bearing the comprehensive judgment of God in his flesh, He liberated mankind. In a much more limited sense, the Israelite who bore the total affliction of leprosy in his own flesh liberated himself judicially from the penalty of exclusion from the city.

Mandatory Atonement

What must be stressed here is that this law was *not* based on considerations of public biological health; it was based on public judicial health. For the individual to be restored to full communion within the congregation, he had to make four of the five sacrifices of Leviticus: the burnt offering (14:13), the cereal offering (14:10), the sin offering (14:19), and the guilt offering (14:13). Only the voluntary peace offering was absent.[4]

The main problem here is to explain the guilt offering. The guilt offering was a reparation offering: the settling of a debt. Why did leprosy involve a debt to God? The commentators have trouble with this question.[5] I see the answer in the way in which this offering was to be administered: anointing the right

4. *Ibid.*, pp. 209-10.

5. *Ibid.*, p. 210.

ear lobe, the right thumb, and the right big toe with oil (v. 17). The boring of the man's ear to the doorpost was the bondservant's mark of his *voluntary adoption as a permanent household servant in another man's family* (Ex. 21:6; Deut. 15:17). The amputation of the right thumb and right big toe was *a mark of a defeated warrior* (Jud. 1:7), leaving him with reduced balance and with the greatly reduced ability to draw a bowstring. The person anointed with oil had his ear, thumb, and toe symbolically restored. *He re-entered the army of the Lord and could lawfully remain inside the camp of God's holy army.* Because he had been outside the camp, and therefore outside the priestly army of the Lord, he had to demonstrate that he was willing to pay a kind of priestly re-entrance fee – a fee analogous to the payments required of those who sought adoption into the family of Levi (Lev. 27:2-8).[6] The reparation offering constituted this payment. The alien seeking adoption had to be circumcised. Because this barrier did not exist for a formerly leprous Israelite, he was required to cross a different barrier.

Disinheritance

This indicates that these specified diseases were primarily regarded as judicial afflictions rather than biological afflictions. *They marked covenantal death: disinheritance.* Furthermore, the requirement that the individual be cast out of the congregation means that he would have to be forced outside the boundaries of any city. On the other hand, a diseased person who lived in a rural area (as did most of the inhabitants of Israel at the beginning) would not have to leave his home or his family. He was not eligible for the army – the camp – being excluded from Passover in Jerusalem and also from the holy camp during wartime, but he could remain in his home. He became the judicial equivalent of an uncircumcised resident alien: a strang-

6. See Chapter 36, below.

er in his own land. He lost his citizenship. But the man who had fled from a blood-avenger and had been cleared by the elders of a city of refuge was in the worst legal condition of all: cast outside the city, he could be lawfully executed by the blood avenger.

Economic Costs

From an economic standpoint, the most significant aspect of all of these laws is that neither the State nor the church was required by God to support the afflicted person financially. An individual could lose his house. Nevertheless, the State was not required to rebuild a new house for him. Similarly, an individual would lose his job, his place of residence, his access to the fellowship of the saints in corporate worship, and almost everything else that an urban resident would enjoy. Nevertheless, neither the State nor the ecclesiastical hierarchy was required to provide any kind of relief or other aid to this individual. This does not mean that voluntary charity was not appropriate. Obviously, it was very appropriate. Nevertheless, the State was not enjoined to compensate the individual for the losses that the individual would sustain. He sustained the losses, not because he was a biological threat to society, but because he was a judicial threat to society. He was a person whose legal status before God had changed. This change had manifested itself as a biological affliction: the mark of covenantal death. No other diseases in the Bible came under the same exclusion rules. This indicates that these diseases were to be regarded as the direct hand of God against an individual. It was not assumed that an individual had caught the disease from another individual. It was not assumed that this individual could pass on the disease to another individual.

The reason why we know this to be the case is that the individual who lived in the countryside was not under the same restraints. Because the individual's presence in the countryside was not a threat to his neighbors, there is reason to believe that the curse of God had something to do with the presence of the city. We may not be able to understand all of these ramifications. The point is, the individual was not quarantined inside the city; he was quarantined by removing him from the city. The one exception to this was King Uzziah (II Chron. 26:21). He was forced to dwell in a separate house, and he was cut off for the rest of his life from the house of God. This judgment had come upon him immediately after his presumptuous sin of offering sacrifice in the temple. It was clear from this incident that the judgment was regarded as judicial – coming directly from the hand of God – and not biological. As the king, he was granted immunity from exclusion from David's city, but only by means of a boundary separating him from the city.

There is no question that quarantine was legal for those dwelling inside the cities of Israel. Men were cut off from their homes, their families, their livelihood, and especially from the household of faith. They could not participate in the covenant rituals and feasts of Israel. This was the ultimate civil quarantine in ancient Israel, other than execution.[7] It meant excommunication from Passover and the loss of citizenship.

To Protect the Public

The justification for quarantine in Leviticus 13 was the need to protect the public. The spread of the disease, or other forms of God's judgment, was to be halted by removing the afflicted individual from the city. The concern was public health, but it was not a concern about biological contagion. It was concern about the willingness of God to afflict other individuals with the disease or other afflictions because of the rulers' unwillingness to enforce God's law. Thus, the quarantining process of Leviticus 13 was primarily judicial. In fact, it would probably be safe to say that it was entirely judicial. Only by the extension of the

7. Being confined to a city of refuge at least had a temporal limit: the death of the high priest (Num. 35:25).

principle of the protection of others within the city is it legitimate to classify today's diseases as being subject legally to the Bible's quarantining process.

Consider a contemporary individual who has contracted a contagious disease. He has become a threat to the community. If the community is required by law to finance this individual until such time as he recovers biologically from the disease, it is less likely that the community will take the necessary steps to isolate him. Common law therefore does not require the civil government to compensate the quarantined individual. Neither does biblical law. This is why quarantine is a devastating event in the life of the individual. Historically, quarantined people have not been permitted to leave their homes. Others have not been able to come into those homes without falling under the ban. While it is assumed that charity will be forthcoming to help the quarantined individual in his time of need, it has been assumed until very recently that the State has no legal obligation to support that person during the period of his confinement. To do so would raise the cost of confining individuals, and it would therefore lead to an unwillingness on the part of public health officials to confine them. This would increase the risk of contagion and disease in the community.

The contagious nature of the disease is, in effect, a form of violence. It is violence conducted by a third party, namely, the biological organisms that transmit the disease, but it is still a form of violence. The carrier places other people at risk. Thus, common law determined that an individual who becomes a threat to the community must be removed from the community so as to reduce the likelihood of this indirect form of violence. Public health measures are directed against the disease primarily and against its carriers secondarily. But with respect to a judicial affliction, this Mosaic law is no longer in effect.[8]

---

8. See North, *Boundaries and Dominion*, ch. 9, section on "Civil Authority."

Conclusion

Wenham has summarized the Levitical laws of quarantine. He correctly relates them to the Levitical holiness laws.[9] The quarantine laws of Leviticus had more to do with quarantining the people from the presence of God than they did with quarantining sick people from healthy people. For example, a blemished priest had to be kept away from God's presence in the temple (Lev. 21:17-21). The laws of leprosy were related to the temple's laws of purity far more than they were to modern public health laws. This is why any conclusions that we attempt to draw from these laws must be done by analogy, not directly.

What can we say with confidence? First, the civil government did possess lawful authority to remove urban residents from their homes in order to protect others in the community from the judgment of God. This judgment came in the form of plague. The contagion was judicial, but the threat did exist.

Second, the priest possessed the civil authority to remove houses and people from a city. His judicial declaration as an ecclesiastical agent had to be enforced by the civil magistrate.

Third, the victim of the plague had to bear the expenses associated with the results of the quarantine. Because there was no command in the Old Testament that the State support quarantined individuals, it is not possible to derive from this law any biblical injunction for State welfare programs. The only legitimate economic conclusion to draw from this law by analogy is that there is no State welfare function. The job of the civil government is to protect people from violence, not support people who have been afflicted, either naturally or judicially. To argue any other way is to make the State into an agency of healing rather than an agency of protection. The State is an agency that is supposed to bring negative sanctions against evildoers. There is no biblical warrant for the concept of the State as a healer. The job of the State is to prohibit behavior that

9. Wenham, *Leviticus*, pp. 213, 214.

threatens other individuals physically. If this threatening behavior is breathing upon others, then the State must see to it that the individuals who are a threat to others are not put into close contact with those who might be injured as a result.

If the State in the Mosaic Covenant was not told by God to support those who fell victim to diseases that mandated quarantine, then there is no biblical case for the State as an agency of tax-financed healing today. If the victim of leprosy in the Mosaic Covenant was forced out of his home by the State, and made to wander outside the city, and still the State was not responsible for his financial support, then the case for modern socialized medicine cannot be based on any biblical text.[10] It must be based on the argument from silence. It must be based on the conclusion that there has been a fundamental change in the function of civil government in the New Testament: from protector (Old Covenant) to healer. We have yet to see the exegetical case for such a change. While the presuppositions of the twentieth century's political order favor such a view of the State – as did the presuppositions of the ancient pagan world – humanist presuppositions are not a valid substitute for biblical exegesis.

10. When I raised this argument in my debate with Ron Sider in the spring of 1981 at Gordon-Conwell Seminary, his rhetorical response was clever. He cried, "Unclean, unclean!" He then admitted that he had never heard anything like this before. But he made no attempt to answer my argument exegetically.

Part 3

SEPARATION
(Lev. 17-22)

INTRODUCTION TO PART 3

Therefore shall ye keep my commandments, and do them: I am the L*ORD. Neither shall ye profane my holy name; but I will be hallowed among the children of Israel: I am the* L*ORD which hallow you, That brought you out of the land of Egypt, to be your God: I am the* L*ORD (Lev. 22:31-33).*

Separation: this is the heart of the Book of Leviticus, the third book of the Pentateuch. The biblical meaning of *holiness* is to be *set apart* by God, i.e., *hallowed*. Separation and holiness are inescapably linked; or, we might say, inescapably *bound*. Leviticus 17-22 presents the laws of separation.

Leviticus 22:31 speaks of profaning God's name in relation to obeying the commandments. This points back to the third commandment, which prohibits the taking of God's name in vain (Ex. 20:7). God places a boundary around His name; to violate this boundary is to profane it. That this law is recapitulated in a passage mandating obedience to God's commandments should not be surprising. Point three of the biblical covenant model, ethics, is related to the third commandment. It is also related to the eight commandment, "thou shalt not steal" (Ex. 20:15), the Bible's supreme affirmation of the rights of private property, i.e., the right of individuals to own, use, and sell (disown) property.[1]

---

1. Gary North, *The Sinai Strategy: Economics and the Ten Commandments* (Tyler,

The separation described in Leviticus is multifaceted. Separation was judicial: sacred, common, and profane. It was geographical: the holy of holies in relation to the temple; the temple area in relation to the rest of the nation; each tribe of Israel in relation to the other tribes; walled cities in relation to the countryside; the very land of Israel in relation to the land outside the boundaries. Tribal separation was in turn prophetic, relating to the promised Seed (Gen. 3:15; 49:10). Separation was priestly: Aaron and Levi; Levi and the other tribes; Israel and the nations. Separation was chronological: the three mandatory yearly feasts, the sabbatical year, and the jubilee year. It was biological: breed vs. breed. It was dietary: clean and unclean. It was physical: clean and unclean. It was ritual: clean and unclean. It was economic: rich and poor. It was political: citizen and non-citizen. It was above all ethical: good and evil.

It is in these chapters that the hermeneutical problem with Leviticus – and with the Mosaic covenant generally – presses the commentator. Which of these laws were cross-boundary laws? Which applied both inside and outside the nation of Israel? The geographically cross-boundary laws were universal moral laws, and as such, their binding character has crossed over into the New Covenant. To use a New Covenant metaphor, these laws were resurrected with Jesus.

Texas: Institute for Christian Economics, 1986), ch. 8.

10

THE PROMISED LAND AS A COVENANTAL AGENT

Defile not ye yourselves in any of these things: for in all these the nations are defiled which I cast out before you: And the land is defiled: therefore I do visit the iniquity thereof upon it, and the land itself vomiteth out her inhabitants. Ye shall therefore keep my statutes and my judgments, and shall not commit any of these abominations; neither any of your own nation, nor any stranger that sojourneth among you: (For all these abominations have the men of the land done, which were before you, and the land is defiled;) That the land spue not you out also, when ye defile it, as it spued out the nations that were before you. For whosoever shall commit any of these abominations, even the souls that commit them shall be cut off from among their people (Lev. 18:24-29).

The theocentric meaning of this passage is that God is the Lord of history. He brings judgments in terms of His covenantal law. History is theocentric. It is therefore to be understood in terms of the covenant.

God, the supreme authority of the covenant (point one), possesses the power to impose sanctions directly (point four), but He usually chooses to use agents in this task (point two). In this passage, He uses an agent to separate covenant-breakers from the society of covenant-keepers (point three).

Leviticus 18, more than any other chapter in the Bible, connects a society's obedience to biblical law and its geography. This chapter describes the land as vomiting out those who disobey God's laws: separation. This graphic metaphor is that of a geographic area that literally forces out of its presence all those who disobey these laws.

The vomiting land of Canaan is one of the most peculiar metaphors in the Bible. Bible commentators do not go into detail on just why it was that the land should be described here as vomiting people from its midst. The reason for the commentators' silence is that they have not recognized that this language is more than metaphorical; it is covenantal. It has to do with a system of boundaries and oaths. The land of Canaan was a covenantal subordinate in a hierarchical system of authority, just as the whole earth has been since the creation of Adam. This language is therefore *judgmental*. It describes a unique hierarchical-judicial relation among God, the land of Israel, and those who lived inside the land's boundaries. The pre-fall hierarchical relationship – God> covenant-keeping man> nature – has been distorted because of sin, although the hierarchical requirement remains the same. The earth brings forth thorns and weeds to thwart mankind; the land of Israel vomited out its inhabitants.

The Promised Land as the Enforcer

Israelites were warned to obey God's laws, "That the land spue not you out also, when ye defile it, as it spued out the nations that were before you." The land is described as serving as *God's sanctioning agent*. Like the hornets that went before the Israelites as they removed the Canaanites (Ex. 23:28), so would the land spew them out if they committed the same sorts of sins that the Canaanites had committed. Historically, the Assyrians and Babylonians spewed them out of the land under the Mosaic Covenant. Yet the land was spoken of as the covenantal agent in the Mosaic Covenant, while the ascended Jesus is spoken of as the agent of spewing in the New Covenant: "So then because thou art lukewarm, and neither cold nor hot, I will spue thee out of my mouth" (Rev. 3:16). The language is both covenantal and symbolic in each case. The land did not have a literal stomach and a literal gullet. Jesus does not literally spew out churches. Yet the language of vomiting is used in both cases. The imagery of vomiting is appropriately disgusting, and it is used throughout the Scriptures to describe sin and its consequences.[1] This imagery is that of a man who has eaten something that he should have avoided, and his stomach rebels. This unpleasant event is supposed to remind him: don't eat this again. The metaphor's message: "Go and sin no more." Israel never learned this lesson.

The imagery of the land's vomiting is closely connected to the Mosaic dietary laws, as we shall see. When those dietary laws ceased to have any covenantal relevance – definitively in Acts 10; finally in A.D. 70 – the Promised Land ceased to perform this covenantal task.

Special Promise, Special Claim

The strategic reality of the symbolism of the land's spewing out the Canaanites was that *Israel possessed a unique legal claim on the land as a result of God's promise to Abraham*. Israel was authorized by God to commit genocide, or mandate total expulsion, against the land's existing inhabitants. God brings negative sanctions in history. He did so with the firstborn of Egypt, and again when Egypt's army perished in the Red Sea. He had shown no mercy to those who rebelled against Him. He would tolerate no mercy on the part of the Israelites against the inhabitants of Canaan. "And thou shalt consume all the people which the LORD thy God shall deliver thee; thine eye shall have no pity upon them: neither shalt thou serve their gods; for that

1. Job 20:15; Prov. 23:8; 26:11; Isa. 19:14; Isa. 28:8; Jer. 48:26; II Pet. 2:22.

will be a snare unto thee" (Deut. 7:16). Why no pity? Because of the abomination of their gods. God's warning: similar worship inside the land will bring similar military sanctions (Deut. 8:19-20). God subsequently raised up Assyria and Babylon to perform an analogous service for Him, which is why this passage warned of a future spewing forth.

The land specified as God's agent was the Promised Land, not Egypt or any other plot of ground. Only the land inside *God's covenantal boundary of separation* served as His agent of negative military sanctions. This leads us to a conclusion: because the Promised Land could serve as a prosecuting witness against Israel, it was unique. The witness for the prosecution is required to cast the first stone (Deut. 17:7). The earthquake is the obvious example of stone-casting by the land (Isa. 29:6; Zech. 14:5; Joel 2:10; Nahum 1:5). This quaking is the language of covenantal judgment. Israel's covenantal agent, Moses, had already experienced this. "And mount Sinai was altogether on a smoke, because the LORD descended upon it in fire: and the smoke thereof ascended as the smoke of a furnace, and the whole mount quaked greatly" (Ex. 19:18). It took place again at the crucifixion of Jesus Christ (Matt. 27:51). Conclusion: If the land's office as *witness for the prosecution* still exists, then its office as *stone-caster* still exists. Because the resurrected Christ appears as the vomiter in New Covenant imagery, I conclude that He is the witness who brings judgment against societies.

What about this prophecy in the Book of Revelation? "And the kings of the earth, and the great men, and the rich men, and the chief captains, and the mighty men, and every bondman, and every free man, hid themselves in the dens and in the rocks of the mountains; And said to the mountains and rocks, Fall on us, and hide us from the face of him that sitteth on the throne, and from the wrath of the Lamb" (Rev. 6:15-16). The reason such language applied to that event is because the prophecy was intended to be fulfilled a few years after it was written. This prophecy of looming covenantal judgment was fulfilled in A.D. 70: the fall of Jerusalem.[2]

Military Sanctions

The Mosaic Covenant's symbolic use of the land as God's agent of negative sanctions represented military conquest: Israel vs. the Canaanites, Moab vs. Israel (Jud. 3), Canaan vs. Israel (Jud. 4), Midian vs. Israel (Jud. 6), Phoenicia and Ammon vs. Israel (Jud. 10; 13), Syria vs. Israel (II Ki. 5:2). In the cases of Assyria vs. Israel and Babylon vs. Judah, the Israelites were actually removed from the land. If someone should argue that the New Covenant has transferred to the earth in general the symbolic authority to serve as an agent bringing negative sanctions, meaning that God still raises up nations to bring military sanctions against His people, he must also insist that genocide is still authorized by God as the mandatory strategy of covenantal conquest by His people. But genocide is not the way of the gospel; persuasion, not military conquest, is its means of evangelism. Conclusion: the land no longer serves as a covenantal agent under the New Covenant except in the general Adamic sense (Gen. 3:17-19). That is, the *symbolism* of the land as God's covenantal agent is no longer valid; *the arena of covenantal conflict is no longer the military battlefield*.

With the abolition of the unique covenantal status of Old Covenant Israel, God ceased to speak of the Promised Land as His covenantal agent. Remember, it did not act as a covenantal agent until the Israelites crossed into the land from the wilderness. Egypt had not spewed out God's enemies. The idea that the land is in some way the bringer of God's military sanctions against covenant-breakers was valid only under the Mosaic Covenant, and only within the boundaries of national Israel.

---

2. David Chilton, *The Days of Vengeance: An Exposition of the Book of Revelation* (Ft. Worth, Texas: Dominion Press, 1987), pp. 196-97.

Ethics and Geography

The issue was ethics, point three of the biblical covenant model. The focus was geography: the Promised Land (Lev. 18:2-5). The laws that God's people must follow in the land should not be the laws of either Egypt or Canaan. While the text does not specifically mention it, it is clear that God's historical sanctions were involved. The Israelites had already seen the sanctions that God had brought against Egypt. First, there were plagues inside the land. Second, the Egyptians had given precious gems and precious metals to the fleeing Israelites. Third, the Israelites had been expelled from Egypt as God's means for providing deliverance and liberation. The Egyptians lost their slave labor force. Similarly, God tells them in this chapter that there will be comprehensive negative sanctions imposed against those who presently dwell in the land of Canaan. The Canaanites will someday be vomited out by the land, i.e., by the invading Israelites. The imagery of *vomiting out* symbolized a military phenomenon – *invasion of the land* – and the cultural phenomenon of *replacement by a new nation*.

The operational factor here was ethics. God promised them that when they entered the land and established residence, the plagues of Egypt would be removed from the land, *if* they remained covenantally faithful (Deut. 7:15). The God of *liberation* they understood as the God who brings *positive and negative sanctions in history*. What is unique about this chapter is that the land itself is described as imposing negative sanctions against law-breakers. The Promised Land would become God's covenantal agent after they invaded Canaan. The land was a surrogate for man.[3] Because of this, living inside the land's boundaries meant that all residents were under a theocratic order.[4]

3. For a detailed discussion, see Gary North, *Boundaries and Dominion: The Economics of Leviticus* (computer edition; Tyler, Texas: Institute for Christian Economics, 1994), ch. 10, section on "The Land as a Surrogate for Man."

4. *Ibid.*, ch. 10, section on "Theocratic Order in the Promised Land."

Strangers in the Land

During the post-exilic era, the same degree of civic evil in the land did not defile the land in equal measure as it had before the exile. There are several reasons for this. Most important, *the exile marked the end of the Davidic theocracy*. Kingship was never again restored politically inside the boundaries of Israel. The highest civil appeals court lay outside the boundaries of the land. The post-exilic period was the era of the empires: Medo-Persia, Macedonia, and Rome. Cyrus of Persia was God's designated anointed agent (Isa. 45:1). This transfer of kingship beyond the land's boundaries led to a fundamental judicial change inside the land. Resident aliens could now inherit rural land permanently (Ezek. 47:23). Also, Greek and then Roman military forces remained in the land. The Samaritans, brought in by the Assyrians after the Northern Kingdom fell, remained as permanent residents within the original geographical boundaries of Israel, accepting a deviant theology that was loosely related to authorized worship (John 4:19-25).

The central judicial manifestation of the sanctuary status of the Promised Land was the temple. There was a *judicial centrality of worship* in the post-exilic era that was even greater than during the pre-exilic era. The Israelites never again indulged themselves in the worship of the gods of Canaan. The purity of the temple, the sacrificial system, and the national synagogue system was primary. *The land is no longer said to be a covenantal agent after the exile*. It did become a covenantal threat one last time in A.D. 70, but this was after the establishment of the New Covenant. The fall of Jerusalem marked the transfer of the kingdom of God to the church (Matt. 21:43): the final annulment of the Promised Land's covenantal status. There were strangers in the land after the Babylonian exile, and these strangers exercised lawful civil authority, but this no longer threatened the sanctuary status of the nation. What would threaten it was the presence of strangers in the temple.

The metaphor of vomiting symbolized a successful military invasion of the land and its subsequent conquest. After the exile, God's people were no longer sovereign over civil affairs in the land. The threat of invasion by a strange nation was no longer a covenantal threat to Israel's civil order, which was not governed by God's covenantal hierarchy. In this sense, a boundary violation of Israel's borders was no longer a major theological problem. Being vomited out of the land was no longer a covenantal threat, except in response to their unsuccessful rebellion against pagan civil authorities who were already in the land. With the replacement of the temple by the church as God's dwelling place in history, it is Jesus Christ who now spews His enemies out of His presence (Rev. 3:16).[5]

The Replacement of the Promised Land

The kingdom of God cannot be confined geographically in New Testament times. Any nation can lawfully covenant with God today.[6] Israel was the single covenanted nation of Old Testament, which alone acknowledged the sanctions of God and the revealed law of God, and which alone required circumcision of all its male citizens. Only one other nation briefly covenanted under God, Assyria (under Jonah's preaching), but this covenant was soon broken.[7] Today, however, there is no monopoly of the Promised Land. All nations are required by God to covenant with Him.[8] Their law structures are supposed to be bibli-

---

5. See North, *ibid.*, ch. 10, subsection on "The Church as the New Temple."

6. Gary DeMar, *Ruler of the Nations: Biblical Blueprints for Government* (Ft. Worth, Texas: Dominion Press, 1987).

7. This seems to have been a common grace covenanting process – formal public obedience to the outward civil laws of the Bible – since there were no covenantal heirs remaining at the time of Assyria's conquest of Israel. Also, there is no indication that they were circumcised as part of their national repentance.

8. Kenneth L. Gentry, Jr., *The Greatness of the Great Commission: The Christian Enterprise in a Fallen World* (Tyler, Texas: Institute for Christian Economics, 1990), ch. 10.

cal. They are to turn to the whole Bible in search of civil laws and civil sanctions.

This is denied by Christian defenders of the polytheistic worldview known as political pluralism. They deny that nations can or should formally make a covenant with the Trinitarian God of the Bible. They argue that Trinitarian oaths remain valid for church and family, but not the State. But Covenant Land status has become a universal promise to all nations rather than a restricted promise to one nation. A nation becomes a biblical sanctuary by means of its covenant. So, where the preaching of the gospel is, there we find a nation being asked to become judicially holy ground. *The gospel has universalized the covenantal promises of God*. But there has been a change in administration because of the missionary work of the church inside non-Christian nations: the land of a covenanted nation is no longer God's covenantal agent, except in the sense that it is the place to which men's bodies return after death (Gen. 3:19). Israel's radical geographical inclusion/exlusion is annulled.

Natural and Supernational Disasters

The land of Israel ceased to be an agent of vomiting when the Old Covenant ended in A.D. 70. After A.D. 70, earthquakes and other geographical phenomena ceased to be relevant covenantally within Palestine, i.e., ceased to be predictable in terms of corporate ethics. This is not to say that earthquakes, like any other kind of disaster, are not signs of God's wrath in general against mankind in general, but there is very little biblical evidence that earthquakes are still part of God's *predictable* covenantal sanctions in history. Jesus is now the agent of judgment, seated on the throne beside God. The land of Israel is no longer an instrument for separating covenant-breakers from covenant-keepers. While nations can lawfully covenant with God in the New Testament order, the lands so constituted judicially are not part of the Abrahamic promise, which was a promise geographically limited to what Abraham could see and walk through (Gen. 13:15-17). Thus, it is fruitless to search the historical records of earthquakes in covenant-keeping nations and covenant-breaking nations in the expectation that a predictable pattern will be discovered.[9]

If I am incorrect about this, then the land still mediates between God and man. We do have such a case in the Old Testament: Cain's curse. "When thou tillest the ground, it shall not henceforth yield unto thee her strength; a fugitive and a vagabond shalt thou be in the earth" (Gen. 4:12). This was a sanction against Cain, whose brother's blood had penetrated the land and testified against Cain (Gen. 4:10). The promised sanction was not active but rather negative: the absence of positive sanctions. The curse in Genesis 4 was agricultural: the land would no longer yield its fruit to Cain. So, Cain built a city (Gen. 4:17). He had been a tiller of the soil; he became a resident of a city. He was not threatened with an earthquake; he was threatened with personal famine. He avoided personal famine by building a city and becoming a trader or other non-agricultural producer. He escaped the curse of the ground by (presumably) switching occupations – he would no longer be a shepherd or a cattle drover – and by changing his residency: rural to urban.

Cain's curse did not speak of earthquakes: the active stone-casting that the land later brought against Israel at the close of the Old Covenant order in A.D. 70. While I believe that God will reveal to covenant-keeping societies techniques that minimize the effects of earthquakes, I do not believe that He will predictably alter their number and intensity in relation to the degree of the societies' obedience to His law.

9. One earthquake that struck a sin center was the 1994 southern California earthquake, which centered in the Canoga Park-Chatsworth area. This is the center for pornographic movie production in the U.S. Models who appear in such movies temporarily became less enthusiastic about their work, according to one agent for these performers. "It's put the fear of God into them." *Christianity Today* (March 7, 1994), p. 57.

The last great wave of such covenantal speculation took place in the aftermath of the Lisbon earthquake of 1755.[10] When rational men concluded that they could make no ethical sense of that momentous event, they ceased searching for such covenantal connections in history. Their initial error in expecting to find specific ethical relevance in the 1755 earthquake led to a rejection of a covenantal worldview in general, a rejection that enhanced the universal triumph of Newtonian rationalism in the late eighteenth century.[11] If earthquakes are irrelevant covenantally, rational men concluded, then so are all the other natural disasters of life, which is why we call them *natural* disasters. This was also Solomon's conclusion in the midst of his existential period: "All things come alike to all: there is one event to the righteous, and to the wicked; to the good and to the clean, and to the unclean; to him that sacrificeth, and to him that sacrificeth not: as is the good, so is the sinner; and he that sweareth, as he that feareth an oath" (Eccl. 9:2). What we should affirm is this: *the arena of God's predictable historical sanctions has moved from geography to society.*

Let me give an example of this move from geography to society. Jesus announced that God does not send more or less rain on a society in terms of its theology or its ethical standards. On the contrary, God "maketh his sun to rise on the evil and on the good, and sendeth rain on the just and on the unjust" (Matt. 5:45b). The positive effects and negative effects of sun and rain fall indiscriminately on the righteous and the wicked. The positive effects of sun and rain are accentuated economically by societies that pursue God's law. Similarly, the negative effects of too much sun and too much rain are minimized in societies that pursue God's law. Matthew 5:45 is a statement regarding God's general laws of covenantal cause and effect; the statement applies to earthquakes as well as to sun and rain. In

10. T. D. Kendrick, *The Lisbon Earthquake* (Philadelphia: Lippencott, 1956).

11. Voltaire included a section on the Lisbon earthquake in *Candide*.

other words, people who build homes in flood plains or on top of major seismic faults will not see their property predictably protected from the effects of flooding or earthquakes merely because they pray a lot or give money to the poor. The best they can legitimately expect from God is better information about controlling floods or better construction methods that resist Richter-7 quakes. I seriously doubt that increased percentages of adultery will produce increased percentages of Richter-9 quakes.[12]

Conclusion

Under the Mosaic Covenant, God dwelt in Israel in a unique way. As men approached God's earthly throne room, they approached holy ground. The extreme edges of this series of concentric holy boundaries were the nation's geographical boundaries. The land of Israel therefore acted as God's covenantal agent. In the New Covenant era, there is no holy ground separate from common ground. We do not take our shoes off when we enter a church, as God required of Moses when he stood on holy ground (Ex. 3:5), and as some Eastern religions and Islam require. We do not have ritual foot washings. The land of the New Covenant no longer serves as a covenantal agent. It no longer brings predictable sanctions in history. It is no longer tied covenantally to military affairs.

Prior to the exile period, the land was spoken of in terms of its covenantal position as God's representing and represented agent. The land was represented by man, but it also represented God when it came time for God to bring His negative sanctions against covenantally rebellious residents inside the land's boundaries. The Promised Land was analogous to God in the

12. If I am wrong, Westminster Seminary West would be wise to move out of Escondido, California to, say, Lynden, Washington. Combine the morality of Southern California and the San Andreas fault, and you have a prescription for disaster if the land is still a covenantal agent.

sense that it is said to vomit the nations out of the land, just as God is also said to be the one who drives the nations out of the land.

In the New Testament, we no longer legitimately speak of the land's vomiting out its inhabitants. Instead, we read of the kingdom and its worldwide expansion. Because the self-consciousness and consistency of the individual is supposed to be greater under the New Covenant than under the Old, the New Testament does not speak of the land as analogous to both God and man. We read instead of the sword of the Lord: the word of God that proceeds out of the mouth of God. "And out of his mouth goeth a sharp sword, that with it he should smite the nations: and he shall rule them with a rod of iron: and he treadeth the winepress of the fierceness and wrath of Almighty God" (Rev. 19:15).

One reason why the land is no longer spoken of as vomiting out its inhabitants is that the progress of the gospel is no longer conducted by means of military conquest. There is no longer a God-sanctioned system for covenant-keeping people to replace covenant-breaking people by means of expulsion. Today, they replace covenant-breakers through performance and productivity. They are to replace them in positions of cultural and political leadership – not by force but by performance.

Covenant-keepers are also to conquer covenant-breakers by means of preaching. Men are to brought into the "Promised Land" today by bringing them into the church, and then by bringing the whole nation under the biblical civil covenant through a democratic vote. This does not equate the visible church with the Promised Land, but it acknowledges that the kingdom of God is primarily manifested in history by the church, and all those who profess to be Christians are supposed to be members of the church. Thus, the land is not the primary agent of enforcement; Jesus Christ is. By purifying the church, He enables His people to purify themselves and to begin the conquest of the earth by means of the preaching of the gospel.

He draws men to Himself rather than casting them out of the land. He does not need to remove covenant-breakers from the land in order to make room for His people. Instead, *the kingdom of God is the Promised Land*, in history and eternity, and by preaching the gospel, we invite all men to enter into that Promised Land. Ultimately, it is the goal of Christianity to bring the whole earth under the dominion of Christ.[13] This means that it would do no good for the land to vomit the inhabitants out because, ultimately, there is no contiguous land to vomit them into. The New Covenant's strategy is *conquest by conversion* rather than conquest by destruction and expulsion.

13. Kenneth L. Gentry, Jr., *He Shall Have Dominion: A Postmillennial Eschatology* (Tyler, Texas: Institute for Christian Economics, 1992).

11

GLEANING: CHARITY WITHOUT ENTITLEMENT

And when ye reap the harvest of your land, thou shalt not wholly reap the corners of thy field, neither shalt thou gather the gleanings of thy harvest. And thou shalt not glean thy vineyard, neither shalt thou gather every grape of thy vineyard; thou shalt leave them for the poor and stranger: I am the Lord *your God (Lev. 19:9-10).*

I have already covered certain aspects of gleaning in *Tools of Dominion*.[1] The theocentric principle that undergirds this law is this: God shows grace to man in history by allowing mankind access to the fruit of God's field, His creation. Put another way, God allows mankind *inside the boundaries* of His field. Fallen man is in the position of the poverty-stricken, landless Israelite or stranger. God does not exclude externally cursed mankind from access to the means of life in history. Neither were landowners in post-conquest Mosaic Israel to exclude the economically poor and judicially excluded residents of the land. *Fallen man is always a gleaner.*[2]

1. Gary North, *Tools of Dominion: The Case Laws of Exodus* (Tyler, Texas: Institute for Christian Economics, 1990), pp. 819-22.

2. Gary North, *Boundaries and Dominion: The Economics of Leviticus* (computer edition; Tyler, Texas: Institute for Christian Economics, 1994), ch. 11, section on

Gleaning was a form of morally compulsory charity. It remains the primary *moral* model for biblical charity, but, as I hope to show, it is not a *literal* model for modern charity. *In a non-agricultural society, gleaning cannot become a literal model for charity*. Morally, however, gleaning is to be our guideline for charity: those in the community who have been called in the West "the deserving poor" are to be allowed to do hard work in order to support themselves and improve their condition. God expects the more successful members of a community to provide economic opportunities for such willing laborers – opportunities for service.

As with every biblical law, this law is ultimately theocentric. The beneficiaries of this law were God's representatives in history, just as victims of crimes are representatives of God. Crime is primarily an assault on God by means of a crime against man, who is made in God's image.[3] Crime is man's attempt to bring unlawful negative sanctions against God by bringing them against one of His representatives. Charity is analogous to crime in this respect, but with this difference: the sanctions are both lawful and positive. What a person does to the poor is counted as if he did it to Jesus (Matt. 25:32-40).

A Lawful Claim: Moral or Legal?

God announced that the poor people and resident aliens in Israel were to be invited in by the landowner so that they could harvest the corners of the field and the fallen grain. This meant that as a class, they had a moral claim on the "droppings" of production. This also meant that they had no legal claim on the primary sources of income of an agricultural community. They were *invited* in. There was no State-financed welfare in Israel.

It would have been difficult for a judge or a jury to identify which individuals in the community had the legal right to bring

---

"We Are All Gleaners."

3. North, *Tools of Dominion*, p. 279.

charges against the landowner as the legal victims of his refusal to honor the gleaning laws. The text specifies no negative institutional sanction that had to be imposed on a landowner who refused to honor the gleaning laws. God is indirectly revealed as the agent who would bring negative sanctions against a landowner who refused to honor the gleaning laws. The State was not authorized by the text to bring these sanctions. This implies that *the sanctions were individual rather than corporate*. God did not threaten the community with negative sanctions. But without the threat of God's negative sanctions against the whole covenanted community, there was no justification for civil sanctions. Civil sanctions were imposed in Israel in order to substitute the State's subordinate wrath for God's more direct wrath against the community. Furthermore, in case of a violation of the gleaning law, there would have been no easy way to determine legitimate restitution. *Where there are no civil sanctions, there is no crime*. God would curse the owner directly, but the society was not at risk. Thus, civil sanctions were inappropriate.[4]

This law applied only to agriculture: field and vineyard. Field and vineyard are the sources of bread and wine: Melchizedek's meal for Abram (Gen. 14:18) and also the Lord's Supper.[5]

The Economics of Gleaning: Who Paid, Who Benefitted?

What were the economics of the gleaning law? In a sense, the requirement that the landowner and professional harvesters leave a small portion of the crop for the gleaners made this portion analogous to the manna that God had supplied to the Israelites during the wilderness wandering. That miraculous though predictable food was a pure gift of God. Similarly, both the produce of the land and God's grace in establishing the

---

4. See my discussion in *Boundaries and Dominion*, ch. 11, subsection on "Individual Sanctions Against Disobedience."

5. *Ibid.*, ch. 11, section on "Bread and Wine."

requirement that the landowners and harvesters share with the gleaners were signs of God's continuing grace to the poor. The gleaners were visibly dependent on God's grace for their survival. This had also been the case for the whole nation in the wilderness.

Gleaning laws were exclusively agricultural laws. God commanded the harvesters of the field and the vineyard to be wasteful – wasteful in terms of their personal goals, but efficient in terms of God's goals. They were to leave part of the produce of both the vineyard and the grain field for gathering by the poor.

This law indicates that *the leftovers of the Promised Land belonged to God*. God transferred the ownership of these high harvesting cost economic assets from the landowner and the harvester to the poor and the stranger. The owner in one sense did benefit, at least those owners who paid their field hands wages rather than by the supply harvested, i.e., piece-rate payment. The obedient owner did not have to pay salaried harvesters to collect marginal pickings. This lowered his labor cost per harvested unit of crop. But the net income loss as a result of gleaning did lower his return from his land and planting expenses. There is no doubt that this economic loss of net revenue constituted a form of compulsory charity. It was a *mandated positive sanction*. This should alert us to the fact that this law was *not* a civil law. It was rather a church-enforced law. The church, not the State, is to bring positive sanctions in history. The church offers Holy Communion, not the State.

The gleaning law was also to some extent an advantage to the piece-rate harvester because he was able to achieve greater output per unit of time invested. He was not expected to spend time gathering the marginal leftovers of the crop. *Marginal* returns on his labor invested were higher than they would have been had it not been for this law. Nevertheless, both the owner of the land and the piece-rate harvesters did suffer a loss of *total* income because of this law. The harvesters saved time but gathered less. They did suffer a loss of income compared to what they would have earned apart from this law.

How did piece-rate harvesters suffer a loss of total income? Because they could not lawfully gather the total crop of the field or the vineyard. Each worker had to leave some produce behind, which means that his income suffered. This also means that the poor of the community were in part funded by the *slightly less poor*: the piece-rate harvesters. The harvesters were reminded of the burdens of poverty. This in effect became an *unemployment insurance* program for the harvesters. They knew that if they later fell into poverty, they would probably be allowed to participate as gleaners sometime in the future. They forfeited some income in the present, but they did so in the knowledge that in a future crisis, they would be able to gain income from gleaning. Both the landowner and the piece-rate worker financed a portion of this compulsory insurance program.

Benefits for the Landowner

The law placed a burden on the landowner. Yet this burden was in fact a form of liberation *if* he acknowledged the covenantal nature of the expenditure. It was analogous to the tithe. By honoring it, he was acknowledging God's sovereign ownership of his land. This act of sharing placed him visibly in the service of the great King. That King was his protector, for he was a vassal. As with rest on the sabbath, the owner could rest confidently in the knowledge that the King would defend his interests as a vassal if he abided by the terms of the King's treaty.

There was another benefit to the faithful owner, according to Aaron Wildavsky, one of the most informed experts in the world on the history of taxation.[6] He was also a student of the Mosaic law. He wrote of the gleaning law that "Compulsiveness

6. Carolyn Webber and Aaron Wildavsky, *A History of Taxation and Expenditure in the Western World* (New York: Simon & Schuster, 1986).

easily converts to fanaticism. The farmer who harvests not 99 percent of his crop but every last little bit becomes consumed by his compulsion. Soon enough excess – getting it all – becomes an overwhelming passion."[7] He quite properly identifies fanaticism as idolatry.[8] The gleaning law restrained the idolatry of greed. It reminded rich men that they did not need to keep everything they managed as God's stewards in order to remain successful. It restrained them from the passion of autonomous man: defining themselves in terms of their wealth rather than their obedience to God.

Hard Work

The gleaner had to work harder than the average worker did in order to gain the same quantity of crops. The "easy pickings" were gone by the time the gleaner was allowed into the fields. This means that he had high marginal labor costs. That is, he had to invest more labor per unit of crop harvested than the piece-rate harvester did. Assuming that the harvester's goal was a higher return on labor invested, it was preferable to be a piece-rate worker than to be a gleaner. To be a gleaner was to be in a nearly desperate condition.

In the case of both piece-rate work and gleaning, most of the labor costs of harvesting were borne by the poor. The rich man did not work in the fields. But there were degrees of poverty. By far, the greater cost per unit harvested was borne by the gleaners. In modern terminology, this might be called a *workfare* program instead of a welfare program. The gleaner was not a passive recipient of someone else's money. He had to work. Furthermore, marketing costs may actually have been borne by the poor. It would have been legal for the poor individual to take whatever pickings he gained from the field and

---

7. Aaron Wildavsky, *The Nursing Father: Moses as a Political Leader* (University, Alabama: University of Alabama Press, 1984), p. 30.

8. *Idem.*

go to a store owner or other purchaser of the crop. The owner of the land did not have the right to compel the gleaner to sell the gleanings to him. This means that the gleaner was enabled to obtain a competitive market price for the output of his labor. Of course, this would have been extra work and risk for the gleaner, and it involved specialized knowledge of markets. Nevertheless, it was a right that the gleaner possessed.

There was another great advantage to this form of morally enforced charity: it brings hard-working, efficient poor people to the attention of potential employers. In effect, employers in Mosaic Israel could "glean" future workers from society's economic "leftovers."

This system produced more food for the community than would have been produced apart from the law, although costs were higher than otherwise.[9]

Subsidizing Localism

Is becoming a low-paid field hand God's universally required on-the-job training system? No. God no longer expects poor people to learn how to become field laborers. In Old Covenant Israel, however, it was important that men learn to serve Him locally. God wanted to preserve localism and tribalism. The tribal system was important for the preservation of freedom in Israel. Tribalism and localism broke down attempts to centralize the nation politically. Thus, the gleaning law was part of the social order associated with Old Covenant Israel. It reinforced the tribal system. It also reinforced rural life at the expense of urban life – one of the few Mosaic laws to do so. The landowner was required by God to subsidize the rural way of life. Local poor people were offered subsidized employment on the farms. Had it not been for the gleaning system, the only rural alternative would have been starvation or beggary in the country.

---

9. North, *Boundaries and Dominion*, ch. 11, section on "More Food for Everyone."

They would have moved to the cities, as starving people all over the world do today.

The jubilee land inheritance laws kept rural land within the Israelite family. This land inheritance was the mark of civil freemanship for every tribe except the Levites. If a daughter inherited land because there was no brother, she could not marry outside her tribe if she wanted to keep the land. "Neither shall the inheritance remove from one tribe to another tribe; but every one of the tribes of the children of Israel shall keep himself to his own inheritance" (Num. 36:9). While a rich man might move permanently to a city, the poor person was encouraged by the gleaning law to stay closer to home.

Cities would inevitably have become the primary dwelling places for most Israelites if they had obeyed God as a nation. Population growth would have forced most people into the cities. The size of family farms would have shrunk as each generation inherited its portion of the land. But until Israel's corporate covenantal faithfulness led to population growth and increased per capita wealth, each tribe's poor members were to be subsidized by the gleaning law to remain close to the tribe's food supplies. This law was a means of retarding the growth of an unemployed urban proletariat. The countryside was to be the place where the poor man received his daily bread. He would have to do simple agricultural labor to receive his food.

This law also promoted localism rather than distant bureaucracy.[10]

No Subsidy for Evil

Another important reason for localism was the concern of God that His resources not be used for evil purposes. Either the provider of this agricultural charity had to reside locally or else his specified agent had to. Local residents in rural Mosaic Israel were more likely to be well known to the landowners.

10. *Ibid.*, ch. 11, subsection on "Localism and Bureaucracy."

Presumably, the cause of their poverty was also well known to the landowners, or at least this could be discovered without much difficulty. The gleaning system reduced the subsidy of evil. The poor person who was poor as a result of his own bad habits did not have to be subsidized by the landowner and the professional harvesters who worked his fields. The landowner had the right to exclude some poor people from access to his fields. Gleaning was therefore a highly personal form of charity, since the person who was required to give this charity was also the person who screened access to the fruit of the land.

This means that the gleaning law was a form of *conditional charity* in each individual recipient's case, although the loss was compulsory from the point of view of the landowner. *Biblical charity is always conditional.*[11] Charity is not to subsidize evil, for it is an act of grace. Unconditional charity is antinomian. In a fallen world, unconditional charity will inevitably subsidize evil.

Strangers

The local member of the landowner's tribe was the primary recipient of charity, but he was not the only one. The other recipient of the grace of gleaning was the stranger. These strangers were presumably resident aliens who had fallen on hard times. They might have been hired servants who could not find employment. They were people who did not want to go back to their home country. They were therefore people who wanted to live under the civil law of God in the Promised Land. These people were entitled to the same consideration that the poor Israelite was entitled to. It is clear that this arrangement would have increased the emotional commitment of the resident alien to the welfare of the community. He was treated justly.

---

11. Ray R. Sutton, "Whose Conditions for Charity?" in *Theonomy: An Informed Response*, edited by Gary North (Tyler, Texas: Institute for Christian Economics, 1991), ch. 9.

The land was God's covenantal agent. This law was agricultural only. It did not apply to urban businesses.[12]

Conditional Charity: Moral Boundaries

The owner of the farm had to acknowledge the sovereignty of God by obeying the gleaning laws. These laws were a reminder to him that *biblical authority always has costs attached to it*. The owner of the land had been given capital that other people lack. He therefore had an obligation to the local poor as God's agent, for the land itself was pictured as God's agent. His obligation was to supply the land's leftovers to the poor.

In making this demand, the gleaning law placed decisive limits (boundaries) on both the poor rural resident and the State. It limited the moral demands that the poor could make on economically successful people in the community. The poor had no comparable moral claim against the successful non-agricultural businessman. This law also limited the demands that the State could make on the community in the name of the poor. Biblical law specified that the man with landed wealth should share his wealth with the deserving poor, but not the poor in general. The deserving poor were those who were willing to work hard, but who could not find work in the normal labor markets. *In short, the gleaning law had conditions attached to it*. The idea of morally compulsory, non-conditional charity was foreign to the laws of the Mosaic Covenant.[13]

---

12. North, *Boundaries and Dominion*, ch. 11, section on "A Law of the Land, Not the Workshop."

13. It is equally foreign to the law of the New Covenant. This assertion appalls Timothy Keller. See Keller, "Theonomy and the Poor: Some Reflections," in William S. Barker and W. Robert Godfrey (eds.), *Theonomy: A Reformed Critique* (Grand Rapids, Michigan: Zondervan, 1990), pp. 273-79. He calls for initially unconditional charity to all poor people. He argues that anyone in need anywhere on earth is my neighbor, thereby universalizing the moral claims of all poor people on the wealth of anyone who is slightly less poor. He writes: "*Anyone* in need is my neighbor – that is the teaching of the Good Samaritan parable." *Ibid.*, p. 275. He rejects the traditional Christian concept of the deserving poor (pp. 276-77). He concludes: "I am proposing

The gleaner had to work very hard, for he reaped only the leftovers. This means his income was lower than would have been the case if he had been a professional harvester. Gleaning provides a lesson to the poor: *there are no free lunches in life*. Someone always has to pay. The economic terms of the gleaning system established that only the destitute members of the community would have become gleaners. If there had been any other source of income, other than begging, they would have taken it. The hard work and low pay of gleaning was an incentive for the individual to get out of poverty.

We must always remember that the gleaning laws operated within the framework of the jubilee land laws. The poorest Israelite in the community at some point would inherit from his father or grandfather a portion of the original family inheritance. The size of that portion of land depended on the number of male heirs. Its value depended on the economic productivity of local residents who could legally bid to lease it.[14] The more productive the heir, the more likely that he would be able to retain control over it.[15] Gleaning gave the poor Israelite an opportunity to gain management and other skills as a landowner prior to the time that he or his children would be given back the original family land grant through the jubilee land law. The gleaning law provided training that could in the future be converted into family capital. The gleaning law was designed to keep poor people in the local agricultural community.

The gleaning law did not apply to non-agricultural businesses or professions. It originated from the fact that God declared

---

that the reconstructionist approach to biblical charity is too conditional and restrictive." *Ibid.*, p. 278. For my response, see North, *Westminster's Confession: The Abandonment of Van Til's Legacy* (Tyler, Texas: Institute for Christian Economics, 1991), pp. 271-73. See also Sutton, "Whose Conditions for Charity?" in North (ed.), *Theonomy*, ch. 9.

14. The economist looks for a price to establish value. The highest market value is determined by the highest market bid by a potential buyer or long-term leaser.

15. This legal right to inherit the family's land did not extend to the stranger until after the exile (Ezek. 47:22-23).

Himself as the owner of the Promised Land. He did not verbally claim an equally special ownership of businesses. The land, not business, was identified as God's covenant agent that brought God's covenant lawsuits in Old Covenant Israel.[16] Any attempt to derive a modern system of charity, public or private, from the gleaning law faces this crucial limitation. It was not intended to apply outside a farm.

The modern welfare State is a perverse mirror image of the gleaning law. It disregards the moral boundaries of charity and substitutes unconditional charity. This has greatly expanded both the political boundaries of charity and the extent of poverty. People get paid by the State for being poor; the market responds: more poor people. The welfare State now faces bankruptcy: the destruction of those dependent on its support.[17]

There are few modern applications of the gleaning law, which was a land law. Modern society is not agricultural.[18] Nevertheless, there is a theological principle that undergirds gleaning: *fallen man is always a gleaner*. But redeemed men will progressively escape their dependence on other men's charity as society advances through God's grace.

Conclusion

The gleaning law was part of an overall system of political economy. Many of the details of this political economy were tied to the Promised Land and the sacrificial system of that land. The economic laws of Leviticus were more closely attached to the Promised Land and the sacrifices than the laws of Exodus and Deuteronomy were. *The Levitical land laws were part of a temporary system of landed familism, tribalism, and localism.*

---

16. See Chapter 10, above.

17. North, *Boundaries and Dominion*, ch. 11, section on "Unconditional Charity: Political Boundaries."

18. *Ibid.*, ch. 11, section on "Modern Applications of the Gleaning Law Are Few."

Localism and tribalism were both basic to the application of the gleaning law in Mosaic Israel. The authority of the local landowner to chose who would glean and who would not from among various candidates – the boundary principle of inclusion and exclusion – transferred great responsibility and authority into his hand. This kind of personalized charity is no longer taken seriously by those who legislate politically grounded welfare State policies in the modern world. Such a view of charity transfers too much authority to property owners, in the eyes of the politicians, and not enough to the State and its functionaries. But it is not the principle of localism that changes in the New Testament era; it is only the landed tribalism that changes. When the kingdom of God was transferred to a new nation (Matt. 21:43), meaning the church, the Levitical land laws were abolished.

Gleaning no longer applies in the New Covenant era. The jubilee land law was annulled by Jesus through: 1) His ministry's fulfillment of the law (Luke 4:16-27); 2) the transfer of the kingdom to the church at Pentecost (Matt. 21:43; Acts 2); and 3) the destruction of Jerusalem in A.D. 70. Can we learn anything from the gleaning law? I think we can, but these lessons are essentially negative. They show us what should not be done, not what must be done, to avoid God's negative sanctions.

The lessons from gleaning are these: 1) all charity is based legally on the fundamental principle that God owns the earth (Ps. 24:1); 2) a third party has no legal civil claim on any asset that he does not own;[19] 3) charity should not create a permanent dependence on the part of the recipient; 4) charity should not subsidize evil; 5) it should involve hard work except in cases

19. In Old Covenant Israel, a person had the right to pluck grapes and corn from a neighbor's fields, though only what he could carry in his hands (Deut. 23:24-25; Luke 6:1). This law increased the likelihood of travel and communications, since visitors would not have to return home to eat or carry food with them everywhere. The economic benefit of being located close to a road – cheap transportation of farm commodities – was partially offset by this open access law.

where the recipient is medically incapacitated; 6) it should not provide living standards that are higher than the poorest workers in society are able to earn.

The fundamental principle learned from the gleaning laws is this: *charity in a biblical social order must not be based on the idea that the State is a legitimate institution of salvation*. The State is not a biblically legitimate agency of social healing. It is an agency of public vengeance (Rom. 13:1-7). It possesses a lawful monopoly of violence. It therefore cannot be entrusted with the authority to take the wealth of successful people in order to reward the poor. If it is allowed to do this, its agents become the primary beneficiaries of the confiscated wealth. Its political and bureaucratic agents will gain power over both the poor and the economically successful. These agents will become permanent spokesmen for the official beneficiaries of the wealth, namely, the poor. They will have no incentive to get poor people as a class permanently out of poverty. A system of legal entitlements for the poor becomes a system of legal entitlements to full-time jobs for those who administer the system. This is the antithesis of the gleaning system of the Mosaic Covenant. In that system, the productive members of the economy all had an economic incentive to get the poor back to work: the landowners, the piece-rate harvesters, and the poor themselves.

12

VERBAL BONDS AND ECONOMIC COORDINATION

Ye shall not steal, neither deal falsely, neither lie one to another. And ye shall not swear by my name falsely, neither shalt thou profane the name of thy God: I am the LORD (Lev. 19:11-12).

Stealing, false dealing, and lying are prohibited. So is swearing falsely by God's name. The latter is worse because it invokes God's name and authority to defend fraud. It compounds the infraction. The passage begins with a judicial boundary that facilitates interpersonal relations: the boundary around private property.

What is the theocentric principle that undergirds this law? *Protecting the name of God*. This passage of Scripture is clearly an application of the third commandment. The third commandment prohibits the profaning of the name of God.[1] That is, *it places a sacred judicial boundary around the name of God* – a boundary that must not be transgressed without permission. The name of God is the protected asset. Like a brand name in advertising, the name of God is strictly licensed by its Owner. Men

1. Gary North, *The Sinai Strategy: Economics and the Ten Commandments* (Tyler, Texas: Institute for Christian Economics, 1986), ch. 3.

are not to swear falsely by the name of God. Swearing in this case is an illegal imitation of a formal act of oath-taking.[2] This form of the violation – swearing falsely – is an aspect of point four of the biblical covenant model: oath/sanctions.

Nevertheless, the primary focus of this text is the profanation of God's name: a *verbal boundary transgression*. This places the law under point three of the biblical covenant model, just as the third commandment is under point three.[3] Additional evidence is the fact that this passage tells us not to defraud a neighbor or rob him. This is a prohibition against theft. The eighth commandment parallels the third commandment.[4] They are both aspects of point three of the biblical covenant model. The theocentric basis of this law is the absolute integrity and inviolability of God's name. A profane act is an act that transgresses a sacred boundary, either judicial or geographical.[5] Therefore, in the Bible, the laws against theft are part of the general law of God that protects His name and His property from any unauthorized invasion.

This commandment has implications that extend beyond the courtroom. Men are not to lie to each other in order to further their own ends at the expense of others. Even when not under oath, their words are to be reliable; other people will plan their own activities in terms of what is said. For example, a physician is not supposed to tell his patients that they are sick when they are healthy, nor is he to tell them they are healthy when they are not. The same rule applies to economic transactions.

Bonds and Promises

"A man's word is his bond." This maxim is a familiar one in Western history. The word "bond" points to a legal transaction.

---

2. *Idem.*
3. *Ibid.*, Preface, p. xvi; ch. 3.
4. *Ibid.*, Preface, p. xx; ch. 8.
5. See Chapter 6, above.

In the Bible, a covenantal bond establishes a formal legal relationship under God: personal, ecclesiastical, familial, or civil. While a promise does not possess the judicial authority of a covenantal bond, since it lacks a lawfully imposed self-maledictory oath, a promise is nevertheless analogous to a covenant bond. It is a verbal contract.

In modern finance, a bond is a promise to pay. A person gives up money in the present in exchange for a specified stream of money in the future, with the return of the principal at a stated date, which will complete the transaction, thus ending the legal relationship.

Promises are a form of inventory. In this sense, they are a form of capital. They serve as substitutes for physically stored assets. Instead of accumulating physical assets for future use, a producer relies on another person to deliver the goods, literally or figuratively.[6] A broken promise in such circumstances is the economic equivalent of an empty storage facility that was thought to be full. Worse; someone had guaranteed that it would be full. The missing good or service creates a kind of falling domino effect: delayed production all down the line. The person who fails to deliver on time produces losses for the person who became dependent on him.

The person who promises to deliver goods or services puts his reputation on the line. The better his reputation, the more business he will generate, other things (such as price) being equal. It pays a person to gain a reputation as one who keeps his word. He tells the truth, and when other people plan their actions in terms of what he says, they are not disappointed (Ps. 15:4). This person lowers the cost of doing business with him. By lowering the price of anything, the seller increases the quan-

6. In the 1980's, the advent of inexpensive computers and the spread of overnight air cargo delivery companies made possible the development of "just in time" manufacturing. Manufacturers can time the delivery of raw materials and parts so that they do not have to invest in large inventories. This has made manufacturing far more efficient.

tity demanded. This is why a person who keeps his word has increased his market value.[7]

The fraudulent person is like a thief who steals the assets stored in a warehouse, and who then swears that the warehouse is full. He posts a verbal bond. Like a bonded warehouse illegally emptied by its manager, the violation of this verbal bond is regarded by God as theft. The promise-giver owes double restitution to his victim.

In this case, the promise-giver has used God's name in his false bonding. This involves an additional infraction. The bond-giver has invoked God as his personal bonding agent. This is a major violation of God's law. "And ye shall not swear by my name falsely, neither shalt thou profane the name of thy God: I am the LORD" (Lev. 19:12). By doing this, the false swearer has placed himself under the sanctions of God. What is said here of individuals is equally true for nations and societies: foreign policy.

What this law prohibits is the illegal transfer of private property. It prohibits a direct transfer in the form of robbery. The law says that we must not steal. There is also an indirect form of theft that is prohibited: fraud. Fraud is false dealing. It involves giving a false report to a buyer. First, fraud means a refusal to abide by one's previous word to another individual. Second, it means the deliberate camouflaging of one's word: to appear to say one thing but in fact mean something else. This is done in order to gain legal control of something that is not lawfully one's own. The other person transfers ownership voluntarily but in confusion. The classic example in the Bible is Satan's deception of Eve: the promise that she would become as God (Gen. 3:5). Third, false dealing is the outright defrauding of the individual. An example of this form of fraud is simple lying. A person says that he is going to do something, but he

7. The market value is an asset's present price. This price is the asset's expected stream of future income, discounted by the prevailing rate of interest.

never intends to do it, and if all the facts were available, it could be proven that he never intended to do it. The deliberate writing of a check drawn against insufficient funds would be such an act of fraud.[8] So would posting as collateral for a loan an asset known by the holder to be worth less than what he insists it is worth. So would gaining multiple loans on the basis of one piece of collateral: fractional reserves.[9]

The Problem of Economic Coordination

The economic issue that must be explained is the problem of the coordination of individual plans. How is this best accomplished: By State compulsion or market coordination? It is clear from both the eighth commandment and the tenth commandment that private property must be honored. Men must neither steal nor covet their neighbor's property. This means that biblical economics rests on the ideal of the legitimacy of private property. "Christian socialism" is an oxymoron.[10]

In a market economy, individuals make plans about the future, and then they act in terms of these plans. They buy or sell or hold in terms of their individual plans. The question then is: How are the millions of individual decisions integrated with each other so that men can participate together in the division of labor? This is the problem of the revision of economic plans. How do people change their plans and expectations in response to the decisions of other individuals? This is the problem of feedback: information coupled with sanctions. In what form does information come to an individual that other participants in the market approve or disapprove of what he is

---

8. In most states in the United States, this act constitutes a felony.

9. Gary North, *Tools of Dominion: The Case Laws of Exodus* (Tyler, Texas: Institute for Christian Economics, 1990), pp. 739-40; North, *Honest Money: The Biblical Blueprint for Money and Banking* (Ft. Worth, Texas: Dominion Press; Nashville: Thomas Nelson Sons, 1986), ch. 8.

10. Gary North, *Boundaries and Dominion: The Economics of Leviticus* (computer edition; Tyler, Texas: Institute for Christian Economics, 1994), Appendix D.

doing or not doing? This is the problem of economic sanctions.[11]

Promise and Dependence

The importance of the division of labor has been emphasized in modern economics ever since Adam Smith wrote his famous first chapter on the production of pins.[12] A highly skilled individual craftsman cannot produce a great number of pins in one day, Smith observed. On the other hand, a small group of relatively unskilled workers can produce thousands of pins if they are given the proper capital equipment. He pointed to the division of labor as the explanation – a fundamental biblical concept (Rom. 12; I Cor. 12). The division of labor allows the increase of output per unit of scarce resource input. Cooperation produces greater wealth than economic autarky can. It is the division of labor which enables us to pool our talents in order to gain much greater output together than we could possibly have achieved as individuals acting in isolation. Because increased cooperation increases individual productivity, it also increases per capita wealth. This increase – a positive sanction – is the incentive for men to cooperate economically with each other. It is a very important aspect of the preservation of society. It allows the pooling of individual talents, and it allows the pooling of capital. This capital can be of three kinds: economic, intellectual, and moral.

Cooperation requires a degree of predictability. First, it requires the predictability of *timing*. Let us consider a business. A business manufactures a particular product. To do so, it requires resource inputs. Because people's knowledge of markets is limited, and because it is expensive to go out and buy exactly what you want exactly when you want it, businesses

11. Gary North, *Inherit the Earth: Biblical Blueprints for Economics* (Ft. Worth, Texas: Dominion Press, 1987), ch. 9.

12. Adam Smith, *The Wealth of Nations* (1776).

carry inventories of raw materials and spare parts. These inventories compensate for men's imperfect knowledge of the future. An inventory of raw materials and spare parts enables the business to expand production without a great deal of warning. An inventory of finished products enables the business to meet the demand without increasing the price of the product. It allows the business to continue operating if there is an interruption of the delivery of materials. In other words, inventories create a production system in which there are fewer bottlenecks. Bottlenecks create "ripple effects," both in the company and in some cases in the economy as a whole. Inventories smooth production. But they must be paid for. They must be "carried." They tie up resources.

Second, the producer seeks predictability in the *pricing* of his resource inputs as a means of gaining predictability of production. If an individual agrees to sell you an item, and you then make plans in terms of the price of that item, you have become dependent on him. Similarly, you have agreed to pay him a money price at a particular time. He has therefore become dependent on you. The free market economy produces a system of independence legally (individualism) and mutual dependence economically (coordination of plans). We are legally free to make our voluntary decisions; therefore, we are judicially independent. At the same time, because of these voluntary agreements, we become mutually interdependent in our economic activities. This is why pricing is so important. It enables us to make decisions rationally in terms of existing conditions of supply and demand.

Third, predictability of *quality* is also important. This one is more difficult to police. What level of quality is good enough at a particular price? This is difficult for the buyer or the seller to specify in a written contract. We seek ways of gaining this information inexpensively, both as buyers and sellers. The existence of brand names is very important in lowering the costs of people's estimates of quality. Pricing also plays an important role.

We are used to the idea that an item that costs five times more than another item is probably of higher quality. We believe that the product will not break readily, and therefore our time won't have to be spent taking the thing in to be repaired. Brand names enable us to make better predictions about the performance of both services and goods.

This is an aspect of the third point of the biblical covenant. God protects His name from profanation. In a similar way, we protect our own names from misuse. We have a property right to our names: other people are not allowed to use our names to promote their ends without our agreement. This is why the existence of brand names and the legal right to property established in a brand name are so important in a society, in order to reduce the uncertainty of the future. People can make decisions based on price and name with respect to the quality of the good or the service.

Contracts

Contracts are a crucial part of this system of economic interdependence. God's goal is greater cooperation among men and a reduction of coercion in economic affairs: peaceful exchange. Peace on earth is a biblical goal. Contracts enable people to specify their own performance more precisely. At least when all parties understand the terms of the contract, contracts reduce the cost of cooperation, and hence increase the quantity of cooperation demanded.

There are always inherent limitations on contracts. One limitation is the difficulty of specifying the conditions of performance. This is why, as societies become more complex, contracts tend to grow longer and in ever-smaller print. Lawyers are the ones today who speak to each other about the nature of the conditions; the actual participants in the contract are rarely able to understand. This has created a new priesthood of lawyers. They speak to each other, and their supposed employers

– clients – have to accept on faith what it is that they have just signed.

Language has limitations. Every possible condition cannot be included in a contract; hence, mutual trust is mandatory. This trust can be abused by one party. So can the contract's language. God serves as the final arbitrator in all contracts. He knows each person's intentions.

Another limit on contracts is the existence of clogged civil courts. A contract may specify exactly what the other individual is supposed to do, but if you cannot get that person into court, the contract does you very little good. This is why mutual trust is important. Nevertheless, people who trust each other should still write contracts in order to settle differences later. Even if the two parties presently agreeing to act together do not get involved in a dispute, their heirs may later get involved in a dispute. Still, we cannot expect contractualism to substitute for trust and moral responsibility. We should not expect words apart from intentions to protect us in all situations. We should not trust the letter of the law to protect us from evil intentions and the skilled misuse of language.

Mutual Trust

The society in which mutual trust is increasing is more likely to be a productive society. Men seek others who will deal honestly with them.[13] The cost of policing contracts is reduced as mutual trust increases. This is a form of *self-government* instead of civil government which becomes dominant. We have appeals courts in a society: both church and State. Less pressure is placed on these courts when mutual trust is increasing. This

13. "And it came to pass at that time, that Abimelech and Phichol the chief captain of his host spake unto Abraham, saying, God is with thee in all that thou doest: Now therefore swear unto me here by God that thou wilt not deal falsely with me, nor with my son, nor with my son's son: but according to the kindness that I have done unto thee, thou shalt do unto me, and to the land wherein thou hast sojourned" (Gen. 21:22-23).

enables a society to achieve its goals with less expenditure than a society in which there is very little mutual trust.

There is another aspect of mutual trust that is important: *historical experience*. When, over a period of time, we have gained the trust of another person, this becomes an asset to us and to him. He has created a mutually beneficial asset. As the record of the participants' past performance becomes available, it makes it less expensive for other individuals to enter into agreements with these individuals.[14] Therefore, a society that has a good record of performance has increased other societies' trust in doing business with it. This is an important aspect of increasing the international division of labor.

The division of labor is a manifestation of the doctrine of the Trinity: unified efforts by more than one person. The Trinity therefore has implications for both social theory and economic theory.[15] Economic theory based on coordination by either the State (macroeconomics) or the market (microeconomics) is incomplete.[16] Theory must be grounded on the idea of the covenant.

Economic Coordination: Covenantal

The free market individualist says that the best economy is the result of human action but not of human design: no central planning by the State. The collectivist says that any economy that is the exclusive result of human action but not of human design is an imperfect economy. It needs the coercive power of the State to right wrongs, correct imbalances, and achieve high employment and sustained economic growth without inflation.

---

14. A word that increases advertising response is "proven."

15. Gary North, *Boundaries and Dominion: The Economics of Leviticus* (computer edition; Tyler, Texas: Institute for Christian Economics, 1994), ch. 12, sections on "The Doctrine of the Trinity and Social Theory" and "The Doctrine of the Trinity and Economic Theory."

16. *Ibid.*, ch. 12, section on "Economic Coordination: State or Market?"

The covenantalist insists that the economy is the result of God's absolute sovereignty through delegated authority. The economy is designed by God. When the human actions of large numbers of the members of society conform to His law, the general economic results will be good, conforming to God's promises (Lev. 26:4-5, 9-10). When men's actions are rebellious, the economic results will be bad (Lev. 25:20, 22, 26). The collective results are determined by God's responses to widespread covenantal faithfulness or rebellion.

This means that there is an all-seeing, omnipotent agent who oversees the "big picture." He does not require or even permit men to usurp His role as overseer. He delegates to individuals the responsibility of planning for the future. He delegates to individuals the authority to bring evil-doers to the attention of civil magistrates. He relies on the individual's self-interest in both cases: the entrepreneur's quest for profit[17] and the victim's quest for restitution.[18]

This system rests on the concept of the honest word: the producer's promise to buy, the seller's promise to sell, and the oath-bound witness' promise to tell the truth to the court. It also rests on the idea of God's predictable corporate sanctions in history: economic, military, and biological-medical.[19] God takes care of the "big picture"; He delegates to individuals and voluntary associations the responsibility of administering the "local picture." This is the biblical doctrine of responsible (hierarchical) stewardship, which is always accompanied by the covenantal doctrines of law, judgment, and inheritance.

---

17. Frank H. Knight, *Risk, Uncertainty and Profit* (New York: Harper Torchbooks, [1921] 1965); Israel M. Kirzner, *Competition and Entrepreneurship* (University of Chicago Press, 1973).

18. North, *Tools of Dominion*, ch. 7. See also Gary North, *Victim's Rights: The Biblical View of Civil Justice* (Tyler, Texas: Institute for Christian Economics, 1990).

19. In Old Covenant Israel, there was another sanctioning agency: the land itself, i.e., the environment. See Chapter 10, above.

Covenantal economics asserts the existence of an original natural harmony of economic interests, but only in the garden of Eden. Since the fall of man, there has not been a harmony of interests. *There can be no permanent harmony of interests between covenant-breakers and covenant-keepers*. There can, however, be temporary cooperation in history based on mutual self-interest. The tares are not uprooted in history; neither is the wheat (Matt. 13:18-23, 36-43). Their cooperation is based either on the willingness of the wheat to abide by the stipulations that are established by the tares or on the willingness of the tares to abide by the stipulations established by the wheat: biblical law. It cannot be based on neutral civil law, since there is no neutral law. There is no neutrality. There is only covenant-breaking and covenant-keeping.

Conclusion

The prohibition against theft and false dealing is here linked to the prohibition against profaning God's name. This points to the parallel between the eighth commandment against theft and the third commandment against taking God's name in vain. The issue in the third commandment is misusing God's name in a formal oath. The issue here is lying. Swearing by God's holy name is prohibited; therefore, so is false dealing and lying.

Men must not deal falsely with each other. In economics, such a law increases the possibilities for cooperation. The division of labor and the specialization of production make possible greater output per unit of resource input. Honest dealing enables men to increase their productivity and their wealth.

"A man's word is his bond." This phrase points to the covenantal grounding of society: a legal bond between God and man, and among God and men, based on a self-maledictory oath. A contract is analogous to a covenant. Men may not use God's name in vain, so they may not swear by God in a contract. But there is an element of self-malediction: the contracting parties agree to submit themselves to an arbitrator or a civil magistrate when signing the contract.

Because of promises, men can cooperate with each other over time. The future becomes less uncertain because of the existence of promises. Thus, if we wish to overcome the economic uncertainties of life, we can enter into agreements with others. But each party to the agreement must deal honestly with the others; otherwise, men's plans regarding the future are undermined by the non-performance of others. The coordination of men's plans then becomes disrupted.

The West has generally been faithful to this law. The result has been the proliferation of contracts, culminating in the highly organized securities markets. These markets have led to a vast increase of wealth in the West. Men have been able to pool their assets, making possible the capitalization of present goods. Capitalization involves placing a present price on an expected future stream of income. If all men were liars all of the time, such capital formation would be impossible.

Because God has delegated authority and responsibility to men, they can cooperate. His system of hierarchical authority is a bottom-up system: men are free to do anything not specifically prohibited. A court system settles disputes between individuals. This is the structural foundation of a free market economy: local responsibility, voluntary cooperation, and hierarchical judgments after the fact. This is the opposite of bureaucracy: a top-down system of controls in which a central planning agency announces goals and standards, modifies them repeatedly, and then evaluates the performance of subordinates in terms of the previous announcements. If all men were liars most of the time, this is the kind of system mankind would be stuck with. It is Satan's system, for he deals with liars. Therefore, when society is marked by widespread lying and fraud, it will either move toward autarky or toward bureaucratic centralization: the many or the one. In both cases, productivity suffers.

13

PROTECTING THE WEAKEST PARTY

Thou shalt not defraud thy neighbour, neither rob him: the wages of him that is hired shall not abide with thee all night until the morning. Thou shalt not curse the deaf, nor put a stumblingblock before the blind, but shalt fear thy God: I am the LORD (Lev. 19:13-14).

The theocentric meaning of this passage is two-fold. First, God pays us what He has agreed to pay us, and He pays us on time; therefore, so should His people. Second, God is a protector of those who cannot protect themselves; therefore, so should His people.

What does a three-part law against fraud, robbery, and the withholding of wages have to do with a two-part law prohibiting an unheard curse against a deaf person and tripping the blind? The connection is not grammatical. These laws are judicially and economically linked. The link is two-fold, as I hope to prove: 1) God's desire to protect the weakest members of society; 2) God's establishment of ways to overcome the inherent limits on men's knowledge, especially limits on judges' knowledge.

This raises an important question. If we are to defend the deaf and the blind because they cannot defend themselves, isn't this a violation of the fundamental judicial principle of Leviticus

19:15, namely, that God does not respect persons? On the contrary, this case law affirms that the deaf and the blind are entitled to the same protection from cursing and tripping that anyone is. But because they cannot bring a lawsuit on their own behalf, a righteous person must do it for them. This upholds the universal authority of God's law.

I. Withholding Wages

The previous section of Leviticus 19 deals with theft through fraud: the deliberately deceptive use of words (vv. 11-12).[1] The first half of verse 13 repeats this warning. The second half adds another form of fraudulent wealth transfer: the withholding of a worker's wages overnight. This act is specified as fraud, and it is also specified as robbery. The question is: Why? If the worker agrees in advance to wait longer than a day for his pay, why should the law of God prohibit the arrangement? Or does it?

It is always helpful in understanding a case law if we can first identify the theocentric principle that undergirds it. Verse 13 deals with paying a debt. The employer-employee relationship reflects God's relationship to man. God provides us with an arena: life and capital. Similarly, the employer supplies an employee with capital that makes the employee more productive. Man is dependent on God. Similarly, the laborer has worked for a full day; the employer is required to pay to him at the end of the work day. The context is clear: *rapid payment for services received*. God employs us as His stewards. He gives us the tools that we need to serve Him and thereby serve ourselves. He always pays us on time. So should the employer. The employer who withholds wages from his employees is making a symbolic statement about God's relationship to man: God supposedly delays paying man what is rightfully owed to him. This symbolism is incorrect. It testifies falsely about God's character.

1. See Chapter 12.

A Position of Weakness

The wage earner in verse 13 is in a position of comparative weakness. He is assumed by God to be in a weaker economic position than the individual who is paying his wages. This employer-employee relationship reflects God's supremacy as the sovereign employer and man's subordination as a dependent employee.

If the wage earner is not paid immediately, then he is being asked by the employer to extend credit to the employer. The employer gains a benefit – the value of the labor services performed – without having to pay for this benefit at the end of the work day. The Bible allows this extension of such credit during daylight hours, but not overnight.[2] This law teaches that the weaker party should not be forced as part of his terms of employment to extend credit to the stronger party. God acknowledges that there are differences in bargaining power and bargaining skills, and He intervenes here to protect the weaker party. This is one of the rare cases in Scripture where God does prohibit a voluntary economic contract.

What if the worker says that he is willing to wait for his pay if he is given an extra payment at the end of the period to compensate him for the time value of his money (i.e., interest)? This would be an unusual transaction. The extra money earned from two weeks of interest would be minimal in comparison to the amount of the wage. In any case, to abide by the terms of this law, such a voluntary agreement would have to be *a legal transaction publicly separate from wage earning as such*. There would have to be a public record of its conditions. It would constitute an investment by the worker. But the worker would have to pay his tithe and taxes on this money before he could legally lend it to the employer.

---

2. By implication, the night laborer is under the same protection: he must be paid before the sun rises. The idea is that he must be paid by the end of the work day.

The law here specifies that an employer who hires an individual to work for a period of time has to have the money available to pay that individual on a daily basis at the end of each work day. This is the employer's standard requirement. There would be no confusion about this in a Christian covenanted society. There is no doubt that in the modern world, such an arrangement is not economically efficient. Checks must be written, checks must be delivered to individuals, account books must be kept, and so forth. If this had to be done daily, it would add to the expense of running a firm.[3] The larger the firm, the more difficult such an arrangement would be. Nevertheless, the employer is required by God to abide by this law. The question is: Can he lawfully substitute a more convenient payment scheme and still meet the requirements of this law?

Debt and Credit: Inescapable Concepts

If the employer decides that it is too much trouble to pay each worker at the end of each work day, he must advance the funds for the period of employment prior to the next payday. Thus, if the average period of employment between paydays is two weeks, the employer must bear the risk of paying an individual for work not yet received. The employer must extend credit to the worker. This is another way of saying that *the worker must assume a debt obligation*: two weeks of agreed-upon labor services.

Payments for a stream of continuous services cannot be simultaneous, although this limitation will change when the use of electronic cash becomes widespread.[4] Therefore, one of the

---

3. In the final stages of the German inflation in 1923, workers were sometimes paid cash in the morning. Wives would accompany them to work, take the cash, and rush to spend it on anything tangible before it depreciated during the day. This inflation devastated workers and employers alike. On the daily payment of wages in the second half of 1923, see Adam Fergusson, *When Money Dies: The Nightmare of the Weimar Collapse* (London: William Kimber, 1975), pp. 149, 191.

4. It is technically possible today to deposit money electronically into a worker's

two parties in this transaction must go into debt in this system, while the other must extend credit. *There is no escape from debt and credit apart from the technology of continuous payments.* What this law authorizes is an extension of credit by the worker to the employer for a maximum of one work day. At the end of the work day, the account must be settled; credit is no longer extended by the worker, so he receives his day's wage.

What if the worker is paid in advance for a week or two of labor? He then necessarily becomes a debtor to the employer. He is required to deliver the work that he has been paid to perform. This places the worker in a debt position, but it is not a long-term debt. It is not considered a form of slavery, but there is no doubt that the worker has voluntarily accepted payment in advance, and this creates an obligation on his part. This debt position is limited, however. The law's presumption is that the employer is not going to pay a person in advance for months of work except in very rare circumstances.

The Bible teaches that we are not to become indebted to others: "Owe no man any thing, but to love one another: for he that loveth another hath fulfilled the law" (Rom. 13:8). This must not be interpreted in an absolutist fashion. We know this because every person is in debt to God, and also to the perfect man, Jesus Christ, as a result of Christ's atoning work at Calvary.[5] This rule of debt-free living should be interpreted in a non-utopian sense. It means that *we are to avoid debt contracts that threaten our continuing legal status as free men.* It does not mean that we are to become hermits who separate ourselves from a

---

account on a moment-by-moment basis, just as it is possible for him to spend it on the same basis, but the cost of doing so is too high to make it feasible. This cost constraint will probably change in the near future as computer technology and the cost of using computer networks both decrease. Kevin Kelly, "Cypherpunks, E-money, and the Techniques of Disconnection," *Whole Earth Review* (Summer 1993).

5. This debt always involves common grace; sometimes it also involves special grace. Gary North, *Dominion and Common Grace: The Biblical Basis of Progress* (Tyler, Texas: Institute for Christian Economics, 1987), ch. 6.

division-of-labor economy. (It surely does not mean that we are required to become household slaves.)

The restraining factor against the extension of too much credit by the stronger party is the employer's fear that the worker will either quit before his term of service ends or else not produce competent work. It is too expensive for the employer to sue the average worker for damages; court expenses plus his own time in court exceed the money owed.[6] The economic judgment of the employer is the restraining factor. He suspects that he will not be repaid if he extends too much credit.

What this text specifies is that the *worker* must not be asked to work for a week or two in order to receive his wage. There is always a risk of default on the part of the debtor, whether he is the employer or the worker. This law specifies that the risk of default for this form of debt – wages beyond one work day – must be born by the employer, not by the worker. This law prohibits a form of robbery: by the employer and also by the employer's accomplice, i.e., the worker who can afford to accept a delayed-payment contract, thereby excluding the poorest workers from the labor market.[7]

The employer must not become a thief by withholding anyone's wages.[8] By forcing the employer to make restitution to his employed workers who had seen their wages withheld, the law reduces the amount of such robbery of those unseen by the judges: future workers who are too weak even to compete for the delayed-payment job.[9]

---

6. God does sue workers who default on His advance payments. Some are sued in history; all are sued on the day of judgment. Court costs are irrelevant to God.

7. Gary North, *Boundaries and Dominion: The Economics of Leviticus* (computer edition; Tyler, Texas: Institute for Christian Economics, 1994), ch. 13, sections on "A Case of Economic Oppression" and "Bargainers: Strong, Weak, and Weakest."

8. *Ibid.*, ch. 13, section on "What Did the Employer Steal?"

9. *Ibid.*, ch. 13, section on "The Limits of Judicial Knowledge."

Worker vs. Worker

In a poor nation, which the whole world was until the nineteenth century, an offer by a worker to accept delayed payment would have given this capital-owning worker a competitive advantage over destitute workers who needed payment immediately. This law establishes that competition among workers must not involve the employer's acceptance of such an offer by any worker. The biblical standard of payment is specified: payment at the end of the day. There may lawfully be payment in advance by the employer but not delayed payment, unless there is a legally separate interest-paying savings plan involved, as mentioned earlier.

Where this law is enforced, destitute workers in the community are not replaced in the labor force by less destitute workers who can afford to forego immediate payment. All workers are to be allowed to compete for jobs, irrespective of any worker's possession of reserves sufficient to tide him over until the next payday. So, one idea behind this law is to make job opportunities available to the destitute workers in the community. Everyone who is physically able to work is to be allowed to compete for a job on a basis independent of his asset reserves. *The destitute man's poverty is not to become the basis of his exclusion from the labor market*. His competitors are not allowed to use their ability to extend credit to an employer as a way to offset his only assets: his willingness and ability to work.

Weaker Parties

The worker needs protection. An employer might hire him for a period and then dismiss him without pay. Jacob's complaint against Laban was that Laban had changed his wages repeatedly, meaning retroactively (Gen. 31:7). To protect the worker from this sort of robbery, the Bible requires the employer to bear the risk of longer-term default on the part of a worker. The employer bears the risk that the worker may turn out to be inefficient and will have to be fired before he has fulfilled his contract. The worker may even cheat the employer by walking off the job before his term of employment is over. That is the employer's problem. He can minimize this risk by paying workers at the end of each day. In doing so, he does not allow them to become indebted to him. If he chooses to have more infrequent pay periods, then he must bear the risk of paying people in advance who turn out to be inefficient or corrupt workers.

It is not immediately apparent that this law deals with the robbery of the poor by the somewhat less poor. This law seems to have only the employer in mind as the agent of theft. But the employer cannot act alone in this act of theft. He needs accomplices, even if they are unaware of their economic status as accomplices. An employer who wants to discriminate against destitute workers by forcing them to extend him credit beyond one working day cannot do so without the voluntary cooperation of other workers. He cannot hire people to work without daily wage payments unless some workers are willing to work on these terms. The text identifies this practice as a form of robbery, but it is not merely the robbery of those workers who voluntarily agree to accept the terms of the contract; it is also the indirect oppression of all those workers who cannot afford to offer their labor services on these terms. It is above all the oppression of those who are *excluded* from the employer's work force, not those who are included. But it requires some knowledge of basic economics to discover this fact. This law's protection of the destitute worker's ability to bid for jobs is implicit in the text, not explicit.

On what legal basis does this law apply to the free market? Why should a voluntary contract – delayed payment – be prohibited by civil law? What makes the practice of delaying payment judicially unique, and therefore legitimately subject to interference by the civil government? Answer: the principle of *priestly pricing*. The closer we get to life-and-death transactions, the less valid is the economic pricing principle, "all the traffic will bear," i.e., "high bid wins." God does not sell salvation by means of "high bid wins." The law against delaying the payment of wages is an application of the ethics of priestly pricing. A destitute worker is not to be excluded from any labor market by an employer's policy of delaying payment. Delayed payment is a policy of excluding workers. *There are biblical judicial limits on voluntarism.*[10] No employment contract contrary to this law is legal in God's eyes. The civil laws of every nation should prohibit such delays in the payment of wages.

The typical employer is trying to minimize his risk when he hires competent workers rather than substandard workers. He delays payment because he wants to see each new worker prove himself before getting paid. This delay in payment pressures workers with little capital to quit early or never even apply for the job. *The practice of delaying wages is therefore primarily a screening device.* It favors workers who have capital in reserve. These capital reserves serve the employer as a substitute for other screening techniques. The employer's economic problem is the his lack of knowledge about the competence of the new worker. *The employer uses a delayed payment scheme in order to minimize his search costs in estimating the competence of new workers.* Accurate knowledge is not a zero-price resource. Employers try to obtain such knowledge as cheaply as possible. They use the new worker's willingness to accept delayed payments as a cost-effective substitute for more detailed information regarding the worker's abilities and his willingness to work.

II. The Deaf and the Blind

Verse 14 deals with the deaf man and the blind man: "Thou shalt not curse the deaf, nor put a stumblingblock before the

---

10. This fact does not constitute a legitimizing of an open-ended socialism, including some modernized version of medieval guild socialism. Biblical law, not socialist slogans, is the source of our knowledge of such limits on voluntary exchange.

blind, but shalt fear thy God: I am the LORD" (v. 14). Neither one of them can defend himself against the specified evil. The deaf man cannot hear the curse; the blind man cannot see the stumbling block. The person who takes advantage of their condition of weakness has broken the law of God.

These are case laws. They are specific applications of more general principles. We are supposed to deduce the general law from the specific conditions described in the case law. What are these conditions? Let us consider the easiest case first.

Tripping the Blind

The blind man must not be tripped, since there is no way that he can adjust for the obstacle. It is not his fault that he cannot see. There is nothing that he can do about his condition. It is not a moral weakness on his part that he is blind (John 9:1-3).

The context of this law is the payment of wages (v. 13). The case law of verse 14 means that the stronger party must not use another person's inherent weakness in order to pay him less than a market wage. By implication, he must not cheat the illiterate man or the mentally retarded person. He must acknowledge the existence of the other person's weakness and not use it to take advantage of him. Where the other person is *biologically unable to compensate for his weakness*, the employer is not to profit from the other person's incapacity.

Cursing the Deaf

A curse under the terms of the Mosaic law was an act of assault.[11] It still is. Modern societies still have laws on the books identifying curses as illegal, although these laws are rare-

11. The curse in this case means "make light," which connotes deliberate humiliation or abuse. Herbert C. Brichto, *The Problem of "Curse" in the Hebrew Bible* (Philadelphia: Society of Biblical Literature and Exegesis, 1963), pp. 120-22. James Jordan provided me with this reference.

ly prosecuted by victims in our day. The Bible regards a verbal curse as a judicial act with consequences in history, just as it regards a verbal blessing.

This outlook is foreign to modern man, both humanist and pietist. Modern man does not believe that God's blessings or curses are called down on others in history because a representative covenantal agent pronounces blessings or curses. The third commandment is clear: God's name must not be taken in vain. The frame of reference is the misuse of God's holy name – a boundary violation – by someone who is not authorized to invoke that name judicially.

Cursing a deaf man is a double violation: calling down God's curses illegitimately, and cursing someone who cannot respond judicially. The deaf man is unaware of the boundary violation. Because God's name has been misused, or at least the violator has judicially misused language, society is at risk. The agent who has been authorized by God to press charges in God's name in an earthly court – the victim – is unaware of the violation. This transfers responsibility for invoking a lawsuit from the victim to the witness.

Pressing Charges

The deaf victim must be informed of the infraction, and the blind person must be informed of the identity of the person who tripped him. The blind person cannot press charges. He did not see who tripped him. Similarly, a deaf person cannot respond to a curse against him, since he did not hear it. Through no fault of their own, these victims cannot bring a lawsuit against the evil-doers who have broken God's law.

But God can. So can His lawfully appointed courts if a representative of the victim either informs the victim or, if the victim cannot press charges himself (e.g., a mental defective), the representative presses charges in the name of the victim. Victims in these cases need spokesmen to act in their behalf.

As in the case of a crime, God is the primary victim.[12] The witness serves as a spokesman for both God and the victim. This law makes it plain that God expects others in the community to take action and serve as covenant agents in the name of the victims. How else could such public infractions of this law be prosecuted? A verbal curse is a public act in defiance of God's law. Such public acts must be prosecuted, not just because they are morally wrong – many immoral acts cannot legitimately be prosecuted under biblical law – but because they are public. The public character of this form of cursing places the integrity of the society on trial, for the victim cannot hear and respond as God's designated agent. If no witness intervenes to bring formal charges, then God will take action against the evil-doer and the society that has failed to protect the handicapped victim from his persecutor.

Conclusion

Grammatically, verses 13 and 14 are not linked; ethically and judicially, they are. The links are: 1) God's protection of the weakest members in society; 2) ways to overcome the limits on men's knowledge, especially the limits on the judges' knowledge. So, the judicial cases are different – theft vs. public assault – but the general prohibition is the same: do not harm the weakest parties.[13]

These case laws prohibit the victimization of the poorest and weakest members of the community. The case law in verse 13 deals with theft from economically weak workers and also (indirectly) the most impoverished workers in the community. The most impoverished workers are those who cannot afford to extend credit to their employer. They need to be paid at the

12. North, *Tools of Dominion*, pp. 279, 296, 300.

13. North, *Boundaries and Dominion*, ch. 13, section on "The General Legal Principle: Protecting the Weakest Party."

end of the work day. The employer is required to do this or else pay them in advance for a longer term of service.

This law proves that Mosaic Israel was not a debt-free society. There were creditors and debtors. A legitimate biblical goal is to reduce long-term debt, but God's civil law does not mandate absolutely debt-free living. Debt is basic to society, for society implies a division of labor. Debt will exist in a division of labor economy until such time as an economically efficient means of making moment-by-moment wage payments becomes universal.

The employer who delays payment to his workers is defrauding them. Verse 13 says this. But to do this, he is inescapably providing an opportunity for some workers to oppress their competitors. The worker who can afford to work without pay for a period is given an opportunity by the employer to steal a job away from a worker so poverty-stricken that he cannot survive without payment at the end of the day. This form of competition is illegitimate, this passage says ("fraud, robbery"). It is unfair competition. God's civil law makes it illegal for an employer to act as the economic agent of any employee against a destitute competitor. There are very few cases of unfair competition specified in the Bible, but this is one of them.

Verse 14 prohibits the active assault on the deaf and blind. We are not to attack defenseless people. The text specifies this. This case law also implicitly condemns all those who sit idly by when others *publicly* assault these defenseless people. We are required by God to become covenantal agents of those victimized people in our presence who are inherently incapable of defending themselves judicially: the deaf and the blind. We are to act as the ears of the deaf and the eyes of the blind whenever we hear or see others assault them. In short, we are to accept our role as covenantal witnesses. God reminds us of who He is: "I am the LORD" (14b).

A delay of payment is described in the text as robbery: a crime. A judge can impose a restitution penalty on the perpetrator. There is also a hidden element of oppression: the excluded workers. To become subject to civil law, oppression must be identifiable as a criminal offense. There must be definable criteria that make the act a crime. The indirectly oppressed, excluded worker is not the victim of a crime. Ironically, the one who has oppressed him, the employed worker, is the victim of a crime: delayed payment. Even more ironically, if the oppressor brings a lawsuit against his assailant, the employer, he thereby makes it less likely that he and his employer will be able to oppress the weakest party: the excluded worker. He therefore may refuse to press charges. This is why I think an excluded worker or the State acting on his behalf can bring a lawsuit against the employer to have the practice stopped.

If it is immoral to discriminate against the weakest worker, then what of trade union practices that exclude these same low-bidding weak parties, referred to by union members as "scabs"? Can this case law legitimately be extended to make all exclusionary trade union screening practices illegal? That is, should we define indirect economic oppression in such a way that all exclusionary hiring practices become crimes? If we do, then we violate a fundamental biblical principle: the predictability of the civil law. The law identified as criminal – robbery – an easily specified act: delaying payment overnight. Only when such oppressive acts are easily specified and prosecution becomes predictable by all parties should this case law be extended to create new civil laws. But the oppressive character of the contract should be recognized, and no legislation should be passed that imitates the "delayed payment" contract, with its exclusionary side effects. This would surely include laws mandating that employers deal with trade unions. The element of State coercion should not be imposed for the benefit of the oppressors, i.e., workers who are members of unions, which gain above-market wages only by excluding others from joining.

14

IMPARTIAL JUSTICE VS. SOCIALIST ECONOMICS

Ye shall do no unrighteousness in judgment: thou shalt not respect the person of the poor, nor honour the person of the mighty: but in righteousness shalt thou judge thy neighbour (Lev. 19:15).

The theocentric meaning of this law is that the State is to imitate God by doing what God does: judge all people without respect to their persons, i.e., their class, status, or power.

This law is one of the two most important laws in the Bible that deal with civil government. The other verse is Exodus 12:49, which insists that civil judgment in the land of the covenant must apply to all men equally, whether strangers or Israelites: "One law shall be to him that is homeborn, and unto the stranger that sojourneth among you." Exodus 12:49 confirms the judicially binding nature of the civil law of God: biblical civil laws are to be applied equally to all people residing within the geographical boundaries of a biblically covenanted society. The same civil laws are to be applied to everyone residing in the land, regardless of race, color, creed, or national origin.[1]

---

1. Gary North, *Moses and Pharaoh: Dominion Religion vs. Power Religion* (Tyler, Texas: Institute for Christian Economics, 1985), ch. 14: "The Rule of Law."

These binding civil laws have been revealed by God directly to mankind in the Bible, and *only* in the Bible.

Almost every legal theorist in Western society accepts the principle of equality before the law. This ideal is one of the bedrock foundations of Western civilization. It comes from the Bible, not from Greek and Roman law, both of which explicitly denied the concept of equality before the civil law. Classical law protected only citizens: males who had lawful access to the religious rites of the city. Women (half the adult population), slaves (one-third of all males), and foreign-born residents were excluded.[2] The ultimate manifestation of the biblical principle of equality before the law in history was God the Father's willingness to place His incarnate son, Jesus Christ, under the negative sanction that had threatened Adam. Paul writes: "He that spared not his own Son, but delivered him up for us all, how shall he not with him also freely give us all things?" (Rom. 8:32). Among these things that God gives is liberty. Liberty is a product, along with other judicial factors, of the ideal of equality before God's law. But Stoic natural law theory is not the source of this ideal; biblical law is. Natural law theory invariably falls into ethical dualism: one law-order for pluralistic society, another for Christians.[3] The natural law theorist prefers Pontius Pilate to Moses as a civil judge. Those Christians who defend natural law theory ignore this biblical judicial principle: any failure to impose God's specified civil sanctions in society necessarily requires the imposition of anti-biblical civil sanctions.

Sanctions: Evaluation and Imposition

Biblical civil justice must seek to apply written laws to public acts. Neither the social status nor the economic class of either

2. Gary North, *Boundaries and Dominion: The Economics of Leviticus* (computer edition; Tyler, Texas: Institute for Christian Economics, 1994), Appendix E: "Greek Mythology: The Myth of Classical Politics."

3. *Ibid.*, ch. 14, section on "Natural Law Theory: Ethical Dualism."

the victim or the accused is to be considered in judicial proceedings. The pronouncement by the judge or the jury regarding the fit between the law and the public act of the accused is to be based solely on the law and the evidence. Justice is never impersonal; it is wholly personal: the law, the act, the evidence, and the court's judgment.

Judgments should involve the imposition of sanctions: blessings (on the victim) and cursings (on the criminal). There is no neutrality. *Any failure to impose biblical sanctions, apart from the permission of the victim, is necessarily the imposition of unbiblical sanctions*. Biblical sanctions are limited. There must be the application of sanctions, but the victim always has the right to reduce the sanctions. Biblical sanctions are always based on the principle of restitution: to God and the victim.[4] The victim is to gain back what he lost plus a penalty payment. But biblical sanctions must not exceed what is legally appropriate to the crime. This places limits on the judges. The judges are not to declare greater sanctions than God's law allows. The judges therefore are under a legal boundary.

The imposition of the sanctions restores the judicial *status quo ante*. Judicially, at the end of the trial and after the sanctions have been imposed, both the victim and the criminal are restored to their original judicial status. Their *economic* status has changed. This is because of the restitution payment. The victim is richer than before the commission of the crime. The convicted criminal is poorer than before the commission of the crime. This fact categorically denies the ideal of economic equality. The economic positions of the two individuals are not equal after the sanctions have been enforced. On the other hand, the judicial positions of the individuals are equal after the sanctions have been imposed. Therefore, *judicial equality before the law* has to mean *economic inequality after the sanctions have been imposed*.

4. Gary North, *Tools of Dominion: The Case Laws of Exodus* (Tyler, Texas: Institute for Christian Economics, 1990), ch. 7.

The civil law determines the maximum extent of the change in economic positions. The victim is entitled to reduce the penalty.[5] Also, under the Mosaic Covenant, the kinsmen-redeemer was entitled to pay the victim in the name of the convicted criminal. If this was not the case, then Jesus Christ, the archetypical Kinsman-Redeemer, cannot lawfully pay for our sins against God. The Mosaic kinsman-redeemer became poorer than he would have been had the crime not been committed. Once the restitution payment was made by anyone, the judicial status of each party was restored to what it had been prior to the commission of the crime. Both the victim and the criminal could return to honest work. Their legal status was restored to what each had been prior to the commission of the crime.

No Respect for Persons

Leviticus 19:15 is an application of Exodus 12:49. Exodus 12:49 insists that the same laws must apply to everyone. Leviticus 19:15 specifically identifies two groups that must be treated equally in civil courts: the poor and the mighty. While Exodus 12:49 refers to covenantal rivals – the stranger in the land and the Israelite – Leviticus 19:15 refers to the legitimate differentiation of wealth and power. *This verse formally legitimizes the simultaneous existence of degrees of power and degrees of wealth within the holy commonwealth.* The poor man is to be judged by the same law as the rich man.

The focus here is not simply on the law itself, but on the person who is actually bringing formal judgment as a member of the court. This is the *judicial agent* who determines the validity of a particular lawsuit. Men are not to respect persons in rendering judgment.[6]

5. *Ibid.*, pp. 294-95, 305-7.

6. Deut. 1:17; 16:19; II Chron. 19:7; Prov. 24:23; Rom. 2:11; Col. 3:25; James 2:9; I Pet. 1:17.

The Theology of the Poor; or, Poor Theology

From the late 1960's through the late 1980's, a movement known as liberation theology had considerable influence on the thinking of highly educated – i.e., humanist-certified – North American evangelical Christians and Latin American Roman Catholic priests.[7] This movement developed out of a self-conscious attempt by Communists and far-Left heretical Christian groups to fuse Marxist social diagnoses and solutions with biblical rhetoric.[8] This phrase became the rallying point of the liberationists: "God is on the side of the poor." Is this phrase true? No, and Leviticus 19:15 is the most obvious passage in the Bible demonstrating the phrase's falsehood. Hardly less powerful in this regard is Psalm 62:9: "Surely men of low degree are vanity, and men of high degree are a lie: to be laid in the balance, they are altogether lighter than vanity." Conclusion: "Trust not in oppression, and become not vain in robbery: if riches increase, set not your heart upon them" (Ps. 62:10). In short, judge righteously.

Whose Side Is God On?

The Bible says specifically that God is on the side of the righteous. Occasionally, the Bible does say that God identifies with certain members of the poor. The poor who are poor not by their own fault, and especially those who are poor because of oppression by others, become identified with God by God's

---

7. The major English-language publishing house for liberation theology is Orbis Books. The major ecclesiastical organization is the Roman Catholic Maryknoll order.

8. Introductory books, critical of the movement, are Michael Novak (ed.), *Liberation North, Liberation South* (Washington, D.C.: American Enterprise Institute, 1980); Gerard Berghoef and Lester DeKoster, *Liberation Theology: The Church's Future Shock* (Grand Rapids, Michigan: Christian Library Press, 1984); James V. Schall, S.J., *Liberation Theology in Latin America* (San Francisco: Ignatius Press, 1982); and Ronald Nash (ed.), *Liberation Theology* (Milford, Michigan: Mott Media, 1984). A neo-orthodox critique is J. Andrew Kirk, *Liberation Theology: An Evangelical View from the Third World* (Atlanta, Georgia: John Knox Press, 1979).

grace. God does care for the righteous. But the Bible makes it clear that God is not on the side of the poor in general. This is why liberation theology is heretical when it is not actually apostate.[9]

Two Kinds of Equality

Which kind of equality do we want? Free market economist and legal theorist F. A. Hayek made it very clear that we can choose between two kinds of equality, but we cannot gain them both simultaneously. We can pursue *equality under the law*, or we can pursue *equality of economic results*, but we cannot rationally pursue both simultaneously. He wrote in 1960: "From the fact that people are very different it follows that, if we treat them equally, the result must be inequality in their actual position, and that the only way to place them in an equal position would be to treat them differently. Equality before the law and material equality are therefore not only different but are in conflict with each other; and we can achieve either the one or the other, but not both at the same time. The equality before the law which freedom requires leads to material inequality."[10]

The Bible requires equality before the law. *The inescapable result of impartial civil justice is economic inequality*. This fact is an affront to all socialists and semi-socialists (i.e., defenders of the corporate State).[11] They want to redistribute wealth by State compulsion, either through State ownership of the means of production (socialism) or though adjusting the incentives of the

9. Most of the time it is apostate. It is too often merely baptized Marxism. Its adherents now face a spiritual crisis: since 1989, Marxism has become terribly passé. For them, this is a far greater psychological blow than mere apostasy. See North, *Boundaries and Dominion*, ch. 14, subsection on "Which Side Is God On?" for a detailed analysis of Ron Sider's version of liberation theology.

10. F. A. Hayek, *The Constitution of Liberty* (University of Chicago Press, 1960), p. 87.

11. George Reisman, *The Government Against the Economy* (Ottowa, Illinois: Caroline House, 1979).

economy, even though legal ownership remains with private individuals or organizations (fascism, Nazism, and Keynesianism).[12] Always, the socialists focus on the supposed need for *specific economic results* rather than the need for an impartial declaration of impartial law and the impartial application of predictable sanctions. Therefore, Sider concludes, "the God of the Bible is on the side of the poor just because he is *not* biased, for he is a God of impartial justice."[13]

This perspective on poverty is basic to all socialist thought. The socialist blames poverty on the capitalist system, not on scarcity and not on immoral behavior on the part of the poor. The phrases that Sider and his colleagues used again and again are "structural injustice"[14] and "structural evil,"[15] meaning unjust institutions. It is therefore not cursed mankind (Gen. 3:16-17) and cursed nature (Gen. 3:18-19) that bring poverty, the socialist insists.[16] Widespread poverty as a social phenomenon is always explained by capitalism's critics as the result of

12. The two systems were linked from the beginning. Keynes admitted in his Preface to the 1936 German language edition of his *General Theory of Employment, Interest, and Money*: "The theory of aggregate production, which is the point of the following book, nevertheless can be much easier adapted to the conditions of a totalitarian state than the theory of production and distribution of a given production put forth under the conditions of free competition and a large degree of laissez-faire. This is one of the reasons that justifies the fact that I call my book a *general* theory." A side-by-side translation of the Preface and the original German edition is found in James J. Martin, *Revisionist Viewpoints* (Colorado Springs: Ralph Myles Press, 1971), pp. 203, 205. The citation appears in *The Collected Writings of John Maynard Keynes* (New York: St. Martin's, 1973), VII, p. xxvi.

13. Ronald L. Sider, *Rich Christians in an Age of Hunger* (Downers Grove, Illinois: InterVarsity Press, 1977), p. 84.

14. *Ibid.*, p. 87.

15. *Ibid.*, ch. 6: "Structural Evil & World Hunger."

16. Mises writes: "Most social reformers, foremost among them Fourier and Marx, pass over in silence the fact that the nature-given means of removing human uneasiness are scarce. As they see it, the fact that there is not abundance of all useful things is merely caused by the inadequacy of the capitalist mode of production and will therefore disappear in the 'higher phase' of communism." Ludwig von Mises, *Human Action: A Treatise on Economics* (New Haven, Connecticut: Yale University Press, 1949), p. 644n.

unjust institutions that are in turn the product of politically powerful rich men who successfully exploit others. This is a vision of a universe not under a curse, not populated by sinners, and not under God's judgments in history – factors that would frequently bring people under the negative sanction of poverty. Proverbs 19:15 – another 19:15 verse that is despised by the socialists – tells us: "Slothfulness casteth into a deep sleep; and an idle soul shall suffer hunger." The socialist discounts this message almost to zero.[17]

God is not on the side of the rich, the poor, or the middle class as such; He is on the side of the covenantally righteous.[18]

The Righteous

God is on the side of the righteous: the righteous poor, the righteous middle class, and the righteous rich. There are few principles in the Bible that are of greater judicial and economic importance. In verse after verse, book after book, the Bible testifies to the fact that God is on the side of the righteous. I offer a long list of supporting verses in the hope that readers will acknowledge the extent of God's commitment to the righteous. Both amillennialism and premillennialism deny the relevance of these verses as they apply to history.[19] But these verses *do* apply to history: "Behold, the righteous shall be recompensed in the earth: much more the wicked and the sinner" (Prov. 11:31). There are dozens of these verses, all ignored by

---

17. So, by the way, did fundamentalist C. I. Scofield, of the *Scofield Reference Bible* fame. Sider quotes him at the beginning of Chapter 9: "The present social order is the most abject failure the world has ever seen. . . . Governments have never learned yet to so legislate as to distribute the fruits of the industry of their people. The countries of the earth produce enough to support all, and if the earnings of each was fairly distributed it would make all men toil some, but no man toil too much." Scofield, *Our Hope*, X (August 1903), pp. 76-77.

18. North, *Boundaries and Dominion*, ch. 14, sections on "Which Poor?" "The Rich," and "The Middle Class."

19. Gary North, *Millennialism and Social Theory* (Tyler, Texas: Institute for Christian Economics, 1990), ch. 6.

liberation theologians. (My favorite is Psalm 58:10, although I do not interpret it literally. It is the thought that counts.) Read them all, so as to drill the basic point into your ethical decision-making: there are predictable covenantal sanctions in history.[20]

There is no escape from this conclusion; the texts are clear: *God is on the side of the righteous as such, not the poor as such*. God is righteous; so, His people should be righteous (Lev. 11:45). God is righteous; so, He brings blessings in history to His people who are righteous. God is righteous; so, He brings negative sanctions against those who are not righteous. God is righteous; so, *some people are deservedly poor*. This is what the socialist does not want to consider.

Sanctions and Inequality

Because God does not respect persons, He rewards and punishes people in terms of their actions and thoughts in history. He rewards individuals in time and eternity in terms of their conformity to His law. He rewards societies in terms of their outward conformity to His law. He brings positive and negative sanctions in history. Therefore, *there is no aspect of God's creation that displays equality of results*. There is no area of God's final judgment that displays inequality of judgment before the law. The *impartiality* of God leads to *disparities of rewards*. Those who achieve a great deal are given great rewards. Those who achieve average results are given average rewards. Those who achieve below-average results receive below-average rewards. Those who are out of covenantal favor with God are said to have nothing, and what they have is taken away from them (Matt. 13:12). That is to say, they are cast out of the presence of God and tortured eternally without mercy. But they are not

20. Gen. 18:23-26; Ex. 23:7, 8; Deut. 25:1; I Kings 8:32; Ps. 1:5, 6; 5:12; 34:15, 17; 34:19; 37:17; 37:25, 29, 39; 55:22; 58:10-11; 92:12; 112:6; 146:8; Prov. 2:7; 10:3, 28; 11:8, 10, 21, 28; 12:7; 13:9, 21, 25; 14:19; 15:6, 29; 28:1; 29:2, 16.

tortured equally (Luke 12:47-48). (Those Christians who are squeamish about the word "torture" may prefer to substitute the word "torment," as in Matthew 18:34 and Luke 16:24.)

Inequality of results is an inescapable outcome of the *inequality of men's productivity*, given the existence of impartial justice. Put another way, impartial justice – justice that does not bring sanctions or evaluate public actions in terms of a person's economic status or legal status – inevitably produces inequality of economic results. When the judge imposes double restitution on the criminal, he inescapably creates inequality of economic results. This is exactly what God does in history. When God brings His judgment into history, there will be unequal economic results.

It is part and parcel of the socialist perspective of all liberation theologians to deny this principle. They seek equality of results, and therefore they inescapably recommend policies that are a flat denial of the biblical principle of impartiality of justice. *Liberation theology is a self-conscious rebellion against Leviticus 19:15.* Its defenders seek to confuse their followers and their readers on this point. Impartial justice that is applied in a world made up of people with differing capacities and differing degrees of righteousness will inevitably produce inequality of economic results. It is this outcome of biblical law which enrages and outrages almost all modern Christian theologians, especially those who are either neo-evangelical college professors (outside of the natural sciences) or liberation theologians. They call for the State to use the threat of violence to steal the wealth of the successful and transfer it to the unsuccessful. They call for socialism: the State's control over resources through bureaucracy. They prefer the political sanctions of bureaucrats to the economic sanctions of consumers.

The law of God testifies against the legitimacy of any society that seeks the equality of results. The law of God testifies against any society that would use the power of the civil government to redistribute wealth on any basis except one: the proportional restitution payment from a criminal to his victim. The liberation theologians, the neo-evangelical theologians, and the humanist-trained and humanist university-certified Reformed theologians who staff and control Reformed seminaries are united on this one point: *there must be equality of ideological results, and therefore there must be respect, if not for persons, then for ideological purity*. This ideological purity is the purity of perspective that says that the civil law of God is no longer to be enforced in the New Covenant era. Anyone who denies this principle will find himself the victim of the seminaries' version of modern academic freedom: "All opinions regarding biblical law are equal, but some are more equal than others."[21]

The Bible is quite clear. There must be no respect of persons. Because individuals have different abilities, there must be inequality of economic results if God's law is enforced without respect of persons. The only justification for the State to intervene to take wealth from one individual and give it to another individual is that the first individual has been convicted in a civil court due process of law for having committed a crime against the second individual. *The quest for restitution for a specific crime is the only legitimate way for an individual to seek the economic intervention of the State against another individual.*

In contrast to this principle of civil justice is the socialist ideal: the equality of economic results. This equality is pursued by using civil power to take wealth from those who have legally gained it through competition in a market with open entry, and to redistribute it to those who have done nothing to receive it other than being statistically classified as poor. Nevertheless, the poor are still with us. So is a growing horde of middle-class bureaucrats who administer the government-mandated anti-poverty programs. The U.S. Federal bureaucracy extracts as

21. Nothing at Westminster Seminary protected Norman Shepherd from being fired in 1982. Gary North, *Westminster's Confession: The Abandonment of Van Til's Legacy* (Tyler, Texas: Institute for Christian Economics, 1991), Appendix E: "A Speech from the Play JULIUS SHEPHERD."

administration expenses at least half of the Federal government's total expenditures on welfare programs.[22]

All of this is rejected by those Christian socialists and Keynesians, who reject – necessarily – the idea of judicially binding biblical blueprints in civil government and economics.[23]

Conclusion

Leviticus 19:15 establishes a fundamental principle of justice: the impartial application of God's legal standards to all men, irrespective of their wealth or status. It proclaims the judicial principle of equality before the law. This biblical principle of civil justice is the antithesis of all socialism. The socialist proclaims the need for the equality of economic results, not equality before the law. There is no way to achieve the former without abandoning the latter, and vice versa. Logically, the socialist has to deny the legitimacy of Leviticus 19:15; logically, the defender of Leviticus 19:15 has to deny socialism. People are not always logical, however. What we find is that defenders of Christian socialism either ignore the existence of Leviticus 19:15 or else reinterpret it to mean the opposite of what it says. They interpret it, as Sider interprets it, to mean that the judge must uphold the poor man in his cause. Upholding the poor man in his cause is as great a sin as upholding the mighty in his cause.

The response of Christian socialists and welfare statists has been to deny that the Bible offers biblical blueprints for economics. Any appeal by a Christian economist to the Mosaic law is rejected as illegitimate. This has to be their response, since the legal order of the Mosaic Covenant, if obeyed, would inevitably produce a free market social order. Without Mosaic law, however, it is not possible to say what kind of social and eco-

22. James L. Payne, *The Culture of Spending: Why Congress Lives Beyond Our Means* (San Francisco: ICS Press, 1991), p. 51.

23. North, *Boundaries and Dominion*, ch. 14, section on "The Rejection of Biblical Blueprints."

nomic order would have to develop from Christianity. Thus, in order to leave the social order biblically open-ended, the Christian defenders of the welfare State are forced to deny that the Bible offers any blueprints at all. Then they tell us what kind of economic order they would like to see established in God's name (by way of Keynes, Marx, or no economist at all).[24]

The issue of wealth redistribution through taxation is never discussed by Christian defenders of the welfare State in terms of Samuel's warning in I Samuel 8: a tyrannical king is marked by his willingness to extract as much as 10 percent of his subjects' net income. To return to such a "tyrannical" tax rate, every modern industrial nation would have to cut its average level of taxation by 75 percent. Yet Christian defenders of the welfare State insist that far too much money is left in the hands of today's citizens. We need more "economic justice" in the name of Jesus, they say. We need greater taxation of the wealthy – and the not-so-wealthy. We need a "graduated tithe."

The biblical solution is to restrict total personal and corporate taxation – national, regional, and local taxation *combined* – to less than 10 percent of net income, just as the tithe lawfully collected by the combined levels of a national church's hierarchy is limited to 10 percent. But this Old Covenant limit on taxation is too confining for welfare statists.

The State today asserts an implicit claim to be the primary judicial agent of God in history. The mark of this presumed primary sovereignty is the lack of biblically revealed limits (boundaries) on the wealth that it is authorized by God to extract from those under its jurisdiction. This is the political doctrine of the divine right of the people – an assertion of the voters' God-granted moral authority to steal from each other by means of the ballot box. "Thou shalt not steal, except by majority vote."

---

24. See the footnotes in the essays other than mine in Clouse (ed.), *Wealth and Poverty*: the absence of economists.

15

LOCAL JUSTICE VS. CENTRALIZED GOVERNMENT

Ye shall do no unrighteousness in judgment: thou shalt not respect the person of the poor, nor honour the person of the mighty: but in righteousness shalt thou judge thy neighbour (Lev. 19:15).

Leviticus 19:15 deals with more than just the principle of impartial civil justice; it also deals with the locus of civil judicial sovereignty: "Ye shall do no unrighteousness in judgment: thou shalt not respect the person of the poor, nor honour the person of the mighty: but in righteousness shalt thou *judge thy neighbour*." This law established the requirement that the citizens of Israel from time to time be required to serve as civil judges in their communities (Ex. 18:21-22). The focus of Leviticus 19:15 is on civil courts within the local community, although the principle of equality before the law also applies to ecclesiastical courts. The verse specifically says, "in righteousness shalt thou judge thy neighbor." There is a very strong emphasis on *ethics*: righteousness. There is also a very strong emphasis on *localism* in this verse: judging a neighbor.

Two issues are fundamental in this verse: equality before the law and local judicial participation. First, *equality before the law*: this points back to Exodus 12:49, where the law of God is identified as the binding judicial standard for all civil judgment, irrespective of the national and covenantal origins of residents within the land.[1] Second, *local judicial participation*: the law is given to people in a particular community. Law enforcement is always to begin with *self-judgment*. The formal exercise of covenantal judgment then extends to local covenantal institutions: church, family, and State. This indicates that jurors and judges in the first stage of civil court proceedings must be recruited from the local community. Their attitudes will inescapably be shaped by that community. Acknowledging both the reality and the legitimacy of this institutional arrangement, Leviticus 19:15 emphasizes the necessity of righteousness. It is this fusion of *God's universal standards* with honest and impartial judgment according to *local customs and circumstances* – the one and the many – that is the basis of the development of the godly civil order.[2]

Judicial Localism

In a political order that is structured in terms of biblical standards, politics is inherently local. The reason why this is true is that politics is an aspect of the civil judicial order. Politics is an aspect of civil judicial sanctions. It is the means by which those who are lawfully represented in the civil realm are given an opportunity periodically to sanction their judicial representatives: legislators, judges, and governors. This is the Bible's authorized means of allocating lawful civil authority. This is why all politics is inherently a form of the judiciary.[3] *Politics is an outworking of the civil office of judge.*

1. See Chapter 14.

2. Gary North, *Moses and Pharaoh: Dominion Religion vs. Power Religion* (Tyler, Texas: Institute for Christian Economics, 1985), ch. 14.

3. On the 60-year transformation of the Massachusetts General Court into a purely legislative body, see Gary North, *Boundaries and Dominion: The Economics of Leviticus* (computer edition; Tyler, Texas: Institute for Christian Economics, 1994), Appendix F: "The Pig That Changed American Government."

Biblical politics is at bottom local because biblical courts are at bottom local. Judicial authority moves from the bottom to the top (local jurisdiction to the more distant center) in a biblical civil order (Ex. 18). Biblical civil justice is exclusively negative: bringing negative sanctions against those who initiate or commit acts that violate fundamental law and its appropriate legislation. An individual defies the legislation by committing a prohibited act. The biblical judicial model places primary responsibility for applying the law within the community in which the prohibited act took place, since the victim was injured while residing under the jurisdiction of a local court. The judicial process of bringing negative sanctions therefore must begin with an investigation of the facts of the case in a particular place and at a certain time. It is least expensive in most judicial conflicts to obtain accurate information about local events in the local jurisdiction. It is also least expensive to obtain accurate information about the local community's interpretation of the law in the local jurisdiction.

The legal issue is *jurisdiction*: speaking (diction) the law. Who possesses the initial right and responsibility for speaking the law and then enforcing it? Exodus 18 is clear: local magistrates.

Tribal Boundaries

The preservation of freedom in Israel's civil order relied on local jurisdiction. Local tribal units helped to maintain this localism. There had to be permanent legal boundaries between each tribe. These boundaries protected Israel from political centralization. Political scientist Aaron Wildavsky writes: "Moses' strategy was to divide the Israelites to keep them whole. Treating the people as a collective unit exposed them to collective punishment." He gives the example of the Levites' slaying of three thousand members of other tribes who had participated in the idolatry of the golden calf (Ex. 32:27-28). "If Moses had not shown that he would punish at least some of the people, the Lord, in whose eyes all were equally guilty, would have done them all in. So Moses had to separate some to save others."[4] Wildavsky could also have offered the example of the tribe of Benjamin, whose rebellion led to the military destruction of almost the entire tribe by the other tribes (Jud. 20). Sin was contained. Israel's tribal boundaries served as restraints against the spread of covenantal rebellion. In this sense, tribal boundaries had a *primary defensive* judicial aspect: preserving the authority of local jurisdictions and outlooks.

These boundaries also had a *secondary expansive* judicial aspect. A local jurisdiction could begin to apply God's law in a new way, and this new application might prove beneficial to the local community. Localism leads to experimentation. A tribal unit could become a kind of judicial laboratory. The rest of the nation could see if God blessed this experiment. (This presumes that God did bring predictable, visible, positive corporate sanctions in history in response to corporate covenantal faithfulness.) At the discretion of the local community, the new judicial practices of another tribe could be imported. But the importing initiative was local, unless the nation's supreme civil authorities mandated the change in the name of God's law. If the nation's appeals court used the local guideline as a judicial standard, it would become a national standard.

Localism in Mosaic Israel was offset in part by the presence of Levites: local advisors who rarely had an inheritance in rural land.[5] Instead, they had income from the tithe (Num. 18:20-21) and urban property (Lev. 25:32-34). They served as specialized judicial agents of God. The tribe of Levi was the only cross-boundary national tribe: the tribe that publicly spoke

---

4. Aaron Wildavsky, *The Nursing Father: Moses as a Political Leader* (University, Alabama: University of Alabama, 1984), p. 112.

5. There were two exceptions: 1) land that had been vowed for use by a priest but then was leased by the vow-taker to someone else; 2) land that had been vowed for a priest which was then voluntarily forfeited by the heirs at the time of the jubilee (Lev. 27:20-21). See Chapter 37, below.

God's law. So, there was both localism and universalism, the many and the one, in the judicial structure of Mosaic Israel.

The Division of Judicial Labor

The organizational problem that Moses faced in applying God's revealed law to specific cases was that there were too many disputes to settle. He was God's only authorized voice of civil authority within the nation, as Korah and Dathan learned the hard way (Num. 16). His word was the final earthly court of appeal in Israel. He therefore became the central civil judicial institution, which is another way of saying that he became the pinnacle (Ex. 18:13-18).

The problem was that Moses, despite his ability to declare the most reliable civil judgments in the land (or in the world, for that matter), had become an impediment to obtaining widespread justice. The reliability and predictability of civil judgment in Israel was no better than the ability of the disputants to get to the front of the line. This allocation system for civil justice rewarded those who were willing and able to stand in line. But standing in line is expensive. It uses up the only truly irreplaceable economic resource: *time*. Jethro saw the problem and recommended a solution: the establishment of a hierarchy of judges (Ex. 18:19-26).

This solution was based on the economic principle of the division of labor. It necessarily relied on the judicial principle of localism. The authority to impose civil and ecclesiastical sanctions moved *upward judicially* (i.e., *inward geographically*, toward the tabernacle, and later, once they were in the Promised Land, toward Jerusalem) from the local jurisdiction to a more distant jurisdiction.[6] This means that the broadest judicial authority in Israel was local. This was where the resident of Israel first encountered God's civil law. Jethro reserved the

6. The "inner circle" of influence or power is therefore at the top of the organizational pyramid, if not formally, then at least informally.

judicial system's scarcest economic resources – those people who possess progressively better-informed judgment – for the progressively more difficult cases.

Judicial resources, being scarce, had to be allocated by means of some principle. This was not the free market principle of "highest bid wins." Civil and ecclesiastical justice may not lawfully be purchased. But without price allocation, there was only one other alternative means of rationing civil justice: standing in line. Jethro's system transformed the single long line in front of Moses' tent into tens of thousands of shorter lines. Rashi,[7] the late eleventh-century French rabbinic commentator, estimated that in Moses' day, there would have been 78,600 judges in four levels.[8]

The Intellectual Division of Labor

Localism is extremely important for the advancement of what I call the division of judicial labor. The concept of the division of labor is basic to the Bible. We see it in a primarily negative sense in the scattering of families at the Tower of Babel.[9] We see it in a positive sense in Paul's injunction that the simple man or the man of one primary skill not feel bad because he does not possess a skill that a more prestigious individual has. In both I Corinthians 12 and Romans 12, Paul

---

7. Rabbi Solomon (Shlomo) Yizchaki.

8. His reasoning: 600 at the top – judges of thousands (600,000 men divided by 1,000); 6,000 in the upper middle – judges of hundreds (600,000 men divided by 100); 12,000 in the lower middle – judges of fifties (600,000 men divided by 50); and 60,000 lower court judges – judges of tens (600,000 men divided by 10). *Chumash with Targum Onkelos, Haphtaroth and Rashi's Commentary*, A. M. Silbermann and M. Rosenbaum, translators, 5 vols. (Jerusalem: Silbermann Family, [1934] 1985 [Jewish year: 5745]), II, p. 95. Rashi served as a rabbinic judge, and difficult cases were continually sent to him from Germany and France. Heinrich Graetz, *History of the Jews*, 5 vols. (Philadelphia: Jewish Publication Society of America, [1894] 1945), III, p. 287.

9. Not entirely a negative sanction. See my comments in *The Dominion Covenant: Genesis* (2nd ed; Tyler, Texas: Institute for Christian Economics, 1987), ch. 15: "The World Trade Incentive."

was speaking of the church as a body. No individual member of the body should feel that he is less important than any other member of the body. The body is governed by its head, Jesus Christ. Therefore, so long as the entire body is honoring its head, no member of the body should feel as though he is less important than any other (I Cor. 12:4-27).

The idea of scarcity is the most fundamental idea of economics: "There is no such thing as a free lunch." Scarcity is defined as follows: at zero price, there is greater demand for a scarce resource than there is supply. Modern economics asks the question: How can men reduce the level of scarcity? This is the question of wealth or economic development. Modern economics began with the observation that the division of labor is society's most important means of reducing scarcity. We date the advent of modern economics with the publication of Adam Smith's *Wealth of Nations* in 1776. Smith began Book I, Chapter I, which is titled "Of the Division of Labour," with these words: "The greatest improvement in the productive powers of labour, and the greater part of the skill, dexterity, and judgment with which it is anywhere directed, or applied, seem to have been the effects of the division of labour." His statement refers to the productivity of labor, but it applies to every area of human endeavor in which cooperative service is beneficial. He was saying that there is a greater output of goods and services for any single input of labor resource when individuals cooperate voluntarily in a division of labor economy.

The application of a biblical truth – the division of labor within the institutional church – is not limited to the church or to economics. It also has important ramifications for politics, social institutions, and all other aspects of life in which men and women cooperate for personal gain, and whose cooperative efforts lead to greater social benefits. The principle is this: through cooperation, the *specialized knowledge* of individuals can be applied more effectively to those areas of life in which this knowledge is most appropriate. Thus, it is possible for individuals to achieve greater output because their unique skills and unique knowledge are most effectively applied to the specific and narrow tasks at hand. This means that through the division of labor, there is a greater output of socially valuable wisdom from a given input of individual knowledge. It is the free market economic order alone that permits the widespread co-ordination of individual plans.[10] By bringing together many minds to deal with particular problems, society gains the benefit of obtaining greater wisdom at any given expenditure – in this context, judicial cases. It also means that there will be a greater number of cases settled by courts when this division of labor is operating. Many courts and many cases mean greater justice within the community (Ex. 18).

The committee is another example of the division of intellectual labor, but it is far more suited to imposing a veto than creating new programs. A committee works better by delegating authority to a representative and then monitoring his performance.[11]

Biblical law was designed by God to spread across borders, increasing the number of people under His jurisdiction, thereby increasing the output of all participants. The law was also intended by God to extend across the judicial border separating the Old Covenant from the New Covenant. The New Covenant's ideal is Christendom: the civilization of God in history.[12]

Judges and Jurors

Localism is the foundation of the biblical judicial system. The primary authority to declare judgment under biblical law is the

---

10. Friedrich A. Hayek, *Individualism and Economic Order* (University of Chicago Press, 1948), chaps. 2, 4. Cf. Gerald P. O'Driscoll, Jr., *Economics as a Coordination Problem: The Contributions of Friederich A. Hayek* (Kansas City, Kansas: Sheed Andrews and McMeel, 1977).

11. North, *Boundaries and Dominion*, ch. 15, subsection on "Committees and Representation."

12. *Ibid.*, ch. 15, subsection on "The Worldwide Extension of God's Law."

local court. *The fundamental agency of corporate judgment is the local court, whether civil or ecclesiastical.* This is an extremely important principle for any system of law designed to resist the centralization of power.

The civil judge in the Mosaic Covenant declared the sentence: negative sanctions. Capital sanctions were carried out by the people, beginning with the witnesses (Deut. 17:6). Case by case, the civil court was to declare judgment. As the cases grew more difficult, they would work their way up the appeals court system. The most difficult civil cases ended up in Jerusalem in the king's courtroom. The king was the Supreme Court of the Israelite civil order. This is why he was commanded to read the law daily (Deut. 17:18-19). Yet even the king could not lawfully declare absolutely final earthly judgment, imposing final earthly sanctions, for there is no final, *institutionalized*, earthly court of appeal in a biblical civil order. Only one person can lawfully declare the final judicial word of the Lord: Jesus Christ. Therefore, the people as a whole could lawfully intervene to restrain the king, as they did when Saul attempted to carry out his judgment against his son Jonathan (I Sam. 14:45). The people placed a judicial boundary around the king, and they were willing to place a physical boundary around him. He relented. On what basis could they overturn the king's sentence? Only as *authorized jurors* who refused to convict Jonathan because the king's verbal legislation on the battlefield had been foolish and therefore unconstitutional. Their declaration of "not guilty" was final, and Saul accepted it.

Nevertheless, the king did lawfully serve as the highest civil judge in Israel. This was the great authority of kingship: exercising the power of speaking in God's name as the single individual who could declare God's final earthly judgment, unless the people lawfully revolted under the direction of the lower magistrates.[13] David's rebellious son Absalom began his revolt

13. See John Calvin, *Institutes of the Christian Religion*, IV:XX:31.

by serving as a lower judge in the gates (II Sam. 15:2-6). But his was a messianic impulse: "Absalom said moreover, Oh that I were made judge in the land, that every man which hath any suit or cause might come unto me, and I would do him justice!" (II Sam. 15:4). He promised justice to all.

To restrain this messianic impulse, the king was not allowed by God to multiply horses (offensive weapons), wives (alliances), or precious metals (Deut. 17:16-17). He was required to study biblical law daily (Deut. 17:18-19). He had to be placed under judicial and institutional restraints in order to restrict the development of a messianic impulse based on concentrated civil authority. *Legitimate authority was not to become illegitimate power*. It is this move from multiple authorities to a single authority – from legitimate, decentralized social authority to centralized State power – that is the essence of the move from freedom to totalitarianism.[14] Biblical law places boundaries around centralized political authority in order to prevent this development.

What, then, was the basis of a judge's authority? We can answer this best by asking: "Biblically, who declared the law in ancient Israel?" The priests did. Yet this office was not limited to ecclesiastical affairs. Israel was a kingdom of priests. "And ye shall be unto me a kingdom of priests, and an holy nation. These are the words which thou shalt speak unto the children of Israel" (Ex. 19:6). This was an office held by all adult circumcised males (age 20+)[15] and all adult women under the authority of a circumcised male.[16]

Civil Priests

There were both civil and ecclesiastical priests. The elders in the gates in ancient Israel were empowered by God to make the

14. Robert A. Nisbet, *The Quest for Community* (New York: Oxford University Press, 1953), ch. 5.

15. Exodus 30:14.

16. The best example is Deborah (Jud. 4).

civil judicial system function. The elders in the gates imposed the negative sanctions of God's civil law. The priests were advisors to the elders (Deut. 17:8-13). The point is, *civil rulership was plural because priestly rulership was plural*. This has not changed. Who are the civil priests – citizens who exercise lawful civil sanctions – in New Testament times? Biblically speaking, in a formally covenanted nation – which all nations are required by God to become[17] – only those adults who are church members and are therefore under church authority.[18]

The fundamental agency of the local court – both civil and ecclesiastical – is the jury. It is the jury that announces guilt or innocence after having heard the arguments of conflicting parties in the courtroom. Its members evaluate the cogency of the arguments and the "fit" between the law and the evidence. The jury places limits on the judge's authority to decide the case. This is especially true in the United States.[19]

The jury system is a necessary outworking of a biblical legal order. It did not appear overnight in the early church, even as slavery was not condemned overnight. But it had to develop in a Christian legal order, even as slavery had to be abolished.[20] *The jury's legal basis is the priesthood of all believers*.[21] The jury is a Christian institution. This is not to say that it is exclusively a Christian institution. Ancient Athens and Rome both had trial by jury.[22]

---

17. Gary DeMar, *Ruler of the Nations: Biblical Blueprints for Government* (Ft. Worth, Texas: Dominion Press, 1987), ch. 4.

18. Gary North, *Political Polytheism: The Myth of Pluralism* (Tyler, Texas: Institute for Christian Economics, 1989), ch. 2.

19. Lawrence M. Friedman, *A History of American Law* (New York: Simon & Schuster, 1973), p. 135.

20. Gary North, *Tools of Dominion: The Case Laws of Exodus* (Tyler, Texas: Institute for Christian Economics, 1990), ch. 4.

21. James B. Jordan, *The Law of the Covenant: An Exposition of Exodus 21-23* (Tyler, Texas: Institute for Christian Economics, 1984), p. 232.

22. North, *Boundaries and Dominion*, ch. 15, subsections of "The Jury" and "Popular Sovereignty in Athenian Democracy."

The Biblical Jury

The goal of the biblical jury system is not to create new laws but rather to apply fixed biblical laws to specific cases. The function of the jury is to bring a small number of individuals into court so they can hear the disputes between individuals who have not been able to settle their disputes outside of the civil court. This is the principle of the division of labor. Many minds are focused on the details of a single case. After hearing both sides, the American jury is sequestered into a private room where members can discuss the case secure from interference or the threat of subsequent retaliation against any individual jury member. Neither the judge nor the agents of the disputants are allowed to enter this room when the jury is in session. This is a sign of its sovereignty. When the common law rule against double jeopardy is honored, the American jury becomes the final court of appeal when it issues a "not guilty" verdict.

The jury publicly announces civil judgment: guilty or innocent. This is the same judicial principle that operates in democratic balloting. It is a manifestation of point four of the biblical covenant model: the imposition of sanctions. The Anglo-American institution of the secret jury rests on the legal principle that no outside agent is authorized to bring pressure of any kind against the decision-makers who sit on that jury. No kind of public pressure, no kind of economic pressure, and no kind of threat is legal to be brought against a jury. Tampering with a jury is a criminal offense. By sequestering the jury – by placing a judicial and physical boundary around the members in their collective capacity as jurors – the judge pressures the members of the jury to focus all of their attention on the details of the particular case, rather than worrying about what their opinions or decisions will produce in response within the community.

This is indirect evidence that the modern political practice of the secret ballot is analogous to the sequestered jury.[23] When

23. The practice first began in Great Britain in 1662, when the Scottish Parlia-

individual citizens bring formal political sanctions against their rulers in a democracy, they are to be left free from subsequent retaliation by politicians. The secret jury and the secret ballot are both basic to the preservation of the institutional independence of the sanctioning agents, and therefore to the preservation of the impartiality of the decision.

The other biblical principle of civil law is the prohibition against double jeopardy. If "not guilty" decisions could be overturned on appeal by a higher court, innocent men could be bankrupted by the State by endless trials for the same accusation.[24]

Men must judge as God's representatives in history. "Judge not!" (Matt. 7:1) is misapplied when it is said to apply to government. This would make all government impossible. This would turn over the office of judge to covenant-breakers.[25] When the judge renders judgment lawfully, he does so as God's agent.[26]

---

ment voted secretly (in disguised hand) on the Billeting Act. This act was repudiated by Charles II. The secret ballot was not used again by the Scottish Parliament until 1705. In the United States, the use of the secret ballot was introduced in the New England colonies, and in Pennsylvania, Delaware, and the two Carolinas at the time of the American Revolution, beginning in 1775. See "Ballot," *Encyclopedia Britannica*, 11th edition (New York: Encyclopedia Britannica, Inc., 1910), III, pp. 279-81.

24. North, *Boundaries and Dominion*, ch. 15, section on "Double Jeopardy." See also Greg L. Bahnsen, "Double Jeopardy: A Case Study in the Influence of Christian Legislation" *Journal of Christian Reconstruction*, II (Winter 1975-76). This protection against double jeopardy does not apply to church courts. First, church membership is voluntary. Second, court costs are minimal. Third, and most important, unlike American civil government, local church government is not divided into judicial, legislative, and executive branches. A church court is unitary. There must be a way to overturn the decisions of such a unitary local power. A local congregation's declaration of "not guilty" can be overturned by a higher court. If this were not true, no liberal clergyman could be removed from office when declared innocent by his liberal congregation, presbytery, or synod. The protection of biblical preaching and the sacraments is more important than the preservation of double jeopardy protection.

25. *Ibid.*, ch. 15, section on "Judge Not!"

26. *Ibid.*, ch. 15, section on "Rendering Judgment: A Voice of Authority."

Conclusion

The Bible specifies the locus of primary judicial sovereignty: the local court. This court has the benefit of better knowledge of the facts and circumstances of any alleged crime. It has a tradition of judicial decisions (precedents) that is familiar to jurors. It is made up of people who speak God's law – jurisdiction – with a familiar local "accent." This enables local residents to forecast more accurately what is expected of them. This reduces forecasting costs.

The jury is the culmination of a long tradition of Christian history. The jury makes possible a greater division of judicial labor. A jury is less likely to be arbitrary than a lone judge. Men can obtain justice less expensively because of the greater efficiency of a jury's collective judgment. The authority of the jury at the local level provides a counter to the decisions of professional bureaucrats.

By lodging in local courts the final authority to declare an accused person "not guilty," God's law provides a check to the centralization of political power. A distant civil government cannot impose its will on local residents without a considerable expenditure of time and money, possibly risking the public's rejection of the central government's legitimacy, the crucial resource of any government.

16

THE STATE'S MONOPOLY OF VENGEANCE

Thou shalt not avenge, nor bear any grudge against the children of thy people, but thou shalt love thy neighbour as thyself: I am the LORD *(Lev. 19:18).*

The theocentric focus of this law is this: only God can know a person's heart (Jer. 17:9-10). Therefore, only God is entitled to judge a person's heart. Because a civil judge is not God, he cannot legitimately claim to be able to search another person's heart in his quest for civil justice. The affairs of the heart and mind are off-limits to the State. There can be no lawful civil sanctions against thoughts or attitudes. We must conclude that the prohibition against holding grudges (Lev. 19:18) cannot be an aspect of the Mosaic civil law.[1] Such a civil law is inherently unenforceable.

Civil law also cannot enforce an attitude of love; hence, civil law is not the focus of the command to love one's neighbor,

1. This is why all polygraph or "lie detector" exams must be submitted to voluntarily. A civil court cannot lawfully use the results of a compulsory lie detector examination as evidence against an individual, nor may any civil court use a person's refusal to submit to such a test as evidence against him. The same principle applies to the use of hypnotism.

except insofar as love is defined judicially: treating the neighbor legally, i.e., love as the fulfilling of God's law (Rom. 13:10). But even in this case, there would have to be an infraction of a specific civil law or an act against another person's rights – lawful immunities (protected boundaries) – in order to enforce this law of compulsory love. Hence, this law, too, is inherently unenforceable by the State.

Nevertheless, this verse begins with a prohibition against individual acts of vengeance. This is clearly an aspect of civil law; the relevant Mosaic case law is the requirement that any man who injures another man in a fight must pay restitution to him (Ex. 21:18-19): no private vengeance. But why is this verse's negative injunction attached to two other injunctions that are clearly individual moral injunctions – aspects of self-government rather than civil government? By prohibiting personal grudges and requiring personal love, this verse makes it clear that the concern of the civil portion of this civil law is the elimination of privately imposed vengeance. The civil prohibition against taking vengeance applies only to individual actions. This prohibition does not apply to the State. Civil law applies negative sanctions to individuals who commit specified prohibited acts; hence, it applies to individual acts of vengeance. Vengeance is legitimate when imposed by the State.

The parallel verse in Deuteronomy is used by Paul in his epistle to the Romans to introduce his discussion of the civil magistrate. "Dearly beloved, avenge not yourselves, but rather give place unto wrath: for it is written, Vengeance is mine; I will repay, saith the Lord" (Rom. 12:19; cf. Deut. 32:35a). Paul's message is *not* that there should be no vengeance in history. On the contrary, he immediately launches into a discussion of the civil magistrate's lawful administration of vengeance: ". . . for he beareth not the sword in vain: for he is the minister of God, a revenger to execute wrath upon him that doeth evil" (Rom. 13:4b). It is a mistake to see Paul's prohibition of vengeance in these verses as applying to the institution of the State, any more than "thou shalt not kill" applies to the State. What Leviticus 19:18 does is to establish the State as the lawful monopolist of covenantal vengeance in history.[2] The Bible is neither pacifistic nor anarchistic; it affirms the legitimacy of the State in seeking public law and order. But both the law and the order must be God's – a covenantal, oath-bound law-order.[3] The State exercises a monopoly over public sanctions.[4]

Establishing the Judicial Conditions of Wealth-Creation

The State makes wealth-creation possible for individuals by protecting private property, i.e., by protecting individuals who own property. The State is required by God to enforce the decisions of property owners to exclude others from using their property. The State is therefore to enforce legal boundaries that are established by private contract. Property owners are given legal immunities – *rights* – by God in history, and these immunities are to be defended by the State whenever the victim of an unauthorized invasion appeals to the civil magistrate. The State is to defend the rights of stewards over the property that God has assigned to them by covenant (lawful inheritance) or by contract. As Rushdoony says, "All property is held in trust under and in stewardship to God the King. No institution can exercise any prerogative of God unless specifically delegated to do so, within the specified area of God's law. The state thus is the ministry of justice, not the original property owner or the sovereign lord over the land."[5]

---

2. The family is not an agency of vengeance. It is an agency of justice only within the boundaries of a covenanted household.

3. Ray R. Sutton, *That You May Prosper: Dominion By Covenant* (Tyler, Texas: Institute for Christian Economics, 1987), ch. 12. Second edition: 1992.

4. Gary North, *Boundaries and Dominion: The Economics of Leviticus* (computer edition; Tyler, Texas: Institute for Christian Economics, 1994), ch. 16, section on "Monopoly Control Over the Sword."

5. R. J. Rushdoony, *The Institutes of Biblical Law* (Nutley, New Jersey: Craig Press, 1973), p. 504.

This means that property rights are human rights. It is true that property rights are not absolute – nothing since the closing of the canon of Scripture is absolute – but they are on the same judicial level as any other human rights except those associated with worship and life. Property rights are not impersonal and therefore are not judicially subordinate to personal rights; property rights are both personal and judicial. The familiar dualism between human rights and property rights should always be resolved in terms of stewardship under God. The key question is this: To whom has God delegated the authority to exercise representative control His property? A discussion of the rights of property should begin with a consideration of God's rights to property.

Positive Benefits Through Negative Sanctions

By remaining exclusively negative judicially, a biblically restricted State serves as a beneficial agency of government within society. This is the only way that it can remain an exclusively positive force in society, given its source of funds. The State is financed by the collection of taxes.[6] Taxes, like the church's tithe, apply legitimately only to individual income and net increases in an individual's wealth (capital gains).[7] The State is an economically dependent institution, not an economically creative institution.

The State has a God-given right to collect taxes by threat of violence. It is therefore not authorized by God to become an

---

6. It can print fiat money, which is a form of taxation: compulsory wealth redistribution from those who gain access to the fiat money before prices rise, from those who gain access to money later in the process. The State can also borrow, but this only transfers wealth from lenders to the State. The State can gain access to credit only by promising to repay the lenders. This means that it must impose taxes (including the inflation tax) later.

7. This means that neither the church nor the State can lawfully tax capital, meaning property. This also means that the State cannot lawfully tax church property. Property, biblically speaking, is tax-immune – not just the church's, but all wealth-producing assets. The fruit may be taxed, not the tree.

agency of positive sanctions, for that would involve asserting its authority as a compulsory agency of healing. There is no *compulsory*, earthly, covenantal agency of healing in history. A compulsory healing agency must be funded by compulsory taxes: anti-healing. Churches and families, while covenantal agencies of healing, are voluntary institutions.[8] The State is compulsory. It can reward one group only by imposing penalties on some other group. God has therefore placed it under strict judicial boundaries. It is not to be regarded by anyone as a creative institution. It is instead exclusively protective. It is a monopolistic agency of vengeance against wrongdoers (Rom. 13:1-7). Its task is not to make men good; rather, it is to penalize biblically identified evil acts. To this end, God has given it the sword.

God is the original source of lawful violence – negative sanctions – in both history and eternity. The State is God's designated monopolistic agent of lawful violence against convicted criminals. God brings negative sanctions; so does the State. God's negative sanctions are physical, in time and eternity. The State's ultimate negative physical sanction is the right of execution: excluding people from continuing access to the blessings of God in history. By executing a person, the State transfers the person's soul into God's heavenly court for final judgment. The State's court thereby becomes the agency of next-to-the-last judgment. God's court brings the final judgment.

Self-Defense

This does not mean that only the State can lawfully possess and use deadly weapons. The person who kills another in self-

8. How can the church be an agency of healing if its only God-mandated income is the tithe? Isn't its dependent condition analogous to the State's dependence on taxes? Doesn't the church also have only two hands: a gentle one and a rough one? This analysis overlooks the positive aspect of the church's covenantal sanctions: the sacraments. Only the church can lawfully confer the sacraments on its members. In contrast, the State is not a means of special grace. It is an agency that administers common grace only to the extent that it confines itself to punishing evil acts.

defense is acting as a lawful agent of God. There are civil laws governing this God-granted authority to kill another person. The case law of Exodus 22:2 allows a householder to kill a burglar if the owner catches him while the intruder is breaking in. The intruder has no legitimate reason to be inside the house. The resident has a legitimate role as a defender of his household's boundaries. God has delegated this authority to him. The occupant cannot know for sure why the invader has entered his home without permission, so he is allowed by God's law to assume the worst: the invader is a potential murderer. He can lawfully be killed by the person who resides there. The mere transgression of the home's boundary is sufficient to remove the protection of God's civil law from the invader. If caught by the homeowner and threatened with a weapon to prevent his flight before the police arrive, the invader is not protected by God's law from execution should he attack the homeowner. Those lawfully inside the house are protected by God's law; therefore, the invader is not. The thief may be struck while breaking in. If he attempts to flee, the resident is not supposed to kill him, for he is no longer breaking in. But the benefit of the doubt is always with the defender. This execution of an illegal invader is not an act of personal vengeance; rather, it is an act that defends a lawful boundary. The defender acts in the name of the State and is authorized by the State because no policeman is available to enforce the law.

By implication, this case law establishes the judicial plea of self-defense. The person who is given cause to believe that an assailant is ready to kill him is entitled to kill the assailant. The civil government is required by God to investigate the reasons for any killing of a human being.[9] The judges must examine the evidence in order to determine whether a murder trial

---

9. The passage that establishes this requirement is Deuteronomy 21:1-9, which requires a special sacrifice when a body is found outside a city, and the elders cannot discover who committed the crime.

should be held.[10] The person who faces a life-threatening assault must decide which risk is greatest: 1) death from the assailant if no action is taken; 2) death from the assailant in a failed self-defense; 3) death from the State for murder of the assailant. There is a slogan used by American defenders of their Constitutional right to own and use guns.[11] "I would rather be tried by twelve than carried by six." When a person is faced with a life-threatening attack, a jury in his future is preferable to pallbearers.

The plea of self-defense is in fact a plea of the right to defend oneself as an authorized agent of the State. Self-defense is not an autonomous act of violence. It is not an act of vengeance. It is a boundary defense.

What is clearly prohibited is vengeance by the victim after the suspect has fled from the scene of the crime. In such a case, there can be no claim of self-defense if the suspect dies as a result of the attack. The victim faces no life-threatening attack. His response is therefore limited to bringing a lawsuit. He may lawfully seek out the civil magistrate as a public avenger, but he is not allowed to impose vengeance unilaterally.[12]

---

10. In common law, this authority to decide to hold a trial belongs to the grand jury, which hands down an indictment. Then the trial is held.

11. This is the Second Amendment of the Constitution: part of the original Bill of Rights. More than any other Constitutional guarantee, this one is under assault by the State in late-twentieth-century America. It was imposed on the Federal government in the 1790's because citizens had achieved parity of weaponry with the State. They were determined to keep this parity, which they recognized as the means of enforcing boundaries on the State. Parity in weaponry was the technical basis of the advent of modern democracy. Carroll Quigley, *Tragedy and Hope: A History of the World in Our Time* (New York: Macmillan, 1966), pp. 34-35. Quigley was an expert in the history of warfare and weaponry and their relation to politics.

12. Some legal codes authorize people to pursue a criminal who is fleeing from the scene of a crime. This is the doctrine of citizen's arrest. Civil government may lawfully authorize such a practice. This law in effect makes the citizen a deputy of the State. If the suspect is injured by the citizen-arrester under such circumstances, the citizen would be at legal risk if the suspect is not subsequently convicted for the crime in question.

God's law places boundaries around men's lives. The State may lawfully deprive a person of his life if the person is convicted of a capital crime, but otherwise he is to be protected. The law is an innocent person's defensive shield because the law is the State's offensive weapon against boundary violators.

Why This Monopoly?

The State possesses a monopoly of vengeance and violence, although in some instances the individual acts as an agent of the State in defending himself and those under his authority. What is the rationale for the creation of such a monopoly? First, to limit the number of people seeking violent vengeance, i.e., *boundary violators*. These State-"anointed" agents can be identified. The agent has the authority to announce himself as an agent of the State. He is usually marked in some way: uniform, badge, or credentials.[13] It is illegal for anyone not so authorized (oath-bound) to wear or bear such marks of authority. The authority to act in an official capacity as God's minister of vengeance is circumscribed by God's law. This limits the number of instances in which violence becomes likely. The goal of any monopoly is to reduce the quantity supplied of some scarce economic resource. In this case, the item to be limited is violence.

By limiting the amount of lawful violence in a society, the law of God channels violence. Residents in a covenanted nation know what to expect from the State. They can identify the lawful uses and applications of violence, and therefore they can identify the unlawful uses. There are far fewer lawful uses than unlawful uses. Biblical law specifies the boundaries of lawful violence and thereby identifies unlawful violence. It includes some violent acts and therefore excludes all other violent acts.

---

13. His vehicle may be similarly marked. Drivers of State-authorized vehicles alone have the right to use flashing red lights and sirens.

It is less costly to specify the legitimate agents of violence than to identify every possible illegitimate agent. By identifying the primary agency of coercion, i.e., the State, biblical law places this institution under greater public scrutiny. By lowering the number of legal public acts, biblical law lowers the cost of publicly scrutinizing the State. More limits are placed around the State as a result of these lower costs of scrutiny. As the agency of violence, the State is feared; a feared agency is likely to be scrutinized more closely by its potential victims. Citizens covenant under God to establish State authority; they monitor the State's activities because of their fear that the State's officers will exceed their lawful boundaries. This is especially true in societies where the State has not become a functional agent of healing. The more acceptable the messianic claims of the State, the less incentive there is for citizens to scrutinize it and limit it. The power to tax is the power to destroy, and the costs of healing must be paid for by higher taxes. The healer State becomes the destroyer State.

The State is required by God to operate under God-revealed biblical law. This biblical law-order is quite specific. The State must apply sanctions specified by the victims. These sanctions are specific. The State is under judicial limits.[14] It is also governed by written law. These laws are supposed to be understood by citizens, which is why the whole law had to be read to the assembled nation every seventh year (Deut. 31:10-13). Citizens are expected by God to know the boundaries that God has placed around them as individuals and also around the State.

This means that the State's sword is to be used sparingly. It is governed by God's civil law. The State is not authorized by God to impose negative sanctions outside the limits of the law. The law circumscribes the application of the sword. Put another

14. Gary North, *Tools of Dominion: The Case Laws of Exodus* (Tyler, Texas: Institute for Christian Economics, 1990), ch. 7.

way, the magistrate's use of violence cannot lawfully be extended to areas that have not been authorized by the law, either explicitly or as extensions of a case law or a judicial principle. In short, *whatever is not prohibited by law is allowed*. This legal principle is derived from God's original command to Adam regarding judicial boundaries placed around a particular tree. Everything else was permitted to Adam; hence, no negative sanctions were threatened in these areas.

Any attempt to substitute other judicial ideals for biblical law is an attempt to substitute either judicial unitarianism or judicial individualism, which in turn move in the direction of international statism or anarchism. The latter ideal in turn devolves into warlordism: rule by private armies. The basis of biblical judicial theory is Trinitarianism.[15]

The Division of Powers

There are several layers of civil government, and in modern Western jurisprudence, several branches within each layer: legislative, executive, and judicial. The delegation of God's unified judicial authority to mankind is always marked by a division of powers, sometimes described as a system of checks and balances.

The existence of a civil covenant, marked by a self-maledictory oath of allegiance, is proof that anarchism is not a biblical ideal. Civil government is a separate jurisdiction from the free market, which is an extension of family government. The State has the God-given authority to settle disputes by force of arms. The free market does not. To argue that it does is to adopt judicial warlordism.[16] While there can be lawful private arbi-

---

15. North, *Boundaries and Dominion*, ch. 16, section on "Trinitarianism, Unitarianism, and Individualism."

16. To argue that no one has the right to impose physical sanctions is to adopt utopian pacifism. It is to reject the idea of God's negative sanctions in history through representative agents. If actually legislated, pacifism would lead to tyranny by Satan's representatives in history: evildoers (Rom. 13:1-7).

tration organizations, they do not possess the covenantal authority to impose the sword, that is, the right to declare guilt and impose mandatory penal sanctions. On the other hand, the existence of multiple levels of civil authority (Ex. 18) is proof that judicial centralism is not a biblical ideal. The biblical system of civil government is Trinitarian, not unitarian or atomistic.

There are two theoretical alternatives to social Trinitarianism: social unitarianism and judicial warlordism. The confessional unitarians – which include Orthodox Jews and orthodox Muslims – deny the doctrine of the Trinity. Unitarianism does not affirm the equal ultimacy of the one and the many. It affirms the ultimacy of the one. A consistent application of this view of God leads to the ideal of a top-down centralized State.[17] God mandated the tribal land ownership system for Mosaic Israel in order to restrain the development of a unitary State, for Israel's confession was, on the surface, unitarian: "Hear, O Israel: The LORD our God is one LORD" (Deut. 6:4). Social unitarianism rejects the ideal of a decentralized theocratic order that is unified by a common confession, where the power to tax the individual directly is exclusively local,[18] and the jury system is also local.

Judicial warlordism, in contrast, rejects the ideal of a central civil government. It offers a theory of truncated courts: no lawful court of appeal above the person of the warlord unless the warlord consents to it. In judicial warlordism, there is only temporary power for imposing order in the case of disputes; there is no legitimate central authority. One form of theoretical

---

17. This may be why Jews continually embrace the State, to their long-term disadvantage. On this political tradition, see Benjamin Ginsberg, *The Fatal Embrace: Jews and the State* (University of Chicago Press, 1993). While there are a few free market economists who are also Orthodox Jews, they generally do their technical economic analyses as secular economists, not as Orthodox Jews.

18. The Articles of Confederation (1781-1788) served as the national constitution of the United States. It restricted tax collection by the national government to assessments made on the states, with the state legislatures actually collecting these taxes (Article VIII).

warlordism (anarcho-capitalism) ends the appeals system with the most militarily powerful individual or with the court of the most powerful private police force in a system of private, competing courts. In the version of truncated courts known as nationalism, appeals end with a national civil court. Both of these truncated judicial systems are associated with the right-wing Enlightenment model. These are polytheistic judicial models: many laws, many gods. Rushdoony writes: "The premise of polytheism is that we live in a multiverse, not a universe, that a variety of law-orders and hence lords exist, and that man cannot therefore be under one law *except* by virtue of imperialism."[19]

Biblical law, being universal in scope, is not polytheistic. It is also not imperialistic. The top-down judicial order of imperialism is Satan's perverse imitation of God's kingdom. Both systems are comprehensive in their claims, but they are structured differently. God's kingdom is a bottom-up system of appeals courts based on binding covenantal oaths. But the biblical system of appeals courts cannot be limited, for the universalism of God's mandatory covenantal oaths cannot be limited. There is no zone of neutrality, no place of refuge outside the jurisdiction of God.

Judicial Trinitarianism proposes the ideal of Christendom. Because it envisions the extension of God's universal kingdom in history, it affirms a confessionally unified pair of appeals systems – ecclesiastical and civil – that transcends national borders. Judicial Trinitarianism is necessarily internationalist because the kingdom of God transcends political borders.[20] Modern Christianity, being antinomian, rejects the ideal of this international kingdom. The churches deny the possibility of internationalism because they deny the universality of God's

19. Rushdoony, *Institutes*, p. 17.

20. Gary North, *Healer of the Nations: Biblical Blueprints for International Relations* (Ft. Worth, Texas: Dominion Press, 1987).

law. Modern Christianity is politically polytheistic.[21] Rushdoony is correct: "To hold, as the churches do, Roman Catholic, Greek Orthodox, Lutheran, Calvinist, and all others virtually, that the law was good for Israel, but that Christians and the church are under grace without law, or under some higher, newer law, is implicit polytheism."[22] This antinomian outlook turns over judicial authority to polytheistic humanist kingdoms as surely as the pacifism of the Mennonite sects causes them to turn over the law-making power, police power, and military authority to others. Thus, modern Christians hail as biblically valid the truncated court systems of modern nationalism. They reject the ideal of Christendom on two accounts: its commitment to universal Christian legal standards and its denial of humanistic nationalism as anything more than a temporary stopgap measure analogous to the scattering at the Tower of Babel. They do not regard Babel's scattering as God's curse on covenant-breakers' confession of autonomy: to make themselves a name. Rather, they see judicial Babel as inherent in the human condition, even if all men were to covenant with God.

Nevertheless, the creation of such a supreme judicial civil court must not precede the creation of a supreme ecclesiastical court. The church is the model for the State, not the State for the church. The church continues into eternity; the State does not (Rev. 21; 22). No agency will then be needed to impose civil sanctions: no sin! Conclusion: to begin to create a supreme civil world court before creating the covenantal foundation of a free world society – Christendom – is to attempt the creation of a secular one-world order. It represents a return to the Tower.

The inherently international ideal of Christendom is denied by right-wing judicial Anabaptists, but they cannot escape the theoretical problem of social order. Traditionally, they have

---

21. Gary North, *Political Polytheism: The Myth of Pluralism* (Tyler, Texas: Institute for Christian Economics, 1989).

22. Rushdoony, *Institutes of Biblical Law*, p. 18.

appealed to civil judicial neutrality – the ideal of either Stoic or Newtonian natural law – in their attempts to deny the ideal of Christendom. They become like the Amish, the archetypal right-wing Anabaptists: trapped in the humanists' judicial order as it moves toward either the one-State world or judicial warlordism. To put it in terms familiar to those living in the 1990's, they find themselves moving toward either the humanists' New World Order or Balkanization.

Conclusion

Vengeance is God's, but He delegates limited authority to the civil government to impose negative sanctions against lawbreakers. The Bible establishes a judicial ideal: the supply of vengeance must be placed under the restraint of Bible-revealed law. This is accomplished biblically by making the State the sole lawful supplier.[23] In the case of negative physical sanctions, except for parental punishing of children, the State is to be the sole supplier of the service.[24]

Biblical law establishes a monopoly of vengeance. The economic function of a monopoly is to reduce the quantity of output of some good or service. The "service" in this case is potentially negative for society: vengeance. There is some socially optimum quantity of this service, but because of the tendency toward autonomy and lawlessness among men, the unrestrained free market would create an oversupply.

The State is required by God to protect private property. The State must honor God-established property rights, i.e., legal immunities – boundaries – against invasion. Stewards over property are to have their rights protected by threat of violence by the State against invaders. Property rights are human rights.

23. In the Old Testament, the kinsman-redeemer was lawfully authorized to act as the State's agent.

24. Personal self-defense should be interpreted as an act of State. The State delegates to the individual the authority to impose this sanction in unique circumstances. It is analogous to "citizen's arrest."

By limiting the number of authorized agents of vengeance, society limits the spread of violence. This also places the State under public scrutiny. The more limited the State, the less it has to be scrutinized.

The State establishes a hierarchical system of appeals courts (Ex. 18). This system parallels the ecclesiastical court of appeals. The church is the model for society, not the State. When the church rejects the covenantal ideal of an international, hierarchical system of appeals courts, both ecclesiastical and civil, it necessarily adopts a rival judicial model: tribalism, regionalism, or nationalism. The biblical goal is world government under God's law, for both church and State. But until the church establishes this in practice, the quest for world civil government under common world law is messianic and a threat to freedom. There must be a common confession among men before there can be a lawful appeals court, and only one confession is valid: Trinitarianism.

17

THE PRESERVATION OF THE SEED

Ye shall keep my statutes. Thou shalt not let thy cattle gender with a diverse kind: thou shalt not sow thy field with mingled seed; neither shall a garment mingled of linen and woolen come upon thee (Lev. 19:19).

The theocentric meaning of this passage is the meaning of the entire Book of Leviticus: God's boundaries must be respected. This case law establishes three boundaries, each referring to a specific economic activity: animal husbandry, agriculture, and textiles. Except for the products of mining and metalworking, these were the primary categories of economic goods in the ancient world. Leviticus 19:19 established rules for all three areas. That world is long gone. Beginning no later than the fifteenth century, A.D., and accelerating rapidly in the late eighteenth century, a series of improvements in all three areas transformed the traditional economy of Europe. The modern capitalist system – with its emphasis on private ownership, the specialization of production, and the division of labor – steadily replaced the older medieval world of the common fields. This comprehensive economic transformation was accompanied by the violation of at least the first two, and seemingly all three, of the statutes of Leviticus 19:19. The question we need to answer is this: Was this law annulled by the New Covenant, or was the

Agricultural/IndustrialRevolution illegitimate biblically? I argue that the law was annulled.[1]

Hermeneutics

I employ a theonomic hermeneutic – a principle of biblical interpretation – that enables me to do three things that every hermeneutic should do: 1) identify the primary function of an Old Covenant law; 2) discover whether it is universal in a redemptive (healing) sense, or whether 3) it was conditioned by its redemptive-historical context (i.e., annulled by the New Covenant). In short: What did the law mean, how did it apply inside and outside Mosaic Israel, and how should it apply today? This exegetical task is not always easy, but it is mandatory. It is a task that has been ignored or denied by the vast majority of Christian theologians for almost two millennia.

The question here is the hermeneutical problem of identifying covenantal continuity and covenantal discontinuity. First, in questions of covenantal continuity, we need to ask: What is the underlying ethical principle? God does not change ethically. The moral law is still binding, but its application may not be. Second, this raises the question of covenantal discontinuity. What has changed as a result of the New Testament era's fulfillment of Old Covenant prophecy and the inauguration of the New Covenant? A continuity – prophetic-judicial fulfillment – has in some cases produced a judicial discontinuity: the annulment of a case law's application. A very good example of this is Leviticus 19:19.

I begin any investigation of any suspected judicial discontinuity with the following questions. First, is the case law related to the priesthood, which has changed (Heb. 7:11-12)? Second,

1. A preliminary version of this chapter appears in *Theonomy: An Informed Response*, edited by Gary North (Tyler, Texas: Institute for Christian Economics, 1991), ch. 10. See also, Gary North, *Boundaries and Dominion: The Economics of Leviticus* (computer edition; Tyler, Texas: Institute for Christian Economics, 1994), ch. 17.

is it related to the sacraments, which have changed? Third, is it related to the jubilee land laws (e.g., inheritance), which Christ fulfilled (Luke 4:18-21)? Fourth, is it related to the tribes (e.g., the seed laws), which Christ fulfilled in His office as Shiloh, the promised Seed (Gal. 3:16)? Fifth, is it related to the "middle wall of partition" between Jew and gentile, which Jesus Christ's gospel has broken down (Gal. 3:28; Eph. 2:14-20)?[2] These five principles prove fruitful in analyzing Leviticus 19:19.[3]

Let us ask another question: Is a change in the priesthood also accompanied by a change in the laws governing the family covenant? Yes. Jesus tightened the laws of divorce by removing the Mosaic law's exception, the bill of divorcement (Matt. 5:31-32).[4] Similarly, the church from the beginning has denied the legality of polygamy even though there is no explicit rejection of polygamy in the New Testament except for church officers: husbands of one wife (I Tim. 3:2, 12). Polygamy is rejected by the church on the same basis that Jesus rejected the Mosaic law's system of easy divorce: "from the beginning it was not so" (Matt. 19:18). Did other changes in the family accompany the New Covenant's change in the priesthood? Specifically, have changes in inheritance taken place? Have these changes resulted in the annulment of the jubilee land laws of the Mosaic economy? Finally, has an annulment of the jubilee land laws annulled the laws of tribal administration?

---

2. This application is especially important in dealing with Rushdoony's theory of "hybridization." See North, *Boundaries and Dominion*, Appendix H: "Rushdoony on 'Hybridization': From Genetic Separation to Racial Separation."

3. There are several other hermeneutical questions that we can ask that relate to covenantal discontinuity. Sixth, is it an aspect of the weakness of the Israelites, which Christ's ministry has overcome, thereby intensifying the rigors of an Old Covenant law (Matt. 5:21-48)? Seventh, is it an aspect of the Old Covenant's cursed six day-one day work week rather than the one day-six day pattern of the New Covenant's now-redeemed week (Heb. 4:1-11)? Eighth, is it part of legal order of the once ritually polluted earth, which has now been cleansed by Christ (Acts 10; I Cor. 8)?

4. Greg L. Bahnsen, *Theonomy in Christian Ethics* (2nd ed.; Phillipsberg, New Jersey: Presbyterian and Reformed, [1977] 1984), p. 99.

Case Laws and Underlying Principles

A law governing agriculture, animal husbandry, and textile production had to be taken very seriously under the Mosaic Covenant. The expositor's initial presumption should be that these three laws constitute a judicial unit. If they are a unit, there has to be some underlying judicial principle common to all three. All three prohibitions deal with mixing. The first question we need to ask is the crucial one: What was the covenantal meaning of these laws? The second question is: What was their economic effect?

I argue here that the fundamental judicial principle undergirding the passage is the requirement of separation. Two kinds of separation were involved: tribal and covenantal. The first two clauses were agricultural applications of the mandatory *segregation of the tribes* inside Israel until a unique prophesied *Seed* would appear in history: the Messiah. We know who the Seed is: Jesus Christ. Paul wrote: "Now unto Abraham and his seed were the promises madc. Hc saith not, And to seeds, as of many; but as of one, and to thy seed, which is Christ" (Gal. 3:16). The context of Paul's discussion is *inheritance*. Inheritance is by promise, he said (Gal. 3:18). The Mosaic law was given, Paul said, "till the seed should come to whom the promise was made" (Gal. 3:18). Two-thirds of Leviticus 19:19 relates to the inheritance laws of national Israel, as we shall see. When the Levitical land inheritance laws (Lev. 25) ended with the establishment of a new priesthood, so did the authority of Leviticus 19:19.

The final clause of Leviticus 19:19 deals with prohibited clothing. This prohibition related not to separation among the tribes of Israel – separation within a covenant – but rather the separation of national Israel from other nations. The principle undergirding second form of separation – clothing – is more familiar to us: *covenantal separation*.

Boundary of Blood: Seed and Land

The preservation of Israel's unique covenantal status was required by biblical law. The physical manifestation of this separation was circumcision. A boundary of blood was imposed on the male organ of reproduction. It was a sign that covenantal life is not obtained by either physical birth or through one's male heirs. Rushdoony has written: "Circumcision witnesses to the fact that man's hope is not in generation but in regeneration. . . ."[5] To escape Adam's legal status as a covenant-breaker, a man must re-covenant with God, a human response made possible by God's absolutely sovereign act of regeneration. The mark of this covenant in ancient Israel was circumcision. Ultimately, this separation was *confessional*. It involved an affirmation of the sovereignty of Israel's God. This was a different kind of boundary from those that divided the tribes, for the tribes were united confessionally: "Hear, O Israel: The LORD our God is one LORD: And thou shalt love the LORD thy God with all thine heart, and with all thy soul, and with all thy might" (Deut. 6:4-5). The nation of Israel was separated from non-covenanted nations by geographical and covenantal boundaries.

Tribal and family units separated the covenant people within Israel. This separation was always to be geographical, usually familial,[6] but never confessional. Every tribe confessed the same confession. They were divided tribally because they would have *different heirs*. Only one tribe would bring forth the promised Seed. Tribal separation was therefore based on differences in inheritance.

Israel's tribal divisions had political implications. They guaranteed localism. This localism of tribal inheritance was the judicial complement of the unity of national covenantal confes-

---

5. R. J. Rushdoony, *The Institutes of Biblical Law* (Nutley, New Jersey: Craig Press, 1973), p. 43.

6. There could be inter-tribal marriages. Daughters received dowries rather than landed inheritance. Dowries could cross tribal boundaries.

sion. Tribal boundaries were part of an overall structure of covenantal unity. This included politics: localism.

Family membership and rural land ownership in Israel were tied together by the laws of inheritance. A rural Israelite – and most Israelites were rural[7] – was the heir of a specific plot of ground because of his family membership. There was no rural landed inheritance apart from family membership. Unlike the laws of ancient Greece, Mosaic law allowed a daughter to inherit the family's land if there was no son. But there was a condition: she had to marry within the tribal unit (Num. 36:8). The landed inheritance could not lawfully move from one tribe to another (Num. 36:9).[8] A man's primary inheritance in Israel was his legal status (freemanship). Land was tied to name. The land of Israel was God's; His name was on it. The family's land was tied to the family's name.[9] Jacob had promised Judah that his blood line would rule until the promised heir (Shiloh) should come (Gen. 49:10). Thus, the integrity of each of the seed lines in Israel – family by family, tribe by tribe – was maintained by the Mosaic law until this promise was fulfilled. The mandatory separation among the tribes was symbolized by the prohibition against mixing seeds. The prohibition applied to the mixing of seeds in one field. The field did not represent the whole world under the Mosaic Covenant; *the field represented the Promised Land*. The husbandman or farmer had to create boundaries between his specialized breeds and between his crops.

So closely were seed and land connected in the Mosaic law that the foreign eunuch, having no possibility of seed, was not

---

7. This is not to say that God intended them to remain rural. On the contrary, the covenantal blessing of God in the form of population growth was to move most Israelites into the cities as time went on. See below, Chapter 25, section on "The Demographics of the Jubilee Inheritance Law," pp. 416-22.

8. The exception was when rural land that had been pledged to a priest went to him in the jubilee year if the pledge was violated (Lev. 27:20-21). See Chapter 37, below: "The Redemption Price System."

9. North, *Boundaries and Dominion*, ch. 17, subsection on "Family Land and Family Name."

allowed to become a citizen in Israel. (The New Testament's system of adoption has annulled this law: Acts 8:26-38.)[10]

Artificial Barriers

The boundaries separating animals had to be there because of the normal sexual bonding that takes place among pairs within a species. So, too, was it normal for members of the same covenantal confession to marry. But Mosaic law established an *artificial barrier* between the tribes. This artificial barrier was both legal and economic: *landed inheritance*. Tribal separation decentralized Israel's economy and politics. There was to be continuity of theological and judicial principles, one tribe to another. Plots of land could not be merged beyond the jubilee. Kings and Levites – the national enforcers of God's law – could not pursue judicial centralization through either land purchase or intermarriage. This prevented what Pharaoh and the priests had done under Joseph (Gen. 47:20-22) – a curse on Egypt consistent with Egypt's theology of the divine Pharaoh.

Thus, the prohibition against the interbreeding of animals and the mixing of seeds had to do with *keeping separate artificially what is normally mixed*. Fenced family fields inside Israel reflected the nation's tribal boundaries. Such tribal separation was abnormal, not normal. What is abnormal is the separation of breeds within a species and the separation of crops within a single fenced field. What is also abnormal is the separation of a biblically covenanted people. This abnormality was essential to the maintenance of the tribal structure in Israel. Inheritance in the land was by tribal separation, but only until Shiloh at last arrived. The internal boundaries would disappear once Shiloh came.[11]

---

10. See below, p. 471.

11. The absence of tribal membership in Judaism indicates that this prophecy was fulfilled prior to A.D. 70.

Leviticus 19:19's prohibition of genetic experimentation was an aspect of the preservation of the national covenant, which included the tribal boundaries. In the *economic trade-off* between the *land's seed* (increased wealth from genetic experimentation) and the *promised Seed* (which required the maintenance of tribal boundaries), the promised Seed had priority. Jacob's prophecy was more important than agricultural production. *We must interpret the seed laws as ritual laws.* Israel had to sacrifice some degree of wealth in order to honor ritually the principle of the promised Seed.

Leviticus 19:19 is part of the Mosaic Covenant's laws governing the preservation of the family's seed (name) during a particular period of history. It was an aspect of the necessary preservation of genetic Israel. The preservation of the separate seeds of Israel's families was basic to the preservation of the nation's legal status as a set-apart, separated, *holy* covenantal entity. This principle of separation applied to domesticated animals, crops, and clothing.

Animals and Crops

Let us begin with the law prohibiting the mixing of cattle. Did this refer to bovines only? No. The plain teaching of the passage indicates that the breeds of all domesticated animals that were common in the Promised Land at the time of the conquest were to be allowed to reproduce. The breeds had to be kept separate, however. There was to be no active breeding of new specialized breeds in order to produce animals that had different characteristics from the land's original breeds. There was to be no man-directed genetic manipulation of animals in Mosaic Israel.

The Mosaic law prohibiting the interbreeding of animals was never part of the creation mandate. It was a temporary law that illustrated an eschatological principle: the fulfillment of God's promise to Abraham regarding the world's deliverance through the Seed, and the fulfillment of Jacob's promise regarding Shiloh, the Messiah.

Separation of the Breeds

The technical possibility of mixing breeds always exists. Mixing will happen without active interference from man. If members of a species are not deliberately kept separate, they will breed together. Thus, to preserve an existing breed genetically, a husbandman must take active steps to keep the breeds separated. He must either build fences or hire drovers to keep them apart.

A law prohibiting random intermixing of breeds really was superfluous. No profit-seeking owner would allow a pair of specialized breeds to intermix randomly. Such progeny would rarely command the same price or produce the same level of output as the progeny of the separate breeds. Even if a more productive offspring would occasionally be produced, this would do the owner no long-term economic good, for he was prohibited from interbreeding the resulting pairs. *So, this law was really a prohibition against scientific breeding aimed at producing a new breed with unique characteristics*. It meant that whatever common animals existed when they entered the land – "mongrels" – could mix freely with other similarly undistinguished animals.

What if the free market began to register demand for a particular kind of animal? This demand would have applied to: 1) a breed that they had brought with them into the Promised Land, 2) a breed already within the land when they invaded, or 3) an imported breed from outside the land after they conquered it. These breeds would have been the modern equivalent of registered animals.

The husbandman would have kept these animals separate from other existing breeds. Obviously, he would have an economic incentive to do this. To sell into a specialized market, his animals would have to be kept away from others not of the same type. So, this law commanded what the economy would have required anyway: separation. *It would have applied only to owners who had begun programs of experimental breeding to produce a separate breed.*

The seed of each breed had to be separated. To obey this law as it applied to "non-mongrels," an Israelite would have had to construct a holding area or pen for each specialized breed. This means that a specific seed or line was associated with a specific place at any point in time. Owners could lawfully move animals to new locations, but there was always to be a geographical boundary associated with each breed (seed). This boundary established a connection between land and seed. This connection was mandatory for both man and beast.

Crops

The same principle of separation – prohibition of genetic experimentation – applied also to crops. The law stipulated, "thou shalt not sow thy field with mingled seed." This means that a specific field had to be devoted to a specific crop at any given point in the growing season. Like the pens for animals, the seeds of the crop had to reside in a particular place. Seed and land had to be linked.

What about genetic experimentation? The same prohibition applied. There could be no lawful, systematic mixing of seeds. An Israelite was not to apply his ingenuity to the creation of new species of plants. Hybrid animals and seeds were illegal to develop. They could be purchased from abroad, but since most hybrids are either sterile (e.g., mules) or else they produce weak offspring, there was little economic incentive to import hybrids except as a one-generation consumer good. Such imports were legal: *with no "inheritance" possible, there was no symbolic threat from hybrids.* A hybrid was not prohibited because of its status as a hybrid. It was illegal to produce them deliberately because of the prohibition against mixing seeds, which was fundamental. The practice of seed-mixing was illegal, not hybrids as such.

This law did not apply to the familiar practice of grafting the branches of one species of fruit tree into the trunk of another.[12] Leviticus 19:19 was specific: it dealt with seeds planted in a field, not with branches grafted into an adult tree. The tree's trunk is the primary agent, symbolic of the covenant itself. The branch would become part of the older tree. It was not a competing seed. The removed branch was "adopted" by the older tree. This was always a legal option in Israel, as the marriages of Rahab and Ruth indicate. The technique of grafting was symbolic of conversion, which was why Paul used this imagery as the archetype in discussing the fate of the old branch of Israel and the grafting in of the gentiles (Rom. 11:17-21). So, tree grafting symbolized covenantal inclusion – adoption by conversion and confession – not tribal mixing.

Some crops do better when mixed, such as fodder. In the modern-day State of Israel, Jewish farmers deal with this problem in a Rabbinically approved way. One man makes a pile of seeds in a public place and covers it with a board. A second person piles up a second seed crop on top of the board. Then a third person comes along and announces in front of witnesses, "I need this board." He removes it. Finally, a fourth man comes along and is instructed to sow the field with the now-mixed crop.[13]

Clothing

Mixed clothing made of linen and wool was under a different kind of prohibition. It was illegal to wear clothing produced

---

12. Rabbinic opinion on this verse forbade grafting. See Nachmanides (Rabbi Moshe ben Nachman, the Ramban), *Commentary on the Torah: Leviticus* (New York: Shiloh, [1267?] 1974), p. 295. He cites the Talmud: *Kiddushin* 39a.

13. Israel Shahak, *Jewish History, Jewish Religion: The Weight of Three Thousand Years* (Boulder, Colorado: Pluto Press, 1994), p. 45.

by mixing these two fibers. There was no law against producing mixed cloth for export, however. Why was wearing it wrong but exporting it allowed?[14]

No other form of mixed-fiber clothing was prohibited by the Mosaic law. Did this case law by implication or extension prohibit all mixed fibers? This seems doubtful. It would have been easy to specify the more general prohibition rather than single out these two fibers. Deuteronomy's parallel passage also specifies this type of mixed fabric (Deut. 22:11) Then what was the nature of the offense? Answer: to wear clothing of this mixture was to proclaim symbolically the equality of Israel with all other nations. This could not be done lawfully inside Israel. But it could be done by non-Israelites outside Israel.

Linen was the priestly cloth. The priests were required to wear linen on the day of atonement (Lev. 16:30-34). Linen was to be worn by the priest in the sacrifice of the burnt offering (Lev. 6:10). During and after the Babylonian captivity, because of their rebellion in Israel, the Levites and priests were placed under a new requirement that kept them separate from the people: they had to wear linen whenever they served before the table of the Lord. They had to put on linen garments when they entered God's presence in the inner court, and remove them when they returned to the outer court. No wool was to come upon them (Ezek. 44:15-19). The text says, "they shall not sanctify the people with their garments" (Ezek. 44:19). Priestly holiness was associated with linen.

Inside a priestly nation, such a mixture was a threat to the holiness of the priests when they brought sacrifices before God. As between a priestly nation and a non-priestly nation, this section of Leviticus 19:19 symbolized the national separation of believers from unbelievers. Deuteronomy 22:11 is the parallel passage: "Thou shalt not wear a garment of divers sorts: [as] of wool and linen together."

14. In biblical law, if something is not prohibited, it is allowed.

Inside the boundaries of Israel the law symbolized sacrificial separation: the tribe of Levi was set apart as a legal representative before God. In this *intra-national* sense, this law did have a role to play in the separation of the tribes. This is why it was connected to the two seed laws in Leviticus 19:19.

It is still prohibited to mix covenantal opposites in a single covenant: in church, State, and family. But is the wearing of this mixture of these two fabrics still prohibited? No. Why not? Because of the change in the priesthood (Gal. 3). Our new covering is Jesus Christ. Paul wrote: "For as many of you as have been baptized into Christ have put on Christ. There is neither Jew nor Greek, there is neither bond nor free, there is neither male nor female: for ye are all one in Christ Jesus. And if ye be Christ's, then are ye Abraham's seed, and heirs according to the promise" (Gal. 3:27-29). Here it is again: inheritance is by God's promise to Abraham. The sign of this inheritance is no longer circumcision; it is baptism. This is our new clothing. The old prohibition against mixing wool and linen in our clothing is annulled. The new priesthood is under a new covering: Jesus Christ.

The Question of Jurisdiction

Was this a civil law or an ecclesiastical law? To identify it as a civil law, we should be able to specify appropriate civil sanctions. The text mentions none. The civil magistrate might have confiscated the progeny of the interbreeding activities, but then what? Sell the animals? Export them? Kill them and sell the meat? These were possible sanctions, but the text is silent. What about mingled seed? Was the entire crop to be confiscated by the State? Could it lawfully be sold? Was it unclean? The text is silent. This silence establishes a *prima facie* case for the law as ecclesiastical.

The mixed clothing law refers to a fact of covenantal separation: a nation of priests. The Israelites were not to wear clothing made of linen and wool. This symbolic mixing testified to the legitimacy of mixing a nation of priests and a common nation. This is why wearing such mixed cloth was prohibited. This aspect of the case law's meaning was primarily priestly. Again, the *prima facie* case is that this was an ecclesiastical law and therefore enforced by the priesthood.

The maximum ecclesiastical sanction was excommunication. This would have marked the law-breaker as being outside the civil covenant. He faced the loss of his citizenship as well as the disinheritance of his sons unless they broke with him publicly. Instead of a mere economic loss, he faced a far greater penalty. This penalty was consistent with the status of this law as a seed law. The prohibition of mixed seeds was an affirmation of tribal separation until Shiloh came. An attack on tribal separation was an attack on Jacob's messianic prophecy. The appropriate penalty was ecclesiastical: removal from both inheritance and citizenship within the tribe.

Conclusion

In this chapter I have attempted to answer three questions: What did Leviticus 19:19 mean? How was it applied? How should it be applied today? This is the three-part challenge of biblical hermeneutics.

The prohibition against the mixing of seeds – animals and crops – was symbolic of the mandatory separation of the tribes. This separation was eschatologically based: till Shiloh came. The prohibition against wearing a mixed cloth of linen and wool was a priestly prohibition: separation of the tribe of Levi within Israel and symbolic of the separation of the priestly nation of Israel from other nations, i.e., a confessional separation.

This three-fold law was temporary. It ended with the death, resurrection, and ascension of Jesus Christ, or, at the latest, at Pentecost. *Spiritual adoption has overcome tribalism as the basis of inheritance in the kingdom of God*. The gift of the Spirit is the basis of Christians' inheritance, not physical reproduction. National

Israel was disinherited in A.D. 70.[15] The kingdom of God was taken from national Israel and given to a new nation, the church (Matt. 21:43). The jubilee land laws (Lev. 25) have ended forever. So have the prohibitions against genetic mixing and mixed crops. When people are baptized into Christ through the Spirit, this new priesthood puts on Christ. The older requirements or prohibitions regarding certain types of garments have ended forever. What remains is the judicial boundary between covenant-breakers and covenant-keepers. This separation is eternal (Rev. 20:14-15).

The biblical principle of not mixing seeds, whether of animals or crops in a single field, applies to us only indirectly. The basic judicial application is that we must be faithful to Jesus Christ, the promised Seed, who has come in history. In Him alone is true inheritance. But there is no application with respect to tribal boundaries. The tribes of Israel are gone forever. Thus, there is no application of this verse genetically. We are allowed to breed animals and plant various crops in the same field at the same time.

The other application of the principle of separation in this verse prohibited the wearing of mixed fiber garments: linen and wool. This applies to us today through baptism, for by baptism we have received our new clothing in Christ. This principle of separation still holds nationally, for it is covenantal, not tribal. It refers to the distinctions between priests and non-priests, between priestly nations (confessionally Christian) and non-priestly nations. It refers to the distinction between Christendom and every other world system. But it has nothing to do with fabrics any longer.

---

15. David Chilton, *The Days of Vengeance: An Exposition of the Book of Revelation* (Ft. Worth, Texas: Dominion Press, 1987).

18

COVENANTAL FRUIT

And when ye shall come into the land, and shall have planted all manner of trees for food, then ye shall count the fruit thereof as uncircumcised: three years shall it be as uncircumcised unto you: it shall not be eaten of. But in the fourth year all the fruit thereof shall be holy to praise the LORD *withal. And in the fifth year shall ye eat of the fruit thereof, that it may yield unto you the increase thereof: I am the* LORD *your God (Lev. 19:23-25).*

When we consider a biblical case law, it is best to begin theocentrically. God established this prohibition, so it must have had something to do with His relation to the land through His agents, men. The problem that the commentator faces is to specify three things: 1) what this relationship involved; 2) which men it applied to, men in general or the Israelites of the Mosaic covenant; 3) its proper application today. Was it a universal prohibition, or did it apply only to the Promised Land under the Mosaic economy?

This is another seed law. *The seed laws were laws of separation.* That is, they placed judicial boundaries around living organisms. We need to determine what this law meant. Because this statute invokes the language of circumcision, it has to refer symbolically (i.e., representatively) to the covenantal separation between circumcised and uncircumcised people. Tribal or family separation within Israel is therefore not in question here. What kind of separation was involved? Did this law refer to the legal boundary separating circumcised and uncircumcised men dwelling in Israel? Did it refer to the separation between circumcised and uncircumcised nations? Or was there some other separation involved? I believe that it referred to a unique form of covenantal separation, one which is represented by no other law in Scripture: a separation whose origins were in Israel's past. This separation was the 40-year period of wandering in the wilderness in which the Israelites of the exodus generation refused to circumcise their sons.

This law applied to orchards. God marked off the fruit of newly planted trees for His own purposes. He set this fruit outside of covenant-keeping man's lawful access. That is, He placed a "no trespassing" boundary around the fruit of newly planted trees for three years after they began to bear fruit. Then he announced that the fruit of the fourth year was holy: set aside for him. This was analogous to what He had done in the garden with the tree of the knowledge of good and evil: setting it aside for a period, keeping men away from it. The question is: Why?

Temporarily Forbidden Fruit

Two facts need to be noted. *First*, this prohibition applied to the first four years of fruit borne by a tree that was planted in the Promised Land after the land had come under the control of the Israelites. As we shall see, the prohibition did not apply to fruit from trees that had been planted by the Canaanites just prior to the invasion of Canaan by Israel. It was not "trees as such" whose fruit came under this ban; it was trees that had been planted after the conquest.

The seeds or cuttings that would serve as the parents of Israel's first crop would have come from the existing trees of Canaan. The new trees' fruit was to be set aside for three seasons and offered to God in the fourth. This indicates that there had to be a discontinuity between the trees and seeds of the old Canaan and the trees and seeds of the new Canaan. Like the leaven of Egypt that had to be purged out during the first Passover, so were the firstfruits of Canaan. The leaven (yeast) of Egypt could not be used as "starter" for the leaven of the conquered Canaan. It was different in the case of Canaan's trees. They had to be used as "starter" for Israel's new orchards. Thus, God prohibited access to their fruit for a period, thereby emphasizing the covenantal discontinuity between the old Canaan and the new Canaan.

Second, God called "uncircumcised" the forbidden fruit of the first three seasons. This is a peculiar way to speak of fruit. Circumcision was the visible mark of the Abrahamic Covenant: the *visible legal boundary* separating the heirs of the promise from non-heirs. That is, circumcision determined inheritance (point five of the biblical covenant model: succession/inheritance). In Mosaic Israel, circumcision separated those who had lawful access to the Passover meal from those who did not (point four: oath/sanctions). The legal basis of separation was inclusion vs. exclusion inside the formally covenanted people of God (point three: boundaries). Incorporation into the covenanted nation was by covenantal oath-sign (point four). The uncircumcised individual was institutionally outside God's covenantal boundary. He was therefore *judicially unholy*, i.e., not set apart legally. He would profane a ritually holy place by crossing its legal boundary. But who was this uncircumcised person? Was he a resident alien? If so, what did the mandatory three years of separation have to do with him?

A judicial separation of this kind implied a threat – negative sanctions – to the violator of the boundary. Whom did the forbidden fruit threaten? Not the birds or other beasts of the land. They had lawful access to the fruit during the first three years. The fruit was not poisonous, obviously. Then why was it prohibited to an Israelite? Why was there a legal boundary placed around it? What did this boundary symbolize?

It could be argued that mankind poses a threat to young trees or to the orchard itself. Perhaps the law was ecological in intent rather than ritual. But then why was the new fruit of young trees that had already been planted in Canaan at the time of the conquest not placed under the ban? And why was the covenantal-legal language of circumcision invoked?

Uncircumcised Fruit

The language of the law is clear: "And when ye shall come into the land, and *shall have planted* all manner of trees for food, then ye shall count the fruit thereof as uncircumcised." The trees of Canaan that were already bearing fruit at the time of Israel's conquest of Canaan were not under any prohibition. They were to be considered by the invading Israelites as part of the spoils of war. "And I have given you a land for which ye did not labour, and cities which ye built not, and ye dwell in them; of the vineyards and oliveyards which ye planted not do ye eat" (Josh. 24:13). This verse does not say that young trees were excluded; it does imply that the whole land was God's gift to Israel. Where a prohibition was placed around spoils, which was uniquely the case with the city of Jericho, God warned them in no uncertain terms through Joshua (Josh. 6:17-19).

Uncircumcised fruit was analogous to an uncircumcised male or a woman who was under the family jurisdiction of an uncircumcised male: outside the covenant. This was a legal issue, not ritual: incorporation. The fruit of the Canaanites' existing orchards was not identified as judicially uncircumcised. It could immediately be consumed or sold by the land's new owners. So, the prohibition had nothing to do with any supposedly ritually polluting effects of the land of Canaan. In fact, the reverse was the case: the land was holy, but the Canaanites were not. The land was part of Abraham's legacy to his heirs (Gen. 15:16). It was judicially holy land. God's promise had made the land *definitively* holy. Subsequently, the land had been *progressively polluted* by the Canaanites (Lev. 18:24-28).

The Canaanites' ethically perverse behavior had defiled the holy land, i.e., *profaned* it. They were unholy men dwelling inside a holy boundary. Finally, the land purged itself of those who had defiled it. It was a holy land, so it vomited out those who were unholy. But why didn't the land do this long before Joshua's generation? Because the cup of iniquity of Canaan ("Amorites") had not been filled up (Gen. 15:16b). A progressive process of profanation had to take place first, just as a progressive process of holiness had to take place among the Israelites. By Joshua's day, this progressive profanation by the Canaanites had reached its fullness (final profanation), as had the progressive sanctification of Israel. It was time for the land to begin vomiting, i.e., time for Israel to invade. The land became *finally* holy at the time of the invasion by a judicially holy nation. *It was circumcised Israel's presence in the land that made the land a finally holy place.* The judicially mandatory cleansing process began. The separation was to be total: the annihilation of the Canaanites (Deut. 7:16).

When the land attained its status as finally holy, it gained its status as ritually holy. The finalization of the land's holy status in history came only with the circumcision of Israel inside the land (Josh. 5). The Israelites had been ritually unholy until they were circumcised at Gilgal. Their circumcision anointed them as a nation of priests, and they could then lawfully offer sacrifice: Jericho, Israel's firstfruits offering to God (Josh. 6:24). The battle of Jericho marked the beginning of the land's vomiting process. The land began serving as God's covenantal agent: "And I will send hornets before thee, which shall drive out the Hivite, the Canaanite, and the Hittite, from before thee" (Ex. 23:28).

It was the presence of the circumcised nation of Israel in the land that made the land and its existing fruits holy. Except for Jericho, which served as the firstfruits for the Lord, none of the land and its fruit was declared off-limits to covenant-keepers. The land had become totally off-limits to the covenant-breaking

Canaanites who were residing in it.[1] When the Israelites inherited the land, the land gained a unique judicial and ritual status as God's dwelling place. It became the land of the tabernacle and, later, the temple. It was the only place on earth where lawful sacrifices to God were offered by God's corporately covenanted people.

Who Planted Which Trees?

Why, then, was the early fruit of newly planted trees identified as uncircumcised? *Uncircumcised* means unholy: not set apart by God, i.e., *not incorporated.* How could the land, which had been made finally holy by the invasion of the Israelites, produce unholy or uncircumcised fruit? Clearly, the new fruit was declared uncircumcised, but the land could not have been at fault. Conclusion: *if it was not the land that was the source of the new fruit's unholy status, then it must have been the Israelites.* But why?

To find the answer, we need first to ask: What was judicially or ritually different about fruit trees that had been planted by the Israelites in the Promised Land, as distinguished from young trees that had been planted by Canaanites immediately prior to Israel's invasion of the land? When an Israelite was the agent who planted seeds in the land, the judicial status of the fruit of the trees changed. The fruit was placed inside a legal boundary for four years. It was declared off-limits. Normally, we would expect any set-apart status to be called *holy* by God, but in this case the fruit was called *uncircumcised.* This is peculiar. What was special about the fruit of young trees planted by Israelites? What was the point, ritually and judicially?

What was God's reason for calling the fruit of the first three years *uncircumcised?* What did circumcision have to do with

---

1. The exceptions, of course, were the Gibeonites (Josh. 9), who lost their land and citizenship, becoming slaves to the Levites (Josh. 9:23, 27), who also owned no land outside cities.

fruit? Biologically, nothing at all; symbolically, everything. In Israel, not to be circumcised was to be judicially unholy, i.e., common or "gentile." Those people who were holy had been set apart judicially by God: incorporated into the covenant people. The new fruit was identified by God as *judicially unholy* – not ritually unclean, but judicially unholy, meaning *common*. The unholy or gentile judicial status of the fruit was not produced by the land, which was itself holy; it therefore had to be produced by the Israelites who did the planting. Conclusion: *the fruit's judicial status of being uncircumcised came from men who were circumcised*. Why was this the case?

Pointing Back to the Wilderness

Obviously, there was nothing unholy about the judicial status of the circumcised Israelite at the time that he planted an orchard. What was it about judicially holy men that produced an opposite judicial status in the fruit of young trees? Here is the dilemma: the Israelite's present judicial status at the time of planting was holy; the land's present judicial status was also holy; yet the fruit would be judicially unholy for three years. The judicial question has to be turned away from the Israelites' present judicial status in Mosaic Israel to their past, their future, or both.

The frame of reference surely was not eschatological in the way that the seed laws of Leviticus 19:19 were. The orchard statute had nothing to do with tribal separation, the way Leviticus 19:19 did. The law of uncircumcised fruit did not refer Jacob's promise to a specific tribe of Israel, nor did it mandate the permanent separation of tribal inheritance until the Promised Seed appeared. I therefore conclude that this statute's primary frame of reference was historical. The anomaly of two holy things – land and circumcised planter – producing something temporarily unholy points back to the generation of the conquest of the land: the fourth generation after Abraham's covenant (Gen. 15:16). Why do I conclude this? First, because that generation was temporarily unholy. Second, because of the *representative* numerical relationship between 40 days (the time the twelve tribal spies spent in the Promised Land: Num. 13), 40 years (the time of the wilderness wandering), and four years (the period of the two-fold boundary around the fruit).

Forty Years

For four decades, the Israelites of the exodus generation had wandered in the wilderness without circumcising their sons. Why 40 years? Because the spies had been in the land for 40 days (Num. 14:28-35). Except for Joshua and Caleb, the men of the exodus generation had been designated by God as unholy because of their disbelief and rebellion. They could not enter the land, which would become finally holy at the time of their sons' mass circumcision at Gilgal. They could not lawfully cross this boundary; to have done so would have been a profane act. Thus, that first generation had to be kept outside the land by God. They were not allowed to profane the holy land by violating its boundaries. When they were all dead, as prophesied, their sons were allowed to cross that boundary. But they, too, were unholy. They had never been circumcised. So, Joshua had them circumcised at Gilgal after they came into the land (Josh. 5:6-12).

The male children in the wilderness should have been circumcised on the eighth day after each was born. Their parents had refused to do this. The text does not say why. I think the most likely economic explanation is that the parents thought they might return to Egypt at some point. They were "keeping their options open" covenantally with respect to their children. The children were not formally placed under the covenantal protection and obligations that God requires of His people. That is, their parents did not incorporate them into the nation.

The parents had been told by God that they would not enter the land (Num. 14:23). The regarded their possession of the land of Canaan as the only meaningful public validation of

God's covenant; their deliverance from bondage in Egypt was not sufficient in their eyes. They were basically announcing: "No immediate payoff in real estate; so, no mark of covenantal subordination in our sons." They wanted an immediate payoff, just as Adam had desired in the garden; they were unwilling to trust God with respect to the inheritance of the land by their children. So, God kept that uncircumcised younger generation in the wilderness until the exodus generation died, except for Joshua and Caleb.

There may also have been a judicial reason for their refusal. The nation had rebelled against Joshua and Caleb, and then against God when they attacked the Amalekites and Canaanites against God's specific command (Num. 14:39-44). The 10 cowardly spies had been killed by God through a plague (Num. 14:37). The nation had become unholy: separated from the definitively holy Promised Land for one generation. The fathers may have concluded that they had lost their status as household priests. So, they refused to circumcise their sons, or have the Levites circumcise them. Whether this was at God's command is not revealed in the text. But these people were cowards, and they had seen what happened to the 10 cowardly spies. They may have decided that discretion was the better part of valor with respect to circumcising their sons.

After entering the land, the sons who had been born in the wilderness were immediately circumcised. At that point, they celebrated the Passover with the existing fruit of the land (Josh. 5:11). Immediately, the miraculous manna ceased. The people lived off the fruit of the land from that time on (Josh. 5:12). They had moved from miraculous food to miraculous warfare (Jericho). After the conquest of the land, they moved to non-miraculous planting.[2]

---

2. There would still be one remaining miracle: the triple harvest just before the seventh sabbatical year (Lev. 25:21).

To recapitulate: Canaan's conquerors had been uncircumcised for up to 40 years. The close of the wilderness period came with their celebration of the Passover as *household priests*: heads of their own households. Then the conquest began. The firstfruits of the conquest was the city of Jericho, which had to be burnt as a whole offering to God. None of its treasure was to be taken by the Israelites personally; everything was either to be burned or used to make the treasures of the tabernacle (Josh. 6:19). Jericho was to be cut off completely: a foreskin.

Four Years

We return to Leviticus 19:23-25. The fruit of newly planted trees was off-limits to them until the fourth year. "But in the fourth year all the fruit thereof shall be holy to praise the LORD withal." The question is: What were they required to do with the fruit in year four? Were they to take it to the priest, as they were required to with the firstfruits offering (Lev. 23:10-11)? Or was it analogous to the required third-year tithe feast in Jerusalem (Deut. 14:22-23)?

Because the forbidden fruit is called uncircumcised, it is best to treat the fourth-year harvest as analogous to the Passover feast. Only after circumcision was Passover legal. This fourth-year feast provided each family with the first lawful occasion for enjoying the fruits of their own labor – the trees they had planted and nurtured – in the Promised Land. What had been uncircumcised fruit and therefore forbidden to them became *circumcised in the fourth year*, and therefore eligible to serve as *food for a mandatory holy feast*. They would have had to invite the Levites to the feast, and presumably also widows and orphans, just as they were required to do in the third-year festival: "And the Levite that is within thy gates; thou shalt not forsake him; for he hath no part nor inheritance with thee. At the end of three years thou shalt bring forth all the tithe of thine increase the same year, and shalt lay it up within thy gates: And the Levite, (because he hath no part nor inheritance with thee,) and the stranger, and the fatherless, and the widow, which are within thy gates, shall come, and shall eat and be satisfied; that the LORD thy God may bless thee in all the work of thine hand which thou doest" (Deut. 14:27-29).

Historical References

It is time to make some connections. We have to ask ourselves: What did this prohibition represent?[3] First, young fruit trees are immature. So were the children born in the wilderness. Such fruit was designated as uncircumcised. The children in the wilderness era had been uncircumcised.

Second, the "harvesting" of Canaan militarily began after 40 years. The unrestricted harvesting of fruit trees began lawfully after four years of fruitfulness.

Third, there is the question of inheritance. Caleb said that he had been 40 years old in the year that he had been sent in to spy out the land (Josh. 14:7). This was one year after the exodus (Num. 10:11-12; 13:17-20). Israel wandered for 39 years after the spying incident before entering Canaan. Caleb was 79 (40 + 39) when the invasion began, and 85 when it ended (Josh. 14:10). So, it took Israel six years to conquer Canaan.[4] The text says that the land then had rest from war (Josh. 14:15). This means that there was rest from war in the seventh year – a sabbatical symbol. Therefore, during the *fifth decade* after the exodus, Israel took possession of the whole land as its inheritance. Similarly, the *fifth year* of fruit was the first year in which the fruit of the trees belonged to the individual.

There is a parallel between the wilderness years the uncircumcised generation of the conquest and the ban on eating the

3. The issue of *symbolism* in the Bible is *judicial representation*, point two of the biblical covenant model. We seek to learn what a particular symbol represented judicially.

4. James B. Jordan, "The Chronology of the Pentateuch (Part 6)," *Biblical Chronology*, VI (Aug. 1994), pp. 3-4.

fruit of new trees planted in Canaan. The fruit did not belong to the owner until after the holy feast of year four. That is, he took possession of the fruit in year five. This parallels Israel's taking possession of Canaan during decade five. This four-year prohibition pointed symbolically back to Israel's rebellion in the wilderness: four decades of deferred possession.[5] This seed law for orchards referred back to the unique historical experience of the conquest generation: Israel's seed.

This ban was not symbolic of the separation between Israelites and resident aliens, a separation that did not involve a four-year waiting period.[6] This law had nothing to do with the agricultural laws of the Hammurabi Code.[7] Contrary to Rabbinical interpretations, it had nothing to do with man's supposedly animalistic nature, which requires the discipline of waiting, i.e., the phenomenon Ludwig von Mises called time-preference.[8]

The Economics of Restricted Access

There is no doubt that one economic effect of this law was to force the orchard's owner to forego three years' worth of the orchard's output before he could celebrate before the Lord in year four. No doubt this law did pressure obedient men to count the costs of their decision: planting an orchard vs. planting something else (or planting nothing). But being required to count the costs of our actions is not in and of itself an incentive

---

5. It also pointed forward to the ministry of Jesus Christ. See Gary North, *Boundaries and Dominion: The Economics of Leviticus* (computer edition; Tyler, Texas: Institute for Christian Economics, 1994), ch. 18, subsection on "Eschatological References."

6. The third-generation circumcised Egyptian or Edomite became a citizen (Deut. 23:8). The third-generation member of these two nations was therefore regarded as the judicial equal of a circumcised Israelite. (He could not inherit land in the countryside, however: Leviticus 25.) But the third-year fruit was still uncircumcised. So, there is no analogy between these two forms of circumcision.

7. *Ibid.*, ch. 18, section on "The Initially Confusing Economics of This Law."

8. *Ibid.*, ch. 18, section on "Rabbinical Interpretations." I refer here to Rashi and S. R. Hirsch.

to become more future-oriented. *No law can force men to become more future-oriented.* The function of biblical civil law is not to make men positively good; it is to reduce the level of public evil. This law merely sorted out those who were more future-oriented (less present-oriented) from those who were less future-oriented (more present-oriented). Those residents of the holy commonwealth who were more future-oriented were more likely to plant orchards. Those who were less future-oriented were more likely to plant a crop that was not under a temporary harvesting restriction. Each man made his choice. So, there was no necessary connection between this case law and a general increase in men's future-orientation. But there was a necessary connection between future-orientation and the kinds of crops individual decision-makers planted.

Edward Banfield has linked time perspective with class position. An upper-class person is someone with low time-preference, i.e., a future-oriented person.[9] A society that views an increase in future-orientation as a virtue – and the Bible indicates that it is a virtue[10] – does pressure individuals to become more future-oriented. But civil law cannot accomplish this.[11] Then what does? Such psychological factors as fear, education, and moral persuasion. At best, widespread obedience to the uncircumcised fruit law would have enabled local residents to identify families whose heads of household were (or had been)

---

9. Edward Banfield, *The Unheavenly City* (Boston: Little, Brown, 1970), pp. 48-50. On the middle class, see pp. 50-53. On the lower class, see pp. 53-59. On the importance of Banfield's book, see Thomas Sowell, "The Unheavenly City Revisited," *American Spectator* (Feb. 1994).

10. At the margin, of course. An increase to total future-orientation is not possible, for we must eat, drink, and be clothed in the present.

11. This includes tax policy. Lowering capital gains tax rates, for example, does not make someone more future-oriented. It merely raises the after-tax return of future profits. The fact that a person can legally keep more in the future than less in the future will affect his present investment decisions, but this change has nothing to do with a change in his time-preference: the discount of future value in relation to present value.

future-oriented. The presence of an orchard on a person's land so identified such an individual, or at least such a family.

In the moral environment of covenantally faithful Israel, the presence of an orchard became a kind of status symbol. The orchard took on the characteristic of a consumer good. Like a very expensive automobile in today's world, the orchard testified to someone who had "made it" because of his (or his father's) diligence and willingness to defer gratification by planting the orchard. In this sense, the uncircumcised fruit law may have indirectly promoted future-orientation, but only because this outlook on deferred gratification was already widely acknowledged to be positive – a sign of character in a person or family. The presence of an orchard became a visible manifestation of a desirable character trait. In short, "if you've got it, flaunt it!"

God told the Israelites to wait, just as He told Adam in the garden.[12]

Conclusion

This law had nothing to do with the sabbath.[13] It also had nothing to do with biological health, contrary to Rushdoony.[14] It had to do with God's special presence in the land. When the temple's sacrifices ended, and God no longer dwelt in the Promised Land, Leviticus 19:23-25 was annulled by God. The land of Palestine today is no longer owed any restitution payment. It no longer spews people out of its boundaries. Its unique covenantal status ended in A.D. 70.

This law was never part of the sabbath rest laws. It was part of the restitution laws. It therefore came under the general

12. North, *Boundaries and Dominion*, ch. 18, section on "Forfeited Income and Class Position," subsection on "When God Says 'Wait!'"

13. *Ibid.*, ch. 18, section on "Which Decalogue Commandment?"

14. R. J. Rushdoony, *The Institutes of Biblical Law* (Nutley, New Jersey: Craig Press, 1973), p. 87.

category of theft laws: the eighth commandment. But the Promised Land's owner was God; thus, this law relates also to the third commandment: the boundary around God's name. God placed a "no trespassing" boundary around the fruit of young trees, just as He had placed such a boundary around the tree of the knowledge of good and evil. He had originally placed no such boundary around the tree of life. It was not trees in general or fruit in general that came under the original ban in Eden; it was only one tree. This Edenic prohibition had nothing to do with soil conservation. It was not universal. It was in fact a temporary ban. So was the Mosaic law's ban on uncircumcised fruit. At the very least, that law ceased to have any judicial authority when circumcision ceased being a covenantally relevant mark (I Cor. 7:19).

The law governing the harvesting of fruit from a young tree was a law unique to ancient Israel. It was not intended for the nations around Israel, for it was part of the seed laws and land laws that applied only to Israel as a holy nation. This law was a negative sanction imposed on Israel by God because of the wilderness rebellion. God imposed this law as a negative sanction because of the failure of the exodus generation to invade the land of Canaan after hearing reports and military analysis from Joshua and Caleb. The land of Canaan had deserved deliverance from the Canaanite rule 40 years before the children of the exodus generation invaded the land. It therefore was owed restitution by the heirs of the exodus generation.

This law was also an aspect of the parents' failure to circumcise their sons in the wilderness. This is why the new fruit was called uncircumcised. This was to remind them of the sons' own temporary status as unholy – *culturally unfruitful* – during the 40 years of wilderness wandering. This law was never designed as a universal statute; it was a specific negative sanction on the people of Israel and a positive sanction on the Promised Land itself. It was not a cross-boundary law. It did not apply outside the Promised Land, so it does not apply today.

19

MEASURING OUT JUSTICE

And if a stranger sojourn with thee in your land, ye shall not vex him. But the stranger that dwelleth with you shall be unto you as one born among you, and thou shalt love him as thyself; for ye were strangers in the land of Egypt: I am the L*ORD your God. Ye shall do no unrighteousness in judgment, in meteyard, in weight, or in measure. Just balances, just weights, a just ephah, and a just hin, shall ye have: I am the* L*ORD your God, which brought you out of the land of Egypt. Therefore shall ye observe all my statutes, and all my judgments, and do them: I am the* L*ORD (Lev. 19:33-37).*

The theocentric meaning of this law is equality before God's law. This includes strangers. The general principle is the familiar guideline known as the golden rule: do unto others as you would have them do unto you (Matt. 7:12).

God reminded the Israelites in this passage that He had delivered them from Egyptian bondage, where they had been strangers. This deliverance had been an application of the fundamental theme of the Bible: *the transition from wrath to grace*. The God who delivered His people in history (point two of the biblical covenant model: historical prologue) is also the God who lays down the law (point three).

One judicial application of God's historical deliverance of His people is the creation of a civil sanctuary: *a place set apart judi-*

cially by God for those who seek liberty under God.[1] The establishment of a boundary is an aspect of point three. In this case, the boundary was geographical. It was to serve as a judicial model for the whole world (Deut. 4:4-8). Strangers in the land were expected to tell "the folks back home" of the benefits of dwelling in God's sanctuary. God prepared a place for strangers to live in peace through justice. This system of justice did not give strangers political authority, for they were outside the ecclesiastical covenant. But the system provided liberty. Conclusion: political pluralism is not biblically necessary for civil liberty.

There is no valid biblical reason to believe that God's ideal of sanctuary for strangers in a holy commonwealth has been annulled by the New Covenant. On the contrary, the sanctuary principle has been extended across the globe through Christ's universal gospel of deliverance (Matt. 28:18-20).[2] *Nation by nation, the whole world is to become such a sanctuary.*[3] But a biblical sanctuary is a theocratic commonwealth. That is to say, the extension of God's theocratic commonwealth means the extension of God's civil sanctuary: *the transition from civil wrath to civil grace*. The judicial evidence of this biblical civil grace is equality before the civil law. To maintain the blessings of liberty, all residents of a holy commonwealth are required to obey the Bible-revealed law of God. God made it quite clear: without corporate obedience to God's Bible-revealed law, no nation can maintain the blessings of civil liberty.[4]

---

1. Gary North, *Political Polytheism: The Myth of Pluralism* (Tyler, Texas: Institute for Christian Economics, 1989), ch. 2: "Sanctuary and Suffrage."

2. Kenneth L. Gentry, Jr., *The Greatness of the Great Commission: The Christian Enterprise in a Fallen World* (Tyler, Texas: Institute for Christian Economics, 1990).

3. Gary North, *Healer of the Nations: Biblical Blueprints for International Relations* (Ft. Worth, Texas: Dominion Press, 1987).

4. Those who seek to defend the ideal of civil liberty – sometimes called "civil liberties" – apart from an appeal to God's Bible-revealed law-order are indulging their preference for humanism: Stoic natural law theology or Newtonian natural law theology. In either case, they have abandoned the Bible's explicit method of retaining the blessings of liberty: Trinitarian, covenantal, oath-bound constitutionalism.

Judicial Love

There are three commands in this passage: to avoid vexing a stranger, to love the stranger, and to use honest weights and measures. We begin with the first. Leviticus 19:33 is a recapitulation of Exodus 22:21: "Thou shalt neither vex a stranger, nor oppress him: for ye were strangers in the land of Egypt." This is followed by the law commanding Israelites to love the resident alien (v. 34). One command is negative: *do not vex*. The other command is positive, or seems to be: *exercise love*. This positive injunction is followed by the phrase, "I am the LORD your God." This was a reminder to Israel of the sovereignty of the ultimate Enforcer.

The third law governs weights and measures. The question is: Are the vexation law (negative) and the weights and measures law (negative) two separate laws? Presumably, they are one law, for they are found in the same section. There is at least one link: the text's stated justification for each of these laws is historical, namely, the Israelites' experience in Egypt and their deliverance by God from Egypt. But these laws seem to be dealing with different issues: 1) the general public's vexing of strangers; 2) sellers' cheating of the general public.

The second law initially appears not to be a civil law, for it commands civility: "Thou shalt love him as thyself." That is, it seems to command a certain attitude toward someone. But biblical civil law does not command righteous behavior; it is limited to forbidding certain kinds of unrighteous behavior. It does not seek to compel goodness; it imposes negative sanctions against certain evil acts. That is to say, *biblical civil law is not messianic*. It establishes no positive civil sanctions for showing love to resident aliens. But without positive civil sanctions for righteous behavior, there is no civil law promoting righteous behavior: *no sanctions = no law*. Thus, if we interpret the command to love someone as meaning the inculcation of a positive attitude toward someone, this command is not a civil law. Also, no civil sanctions are attached to this law.

In apparent contrast, the third law is at the very heart of civil law: the enforcement of universal public standards of weights and measures. It forbids a public evil: "Ye shall do no unrighteousness in judgment." This is a restatement of Leviticus 19:15: "Ye shall do no unrighteousness in judgment: thou shalt not respect the person of the poor, nor honour the person of the mighty: but in righteousness shalt thou judge thy neighbour." The principle of the rule of law is publicly displayed in the enforcement of just weights and measures.

The Example of Egypt

The text's historical references to Egypt are two-fold: residence in Egypt and deliverance out of Egypt. The Israelites had not been loved in Egypt. The mark of that lack of love was their enslavement. They had been vexed by their one-time hosts, whose fathers' lives Joseph had saved. They had not been treated fairly. So perverse were the Egyptians – so unloving – that God intervened to deliver His people. In doing so, He imposed negative historical sanctions against the Egyptians. The warning in this case law is clear: those who refuse to honor God by loving their neighbors will be placed under God's negative historical sanctions.

But this raises a question: If the sin of the Egyptians in not loving the Israelites was their act of enslaving the Israelites, rather than a mere negative attitude toward the Israelites, then the focus of the anti-vexation law may be judicial rather than psychological. This is my interpretation of the law. *Love* in this case can legitimately be understood as *treating people lawfully* – as Bahnsen has put it, "showing love to our fellow men (by protecting them from theft, rape, slander, abortion, sexual deviance, etc.). . . ."[5] If so, then the two laws are doubly linked:

5. Greg L. Bahnsen, *No Other Standard: Theonomy and Its Critics* (Tyler, Texas: Institute for Christian Economics, 1991), p. 205.

both prohibit evil public actions; both are justified in terms of the Israelites' experience in Egypt.

The State as Savior

The State is authorized by God to impose only negative sanctions. The modern welfare State ignores this restriction. It attempts to benefit some groups at the expense of others. It has become the Savior State, a plundering State. It seeks to act messianically: a healer in history. It seeks to make men good rather than to restrict its activities to preventing designated evil acts.[6]

Corporate Sanctions

The State imposes negative physical sanctions as God's delegated agent in history. If Israelite magistrates failed in this task with respect to individual law-breakers, God would raise up other agents of His justice to impose negative sanctions on the whole society. For example, when Judah refused to honor the sabbatical year of rest for the land, God raised up Babylon – strangers – to carry His people into captivity, so that the land would receive its long-awaited lawful rest. God's law had specified this as the appropriate negative sanction (Lev. 26:32-35; fulfilled in II Chron. 36:17, 21).

The biblical justification for the State's imposition of negative sanctions against individual law-breakers is God's threat to impose negative corporate sanctions against the entire society if His Bible-revealed civil law is not enforced by civil magistrates. This is *the* distinctive principle of biblical civil government. I keep returning to this theme because it is central to biblical political economy. God's negative historical sanctions *will* be applied. The question is: By God or by the civil magistrates?

6. Gary North, *Boundaries and Dominion: The Economics of Leviticus* (computer edition; Tyler, Texas: Institute for Christian Economics, 1994), ch. 19, section on "Negative Sanctions: The State as Intermediary."

Those in society who are innocent of a particular crime deserve protection from God's corporate sanctions.[7] The State is therefore authorized to impose negative sanctions on convicted lawbreakers.

To Love the Imperfect Stranger

"Thou shalt love him as thyself." Why does this positive injunction to love the stranger appear in a list of civil laws? There are no non-judicial criteria listed that indicate how the covenant-keeping individual can show love to the stranger. There are no negative civil sanctions for a refusal to perform positive acts of charity, let alone for not displaying a positive mental attitude toward strangers. Therefore, love in this case law must be interpreted judicially: *treating the stranger lawfully*, as if he were a full citizen of the holy commonwealth. It is the same meaning that Paul attributed to love: "Love worketh no ill to his neighbour: therefore love is the fulfilling of the law" (Rom. 13:10). Fulfilling the terms of the law is the public manifestation of love. This is what the civil law requires of the covenant-keeper.

What was the *representative illegal act* of not showing love in Israel? *The oppression of strangers, widows, and orphans*.[8] How men treated the least powerful members of society served as a representation of their covenantal status before God, just as Jesus warned regarding the final judgment (Matt. 25:34-40).

But was there a specific *representative public act* in Israel that defined a *prosecutable* oppression? Yes. The next case law identifies it: *using rigged weights and measures*. A seller of goods was not allowed to use one set of weights for buying goods and

---

7. This is why, in the case of an unsolved murder in a field, civil magistrates from the nearest city were required to kill a heifer and have the priests sacrifice it in a nearby valley (Deut. 21:1-9). The blood covering had to be made, either by the shed blood of the convicted murderer or by the heifer.

8. Gary North, *Tools of Dominion: The Case Laws of Exodus* (Tyler, Texas: Institute for Christian Economics, 1990), ch. 22.

another set for selling these goods. He was not allowed to use one set of weights for some customers and another set for other customers. To do so would have testified to the existence of a God who imposes His law's standards in a partial manner. That is, it would have pointed to a God who shows favor to certain persons: one law for one group, another law for a different group. Again and again in Scripture, this is denied emphatically.[9] The essence of God's moral character, and therefore of His character as a judge, is the consistent application of His law.

Accompanying this law was an affirmation of God's character as a *consistent judge*, which also served as an implicit warning to the nation of Israel: "I am the LORD your God, which brought you out of the land of Egypt." God had brought negative sanctions against the Egyptians for their unrighteous behavior; He would do the same to Israel. He said this explicitly just before the next generation entered the land of Canaan: "And it shall be, if thou do at all forget the LORD thy God, and walk after other gods, and serve them, and worship them, I testify against you this day that ye shall surely perish. As the nations which the LORD destroyeth before your face, so shall ye perish; because ye would not be obedient unto the voice of the LORD your God" (Deut. 8:19-20).

A State that applies God's law impartially on all has obeyed the injunction to love men. It must provide equal access to justice.[10]

Just Measures and a Just Society

The familiar Western symbol of justice is the blindfolded woman holding a balance scale. The blindfold symbolizes the court's unwillingness to recognize persons. The scale symbolizes

---

9. See the citations in Chapter 14, p. 239, footnote 6.

10. North, *Boundaries and Dominion*, ch. 19, section on "Open Access and Impartial Justice."

fixed standards of justice: a fixed law applied to the facts of the case. Justice is symbolically linked to weights.

Justice cannot be quantified,[11] yet symbolically it is represented by the ultimate determinant of quantity: a scale. An honest scale registers very tiny changes in the weight of the things being weighed. A scale can be balanced only by adding or removing a quantity of the thing being measured until the weights on each side are equal, meaning as close to equal as the scale can register.[12] Even here, the establishment of a precise balance may take several attempts. An average of the attempts then becomes the acceptable measure.

The ability of men to make comparisons is best exemplified in the implements of physical measurement. The language of physical measurement is adopted by men when they speak of making historical or judicial comparisons. For example, the consumer *balances* his checkbook. This does not mean that he places it on a scale. Or he *weighs* the expected advantages and disadvantages of some decision.

The language of measurement is inescapable, whether in economics (giving proper "weight" to goods and services in constructing a price index) or politics ("checks and balances"). This is an implication of point three of the biblical covenant model: standards.[13] As surely as societies create bureaus that establish standards of measurement, so God has established permanent judicial standards. Both kinds of standards must be observed by law-abiding people.

---

11. See below, "Intuition and Measurement," pp. 317-21.

12. There are physical limits on the accuracy of scales. The best balance scales today can measure changes as small as one-tenth of a microgram. *Grolier Encyclopedia* (1990): "Weights and Measures." God's civil law calls for equal justice, not perfect justice. Cf. Gary North, *Moses and Pharaoh: Dominion Religion vs. Power Religion* (Tyler, Texas: Institute for Christian Economics, 1985), ch. 19: "Perfect Justice."

13. Ray R. Sutton, *That You May Prosper: Dominion By Covenant* (2nd ed.; Tyler, Texas: Institute for Christian Economics, 1992), ch. 3.

The Representative Case

The preservation of just weights and measures in the Mosaic Covenant was important for symbolic reasons as well as economic reasons. As a case law, it represented a wider class of crimes. It was important in itself: prohibiting theft through fraud. But there was something unique about the case law governing weights and measures: *it was representative of injustice in general*. "Ye shall do no unrighteousness in judgment, in meteyard, in weight, or in measure." The language of unrighteousness and judgment has a wider application than merely economic transactions. "Ye shall do no unrighteousness in judgment: thou shalt not respect the person of the poor, nor honour the person of the mighty: but in righteousness shalt thou judge thy neighbour" (Lev. 19:15). This states the fundamental principle of all biblical justice.

Injustice is also linked with false weights and measures. Isaiah made all these connections clear in his initial accusation against the rulers of Israel: "Thy silver is become dross, thy wine mixed with water: Thy princes are rebellious, and companions of thieves: every one loveth gifts, and followeth after rewards: they judge not the fatherless, neither doth the cause of the widow come unto them" (Isa. 1:22-23). False measures in silver and wine; princes in rebellion against God but companions of thieves; universal bribe-seeking; oppression of widows and orphans: all are linked in God's covenant lawsuit brought by the prophet. It was all part of *a great spiritual apostasy* – an apostasy that would be reversed by the direct intervention of God: "Therefore saith the Lord, the LORD of hosts, the mighty One of Israel, Ah, I will ease me of mine adversaries, and avenge me of mine enemies: And I will turn my hand upon thee, and purely purge away thy dross, and take away all thy tin: And I will restore thy judges as at the first, and thy counsellors as at the beginning: afterward thou shalt be called, The city of righteousness, the faithful city" (Isa. 1:24-26).

Because weights and measurements are representative of the moral condition of society in general, the prophets used the metaphor of weights and measures in bringing their covenant lawsuits against individuals and nations. The Psalmist had set the example: "Surely men of low degree are vanity, and men of high degree are a lie: to be laid in the balance, they are altogether lighter than vanity" (Ps. 62:9). Micah castigated the whole society, warning of judgment to come, for they honored "the statutes of Omri" and did the works of his son Ahab (Mic. 6:16; see also 6:9-12). The essence of their rebellion, Micah said, was *the injustice of the civil magistrates*: "The good man is perished out of the earth: and there is none upright among men: they all lie in wait for blood; they hunt every man his brother with a net. That they may do evil with both hands earnestly, the prince asketh, and the judge asketh for a reward; and the great man, he uttereth his mischievous desire: so they wrap it up" (Mic. 7:2-3).

Daniel's announcement to the rulers of Babylon regarding the meaning of the message of the handwriting on the wall is perhaps the most famous use in Scripture of the imagery of the balance. "And this is the writing that was written, MENE, MENE, TEKEL, UPHARSIN. This is the interpretation of the thing: MENE; God hath numbered thy kingdom, and finished it. TEKEL; Thou art weighed in the balances, and art found wanting. PERES; Thy kingdom is divided, and given to the Medes and Persians" (Dan. 5:25-28).

Corrupt measures are a token – *representative* – of moral corruption. To be out of balance judicially is to be out of covenantal favor. The representative civil transgression in society is the adoption of false weights and measures.

Intuition and Measurement

"Add a pinch of salt." How many cooks through the centuries have recommended this unspecific quantity? There are cooks who cannot cook with a recipe book, but who are master chefs without one. Their skills are intuitive, not numerical. This is true in every field.

There are limits to measurement because there are limits to our perception. There are also limits on our ability to verbalize or quantify the measurements that we perceive well enough to act upon. Oskar Morgenstern addressed this problem in the early paragraphs of his classic book, *On the Accuracy of Economic Observations*.[14] Our economic knowledge is inescapably a mixture of objective and subjective knowledge.[15] That is to say, we think as persons; we are not computers. We do not think digitally. We think analogically, as persons made in God's image. We are required to think God's thoughts after Him. To do this, we need *standards provided by God* that are *perceptible to man*. God has given us such standards (point three of the biblical covenant model). We also need to exercise judgment in understanding and applying them (point four). This judgment is not digital; it is analogical: thinking God's thoughts after Him. We are required by God to assess the performance of others in terms of God's fixed ethical and judicial standards.

In order to achieve a "fit" between God's standards and the behavior of others, we must interpret God's objective law (a subjective task), assemble the relevant objective facts (a subjective task), discard the irrelevant objective facts (a subjective task), and apply this law to those facts (a subjective task). The result is a judicially objective decision. At every stage of the decision-making or judgment-rendering process, there is an

---

14. Oskar Morgenstern, *On the Accuracy of Economic Observations* (2nd ed.; Princeton, New Jersey: Princeton University Press, 1963). Morgenstern wrote a book on game theory with John von Neumann, one of the most gifted mathematicians of the twentieth century. Morgenstern was aware of the limits of mathematics as a tool of economic analysis. A more recent treatment of the problem is Andrew M. Kamarck's *Economics and the Real World* (Philadelphia: University of Pennsylvania Press, 1983). See also Thomas Mayer, *Truth versus Precision in Economics* (Hampshire, England: Elgar, 1993).

15. Morgenstern, *Accuracy*, pp. 3-4.

inescapably personal element, for which we are held personally responsible by God.[16]

Objective Facts Interpreted Subjectively

When we speak of objective facts, we often invoke the language of physical measurement. This is because we think analogically. Making subjective judgments is analogous to measuring things objectively. Yet we never measure things objectively, meaning *exclusively* objectively. It is men who do the measuring, and men are not machines – and even machines have limits of perception. We ask: "Is the balance even?" "Is the bubble in the level equidistant between two points?" At some point, we say: "It's a judgment call." Analogously, we ask of other men's offers: "Is this on the level?" Discovering the answer is a judgment call: an evaluation based on one's observation of something that is beyond the limits of one's ability to perceive distinctions.

To make a biblically valid judgment regarding the public record of the event under scrutiny, judges must perceive the limits of the law and the limits of the records. In the language of the common law courts, an illegal act must have violated the law's boundary "beyond reasonable doubt." *The language of the law is imprecise here because the act of rendering judgment is imprecise.* Yet juries decide, judges hand down punishments, and society goes on.

Spiritual maturity is the ability to make biblically well-informed judgments. Christians must presume that intuitive judgments that come after years of studying God's Bible-revealed laws and making decisions in terms of them will be more reliable – i.e., more pleasing to God – than intuitive judgments that come from other traditions or that are the products of

---

16. North, *Boundaries and Dominion*, Appendix G: "The Covenantal Structure of Judgment."

unsystematic approaches.[17] There is no way to test the accuracy of this presumption except by observing God's sanctions in history on those groups that are under the authority of specifically covenanted judges.[18]

God is the Supreme Judge. He makes objective judgments, yet He makes them subjectively. We must think His thoughts after Him. We must render subordinate judgment. We must not cheat. The free market's competition establishes limits to cheating by sellers of goods and services, who are more capable of cheating, given their specialized knowledge of what is being sold.[19] Sellers will compete against sellers, thereby improving the public's access to honest standards.[20] In a similar way, a form of competition – immigration – brings "buyers of justice" into the courtrooms of honest judges.[21] Honest courts that predictably enforce law reduce the costs of justice and thereby create conditions of prosperity.[22] But when the rules are in flux, the quest for power through politics increases.[23] The rights of victims are no longer upheld.[24]

Eternally objective standards of justice are found in the Bible, not in natural law. All other standards are subject to the flux of history and man's subjectivity.[25] God declares the truth objectively.

---

17. *Ibid.*, ch. 19, section on "Intuition and Measurement," subsection on "Intuition and Creation."

18. If God's sanctions in history are random in the New Covenant era, as Meredith G. Kline insists that they are, then there is no way to test this presumption. Intuition-based decisions would become as random in their effects as God's historical sanctions supposedly are. See Meredith G. Kline, "Comments on an Old-New Error," *Westminster Theological Journal*, XLI (Fall 1978), p. 184.

19. North, *Boundaries and Dominion*, ch. 19, section on "Objective Standards."

20. *Ibid.*, ch. 19, section on "Competition and the Margins of Cheating."

21. *Ibid.*, ch. 19, subsection on "The Scales of Justice."

22. *Ibid.*, ch. 19, section on "A Final Sovereign."

23. *Ibid.*, ch. 19, subsection on "Justice in Flux."

24. *Ibid.*, ch. 19, section on "Victim's Rights and Restitution."

25. *Ibid.*, ch. 19, section on "Evangelical Antinomianism and Humanism's Myth of Neutrality."

Conclusion

"Let me be weighed in an even balance, that God may know mine integrity" (Job 31:6). The imagery of the balance scale is basic to understanding each person's relation to God, either as a covenant-keeper or a covenant-breaker. Weights and measures are also representative biblically of the degree of civil justice available in a society. If those who own the measuring instruments of commerce tamper with them in order to defraud consumers, either specific groups of consumers – especially resident aliens – or consumers in general, they have sinned against God. They have stolen. If the civil government does not prosecute such thieves, then the society is corrupt. The continued existence of false weights and measures testifies against the whole society.

There are limits to our perception; there are limits to the accuracy of scales. This applies both to physical measurement and civil justice. Society cannot attain perfect justice. There must always be an appeal to the judge's intuition in judicial conflicts where contested public acts were not clearly inside or outside the law. This does not mean that there are limits to God's perception and God's justice. Thus, there will be a day of perfect reckoning. Over time, covenantally faithful individuals and institutions approach as a limit, but never reach, the perfect justice of that final judgment. This brings God's positive sanctions to covenant-keeping individuals and institutions, making them more responsible by making them more powerful. Progressive sanctification, both personal and corporate, necessarily involves an increase in God's blessings and also personal responsibility.

The State is required by God to enforce His standards. The free market social order – a development that has its origins in the twin doctrines of personal responsibility and self-government – requires civil government as a legitimate court of appeal. But the bulk of law enforcement has to be individual: "Every man his own policeman." No other concept of law enforcement will suffice if a society is not to become a society of informants and secret police. Secondarily, law enforcement must be associative: market competition. Buyers and sellers determine the degree of acceptable fluctuation around agreed-upon standards. Only in the third stage is law enforcement to become civil. Here, the standards are to be much more precise, much more rigid, and much more predictable. Representative cases – legal precedents – are to become guidelines for self-government and voluntary associative government.

20

INHERITANCE BY FIRE

Again, thou shalt say to the children of Israel, Whosoever he be of the children of Israel, or of the strangers that sojourn in Israel, that giveth any of his seed unto Molech; he shall surely be put to death: the people of the land shall stone him with stones. And I will set my face against that man, and will cut him off from among his people; because he hath given of his seed unto Molech, to defile my sanctuary, and to profane my holy name. And if the people of the land do any ways hide their eyes from the man, when he giveth of his seed unto Molech, and kill him not: Then I will set my face against that man, and against his family, and will cut him off, and all that go a whoring after him, to commit whoredom with Molech, from among their people (Lev. 20:2-5).

The theocentric principle governing this statute is God's jealousy against all rival gods. More specifically, God in the Old Covenant era held the office of "Father of the sons of Israel." The nation of Israel was His son (Ex. 4:23), adopted by His grace. So, God as Father demanded that the sons of Israel acknowledge this fact ritually by circumcising their sons.

The practice of sending children through a ritual fire was a denial of God's fatherhood and therefore also Israel's sonship. This two-fold ritual denial called forth the threat of disinheritance by God. The required means of this disinheritance was public execution by stoning, a penalty that outrages modern

Christians, who regard it (and, by implication, the God who required it) as barbaric. The penalty was not execution by fire – or, for that matter, by drinking hemlock.

Godly inheritance in history is always by fire. This fire is covenantal: placing God's people in trials and tribulations – historical sanctions – in order to purge them of their sins (Isa. 1:25-26). The imagery is that of metal-working (Isa. 1:22a). One pagan version of this imagery of metal-working is alchemy.[1] Another was the practice of passing children through a fire.

The sanction of execution makes it clear that this was a civil law. As a civil law, it applied to all those residing within the jurisdiction of the State. It applied equally to covenanted Israelites and "strangers that sojourn in Israel" (v. 2). If the civil magistrate refused to prosecute, or if the civil judges refused to convict, or if the capital sanction was not imposed, God threatened the practitioner with excommunication: cutting off (v. 5). Since this would be God's act rather than the priests' act, the implication is that God would intervene directly to kill him.

Here is another seed law, or so the language indicates: "any of his seed." This seed law applied to a parent's dedication of a son or daughter to a specific foreign god, Molech. First, the seed laws were part of the laws governing inheritance and disinheritance. Second, as a seed law, it was part of the laws governing the land. These land laws were necessary because of the presence of God's temple within the land. The temple had to be protected from defilement. Third, this statute was part of the laws prohibiting blasphemy: prohibiting the profanation of God's holy name. The *judicial boundary around God's name* was as important as the physical boundaries around the temple and its environs. This boundary extends into the New Covenant, unlike the land-based boundaries of the Mosaic Covenant. This third aspect of the law is therefore a cross-boundary law.

---

1. Mircea Eliade, *The Forge and the Crucible: The Origins and Structures of Alchemy* (New York: Harper Torchbooks, [1956] 1971).

This God Molech

Molech was the god of Ammon, the incest-conceived, bastard cousin of Israel (Gen. 19:38). "Then did Solomon build an high place for Chemosh, the abomination of Moab, in the hill that is before Jerusalem, and for Molech, the abomination of the children of Ammon" (I Ki. 11:7). His name came from the Hebrew word for king, *Melek*. This deity was also known as Milcom and Milcham. He was a fire god, essentially the same as the Moabites' deity, Chemosh (I Ki. 11:5; cf. v. 7).[2] Stephen referred to Molech as a god worshipped by the Israelites in the wilderness: "Then God turned, and gave them up to worship the host of heaven; as it is written in the book of the prophets, O ye house of Israel, have ye offered to me slain beasts and sacrifices by the space of forty years in the wilderness? Yea, ye took up the tabernacle of Moloch, and the star of your god Remphan, figures which ye made to worship them: and I will carry you away beyond Babylon" (Acts 7:42-43). Molech was a major rival god in the history of Israel.

Molech required a specific form of dedication: passing children through a fire. "And thou shalt not let any of thy seed pass through the fire to Molech, neither shalt thou profane the name of thy God: I am the LORD" (Lev. 18:21). Israel ignored this law, among many others, and God cited this in His covenant lawsuit against Jerusalem. Jerusalem would pass through the Chaldeans' fire: fire for fire (Jer. 32:29, 35). This indicates that God's negative sanctions against this crime were not limited to the family that practiced it. As with all ritual abominations, if the civil authorities allowed the practice to continue unopposed, God would bring His corporate sanctions against the nation as a whole. But it was this ritual abomination that was identified by God through Jeremiah as *the representative evil in the land*.

---

2. "Molech," in *Cyclopaedia of Biblical, Theological, and Ecclesiastical Literature*, edited by John M'Clintock and James Strong, 12 vols. (New York: Harper Bros., 1894), IV, p. 437.

Their crimes were comprehensive: "Because of all the evil of the children of Israel and of the children of Judah, which they have done to provoke me to anger, they, their kings, their princes, their priests, and their prophets, and the men of Judah, and the inhabitants of Jerusalem" (Jer. 32:32). Their worship of Molech was representative: "And they built the high places of Baal, which are in the valley of the son of Hinnom, to cause their sons and their daughters to pass through the fire unto Molech; which I commanded them not, neither came it into my mind, that they should do this abomination, to cause Judah to sin" (Jer. 32:35).

Molech required the shedding of innocent blood. The Israelites worshipped Molech as he required: "Yea, they sacrificed their sons and their daughters unto devils, And shed innocent blood, even the blood of their sons and of their daughters, whom they sacrificed unto the idols of Canaan: and the land was polluted with blood" (Ps. 106:37-38). "Moreover thou hast taken thy sons and thy daughters, whom thou hast borne unto me, and these hast thou sacrificed unto them to be devoured. Is this of thy whoredoms a small matter, That thou hast slain my children, and delivered them to cause them to pass through the fire for them?" (Ezek. 16:20-21). "That they have committed adultery, and blood is in their hands, and with their idols have they committed adultery, and have also caused their sons, whom they bare unto me, to pass for them through the fire, to devour them" (Ezek. 23:37). "Moreover he [King Ahaz] burnt incense in the valley of the son of Hinnom, and burnt his children in the fire, after the abominations of the heathen whom the LORD had cast out before the children of Israel" (II Chron. 28:3). This was not an occasional practice in Israel; it became a way of life through death.

Five Questions

This law raises at least five questions. First, exactly what did "giving one's seed to Molech" involve? Was it a formal dedication service comparable to circumcision? Second, why did the ritual offering of a child defile the sanctuary of God? Why was this a uniquely profane act? Third, why was this forbidden to resident aliens? The specified negative sanction, death by stoning, if ignored by the judges, would be followed by God's intervention against that family and all those who joined with that family. The law here says nothing about a threat to the Israelite community at large. Why, then, should resident aliens be prohibited from performing such a rite? Fourth, was this law a law governing false worship in general, or was it confined to Molech worship only? Fifth, does it still apply in New Covenant times? Was it a cross-boundary law? Let us consider each of these questions in greater detail, one by one.[3]

1. Rites of Dedication

There is no question that some sort of cultic rite was involved in this crime. It was a formal, covenantal transgression of the first commandment: "Thou shalt have no other gods before me" (Ex. 20:3). The legal question is: Did this act become a crime only when committed outside of a household? No; it was a crime for an Israelite no matter where it took place. False worship within an Israelite household was a capital crime in Mosaic Israel (Deut. 13:6-11).

Molech's required ritual was a perverse imitation of Jehovah's require rite of circumcision. Instead of physically marring the organ of generation as a symbol of physical death but also covenantal life, the child was actually passed through a literal fire. The child who survived this ordeal was therefore assumed to be blessed covenantally by Molech. He had passed the deadly initiation rite by means of supernatural intervention. This ritual was covenantal, but rather than being ethical in its focus, it was

---

3. A far more detailed discussion appears in Gary North, *Boundaries and Dominion: The Economics of Leviticus* (computer edition; Tyler, Texas: Institute for Christian Economics, 1994), ch. 20, sections I-V.

magical. Its mark of supernatural power was the survival of the child.[4] If the child died, the parents had to regard this as the god's required sacrifice. Thus, the idea of covenantal inheritance in Molech worship was magical rather than ethical. Molech religion was power religion.

In both dominion religion and power religion, the seed is central to the rites of initiation. The seed represents the future. The seed is the means of expansion. If there is no growth, there can be no expansion. If the seed does not grow, or does not reproduce itself, the covenantal future is cut off. In biblical religion, children are seen as children of God ethically. He who obeys God's law is the true son of God. In power religion, children are seen as children of god ritually. He who observes the details of the rites is the true son of the god. Such a view is antithetical to biblical religion (Mic. 6:6-8).

To remove the child from the covenantal authority of Molech-worshiping parents, the State was required by God to execute the parents. A child who survived this rite of fire would become an orphan when the mandatory civil sanction attached to this law was applied by the civil magistrate. God's law made it clear: better to become an orphan and live under the authority of covenantally faithful foster parents than to live under the authority of Molech-worshipping parents. The family's inheritance was immediately transferred to the child or children (if there were older siblings) for this sin by the parents. This transfer was a positive side-effect of this statute; it was not a specified goal of the law. This means that the covenantal authority of the parents was never absolute in the Mosaic economy. The parents were to be disinherited by execution because of their false

4. In modern times, the peculiar practice of fire-walking has again become a popular initiatory rite, this time among business executives. Certain management training programs end with the participants' walking over hot coals as a sign of their confidence in themselves and their new-found ability to manage other people through techniques of power. The fire-walkers never attempt to walk on sheet metal placed on top of the hot coals; metal is a very efficient heat transmitter.

theology of inheritance, ritually manifested in strange fire. The Israelite family was not autonomous. The father's authority was bounded.

2. *Strange Fire: Defiling the Sanctuary*

A murder in Israel defiled the land, which is why God required certain rites of purification in cases where the murderer could not be located (Deut. 21:1-9). But a murder committed outside God's sanctuary did not defile the sanctuary. The question arises: Why did this ritual offering of a child defile God's sanctuary? The act took place away from the sanctuary. Why was this a uniquely profane act?

There are at least two reasons. First, because this form of ritual murder, or potential ritual murder, involved the use of a fiery altar, meaning a rival to God's altar. Second, because it was an assault on the Seed, meaning the prophesied future Messiah.

3. *Resident Aliens and Biblical Pluralism*

This law specified that a stranger in the land was to be executed by the citizens of Israel if he was caught performing a specific rite of Molech worship: giving his seed to Molech. The reason why strangers were under this law is stated clearly in the statute: such an act defiles God's sanctuary and profanes His holy name. No one inside the boundaries of Israel was allowed to do this. But God regarded household false worship by resident aliens as peripheral to the national covenant. Only when the stranger ritually threatened the survival of his own child did he defile God's sanctuary. The judicial foundation of the rights of resident aliens – their immunity from State sanctions – was the possibility that they or their children might covenant with God. Justice in Israel was a major form of evangelism, both inside and outside the land (Deut. 4:4-8). Allowing aliens to see God's law in action was a way to persuade them of the righteousness of God. Israel's system of civil justice was unique in the ancient world: a single legal order for all residents.

Today, we call such a judicial system pluralistic, but biblical pluralism has limits. All pluralism has limits. Pluralism can never be unbounded; someone's religious principles or practices will always be threatened by one or another aspect of any society's legal order. The resident of Israel could not lawfully claim religious freedom as authorization for exposing his children to the risk of death, even though his god required such a rite. The ideal of biblical pluralism extended to the resident alien the right to worship family gods in peace *within the boundaries of their homes*, but it did not authorize heads of households the right of literally sacrificing their children. The seal of a household's religion could not lawfully be death or the risk of death. The household in Israel was a limited sanctuary: a place set aside, protected judicially from outside interference from the State. There was a boundary on State power. But passing a child through Molech's fire was regarded by God as strange fire: a transgression of His sanctuary's monopoly. There was no right – no legal immunity from the sanctions of civil government – for anyone to light a strange fire in Israel: a ritual fire that literally invoked death as a means of sanctioning a covenant.

4. The Limits of Biblical Pluralism

The State was required to intervene and execute any Israelite who could be proven to have attempted to lure one of his family members into a rival covenant (Deut. 13:6-11). "And thou shalt stone him with stones, that he die; because he hath sought to thrust thee away from the LORD thy God, which brought thee out of the land of Egypt, from the house of bondage" (v. 10). The general crime was false worship, but the specific reason given was God's deliverance of the Israelites out of Egypt. This clearly had nothing to do with resident aliens.

False household worship was not generally a crime for resident aliens.

Specifically, false worship was a crime if they participated in a ritual offering of a child to Molech. Even if the child survived the ordeal, the parent or parents were to be executed. The crime was not murder or attempted murder; it was the profanation of God's boundary: the altar of sacrifice. The attempted sacrifice of a child on such an altar was a capital crime. It was this crime that God specified through Jeremiah as *the* crime of Israel and Judah, leading to their captivity in Babylon. This was the abomination that God would not tolerate when His covenant people did tolerate it (Jer. 32:35).

5. Is This Law Still in Force?

What principle of interpretation would lead us to conclude that this law is not still in force? The Bible-affirming expositor who claims that there is a total judicial discontinuity between the two covenants with respect to this law needs to identify the biblical basis of this alleged discontinuity.

The covenantal principle of inheritance teaches that the heirs of covenant-keepers will inherit the earth progressively over time. "His soul shall dwell at ease; and his seed shall inherit the earth" (Ps. 25:13). This is clearly one aspect of the seed laws, which were all fulfilled in Christ. *Covenant-breakers are progressively disinherited*. "For evildoers shall be cut off: but those that wait upon the LORD, they shall inherit the earth" (Ps. 37:9). The practice of Molech initiation reverses this principle of inheritance: infanticide, either physical or covenantal. It is therefore an abomination before God.

To the extent that the initiatory practice relies on demonic intervention to protect the child, this ritual will kill off more and more children as the demonic realm becomes weaker. When demons can protect no child from the fire, the participants will disinherit themselves. Presumably, this will reduce the number of participants over time. Also, the death of a child would subject the parent(s) and any cooperating priests to the civil law against murder. So, we would not expect to find large numbers of participants in such a religion. But the question still remains: What is the valid civil sanction against a participant whose child survives intact? If the rite really did threaten the survival of the child, what is the appropriate civil sanction?

Biblically, the answer is obvious: *public execution by stoning*. How much clearer could God's law be? But God's word is not taken seriously in this matter. Its very clarity constitutes an embarrassment for those who call themselves Christians. They would much prefer a bit of vagueness. Despite these preferences, the profaning of God's holy name is still the judicial issue: a special profaning far worse than mere verbal profanity. The issue is blasphemy and its appropriate civil sanction.

Citizenship and Separation

Then what of religious toleration? This raises the question of the existence of civil laws that are in no way religiously intolerant – religiously neutral laws. Such laws are not even conceptually possible, let alone practical. But if this is the case, then what happens to the concept of citizenship?

Citizenship is inherently covenantal.[5] The citizen acknowledges the legitimacy of a sovereign, subordinates himself to the agents of that sovereign, agrees to obey the laws of that sovereign, swears allegiance to that sovereign, and inherits in terms of that sovereign. The Israelites were told by God that the Canaanites could not lawfully occupy the land even as resident aliens. There could be no lawful toleration of Canaanites within the land, for this would have meant toleration of the previous regional gods of the land. Only aliens from outside the land were to be allowed to dwell in the land. They could not become citizens except by becoming Israelites: through circumcision.

---

5. Ray R. Sutton, *That You May Prosper: Dominion By Covenant* (2nd ed.; Tyler, Texas: Institute for Christian Economics, 1992), ch. 12.

The Gods of the Land

The gods of the ancient Near East were local. This is why there could be no lawful toleration of Canaanite religion in Mosaic Israel. Genocide was God's required means of removing even the opportunity to tolerate a Canaanite. "And thou shalt consume all the people which the LORD thy God shall deliver thee; thine eye shall have no pity upon them: neither shalt thou serve their gods; for that will be a snare unto thee" (Deut. 7:16). This era of total intolerance toward Canaanites was limited to the era of the Mosaic law; intolerance was tied to the land's sacred boundaries. The land was the dwelling place of God in His temple. The land was the place of lawful sacrifice. That is, the land was sacred. No rival god that had previously been associated with this unique piece of real estate could be allowed to manifest itself through the presence of its representatives in Mosaic Israel.

This was a prohibition against Canaanitic gods, not the gods of immigrants. Why the distinction? Because of pagan theology in the ancient world. Except in Israel, a god in the ancient world was regarded either as a household god or the god of a particular nation.[6] There was always a danger that the Israelites would succumb to this false theology; thus, the gods of Canaan were to be destroyed, along with their representatives (once). Immigrants' gods were clearly regarded by their adherents as household gods, not gods of the land. Immigrants had left their respective homelands. They had to view their idols as possessing power only within the boundaries of the household.

---

6. We can see this false theology of local divinities in the disastrous analysis of Ben-hadad's advisors: "And the servants of the king of Syria said unto him, Their gods are gods of the hills; therefore they were stronger than we; but let us fight against them in the plain, and surely we shall be stronger than they" (I Kings 20:23). "And there came a man of God, and spake unto the king of Israel, and said, Thus saith the LORD, Because the Syrians have said, The LORD is God of the hills, but he is not God of the valleys, therefore will I deliver all this great multitude into thine hand, and ye shall know that I am the LORD" (I Ki. 20:28).

Immigrants were welcome in Israel, but the price of immigration was the forfeiture of the right to proselytize among the Israelites. The household gods of immigrants could not lawfully leave their households. They could not become public gods in Israel. That is, they could not lawfully take on the status of national gods. There was to be no public polytheism in Israel, political or otherwise.

The God Who Imposes Boundaries

Rushdoony's discussion of laws of separation is correct: "God identifies Himself as the God who separates His people from other peoples: this is a basic part of salvation. The religious and moral separation of the believer is thus a basic aspect of Biblical law."[7] Separation can be achieved in several ways, however. *First*, the believer can join other believers in a religious ghetto. This ghetto can be geographical, as in the case of certain Amish and Mennonite sects. It can be cultural, as in the case of much of modern fundamentalism and immigrant religious groups. It is always psychological, what Rushdoony has called the permanent remnant psychology.[8] *Second*, the believer can seek the physical removal of unbelievers from the community, either through execution or expulsion. This was God's required method with respect to the Canaanites. The problem here is honoring the biblical judicial concept of "the stranger within the gates": preserving liberty of conscience without opening the social order to a new law-order, which means a new god. The radical Anabaptists in Münster in 1533-35 and the Puritans in New England, 1630-65,[9] made the mistake of exiling residents

7. Rushdoony, *Institutes*, p. 294.

8. R. J. Rushdoony, *Van Til* (Philadelphia: Presbyterian and Reformed, 1960), p. 13.

9. A 1662 letter from Charles II to Massachusetts established liberty of conscience. It was not read in the Massachusetts General Court until 1665. In that year, the General Court repealed all laws that limited the vote to Congregational church members. The Court determined that citizens in the colony henceforth did have to

for their failure to adhere to the community's religious and ecclesiastical confession. This practice denied the biblical legal status of the resident alien. *Third,* separation can be achieved covenantally: the removal of unbelievers from citizenship. This is what the New Testament mandates for covenant-keeping nations.

The New Testament does not break from the Old Testament with respect to denying judicial participation – citizenship – to those unwilling to affirm a Trinitarian covenant in both church and State.[10] In this sense, the New Covenant is intolerant. But every civil order is intolerant. Intolerance is an inescapable concept.[11]

Conclusion

The law prohibiting the dedication of children to Molech through initiation was a *seed law.* It was a law that governed inheritance and disinheritance, for it dealt with a pagan rite governing inheritance and disinheritance. Because of the presence of the temple sanctuary in the holy land of Israel, this law was also a *land law.* It was required to restrain the creation of alternative centers of worship: specifically, it prohibited strange fire. Strange fire defiled the sanctuary, even at a distance. Next, this law reduced the likelihood of the profanation of God's name. It was therefore a *blasphemy law.* Finally, because the child's life was placed at risk, it was a law against *attempted murder*. As a seed law and a land law, it is no longer judicially binding in New Covenant times. As a law against blasphemy, it is still judicially binding. But if the law is still binding, so is the

---

be "orthodox in religion" and "not vicious in conversation," but they could be "of different persuasions concerning church government. . . ." Cited in Kai T. Erikson, *Wayward Puritans: A Study in the Sociology of Deviance* (New York: Wiley, 1966), p. 135.

10. Gary North, *Political Polytheism: The Myth of Pluralism* (Tyler, Texas: Institute for Christian Economics, 1989), ch. 2.

11. North, *Boundaries and Dominion,* ch. 20, section on "Intolerance: An Inescapable Concept."

biblically specified sanction: death by stoning.[12] The blasphemy aspect of the law takes precedence over attempted murder. God is the intended victim of blasphemy: treason against God. The victim of attempted murder can refuse to press charges. He can specify a lesser penalty than God's law allows. Not so with blasphemy. The mandatory penalty is clear.

---

12. God's mandated method of execution – public stoning by the witnesses whose words condemned the criminal – is regarded as perverse even by those few Christians who still defend the legitimacy of the death penalty. They do not believe that God requires the trial's hostile witnesses to cast the first stones. But He does: "The hands of the witnesses shall be first upon him to put him to death, and afterward the hands of all the people. So thou shalt put the evil away from among you" (Deut. 17:7). Like twentieth-century humanists, Christians today regard God's mandated sanctions as barbaric; in this case, public execution by citizens. Why is this regarded as barbaric? The critics do not say. They do not think that have to say. "Everyone can see that such a thing is barbaric!" And such a God.

This law, if enforced, would place enormous responsibility into citizens' hands, both literally and figuratively. Christians today want to avoid such a fearful responsibility. They want the execution performed by some faceless bureaucrat behind closed doors, which is what God's law prohibits. Christians do not want the witnesses – those whose public words condemned the person to death – to suffer the psychological pressure of having to enforce their own words of condemnation. The witnesses' public judicial words are not to be enforced by their public judicial sanctions. Their words killed the person judicially, but the work of their hands is not supposed to kill the person biologically. The witnesses must not be burdened by the enormous emotional pressure of having to act out in public the judicial implications of their words. Word and deed are to be kept radically separate. The dirty work is to be done by a hireling, a professional executioner paid by the State.

God's law identifies the witnesses as God's agents, as well as the victim's agents. They are His agents both in their capacity as bringers of a lawsuit and as public executioners. They are to deliver the condemned person into God's heavenly court. In contrast, modern jurisprudence sees the witnesses as agents solely of the State. Then the State hires its own sanctions-bringer to execute judgment. The State consolidates its power by relieving the citizenry of their responsibilities. Not all of these responsibilities are economic.

Once the citizen is relieved of his judicial responsibility to cast stones against criminals, the State can then take the next step: confiscate his weapons. Step by step, humanism's civil authority lodges at the top of the hierarchy. First, stoning by witnesses is eliminated. This removes the mark of judicial sovereignty from the citizen-witness: God's mandated sanctions-bringer. Second, God is eliminated by removing self-maledictory oaths under God by the witnesses. This makes the State the new god: defender of the oath. Third, gun control laws are legislated: the visible monopolization of sovereignty in the State. The State is no longer confessionally in between God and the oath-bound citizen. It is over the citizen and under no one.

21

INHERITANCE THROUGH SEPARATION

Ye shall therefore keep all my statutes, and all my judgments, and do them: that the land, whither I bring you to dwell therein, spue you not out. And ye shall not walk in the manners of the nation, which I cast out before you: for they committed all these things, and therefore I abhorred them. But I have said unto you, Ye shall inherit their land, and I will give it unto you to possess it, a land that floweth with milk and honey: I am the Lord *your God, which have separated you from other people. Ye shall therefore put difference between clean beasts and unclean, and between unclean fowls and clean: and ye shall not make your souls abominable by beast, or by fowl, or by any manner of living thing that creepeth on the ground, which I have separated from you as unclean. And ye shall be holy unto me: for I the* Lord *am holy, and have severed you from other people, that ye should be mine (Lev. 20:22-26).*

The theocentric foundation of this law was God's act of covenantal separation: "I am the Lord your God, which have separated you from other people" (v. 24b). The Creator God has separated His people from all other people. This separation is not only historical; it is eternal. It is above all covenantal. It has ethical and judicial implications. The fundamental issue is *holiness*: the set-apartness of God and also of His people. This law was one of these implications of holiness. Some of these implications are still in force judicially; others are not. It is the task of the expositor to sort out – separate – these implications in terms of the biblical principle of holiness.[1]

This law recapitulates the warning in Leviticus 18:28: if they commit the evil acts that the Canaanites committed in the land, the land will vomit them out. They were required to obey God's revealed law. I have argued that this threatened negative sanction was an aspect of the land laws of Israel, confined geographically to the Promised Land, and annulled in A.D. 70 with the final annulment of the Old Covenant.[2] The office of "covenantal vomiter" has been taken by the resurrected Christ (Rev. 3:16). The land no longer acts as a covenantal mediator between God and man, either in Palestine or elsewhere. It does not provide *covenantally predictable sanctions* in the New Covenant era. But the Promised Land did do this under the Mosaic Covenant.

A Separate Land for a Separate Nation

In this passage, we find four basic themes of the Book of Leviticus: obedience to God's revealed law, covenantal separation, national holiness, and the inheritance of the land. Actually, the third theme, national holiness, is another way of expressing the first two themes. God compares the religious boundary around the people of Israel with the geographical boundary around the land itself. The continuing covenantal separation of the nation of Israel could be secured only by obedience to God's law, not by a strictly military defense of the nation's geographical boundaries. Secure geographical boundaries for Israel would be the product of covenantal faithfulness, not military strength as such (Ps. 20:7; Isa. 31:1).

The Promised Land's geographical boundary had formerly surrounded the nation – singular – that had occupied the land.

---

1. Rival principles of interpretation have divided me from Rushdoony at this point: the interpretation of the dietary laws.

2. See above, Chapter 10: "The Promised Land as a Covenantal Agent."

The Canaanite nations are spoken of here in the singular, as a single culture: "ye shall not walk in the manners of the nation." According to the definition in Strong's *Concordance*, the Hebrew word translated here as "nation," commonly transliterated as *goy* (more accurately, *go'ee*), is apparently derived from the same root as the Hebrew word for massing: "a foreign nation; hence a Gentile; also (fig.) a troop of animals, or a flight of locusts: Gentile, heathen, nation, people." It is the most commonly used Hebrew word for "nation" in the Old Testament. The Canaanites had served as God's stewards over the land for generations; their rebellion had now come to fruition.[3]

Sustaining Grace

The Promised Land was already a land flowing with milk and honey when the Israelites arrived. This material wealth had been set aside by God in Abraham's day as His gift to Abraham's heirs. The land contained raw materials of great value: original capital (Deut. 8:7-9). Furthermore, it contained secondary capital: marketable wealth which was the product of other men's thrift and vision over several generations (Deut. 6:10-11). This combined capital value – land plus labor – could be maintained intact long-term only by obeying God (Deut. 6:12-15).

The capitalized value of the land was part of God's promise to Abraham. It was therefore not earned by the Israelites. It was an *unmerited gift*: the biblical definition of grace.[4] But once delivered into the hands of Abraham's heirs, possession of the land could be maintained only by national covenantal faithfulness, as manifested by the Israelites' outward obedience to

3. Gary North, *Boundaries and Dominion: The Economics of Leviticus* (computer edition; Tyler, Texas: Institute for Christian Economics, 1994), ch. 21, subsection on "Removing the Evil Stewards."

4. Gary North, *Dominion and Common Grace: The Biblical Basis of Progress* (Tyler, Texas: Institute for Christian Economics, 1987), p. 4. By unmerited, I mean unmerited by the recipient. It was merited by Jesus Christ.

God's statutes. Public obedience to the Mosaic law was to remain the mandatory manifestation of their service to Him and fear of Him.

The familiar Christian hymn, "Trust and Obey," expresses the ethical nature of covenantal inheritance: "for there's no other way" to maintain this inheritance. (This hymn is sung enthusiastically by Protestants whose churches officially deny its theology of sanctification.) Abraham was told to trust God. This meant trusting God's promises. His heirs were also to trust these promises. The outward manifestation of this trust was circumcision. Without this outward act of obedience, the Israelite ceased to be an Israelite, and therefore he removed himself and his heirs from the promised inheritance. So, the inheritance of the land was a pure gift from God, but to remain the beneficiary of this unmerited legacy, the recipients of the promise had to obey the terms of the covenant. It was not that their obedience was the legal foundation of the promise. The promise of God was its own legal foundation. But obedience was the legal basis of their remaining in the will of God, in both senses: the moral will and the testamentary will. A refusal to place the mark of the covenant – a symbolic boundary – on the flesh of all one's male heirs was an act of *self-disinheritance*. Excommunication became mandatory: a cutting off from the people, i.e., a kind of *judicial circumcision of the nation*. Covenant-keepers who broke this commandment were to be treated as foreskins.[5]

The Dietary Laws

The prohibition against eating certain foods was part of the land laws of Israel. This passage makes it clear that the reason why God imposed the food laws was to preserve the nation's separation. "Ye shall therefore put difference between clean beasts and unclean, and between unclean fowls and clean: and

5. Saul's demand that David provide a bride price for Michal of a hundred Philistines' foreskins points to this judicial meaning of the foreskin (I Sam. 18:25).

ye shall not make your souls abominable by beast, or by fowl, or by any manner of living thing that creepeth on the ground, which I have separated from you as unclean" (v. 25). These animals had not been prohibited before God led them out of Egypt. The distinction between clean and unclean had been present in Noah's day (Gen. 7:2, 8), but no prohibition against eating unclean beasts was announced at that time. In this sense, the clean-unclean distinction was prophetic for Noah. The distinction was established so that Noah would take seven times as many pairs of clean beasts into the ark (Gen. 7:2). The distinction had significance for the future of Israel – the increased likelihood of the survival of clean beasts – but not for Noah's day. Otherwise, the detailed food laws of Leviticus would have been given to Noah. But they weren't. "Every moving thing that liveth shall be meat for you; even as the green herb have I given you all things" (Gen. 9:3).[6] Abraham was under no dietary restrictions; God's promise of the land did not involve dietary separation. Joseph was under no dietary restrictions in Egypt. Clearly, the dietary laws were not cross-boundary laws.

A society's diet separates it from other societies almost as completely as its language does. It is very difficult for overweight people to lose weight permanently because of people's almost unbreakable eating habits. To change a society's eating habits takes generations, even assuming extensive contact with foreigners (which Israel did experience because of her open borders). Immigrants, or the children of immigrants, slowly adopt the foods of their host nation. The Mosaic dietary laws forced a major cultural break with the home nation for all those who became circumcised resident aliens in Israel.

---

6. Given his insistence of the authority of the Mosaic food laws in the New Testament, Rushdoony should have commented on Genesis 9:3 in *The Institutes of Biblical Law* (Nutley, New Jersey: Craig Press, 1973). There is only one reference to this verse, in the middle of a block quotation from another author (p. 36). The verse is not even cited in the Scripture Texts index in volume 2, *Law and Society* (Vallecito, California: Ross House, 1982).

Covenantal Separation or Biological Health?

Covenantal separation inside the Promised Land was the goal of these laws, not dietary health as such. What about outside the Promised Land? The young Israelites in the court of Nebuchadnezzar refused to eat any food prepared by the Babylonians except vegetables and water. These self-imposed restrictions had not been mandated by the dietary laws of Leviticus. It was the king's choice food and wine that they refused to eat, not unclean or abominable animals. Wine had not been prohibited to them by the Mosaic law, but they refused to drink the king's wine (Dan. 1:8). Despite their diet of vegetables and water – no fat – the four Israelite youths looked fatter at the end of 10 days than those Babylonian youths who had been eating from the king's menu (Dan. 1:15). This was nothing short of miraculous. That, of course, was the whole point: a visible demonstration of the sovereignty of God in the lives of the four youths. The prescribed food of the supposedly divine king of Babylon produced a less healthy appearance in his servants than the uncharacteristically restricted diet produced in the four judicial representatives of Israel.

There are vegetarian cultists today who point to this incident as proof of the superiority of vegetarianism. This is a misapplication of the text. What the Hebrew youths and their captors all knew was that *the diet decreed by the king was superior fare by conventional Babylonian and Mosaic standards*, yet it produced visibly inferior results. The fundamental issues in this unique case were separation (holiness) and the sovereignty of God, not the comparative caloric or nutritional content of the rival diets. The four youths demonstrated publicly that *their God, not their diet, was the source of their physiological advantage*.

Why didn't the four youths insist on a conventional Levitical diet? Had the issue been comparative nutrition, this would have been the public test of the two diets. But they did not request such a test. They simply wanted their rulers to see that a minimal diet – not a uniquely Levitical diet – would produce visibly superior results in the lives of covenant-keeping people. Insisting on a Levitical diet would have been an act of religious and political rebellion: the preservation of a defeated nation's diet. That was not their point. It was not that the Israelites possessed a uniquely healthy diet that had to be preserved outside the land; rather, it was the preservation of their covenantal commitment to the God of Israel, whose sovereignty extended beyond the land. While the young men did not request food that was prohibited by Leviticus, they also did not request the blessings – "fat" – of the Levitical diet: the best of the land. This should warn us: *the Levitical dietary laws were laws furthering covenantal separation inside the Promised Land, not universal laws of health.* To misunderstand this is to misunderstand covenant theology. To deny this is to deny covenant theology and replace it with "taste not–touch not" religion.

If the captive Israelites were required to honor the Mosaic dietary laws outside the Promised Land, how did Esther conceal her identity from her husband and Haman? Or was she in rebellion? Did God deliver His people from their enemies by means of a woman who openly defied God's law? Or is there a theologically simpler answer, namely, that the Israelites lawfully ignored the dietary law's requirements when they were in captivity outside the land, i.e., under the God-ordained authority of a rival civilization?

A Temporarily Marked-Off Nation

The dietary laws were imposed by God before the nation came into the Promised Land but after the Israelites had left Egypt. These laws were given early in the wilderness experience. Throughout the 40 years, the people ate mostly manna. They were forced to refrain from newly prohibited foods, whatever their dietary tastes had been in Egypt. Therefore, these food laws were preparatory for the invasion. Manna, coupled with the food laws, forced the younger generation to grow up completely unfamiliar with the taste of covenantally prohibited animals. The manna ceased when the entered the land. After they conquered the land, they would have no eating habits to overcome, and therefore no gastronomical temptation to mix with any of the remaining tribes of Canaan.

These laws marked off the Israelites gastronomically, just as circumcision marked them off physiologically. The Levitical dietary laws were no more permanent than the Passover law – and no less permanent. In captivity, they could not journey to Jerusalem to celebrate the mandatory feasts. Abraham had been instructed to circumcise those males under his household authority, but he received no instruction regarding his diet. Why not? Because he did not dwell in the land of Canaan as a permanent owner. He was still a stranger in a strange land. He was a pilgrim. A pilgrim has no geographical headquarters, no geographical home. Abraham's earthly home was eschatological. God told him that his family's inheritance of the land would not take place until the fourth generation after him (Gen. 15:16). So, he did have to honor the law of circumcision, for circumcision identified who his heirs were: a law of covenantal separation. The Israelites in Joshua's day crossed the Jordan, camped and Gilgal, were circumcised, and celebrated the Passover in the land (Josh. 5:2-10). Then they ate the corn of the land: the spoils of conquest (v. 11). They thereby also claimed their inheritance. They thereby claimed their national headquarters. "And the manna ceased on the morrow after they had eaten of the old corn of the land; neither had the children of Israel manna any more; but they did eat of the fruit of the land of Canaan that year" (v. 12). At that point, they had the option of violating the dietary laws that Moses had announced four decades earlier. Their testing began at Gilgal.

The laws governing Passover had been given in Egypt before they crossed the boundary out of Egypt to enter the wilderness (Ex. 12). Passover's laws were primary in Mosaic Israel. They established the rite that would henceforth celebrate their deliverance from Egypt. Passover was celebrated inside Egypt. Passover announced symbolically points one and two of the biblical covenant: the sovereignty of God and His authority over the gods of Egypt. The dietary laws were secondary to the Passover laws, for they were given in the wilderness after the Israelites had crossed over Egypt's boundary. Like the laws of clean and unclean beasts for Noah, these laws were prophetic: tied to the fulfillment of Abraham's promise. These dietary laws had little immediate relevance in the wilderness; the nation survived on manna. Only when the Israelites crossed over the Promised Land's boundary, and were circumcised, did the manna cease. At that point, the dietary laws became relevant. This is why I argue that the dietary laws were tied to the land and the Levitical laws of inheritance. The dietary laws lost all covenantal relevance once the land of Canaan ceased to be an aspect of the Abrahamic promise: in A.D. 70.

The dietary laws reinforced point three of the covenant: covenantal boundaries. For as long as the boundaries of the Promised Land remained intact covenantally, Israelites were required to honor the dietary laws. *The Levitical dietary laws were expressly historical: honoring the fulfillment of God's promise to Abraham regarding the land.* They were laws that reinforced the Levitical laws governing landed inheritance. When the Levitical inheritance laws ceased, meaning when the Jubilee land laws definitively ceased, the dietary laws also ceased. This is why Jesus laid down a challenge to the Pharisees, who were the defenders of the dietary laws: "Not that which goeth into the mouth defileth a man; but that which cometh out of the mouth, this defileth a man. Then came his disciples, and said unto him, Knowest thou that the Pharisees were offended, after they heard this saying? But he answered and said, Every plant, which my heavenly Father hath not planted, shall be rooted up. Let them alone: they be blind leaders of the blind. And if the blind lead the blind, both shall fall into the ditch" (Matt. 15:11-

14). There would soon be a rooting up of the nation of Israel.[7] The old nation of priests (Ex. 19:6) was about to be replaced by a new nation of priests (I Pet. 2:5, 9). A change in covenantal law is accompanied by a change in the priesthood (Heb. 7:12). This is why Peter was told repeatedly by God in a vision to eat unclean foods (Acts 10:15). The covenantal separation between Jews and gentiles had ended forever (Eph. 2). A new covenantal separation had arrived: Christian vs. non-Christian. A new dietary law accompanied this new form of covenantal separation: the Lord's Supper – a new dietary boundary.

Covenant-keeping man's defilement by unclean or abominable meats ceased as soon as the Lord's Supper replaced Passover. Gentiles outside the land were never under its restrictions. There was nothing intrinsically evil or unclean in any food; there was only *temporary uncleanness* – as temporary as the covenantal status of the boundaries of the Promised Land. When Jesus announced that there has never been anything intrinsically unclean or defiling about any food, He was also announcing that there was nothing intrinsically sacrosanct about the boundaries of geographic Israel.

The Jews of Jesus' day thought that Israel's dietary laws, like Israel's geographical boundaries, would last forever. Today, Jews and Anglo-Israelites suppose that the Mosaic dietary laws are still binding. But the covenantal significance of Israel's geographical boundaries and the dietary laws ended together: the demise in A.D. 70 of national Israel and the temple sacrifices. As Paul wrote to a gentile church, "Wherefore if ye be dead with Christ from the rudiments of the world, why, as though living in the world, are ye subject to ordinances, (Touch not; taste not; handle not; which all are to perish with the using;) after the commandments and doctrines of men? Which things have indeed a shew of wisdom in will worship, and hu-

7. David Chilton, *The Days of Vengeance: An Exposition of the Book of Revelation* (Ft. Worth, Texas: Dominion Press, 1987).

mility, and neglecting of the body; not in any honour to the satisfying of the flesh" (Col. 2:20-23). Apart from national Israel under the Mosaic law, such commandments regarding unclean food have always been "the commandments and doctrines of men." When the temple's veil was torn immediately after Christ's death (Matt. 27:51), de-sanctifying the holy of holies, the Mosaic Covenant's dietary laws became the commandments and doctrines of men. Honoring the dietary laws today is only "a shew of wisdom in will worship, and humility, and neglecting of the body." This is false wisdom and false humility.

When the promised Seed arrived (Gal. 2:16), instituting His new covenant, the circumcision law was annulled, replaced by the rite of baptism. Similarly, when the Holy Spirit arrived, the Lord's Supper replaced Passover and its ancillary dietary laws. Covenantal separation was not annulled; its Abrahamic Covenant ritual marks were annulled. Then God announced to Peter the annulment of the dietary laws (Acts 10:15). This marked the end of the Mosaic land laws and the end of Israel as national headquarters. Henceforth, there would be no national headquarters for God's covenant people. The church replaced Israel as headquarters. Henceforth, the pursuit of the Great Commission would no longer be restricted by national headquarters or dietary restrictions.[8]

Conclusion

The inheritance of the land by the Israelites was part of God's promise to Abraham. To maintain this inheritance, the Israelites were required to obey God's laws. The covenantal mark of such obedience was circumcision. They also had to honor Passover and the dietary laws. These were laws of separation. A separate land required a separated people. But this Mosaic separation was temporary.

---

8. North, *Boundaries and Dominion*, ch. 21, section on "Rushdoony on the Dietary Laws."

God is holy – set apart – from all other gods (Ex. 20:2-3). The people of Israel were therefore set apart by God from all other nations on earth. Israel's national boundaries were sacred. That is, they were tied to the sacrificial system. A series of boundaries surrounded (marked off) the temple in which God's authorized sacraments were performed by His authorized agents. God established three separate covenantal jurisdictions – ecclesiastical, civil, familial – to be maintained within these national boundaries. The Israelites were given a *sanctuary* from the rest of the world: a place where God's judicial sanctions would be applied in terms of His law.

Their ethical, judicial, and geographical holiness was to be manifested by what they ate and did not eat: primarily at the Passover meal and secondarily by the dietary laws. This holiness or separation was ritually reinforced by the Passover meal and the special dietary restrictions. The Passover laws were both positive and negative. At the Passover, Israelites were *required* to eat certain foods and *forbidden* to eat leavened bread. The dietary laws were exclusively negative. Neither of these food laws was a civil requirement. The Passover laws and the dietary laws were to be enforced only by family and ecclesiastical governments.

With the abrogation of the Old Covenant order came the abrogation of the Mosaic food laws: Passover and the "pork" laws.[9] This abrogation ended with the abrogation of the Promised Land's historically unique position as an agent of God's sanctions. That is to say, the positive and negative sanctions associated with the Abrahamic promise regarding the land ceased to be relevant in history. Prior to the fall of Jerusalem in A.D. 70, the Promised Land was said to spew out evil-doers: symbolically, *disgorging something that should not have been eaten*. This meant that the land was an arena of covenantal confronta-

9. James B. Jordan, *Pig Out? 25 Reasons Why Christians May Eat Pork* (Niceville, Florida: Transfiguration Press, 1992).

tion: sanctions that were primarily military in nature. The Israelites would drive out the Canaanites; if they subsequently rebelled, other nations would drive them out.

After A.D. 70, the land of Israel lost its special covenantal status. The Mosaic sacrificial system was cut off.[10] In no sense – militarily or environmentally – is land to be regarded today as a covenantal agent. Under the New Covenant, common grace and common curses have completely replaced special grace and special curses with respect to the climate: sunshine and rain, drought and flooding. God the Father "maketh his sun to rise on the evil and on the good, and sendeth rain on the just and on the unjust" (Matt. 5:45). Only to the extent that climate is directly influenced by man's science and practices does it manifest covenantally predictable sanctions: blessings and cursings.

---

10. One result of this was the appearance of a new religion, Judaism.

Part 4

COVENANTAL ACTS
(Lev. 23-24)

INTRODUCTION TO PART 4

And the LORD spake unto Moses, saying, Speak unto the children of Israel, and say unto them, Concerning the feasts of the LORD, which ye shall proclaim to be holy convocations, even these are my feasts (Lev. 23:1-2).

And thou shalt speak unto the children of Israel, saying, Whosoever curseth his God shall bear his sin. And he that blasphemeth the name of the LORD, he shall surely be put to death, and all the congregation shall certainly stone him: as well the stranger, as he that is born in the land, when he blasphemeth the name of the LORD, shall be put to death (Lev. 24:15-16).

Leviticus 23 and the first section of Leviticus 24 are concerned with corporate religious feasts. The second half of Leviticus 24 deals with blasphemy. The judicial link between these passages is point four of the biblical covenant: sanctions. The first section deals with covenant renewal through participation in corporate covenant-renewal celebrations. The second section deals with individual covenant-breaking by oath.

Leviticus 23 lists the three national covenant-renewal celebrations: Passover (vv. 4-8); Firstfruits (vv. 10-21); and Tabernacles or booths (vv. 23-44). Verse 22 is seemingly a textual anomaly: "And when ye reap the harvest of your land, thou shalt not make clean riddance of the corners of thy field when thou reapest, neither shalt thou gather any gleaning of thy harvest:

thou shalt leave them unto the poor, and to the stranger: I am the LORD your God." I discuss in Chapter 22 the reason why the gleaning law of Leviticus 19:9 is recapitulated in the middle of the section on the three feasts.

Covenant is an inescapable concept. A man must affirm a covenant of some kind. He is, in Meredith G. Kline's words, by oath consigned. Covenantal affirmations in the modern world are usually implicit rather than explicit. Civil covenants are not normally established by explicit public oath except for political office-holders and members of the military. Marriage is today regarded as a contract rather than an oath-bound institution under God's sanctions in history. Baptism is also not regarded as an oath-sign, nor is the Lord's Supper regarded as an act of covenant-renewal. People make and break covenants without knowing what they are doing.

Blasphemy, however, is a far more self-conscious violation of God's covenant: a covenant-breaking verbal oath. No one is allowed to assault God's name verbally, whether he is a covenant-keeper under special grace or a covenant-breaker under common grace. The mandatory sanction is public execution (Lev. 24:15-16). This is the ultimate reparations payment to God in history: a forcible crossing of the ultimate boundary in history, death.

22

MUTUAL SELF-INTEREST: PRIESTS AND GLEANERS

And when ye reap the harvest of your land, thou shalt not make clean riddance of the corners of thy field when thou reapest, neither shalt thou gather any gleaning of thy harvest: thou shalt leave them unto the poor, and to the stranger: I am the LORD your God (Lev. 23:22).

The gleaning statutes reflected the theocentric principle of God as the absolute owner of the land, who possessed the authority to set the terms of management for His "sharecroppers," the Israelites. This passage comes in between sections on two required national feasts: Pentecost or "weeks" (vv. 15-21) and Tabernacles or "booths" (vv. 34-43). Pentecost was the celebration of the harvest. It took place 50 ("*pentekosté*": fiftieth) days after Passover. As in all the other national festivals, sacrifices to God were required. What made this feast unique were two things: it was a one-day festival rather than a full week, and it mandated the use of leavened bread (v. 17).

Passover prohibited all leaven (Ex. 12:15). Leaven's symbolism of growth is the reason for both the prohibition and the subsequent requirement at Pentecost. It was Egypt's leaven that was prohibited at Passover: the covenantal necessity of ethical discontinuity with evil. It was Israel's leaven – the product of the Promised Land – that was mandated at Pentecost: the covenantal necessity of ethical continuity with righteousness.

Pentecost was understood by the rabbis as the anniversary of the giving of the Ten Commandments.[1] It was a third-month feast in the sanctuary calendar. There were two overlapping systems used in Israel for measuring the year: sanctuary and ordinary.[2] The religious year began in the spring: the first month, Nisan (Esth. 3:7), when Passover was celebrated (Ex. 12). The civil year began in the fall: on the first day the seventh month of the religious calendar (called Tishri in the Talmud).[3] This month began with a day of sabbath rest (Lev. 23:24-25). Ten days later, the day of atonement took place (Lev. 23:27-28).[4] In terms of the sanctuary calendar, the law was given to Moses in the third month (Ex. 19:1) on the third day of the week (Ex. 19:16). Tabernacles was a seventh-month feast (Lev. 23:24). It completed the annual cycles of three feasts.[5]

The Festival of Pentecost

Pentecost was closely associated with the harvest.[6] It was a grain-related feast. The festival required the following: "Ye shall bring out of your habitations two wave loaves of two tenth deals: they shall be of fine flour; they shall be baken with leav-

---

1. Alfred Edersheim, *The Temple: Its Ministry and Services As They Were in the Time of Jesus Christ* (Grand Rapids, Michigan: Eerdmans, [1874] 1983), p. 261.

2. James Jordan, "Jubilee, Part 2," *Biblical Chronology*, V (March 1993), p. 1.

3. *Rosh. Hash.*, 1:3; cited in "Month," *Cyclopaedia of Biblical, Theological, and Ecclesiastical Literature*, edited by John M'Clintock and James Strong, 12 vols. (New York: Harper & Bros., 1876), IV, p. 547.

4. Jordan notes that the official first year of the reign of a king of Judah ran from the first day of the seventh month of the religious year to the last day of the sixth month of the next religious year.

5. This structure parallels the week of purifications for the person who had come in contact with a dead body: third-day purification and seventh-day release (Num. 19:11-12). James Jordan, *The Law of the Covenant: An Exposition of Exodus 21-23* (Tyler, Texas: Institute for Christian Economics, 1984), p. 57.

6. Gordon J. Wenham, *The Book of Leviticus* (Grand Rapids, Michigan: Eerdmans, 1979), p. 304.

en; they are the firstfruits unto the LORD" (v. 17). These loaves were separate representative offerings made by the priests. All of Pentecost's offerings had to take place on one day. To offer 1.2 million loaves of bread before (not on)[7] the altar in one day was not possible. Also, in addition to the loaves were required seven lambs, two rams, and a young bullock (v. 18), plus a goat kid and two more lambs (v. 19).[8] These animal sacrifices were corporate sacrifices. There is no way that these offerings were required from every family.

Edersheim says that the temple's doors were opened at midnight. The offerings had to be made before sunrise: the time of the mandatory morning offering.[9] Men were required to bring free will offerings (Deut. 16:10). Presumably, during the period from midnight to sunrise, they brought these offerings into the tabernacle or temple.

A family's main cost of the feast of Pentecost was not the value of the free will offering. It was the cost of the journey itself.

Gleaning, Again

Leviticus 23:22 is a recapitulation of the gleaning law of Leviticus 19:9. The question is: Why did God here remind the Israelites of the landowners' responsibility to the landless poor, at the end of the passage that set forth the laws governing Pentecost ("weeks")? This question has baffled orthodox Bible commentators. S. H. Kellogg offers comments on Pentecost (vv. 15-21), but then skips verse 22 to begin commenting on the

---

7. Leaven was not allowed on the altar (Lev. 2:11).

8. The Jews doubled the number of sacrifices by offering separately those required in Numbers 28:26, 27, 30 and Leviticus 23:18. On this point, Josephus' first-century observations and Maimonides' evaluation of rabbinical texts agree. "Pentecost," *Cyclopaedia of Biblical, Theological, and Ecclesiastical Literature,* VIII, pp. 925-26.

9. Edersheim, *Temple,* p. 263.

convocation of trumpets (vv. 23-25).[10] Andrew Bonar refers back to Leviticus 19:9 and concludes: "In this manner, *love to man* was taught in these thanksgiving feasts, at the very time that *love to God* who so kindly gave them their plenty was called forth and increased." He then goes on to offer an allegorical interpretation, with the gleaners as members of a remnant: gentiles in the Old Covenant, Jews in the New Covenant. "A feast is coming on that will unite Jew and Gentile in equal fulness."[11] But this does not explain why the gleaning law for the fields was repeated here, or perhaps more to the point, why it first appears in Leviticus 19:9 rather than here. Gordon Wenham thinks that the connection between Leviticus 19:9 and 23:22 may be the requirement to care for the poor: the Levites, the poor, and the stranger. There may be a link here: shared poverty.[12] But why should the Levites and priests have been poor? They received the tithes and sacrifices of the tribes. They could also own real estate in the cities. The commentators are confused about the reason behind the recapitulation.

There is a reason for this recapitulation: a shared economic link. There is also a reason for the confusion of the commentators. The reason is their lack of knowledge about, or interest in, economic theory. This lack of knowledge has left gaps in our understanding of biblical law.

Laws of Inheritance

To begin to understand the relationship between the gleaning laws and the feasts, we first need to recognize that the land of Israel was an inheritance from God. Landownership in Israel was part of the original spoils of war. Only those who fought

---

10. S. H. Kellogg, *The Book of Leviticus* (Minneapolis, Minnesota: Klock & Klock, [1899] 1978), pp. 459-61.

11. Andrew Bonar, *A Commentary on Leviticus* (London: Banner of Truth, [1846] 1966), p. 411.

12. Wenham, *Leviticus*, p. 305.

the Canaanites could claim an inheritance in the land (Num. 32:16-23). Before the conquest began, God set forth the laws governing landownership after Israel took possession. These laws were laws of *landed inheritance*. The Levitical priesthood possessed the authority to declare these laws and apply them to specific cases.

The special judicial status of the nation of Israel depended on the presence of an absolutely sovereign God (point one of the biblical covenant model).[13] The Levites and priests were God's primary representatives (point two)[14] because the priesthood had the primary responsibility of defending the moral purity of the land (point three).[15] The priests possessed only one final sanction: excommunication (point four).[16] They could disinherit covenant-breakers (point five).[17] Inheritance is the key to a proper understanding of the economic link between the priesthood and the gleaners. The poor had been temporarily disinherited by economic events or some other reason: no income from their family land. The Levites and priests had no landed inheritance in rural Israel; their inheritance was the tithe. Between the two groups there was a shared economic goal: the maintenance of income from rural land. The gleaners were poor; the Levites and priests did not want to become poor. The gleaners wanted a share of the crop; the Levites and priests wanted a share of the crop. Because of the structure of the laws governing gleaning, each group helped the other to achieve its economic goal.

Biblical law mandated gleaning in Israel. A landowner's refusal to honor the gleaning law, like his refusal to honor the tithe, was an excommunicable offense. The threat of this shared

---

13. Transcendence/presence. See Ray R. Sutton, *That You May Prosper: Dominion By Covenant* (2nd ed.; Tyler, Texas: Institute for Christian Economics, 1992), ch. 1.

14. Hierarchy/representation. *Ibid.*, ch. 2.

15. Ethics/boundaries. *Ibid.*, ch. 3.

16. Oath/sanctions. *Ibid.*, ch. 4.

17. Succession/inheritance. *Ibid.*, ch. 5.

negative sanction – reduced income – is what linked the Levitical priesthood to the gleaners.

Economic Motivation

The landowner sent his harvesting crew into the fields before the gleaners gained access. Gleaners got only the leftovers. Landowners were required by God's law to honor the laws of gleaning. They could not lawfully have their economic agents harvest the corners of the fields. That portion of the crop belonged by law to the gleaners. The poorest members of the able-bodied community had a legal right to this portion of the crop.

The question is: Which covenantal agency possessed lawful authority to enforce this law? Was it the State or the church? I have already announced my opinion: this legal right of the poor was not to be enforced by the State.[18] The State was not an agency of charity under the Old Covenant. It was an agency of compulsion: negative sanctions. It was not an agency authorized by God to bring positive sanctions. To gain ownership of assets, or the power to direct assets, necessary for bringing positive sanctions to one group, the State would have had to threaten negative sanctions against others. This was not allowed by God's law: the same laws had to apply equally to all residents of the nation (Ex. 12:49). Civil judges were not to discriminate between rich and poor (Lev. 19:15). The church, however, can lawfully bring positive sanctions as the agency of reconciliation – man and nature's reconciliation to God – and as an agency of healing: man and nature.

Self-Interest and Law Enforcement

My assertion of the designation of the priests as the enforcers of the gleaning law raises the question of economic motiva-

18. See above, Chapter 11, pp. 196-97.

tion. While there may be individuals who at times place the interests of the community, or some segment of the community, above their own personal self-interest, no society can safely be constructed which relies exclusively on the widespread *voluntary* suppression of personal self-interest among those who are given monopolistic authority to impose negative sanctions on others. Liberty and justice require that the legal order acknowledge the fact that the personal self-interest of judges must be dealt with institutionally. Negative sanctions must be brought against those officials who make decisions that favor their interests at the expense of segments of the general public.

This institutional guideline is true for non-profit organizations, not just civil governments. I would not go so far as to say that it is equally true of priesthoods, since priesthoods formally are committed to a doctrine of sanctions beyond physical death, either a final judgment imposed by a divinity or the judgment of the impersonally applied moral laws of karma: an extension of the results of personal behavior through reincarnation. Thus, a priest may have a concept of personal self-interest that is longer or more apocalyptic than that adopted by a civil judge, or even more to the point, by a twentieth-century academic economist. But even non-profit organizations and priesthoods must acknowledge the potential conflict of interests between the power to impose negative sanctions and the public interest. Rewards and punishments must be built into the institutional system in order to reduce the profitable exploitation of such conflicts of interest, since the public interest will normally be sacrificed in these conflicts.

Public Choice Theory

In order to understand and then predict the decisions made by sanctioning agents, we need to consider the influence of self-interest. If we want to increase the likelihood that people will act in a particular way, we must see to it that they are rewarded for performing in the preferred way and punished for deviating. This includes government officials – those who possess the right to impose sanctions. This was the insight by economist James Buchanan that won him a Nobel Prize in economics in 1986. Buchanan and his associate, legal theorist Gordon Tullock, pioneered a specialty in economics called public choice theory.[19] This economic approach to understanding institutions assumes that 1) all institutions, including political and judicial institutions, are the product of individual decisions, and 2) official decisions of organizations are based on the personal self-interest of those vested with the institutional authority to make them. In an introductory economics textbook committed to public choice theory, Gwartney and Stroup write: "The government is *not* a supraindividual that will always make decisions in the 'public interest,' however that nebulous term might be defined. It is merely an institution through which individuals make collective decisions and through which they carry out activities collectively." They continue: "The basic postulate of all economics is that changes in expected costs and benefits will cause decision-makers to alter their actions in a predictable way. Specifically, as the personal costs of an event increase (and/or the benefits decline), decision-makers will be less likely to choose the event. As costs decline and benefits increase, the opposite tendency will be true. This postulate will be maintained throughout our analysis of market behavior. Similarly, it will be utilized to yield insight on the organization and functioning of the public sector."[20]

This insight on at least one set of human motivations governing institutional action – costs and benefits – must be re-

---

19. James Buchanan and Gordon Tullock, *The Calculus of Consent: Logical Foundations of Constitutional Democracy* (Ann Arbor: University of Michigan Press, 1962). Tullock did not win the Nobel Prize with Buchanan in 1986, he believes, because he has never taken an economics course. I discussed this with him in 1988 at an Eris Society meeting in Aspen, Colorado.

20. James D. Gwartney and Richard Stroup, *Economics: Private and Public Choice* (2nd ed.; New York: Academic Press, 1980), p. 75.

spected by the social theorist. We must apply this insight to the behavior of those people who have been invested by God with covenantal authority. We therefore need to pursue the question of law-enforcement in Old Covenant Israel. If the Levites and priests were in fact the covenantal agents assigned by God to enforce the gleaning laws, then we should not expect God's law to rest on the assumption that the Levites and priests would normally carry out this assignment against their personal self-interest. We should expect rather to find judicial safeguards that protected their interests as they went about their judicial assignments. This is exactly what we find in the case of the gleaning laws.

How to Pay Judges

Judges should not take bribes (Ex. 23:8; Deut. 16:19). Judges should declare God's law and apply it to specific cases that come before them. This is a basic operating premise of biblical jurisprudence. The availability of personal gain is not to influence the judges' decisions. Having said this, we should also acknowledge the bribery law's economic corollary: judges should not suffer losses because of their decisions. Their decisions should not make them poorer. Thus, we conclude, *judges' income should not be affected positively or adversely by their decisions.* This is why they should be paid agreed-upon salaries by the sanctioning institution irrespective of their decisions for as long as they are employed by that institution. This rule governs both church and State. This is also why they should not be allowed to judge cases in which they are uniquely in a position to gain or lose because of their decision.

The question then arises: Were the Levites and priests threatened economically by their honest enforcing of the gleaning law? If they did enforce it, did they or the priesthood in general risk a loss of income? Even more to the point, would their income automatically have been reduced? *Specifically, did the enforcement of "gleaner's rights" reduce the priesthood's portion of the crop collected from the landowners?* If their income would have been automatically reduced by their commitment to upholding the gleaning laws, then we must conclude one of two things: 1) Mosaic Covenant law rested on the assumption that judges would consistently hand down impartial decisions that were against their economic self-interest, or 2) the Levites and priests were not the authorized covenantal agents to enforce the gleaning laws.

Not a Threat

Leviticus 23:9-22 makes it clear that the Levites and priests were not threatened economically by the enforcement of the gleaning law. Their share of the crop during the two feasts was not reduced by whatever percentage was harvested by the gleaners. The landowner had to bring a specified quantity of the best of his crop as an offering to God, by way of the priesthood. This payment was owed to the Levites irrespective of the percentage of the crop harvested by the landowner's crew.

This payment was not part of the tithe; it was a separate offering. To understand the implications of this fact, consider the collecting of the tithe. Enforcing the gleaning law would not have threatened the church's income from tithes, since gleaners also owed a tithe, just as landowners did. A Levite's insistence that the gleaners be given access to the fields would not have threatened that portion of the tithe paid by gleaners. *The gleaners would have understood to whom they owed the enforcement of this law.* Furthermore, the Levite's enforcement of the gleaning law would have tended to ensure the collection of the tithe from the landowners. The requirement of gleaners on a farm created a class of outside agents who had knowledge of the size of the landowner's crop. This would have helped solve a fundamental problem for all agricultural tax collecting: cheating. *Gleaners would have been potential monitors for the church's interests.* Any landowner would have known this. In short, there was a meshing of economic interests between the Levites and honest gleaners in the case of tithe-collecting. The more gleaners in the fields, the more likelihood that two or more of them would have told the truth to the church's officers about the size of the crop.

Reducing the Costs of Monitoring Cheaters

If a landowner did not allow any gleaners to glean, one or more of them could lawfully complain to the Levites. This would alert the Levites to the possibility of an infraction: if the landowner was willing to cheat God by cheating the gleaners, he was perhaps equally willing to cheat God by cheating the Levites of their tithe. The presence of gleaners meant the presence of *monitoring agents* whose self-interest coincided with the priesthood's self-interest.

These agents were not paid by the priesthood. This points to the priesthood as the authorized agency for enforcing the gleaning laws. Why not the local civil magistrate? Because the Levites received a greater percentage of the crop than a God-honoring civil magistrate would. The Levites lawfully received a full 10 percent of the increase in the crop; only a corrupt king would demand this much (I Sam. 8:15, 17). The Levites had to give only 10 percent to the priests, retaining 90 percent for themselves (Num. 18:26-28). There was no similar kingly guarantee for the percentage retained personally by local magistrates. Thus, local Levites had a far greater economic incentive under Mosaic law to monitor the output of the fields than the local civil magistrates did. The Levites had the greater economic incentive under biblical law to seek out zero-price agents to monitor the output of the farms. This incentive structure indicates that the church was where God lodged the judicial authority governing the gleaning law. The church could do very well – collect the full tithe owed to it – by doing good: defending the gleaners.

The recapitulation of the gleaning law in the section of Leviticus dealing with two fixed-payment grain offerings – the firstfruits – also points to the priesthood as the agency of enforcement for the gleaning law. The priests are identified in this passage as being guaranteed a fixed payment at the feasts, irrespective of the size of any farm's crop. As judges, their economic self-interest was in no way threatened by the gleaners. The Levites and priests could enforce the gleaning law without worrying that their very diligence would automatically reduce their income. The costs of the gleaning program would be borne by the landowners.

What we have here is a system of mutual self-interest between the priestly tribe and the gleaners. The Levites and priests gained allies among the gleaners during the season of the tithe – zero-price (to the priestly tribe) monitors in the fields – while being exposed to no economic threat from their allies during the seasons of the feasts. Simultaneously, the gleaners gained allies – a priesthood with the power to excommunicate uncooperative landowners – during the season of the tithe, while being exposed to no economic threat from their allies during the seasons of the feasts.

This mutually beneficial arrangement worked well in normal years. It broke down, however, during sabbatical years (Lev. 25:4-5, 20). In sabbatical years, the priesthood had a short-term financial interest in seeing a normal harvest rather than idle (resting) land. Priests and landowners did not acknowledge the long-term agricultural productivity benefits of resting the land one year in seven. Their shortened time perspective persuaded them not to honor the sabbatical year of rest for the land.[21] This seems to me to be the most likely reason why the sabbatical year of rest for the land was not enforced in Israel for almost five centuries (II Chron. 36:21). The Levites defected. But it was the priesthood, not the State, that was authorized by God to enforce the gleaning law.[22]

---

21. See below, p. 404.

22. Gary North, *Boundaries and Dominion: The Economics of Leviticus* (computer

Conclusion

The gleaning law was recapitulated in this section because gleaning was connected judicially to the Levites, the mandated participants and beneficiaries at the national feasts. Gleaning pointed to the priests and Levites as God's designated agents of enforcement for the gleaning law. There was a mutually beneficial relationship between the Levites and the gleaners. The gleaners could serve the Levites as monitors of the size of the landowner's crop. This assured the priestly tribe of receiving a more honest tithe. The gleaners also had to pay the tithe, but they had allies in the Levitical priesthood. Their priestly beneficiaries possessed the authority to declare a person excommunicate, including a cheating landowner or a landowner who refused to honor the gleaning law.

This arrangement was mutually beneficial. The priestly tribe had an incentive to see to it that gleaners received access to the leftovers of the crop, and the gleaners had an incentive to see to it that the local Levites were appraised of the size of the crop if cheating was going on. This mutually beneficial economic arrangement placed *information boundaries* around cheaters.

This arrangement also kept the State under appropriate boundaries. The local agents of enforcement, the priests, could not normally inherit rural land.[23] This reduced the threat of confiscation for both landowners and gleaners. It also tended to keep the politics of plunder at bay. With the priesthood as the agents of enforcement, no one was tempted to seek political power in order to increase his group's share of the plunder.

---

edition; Tyler, Texas: Institute for Christian Economics, 1994), ch. 22, section on "Church or State?"

23. For the two exceptions, see Leviticus 27:20-21. See Chapter 37, below.

23

BLASPHEMY AND CIVIL RIGHTS

Bring forth him that hath cursed without the camp; and let all that heard him lay their hands upon his head, and let all the congregation stone him. And thou shalt speak unto the children of Israel, saying, Whosoever curseth his God shall bear his sin. And he that blasphemeth the name of the LORD, he shall surely be put to death, and all the congregation shall certainly stone him: as well the stranger, as he that is born in the land, when he blasphemeth the name of the LORD, shall be put to death. And he that killeth any man shall surely be put to death. And he that killeth a beast shall make it good; beast for beast. And if a man cause a blemish in his neighbour; as he hath done, so shall it be done to him; Breach for breach, eye for eye, tooth for tooth: as he hath caused a blemish in a man, so shall it be done to him again. And he that killeth a beast, he shall restore it: and he that killeth a man, he shall be put to death. Ye shall have one manner of law, as well for the stranger, as for one of your own country: for I am the LORD your God (Lev. 24:14-22).

Basic to the concept of every social order is the sanctity of the god that is believed to defend it. The source of a society's law is the god of that society.[1] For example, no political order exists that does not have a concept of treason. As Rushdoony

1. R. J. Rushdoony, *The Institutes of Biblical Law* (Nutley, New Jersey: Craig Press, 1973), p. 4.

says, "there can be no tolerance in a law-system for another religion. Toleration is a device used to introduce a new law-system as a prelude to a new intolerance. . . . Every law-system must maintain its existence by hostility to every other law-system and to alien religious foundations, or else it commits suicide."[2]

Historical Context

The Israelites faced a problem: What should be done with a blasphemer who was half Israelite and half Egyptian? "And the son of an Israelitish woman, whose father was an Egyptian, went out among the children of Israel: and this son of the Israelitish woman and a man of Israel strove together in the camp; And the Israelitish woman's son blasphemed the name of the LORD, and cursed. And they brought him unto Moses: (and his mother's name was Shelomith, the daughter of Dibri, of the tribe of Dan:) And they put him in ward, that the mind of the LORD might be shewed them" (Lev. 24:10-12). God's answer would establish a precedent by means of this case law application.

The historical context of his blasphemy was a fight. The blasphemer had uttered his curse against God in the midst of a physical struggle with an Israelite. This context points to the nature of blasphemy: *a verbal attack on God by means of an attack on a representative of God*. The blasphemer had verbally assaulted God in the presence of a covenanted follower of God. In effect, the act had publicly challenged God and His representatives to do something about it. The blasphemer had announced by his curses that neither God nor God's people possess lawful authority in history. He broke the national covenantal oath, not merely by renouncing his citizenship through renouncing faith in God, but by uttering a curse against God. He had profaned

2. *Ibid.*, pp. 5-6.

God's name. This was an active assault, which was not tolerated in Israel. It was a capital crime.

Penalty

God's required civil sanction against blasphemy is clear from His answer to Moses' inquiry: "Bring forth him that hath cursed without [outside] the camp; and let all that heard him lay their hands upon his head, and let all the congregation stone him" (Lev. 10:14) This verbal assault had been an act of rebellion, of treason. It had been a public challenge to the legitimacy of the social order. The legitimacy of the covenanted social order had to be maintained by the State. The proper civil sanction, God insisted, was public stoning: the corporate execution of the blasphemer.

No society in the West enforces this statute in modern times, or even thinks about it. No society in the West requires witnesses to participate in the public stoning of those who have committed a capital crime. This biblically mandated sanction has never been taken seriously by church or State in New Covenant times. Indeed, even to suggest that stoning is a legitimate form of execution, let alone required by God, is to risk bringing down the negative sanction of public ridicule on the head of the person who suggests this, and ridicule by Trinitarian theologians at that.[3] The modern world, including the modern Christian world, takes offense against the very idea of negative sanctions imposed by God, whether Mosaic, historical, or eternal.[4] Nevertheless, the fundamental issue of blasphemy is the

---

3. In their attempt to establish a dispensational case against capital punishment for any crime except murder, H. Wayne House and Thomas D. Ice refer to my five-point defense of public stoning as God's specified means of execution. They seem to believe (perhaps correctly) that this will seal their case in modern fundamentalist circles against the theonomists' defense of the Mosaic penal sanctions. House and Ice, *Dominion Theology: Blessing or Curse?* (Portland, Oregon: Multnomah Press, 1988), p. 73.

4. At a meeting in May, 1989, a majority of a group of 385 neo-evangelical theologians of the National Association of Evangelicals voted against the doctrine of

binding character of the respective sanctions: verbal sanctions against God, civil sanctions against blasphemers, and divine sanctions against societies that ignore these sanctions.

What is – not merely *was* – the judicial issue of blasphemy? It is treason against God.[5] Such treason is no longer regarded as a crime. As Levy writes: "In the twentieth century, scorning God, even reviling Him, T. S. Eliot reflected, is merely a breach of good taste, not of deep-seated faith."[6] A violation of etiquette is not considered valid legal grounds for calling in the civil magistrate.

Levy correctly points out that there are very few accounts in the Old Testament of the crime of blasphemy and its punishment. Idolatry was continual (at least prior to the exile), but blasphemy played little role.[7] He is also correct that with the advent of the Christian political order, blasphemy was defined broadly, encompassing "not only verbal abuse or denial of Christianity but even the expression of a difference of opinion about it."[8] It was equated with heresy. This was an illegitimate application of the biblical blasphemy law, for blasphemy is a verbal assault on God's ethical character, not an intellectual proposition about His nature. It is a public curse, not an intellectual error. To charge someone with blasphemy when he is only theologically incorrect is a form of slander.[9] This case

---

eternal punishment. They proclaimed instead the Seventh-Day Adventist and Jehovah's Witness doctrine of "conditionalism" or soul-sleep. See *World* (June 3, 1989).

5. Leonard W. Levy, *Treason Against God: A History of the Offense of Blasphemy* (New York: Schocken Books, 1981). Schocken Books is a Jewish publishing house. See also Gary North, *Boundaries and Dominion: The Economics of Leviticus* (computer edition; Tyler, Texas: Institute for Christian Economics, 1994), ch. 23, section on "Treason Against God."

6. *Ibid.*, p. 3. He cites Eliot's *After Strange Gods* (1934), pp. 55-57.

7. *Ibid.*, p. 331.

8. *Idem.*

9. Rushdoony is categorically wrong to invoke the charge of blasphemy against all amillennialists and premillennialists: "Amillennialism and premillennialism are in retreat from the world and blasphemously surrender it to the devil." R. J. Rushdoony, "Postmillennialism versus Impotent Religion," *Journal of Christian Reconstruc-*

law's context in Leviticus 24 is that of physical crimes: murder, physical assault, and killing a neighbor's animal.

Blasphemy and Negative Sanctions

What is the mandated biblical penalty? Restitution. When a direct attack against God takes place in public, the restitution payment is the forfeiture of one's life. This is why blasphemy is a capital crime. But few, if any, Christian commentators are willing to discuss blasphemy in terms of judicial categories.

Whenever and wherever the doctrine of a personal God or gods is regarded as irrelevant to the legal order, blasphemy is assumed to offer no threat to the integrity or survival of the social order. It steadily loses its status as a crime. Virtually no one in a position of leadership in the West today believes that there is a personal God who brings predictable negative corporate sanctions in history against those societies that tolerate blasphemy. This includes those who identify themselves as Christians. Muslims do not agree with the Christians on this point. Muslims take God's corporate sanctions seriously; they take blasphemy seriously.[10]

---

tion, III (Winter 1976-77), p. 126. On dispensationalists: "I have had some of these escapists tell me that if the Lord will not rapture them out of the 'tribulation,' they see no point in being a Christian! This is not faith: it is blasphemy." *Chalcedon Report* (June 17, 1968); reprinted in Rushdoony, *The Roots of Reconstruction* (Vallecito, California: Ross House, 1991), p. 640. More generally: "If, for example, we refuse to work, and then pray to God for food for our family, we are doubly guilty before God, guilty of improvidence and blasphemy." *Chalcedon Report* (Jan. 1, 1966); *ibid.*, p. 547.

10. The liberal ex-Muslim novelist Salmon Rushdie wrote *The Satanic Verses* (1989), a book that impugned the character of Muhammed. Iran's political leader, the Ayatollah Khomeini, immediately issued a death warrant against Rushdie, offering $5 million to anyone who would assassinate Rushdie, despite the fact that Rushdie was an Indian expatriate living in England. Khomeini died a few months later. Rushdie went into hiding, then publicly apologized, and finally reaffirmed his faith in Islam, but the death warrant has not been repealed. The idea that a Muslim leader can legitimately hire assassins to kill a resident of another national jurisdiction indicates how committed radical (i.e., original) Islam is to the ideal of conquest by the sword.

Blasphemy is cursing: a verbal attack on God, comparable to assault. Blasphemy calls down on God some sort of implicit negative sanction for having misrepresented Himself. Blasphemy is the opposite of the positive sanction: "Bless God." The classic example of blasphemy in the Bible is the statement by Job's wife: "Curse God, and die" (Job 2:9b). The two events are associated: cursing God and death.

It is almost universally assumed today that God's name needs no civil protection. God is not regarded as a person in the legal order. He therefore is entitled to no judicial protection. This means that men are not to be threatened by the State for cursing God, i.e., publicly saying that the God of the Bible is a liar, or a cheat, or some other kind of reprobate being, and therefore deserving of contempt.

Treason against God is considered judicially irrelevant. Treason against the State is regarded as serious, but concern over even this form of treason has faded in recent decades. Treasonous acts that would have led to execution in 1950 today result in life imprisonment with no possibility of parole, which means parole will be possible a decade later. There is a judicial reason for this: wars fought by the United States after World War II have not been formally declared wars. The U.S. Congress has not formally declared war, which Constitutionally is the only legal basis of war. With no formally declared enemy, it has been difficult to prosecute treason.[11] With the demise of the Soviet Union in 1991, it is likely that another round of reduced sanctions for treason will result: the West's primary enemy has

11. The obvious example was the popular actress Jane Fonda during the Vietnam "war." Legally, she did not commit treason. Conservatives ridiculed her as "Hanoi Jane," but they could not say that she was treasonous, despite her public endorsement of Communism. Her career soared during and after the conflict. Similarly, American pilots captured by the North Vietnamese were not entitled to Geneva Convention protection because the United States had not declared war against North Vietnam. The North Vietnamese treated them as spies who have no rights. They were tortured without legal appeal. See Jeremiah A. Denton, Jr., *When Hell Was in Session* (Clover, South Carolina: Riverhills Plantation, 1976).

disappeared. But treason is an inescapable concept. It is correlative to the concept of final sovereignty. Where there is an acknowledged final sovereignty, there will always be laws against treason. It is only during temporary periods in which final sovereignty is not widely agreed upon that we see the relaxation of the treason laws.

Restitution and Rights

The text of this case law continues:

> And he that killeth a beast shall make it good; beast for beast. And if a man cause a blemish in his neighbour; as he hath done, so shall it be done to him; Breach for breach, eye for eye, tooth for tooth: as he hath caused a blemish in a man, so shall it be done to him again. And he that killeth a beast, he shall restore it: and he that killeth a man, he shall be put to death. Ye shall have one manner of law, as well for the stranger, as for one of your own country: for I am the LORD your God (Lev. 24:18-22).

By presenting a discussion of the civil laws governing restitution within the context of the blasphemy laws, the Book of Leviticus makes it plain that the fundamental legal issue here is *restitution*: the imposition of appropriate sanctions. This restitution case law governs murder: "And he that killeth any man shall surely be put to death" (v. 17). The death penalty is God's required means of enforcing earthly restitution for certain crimes, irrespective of the opinion of any victim.[12] The convicted criminal is to be transferred from the civil court to God's heavenly court. The means of this transfer is execution.

---

12. Murder (Ex. 21:12), bestiality (Ex. 22:19), passing children through Molech's fire (Lev. 18:21; 20:2), homosexual acts (Lev. 20:13), wizardry (Lev. 20:27), and blasphemy (Lev. 24:16). Gary North, *Tools of Dominion: The Case Laws of Exodus* (Tyler, Texas: Institute for Christian Economics, 1990), pp. 318-20. Sabbath-breaking was a capital crime under the Mosaic Covenant (Ex. 31:14-15), but not under the New Covenant: Gary North, *The Sinai Strategy: Economics and the Ten Commandments* (Tyler, Texas: Institute for Christian Economics, 1986), ch. 4, Appendix A.

Strangers

The ultimate foundation of biblical law is the sovereignty of God. The original sin of mankind was to transgress the word of God by physically transgressing the "No Trespassing" injunction regarding the forbidden fruit. The appropriate sanction was death, both physical and spiritual. Yet the crime visibly was trespassing: the transgression of a barrier. Then why death? Why not some sort of restitution? This is the wrong way to phrase the question. *Death is restitution to God.* Eternal death is God's ultimate sanction, and it is applied to every infraction. "For whosoever shall keep the whole law, and yet offend in one point, he is guilty of all" (James 2:10). The negative sanction is death. "For the wages of sin is death; but the gift of God is eternal life through Jesus Christ our Lord" (Rom. 6:23). It was not simply that Adam was not to transgress God's property; he was not to defy God by ignoring His threatened negative sanction: death. Satan promised positive sanctions to man: to become as God, knowing good and evil. God threatened a negative sanction: death. Which voice of authority would man obey? His outward actions would determine whose covenant he would affirm: God's or Satan's.

Why did this case law apply to strangers in the land? Because the whole of the Mosaic civil law applied to strangers. "One law shall be to him that is homeborn, and unto the stranger that sojourneth among you" (Ex. 12:49). Restitution was owed to the victimized stranger in Israel as much as to the victimized Israelite. The civil law was not to discriminate in the application of sanctions. This civil protection of the stranger rested on a presupposition: the civil protection of God's name. A society that refuses to protect the integrity of God's name is not going to protect the stranger very long. The theocentric nature of God's law is inescapable. What men do "unto the least of these," they do unto God (Matt. 25:40, 45). This is the biblical doctrine of representation. Similarly, and even more surely, what men seek to do to God, they will eventually do to the least member of the commonwealth. Christians in modern times generally believe the first version of the equation – "from the least of these to God" – but not the second version: "from God to the least of these." They are not particularly concerned about the annulment of civil laws against blasphemy. They are much more concerned about civil rights of minorities. The problem is, *there can be no long-term extension of civil rights to minorities without an equal extension of civil rights to God*. God is much more concerned about His own civil rights than about man's presumed civil rights. God is more concerned about the legal immunity of His name from public desecration than He is about a man's supposed autonomy from both God and other men in desecrating God's name. This perspective is the antithesis of the pluralistic religion of our day, but it is true nevertheless. God is theocentric in His perspective.

Rights

What are legal rights? They are boundaries of individual thought and action that may not be lawfully transgressed or interfered with apart from the permission of the individual who has been granted a legitimate sphere of authority. A civil right is a boundary protected by the threat of civil sanctions. Covenantally, any society that does not honor God's boundaries will find itself under God's negative corporate sanctions. The most appropriate negative sanctions are boundary violations: pestilence, foreign invaders, wicked rulers, and well-meaning bureaucrats. "I'm from the government, and I'm here to help" are among the most ominous words of modern life. They announce the initial stage of servitude.

Civil rights in a society must begin with the blasphemy law. If God's name and reputation are not protected by law, then no man's name and reputation will be protected for very long. A man's name and reputation are more important than his physical property. Shakespeare's lines in *Othello* are true:

Good name in man and woman, dear my lord,
Is the immediate jewel of their souls:
Who steals my purse steals trash; 'tis something, nothing;
'Twas mine, 'tis his, and has been slave to thousands;
But he that filches from me my good name
Robs me of that which not enriches him,
And makes me poor indeed.

If God is regarded as either unwilling or incapable of bringing negative sanctions against those who violate His name, then why should His judicial representatives bother to press God's case in a civil court? They do not, and no century proves this more conclusively than the twentieth: Christian theologians have abandoned hope or belief in God's predictable historical sanctions,[13] and they have also abandoned any belief in the legitimacy of the blasphemy law, let alone its biblically mandated sanction. No ordained officer of church or State wants to bring a covenant lawsuit against a rebellious society if he also firmly believes that God will not prosecute that lawsuit in history. But if God's judicial representatives are unwilling to press His case, then covenant-breakers should not be expected to.

This raises the issue of the prophetic office. The Old Covenant prophet brought a covenant lawsuit against individuals and societies. He declared God's law; then he announced God's sanctions. "Thou art the man," Nathan told David; then he announced God's sanctions. These sanctions would be visible: "I will do this thing before all Israel, and before the sun" (II Sam. 12:12b). God honored Nathan's word. This was verification of Nathan's office as a true prophet. With the final Mosaic sanctions against Israel in A.D. 70, this office ceased. Today, God's people act in a prophetic fashion, but they are not prophets. They declare God's law and His covenantal sanctions in history,

13. Gary North, *Millennialism and Social Theory* (Tyler, Texas: Institute for Christian Economics, 1990), ch. 7.

but they cannot say precisely which sanctions will be imposed and when. But to deny that God's sanctions are in any way predictable in history in terms of His law is to deny the prophetic function altogether. If this theology were true, the gospel would lose its status as prophetic. Its proclamation would become a matter of personal opinion in history regarding sanctions in eternity. The covenantal link between history and eternity would be broken because the covenantal link between historical and eternal sanctions is broken. To a great extent, this is the gospel of modern evangelicalism. Denying God's law and especially its mandated civil sanctions, and denying also God's predictable corporate sanctions in history, modern evangelicalism has stripped the gospel of its prophetic character.

Thus, a society that has disallowed the Bible's blasphemy law is not in a position to defend itself against the extension of the society of Satan: the triumph, judicially and culturally, of Satan's representatives in history. If God's name is not worth defending through civil law, neither is anyone else's. It should come as no surprise that we have seen the virtual annulment of civil laws in the United States that once protected public figures from libel.[14] It is not enough for a victim to prove that someone has lied about him; he must also prove malice on the part of the liar.[15] This erosion of protection has escalated in the final third of the twentieth century, paralleling the systematic removal of God's name from all public institutions and space in the U.S. We have also seen the rise of gossip as a major political force. This has tarnished the reputations of politically liberal

---

14. *New York Times Co. v. Sullivan* (1964). Cf. *The Constitution of the United States of America: Analysis and Interpretation*, prepared by the Congressional Research Service, Library of Congress (Washington, D.C.: Government Printing Office, 1972), pp. 1003-7. The case was handed down by the U.S. Supreme Court two years after *Engel v. Vitale*, in which prayer in public schools was outlawed by the Court. In 1963 came *Abington School District v. Schempp*, in which Bible reading in public schools was outlawed. Cf. *Constitution*, pp. 920-22.

15. A very fine movie that examines the crisis produced by the annulment of the libel laws is *Absence of Malice* (1981).

adulterers – to a man, the public defenders of civil rights and opponents of anachronisms like the blasphemy laws – far more than it has damaged conservatives.[16]

Conclusion

What kind of crime is blasphemy? The Bible's discussion of the appropriate sanction against blasphemy appears in a passage that raises the question of restitution: killing animals, injuring men. This indicates that blasphemy is judicially the equivalent of an assault. The resolution of the incident rests on the idea that the State must intervene and impose the ultimate form of restitution: the death penalty. The criminal is thereby delivered into God's heavenly court for final judgment.

Blasphemy is a public attack on the character, integrity, and final authority of the God of the Bible. The attack may call down a formal curse on God. It may describe God in obscene or perverse language or imagery. It constitutes a public assault against a biblically covenanted Christian social order. Treason against God is treason against a biblical covenantal order, for it

16. The reputation of President John F. Kennedy (1961-63), literally a daily adulterer, has been tarnished retroactively. In his day, however, the press still covered up for him. No longer. U.S. Senator Gary Hart, the leading candidate for the Democratic Party's nomination for President in 1988, went down to defeat when his suspected adultery with Donna Rice became public. A photograph of Miss Rice sitting on his lap on the pier next to the rented boat "Monkey Business" ended his campaign. Miss Rice had the good grace to disappear very quietly into religious service work after the scandal died down.

A quarter century earlier, so had England's Member of Parliament and Secretary of War, John Profumo, whose scandal regarding a prostitute brought down the Conservative government in 1963. It was not that he had committed adultery that destroyed him; it was that he had lied on the floor of Parliament about the affair. Lying publicly to one's colleagues is taken very seriously by Parliament; adultery isn't. If the prostitute had not also been close to a known Russian agent, Profumo probably would have had no problem. He worked nearly anonymously for the next two decades, helping juvenile offenders, for which he was eventually granted national honors by the Queen. What is not remembered is that the conservative journalist who first broke the story in a small-circulation newsletter went to jail for violating the government's secrecy laws by exposing Profumo. English common law is more concerned about protecting the civil government than protecting God's name.

undermines the legitimacy of the covenantal family, church, and State. But the State in the West today is regarded by political pluralists as neutral theologically. This is why political pluralists have been forced to abandon the enforcement of the crime of blasphemy. The crime of blasphemy is no longer regarded as a crime because the ideal of a biblically covenanted social order is no longer taken seriously. With the political triumph of the humanistic theology of political pluralism, all supernatural gods and laws have been relegated to the realm of *adiaphora*: issues not fundamental to the true faith, namely, the religion of humanism.

The biblical legal foundation of the concept of civil rights rests on a more fundamental concept: *unlawful trespass*. What belongs to God cannot lawfully be stolen or misused. What belongs to God's agent, man, also cannot be lawfully stolen or misused. The primary form of ownership is ownership of one's own name. God identified Himself to Moses as "I AM THAT I AM" (Ex. 3:14): the self-defined, self-contained Creator God. The authority to name something is a mark of hierarchical authority. God named Adam; Adam named the animals (Gen. 2:20) and then Eve (Gen. 3:20). The name of God must be defended. So must the name of man. Thus, an attack on a person's good name is a crime, but only because an attack on God's name is a more serious crime. Biblical law is theocentric. A crime is primarily an attack on God; secondarily, an attack on man as God's representative. A public assault on God's name is therefore a capital crime, the archetype of all civil rights laws. If God's rights are not defended by the civil order, then no one's rights are safe. When a man's good name can be publicly tarnished, his purse is not safe either. That the libel laws should have been weakened in this, the century of massive taxation, compulsory wealth redistribution, and political pluralism, should come as no surprise. The present age of legislated envy began with an attack on the authority of God during the French Revolution. Envy has spread to every institution, including even the State. If God's name is not safe from public vilification, then nothing is safe.

Blasphemy is associated with a curse, not with theological error as such. Heresy is not a crime. It is not a direct public assault on the character of God. It is a serious error to equate blasphemy with heresy.

Part 5

INHERITANCE
(Lev. 25-27)

INTRODUCTION TO PART 5

And ye shall hallow the fiftieth year, and proclaim liberty throughout all the land unto all the inhabitants thereof: it shall be a jubile unto you; and ye shall return every man unto his possession, and ye shall return every man unto his family (Lev. 25:10).

The fifth section of Leviticus begins with Chapter 25, which lists the laws governing the jubilee year: inheritance inside the land's boundaries. The remainder of Leviticus deals with inheritance.

Modern evangelical theologians remain totally hostile to the theonomists' principle of biblical interpretation: any Mosaic law not annulled by the New Covenant is still judicially binding on church, State, or family. Nevertheless, prominent evangelical social commentators – though not the theologians – of the far right and the far left remain fascinated with the jubilee laws of Leviticus 25.

This is a very curious phenomenon. The jubilee laws were explicitly tied to the Promised Land. They were laws governing the sale of real estate and people. They were not revealed by God prior to the exodus, and they applied to no region on earth prior to the conquest of Canaan. Why should evangelical Protestant social commentators who denounce theonomy's hermeneutic of judicial continuity also proclaim the benefits of the jubilee laws? Is there some hidden agenda at work here?

There are two approaches taken by the evangelical commentators. Right-wing evangelicals argue that the jubilee's 50-year cycle was related to inherent limits on debt. Thus, we should in some way honor the jubilee's principle of debt limits. If we fail to do this through some sort of national bankruptcy law, a built-in economic cycle of economic depression and bankruptcy will do it for us. Far-left evangelicals argue that the jubilee law governed ownership in the broadest sense, not just real estate. Mosaic civil law specified that every rural plot be returned to its original family every 50 years. They conclude from this that the modern State should legislate a massive, compulsory redistribution of capital from the wealthy to the poor.

Both groups are wrong. Neither group comes close to the specifics of the jubilee law. Neither group comes close to the meaning of this law. This is because neither group actually goes to the actual jubilee law with the assumption that every aspect of this law *as well as its Mosaic judicial context* is judicially binding in the New Covenant. Neither suggests a principle of judicial continuity. Each side has an economic agenda, and each misuses the texts of Scripture to promote this agenda.

First, with respect to the right-wing analysis, the jubilee year had very little to do with debt limitation except insofar as a 50-year lease for land is a form of debt. How relevant is it today? Hardly anyone today signs a 50-year lease. This law had nothing to do with consumer debt or business debt for capital equipment, or anything besides Israelite bondservants, land outside of walled cities, and Levites' houses.

Second, with respect to the left-wing analysis, the jubilee law rested legally on God's mandate that Israel invade Canaan and wipe out all of its inhabitants. That is to say, *the jubilee law rested on genocide*. It was an aspect of the original spoils of war. It had nothing to do with a government program of systematic wealth redistribution from the rich to the poor. The jubilee law established that the conquering families of Joshua's era would permanently retain title to their land. This law was announced four decades before the conquest began. The return of rural land to the heirs of these original families every 50 years was not statist wealth redistribution; rather, it was the judicial defense of original title: a defense of private property.

The Meaning of the Jubilee

The Mosaic law guaranteed that the Israelites would multiply if they obeyed God's law: longer life spans (Ex. 20:12) and zero miscarriages (Ex. 23:26). But a multiplying population leads to ever-shrinking land holdings. As time passed and the population grew, each family plot in Israel would shrink to the point of near-invisibility. Given the fact that the average family allotment at the time of the conquest was under eleven acres, a population that doubled every quarter century (3 percent growth per annum) could not remain an agricultural society for very long. Every 24 years, the average family's share of the farm would shrink by half. The average allotment would have been down to a little over an acre within a century with a population growth rate of 3 percent a year.

The jubilee law had nothing to do with the equalization of property except in the peculiar sense of eventually producing plot sizes so tiny that the value of any given family's landed inheritance was so small that it really did not make any difference. In today's world, an inheritance worth two dollars is twice as large as an inheritance worth one dollar, but in terms of what either inheritance will buy, the percentage difference between them really does not matter.

Then what was the jubilee law all about? First, it was a law that decentralized politics: every heir of a family of the conquest could identify his citizenship in a particular tribe because every family had an inheritance in the land. Ownership stayed inside the tribes. Second, it restricted the accumulation of rural land holdings by the Levites, who could never buy up the land. This geographically dispersed urban tribe would remain dispersed. Third, it kept the State from extending its land holdings on a permanent basis. Fourth, it kept foreigners from buying permanent residences outside of walled cities where homes were not under the jubilee law. Fifth, it pressured the nation to move into walled cities or emigrate out of Israel when population growth had its effect on farm size.

There was an overall economic principle at work here: those outside the covenants – civil, familial, and ecclesiastical – should be kept economically and numerically subordinate to those inside the covenants. This is not discussed by commentators.

If Israel remained covenantally faithful as a nation, the life style of the typical Israelite would not remain agricultural. A few generations after the conquest, the nation would have become an urbanized center of commerce. More than this: the old wineskin of the original grant of territory to Joshua's generation could not long hold the new wine of population growth. The Promised Land's boundaries would be breached. The Israelites would spread beyond the nation's borders.

Having said all this, now I must prove it. But there really isn't very much to prove regarding the fundamental economic aspect of this law. It is simple to comprehend. The economic value of each family's plot would have decreased over the generations, as covenant-keeping families multiplied. Yet for over two millennia, the commentators have ignored the obvious: a growing population will eventually fill up the land.

There is a reason for this error: those who write Bible commentaries rarely take the Mosaic law seriously. They pay little attention to the coherence of its details. They refuse to ask themselves the crucial question: *How did each law actually work in relation to the other laws?* The liberals assume that the judicial system could not have functioned coherently because multiple authors wrote the Pentateuch. A coherent system of law would undermine their presupposition of judicial incoherence. They discover what they assume: a patchwork of uncoordinated laws. They do not seek to discover the meaning of any law in terms of the whole. Meanwhile, the conservatives feel justified in ignoring the details of the law because they assume that the Mosaic law isn't relevant under the New Covenant. This almost contemptuous attitude toward the Mosaic law has hampered Christian scholarship. It is time for this contempt to end. It is time to search the law in depth to discover what God expects from us, just as David did (Ps. 119). The jubilee law is a better place than most to begin because it is clearly a coherent series of laws with many ramifications.

A Matter of Holiness

God required the nation of Israel to hallow – set apart – the fiftieth year. This identified the fiftieth year as uniquely holy. It was the jubilee year. It was to be inaugurated by the blowing of the trumpet on the day of atonement (Lev. 25:9). The jubilee year was to be the year for claiming one's inheritance: of land, but far more important, of legal status as a citizen. Those circumcised men who were heirs of the original holy army that had conquered Canaan could not legally be disenfranchised except through the loss of their landed inheritance outside a walled city, or, in the case of the Levites, of their homes in Levitical cities.

Citizenship (freemanship) in Mosaic Israel was based on three religious factors: confession, circumcision, and lawful participation in God's holy army. One mark of citizenship was ownership of a share of the land that had been possessed by a conquering family under Joshua. This was not the only proof of citizenship, but it was the most universal. A man who had been judicially severed from ecclesiastical participation in the congregation could not retain his family's landed inheritance beyond the next jubilee. He became disinherited. His property would go to his next-of-kin: his kinsman-redeemer. He could legally buy title to a residence in a walled city, since this property was not governed by the jubilee law, but he might have to sell it in a crisis. It was risky to be excommunicated.

As an excommunicate, he was no longer an Israelite. He was a resident alien. As such, he became subject to the threat of lifetime servitude. So did his minor heirs (Lev. 25:44-46). He was no longer a freeman. In an economic crisis, he might also lose his status as a free man.

If Israel did not honor God's law, God threatened national disinheritance (Deut. 8:19-20). This placed every Israelite in jeopardy of becoming a slave. Slavery was a permanent sanction. A slave could not buy his way out of slavery. There were only three ways for a slave to escape his legal condition and still remain inside the land: 1) manumission, 2) liberation by an invading foreign army, or 3) adoption, either by his owner or some other Israelite.

The legal issue of inheritance is, in the final analysis, the theological issue of adoption by God (Ezek. 16). So is the legal issue of liberty. In this regard, consider the New Testament's doctrine of adoption through God's grace (John 1:12; Eph. 1:5): an act of the ultimate Kinsman-Redeemer.

Enforcement

Was the jubilee law actually enforced? It is not clear from the historical sections of the Bible whether or not Israel ever observed the jubilee year. The Bible's silence indicates that it may not have been enforced, but we cannot be certain about this. Consider Ahab's theft of Naboth's land (I Ki. 21). On the one hand, Naboth refused to sell his land to King Ahab. This is evidence of one man's commitment to the Mosaic law's principle of jubilee inheritance. On the other hand, the fact that Ahab thought he could permanently steal the land from Naboth by having him executed indicates that the enforcement of the jubilee was sporadic or nonexistent in his day. Surely, Ahab was not Naboth's kinsman-redeemer. The incident reveals no clear-cut evidence with regard to the entire history of Israel.

The Mosaic law provided economic incentives for those who possessed the authority to declare the jubilee year to do so: the

Levites. Because the homes of the Levites in Levitical cities were governed by the jubilee (Lev. 25:32-33), the Levites had an economic incentive to declare the jubilee on schedule twice per century – far stronger than the incentive for them to declare a sabbatical year. Did they nevertheless defect? If so, why?

Conclusion

The jubilee year was a year of liberty for all the inhabitants of Israel (v. 10). But there was an exclusionary clause in the jubilee law: the enslavement of heathens (vv. 44-46). The best way to avoid slavery was to become a citizen of the holy commonwealth. Unlike the other ancient nations, citizenship in Israel was open to any resident alien, or at least to his heirs (Deut. 23:2-8). The blessings of liberty could be secured through confession of faith in God, circumcision, and eligibility to serve in God's holy army. This was the Mosaic law's incomparable promise to all resident aliens. But to attain citizenship, a family would have to remain economically productive until the heirs of the promise could secure their claim. This promise was conditional: remaining productive and avoiding being sold into servitude.

The jubilee law pointed to the conditional nature of Israel's very existence as a nation: God's threat of disinheritance, which was a threat of servitude to foreigners. There were conditions attached to citizenship: covenantal stipulations. The jubilee law's stipulations (Lev. 25) – point three of the biblical covenant – were immediately followed by a list of promised sanctions (Lev. 26): point four.

Every true prophet of Israel came before the nation to bring a covenant lawsuit. This reminded them of the ethical basis of liberty. Israel's final prophet would bring Israel's final covenant lawsuit. He would declare liberty for the enslaved and slavery for the rebellious slavemasters. He would serve as the final *go'el*: the kinsman-redeemer and the blood avenger. He would adopt many and disinherit others. He would bring sanctions. He would announce the final jubilee year: "The Spirit of the Lord is upon me, because he hath anointed me to preach the gospel to the poor; he hath sent me to heal the brokenhearted, to preach deliverance to the captives, and recovering of sight to the blind, to set at liberty them that are bruised, To preach the acceptable year of the Lord" (Luke 4:18-19). Fulfilled!

24

THE SABBATICAL YEAR

And the Lord *spake unto Moses in mount Sinai, saying, Speak unto the children of Israel, and say unto them, When ye come into the land which I give you, then shall the land keep a sabbath unto the* Lord. *Six years thou shalt sow thy field, and six years thou shalt prune thy vineyard, and gather in the fruit thereof; But in the seventh year shall be a sabbath of rest unto the land, a sabbath for the* Lord: *thou shalt neither sow thy field, nor prune thy vineyard. That which groweth of its own accord of thy harvest thou shalt not reap, neither gather the grapes of thy vine undressed: for it is a year of rest unto the land. And the sabbath of the land shall be meat for you; for thee, and for thy servant, and for thy maid, and for thy hired servant, and for thy stranger that sojourneth with thee, And for thy cattle, and for the beast that are in thy land, shall all the increase thereof be meat (Lev. 25:1-7).*

This law is a recapitulation and extension of the sabbath laws of Exodus 23:10-12. It was not in origin a law of the jubilee, although it was tied to it; it was a law of the sabbath. This leads us to an important implication: *the law of the jubilee was an extension of the sabbatical principle of rest*. The sabbatical year law was primary; the jubilee land laws were secondary. *The sabbatical year law was more fundamental than the jubilee land laws.*

We begin our study of the jubilee laws with a consideration of the meaning of the sabbath: rest for land as well as for man.

We need to discover the meaning of "rest" in the context of the sabbatical year. We also need to recognize that this law was a Mosaic land law: an aspect of the land as God's covenantal agent (Lev. 18:25, 28).

Sabbath and Capital Preservation

The law of God is theocentric. Whatever secondary applications it may have, a law's primary application always relates to God. This law focused on the mandatory resting of the land of Israel, but its ultimate reference point was the sovereignty of the Creator God of the covenantal promise.

The Bible introduces the subject of the sabbath in relation to the story of the creation. God created the world in six days; then He rested (Ex. 20:11). Whenever the Israelites observed this law, they were acknowledging the sovereignty of God as both the Creator and the original owner. Bonar comments: "It has been well said that by the weekly Sabbath they owned that they themselves belonged to Jehovah, and by this seventh-year Sabbath they professed that their land was His, and they His tenants."[1]

God deals with men as an absentee landlord deals with leaseholders who use his property. He gave Adam an assignment; then He left the garden. This is a continuing theme in the Bible. The Book of Job pictures God as normally distant from man. Jesus used the theme of the absentee landlord in several of His parables. While God dwells in the midst of men judicially, especially during ecclesiastical feasts, He does not dwell in their midst physically. The dominion covenant (Gen. 1:26-28) is supposed to be fulfilled by men acting as responsible managers, not as supervised coolies in a field. The managerial model in the Bible is that of a sharecropper or tenant farmer who pays 10 percent of his net income to the landowner.

---

1. Andrew Bonar, *A Commentary on Leviticus* (London: Banner of Truth Trust, [1846] 1966), p. 446.

The Terms of the Lease

Leasing land is a very difficult proposition for a landlord. For an absentee landlord, it is even more difficult. The problem is to establish leasing terms that preserve economic incentives that achieve three goals: 1) keeping a competent lessee on the property by allowing him to maximize his income; 2) maintaining or increasing the capitalized value of the land; 3) maximizing the landlord's lease income. The absentee landlord must discover a way to achieve all three goals without a great expenditure on local monitors. Inexpensive monitors are valuable.

God established the laws governing the Promised Land because He delivered it into their hands. As its owner, He had the authority to establish the terms of the leasehold. If the people did not like the terms of the lease, they could live elsewhere. So, one foundation of this law is God's ownership. (The other foundation is the principle of sabbath rest.)

The terms of God's lease are generous to the lessee, who keeps nine-tenths of the net income of the operation. This is the principle of the tithe. The tithe is paid to God's designated agency of collection, the church.[2] The church acts as God's accountant and crop-collector. The payment of the tithe is a public acknowledgment by the lessees of God's ultimate ownership of the original capital: land (rent) plus labor (wages) over time (interest). This original grant of capital is also accurately described by John Locke's three-fold classification: life, liberty, and property.[3]

---

2. Gary North, *Tithing and the Church* (Tyler, Texas: Institute for Christian Economics, 1994).

3. He never used this phrase exactly as quoted. He wrote of property in general as "life, liberty, and estate." John Locke, *Second Treatise on Government* (1690), paragraph 87. He spoke of "life, liberty, or possession" in paragraph 137. Exactly one century later, Edmund Burke wrote of "property, liberty, and life." *Reflections on the Revolution in France* (1790), paragraph 324. The U.S. Constitution adopted "life, liberty, or property" in Article V of the Bill of Rights (1791), and also in Article XIV:1 (1868).

God's Land Grant

Consider the grant of capital in the form of developed land. God gave His people the Promised Land as their inheritance. This was an aspect of the promise given to Abraham (Gen. 15:13-16). Also included were existing houses and fields. "And I have given you a land for which ye did not labour, and cities which ye built not, and ye dwell in them; of the vineyards and oliveyards which ye planted not do ye eat" (Josh. 24:13). They inherited the capitalized value of the houses and planted fields of the Canaanites. The Canaanites had unknowingly served as stewards of the land, building up its value until the fourth generation after Israel's subordination to Egypt (Gen. 15:16).

Having delivered a capital asset into their hands, God specified that they must, as a nation, rest the land every seventh year. This was to be a national year of rest. The law applied only to agricultural land. It did not restrict commerce, manufacturing, equipment repair, or anything except planting and harvesting by owners. Urban occupations were not under the terms of this law. This law granted a year of rest from field work to all those under the household authority of landowners, including hired servants.

The year of rest was an acknowledgment of the limits on man's knowledge. Man cannot know everything about the land. He therefore was not allowed to treat the land indefinitely as if it were a mine. The "mining" of the soil could go on for six years in seven, but not in the seventh year. He was not allowed to strip the soil of its productivity. The seventh year was a rest period for the land in the broadest sense, including worms, bugs, birds, weeds, and every other living creature that dwelled on or in the land. *This would preserve the land's long-run value*.

This limitation on the landowner's extraction of present income from the land was a means of preserving the capitalized value of the land over time. This placed a limit on both man's greed and ignorance. It forced the landowner to honor the future-orientation of God's covenant. It preserved the landed inheritance for future generations. God's sharecroppers in one generation were not allowed to undermine the future value of the land by overproduction in the present. God, as the land's ultimate owner, was thereby able to maintain a greater percentage of the land's original capitalized value.

The Israelites did not always enforce the provisions of the sabbath land law prior to the exile. In other words, they did not enforce the terms of the original lease. God allowed this infraction to continue for almost five centuries. Then He collected payment from a later generation. "And them that had escaped from the sword carried he away to Babylon; where they were servants to him and his sons until the reign of the kingdom of Persia: To fulfil the word of the LORD by the mouth of Jeremiah, until the land had enjoyed her sabbaths: for as long as she lay desolate she kept sabbath, to fulfil threescore and ten years" (II Chron. 36:20-21).[4] Two generations of sharecroppers then learned a judicial lesson in Babylon: God has a long memory for the details of His law. Those who violate it will eventually pay restitution to Him by paying restitution to their victims. In this case, they paid to the land, which rested.

A Year of Gleaning

There appears a problem with the translation in the King James Version. Actually, there is no problem, but there is a problem for interpreters who do not take the text literally. Verse 5 says: "That which groweth of its own accord of thy harvest thou shalt not reap, neither gather the grapes of thy

4. By the time of Jeremiah, the Israelites had been in the Promised Land for almost eight centuries. Of this period, 490 years (70 x 7) had been spent without a sabbatical year. Jeremiah did not say when this period of law-breaking began. I presume that it began 490 years before the Babylonian captivity, i.e., sometime late in Saul's kingship. I am using James Jordan's chronology: "The Babylonian Connection," *Biblical Chronology*, II (Nov. 1990), p. 1: 3426 Anno Mundi = 586 B.C. The accession of Saul was 2909 AM. Jordan, "Chronologies and Kings (II)," *ibid.*, III (Aug. 1991), p. 2. Computation: 586 + 490 = 1076 B.C., i.e., 3426 AM - 490 AM = 2936 AM. David came to the throne in 2949 AM, i.e., 1063 B.C.

vine undressed: for it is a year of rest unto the land." Conclusion: someone was prohibited from reaping the fields. The next two verses are translated as follows: "And the sabbath of the land shall be meat for you; for thee, and for thy servant, and for thy maid, and for thy hired servant, and for thy stranger that sojourneth with thee, And for thy cattle, and for the beast that are in thy land, shall all the increase thereof be meat" (vv. 6-7). Conclusion: the produce of the field served as food for someone. But if the increase is identified as meat (i.e., food),[5] then what about the prohibition? "That which groweth of its own accord of thy harvest thou shalt not reap, neither gather the grapes of thy vine undressed." How could the increase serve as food if the crop could not lawfully be harvested?

To solve this problem, the New American Standard Version inserts a word in verse 6: *products*. "And all of you shall have the sabbath products of the land for food. . . ." The Revised Standard Version translates it as follows: "The sabbath of the land shall provide food for you. . . ." None of this is satisfactory. Why not? Because the text of verse 5 is too specific: "That which groweth of its own accord of thy harvest thou shalt not reap, neither gather the grapes of thy vine undressed." Someone was prohibited from harvesting. The question is: Who?

The solution is found in the word *thy*. The law was addressed to landowners. It applied to those identified in verse 4: "Six years thou shalt sow *thy* field, and six years thou shalt prune *thy* vineyard, and gather in the fruit thereof." Those who owned the fields and vineyards were not allowed by God to reap them in the seventh year. This prohibition did not apply to their hired servants, strangers in the community, poor people, and the beasts of the field. "But the seventh year thou shalt let it rest and lie still; that the poor of thy people may eat: and what they leave the beasts of the field shall eat. In like manner

5. The Hebrew words translated as "meat" in verses 6 and 7 both can be translated as "food."

thou shalt deal with thy vineyard, and with thy oliveyard" (Ex. 23:11). *The prohibition did not apply to those who did not own the land.*

What this law established was *a year of unlimited gleaning.* Hired harvesters were not allowed into the fields and vineyards as employees of the landowners. Instead, they were given free access as independent agents. On the one hand, landowners did not invest any money or time in seeding the fields, pruning the vineyards, or caring for the land. This cut their expenses in year six. On the other hand, they reaped no crops. The crops were reaped in year seven by non-owners. Like the leftovers that were collected by the gleaners annually, so were the crops that grew by themselves. The land's rest was specific: rest from the activities of its owners, not rest from harvesting by non-owners.

Independence

What was the point? Rushdoony argues that this law was not humanitarian, meaning (I give him the benefit of the doubt) uniquely humanitarian, because gleaners had access to the fields every year.[6] This interpretation is incorrect. This law was obviously a humanitarian law, for it singled out the poor and strangers. They would receive something from the landowner that otherwise would have been kept by him. A transfer of wealth was involved. The sabbatical land law was as much a humanitarian law as the annual gleaning law was. It treated the beasts of the fields as if they were gleaners. It treated them as servants on the weekly sabbath. In other words, the sabbatical rest forced landowners to let the land alone and allow human and animal gleaners into the fields. The landowners were not allowed to use land, man, or beast for their purposes. Non-owners were allowed by God to do whatever they wanted: to

6. R. J. Rushdoony, *The Institutes of Biblical Law* (Nutley, New Jersey: Craig Press, 1973), p. 140.

glean or not to glean. It was not that they were required to rest from self-employment as harvesters. They were not to be compelled by economic circumstances to work for landowners. God provided them with a source of income to offset the absence of wages. This was a compulsory wealth-redistribution program: from landowners to non-owners. The question is: Who imposed the negative sanctions? Answer: the Levites.[7]

In the sabbatical year, all charitable, morally obligatory, zero-interest loans had to be canceled (Deut. 15:1-7). This means that the debtor who had been forced to labor for another landowner because he had gone into debt and then had defaulted on this charitable loan had to be released from bondage. But this release from bondage did not relieve him from the personal economic necessity of participating in the harvesting of the crop of his former creditor and perhaps harvesting part of his own land's crop, which was also to lie fallow. He achieved his release from debt in a year of heavy national dependence on God. There was not supposed to be any planting in the season prior to the sabbatical year. The land was to receive its rest. So, the released debtor faced a problem: how to get enough to eat.

He would have faced high demand for food from the free market. If he could harvest anything, he could either consume it or sell it. He would possess a valuable asset – food – in a year of above-average scarcity. This was an advantage for him. But without the landowner to serve as his intermediary, the newly debt-free Israelite would begin to regain his confidence as a free man. He would be forced to learn marketing in the year that he would plant the eighth-year crop on his own land, except in jubilee "weeks," when the law also prohibited planting in the year after the sabbatical year. The year of his release from debt or even servitude would also be a difficult year economically. It was a year in which Israelites were supposed to rely on God's grace and their own previous thrift. This was why

7. See below: "The Defection of the Levites."

the newly resealed Israelite had to be liberally provided with food (Deut. 15:13-14): to get him through the sabbatical year. The fruit of his own field would belong to non-owning harvesters and beasts.

The sabbatical year was a system for forcing men to become self-consciously dependent on God's grace. Dependent on Him, they were to become dominion-minded. *Subordinate to God, they were to become active toward the creation.* (This is the mandated pattern for the dominion covenant.) The year of debt release was to be the year of open access to the fields for non-owners. It was a year of hard work for harvesters, for they harvested on their own and for their own. A new master told them to do this: the market.

Because independent harvesters were given free access to the land's unassisted production one year in seven, they had an incentive to recommend land management practices that would maximize output in the seventh year: crop rotation, fertilization, irrigation, etc. This does not mean that landowners were required to follow the suggestions of the full-time harvesters, but to the extent that owners deferred to harvesters in gathering information and assessing its value, the sabbatical year law encouraged agricultural practices that did not strip the land of its long-run productivity. This law, when enforced, created a class of preferred workers who had an incentive to act as *economic agents of the land*, and therefore as *economic agents of the future*.

We do not know for certain whether the gleaners would have received more income as secondary harvesters in a year following an investment of capital or as primary harvesters in a year following an investment of zero. As I hope to show, it is quite likely that the total output of the fields was greater in a normal harvest year than in a sabbatical year.[8] What we do know is that when this law was enforced, the land received its

---

8. See below, "The Defection of the Levites."

rest, and the poor had access to the fields. God therefore placed self-interested monitors in the midst of the community. The question was: Would these monitors possess sufficient power or influence over landowners through the priesthood? The answer for 490 years: no.

The Threat of Debt

Because this law pressured landowners to save for six years in preparation for the sabbatical year, it subsidized those who possessed an attitude favorable to thrift, i.e., future orientation. Simultaneously, this law threatened improvident landowners with debt servitude, beginning in the year of release.[9] In the seventh year, all charitable, zero-interest loans to poor Israelites became null and void (Deut. 15:1). Creditors could not legally collect from impoverished debtors. Meanwhile, the economy grew tight: reduced food production. Improvident landowners went looking for loans to get them through the year. There would have been greater-than-normal demand for interest-bearing loans, i.e., higher interest rates. This would have tended to squeeze the weakest borrowers out of the loan market. Lenders prefer to lend to those who are likely to repay. On the other hand, if an evil man wanted to trap a weak debtor in order to gain control over his labor if he defaulted, the year of national gleaning would have been an ideal time. The recently liberated debtors would have known this. Their memory of their previous bondage was to keep them from succumbing to this temptation. The poor had access to the untilled fields of the landowners. They were to take advantage of this unique situation and stay out of debt. They were not to "return to Egypt" by going into debt and risking another round of bondage.

---

9. Gary North, *Boundaries and Dominion: The Economics of Leviticus* (computer edition; Tyler, Texas: Institute for Christian Economics, 1994), ch. 24, section on "The Pressure on Landowners to Save."

Any landowner who had not planned carefully would face a crisis in year seven. Without sufficient thrift in the previous six years, he might have been forced to enter the debt market to save his business. But he would have come to a lender as a businessman, not as a poverty-stricken brother in the faith. There was no moral pressure on anyone to lend to him. Such moral compulsion to lend applied only to loans to the poor (Deut. 15:7-10). A land-secured loan threatened the borrower greatly: to default the loan meant the forced sale of his land until the loan was repaid or until the next jubilee year.

Lenders would have been more ready to lend to landowners than to most poor men: secure collateral. This gave landowners an advantage in the loan markets. But there was great risk for the debtor. There was also the embarrassment of having to mortgage the family's property. The present-oriented landowner would then face the need to repay the loan, making preparation for the next sabbatical year even more burdensome. The debt trap loomed much larger to the person who fell behind. This is the grim reality of debt.

The sabbatical year was therefore a major burden on landowners. There is little doubt that they would have preferred to avoid this burden. If this law was going to be enforced, there had to be an agency of enforcement that had an economic incentive to do so. Which agency was it? And why did it fail to enforce the law prior to the Babylonian exile?

The Defection of the Levites

We know that this law was not enforced for centuries prior to the exile. Jeremiah identified their failure to honor the year of release as the cause of the exile: "At the end of seven years let ye go every man his brother an Hebrew, which hath been sold unto thee; and when he hath served thee six years, thou shalt let him go free from thee: but your fathers hearkened not unto me, neither inclined their ear" (Jer. 34:14).

The enforcing agents, the Levites (gleaning law) and civil magistrates (land law), did not assert their authority. Why not? We do not know. This may be one of those cases in which they had a short-term incentive not to enforce the law. In a normal year, they were entitled to tithes and taxes from landowners and gleaners. In a sabbatical year, only the gleaners paid. The landowners harvested nothing for their own account. Perhaps the collectors of tithes and taxes did not consider the soil's long-term output, allowing landowners to plant and harvest.

I conclude that the total output of the land in a normal year was greater than during a sabbatical year. Levites and civil magistrates received a larger tithe in non-sabbatical years. Thus, they had less short-term economic incentive to see that the sabbatical year law was enforced. They had to enforce the law because God required them to do so, not because they were paid to do so. The tribe of Levi was to cooperate with the local monitors: hired hands, the poor, and strangers. Levites were required to see to it that the sabbath year's gleaning law was enforced. They refused. They forfeited their position as sanctioning agents on this issue. As a result, the nation went into captivity. After their return, Israel honored this law (I Macc. 6:49, 53). Ezekiel had prophesied that heathen residents in the land would participate in a new allocation of land (Ezek. 47:21-23), but we do not know if the jubilee laws were honored.

Because this law is sabbatical, it extends into the New Covenant. But its enforcement is no longer either ecclesiastical or civil; rather, it is individual. The locus of sabbath enforcement has shifted under the New Covenant. The individual conscience today governs the observation of the sabbath.[10] The land no longer serves as God's covenantal agent. While there may be good ecological reasons for resting the land every seventh year – this is a scientific question, not theological – the decision-

10. Gary North, *The Sinai Strategy: Economics and the Ten Commandments* (Tyler, Texas: Institute for Christian Economics, 1986), Appendix A.

maker with the authority to rest the land is the landowner.[11] The issue of resting the land has moved from covenant law to science.

The modern State of Israel pretends to honor this law, and has since the 1880's. Every seventh year, the farmland of the nation is transferred by the Minister of Internal Affairs to the Chief Rabbinate, which sells title to an anonymous gentile, usually an Arab, who retains formal ownership for one year. Then he sells it back. By Rabbinic law, he is outside the sabbatical year's requirements, so he does not enforce this law. He sells back the land to the Chief Rabbinate at the end of the sabbatical year, which in turn returns formal ownership to the *de facto* owners. "If we were to stop marketing our products to Europe even for one year, we'd be finished," according to the Director General of the Ministry of Agriculture.[12] Non-zionist Orthodox Jewish rabbis refuse to go along, however, since by Jewish law, Jews are not allowed to sell land in Palestine to gentiles.[13] They organize special shops in sabbatical years that sell fruits and vegetables grown by Arabs on Arab land.[14]

(A similar strategy is used during Passover week. The law requires all leaven to be removed from every Jewish household. This makes it difficult for grain merchants. Solution: observant Jews sell all of these prohibited substances to the local rabbi, who sells them to the Chief Rabbinate, which sells them to a gentile for a week. Then he sells them back. By a special dispensation, these multiple sales are presumed to include the leavened substances of non-practicing Jews, too.)[15]

---

11. North, *Boundaries and Dominion*, ch. 24, section on "New Testament Applications."

12. Clyde Haberman, "The Rabbis' Almanack of Seventh-Year Farming," *New York Times* (Dec. 10, 1992). The year 1992 was the sixth year in the cycle.

13. Israel Shahak, *Jewish History, Jewish Religion: The Weight of Three Thousand Years* (Boulder, Colorado: Pluto Press, 1994), p. 43.

14. *Ibid.*, p. 108, n. 17.

15. *Ibid.*, p. 45.

Conclusion

The judicial foundations of the sabbatical year of rest were two-fold: 1) the sabbath rest principle; 2) God's original ownership of the land. At the time of the conquest, God transferred control over the land to families that held legal title on a sharecropping basis, operating under specific terms of the original leasehold agreement. The lease provided a payment to God (the tithe), i.e., a high percentage return to God's authorized sharecropper-owners (90 percent before taxes), and a provision for the maintenance of the long-term capital value of the land (the sabbatical year). Those residents in Israel who did not own the land had legal title to the output of the land: unrestricted harvest in sabbatical years. This legal title was to be enforced by the Levites and priests, not the civil government.

The judicial issue of the sabbatical year was rest: rest for the land, hired workers, and animals. This also included release from the requirement to repay charitable debts (Deut. 15). By "rest," the law meant *a respite for the landless from the requirement to work for the landed*. This law governed agricultural land and those who worked it. There is nothing in the Bible to indicate that it governed any nonagricultural occupation.

This law pressured landowners to plan and save for the sabbatical year. They had to store up both food corn and seed corn. When this law was enforced, it forced them to develop the habit of thrift, i.e., future-orientation. The law also required landowners to forfeit the automatic (though not "natural") productivity of the land in the seventh year. The poor, the stranger, the field animals, and the regular harvesters all had a legal claim on this production, if they were willing to do the work to glean it.

The Levites were the enforcers of this law as it applied to the gleaners' lawful access to the fruits of the land. The Levites refused. This indicates they had little or no short-term economic incentive to enforce it. This in turn indicates that their tithe income was greater when the land was planted and harvested.

Finally, this indicates that there was less net agricultural output in the seventh year than in the other six.

This law was good for the land and all the creatures great and small that inhabited it. Owners were restrained in their use of God's land. Agricultural practices that overworked the land were restrained by this law. The land, as God's judicial agent, deserved its rest. This law mandated it. If this land-protecting aspect of the law was enforced by the State, as I believe it was, it rested on the legal status of the land as God's judicial agent, not on the State as an agency of wealth redistribution to the gleaners. This law is no longer in force in the New Testament era because the land ceased to be a covenantal agent in A.D. 71.

The sabbatical year law was enforced after the Babylonian exile (I Macc. 6:49, 53). The fear of God is a great incentive. During the exile, God had substituted His negative sanctions in history for the failure of the priesthood and the State to enforce the sabbatical year law. Exile was God's partial disinheritance of Israel. It warned Israel of *comprehensive disinheritance*, should the nation continue to rebel. The exile altered land tenure: a new distribution replaced the original distribution under Joshua. The exile had severed the judicial link between each family's plot and Joshua's distribution. The jubilee land laws had been established by genocide, but genocide was neither authorized by God nor possible after the exile. The jubilee's heathen slave laws remained in force, but the residents who participated in any post-exilic distribution were to become immune to the threat of permanent servitude by Israelites.

The sabbatical land law was an extension of the law of the sabbath. It was not a subset of the jubilee land laws; on the contrary, the jubilee land laws were temporary applications of the sabbath law's principle of rest. If there are any New Testament applications of the sabbatical year of rest for the land, they are based on ecology or the general authority of sabbath rules, not on the jubilee's military conquest. This transfers the locus of authority to the landowner: individual, not corporate.

25

BOUNDARIES OF THE JUBILEE LAND LAWS

And thou shalt number seven sabbaths of years unto thee, seven times seven years; and the space of the seven sabbaths of years shall be unto thee forty and nine years. Then shalt thou cause the trumpet of the jubile to sound on the tenth day of the seventh month, in the day of atonement shall ye make the trumpet sound throughout all your land. And ye shall hallow the fiftieth year, and proclaim liberty throughout all the land unto all the inhabitants thereof: it shall be a jubile unto you; and ye shall return every man unto his possession, and ye shall return every man unto his family. A jubile shall that fiftieth year be unto you: ye shall not sow, neither reap that which groweth of itself in it, nor gather the grapes in it of thy vine undressed. For it is the jubile; it shall be holy unto you: ye shall eat the increase thereof out of the field. In the year of this jubile ye shall return every man unto his possession (Lev. 25:8-13).

The theocentric meaning of the jubilee law was God's ownership of both the land and the people. He reserved the right to dictate the terms of inheritance to the Israelites. This inheritance included rural land, heathen slaves, and homes owned by Levites in Levitical cities.

First, for reasons that I survey in *Boundaries and Dominion*, I accept the view of those commentators who argue that year 50 served as the first year in the next sabbath cycle.[1] We cannot appeal to historical records of the jubilee as empirical tests of this theory because there is no biblical record or any other ancient contemporary record of Israel's ever having celebrated a jubilee year.[2]

Second, we need to consider the timing of the day of jubilee. It is not generally recognized that there were two calendars in ancient Israel: priestly and kingly, sanctuary and land. They corresponded to the two shekels: sanctuary (Lev. 27:3, 25) and ordinary. Jordan believes that the two calendars corresponded to two separate government systems.[3] The religious year began in the spring: the first month, Nisan (Esth. 3:7), when Passover was celebrated (Ex. 12). The civil year began in the fall: on the first day the seventh month of the religious calendar (called Tishri in the Talmud).[4] This month began with a day of sabbath rest (Lev. 23:24-25). Ten days later, the day of atonement took place (Lev. 23:27-28).[5] As we shall see, the jubilee was tied to the civil (land) year. This is why the jubilee was a predominantly civil event. It launched the next cycle of inheritance. This inheritance was predominately civil: a matter of citizenship. Those who were heirs of the generation of the conquest were citizens; the jubilee restored them to their judicial tokens of citizenship: their land. On the fifteenth day, the feast of booths or Tabernacles took place (Lev. 23:34-36, 39-43).

---

1. Gary North, *Boundaries and Dominion: The Economics of Leviticus* (computer edition; Tyler, Texas: Institute for Christian Economics, 1994), ch. 25, introductory remarks.

2. A. Löwy, *A Treatise on the Sabbatical Cycle and the Jubilee* (New York: Hermon, [1866] 1974), p. 19.

3. James Jordan, "Jubilee, Part 2," *Biblical Chronology*, V (March 1993), p. 1.

4. *Rosh. Hash.*, 1:3; cited in "Month," *Cyclopaedia of Biblical, Theological, and Ecclesiastical Literature*, edited by John M'Clintock and James Strong, 12 vols. (New York: Harper & Bros., 1876), IV, p. 547.

5. Jordan notes that the official first year of the reign of a king of Judah ran from the first day of the seventh month of the religious year to the last day of the sixth month of the next religious year.

The Day of Atonement

In the jubilee year, trumpets were to be blown throughout the land on the tenth day of the seventh month. This marked the great year of release. It was also a day of rest because it was the day of atonement (Lev. 23:28). The next day, men dwelling near the borders of Israel had to begin their walk to Jerusalem to celebrate Tabernacles (booths): the feast of ingathering. In no more than four days, they had to complete their journey. This time requirement restrained any major extension of the geographical boundaries of Israel. On the day above all other days in Israel's life that was tied to geographical boundaries – jubilee's day of landed inheritance – the timing of the jubilee and Tabernacles established tight limits on the size of the nation. *Israel could never become an expansionist territorial empire and still honor the day of atonement (rest), the jubilee year (inheritance), and the feast of Tabernacles (celebration).* When the Israelites walked to Jerusalem in the jubilee year, all but the Levites went as rural land owners and citizens, even urban dwellers who had leased out their land to others. But they could never lawfully walk from an inheritance located very far from Jerusalem. If Israel ever became an empire, Israelites living near the outer boundaries would forfeit their inheritance in the original land.[6]

The year of jubilee was to begin on the day of atonement (*yom kippur*). The theological significance of this is readily apparent: the day of atonement was the day on which the people of Israel made a formal public acknowledgment of their dependence on the grace of God in escaping from God's required punishment for sin. There had to be an animal sacrifice as part of this formal worship ceremony. It was a day of affliction: death for an animal and public humility for the participants.

6. The reader may think: "This is obvious. What is the big deal?" Try to find any commentary on Leviticus that discusses the relationship between the timing of the day of atonement-jubilee and the growth of empire. The silence of the commentators is testimony to their unwillingness to take the Bible's literal texts seriously (theological liberalism) or to take political theory seriously (theological conservatism).

No work was allowed on that day. *The day of atonement was a day of rest – the ultimate day of rest in ancient Israel, symbolizing covenant-keeping man's rest from the curse of sin*. It was a day set apart for each person's examination of his legal state before God and the self-affliction of his soul (Lev. 16:30-34; 23:27-31).

Once each half century, the day of affliction was to become the day of liberation. The meaning of the Hebrew verb for "afflict" is submission or humility. The day of national liberation and family inheritance took place on the day of formal subordination to God. The imagery is obvious. *Only through submission to God can man experience liberation*. Autonomy is not liberation. It is the antithesis of liberation. This is why modern humanism's free market economic theory, which is both agnostic and individualistic, is not the source of the free society that its defenders proclaim. If we begin our economic analysis with the presupposition of the autonomous individual in an autonomous cosmos, we begin with a hypothesis that cannot lead to liberty and maintain it.

A Question of Subordination

The year of jubilee began with the blowing of a trumpet, a trumpet announcing the day of atonement. The ram's horn, *yobale* (Josh. 6:4-5), is the origin of the English transliteration, *jubilee* (Lev. 25:10-13). The covenantal basis of dominion is formal, oath-bound subordination to God. The jubilee year began with the sound of a trumpet: the audible symbol of the final judgment (I Cor. 15:52). The day of atonement was to remind the Israelite nation of its unique corporate subordination to God. This ritual subordination was to serve as the foundation, both judicially and psychologically, of each Israelite's tasks of leadership. Humble before God, they were to be aggressive toward the world. This is the meaning of the New Testament statement, "Blessed are the meek: for they shall inherit the earth" (Matt. 5:5). They are meek before God, not meek before covenant-breaking men.[7] To be compelled to be meek before covenant-breaking men is evidence of God's temporary chastisement of His covenant people. It is to be forced to adhere to an illegitimate civil oath.[8]

On the day above all other days in which each Israelite publicly manifested his subordinate position before God, the *day of atonement* also served, twice per century, as the *day of inheritance*, the day on which a man's inheritance was returned to him. He would henceforth regain *legal authority* over a piece of land. He would then discover if he had the skills and foresight as an entrepreneur – a future-predicting planner and executor of plans[9] – to retain *economic authority* over it as an economic representative of God, his family, and the consumers in the marketplace. The hierarchy of consumer's sovereignty would henceforth operate though the land's owner, not through a leaseholder.[10] This would be a subordination based on the principle of sabbatical rest.[11]

The Spoils of War

"In the year of this jubile ye shall return every man unto his possession" (Lev. 25:13). This provision applied to rural land. It did not apply to property in walled cities (Lev. 25:29-30). It did not apply to non-agricultural property.

What was the historical origin of this law? Judicially, it was an application of the Mosaic sabbath (Ex. 23:10-12). But histori-

7. Gary North, *The Dominion Covenant: Genesis* (2nd ed.; Tyler, Texas: Institute for Christian Economics, 1987), pp. 436-39.

8. Gary North, *Political Polytheism: The Myth of Pluralism* (Tyler, Texas: Institute for Christian Economics, 1989).

9. Ludwig von Mises, "Profit and Loss" (1951), in *Planning For Freedom* (4th ed.; South Holland, Illinois: Libertarian Press, 1980), ch. 9; Frank H. Knight, *Risk, Uncertainty and Profit* (New York: Harper Torchbooks, [1921] 1965). Cf. North, *Dominion Covenant*, ch. 23.

10. North, *Boundaries and Dominion*, ch. 25, section on "A Question of Subordination."

11. *Ibid.*, ch. 25, subsection on "Rest and Subordination."

cally, it was part of the promised spoils of war. God offered land only to those families that would participate in the military conquest of Canaan. Families that refused to join the battle could not participate in the post-conquest distribution of land. This was never stated explicitly, but we can safely conclude that this was the case because of Joshua's dealing with the Reubenites, the Gadites, and half the tribe of Manasseh. These tribes had already inherited property outside the Promised Land, across the Jordan River. This inheritance was an aspect of the spoils of war. Moses had announced: "And when ye came unto this place, Sihon the king of Heshbon, and Og the king of Bashan, came out against us unto battle, and we smote them: And we took their land, and gave it for an inheritance unto the Reubenites, and to the Gadites, and to the half tribe of Manasseh" (Deut. 29:7-8). However, for them to inherit this recently promised land, Joshua insisted, they would have to fight the Canaanites alongside the other tribes, despite the fact that they had already fought Sihon and Og for their land, and Moses had passed title to them. In short, *there would be no transfer of lawful title prior to the final battle*. That is to say, there would be no rest for any until after the labor of war was over for all. What had been given to these tribes definitively could not be claimed by them finally until after the conquest was over (Josh. 1:10-17).

If militarily victorious tribes had to wait for the transfer of title to land already verbally promised – land located across the Jordan and therefore not part of God's promise to Abraham – then what of lawful title to land within the boundaries of the Jordan? Surely the basis of landed inheritance inside the Promised Land would also be based on military conquest. Yet it is unheard of for any commentator to discuss the jubilee year in terms of its historical basis: the distribution of spoils after the military conquest of Canaan.[12] This is why the jubilee inheri-

12. Robert North's seemingly exhaustive and mentally exhausting study, *Sociology*

tance laws are so frequently misinterpreted, including their various applications to areas completely outside of the jubilee land law's agricultural frame of reference.

Genocide and Burnt Offerings

For the Israelites to inherit the land, they were required to kill everyone who had previously occupied the land. "And thou shalt consume all the people which the LORD thy God shall deliver thee; thine eye shall have no pity upon them: neither shalt thou serve their gods; for that will be a snare unto thee" (Deut. 7:16a). Note that the key issue was theology: the gods of the land's previous owners. The people of Israel were to be kept away from these alien gods.

God required a bloody burnt sacrifice as the covenantal foundation of the national inheritance: the genocide of the residents of Jericho and the city's subsequent burning. This mandatory ritual sacrifice[13] was to be followed by the total annihilation of all other residents of the Promised Land. To the degree that the Israelites in any way pitied the existing inhabitants, they would thereby compromise their inheritance. They would have to share the land with others.

Recent commentators have attempted to apply the jubilee laws to the modern world as if these laws had not been grounded in genocide. The original promise had been given to Abraham, but it was conditional on the heirs' continuation of the ritual of circumcision: a bloody rite symbolizing the cutting off of a man's biological heirs. This is why the generation of the conquest had to be circumcised before the conquest could begin (Josh. 5). Commentators who do not trace the origin of the

---

of the Biblical Jubilee (Rome: Pontifical Biblical Institute, 1954), is a good example of modern scholarship. Based on higher critical assumptions and methodology, it never mentions the jubilee in relation to the conquest of the land.

13. Achan and his entire family, including their animals, were executed for his having thwarted this required burnt offering. See North, *Boundaries and Dominion*, Appendix A: "Sacrilege and Sanctions."

jubilee to the Israelites' genocidal conquest of the land also refuse to discuss the jubilee in terms of the unique, one-time nature of the conquest and the subsequent distribution of military spoils. To discuss the jubilee laws without also discussing the God-mandated genocide that implemented these laws is the equivalent of discussing the Christian ideal of heaven without discussing the cross, hell, and the lake of fire. The legal issue is the same: eternal genocide and eternal burnt offerings – not *by* covenant-breakers; rather, *of* covenant-breakers.[14]

Dominion, Ownership, and Rest

Notice the phrase, "The LORD your God hath given you rest, and hath given you this land" (Josh. 1:13b). *Rest was associated with lawful inheritance.* These two and a half tribes had fought and won their land outside of the Promised Land, but they would now have to fight and win again in order to seal their lawful inheritance: "Until the LORD have given your brethren rest, as he hath given you" (Josh. 1:15a). *To seal the tribal promise, there had to be a national victory.* Only a comprehensive military victory would bring the nation the rest that would become the basis of tribal inheritance. *Only on the basis of military peace can private property be secured.* This is an eschatological reality: when the implements of war disappear, God's covenant people will then possess lawful title to their property in peace. This can come only when nations universally conform themselves to the terms of God's covenant law (Mic. 4:1-4).

There are three primary goals of war: victory (dominion), spoils (inheritance), and peace (rest). The greatest of these is peace, if the peace is secured on God's terms. Permanent peace can be attained only when the law-order of the victors replaces the law-order of the losers. Victor's justice is the only form of justice after the war ends. But without a change in law, there

14. Gary North, "Publisher's Epilogue," in David Chilton, *The Great Tribulation* (Ft. Worth, Texas: Dominion Press, 1987).

has been no victory. There has only been assimilation by the defeated culture.[15] Legal scholar Harold Berman has put it well: without a change in law, there is no revolution, only a successful *coup* or rebellion.[16] It takes more than one generation to produce a genuine revolution, he says.[17] In Israel, it took two generations: the generation of the exodus, all but two of whom died in the wilderness, and the generation of the heirs, 40 years spent growing up in the wilderness. Because God ordered the total annihilation of the Canaanites, this revolution in law was not supposed to take another generation. Canaan could not be persuaded by the law, so it was to be destroyed by the law's designated sanctioning agent: the land itself, operating through the nation of Israel. God's grace to the Israelites mandated His wrath to the Canaanites.

All three goals – victory, spoils, and peace – were encapsulated in the conquest of Canaan. The conquest of Canaan did not rival the exodus as the archetype of God's dealings with His people, but it did govern that most crucial aspect of a rural civilization: the inheritance of land. The specific terms of land ownership and inheritance in Israel, which in turn established the judicial basis of citizenship, did not derive from the Old Covenant era prior to the exodus, but were announced after the exodus and were ratified in history by the conquest.

The Demographics of the Jubilee Inheritance Law

The year of jubilee nullified all existing rural land lease contracts. On what legal basis? *Assertion of original title*. God, as the primary owner, transferred the leaseholds back to the heirs of the original conquering families. God, as the primary owner

---

15. The classic examples of this in Western European history were the military victories by the Goths over Rome. The Goths were steadily assimilated both theologically and judicially by the Christian order that had prevailed in Rome.

16. Harold J. Berman, *Law and Revolution: The Formation of the Western Legal Tradition* (Cambridge, Massachusetts: Harvard University Press, 1983), pp. 19-20.

17. *Ibid.*, p. 20.

of the land, announced in advance of the conquest the terms of His leasehold contracts. These leases were to be periodically re-established with members of the families of the original invasion and conquest. There could be no other lawful basis of inheritance in the Promised Land. Eventually, a future generation of those families whose members were unwise enough not to honor these terms would find itself dispossessed through captivity (Lev. 26:33-35).

The terms of the leases created a monopoly of family ownership. No foreigner prior to the exile could ever hope to establish a landed inheritance outside of a walled city except by adoption into an Israelite family. This law tended to keep foreigners inside cities. They would have been restricted to such occupations as merchants, craftsmen, and bankers. They could become landed heirs outside the cities only through adoption by an existing Israelite family.[18] On the other hand, they themselves could become the inherited property of Israelites, for the jubilee land law established permanent, inter-generational chattel slavery for foreigners (Lev. 25:44-46). The jubilee laws therefore made it difficult for foreigners to achieve a permanent cultural presence in the land. It kept them as outsiders, except as temporary leaseholders, hired workers, slaves, and residents of walled cities.

Population Growth

Simultaneously, the jubilee inheritance law created demographic pressure for expansion beyond the boundaries of the Promised Land. No commentator ever discusses this obvious aspect of the jubilee. First, Mosaic law established the possibility of zero miscarriages: "There shall nothing cast their young, nor be barren, in thy land: the number of thy days I will fulfil" (Ex. 23:26). It therefore established the possibility of high birth

18. This included adoption through marriage for women, as the cases of Rahab and Ruth indicate.

rates. Second, it established the possibility of longer life spans: "Honour thy father and thy mother: that thy days may be long upon the land which the LORD thy God giveth thee" (Ex. 20:12). Third, the law allowed the adoption by Israelites of circumcised foreigners, a practice that had taken place widely in Egypt before the persecutions began.[19] This was a covenantal formula for blessings that would produce "explosively" high population growth.[20] The rapid population growth they had experienced in Egypt, which had so terrified the Pharaoh of the oppression (Ex. 1:7-10), was the model.

When a high population growth rate is combined with a fixed supply of land, societies become progressively urbanized and progressively engaged in foreign trade. The model in the early modern period of Europe is the tiny nation of the Netherlands. The twentieth-century model is the even tinier nation of Hong Kong.[21] If residents of a small, formerly rural nation are unwilling to become urbanized, they must emigrate to less densely populated nations. The land at home fills up.

Small Farms and Large Families

In ancient Israel, the land was to be transferred back to the original families. The geographically bounded nation was small when they invaded, yet they came in with at least two million people. There were 601,730 adult males at the time of the conquest (Num. 26:51), plus 23,000 Levites (Num. 26:62). Since this was approximately the same number that had come out of Egypt (Ex. 12:37), there had been no population growth for 40 years. This meant that they were reproducing at the replacement rate level: 2.1 children per family. (Some children do not

---

19. Gary North, *Moses and Pharaoh: Dominion Religion vs. Power Religion* (Tyler, Texas: Institute for Christian Economics, 1985), pp. 23-25.

20. Populations do not explode except when bombed. The language of modern growth theory has attached the metaphor of explosives to the metaphor of growth.

21. Alvin Rabushka, *Hong Kong: A Study in Economic Freedom* (University of Chicago Press, 1979).

marry, which is why the replacement rate is not 2.0 children.) So, there must have been about 2.4 million people at the time of the exodus: two adult parents and about two children per family.[22]

They entered a land of about six and a half million acres.[23] This meant that the average family, had there been no cities, would have owned about 11 acres.[24] Not all of this land was arable. Some of it was taken up by cities, where the Levites lived. Over time, the number of acres per "nuclear" family unit[25] would have declined as population rose. If Israel had remained faithful to God's law, miscarriages would have ceased. The early Egypt-era rate of growth of Israelite nuclear families would have resumed. No nuclear family could have inherited more than a declining number of acres as time went on. Eventually, no farm would have been large enough to support all the heirs.

Consider a rate of population growth of 3 percent per annum, which has been sustained by many agricultural nations in the twentieth century. This rate of increase would have doubled the size of the population in a quarter of a century.[26] By the first jubilee, the average farm would have been down to just under three acres (11 divided by 4). By the second jubilee, the average farm would have been under .7 acre. And so on.

This would have forced the creation of extended family agricultural corporations, with one or two nuclear families (or

---

22. North, *Moses and Pharaoh*, ch. 1.

23. The land was no more than 10,330 square miles. Barry J. Beitzel, *The Moody Atlas of Bible Lands* (Chicago: Moody Press, 1985), p. 25. There are 640 acres per square mile. This means 6,661,200 acres.

24. 6,661,200 acres divided by 601,730 families = 10.98 acres per family. This was comparable to the 4 to 15 acres owned by the average Roman farmer around 200 B.C. "Agriculture, history of," *Software Toolworks Illustrated Encyclopedia* (1990). This is *Grolier's Encyclopedia* on a CD-ROM disk.

25. Contrasted with the extended family.

26. This is based on the "law of 73": divide the annual rate of growth into 73 in order to discover the doubling period.

even foreign sharecroppers) running the farm in the name of the extended family's members, most of whom would have moved to cities or abroad. There would be no mass exodus back to the original family plots of the conquest era. Only moral rebellion could have kept the land of Israel sufficiently empty of residents to have allowed each family's return to the family plot.

Any discussion of this law as if it were a way to maintain small family farms must discuss in detail how very small these farms would have been within a century or two of rapid population growth. The point is, this law did not guarantee the continuation of agricultural life for a significant percentage of the population. There was no way for any law to assure such a way of life to a growing population in a very small nation. What the jubilee inheritance law did was *to cut off all reasonable hope that a family had any economic future in farming*, except in those periods in which the nation was in rebellion, when God would respond by sending plagues, famines, miscarriages, and other negative demographic sanctions. But in such deplorable ethical conditions, it would have been highly unlikely that the jubilee inheritance law would have been honored anyway. The system of covenantal law and covenantal sanctions in Mosaic Israel points to a conclusion that the commentators never mention: *the anti-rural implications of the Mosaic law*. It did not despise farming; it simply made clear that hardly anyone in a God-honoring society is expected to be a full-time farmer. The urban family garden, not the family farm, is the biblical ideal.[27]

---

27. When Wilhelm Röpke was visited by a free market economist, the visitor pointed to Röpke's traditional Swiss garden and said: "That is an inefficient way to produce food." Röpke's answer was classic: "It is an efficient way to produce men." I was told this story by Patrick Boarman, who studied under Röpke and translated his *Economics of the Free Society* (Chicago: Regnery, 1963) into English. I do not know if this visitor was Ludwig von Mises, as Russell Kirk claims it was in his Foreword to the re-issue of Röpke's 1942 book, *The Social Crisis of Our Time* (New Brunswick, New Jersey: Transaction, 1992), p. ix.

Declining Per Capita Farm Income

The jubilee inheritance law was a way to guarantee every head of household a small and declining share of income from a family farm. Most heirs would have become urban residents in Israel or emigrants to other nations. The promise of God regarding population growth – being fruitful and multiplying – was a guarantee that covenantal faithfulness would lower the proportion of per capita family income derived from farming. The law made it plain to everyone except modern Bible commentators that if the nation's numbers grew as a result of God's blessing, Israelites could place little hope in the possibility of supporting themselves financially as farmers. Far from being a guarantor of egalitarianism, *the jubilee inheritance law was a law forcing covenant-keeping people into the cities or out of the nation.*

Real estate located inside walled cities did not come under this law. Neither did property owned or leased outside the boundaries of Israel. This law warned them that *a covenantally faithful nation would become an urbanized nation and/or a nation of emigrants*. The law made it plain that their lives as farmers could continue only if they were not faithful to God's law. If the nation remained primarily agricultural, this was God's visible curse against them.

The jubilee land inheritance law was designed to force the Israelites to plan for a very different future. They were to become city dwellers as a people within the Promised Land, and traders, bankers, and skilled manufacturers outside the land. There could be no legitimate hope in remaining farmers in the Promised Land. The boundaries of the land were fixed; their population size was not. There would eventually have to be expansion beyond the boundaries of Israel, and there would have to be a concentration of population in Israel's cities. Like the garden east of Eden, the family-owned gardens of Israel would be temporary dwelling places of preliminary training for worldwide dominion. The faster the population grew, the faster their life as farmers and animal herders would disappear. What the West has experienced since the late eighteenth century is what God had in mind for Israel from the time of the conquest, namely, *rapid growth* – of population, cities, specialization, manufacturing, trade, emigration, and per capita wealth. To the extent that they did not experience this, they would know that they were under God's national curse.

The jubilee inheritance law was designed to promote emigration out of Israel and urban occupations inside the land that relied on foreign trade. The rural land inheritance law promoted contact with foreigners. This was an aspect of the dominion covenant. It was to serve as a means of evangelism. The story of Israel, her laws, and her God was to spread abroad (Deut. 4:5-8). The jubilee law was in no sense a law mandating the State-enforced equalization of wealth, contrary to that peculiar late-twentieth-century theology known as liberation theology (socialism for evangelical Christians).[28]

Aliens and Inalienable Land

We can discover the fundamental jubilee principle by beginning with God's own statement regarding the reason for the jubilee law: "The land shall not be sold for ever: for the land is mine; for ye are strangers and sojourners with me" (Lev. 25:23). Problem: God owns all the earth, then and now. "For every beast of the forest is mine, and the cattle upon a thousand hills" (Ps. 50:10). Yet this very ownership of the world is what led to the special position of the land of Canaan and its conquerors: "Now therefore, if ye will obey my voice indeed, and keep my covenant, then ye shall be a peculiar treasure unto me above all people: for all the earth is mine: And ye shall be unto me a kingdom of priests, and an holy nation. These are the words which thou shalt speak unto the children of Israel" (Ex. 19:5-6). It was the Israelites, and *only* the Israelites, who

28. North, *Boundaries and Dominion*, ch. 25, section on "The Myth of Jubilee Egalitarianism."

were to be owners of rural land in Israel – not the immigrant stranger, and surely not the Canaanite.

Only the Israelites were strangers and sojourners with God. Therefore, for as long as God dwelled uniquely in the land, only His covenant people were allowed to remain agricultural owners. They would police the land's boundaries, keeping strangers out except on God's terms: inside walled cities, inside Israelite households as slaves, as leaseholders, and as free agricultural laborers. Far from being sojourners in the sense of "wanderers in the land," Israelites were to become the only permanent owners of rural land. They would be strangers and wanderers outside the Promised Land, but permanent owners inside. The Promised Land was to serve as "home base" in a worldwide program of trade and evangelism. To be a perfect stranger to the covenant-breaking world outside the geographical boundaries of Israel, one had to be: 1) a covenanted member of an Israelite family that had participated in the conquest, or 2) an adopted member of a walled city's tribe. This was the meaning of "strangers and sojourners with me": strangers to the world but perpetual land owners inside rural Israel. Then as now, the concept of *stranger* was an inescapable concept. A person was either a stranger *with* God or a stranger *from* God. The physical mark of circumcision and lawful inheritance inside Israel identified a man as being a stranger with God.

So, God set apart the Promised Land as His holy dwelling place. He sanctified it. He placed boundaries around it. Thus, the fundamental covenantal principle of the jubilee law was holiness: the separation of *covenantally unequal* people from each other.

The Principle of Inequality

God established His people as owners of the land through an historically and judicially unique program of genocide. The covenantal principle of the jubilee is simple: those who worshipped false gods within the geographical boundaries of Israel could not own agricultural land. The original Canaanites had to be killed, God insisted, while future immigrants from pagan nations would have to be confined geographically. For as long as they dwelt within the land's geographical boundaries under the terms of the original distribution, Israelites had to keep strangers from inheriting agricultural land. Strangers could inherit houses only inside walled cities. The walls were symbols of the covenantal restraints on them. They could also lawfully be enslaved on a permanent basis if they ever sold themselves to an Israelite family. This means that the primary economic concern of the jubilee laws was not the equalization of property, or even equality of opportunity; it was, on the contrary, the establishment of the principle of *inequality of opportunity* for those outside the covenant.

The economic principle is clear: those who did not worship the God of the Bible, as well as the heirs of those who had not proven their devotion to God by participating in national genocide, had to be restricted economically (no landed inheritance) or geographically (inside walls). There was a corollary: the vast majority of the covenantally faithful nation would eventually move into walled cities, which would have made it less likely that strangers would become economically influential there. *The fundamental economic principle of the jubilee laws was that those outside the covenants – civil, familial, and ecclesiastical – should be kept economically and numerically subordinate to those inside the covenants.*[29] But this raises a fundamental question: How can we apply these jubilee principles in New Covenant times?

Citizenship

In ancient Israel, citizenship was by formal covenant.[30] It was not by property ownership. The stranger could be circum-

---

29. They were always subordinate politically: North, *Political Polytheism*, ch. 2: "Sanctuary and Suffrage."

30. *Idem.*

cised, but he could not inherit rural land. He could therefore not become a judge in the Promised Land as a member of the congregation unless he was adopted into an Israelite tribe (walled city) or family. Only if adopted could he become eligible to serve in God's holy army, which was the mark of citizenship.

The strangers' economic and cultural influence was to be offset by a growing concentration of Israelites living in walled cities. The walled cities were places of refuge for immigrants (as cities become in nations that open their borders to immigrants), but walled cities were not to become strongholds of foreign influence, either political or economic. Any city in Israel that covenanted with a foreign god was to be totally destroyed (Deut. 13:12-17).

The interactions between foreign cultures (plural) and domestic culture (singular) would take place mainly in the walled cities of Israel and in the commercial cities of other societies. The kingdom (civilization) of God was to overwhelm the kingdoms of all other gods. Cities would be the places where the confrontation between God's kingdom and all others would take place. The jubilee inheritance law, when coupled with a rising Israelite population, insured that there would be a strong and growing presence of covenant-keepers in the walled cities of Israel. This reinforced a fundamental principle of the Mosaic law: the geographical holiness of Israel.[31]

The Promise of Sanctuary

The law required that "ye shall return every man to his possession, and ye shall return every man unto his family" (Lev. 25:10b). This was why it was illegal to enslave an Israelite permanently. *The family plots served as legal sanctuaries*. An Israelite's legal claim to eventual freedom and his legal claim to landed inheritance were both aspects of the same covenantal grant. An Israelite could not legally alienate his freedom, his heirs' free-

31. North, *Boundaries and Dominion*, ch. 25, section on "Geographical Holiness."

dom, or his share in the land.[32] Civil freedom and rural land ownership were linked. Any unwillingness on the part of the civil magistrates to enforce the jubilee land laws was implicitly *a denial of sanctuary* to the heirs of the Abrahamic promise and also a denial of the original terms of the conquest.

The legal justification for the right of the Israelites to buy resident aliens on a permanent basis (Lev. 25:44-46) was the fact that resident aliens were not citizens of the commonwealth. They could not serve as civil judges or as warriors in God's holy army. They were outside the civil covenant. They were guaranteed sanctuary from pagan lands, but not sanctuary within the land. They could be sold into slavery to pay their debts, including especially debts to victims of their crimes.[33] Their heirs – the fruit of their loins – were sold with them.[34]

A family's original grant of land at the time of the conquest established a legal claim to sanctuary from permanent enslavement for its heirs. The land was holy, sanctified by God's presence. The Israelites were holy, sanctified by God's promise to Abraham and also by their obedience to the requirement of the covenant: circumcision.[35] The family plots were sanctuaries, sanctified by God's original ownership of the land and by the terms of his leasehold with Israel at the time of the conquest.

When Jesus declared the jubilee fulfilled by Him (Luke 4:18-21), He granted universal sanctuary. The land of Israel would no longer serve as a place of sanctuary in history, sanctified by the special presence of God. The kingdom of God has become

---

32. The one exception involved the transfer of ownership to a priest (Lev. 27:20-21). See Chapter 37.

33. It was therefore very risky for foreigners to commit major crimes in Israel. Making restitution could lead to his children's permanent enslavement if the criminal could not buy his way out before he died.

34. Adult male children of pagans presumably were not sold into slavery with their parents. Neither were their married daughters or their aged parents. Adults had already established separate family jurisdictions. But those children who were still under the covenantal jurisdiction of alien parents went into bondage with them.

35. The promise was obviously conditional.

the New Covenant's place of sanctuary – not merely the institutional church, but the civilization of God. The whole world of paganism is required by God to seek sanctuary in Christ's church. This substitution of a new sanctuary annulled the jubilee land laws, and thereby also annulled the jubilee's permanent slave law.

The alternative to this interpretation of the New Covenant is the long-held defense of slavery made by Christian commentators. Their interpretation – never explicit but necessarily implicit – is that the annulment of the jubilee land laws did not also annul the slave law. This leads to the conclusion that God's law no longer makes provision for those seeking geographical sanctuary. In other words, when national Israel ceased to offer sanctuary to the lost or the righteous foreigner, geographical sanctuary ceased in history. The argument runs as follows: "The Israelites no longer possessed a guarantee of jubilee liberty; therefore, the liberty announced by Christ must have constituted the annulment of Mosaic liberty. God has annulled the land-sanctuary-liberty connection, but nothing has taken its place. Thus, slavery is validated as a universal institution."

The only New Testament-based alternative to this unpleasant interpretation is to conclude that liberty has been validated by the work of Jesus Christ, and the mark of this validation is the abolition of slavery in Christian nations. The church has never publicly acknowledged the abolitionist implications of Jesus' fulfillment of the jubilee law. His announcement was not, to my knowledge, ever cited by any abolitionist of the late eighteenth and nineteenth centuries. But after 1780, pressure to abolish slavery increased within many Anglo-Saxon Protestant churches located outside of the slave-owning regions. By the end of the 1880's, slavery had been abolished in the West.

Meanwhile, national sanctuaries for the oppressed and poor were opened: free emigration and immigration. But after World War I, this open access was steadily closed by legislation. Immigration barriers were erected everywhere. The modern passport is one of humanism's important covenantal marks: a progressive contraction of international sanctuaries. Political liberals as well as political conservatives have affirmed the legitimacy of these immigration barriers.[36] When nations are no longer covenantally Christian, i.e., when they adopt religious pluralism and other marks of citizenship besides church membership, and when they replace voluntary charity with welfare State entitlements, the Christian evangelist's call to the lost in the name of Christ steadily fades. "Come unto me, all ye that labor and are heavy laden, and I will give you rest" is replaced by "Keep out those welfare-seeking bums!" Finally, when mandatory identification cards are issued by the State to every resident in order to "reduce welfare fraud," all remaining sanctuaries tend to disappear: in churches, regions, and families.

Land Ownership by Foreigners: Then and Now

Under the initial distribution of the land under Joshua, no non-citizen could own rural land. Not every citizen had to own rural land – most notably, a circumcised immigrant or his heir who was eligible to serve in the army – but every rural land owner had to be a citizen.

The primary legal issue for rural land ownership in Mosaic Israel was adoption, not confession. Both the confessing resident alien [*geyr*] and the non-confessing resident alien [*nokree*] could buy inheritable residential real estate inside walled cities. Confession had nothing to do with urban residential ownership. On the other hand, covenant-keeping converts to the faith had no access to rural land ownership apart from their adoption into a family of the conquest generation. The resident alien's orthodox confession had nothing to do with inalienable rural ownership except insofar as such confession was necessary for legal adoption into an Israelite family.

36. The ultimate immigration barrier is abortion.

Then there was Ezekiel's prophecy of a new law that would prevail after their return to the land: "So shall ye divide this land unto you according to the tribes of Israel. And it shall come to pass, that ye shall divide it by lot for an inheritance unto you, and to the strangers that sojourn among you, which shall beget children among you: and they shall be unto you as born in the country among the children of Israel; they shall have inheritance with you among the tribes of Israel. And it shall come to pass, that in what tribe the stranger sojourneth, there shall ye give him his inheritance, saith the Lord GOD" (Ezek. 47:21-23). The old prohibition against land ownership by the circumcised resident alien ended after the exile. This had nothing to do with marriage to an Israelite. The circumcised stranger was the covenantally faithful resident alien [*geyr*], the one from whom it was illegal to take interest (Lev. 25:35-37), not the resident who was not part of the covenant [*nokree*] from whom it was legal to take interest (Deut. 23:20).

The civil enforcement of property rights to land in the New Covenant era has nothing to do with either theological confession or bodily residence. The jubilee land laws of Israel have all been annulled. They were never cross-boundary laws; they applied only to the land and heirs of the conquest. No judicial appeal to any of those laws is valid today. Those who appeal to them risk placing us in bondage: the revival of permanent chattel slavery or the imposition of permanent slavery to the messianic welfare State (liberation theology).

Conclusion

The jubilee year began with the day of atonement. This was a day of public submission to God, invoking His grace: a positive sanction. The judicial issue of the day of atonement was man's subordination to God. There could be no profit-seeking work on that day. Men had to rest contentedly in God's grace.

The jubilee year was the culmination of the cycle of sabbatical years. Sabbatical years were mandated by God in order to train landless Israelites and poor strangers how to produce for a market. The Mosaic law identified harvesters as landless or impoverished people who worked as harvesters or gleaners in six years out of seven. In sabbatical years, they became dependent on whatever it was that God would allow the fields to produce apart from cultivation. In those years, harvesters learned to make decisions without a land owner or his supervisor ruling over them.

The jubilee inheritance law applied to rural land inside the boundaries of Israel. It did not apply to houses within the walled cities of the nation except Levitical cities (Lev. 25:32-33). It also did not apply to property outside the Promised Land. This law had been given to the people by God because He was the owner of the land (Lev. 25:23). It was part of the terms of God's lease under which they held rights of administration as sharecropping tenants, with 10 percent of any increase owed to God through the Levites and priests. It was also part of the spoils of war.

A Question of Sanctification

God is owner of all the earth, not just the Promised Land. Why did the jubilee laws not apply to all other nations? Because these laws applied only to His special dwelling place. They were an aspect of God's holiness, which is why the jubilee laws appear in Leviticus, the book of holiness. The Promised Land was to be kept holy: set apart judicially from all other nations. How? Initially, this separation began with God's promise to Abraham: definitive holiness, i.e., definitive sanctification.

The second phase of the process of separation began with the conquest: progressive holiness, i.e., progressive sanctification. God cleansed the land of His enemies by means of total war: the annihilation of His enemies. He required the extermination of the gods of Canaan by means of an original program of genocide. He promised to dwell in the land that contained the tabernacle and temple; He would not permit any other god to be worshipped publicly in Israel. Thus, the gods of the land had to be removed from public view. To achieve this initially, the Israelites were told by God to exterminate or drive out every person dwelling in the land. Only Rahab and her family would be allowed by God to escape this judgment, for she had established a pre-invasion covenant with God.[37]

Third, His holiness was to be defended by enforcing a law that kept post-conquest immigrants from ever owning property in Israel except inside Israel's walled cities. The families of the conquest received an inheritable lease that could not be alienated beyond 49 years. Later immigrants could sublease rural property if they were sufficiently productive, but they could not leave an inheritance beyond the jubilee year.

Fourth, God established a law that removed from the majority of the population any legitimate hope of remaining farmers in Israel if His blessings were forthcoming in response to their covenantal faithfulness as a nation. They surely knew that, as Israel's population expanded, no branch of any extended family could retain economic control over of a particular plot of rural land apart from the compliance of all the other members of the family, except perhaps as a small recreational property (a consumer good). If they wanted income from the land, they could attain it only through its productivity. Small, isolated plots are not very productive. If they wanted to maximize their passive income from their portion of the extended family's land, they would have to cooperate with other members of the extended family in selecting representative managers, either from within the extended family or from outside its legal boundaries. If any nuclear family unit wanted to farm all of the

37. It is worth noting that members of Rahab's family never formally voiced their individual support of this covenant, but by remaining silent before she made it, when the civil authorities had questioned her regarding the spies (Josh. 2:3), they became lawful residents of Israel through their adherence to the external demands of Rahab's covenant. If they remained inside their section of the wall, despite the collapse of the remainder of the wall, they could remain in the Promised Land (2:19).

original "eleven acres" for the others, it would have to meet the competition of any other members of the extended family who might offer to serve as the family's representatives on the farm.

Fifth, wealthy immigrants and strangers in the land would have tended to dwell in walled cities, where they could own homes. This is where the population of the Israelites was intended by God to be channeled over time. This process was intended to keep strangers and foreigners from gaining too much influence in the cities. They would have been outnumbered by immigrants from rural areas.

Sixth, God kept the geographically dispersed family of the Levites from gaining political control through land purchases. Their cross-tribal boundary judicial influence had to be advisory. The jubilee land law made it impossible for Levites to centralize land ownership in Israel. They could only rarely inherit rural land (Lev. 27:20-21).[38] But to make sure that they would not abandon their support of the jubilee year because of their desire to inherit rural land, they were given jubilee privileges in the cities: reversion in the jubilee year (Lev. 25:32-33). When enforced, this aspect of the jubilee land laws would have tended to confine their political power to cities, but it also balanced the jubilee law's economic costs and benefits for them. Over time, their influence would grow with the population, as more people congregated in cities, assuming that they could find ways of maintaining the people's theological allegiance in a progressively urbanized culture. Ultimately, the cities would have become economically dominant, and therefore politically dominant, just as they have become all over the world in modern times. But the Levites were not supposed to centralize political and economic power during the rural phase of the Israelite kingdom.

The primary covenantal issue of the jubilee laws was holiness. The jubilee inheritance law had little or nothing to do with assuring economic equality, except in times of national

38. Chapter 37.

covenantal cursing: stagnant population. The law had everything to do with the mandating of political and cultural *inequality*: giving a permanent head start to heirs of the conquest over immigrants, even those immigrants who became members of the covenant through circumcision, but not members of land-inheriting families. Only through adoption, either directly or through marriage (for females), could immigrants gain this advantage.

26

ECONOMIC OPPRESSION BY MEANS OF THE STATE

And if thou sell ought unto thy neighbour, or buyest ought of thy neighbour's hand, ye shall not oppress one another: According to the number of years after the jubile thou shalt buy of thy neighbour, and according unto the number of years of the fruits he shall sell unto thee: According to the multitude of years thou shalt increase the price thereof, and according to the fewness of years thou shalt diminish the price of it: for according to the number of the years of the fruits doth he sell unto thee. Ye shall not therefore oppress one another; but thou shalt fear thy God: for I am the Lord *your God (Lev. 25:14-17).*

The theocentric message of this passage is that God is not an oppressor. Though He is the author of the law, as well as the final judge, He does not use His authority to do injustice. He does not seek unfair advantage. Neither should those who act in His name as His stewards.

In buying and selling, both parties were required to honor the limiting factor of the jubilee year. This raises important questions. First, what is oppression, biblically speaking? Second, is oppression here merely the failure to write contracts whose provisions ended with the advent of the jubilee year? Third, did this warning refer only to rural land sales?

The context indicates that rural land was the thing being bought and sold. But the legal restriction on the leasing of land would also have applied to the leasing of men. If, for example, an Israelite was sold into bondage because of his failure to repay a business debt, his term of servitude could not extend beyond the jubilee year.[1] The law required that "ye shall return every man to his possession, and ye shall return every man unto his family" (Lev. 25:10b). Business debt could not be collateralized by land or servitude beyond the jubilee.

The first question is more difficult to answer. What is *oppression* in this context? Has it anything to do with pricing? The text indicates that it has everything to do with the *period of time* in which the terms of the contract will apply. Time has something to do with pricing, but what? "According to the multitude of years thou shalt increase the price thereof." The question arises: Increase the price from what? What were the *price floor* and *price ceiling* that governed the pricing of additional years? How were they established? To answer these questions in the absence of historical records, we need to understand something about modern capital theory.

Pricing a Factor of Production

The text speaks of *the years of the fruits*. "According to the number of years after the jubile thou shalt buy of thy neighbour, and according unto the number of years of the fruits he shall sell unto thee" (v. 15). This is a very important economic concept. Capital theory is dependent on it. Land and labor produce fruit over time. This is what makes land and labor valuable. Modern economic theory, beginning with the marginalist revolution of the early 1870's,[2] attempts to explain the

1. If he was being sold to repay a zero-interest charitable loan, his term of servitude could not extend beyond the sabbatical year (Deut. 15:12).

2. The simultaneous and independent work of William Stanley Jevons, Leon Walras, and Carl Menger. See *The Marginalist Revolution in Economics: Interpretation*

relationship between the market value of the fruits of production and the market value of the economic inputs that produce these fruits.

What does modern economic theory teach? First and foremost, it teaches that all economic value is *subjective value*. Economic value is imputed, i.e., it is subjectively determined. Economic value is not the product of labor; on the contrary, labor is valuable because of the value of labor's output.[3] Economic value is also not the product of objective costs of production. The classical economists, from Adam Smith to Karl Marx and John Stuart Mill, argued for objective value theory – labor theory of value or cost-of-production theory of value – but the marginalist or subjectivist revolution rejected this approach to value theory.[4] The classical economists did not trace market exchange, production, and the formation of prices solely to the actions of consumers. They did not construct a general theory of value.[5]

Consumer Sovereignty[6]

The subjectivists concluded that economic inputs possess value only in relation to the value of their output. The question immediately arises: *Value to whom?* Concluded the subjectivists:

---

and Evaluation, edited by R. D. Collison Black, *et al.* (Durham, North Carolina: Duke University Press, 1973).

3. Any scarce economic resource with a market price is in part the product of labor. If it is not yet the product of labor, such as a waterfall, it will have to have labor (including intellectual labor) added to it before its fruits can be appropriated. Before any asset can be appropriated and used by an owner, he must perform some kind of labor.

4. Mark Skousen, *The Structure of Production* (New York: New York University Press, 1990), ch. 2.

5. Ludwig von Mises, *Human Action: A Treatise on Economics* (New Haven, Connecticut: Yale University Press, 1949), p. 63.

6. The phrase is generally attributed to W. H. Hutt. Hutt, "The Nature of Aggressive Selling" (1935), in *Individual Freedom: Selected Works of William H. Hutt*, edited by Svetozar Pejovich and David Klingaman (Westport, Connecticut: Greenwood Press, 1975), p. 185.

value is imputed subjectively by an imputing agent – the consumer – to the fruits of production. The persons who are the last to acquire anything are called *consumers*. If all potential consumers refuse to pay for some asset's fruits of production, these fruits have no economic value.[7] Neither will the specific factor of production, assuming that all producers recognize that no future consumer will pay for this output. Thus, "The consumers determine ultimately not only the prices of the consumers' goods, but no less the prices of all factors of production."[8] Regarding capital goods, Mises wrote: "The prices of the goods of higher orders are ultimately determined by the prices of the goods of the first or lowest order, that is, the consumers' goods. As a consequence of this dependence they are ultimately determined by the subjective valuations of all members of the market society."[9] This is why he concluded: "The pricing process is a social process."[10]

But don't producers have more money than consumers? Can't they impose their will on consumers? On the contrary, producers have far less money than consumers, which is why producers are vulnerable to shifts in consumer demand. Producers own inventories of highly specialized consumer goods and even more specialized producer goods (capital equipment). Consumers own the most marketable commodity, money. They have the competitive advantage. Think of a producer of shoes. If consumers decide they do not like the style of these shoes, what can the producer do with these shoes? Spend a fortune on advertising to change consumers' minds? I am in the advertis-

---

7. In another place, I have discussed why value theory in economics requires the doctrine of an imputing sovereign God in order to avoid the incoherence produced by pure subjectivism's theory of autonomous man. See Gary North, *The Dominion Covenant: Genesis* (2nd ed.; Tyler, Texas: Institute for Christian Economics, 1987), ch. 4: "Economic Value: Objective and Subjective."

8. Mises, *Human Action*, p. 271.

9. *Ibid.*, p. 330.

10. *Ibid.*, p. 335.

ing business; let me assure you, most producers do not have sufficient funds to change the minds of many consumers.[11] All the shoe manufacturer can do is lower the price of his inventory, even if he does not regain his costs of production. After all, some income is better than no income. Some money is better than a pile of unsold shoes that must be stored somewhere.

Consumers can buy many things with their inventory of unspecialized money; producers cannot buy many things with their inventory of specialized goods. This is why consumers are *economically sovereign* over producers, even though consumers and producers are equally sovereign legally. The hierarchy of control under capitalism is economic. Consumers "hold the hammer": money (the most marketable commodity) plus the legal authority to buy or not to buy from any producer.

Market theory rests on the insight that the consumer is *economically* sovereign, even though the owner of a tool of production is *legally* sovereign. The owner lawfully can do whatever he pleases with his property, so long as he does not physically injure someone else, but *he cannot thwart the consumer at zero cost.* If he thwarts the demand of the highest-bidding consumer by not selling the capital good's final output to him, he thereby forfeits the extra amount of money which that consumer would have paid him. The owner's inventory cost is not just the cost of storage and insurance, but also the forfeited income.[12]

In the expectation that a particular piece of capital equipment will produce something of value to future consumers – something they will pay for – producers today impute value to capital equipment. They do the same with land, labor, and raw materials. *They do this as present economic agents of future consumers.* The sovereign consumers in a supplier's plans are not present

11. The classic example is Ford Motor Company's introduction of the Edsel automobile, 1958-60. Ford could not sell enough cars to make a profit.

12. The cost of production is not an aspect of economic cost. What is spent is spent: sunk costs. Once spent, the producer's past costs are irrelevant to the crucial question: What can I get for my stock of goods?

consumers, for production is always aimed at the future. *The consumers who control production are in the minds of the producers.* A particular producer – the capitalist entrepreneur – may discover later that the actual consumers do not act in the way that his mental consumers did. He will then suffer losses, either because he has to sell his output for less per unit than he planned, in order to unload his inventory, or else he sells it at the expected price per unit, but then discovers that he could have charged more.[13] In either case, he experiences a loss. The ability to impose this loss is the consumer's "hammer." Consumers, not producers, impute economic value to consumer goods; this act of imputation extends to producer goods and raw materials.[14]

An Expected Stream of Net Income

When a person purchases a piece of property, he is buying legal ownership over what the text in Leviticus calls the years of its fruitfulness. The buyer is buying an expected *stream of production* when he buys a piece of land, but he cannot know for sure that this stream of income will persist in the future. As Knight wrote in 1933, "The basic economic magnitude (value or utility) is service, not good. It is inherently a stream or flow in time. . . ."[15] To put it bluntly, *streams can dry up.*

---

13. An interesting epistemological question can be asked at this point: If the producer and his competitors never discover that he could have charged more, has he suffered an economic loss? If pure subjectivism is true, and if God's omniscience is not part of the theoretical explanation of value, then on what basis can the economist say that the producer has suffered a loss? If there is no objective value, then there cannot be an objective loss. But if there is no subjective perception on the part of the producer or his competitors that he has sustained a loss, has he in fact sustained it? This is an unsolved theoretical dilemma of modern humanistic economics.

14. Gary North, *Boundaries and Dominion: The Economics of Leviticus* (computer edition; Tyler, Texas: Institute for Christian Economics, 1994), ch. 26, subsection on "Economic Imputation."

15. Knight, "Preface to the Re-issue," *Risk, Uncertainty and Profit* (New York: Harper Torchbooks, [1933] 1965), p. xxvi. Mises rejected the whole concept of a stream of income: "There is in nature no such thing as a stream of income. Income is a category of action; it is the outcome of careful economizing of scarce factors."

The jubilee law limited its discussion of fruits to agricultural land located in Israel, but the same principle of ownership always governs the purchase of any scarce economic resource: the owner has purchased legal control over an expected stream of net productivity (a capital good) or over an expected stream of passive income (a bond).

If a person buys a capital good for a cash payment, he becomes its permanent owner. If he rents it for a specified period of time, he becomes a lessee. Because the capital good is physical, people without training in economics tend to think of it differently from the way they think of a promissory note. But the present value of the note is not derived from the physical piece of paper or a blip in a computer memory device; rather, it is derived from the estimated value of the money it promises to repay in the future, discounted by the prevailing rate of interest.[16] Similarly, the present value of a capital good is not derived from its physical make-up; rather, its present value is the estimated value of what it is expected to produce, discounted by the prevailing rate of interest. *The economic issue is value, not physical make-up*. The economic issue is the market's present imputation of future value, discounted by the prevailing rate of interest. Thus, the same process of imputation (valuation) applies equally to promissory notes, land, and capital equipment.[17] Prior to the abolition of slavery in the nineteenth century, it also applied to human labor. We call this imputation process *capitalization*.

Consider the case of a person who leases a piece of equipment but whose lease contract permits him to sublease it to

---

Mises, *Human Action*, p. 390. The stream of income concept has nevertheless proven useful in discussing the discounting process of time-preference or interest: a discount applied to expected income over time. We speak of time as flowing; the same language of continuity applies equally well to the arrival of income over time.

16. On the interest rate (time-preference), see Murray N. Rothbard, *Man, Economy, and State* (Auburn, Alabama: Mises Institute, [1962] 1993), pp. 319-23.

17. On the discounting process, see *ibid*., ch. 7: "Production: General Pricing of the Factors."

someone else. A second person agrees to make a cash payment or else a periodic payment to the person who leased the equipment first. The person who leased the asset first has now become a recipient of money income. It is now the same as if he had purchased a bond in the first place instead of leasing a piece of equipment from someone else. He now owns a piece of paper issued by a third party who promises to pay him in the future. So, there is no *economic* difference between buying a stream of *net future income* in the form of a piece of capital equipment or a written promise to pay (IOU).

Economic Oppression

The text warns against becoming an economic oppressor. What must be recognized from the beginning is that in the case of buying and selling rural land in Israel, *economic oppression was a two-way street*. Whether a person was a seller of land (buyer of money) or a buyer of land (seller of money) – i.e., whether a lessor or lessee – he could become an oppressor, according to this passage. "And if thou sell ought unto thy neighbour, or buyest ought of thy neighbour's hand, ye shall not oppress one another" (Lev. 25:14). This should warn us against any thought that the potential oppressor is always a buyer of some asset, or that a seller is always the potential oppressor.

This is especially relevant with respect to buyers of labor services (sellers of money) and sellers of labor services (buyers of money). It has been assumed by those who favor civil legislation that "protects labor" that employers are almost always the oppressors. Similarly, it has been assumed by those who oppose trade unions that the unions are normally the oppressors. Neither assumption is valid. What is valid is the conclusion that when the civil government interferes in the competitive market process of making voluntary contracts, *the group favored by the legislation becomes the economic oppressor*. This oppression is established by positive sanctions (subsidies) and negative sanctions (restraints against trade). The element of *civil compulsion* is the most important aspect in identifying the Bible's concept of *economic oppression.*[18]

The State and Economic Oppression

The person who leases a piece of land from an owner can become an oppressor, but so can the owner who leases it. The ethical and judicial question is this: What is economic oppression? This is not so easy to answer as Christian social commentators and humanistic legislators have sometimes imagined. In *Tools of Dominion,* I argued that neither the Bible nor economic theory provides a legally enforceable definition of economic oppression that is based on price. I argued rather that the State creates the conditions for economic oppression: injustice.[19] This is affirmed by Psalm 82, which refers to rulers of the congregation, which was the nation as a whole.[20] "God standeth in the congregation of the mighty; he judgeth among the gods. How long will ye judge unjustly, and accept the persons of the wicked? Selah. Defend the poor and fatherless: do justice to the afflicted and needy. Deliver the poor and needy: rid them out of the hand of the wicked" (Ps. 82:1-4).

Oppression and the Jubilee Land Law

We now return to the text of the jubilee land law. Who is likely to become the victim of oppression? Answer: the person with less reliable information about alternative offers and future economic *and legal* conditions. This can be either party. In an overwhelmingly agricultural community, both parties probably

---

18. For a discussion of State-enforced compulsory trade unionism as an aspect of oppression, see North, *Boundaries and Dominion*, ch. 26, subsection on "Things Seen and Unseen."

19. See Gary North, *Tools of Dominion: The Case Laws of Exodus* (Tyler, Texas: Institute for Christian Economics, 1990), pp. 683-84.

20. James B. Jordan, *The Sociology of the Church* (Tyler, Texas: Geneva Ministries, 1986), Appendix A: "Biblical Terminology for the Church." See Chapter 4, above: section on "Ritual Cleansings," pp. 91-92.

have equally good information about the value of the fruits of production. The person who wants to lease the land probably has somewhat poorer information about the physical details of the property. On the other hand, the land owner may have fallen into debt. Perhaps he is not a good manager of his money. He may be a poor farmer. He may have poor information about the value of the stream of *net* income from the land. So the text does not specify one of the two parties as the more likely oppressor.

To identify the oppressor here, we need to identify the person who uses the State, or his knowledge about the most likely future actions of the State, in order to gain a competitive advantage over the other person in a voluntary transaction. It is rare for biblical law to specify pricing as *judicable* economic oppression except in life-and-death situations – what I call "priestly pricing." Biblically defined economic oppression through price-setting is usually based on a person's efficient use of illegitimate power by the State. The oppressor and the civil magistrates act in collusion to oppress someone or some group.

A Question of Knowledge

The law of the jubilee was clear: in year 50, Israel's agricultural land was to revert to the original owners or their heirs. This leads me to ask: On what basis could anyone not know what to pay for or charge for leasing the land? All land was not equally valuable. To the extent that one piece of land was more productive, net, than another, to that extent the lease price would have been higher than less productive land. For example, a farm with a well-developed orchard would have brought a higher price than a farm whose income was dependent on farming that required higher inputs of labor and capital. The net income from the fruit of the orchard probably would have exceeded the net income from grain farming. So, the existence of variously priced annual leasehold rents was not necessarily evidence of economic oppression by anyone.

Then what was? A cash payment or long-term annual rent agreement that was either too high (an exploiting lessor) or too low (an exploiting lessee) for the number of years remaining before the jubilee. But since everyone knew the number of years remaining, how could there be any doubt about this? The answer should be clear to anyone who has followed my logic so far: *one of the parties knew that this statute would probably not be honored by the civil magistrates when the year of jubilee arrived.*

Which of the two would become the beneficiary if only one of them knew the truth? In the case of an advance cash payment for the full term of the lease, the party making the payment would have benefited. The person giving up control over the property would have asked a price on the assumption that the property would return to him or his heirs in the jubilee year. But this price was too low if the person gaining control would not in fact be required to relinquish control at the jubilee.

In the case of a long-term lease arrangement, however, the person agreeing to pay the existing owner an annual payment until the next jubilee year would have taken on an obligation longer than he had suspected. If the civil courts enforced the payment of the terms of the lease, but refused to enforce the jubilee, the person obligated to pay could become the oppressed party. If the land became less productive or its fruits less valuable in the market, the person who leased the land was stuck. The owner would collect his rental payment indefinitely.

The Civil Magistrates as Enforcers

The decisive factor, then, was the covenantal faithfulness of the civil rulers. Their decision to neglect the enforcement of the jubilee year would create conditions for economic oppression by one of the two contracting parties. Each party in the transaction was therefore warned in advance by God: do not become an oppressor, *even if corrupt civil magistrates make such oppression possible* by refusing to enforce the terms of the jubilee land law.

God warned everyone to abide by the jubilee law even if the civil rulers did not enforce it.

If I am correct in my analysis of this passage, then we have additional evidence that *economic oppression in a free market is usually the result of civil magistrates who refuse to enforce God's revealed law.* It is rarely the process of voluntary pricing in a free market that constitutes economic oppression; it is rather pricing in a society in which civil magistrates favor a particular individual or class by means of economically discriminatory legislation or economically discriminatory court decisions. *State subsidies of all kinds enable people to oppress each other economically.* The incentive to oppress others in this way is universal; the ability to do so is very limited when the civil magistrates restrict their actions to enforcing the laws of God by imposing the sanctions specified by His law. The State initiates economic oppression by creating the legal conditions in which such oppression is profitable. In short, *the State subsidizes economic oppression.* As in the case of any State subsidy, this increases the supply of the item being subsidized: economic oppression.

Contrary to utopian Christian non-economists, oppression has nothing to do with rental income or interest income, which tend toward an equal rate of return in a free market economy. The jubilee law authorized long-term lease contracts, which are a form of rent; it therefore by implication also authorized interest payments.[21]

Conclusion

The jubilee land law prohibited oppression in the writing of land lease contracts. Oppression resulted when one of the two parties to the transaction used specialized knowledge to take advantage of the other. The kind of knowledge was quite speci-

---

21. North, *Boundaries and Dominion*, ch. 26, section on "The Legitimacy of Rent and Interest." Cf. North, *Tools of Dominion*, Appendix G: "Lots of Free Time: The Existentialist Utopia of S. C. Mooney."

fic: *knowledge of future decisions by the civil magistrates not to enforce the terms of the jubilee land law.*

Either party to the transaction could become an oppressor under this definition. The land owner might persuade the lessee to agree to a contract in which the lessee promised to make regular payments until the jubilee year was declared. If it was not declared, and the magistrates refused to allow him to escape from the terms of the contract, the lessee would find himself locked into the contract. Under some economic conditions (e.g., a long-term fall in the money price for agricultural products), this would defraud the lessee. On the other hand, the lessee might be able to get the land owner to accept a cash payment in advance for legal control over the land's production. If the jubilee land law was not enforced, the lessee would be able to extend his control over the land indefinitely. This would defraud the land owner. Conclusion: the State was the source of the opportunity for oppression.

Both parties were warned to honor the terms of the jubilee land law whether the civil magistrates did or not. God placed the primary responsibility for law enforcement on the contracting parties. He warned them both: "Honor the terms of the leasehold that I have made with Israel for control over My land."

The issue of economic oppression in this law was not the actual pricing of the factor of production: land. This decision was left to the contracting parties. Each looked at the expected future stream of income from the land. Each would apply the prevailing market discount of the price of future goods in relation to present goods to this stream of income: interest. Then they would decide what to offer each other. The agreed-upon price, however, had to take into consideration the irrevocable date for the termination of the contract: the jubilee year.

The existence of a law governing land leases in Israel testifies to the error of interpreting the Bible's prohibition against usury in charitable loans as a prohibition against all forms of interest payments. The decision to make a cash payment in order to acquire legal ownership of a stream of resource-generated income over a fixed period of time is identical economically to making a cash payment to buy an interest-paying bond with the same expiration date as the lease. This means that a prohibition against all interest payments must also be a prohibition against all rent payments. Yet this law establishes the legality of rent. I therefore conclude that the Bible does not prohibit interest in non-charity loans.

There is no evidence that the jubilee laws were ever enforced in Israel. This may indicate that the jubilee laws sometimes were not enforced. Probably they were not enforced prior to the exile, for the seventh year of release was not honored, which is why God sent Israel into exile (II Chron. 36:21). Thus, every Israelite could safely assume that other laws beside the jubilee land law would govern leasehold contracts. Other civil laws would provide differing authority to magistrates to decide which leases would be honored and which would not. The magistrates of Israel arrogated authority to themselves to disobey God regarding the sabbatical year. How far could they safely be trusted to honor the terms of other laws? The opportunities for economic oppression must have increased, compared to rule by the sabbatical law and the jubilee land law, for there would have been less certainty about the enforcement of the civil law. The greater the degree of judicial uncertainty, the greater the amount of resources necessary to protect oneself: better lawyers, larger bribes, and higher expenditures on searching out information regarding the integrity of one's trading partners and also the moral integrity of their legal heirs. These were long-term lease contracts.

27

FOOD MIRACLES AND COVENANTAL PREDICTABILITY

> *Wherefore ye shall do my statutes, and keep my judgments, and do them; and ye shall dwell in the land in safety. And the land shall yield her fruit, and ye shall eat your fill, and dwell therein in safety. And if ye shall say, What shall we eat the seventh year? behold, we shall not sow, nor gather in our increase: Then I will command my blessing upon you in the sixth year, and it shall bring forth fruit for three years. And ye shall sow the eighth year, and eat yet of old fruit until the ninth year; until her fruits come in ye shall eat of the old store (Lev. 25:18-22).*

The theocentric meaning of this passage is that God sustains His people, and more than sustains them. He offers them plenty. They are required to acknowledge this fact by trusting His promises. They display this trust through their obedience to His law.

This passage begins with a re-statement of the familiar cause-and-effect relationship between corporate external obedience to God's covenant law and corporate external blessings. We know that the frame of reference is corporate blessings because of the use of the first person plural: "What shall *we* eat the seventh year? behold, *we* shall not sow, nor gather in our increase." In this case, the text focuses on two blessings: peace and food.

"Wherefore ye shall do my statutes, and keep my judgments, and do them; and ye shall dwell in the land in *safety*. And the land shall yield her fruit, and ye shall *eat your fill*, and dwell therein in safety." This is a repeated theme in the Bible. "But they shall sit every man under his vine and under his fig tree; and none shall make them afraid: for the mouth of the LORD of hosts hath spoken it" (Mic. 4:4).

Universal Benefits: Peace and Food

If this dual promise of peace and food were found only in Leviticus 25, it could be discussed as an aspect of the jubilee laws and therefore no longer in force. But the list of God's positive sanctions in Leviticus 26:3-15 indicates that this pair of positive sanctions was not uniquely tied to the jubilee. The promise of peace and food is more general than the jubilee law, since it refers to "my statutes" and "my judgments." God refers Israel back to His revealed law-order. It is their covenantal faithfulness to the stipulations of this law-order which alone serves the basis of their external prosperity. Without obedience, they can have no legitimate confidence in their earthly future in the land. This law has a broad application. It undergirds the observation by David: "I have been young, and now am old; yet have I not seen the righteous forsaken, nor his seed begging bread" (Ps. 37:25). The link between obedience to God's statutes and eating is reflected in David's observation: righteousness and the absence of begging.

Why is this passage found in the jubilee statutes? Because of the unique place of both the land and the harvest in the jubilee laws. Preceding this section are laws that deal with the transfer of a family's land to the heirs: the return – legally, though not necessarily physically – of each man to his father's land (v. 13). This was *a testament of liberation*. Because of this law, there could be no permanent legal enslavement of Israelites inside the land.[1] The jubilee law also established an obligation for all leasehold contracts to be based on the jubilee year's requirement of rural land's reversion to the original family (vv. 14-17). Following the announcement of the dual blessing of peace and food is another promise: a triple crop in the sixth year of the seventh cycle of sabbatical weeks of years (vv. 20-22).

The promise of peace and food points the reader's attention to the author of the law. God is sovereign. He promised to bring them national prosperity in response to their adherence to His laws. This promise was conditional: no obedience, no prosperity. This fact of covenantal life becomes clear in the next chapter of Leviticus. In order to demonstrate the reliability of His promises on a year-to-year basis, He promised a manifestation of His supernatural sovereignty: a miracle year.

The Miracle Year

To the jubilee year was attached a miracle. God promised to deliver a triple crop in the sixth year of the seventh sabbatical cycle of years. "And if ye shall say, What shall we eat the seventh year? behold, we shall not sow, nor gather in our increase: Then I will command my blessing upon you in the sixth year, and it shall bring forth fruit for three years. And ye shall sow the eighth year, and eat yet of old fruit until the ninth year; until her fruits come in ye shall eat of the old store" (vv. 20-22). This triple portion was God's way of announcing His presence with His people. They would be given sufficient crops to sustain them through the sabbath year and the jubilee year. Then, at

1. The law applied to all Israelites. Aliens could become heirs of this promise through adoption, either into a family (rural) or tribe (walled city). Excommunication removed an heir from his landed inheritance and his citizenship. This is why a excommunicant's adult sons had to break publicly with him and his rebellion in order to preserve their own inheritance. Although there is no law governing this, I presume that minor sons of an excommunicated father could inherit upon their majority at age 20 if they broke with their father publicly when they turned 20. At age 20, they became eligible for military numbering (Ex. 30:12): citizenship. The Mosaic law always had covenantal resoration as its goal.

the end of the jubilee (eighth) year, they were to plant for the next year.

The Miraculous Manna

In the wilderness period, they had been given the almost daily miracle of the manna. The exception to this miracle was itself an even greater miracle. On the day before the sabbath, they could gather a double portion. The manna in jars would not rot on the sabbath (Ex. 16:22). On every other day of the week, any manna that was left in a jar overnight would rot (Ex. 16:20).

As I have written in my commentary on Exodus, the manna had a function beyond the mere provisioning of the people with their daily bread. It was given to them in order that they might develop confidence in God as a sovereign provider. His provision of manna was miraculous. It was also regular. They had to trust God to bring the manna the next day, for it could not be stored overnight. Then, once a week, the regularity of the miracle was manifested in a different way: the miraculous rotting of the manna miraculously ceased. They could store it overnight, so that they would not have to labor to harvest it on the sabbath. So, the miracle was to teach them about the regularity of God's provisioning, as well as their total dependence on His grace.[2]

When they came into the land, the manna ceased forever: "And the manna ceased on the morrow after they had eaten of the old corn of the land; neither had the children of Israel manna any more; but they did eat of the fruit of the land of Canaan that year" (Josh. 5:12). The fruit of the land would henceforth sustain them. But this did not mean that they were any less dependent on God for their food. Now, however, their

2. Gary North, *Moses and Pharaoh: Dominion Religion vs. Power Religion* (Tyler, Texas: Institute for Christian Economics, 1985), ch. 18: "Manna, Predictability, and Dominion."

food would come predictably in terms of their corporate covenantal conformity to His law: the greater their obedience, the more predictable their food.

The Miraculous Triple Crop

In order to remind them of their continuing need to obey Him, as the sovereign provider of food, God did not totally remove His miracles from the land. Twice per century, God promised to provide them with bread in a miraculous way: the triple crop of the sixth year in the seventh cycle of the sabbatical week of years. This would be the equivalent of manna.

The Self-Discipline of Thrift

In a normal cycle of seven years, the Israelites had to save enough grain over six years to get through the seventh (sabbatical) year and half way through the eighth year, until the eighth-year crop could be harvested.[3] But this was not the case in jubilee year periods. In the sixth year would come a triple crop. That crop would feed them in the second half of year six, all of year seven (sabbatical), all of year eight (jubilee), and half way through year nine.

This means that in the six years prior to a jubilee year, farmers did not have to store up crops in order to carry themselves through the sabbatical year, the jubilee year, and half way through the ninth year until the crop came in. This triple crop was Old Covenant Israel's equivalent of the manna of the wilderness: a miraculous gift from God. It was the bread of life.

In escaping the production restraints of a normal sabbatical cycle, they acknowledged their dependence on the grace of God. The thrift that was agriculturally necessary during normal sabbatical periods was not required during the jubilee's week of

3. Gary North, *Tools of Dominion: The Case Laws of Exodus* (Tyler, Texas: Institute for Christian Economics, 1990), pp. 816-17.

years. Each farm could safely consume or sell one-sixth of each year's crop during the final sabbatical cycle. This income would otherwise have had to be stored or sold for cash and retained in that form in preparation for the sabbatical year. This pre-jubilee miracle would have made it possible for thrifty farmers to increase their purchase of farming tools, or make investments in urban industries, or make foreign investments. This extra marketable output of food would have tended to lower the price of food in Israel during jubilee periods, thereby stimulating the export of food to nations where food prices were higher.[4] Meanwhile, not-so-thrifty Israelites could have enjoyed more food, or else they could have sold the agricultural surplus in order to buy urban-produced consumer goods or imported consumer goods. To both the thrifty and the less thrifty, God promised six consecutive years of relief from the pressure to save for the normal sabbatical year.

To take advantage of this miraculous gift from God, the Israelites had to trust God to deliver on His promise to the nation. If they refused to save for six years in preparation for the arrival of a sabbath year of rest and the jubilee year, back to back, a refusal of God to deliver the triple crop would have created near-famine conditions by the ninth year. Many people would have been forced to sell their family lands or even sell themselves into slavery – in the very period that God set aside for the recovery of family lands and the release of bondservants. Thus, they had to exercise faith that the triple crop would arrive on schedule.

On the other hand, if God delivered on His promise, but the people then refused to honor the sabbatical year and/or the jubilee year, planting and harvesting instead, this would have constituted a misuse of the jubilee miracle. It would have constituted theft from God through the economic oppression of

4. Because of the high cost of ground transportation, these exported crops would normally have gone by boat.

hired harvesters, strangers, and gleaners. It is clear from the message of Jeremiah that the nation did not honor the sabbatical years for 70 sabbatical cycles, or 490 years. This is why they were sent into captivity. "To fulfil the word of the LORD by the mouth of Jeremiah, until the land had enjoyed her sabbaths: for as long as she lay desolate she kept sabbath, to fulfil threescore and ten years" (II Chron. 36:21).

There is no unambiguous biblical record that the jubilee law was ever honored in Israel. We know that the sabbath year of release was not honored for 490 years prior to the exile. Since they did not honor the sabbath year of release, it is highly doubtful that God ever gave them the promised triple crop in the seventh sabbatical cycle. Without the triple crop, perhaps they chose to ignore the jubilee law. The Bible does not say.

Miracles, Sanctions, and Mysticism

When Jesus announced His fulfillment of the jubilee year (Luke 4:18-21), He was announcing the end of the miraculous jubilee year. Under the New Covenant, there is no triple crop in the sixth year of the seventh "week of years." The faith of New Covenant-keepers has been stripped of a national miracle that demonstrated the reliability of God's providential and *law-bounded* covenantal order, just as a similar faith during the wilderness era was stripped of a daily miracle when the manna ceased upon the nation's entry into Canaan. As the spiritual maturity of covenant-keepers advances, miracles steadily cease.[5]

The question arises: What about the covenantal cause-and-effect connection between corporate external obedience and corporate blessings? Are covenant-bound societies still promised peace and agricultural prosperity if they adhere to the external

5. This has been the case in the history of Christianity. In the early church, the miracles of healing and exorcism were important in evangelism. Today, both of these gifts are far less evident in advanced industrial nations, although both still are used by some fundamentalist missionaries working in primitive societies or in societies deeply in bondage to a rival supernatural religion.

requirements God's revealed law? Was this annulled by Jesus in His fulfillment of the jubilee year? No. In Leviticus 26, which appears after the close of the jubilee laws, we read: "And I will give peace in the land, and ye shall lie down, and none shall make you afraid: and I will rid evil beasts out of the land, neither shall the sword go through your land" (Lev. 26:6). This recapitulation of the promise of Leviticus 25:18-19 indicates that this aspect of the jubilee law was broader than an aspect of the jubilee law. But was it a cross-boundary law? Did it apply outside the Promised Land? The recapitulation in Leviticus 26 is paralleled in Deuteronomy 28, and is mentioned as a testimony to enemy nations, which would fear them (Lev. 26:7-10).

Why should these enemies be afraid of Israel if they did not interpret the visible predictable sanctions in Israel as proof of God's unique presence with Israel? Did this fear apply only to the risks of invading Israel? Were the nations not also to fear a counter-invasion by Israel?[6] Deuteronomy 20:10-20 lists the laws of siege. These laws did not apply to Israel's invasion of Canaan, for they established legitimate terms of surrender, which were not options during the conquest. Therefore, these military laws had to apply to warfare outside the land. They were cross-boundary laws. Since Israel was to be feared by foreign nations, the corporate covenantal sanctions visible to foreigners inside the land had to be presumed by them to apply outside the land, too (Deut. 4:4-8).

Without the miracle of manna or the miracle of the triple crop, New Covenant Christians are thrown back on their faith in God's revealed word. The compelling evidence of God is supposed to be God's word. This always was the case, but the miracles were added to overcome the Israelites' weakness of faith. Old Covenant believers in the wilderness had daily edible reminders of God's presence. In the Promised Land, these

6. Israel was not to initiate foreign wars. The Mosaic festival laws made empire impossible. There was no permanent payoff in launching foreign wars.

reminders were reduced numerically to twice per century. In the New Covenant, the miracle of food is restricted to the Lord's Supper. This miracle – co-participation in heavenly worship by the earthly church and the heavenly church – must be accepted on faith.[7]

Covenantal Predictability

Has God reduced His covenantal predictability in history along with His reduction of miracles? For instance, does it take longer today than it did in Mosaic Israel for God to bring his negative sanctions in history? No evidence that I am aware of suggests this. Sometimes, the negative sanctions came soon. God was angry with Israel, so He moved David to take an illegal holy census (I Sam. 24:1).[8] David's sin in numbering the nation brought an immediate plague on 70,000 people (II Sam. 24:15). Rapid judgment was the threat that Nineveh faced; the nation therefore repented. Covenant-breakers outside the land understood the cause-and-effect connection between corporate sin and God's wrath in history. In other cases, judgment was delayed for centuries. In Mosaic Israel, the nation violated the sabbatical year laws for centuries. Not until Jeremiah's day were they told that God would soon bring His corporate wrath against the nation for this long-term act of rebellion by sending them into captivity (I Chron. 36:21).

While miracles steadily disappear, the covenantal promise of God's predictable corporate sanctions remain in place. If this were not the case, the sanctions aspect of the Lord's Supper (I

7. New Covenant Christians have gone in three directions to explain this miracle. Roman Catholics have turned to philosophical realism: the literal, bodily presence of Christ in the sacrament. The Lutherans also are realists, defending the body and blood of Christ as being substantially present: Formula of Concord (1576), Art. VII, Sections. 1, 2. Anabaptists have adopted nominalism: the Lord's Supper as a mere memorial. The biblical view is neither realism nor nominalism but covenantalism: God's special *judicial presence* in the eating of the meal. It is a meal eaten on the Lord's Day, or Day of the Lord, or judgment day.

8. The census was to be taken prior to holy war (Ex. 30).

Cor. 11:30) would be transferred completely out of history. While a man's verbal oath and the physical sacraments are part of history, the oath is taken under God, who is in eternity. Some of the personal sanctions are both predictable and eternal, but corporate negative sanctions are exclusively historical (no sin beyond the resurrection). On what exegetical basis can the sacrament's sanctions be said to be predictable only outside of history and apply only to individuals?

This raises the question of civil oaths. Nations take oaths (Ex. 19). Are these oaths enforced exclusively by men rather than God? Political pluralists are logically compelled to answer *yes*: no God enforces corporate civil oaths with covenantally predictable historical sanctions invoked by the oaths. If pluralists were to answer *no*, thereby affirming God's predictable, corporate, covenantal, historical sanctions, they would have to abandon their pluralism. Their religion forbids them to answer otherwise: no supernatural frame of reference for civil oaths.

If God's predictable, corporate, covenantal sanctions in history were to disappear, just as predictable corporate miracles such as manna and the triple crop have disappeared, Christianity would necessarily be progressively absorbed into the larger covenant-breaking culture. Whatever regularity in corporate sanctions that might be said to exist in history would be based on shared, universal categories of social and political ethics, e.g., natural law theory. There would be no way for the kingdom of God to manifest its presence among men except through the verbal testimony of individuals regarding totally invisible, subjectively discerned patterns of predictability, e.g., "I feel all tingly when I pray." For those people who have no desire to feel tingly, or who are content to take niacinamide whenever they want to feel tingly, such verbal testimony carries no weight. Christian culture could be differentiated from pagan culture only through the personal mysticism of its members. But mysticism is inherently without theological and judicial content – beyond the realm of creeds and intellectual categories. So-called Christian mysticism cannot be distinguished judicially from pagan mysticism. In short, if neither revelational ethics and its attached sanctions nor miracles identify the historical presence of the kingdom of God, the institutional church ceases to have a role to play in history visibly different from any other charitable or salvationist organization. This lack of distinction has overtaken most evangelical churches in the twentieth century. Christianity is regarded by covenant-breakers as just one more ameliorative-mystical tradition among thousands.

The way to restore the church to its position as society's central institution is to preach a separate biblical worldview based on biblical law and biblical sanctions. The other avenue for distinguishing the church from the world – the quest for miracles or continuing revelation – in the twentieth century has been the differentiating mark of pentecostals and charismatics.[9] The third path is mysticism.

Covenantal corporate predictability in history is mandatory if Christians are to reconstruct social theory. If such regularity did not exist in New Covenant history, then society could not be reformed on a uniquely Christian basis. The church would then seek to avoid social transformation. It would retreat from the world (discontinuity) or conform itself to the world (continuity). It would go fundamentalist-mystical or liberal. This is generally what happened in the United States, 1900-1975. As Rushdoony says, the fundamentalists believe in God but not in history, while the liberals believe in history but not in God. In either case, the world is abandoned to the covenantal representatives of Satan. There is no neutrality.

Miracles of Feeding

The law of God is given to all men so that they will learn to obey the God of the Bible. If they live in societies that are

9. Katherine Kulhman, *I Believe in Miracles* (New York: Pyramid Books, [1962] 1964).

marked by widespread obedience to the external laws of God, they will experience widespread external blessings, among which are peace and food.

To prove that this promise can be trusted, God on occasion has established *miracles of feeding*. The first time was in the wilderness period: the manna. When they entered the Promised Land, they initially lived off the crops of their defeated enemies. Then, as they began to plant and reap, they were to become thrifty: saving, not for a rainy day, but for the sabbatical year. But in the seventh cycle of sabbatical years, God promised to give them a miracle: the triple crop of the sixth year.[10]

The triple crop was also to remind them that God's blessings are predictable in history. It would remind them that the source of their prosperity was not thrift as such, but thrift within the framework of God's covenant. They were warned not to draw a false conclusion, one based on the humanist presupposition of the autonomy of man: "And thou say in thine heart, My power and the might of mine hand hath gotten me this wealth. But thou shalt remember the LORD thy God: for it is he that giveth thee power to get wealth, that he may establish his covenant which he sware unto thy fathers, as it is this day" (Deut. 8:17-18). Covenantal blessings are given to confirm the covenant.

Conclusion

The miracle of the triple crop was promised to Israel in order to confirm visibly: 1) the sovereignty of God over nature; 2) the predictability of God's covenant-based blessings in history. The Israelites were not to capitulate to the temptation of worshipping another god, either a god of nature or a god of

10. The prophets used the miracle of feeding on numerous occasions. The pagan widow of Zerephath had two containers that filled daily, one with oil and the other with meal, when Elijah lived in her home (I Ki. 17:14-15). In the New Testament, Jesus used the miracle of feeding on at least two occasions.

history – the only two kinds of idols available to covenant-breaking man.[11]

Modern covenant-breaking man denies the reality of miracles, then and now. He wishes to divinize either nature or history or both (Darwinism). To do this, he must deny all traces of God's authority over nature and history. Modern man has chosen evolution as his god, meaning his source of law. Evolution is said to govern both nature and historical process. Evolution is regarded as impersonal except when man, meaning elite men, learn the secrets of evolution and then direct both nature and history.[12] A major appeal of evolution is power.

Modern Christians reject evolution in its humanist form. They insist that God is still sovereign over history, although Augustinians and Calvinists alone insist that God predestines everything that comes to pass in history. There are virtually no visible traces of Catholic Augustinianism and very few traces of Calvinism. Furthermore, most Calvinists in the late twentieth century have explicitly or implicitly denied the existence of covenantal predictability in New Covenant times. They openly reject the idea of a national civil covenant under God. They are political pluralists.[13] They do not believe that God brings predictable corporate sanctions, positive or negative, in terms of a nation's obedience to God's Bible-revealed law.[14]

This belief leaves them without any miracles with which to challenge humanists and other covenant-breakers. This belief also provides them with a theological explanation for the seeming helplessness of Christianity to transform culture by estab-

---

11. Herbert Schlossberg, *Idols for Destruction: Christian Faith and Its Confrontation with American Society* (Westchester, Illinois: Crossway, [1983] 1993), p. 11.

12. Gary North, *The Dominion Covenant: Genesis* (2nd ed.; Tyler, Texas: Institute for Christian Economics, 1987), Appendix A: "From Cosmic Purposelessness to Humanistic Sovereignty."

13. Gary North, *Political Polytheism: The Myth of Pluralism* (Tyler, Texas: Institute for Christian Economics, 1989), chaps. 3-5.

14. Gary North, *Millennialism and Social Theory* (Tyler, Texas: Institute for Christian Economics, 1990), ch. 7.

lishing the civilization of God in history: God's kingdom. This in turn creates a deep psychological need to find personal solace in the midst of inevitable cultural defeat: pietistic ecclesiastical ghettos. Finally, their widespread acceptance of life in these ghettos has led to the development of ghetto eschatologies.[15]

Without a concept of God's covenant in history, Christians have not been able to develop an explicitly Christian social theory. They have relied on imported pagan natural law concepts to develop what few social ideas they possess. All of this has been the product of the widespread acceptance of the original theological assumption, namely, that God in the New Covenant era has annulled the covenantal predictability of Leviticus 26 and Deuteronomy 28. With neither widespread faith in the miracle of covenantal predictability nor the presence of earlier covenantal miracles of food and healing, modern Christians have become almost totally defensive in their thinking. Ideas have consequences.

15. Gary North, "Ghetto Eschatologies," *Biblical Economics Today*, XIV (April/May 1992).

28

THE RIGHT OF REDEMPTION

The land shall not be sold for ever: for the land is mine; for ye are strangers and sojourners with me. And in all the land of your possession ye shall grant a redemption for the land (Lev. 25:23-24).

We begin with a theocentric analysis of this passage. The prohibition against the permanent sale of rural land was connected to the nation's judicial status as strangers and sojourners with God. What did this mean? God began to dwell in the land of Israel when the conquest began, i.e., after the nation had crossed Canaan's border. This means that He lived among them *judicially*. He did not take up residence with them physically. His unique judicial presence in the land was marked physically by the presence of the two tablets of the law inside the Ark of the Covenant. Even this testimony had to be taken on faith; no one was allowed to look inside the Ark. When this law was violated by the men of Bethshemesh, God killed 50,070 of them (I Sam. 6:19). Negative corporate sanctions came immediately after God allowed the corporate infraction to take place.[1]

1. Had the first three or four people who looked inside the Ark immediately been stricken with leprosy, as Miriam was stricken in the wilderness (Num. 12:10), the infraction would have ceased.

The special judicial presence of God among them had been manifested historically to Israel by the genocide of the Canaanites. God had used His people – a royal priesthood (Ex. 19:6) – to bring negative historical sanctions against His enemies. They had served in a holy army. They had inherited the land of God's enemies. This was *inheritance through corporate execution.* Their landed inheritance began with their obedience in committing genocide.[2] It ended with their national disinheritance at the fall of Jerusalem in A.D. 70.

The Kinsman-Redeemer

The person who is identified in Leviticus 25 as the person with the authority to buy back a poor man's land is the kinsman (Lev. 25:25-26). The same root word in Hebrew is used for the verb for purchasing: "And if it be not *redeemed* within the space of a full year, then the house that is in the walled city shall be established for ever to him that bought it throughout his generations: it shall not go out in the jubile" (Lev. 25:30). "And if a man *purchase* of the Levites, then the house that was sold, and the city of his possession, shall go out in the year of jubile: for the houses of the cities of the Levites are their possession among the children of Israel" (Lev. 25:33).

The office of kinsman-redeemer was based on a messianic model (Ps. 72:11-14). The kinsman-redeemer was the same office as the blood-avenger, the *go'el* (sometimes transliterated

---

2. None of this is visible in W. Brueggemann's book, *The Land* (London: SPCK, 1978). He writes the following: "But Israel's Torah is markedly uninterested in a religion of obedience as such. It is rather interested in care for land. . ." (p. 60). Thus, he interprets the Mosaic law's universally acknowledged concern for ethics as a concern for ecology. You would be hard-pressed to find any interpretation of the Pentateuch more bizarre and misleading than this one. Then he quotes Joshua 1:7-8, God's command to be strong and courageous in the conquest of the land. Concludes Brueggemann: "The rhetoric is peculiar because it is an imperative to martial bravery and courage. But what is asked is not courage to destroy enemies, but courage to keep Torah" (p. 60). It is not the Bible's rhetoric that is peculiar. What is peculiar is Prof. Brueggemann's hermeneutic.

as *ga'awl*). "But if the man have no kinsman [*go'el*] to recompense the trespass unto, let the trespass be recompensed unto the LORD, even to the priest; beside the ram of the atonement, whereby an atonement shall be made for him" (Num. 5:8). God identified Himself as Israel's Kinsman-Redeemer (Ex. 6:6).

The blood avenger was the nearest of kin. It was he who had the responsibility of pursuing and then slaying anyone suspected of having murdered his kinsman. The cities of refuge were built in order to provide a place for suspected murderers to flee. The city of refuge was a legal boundary into which the authority of a blood avenger from outside the city did not extend (Num. 35:12). Outside the boundaries of a city of refuge, "The revenger of blood himself shall slay the murderer: when he meeteth him, he shall slay him" (Num. 35:19). After a trial in the city, a man convicted of murder (as distinguished from accidental manslaughter) was placed outside the city, to be executed by the blood avenger (Num. 35:25). A man convicted of accidental manslaughter could lawfully be killed by the blood-avenger at any time outside the city of refuge, until the high priest died. Here the language of release is the same as the language of the jubilee year: returning to the family's land: "Because he should have remained in the city of his refuge until the death of the high priest: but after the death of the high priest the slayer shall return into the land of his possession" (Num. 35:28). In the captivity of Israel, God acted as their kinsman (Isa. 48:20). In doing so, God acted as blood-avenger (Isa. 49:26).

After his redemption by the kinsman-redeemer, the redeemed relative would then have served as the employee of the kinsman-redeemer – his bondservant, in other words – until the jubilee year.[3]

---

3. Gary North, *Boundaries and Dominion: The Economics of Leviticus* (computer edition; Tyler, Texas: Institute for Christian Economics, 1994), ch. 28, subsection on "Why Redeem Another Man's Land or Person?"

Walled Cities

The law of redemption applied inside the walled cities of Israel in a different way: the seller or his kinsman had only one year to redeem a home (dwelling place). Once this year had passed, the buyer became a permanent owner (Lev. 25:29-30). Notice: this law applied only to homes. It did not apply to other kinds of urban real estate. Only a residence was protected by the year of grace. Title to other real estate passed at the time of sale. Title to urban real estate was *alienable*: for sale to aliens. Outside the boundary of the wall, the Israelite's right of redemption was universal, bounded by a 50-year limit (v. 31).

Was it legal for subsequent generations to build walls around unwalled cities? Yes. Would this new wall have changed the legal status of the heirs of the original families? No. An unwalled city of Joshua's day, with the exception of the cities of the Levites, came under the jubilee's rural land law. The inheritance left by the original generation could never be alienated by contract.[4] The inheritance could only be alienated by God, through corporate covenantal execution. So, a wall could be built for the sake of military defense, but this would not have changed the legal status of the heirs of the original families. No alteration of the inheritance of the original families was allowed; the defensive wall was not a judicial wall.

Citizenship could not be revoked for any reason other than excommunication. This means that the priests, through their delegated authority to the Levites, could alone revoke citizenship. This is the mark of a biblical civil order. The biblical civil order does not autonomously establish or enforce the criteria of citizenship. Citizenship is creedal, and the church enforces the content of the creed. A biblical civil order cannot become autonomous; biblical political theory reflects this fact.

---

4. Rabbinical opinion was that only the walled cities in the era of Joshua's conquest were exempted from the jubilee rural land law. *Arakhin* 9:6; *The Mishnah*, trans., Herbert Danby (New York: Oxford University Press, [1933] 1987), p. 553.

Who would have chosen to live in a walled city in the era of the conquest? Any Israelite family would have had the right to participate in the distribution of rural land. This would have been that family's permanent inheritance. The urban residents would then have been made up of the following: 1) land-owning Israelites who became absentee landlords; 2) permanent resident aliens who had been adopted into the tribe of a city; 3) permanent resident aliens who had not been adopted by an Israelite family or tribe; 4) traders who would reside there relatively briefly; 5) Levites who were not residents of a Levitical city; 6) soldiers or other officials from the central government; 7) Israelites who had been excommunicated (i.e., circumcised strangers: *nokree*); 8) convicted Israelite criminals who had been sold into servitude to someone in a walled city.[5]

The Terms of Sale

The text does not speak of a deferred payment, i.e., a mortgage beyond one year. The right of redemption was one year. There is no indication that this means anything except one year from the time that the transfer of ownership took place. Ownership transfers with responsibility over the property. Ownership is a judicial concept: the identification of the legally responsible agent. The owner has the right to disown the property.

---

5. The Bible does not say whether convicted criminals were part of the jubilee land law's primary benefit: a judicial return to the family's land, i.e., liberation from bondage. This would have meant freedom for all criminals in the jubilee year. This, in turn, would have created a subsidy to crime as the jubilee year approached: a conviction would not have led to a high price for his sale into bondage, since the time of potential servitude was steadily shrinking. The victims would have been short-changed. Because God defends the victim, it seems safe to conclude that there were two exceptions to the jubilee law of liberation: the apostate who had forfeited his inheritance and the criminal who was still under the requirement to pay off his victims or the person who bought him, with the purchase price going to the victims. This conclusion follows from two general principles of biblical law: 1) God does not subsidize evil; 2) victim's rights. If this is correct, then the criminal who was released from bondage would have had to wait until the next jubilee year to reclaim his land.

Could there have been home mortgages under such a legal system? Yes, but the original owner had only one year to reclaim his property unless the buyer subsequently defaulted on his payments. He would have had to repay to the new buyer whatever the new buyer had paid him during the interim. The purchaser had to forfeit the use of the assets or money that he used to buy the house. This is what the seller owed him if the former wanted to reclaim the house. The buyer remained a renter for up to one year; his eviction through re-purchase was possible at any time. Under open competition, the lease payment would therefore have tended to equal the rate of interest/rent: whatever the lessor gained by occupying the house – psychic income – was offset by the payments he had made to the original owner. On the other side of the transaction, whatever the seller had gained from holding the item used to purchase the house was paid for by his loss of control over the house.

A Stake in Society

No explicit reason is provided in the Bible to explain this judicial difference: wall vs. no wall. The judicial boundary established by the city's wall provided an exemption from the jubilee land law after 12 months.[6] Inheritance there was based on secondary purchase rather than original conquest. It was based on economics rather than ecclesiastical confession. This made possible a place for resident aliens or post-conquest converts to the faith to gain what is sometimes called a stake in society. A stake is a marker that establishes the edge of a boundary in land, but it is used here more broadly: a permanent residence or a permanent possession of value that is tied to a specific place. A stake in society is therefore a *legal claim*, some-

6. Though not interest-free: see above. There is no escape from the phenomenon of interest: a discount of future goods as against those same goods in the present.

thing that at some price is worth defending, either in a court or on a battlefield.

Would resident aliens have been required to fight to defend the city? Not unless they were citizens. They did not possess membership in an Israelite family. The military numbering process would not have touched them (Ex. 30). Presumably they could volunteer, but only if they professed the required national confession of faith, the *shema Israel*: "Hear, O Israel: The LORD our God is one LORD" (Deut. 6:4). There were many instances of foreign soldiers in Israel's holy army, Uriah the Hittite being the most famous. Citizenship was probably a reward granted to circumcised resident aliens who volunteered for military service. If you could be legally numbered, you were a citizen; conversely, if you could not legally be numbered, you were not a citizen.[7]

Was confession, circumcision, and eligibility for service in the Lord's army sufficient to establish an inheritable claim of citizenship? Yes. Was this citizenship inalienable? Yes. Citizenship was covenantal. Covenantal inheritance was by confession, circumcision, and eligibility to bring sanctions: as a holy warrior and therefore as a judge.[8] Once a citizen of Israel, a person could not become a permanent bondservant under Mosaic law.

Post-Exilic Israel

This raises an extremely important point: the alteration of land ownership after the exile. Ezekiel prophesied that after Israel's return from exile, strangers in the land would participate in a second division of the land by lot. These strangers would gain permanent possession in the land. Strangers who

7. See Chapter 30, below, under the heading, "Holy War, Citizenship, and Liberty," pp. 503-5.

8. Deborah, a prophetess, also served as a judge (Jud. 4:4). She served functionally as a holy warrior: senior in command (Jud. 4:8). As the sanctions-bringer against Sisera, Jael also served as a holy warrior (v. 22). Neither was circumcised, but both were under legal authority of circumcised males: husbands.

resided within the jurisdiction of a particular tribe at the time of the reclaiming of the land by that tribe would become part of a new land allocation (Ezek. 47:21-23). They could not be disinherited. But if that was true, then they could not be enslaved.

There is no indication that the jubilee's heathen slave law was annulled after the exile. Jesus announced His ministry in terms of jubilee liberation (Luke 4:18-21). This assertion rested on the continuing authority of the jubilee slave law. That aspect of the jubilee was related to family ownership and citizenship, not the original distribution of the land under Joshua. But a new land allocation would free participating heathen families from any threat of inter-generational bondage. Those who resided in the land at the time of the return could not lawfully be enslaved.

This was the source of the lawful continuing presence of Samaritans in the land. These foreigners had been brought into the Northern Kingdom by the Assyrians to replace the captive Israelites. The returning Israelites were not authorized to kill or exile these people. There would never again be a lawful program of genocide to establish original title in Israel. Rather, the resident alien at the return would receive an inheritable grant of rural land. The worship of Canaanite gods and religion never reappeared. The gods of Canaan had been gods of the land, meaning gods of the city-state. Those gods were no longer relevant in a nation under the authority of Medo-Persia, then Hellenism, and finally Rome. In contrast, Persian dualism, Hellenism, and Talmudism were not bound by geography. These became the main threats to biblical orthodoxy.

The returning Israelites took centuries to reconquer the land. The reconquest was never completed, nor was Mosaic civil authority ever re-established. The tribes did not re-establish their original borders, nor were they ever again totally free from foreign civil rule. But the Jews did come close to re-establishing their pre-exilic political power and national boundaries in the decades prior to Rome's invasion, which led non-Jewish inhabitants of Palestine to welcome the Romans.[9] Because the physical boundaries of the Promised Land had been breached during the exile, never to be healed, and because the pre-exilic judicial boundaries were never again established, the original land distribution of the era of the conquest lost its judicial relevance. Israelite citizenship therefore lost most of its judicial relevance except during periods of civil revolt. Confession, circumcision, and adoption remained the basis of this much-reduced citizenship. God's holy army had ceased to exist.

Urban Citizenship

Ammonites and Moabites could become members of the congregation after 10 generations (Deut. 23:3). This was citizenship, for the same 10-generation limit applied also to Israelite bastards (Deut. 23:2). The question is: Where would these new citizens have exercised their judicial powers? I think it must have been inside walled cities. The cities were tribal affairs. They had been parcelled out to the tribes under Joshua (Josh. 13:23-32; 15). Citizenship in a city must have been tribal. But judges in cities probably resided in those cities. Local urban residents possessed knowledge of local affairs.

The question is: Was real estate ownership required to be an urban citizen? Did an urban resident lose his citizenship if he lost ownership of his home? That could happen in one year. Was the threat of disenfranchisement hanging over the head of every urban real estate owner who did not have an inheritance in rural Israel? The Bible does not say. Any answer is speculative. But since lawful participation in holy warfare seems to be the best way to define the mark of citizenship, my conclusion is that aliens could become eligible for citizenshop as adopted

9. The one city that refused to submit to the Jews was Pella. W. H. C. Frend, *The Rise of Christianity* (Philadelphia: Fortress, 1984), p. 19. It was to Pella, located beyond the Jordan, that the Jerusalem church supposedly fled just before the siege of the city by Rome in A.D. 69. Eusebius, *Ecclesiastical History*, III:V.

members of the tribes governing walled cities. Citizenship did not require the ownership of a home in a walled city. Urban citizenship was by confession, circumcision, and eligibility for holy war. It was not based on landed inheritance.

For an alien to become a citizen in Israel meant that he became a free man. Israelites were not allowed to own Israelite slaves as inheritable property (Lev. 25:46b). By becoming a citizen, the alien permanently established his legal claim as an Israelite.

This raises the question of access to citizenship. Deuteronomy 23 is the main section dealing with this. The context is that of an outsider wanting in. Deuteronomy 23:1 lists the eunuch. I think this refers to a foreign eunuch, not an Israelite.[10] If an Israelite warrior, for example, received such an injury, was he expelled from the congregation? Did he cease to be an Israelite? Did he become a heathen subject to permanent bondage? This does not seem reasonable. The passage refers to outsiders wanting in, including bastards, i.e., outsiders to the covenantal family. The context is not of an insider who is being forced out. In any case, adoption into an Israelite family could always overcome this restriction.[11] Caleb, the son of a Kenizite (Num. 32:12), was surely a citizen. He must have been adopted into the tribe of Judah (Num. 13:6), the tribe of Jacob's messianic promise (Gen. 49:10).[12]

Circumcised resident aliens were not citizens unless they were eligible to serve in God's holy army: adoption into the tribe under whose authority they fought. They did not otherwise possess the legal right to impose judicial sanctions as judg-

---

10. Rushdoony argues that it was an Israelite who became a eunuch. R. J. Rushdoony, *The Institutes of Biblical Law* (Nutley, New Jersey: Craig Press, 1973), p. 84.

11. The adoption of the Ethiopian eunuch – a foreigner – into the New Covenant church (Acts 8:26-40) is indicative of the law of adoption.

12. He may not have been adopted into a family. This took place prior to the conquest of Canaan, so the issue of family adoption and landed inheritance was not yet relevant.

es in Israel. Only citizens possessed this right. In other words, resident aliens could never become citizens except by adoption: the implicit or explicit acceptance of military service. Urban adoption was tribal, not familistic.

Uriah was called a Hittite. This may have meant that he was not a third-generation circumcised resident, and therefore not normally eligible for citizenship. But he was a warrior in God's holy army. This indicates that the resident alien could become a citizen through military service in the defense of Israel during wartime, even if he was not a third or tenth generation circumcised resident. If a circumcised alien was willing to risk dying for God in defense of Israel's boundaries, and if his offer to serve was accepted by the military, this made him a citizen: a man with the right to the office of judge – a sanctions-bringer.

The Sociology of Home Ownership

Poor people rent; rich people own; middle-class people pay off mortgages. Economic freedom produces incentives for owners to build housing for poorer people to rent. Poor people rent new quarters when they grow richer. People move to better quarters when they grow richer. Only the richest sons of the richest families stay put, decade after decade. They move from their palatial summer homes to their palatial winter homes. They are mobile; ownership is not. Permanent landed estates are an important mark of "old money." The dispersal of landed estates in Europe in the twentieth century through the drastic taxation of large inheritances was an aspect of class warfare: the middle classes, in the name of the poorer classes, voted away the wealth of the landed classes, whose heirs could no longer afford to inherit.[13]

---

13. In the late 1980's, I was told by a Scottish-American Jacobite (a defender of the English crown rights of the heir of James II, who fled in 1688) that members of every Jacobite family that retains control through the National Trust of a Scottish or English castle are expected to volunteer their services for two years to serve as residents of these castles to oversee the tourists. Any time a family member is not a

In walled cities, the kinds of people who would have wound up as owners of urban housing would have been the same kinds of people who own urban property today. Richer people would have been dominant home owners. That is, those who were the most productive people in the economy would have been most likely to buy a home and retain a stake in society. This property right, irrespective of family creed and ritual, to buy and inherit housing in Mosaic Israel's walled cities was an important way for Israel to attract and keep very productive people from abroad. It would have made Israel's walled cities centers of entrepreneurship and trade.

Turnover of ownership would initially have been much more rapid in walled cities than in rural settings or in unwalled cities. Nineteenth-century American capitalism's story of "poor man to rich man to poor man" in three generations would have been much more common in Israel's walled cities than outside them, at least until population growth shrank the size of the average farm.[14]

The walled cities of the Canaanite era became the walled cities of Israel. Which cities would have been the walled cities of Canaan? First, cities that housed cultures with military aspirations: city-state empires. Second, cities with wealth to protect from invasion: trade centers. Third, cities with unique religious icons or practices that served the needs of a particular region: religious centers. Walled cities would have tended to be cities on the crossroads of trade. Their architecture, water systems, and similar "infrastructure" would have been suited to trading centers. Thus, their character as crossroad cities would not have been radically altered by Israelite civilization. This means that walled cities would have become cosmopolitan: world (cosmos)

---

resident, he said, the hated Windsor family inherits the castle.

14. Tocqueville commented on the United States in the 1830's: "But wealth circulates there with incredible rapidity, and experience shows that two successive generations seldom enjoy its favors." Alexis de Tocqueville, *Democracy in America*, edited by J. P. Mayer (Garden City, New York: Doubleday, [1835] 1966), I:3, p. 54.

cities (polis = city). This raises the question of citizenship. It also raises the question of pluralism.

Pluralism: Cultural, Not Judicial

The walled city would have been the preferred place of residence for wealthy aliens and wealthy covenant converts who were not heirs of the generation of the conquest. These cities would have been the centers of cosmopolitan life, where ideas and customs from outside the land would have intermingled. This means that the ideas and customs of a particular foreign god would always have had competition from people who had faith in other gods. This would have created a true cultural pluralism within the legal framework of a biblically covenanted community. The walled cities would have been testing areas – social laboratories – for many ideas and practices, but always within the judicial boundary of God's law.

These testing areas were sealed off judicially from the land outside their walls. This seal was not absolute. Resident aliens could lease agricultural property outside the walls, but they had no assurance of being able to renew these leases, nor could they pass on legal access to rural land to heirs. The jubilee was designed to cut short any attempt by foreigners to colonize the land of Israel. Even urban colonization would have been restricted to ideas and customs that were not in violation of the laws of God. Urban aliens were not citizens. They could not serve as judges.

Not being citizens, resident aliens could not impose judicial sanctions in Mosaic Israel. They could not lawfully seek converts to their imported religions. Only the non-confessional expressions of these imported religious worldviews were legal in the public square. This is why cultural pluralism is not the same as judicial pluralism. Cultural pluralism within a holy commonwealth is stripped of theological confession and judicial sanctions.

The modern humanist world has made politics formally as pluralistic as culture is. This has created a situation in which politics has become polytheistic.[15] Beginning at the outbreak of World War I in 1914, Western nations have imposed immigration barriers in order to keep out foreigners, for fear of losing both culture and politics to hordes of aliens. The expansion of the welfare State has made such restrictions even more important: keeping aliens away from the public treasuries. But "alien" is not defined covenantally; it is defined culturally. National boundaries become walls barring too great a disruption of the established culture, however pluralistic it may already be. Barbed wire has replaced theological confession as the preferred means of discouraging immigrants.

In Mosaic Israel, foreign culture was bounded by urban walls, physiological walls (circumcision), and confessional walls. When the law was enforced, immigrants from foreign cultures (plural) could not become threats to Israel. God's word alone had judicial authority, so imported cultures had to conform to the covenant. The ethical and judicial terms of the covenant became filtering devices for sifting through the wheat and the chaff in every cultural import. There was no need for immigration barriers. There is no evidence that such barriers ever existed. Mosaic law does not authorize them, precisely because it does not authorize political pluralism.

Lest we forget: the ultimate immigration barrier is abortion.

The Levites' Cities

There was one additional aspect of the jubilee land law: Levitical cities. There were 48 of these cities, six of which were cities of refuge (Num. 35:6-7). "Notwithstanding the cities of the Levites, and the houses of the cities of their possession, may the Levites redeem at any time. And if a man purchase of the

---

15. Gary North, *Political Polytheism: The Myth of Pluralism* (Tyler, Texas: Institute for Christian Economics, 1989), Part 3.

Levites, then the house that was sold, and the city of his possession, shall go out in the year of jubile: for the houses of the cities of the Levites are their possession among the children of Israel. But the field of the suburbs of their cities may not be sold; for it is their perpetual possession" (Lev. 25:32-34).

The Levites were therefore likely to be urban dwellers at any point in Israel's history. They could not become owners of rural land, which was the inheritance of other tribes.[16] Their presence in a region would have been concentrated in a local tribal city. At the same time, they were dispersed as a tribe throughout the land, just as their cities were. This kept all of the tribes in close proximity to specialists in covenantal law and ritual. This also kept the nation free from priestly attempts to centralize rural land ownership, except in periods in which the jubilee inheritance laws were not enforced. Even in such rebellious periods, there was always the possibility that some subsequent generation would enforce the law. Anti-jubilee legal title was always at risk.

A Nation of City Dwellers

The Levites would have been urban residents. They advised rural people, but they lived primarily in cities. Their "home base" was urban. This fact should tell the commentators something, but none of them ever mentions it. *Israel's legal structure was designed to produce an urban society*. Covenant-keeping would bring rapid population growth. In a growing economy, wealth is increasingly based on intellectual labor and creativity, not on raw materials.[17] As agriculture becomes more efficient, fewer people need to work the land, or can afford to. Thus, the struc-

---

16. Priests occasionally could. See chapter 37.

17. Julian Simon, *The Ultimate Resource* (Princeton, New Jersey: Princeton University Press, 1981); Warren T. Brookes, *The Economy in Mind* (New York: Universe, 1982); E. Calvin Beisner, *Prospects for Growth: A Biblical View of Population, Resources, and the Future* (Westchester, Illinois: Crossway, 1990).

ture of jubilee ownership led the Levites to live in cities, which is where a growing percentage of the population of covenant-keeping Israel was expected by God to dwell as time went on – and outside the Promised Land, also in cities. The Levites would become the major urban real estate owners except in non-Levite walled cities. Most people would have to rent or lease housing from them.

Let us not mistake what this would have meant: *the accumulation of urban wealth by one tribe*. Urban wealth would increasingly have become the dominant form of wealth in a growing economy, as it is today. Unless Israel conquered new lands, Israelites had only four places to go if they wanted to escape rural life: the original walled cities, unwalled cities, Levitical cities, and other nations. They could not permanently own homes in unwalled cities: a disadvantage. In the original walled cities, the influence of the Levites as advisors would have been strong. In Levitical cities, they would have been the predominant home owners, renting space to poorer residents. *Thus, the structure of land ownership favored the Levites above all other tribes in times of righteousness*. They were the most mobile tribe, the most urban tribe, and the most educated tribe. They had the greatest number of personal contacts across the nation. They would steadily have become the dominant tribe and the wealthiest tribe in a covenantally faithful society.

Why did God subsidize the Levites in this way? One economic reason was the fact that the Levites had an incentive to make sure that the jubilee laws were enforced. They had the authority to excommunicate civil rulers who refused to enforce God's civil law. Levitical families would receive back their homes in the same year that the other tribes' families received back their lands. But did they do this? It seems more likely that they refused to pressure civil magistrates to enforce the jubilee. If they did refuse, there would have been a class of homeless Levites who had to rent housing in their own cities. This would have led to class division within the priestly tribe. If the civil authorities enforced the jubilee only in Levitical cities, there would have been widespread resentment among the other tribes.

Conclusion

This law had to be temporary. The tribal structure was not designed to be permanent; its purpose would end after Shiloh (the Messiah) had come: a member of the tribe of Judah. When the redeemer came, the right of redemption would end. The ideal of the city of God would then replace the ideal of the land of God.

The structure of land ownership under the jubilee system was clearly a wineskin destined to be broken, either through God's blessing – urbanization and/or the conquest of new lands – or God's cursing: conquest by other lands and dispersion. The inheritance of Joshua's day would fade into insignificance: through urbanization; through the extension of the boundaries of Israel outward, beyond the original land grant and the jubilee law; or through emigration, either voluntary or forced. In any case, the importance of the right of redemption would fade.

The right of redemption meant different things to different people in ancient Israel. For the rural land owner, it meant that he could collateralize a business loan or lease his property without the risk of disinheriting his children. An urban home could become the property of the lender if the borrower defaulted. It could become part of the lender's permanent legacy to his children. Also, an urban house was located in a commercial center. The benefits of lending to the urban real estate owner were greater than lending to a rural family with the land as collateral. This meant that a rent-seeking lender might not lend him so much, or at so low an interest rate, as he would lend the home-owning resident of a walled city. The collateral value of a home in a walled city was probably greater than the collateralized value of a dozen acres in the country.

The resident of a walled city lived in an economically active trading center that was cosmopolitan. Resident aliens could buy permanent ownership of homes in such cities. They could even become citizens. The influence of resident aliens in Israel was concentrated here, for only here could they buy homes and pass them to their children. The buying and selling of homes would have concentrated home ownership into the hands of rich families irrespective of their religion. There would have been considerable turnover in ownership, with successful merchants buying or foreclosing on the homes of the less successful. It would have been difficult for any family residing in a walled city to retain ownership of a home through several generations. In other words, home ownership in a walled city in Israel was far more like the modern world than home ownership was elsewhere in Israel. As we have seen, a growing Israelite population would have pushed the population out of rural Israel and into walled cities or outside the nation.

For the Levite, the jubilee redemption law was limited to Levitical cities. This would have tended to tie Levitical families to certain cities. A Levite could also buy a permanent home in a walled city, although he had no competitive advantage over any other buyer. He had no inheritance in the land outside the cities. This structure of inheritance would have made the Levite primarily an urban figure. If the economy and the population grew, the Levites would become the principal Jewish home owners in Israel. But since God's law is not designed to favor one family over another, long-term, we can safely conclude that the jubilee inheritance laws were not designed to be permanent. They would end when the Kinsman-Redeemer finished His work. As it turned out, it was in His office of Blood-Avenger that He ended the jubilee laws: in A.D. 70.

29

POVERTY AND USURY

And if thy brother be waxen poor, and fallen in decay with thee; then thou shalt relieve him: yea, though he be a stranger, or a sojourner; that he may live with thee. Take thou no usury of him, or increase: but fear thy God; that thy brother may live with thee. Thou shalt not give him thy money upon usury, nor lend him thy victuals for increase. I am the LORD *your God, which brought you forth out of the land of Egypt, to give you the land of Canaan, and to be your God (Lev. 25:35-38).*

The theocentric basis of this law was God's role as the liberator. Men are to fear God. This fear of God should overcome men's fear of nature and history. Fear of God is liberating; fear of the creation is paralyzing.

This law is an extension of Exodus 22:25: "If thou lend money to any of my people that is poor by thee, thou shalt not be to him as an usurer, neither shalt thou lay upon him usury." The Hebrew word translated here as *usury* means *bite*. "And the LORD sent fiery serpents among the people, and they bit the people; and much people of Israel died" (Num. 21:6). In both Exodus and Leviticus, the borrower is described as being a poor brother in the faith, i.e., under God's covenant. The heart of the matter in Leviticus 25:35-38 and Exodus 22:25 is the establishment of judicial conditions for charitable, interest-free loans: poverty, covenantal brotherhood, and geographical proximity. As we shall see, these conditions had to be legally identifiable in order for the prohibition against usury to be enforced by a civil court. It was this aspect of conditionality that medieval theologians failed to recognize when they issued prohibitions against taking interest in all loans. The biblical texts are clear; it is the theologians who have been muddled.[1]

Usury Defined

What is usury? Both texts are quite clear about the definition: *usury is any positive rate of return taken from a loan*. There is no universal prohibition in the Bible against interest. This is clear from the text in Deuteronomy that authorizes covenant-keepers to make interest-bearing charitable loans to covenantal strangers. "Thou shalt not lend upon usury to thy brother; usury of money, usury of victuals, usury of any thing that is lent upon usury: Unto a stranger thou mayest lend upon usury; but unto thy brother thou shalt not lend upon usury: that the LORD thy God may bless thee in all that thou settest thine hand to in the land whither thou goest to possess it" (Deut. 23:19-20). In fact, God encourages His people to lend to those outside the faith; it is a means of subduing them. "For the LORD thy God blesseth thee, as he promised thee: and thou shalt lend unto many nations, but thou shalt not borrow; and thou shalt reign over many nations, but they shall not reign over thee" (Deut. 15:6). Lending at interest is an aspect of the dominion covenant. Biblically, there is no universal prohibition against this.

Medieval Christian expositors concluded, following Aristotle rather than Moses, that interest is always prohibited.[2] It is not.

---

1. The non-theologians have been even more muddled. See, for example, S. C. Mooney, *Usury: Destroyer of Nations* (Warsaw, Ohio: Theopolis, 1988). For my response, see Gary North, *Tools of Dominion: The Case Laws of Exodus* (Tyler, Texas: Institute for Christian Economics, 1990), Appendix G: "Lots of Free Time: The Existentialist Utopia of S. C. Mooncy."

2. The prohibition against interest (usury) began with the Council of Nicea (325): clerics were prohibited from making interest-bearing loans. J. Gilchrist, *The Church*

What was prohibited under Mosaic law was interest taken from a poor brother in the faith or a poor resident alien who had subordinated himself to the civil covenant, presumably by submitting to circumcision. The lender, then as now, was not to take advantage of certain poor people: those who had submitted themselves to the terms of the covenant. He was required by God to make a charitable loan. He would thereby forfeit the interest he might have earned from a business loan. Forfeited interest was the charitable component of his act. *If interest were universally prohibited, then all legal loans would be charitable.* There would then be no economic distinction between charity loans and business loans, or between dominion by restoring the covenant-keeping poor and dominion by subordinating the covenant-breaking poor. The Bible teaches otherwise.

Charity: Conditional vs. Unconditional

Charitable loans are part of God's program to provide help to honest, covenant-keeping people who have fallen on hard times. These loans are not supposed to subsidize sloth or evil. God does not want us to subsidize evil with the money or assets that He has provided for us.[3] In this sense, *biblical charity is necessarily morally conditional*.[4] Biblical charity is never a judicial-

---

and Economic Activity in the Middle Ages (New York: St. Martin's, 1969), p. 155. This prohibition was gradually extended by the theologians after 800. *Ibid.*, p. 63. The Second Lateran Council (1139) was especially hostile, going so far as to prohibit usurers from being granted Christian burial. *Ibid.*, p. 165. The Council at Vienna (1311-12) mandated the excommunication of civil rulers who permitted usury within their jurisdictions. *Ibid.*, p. 206. Gilchrist's excellent book did not receive the audience that it should have. It includes translations of the texts of the general councils. This makes it invaluable.

3. R. J. Rushdoony, "Subsidizing Evil," in Rushdoony, *Bread Upon the Waters* (Nutley, New Jersey: Craig Press, 1969), ch. 3.

4. Ray R. Sutton, "Whose Conditions for Charity?" in *Theonomy: An Informed Response*, edited by Gary North (Tyler, Texas: Institute for Christian Economics, 1991), ch. 9. Sutton is responding to Timothy J. Keller, "Theonomy and the Poor: Some Reflections," in *Theonomy: A Reformed Critique*, edited by William S. Barker and W. Robert Godfrey (Grand Rapids, Michigan: Zondervan Academie, 1990), ch. 12.

ly automatic "entitlement," to use the terminology of the modern welfare State: a compulsory redistribution of wealth from the successful to the unsuccessful (minus approximately 50% for "handling" by government bureaucrats[5]). It is this element of covenantal conditionality which distinguishes biblical charity from humanist compulsion.[6]

The modern welfare State does not distinguish judicially between faith and unbelief, or between righteousness and moral rebellion, as primary factors underlying both wealth and poverty. The Bible's ethics-based correlation is an implicit denial of the very foundation of humanism's welfare State. The welfare State rests on two rival theories of the origin of wealth and poverty, held together dialectically in most humanist explanations of economic inequality: 1) the chance distribution of economic assets and personal skills; 2) the exploitation of the poor by the economically and politically successful. The State is seen as the most powerful agency that possesses a moral and legal obligation to offset the effects of either chance or exploitation. The welfare State therefore in theory looks only at the numbers, not at the moral condition of the recipients of State money: their reported income in relation to statute law. Being bureaucratic, the West's welfare State must by law ignore moral criteria and respond strictly in terms of formal criteria: so much income; so many children in the household under age 18, irrespective of the mother's marital status; and so forth. *The welfare State is to biblical charity what fornication is to biblical marriage*. It literally subsidizes fornication by subsidizing the bastards who are produced by fornication, thereby swelling the ranks of the government-dependent children of the morally corrupt.[7] This creates lifetime employment for the next gener-

---

5. James L. Payne, *The Culture of Spending: Why Congress Lives Beyond Our Means* (San Francisco: ICS Press, 1991), p. 51.

6. Marvin Olasky, *The Tragedy of American Compassion* (Westchester, Illinois: Crossway, 1992).

7. Charles Murray, "The Coming White Underclass," *Wall Street Journal* (Oct. 29,

ation of welfare State bureaucrats – the unstated but inevitable goal of the welfare State. Yet so powerful is humanism today in the thinking of academically trained Christians that they have become open defenders of the legitimacy of the modern welfare State's system of compulsory wealth redistribution, despite the fact that it rests on a theory of unconditional legal entitlement.[8]

Reducing Our Fear of the Unknown

Biblical charity is essential for building God's kingdom on earth, for it reduces our fear of the unknown. We are not to live in fear of the unknown. We are to live in the fear of God, which is the beginning of wisdom (Prov. 1:7; 9:10). Intense fear of any aspect of the creation tends to paralyze men, to keep them in bondage to the creation. Fear and paralysis are what the biblical covenant was designed to overcome.

Bad things can and do happen to good people from time to time, while good things happen to the unrighteous (Ps. 73). The world sometimes appears to be governed by a system of perverse historical sanctions. Schlossberg is correct: "The Bible can be interpreted as a string of God's triumphs disguised as disasters."[9] Covenant-keepers are not immune from the corpo-

---

1993), editorial page.

8. Ronald J. Sider, *Rich Christians in an Age of Hunger: A Biblical View* (Downers Grove, Illinois: Inter-Varsity Press, 1977). For a line-by-line refutation of Sider, including his revised second edition (1984), see David Chilton, *Productive Christians in an Age of Guilt-Manipulators* (3rd ed.; Tyler, Texas: Institute for Christian Economics, [1985] 1990). Sider did not reply to Chilton in his third edition, either (Waco, Texas: Word, 1990). He did not even mention Chilton's book in his extensive bibliography. Sider has treated Chilton's book in the way that Winston Smith was instructed to deal with inconvenient facts in *1984*: he drops them down the memory hole. Yet Trinity College's Kenneth Kantzer writes in the third edition's Foreword that every North American Christian ought to read the book. "It is an honest exposition and condemnation of our rampant materialism" (p. xi). Condemnation, yes; honest, hardly. Thankfully, the printing quality of the third edition is so bad that very few readers will get through it.

9. Herbert Schlossberg, *Idols for Destruction: Christian Faith and Its Confrontation with American Society* (Westchester, Illinois: Crossway, [1983] 1993), p. 304.

rate curse that God has placed on the creation. We are also not immune to the corporate curses He places on the covenant-breaking society in which we live. So, as a way to reduce our fear of the unknown, God commands us to be generous to others in the faith during their time of need.

Biblical charity is a form of social insurance – not State insurance, but social insurance: provided through voluntarism without any threat of civil sanctions. Biblical charity begins with those who labor in the work of building God's kingdom on earth who voluntarily support other covenantally faithful people who share in this work. Biblical charity is therefore part of God's system of corporate covenant sanctions – in this case, positive sanctions, beginning with covenant-keepers and extending to covenant-breakers only after those inside the household of faith have been assisted.

The State as Insurer

Charity creates dependence. This dependence is to be temporary except in cases of permanent physical or mental helplessness. The biblical goal is dominion by covenant, not by permanent dependence. This is why State charity is so dangerous to biblical dominion and therefore to liberty. It creates a permanent political base of dependents and also a permanent corps of State-funded welfare agents whose income depends on the maintenance of poverty to relieve. For this corps of welfare agents, poverty is where the money is.[10] The positive sanction of charity is not to be provided by the State, which must impose compulsory negative sanctions (taxes) on some people in order to extend positive sanctions (welfare) to others. The State is to promote the general welfare only by punishing criminals and defending the nation from invasion. A biblical positive sanction

---

10. Shirley Scheibla, *Poverty Is Where the Money Is* (New Rochelle, New York: Arlington House, 1968).

– the general welfare – is the social result of the State's exclusively negative sanctions.

The State is required by God to defend the legal boundaries that establish private property, not invade these boundaries in an illegitimate messianic quest to bring positive sanctions to the poor. The civil magistrate is figuratively to stand inside the boundaries beside of the property owner to defend him against any threat of invasion by a non-owner. He is not to stand outside the boundaries by the side of the non-owner, threatening to invade. Defenders of the welfare State reject this view of the civil magistrate. Because so many of these defenders are orthodox theologians and church leaders, Christian social theory today is either non-existent (baptized humanism) or undermined by humanism.

Strangers and Neighbors

This text says that we are to relieve the stranger and the sojourner. The text in Deuteronomy 23:20 says that we may lawfully charge strangers interest. How can this apparent contradiction be resolved? Answer: by going to the Hebrew text. I have dealt with this issue in *Tools of Dominion.*[11] There were two kinds of foreigners in Israel: 1) permanent resident aliens who had placed themselves under God's law (Hebrew words transliterated *toshawb* and *geyr*); 2) traders and other temporary residents (*nokree*). The former were to be treated as if they were Israelites; the latter were not.

The resident alien was to be treated as a neighbor. The neighbor was a local resident. There is proximity in life. The neighbor is the person we meet in our daily walk, like the

11. North, *Tools of Dominion*, pp. 708-16. Reprinted with a few modifications in Gary North, *Boundaries and Dominion: The Economics of Leviticus* (computer edition; Tyler, Texas: Institute for Christian Economics, 1994), ch. 29, section on "Strangers and Neighbors."

Samaritan met in Jesus' parable of the Good Samaritan (Luke 10:30-35).

The destitute neighbor has a moral right to a zero-interest charitable loan, the law says (Deut. 15:7-10). This is not a legal claim enforceable in a civil court. The Mosaic law imposed moral obligations on Israelites – obligations that were not civil requirements.

A person who was destitute by Mosaic statute was someone who could be put into temporary bondservice for up to six years, until the beginning of the next sabbatical year, when all charitable debts were cancelled. A non-charitable debt contract could lawfully impose a longer term of bondage for bankruptcy, but such a debt contract was not morally obligatory on the part of the lender, and it could and certainly would extract an interest payment.

Interest and Inflation

In *Tools of Dominion,* I went into considerable detail about the economics of time-preference: the originary interest rate. I also discussed the thousand-year history of the church's false interpretations of the usury prohibition as a universal prohibition against all forms of interest. I do not need to reprint the entire chapter here. Those readers who want a detailed treatment may consult that chapter. Warning: it is a long chapter.[12]

It is necessary, however, to remind the reader at this point that *the interest rate is a universal category of human action.* It is not a purely monetary phenomenon. It results from the inescapable discount that acting men place on the future. For example, a brand new Rolls-Royce automobile is worth more to me today than the same Rolls-Royce delivered a year from now is worth to me today.[13] A bird in hand today is worth more than the

12. *Ibid.*, ch. 23.

13. I use the Rolls-Royce example because its style does not change very often, and older models retain their market value.

same bird in hand in a year.[14] This *rate of discount* of future goods as against physically identical goods that are in our possession today is the *rate of interest*.[15] It does not apply to money alone, just as the text in Leviticus indicates; it applies to food and, by extension, all goods and services. Interest on charitable loans is prohibited in the case of money, services, or goods – a recognition in God's law of the universality of the interest rate phenomenon.

Monetary Policy

In a period of rising prices (i.e., falling value of money), an astute charitable lender prefers to lend food ("victuals," or "vittles," as the word is pronounced) rather than money.[16] He cannot lawfully charge interest on such loans. A loan "in kind" – a consumer good rather than money – means that the lender will receive back the physical equivalent of whatever he gave up temporarily to the borrower. He will not suffer an additional loss from the debtor's repayment of the loan in money of reduced purchasing power. Since he cannot lawfully charge interest, he does not tack on what is called an *inflation premium* to the loan: an extra payment to compensate him for the fall in the value of money. There is little doubt that price inflation in Israel would have increased the number of loans in kind compared to money loans. A charitable loan made in money would have produced a loss of more than the forfeited interest; it meant the loss of capital.

On the other hand, in a time of falling prices (rising money value), either as a result of an economic depression or because of added economic output, an astute lender would prefer to

14. This assumes that the bird's species is not known to be facing extinction or some tremendous fall in numbers next year.

15. Ludwig von Mises, *Human Action: A Treatise on Economics* (New Haven, Connecticut: Yale University Press, 1949), ch. 19.

16. The word is seldom used outside of backward rural areas.

lend money rather than goods. He would then receive an implicit interest return on the loan: added capital (purchasing power) despite the numerical equality of the monetary units repaid. The Bible allows this. In times of falling prices, an astute borrower will prefer a loan in goods rather than money, but he is not in a position to demand such a loan. "Beggars can't be choosers," as the saying goes. However, in most periods in history, this added return on money loans is very low, since prices rarely fall rapidly except following a period of high monetary inflation. Economic output grows slowly most of the time; prices therefore fall slowly.[17]

There is no question that the lender's decision to loan in money or in goods is heavily dependent on the civil government's monetary policies. Because monetary policy cannot be economically neutral,[18] to some extent there will always be profits and losses in debt arrangements. Either the lender loses or the debtor loses, depending on the terms of the contract and monetary policy. The key judicial issue, however, is that in a covenanted Trinitarian nation, the contract for a charitable loan must not impose an explicit interest payment.

Conclusion

Usury from the poor brother is prohibited by the Bible. In the Mosaic Covenant, this poor person had to be willing to risk going into bondservice for up to six years if he defaulted on such a zero-interest loan. The civil courts were required to enforce this provision of a charitable loan. This bondservice provision was assumed in every zero-interest loan, which the court could safely assume was a charity loan. It was this willingness on the poor person's part to risk bondservice that identi-

---

17. This is not true of computer chips, whose speed doubles every 18 to 24 months: Moore's Law.

18. Murray N. Rothbard, *Man, Economy, and State: A Treatise on Economic Principles* (Auburn, Alabama: Mises Institute, [1962] 1993), p. 715.

fied him as a needy person. Accepting such a loan was a last resort. It was this degree of poverty, and *only* this degree of poverty, that created a moral obligation on the lender to lend.

This usury prohibition has nothing to do with interest on business loans or consumer loans, whether or not they are collateralized, although large loans normally will be. Commercial loans possess no element of moral obligation. Such interest-bearing loans in Mosaic Israel were not under the cancellation provisions of the sabbatical year, but the collateral for the loan could not be perpetual bondservice, for only heathens could be enslaved permanently in Israel. The Israelite bondservant had to be paid a wage, enabling him to buy his way out.[19]

The Pentateuchal texts are clear: covenant-keepers do not owe interest-free charitable loans to those who are not under the jurisdiction of either God's ecclesiastical covenant or God's civil covenant. This means that Christians who live under a civil government in which citizenship is not based on taking or implicitly accepting a formal Trinitarian oath owe no loans to resident aliens, i.e., non-believers. Why not? Because, covenantally speaking, *Christians have become the resident aliens*. We are the strangers in a strange land. We live as Abraham lived in Canaan, not as Joshua's heirs lived in Israel.[20] The difference is, Abraham looked forward to deliverance and victory during Joshua's generation (Gen. 15:16). Today, the vast majority of Christians praise their permanent resident-alien status as God's plan for the New Covenant era: political pluralism.[21] What Jews in Jesus' day correctly regarded as civil tyranny – subservience to Rome's pantheon of gods, incarnated in the State – today's Christians regard as political freedom. Even Calvinists, Protestantism's historic defenders of theocracy, from Calvin's

19. See Chapter 30.

20. Martin E. Marty, *Pilgrims in Their Own Land: 500 Years of Religion in America* (Boston: Little, Brown, 1984).

21. Gary North, *Political Polytheism: The Myth of Pluralism* (Tyler, Texas: Institute for Christian Economics, 1989).

Geneva through Cromwell's England to Puritan New England, have fallen into this humanist mind-set.[22] The Greek rationalism of the medieval university's curriculum has triumphed over whatever biblical elements had been sporadically tacked on by wishful Scholastic thinkers.

Today, the State does not recognize the legitimacy of temporary servitude in order to repay loans. The modern State has annulled the defining legal condition under which God established the Mosaic law's compulsory charitable loans. What about the New Covenant? Jesus set forth this rule: "And if ye lend to them of whom ye hope to receive, what thank have ye? for sinners also lend to sinners, to receive as much again. But love ye your enemies, and do good, and lend, hoping for nothing again; and your reward shall be great, and ye shall be the children of the Highest: for he is kind unto the unthankful and to the evil" (Luke 6:34-35). The law has been extended to God's covenantal enemies even when the threat of servitude for default has been eliminated. The law is broader and more rigorous in the New Covenant. But it is still conditional: no subsidy of evil. It is part of God's judgment: "Therefore if thine enemy hunger, feed him; if he thirst, give him drink: for in so doing thou shalt heap coals of fire on his head" (Rom. 12:20).

---

22. Gary Scott Smith, *The Seeds of Secularization: Calvinism, Culture, and Pluralism in America, 1870-1915* (Grand Rapids, Michigan: Christian University Press, 1985).

30

PROMISE, ADOPTION, AND LIBERTY

And if thy brother that dwelleth by thee be waxen poor, and be sold unto thee; thou shalt not compel him to serve as a bondservant: But as an hired servant, and as a sojourner, he shall be with thee, and shall serve thee unto the year of jubile: And then shall he depart from thee, both he and his children with him, and shall return unto his own family, and unto the possession of his fathers shall he return. For they are my servants, which I brought forth out of the land of Egypt: they shall not be sold as bondmen. Thou shalt not rule over him with rigour; but shalt fear thy God (Lev. 25:39-43).

The theocentric principle is clear: God is the master. He sets the terms for bondservice. What was a bondservant in Mosaic Israel? The Hebrew words used in this passage, *'abodah* and *ebed*, cannot be distinguished by grammar.[1] Both of these Hebrew words are analogous to the Greek word *doulos*, which is sometimes translated *slave* and other times as *servant*. We must therefore turn from grammar to context in our search for meaning. The context of this passage is twofold: poverty and permanent slavery. The preceding section in Leviticus 25 deals

1. See the introductory remarks in Gary North, *Boundaries and Dominion: The Economics of Leviticus* (computer edition; Tyler, Texas: Institute for Christian Economics, 1994), ch. 30.

with zero-interest charitable loans to poor people, either Israelites or resident aliens (vv. 35-38). The succeeding section deals with inter-generational slavery: a legal condition exclusively of non-Israelites (vv. 44-46). In between is this section: how to treat a poor Israelite.

Two Forms of Bondservice

In the previous chapter, I argued that the identifying mark of a person who was morally entitled to consideration for a zero-interest charitable loan was his willingness to become a bondservant if he did not repay the debt on schedule. In the sabbatical year, charitable debts were cancelled (Deut. 15:1-7). So was bondservice (Deut. 15:12). The two obligations were linked judicially. When the legal obligation to repay a charitable loan ceased, so did the obligation to serve as a bondservant for having defaulted on a charitable loan.

Leviticus 25:39 states that an Israelite could be sold into bondservice. He would not automatically go free until the jubilee year. The sabbath-year release did not apply to him. I call this jubilee bondservice, in contrast to sabbatical. I argue in this chapter that both forms of bondservice were likely to have been legal penalties for personal bankruptcy. There was always the threat of debt bondage in Mosaic Israel. The differences between the two forms of bondservice were the results of two different types of loans: charitable vs. non-charitable. There was a much greater threat of long-term bondage for having defaulted on a non-charitable loan than a charitable loan. A person entered a business debt contract with open eyes. A poor man who sought a charitable loan was under greater external constraints. God imposed reduced risks of servitude on him.

Bondservice as Collateral

A man's unwillingness to bear the risk of up to six years of bondservice for his failure to repay a loan established the loan as a morally compulsory, zero-interest, charitable loan. Unless the poor borrower were willing to take this risk, he had no moral claim on the lender. Yet it is clear from the text that Israelites could lawfully be sold into servitude until the next jubilee year. This bondage was a means of debt repayment. So, if servitude of up to 49 years was possible, why did the threat of no more than six years of bondservice judicially identify a morally compulsory charitable loan?

The answer is found in the issue of legal access to the inheritance. A man who was so poor that he was willing to risk bondservice until the next sabbatical year, but who was unwilling to put up his land as collateral, had a moral claim on a zero-interest charitable loan. He had a property to return to. He was poor, but he was obviously not so present-oriented or risk-oriented that he would use his inheritance as collateral. His poverty was temporary. He had an inheritance to return to in the sabbatical year after a period of bondservice. His post-crisis goal was liberty and dominion: self-government. So, he used his own potential servitude as collateral to secure the charitable loan.

The borrower who was willing to use his inheritance as collateral in a business loan, or one who had already leased out his land until the next jubilee year, was not equally protected by the Mosaic law. He had no moral claim on a zero-interest charitable loan. Either this was a business loan, in which the element of moral obligation was not involved, or else the person was economically incompetent: he had already leased his inheritance, yet he still wanted a loan. For this person, the time limits on bondservice that were offered by the sabbatical year of release were inoperative. He could be placed into bondservice until the next jubilee year.

Access to the inheritance served as the debtor's sanctuary. If he had not leased out his land, or if he had not lost it because he had used it as collateral to secure a non-charity loan that later went bad, he could not be placed in bondservice for longer than six years. God reminded the debtor that retaining possession of his inheritance – guaranteed citizenship as a warrior in God's holy army – was very important in God's eyes. Debtors who were willing to place their inheritance at risk to secure a business loan, or who had already leased out their land, were regarded by the Mosaic law as second-class debtors. They had no moral claim on a zero-interest loan; they also did not possess a sanctuary from bondage until the next jubilee trumpet sounded.

Bondservice and Boundaries

An impoverished Israelite who had been sold into jubilee bondservice was not to be treated as a bondservant by a fellow Israelite; instead, he was to be treated as a hired servant. This passage indicates that being a hired servant was preferable to being a bondservant. An Israelite was not to *compel* a fellow Israelite to serve as a bondservant. We need to ask: What was the difference between a bondservant and a hired servant?

There were exclusionary boundaries on hired servants and sojourners that did not apply to bondservants. A sojourner and a hired servant could not eat a holy meal with a priest; the priest's household bondservant could (Lev. 22:10-11). What was different between the two? The sojourner and hired servant were not owned, and therefore they could leave the household; the household's boundary did not restrict them. The slave could not leave; the boundary did restrict him. He therefore had legal access to the ritual meal of the priest's household. He was judicially inside the household's boundary.

The shared judicial status of sojourners and hired servants in Mosaic Israel seems to have been two-fold: first, they could leave the household of the employer; second, in some instances they were uncircumcised. We see this in the law of the Passover: it prohibited strangers and hired servants from eating, yet it allowed circumcised strangers to eat (Ex. 12:43-48).

The defining judicial issue in the Passover law was an individual's circumcision, not his right of mobility. In contrast, the definition of "sojourner" and "hired servant" applicable to Leviticus 25:40 is based on the existence of a household boundary. The sojourner and the hired servant could legally leave the jurisdiction of the household at the end of their voluntary, contractual service. The bondservant could not. The jubilee law did not require the Israelite to treat his impoverished brother as an uncircumcised person; it therefore must have required the owner to treat his fellow Israelite as well as he would treat a geographically mobile person. The poor Israelite was to be protected. He was defined judicially as a man who had temporarily lost possession of his landed inheritance. Economically, he was poor, but this was not a judicially binding definition.[2]

To Buy a Brother

This passage governs the treatment of an Israelite who had been sold to another Israelite. He had to serve the purchaser until the jubilee unless his kinsman-redeemer bought him out of bondage. This means that he was not under the protection of the sabbatical year of release (Deut. 15). What is the judicial distinction between the two conditions of household servitude? The Bible is not explicit, but the difference appears to relate to lawful immediate access to rural land. The poor man in Deuteronomy 15 was to be sent away with sheep, grain, and wine (Deut. 15:13-14). This indicates that he had a home to return to. The poor man in Leviticus 25 was to be sent back to his land only with his family. Nothing is said of his buyer's responsibility to provide him with any economic resources (Lev. 25:41). His judicial status as a free man was his primary resource; his landed inheritance was his economic resource; and his family went free with him. This distinguished him from both the poor man who had defaulted on a zero-interest, mor-

---

2. North, *Boundaries and Dominion*, ch. 30, section on "Who Were the Poor in Israel?"

ally mandatory charitable loan (Deut. 15:12) and the pagan slave who never departed, and whose children became the property of the Israelite who had bought him (Lev. 25:44-46).

The poor man in Leviticus 25 had already been legally stripped of immediate access to his land. Until the jubilee, he became as a poor resident alien in the land. He did not own a home in a walled city. He was landless. But this landless condition was economic, not judicial. *His judicial status as a free man was guaranteed by his legal claim as a member of God's holy army.* The jubilee year would reinstate him as owner and legal occupier of his family plot. He had no claim to his family's land in the present, but he had permanent title as a citizen. The year of jubilee guaranteed this. But if he became a bondservant, he forfeited his judicial status as a freeman until he was released. He could no longer respond to a call to be numbered without his master's permission.

Unlike the foreign slave, who was the property of the family that bought him or inherited him, the temporarily landless Israelite in bondage had to be paid a wage by his Israelite master.[3] At the very least, he had to be treated as well as a hired man was treated. The hired man could walk away from a tyrant. The permanent slave could not. So, the master was not allowed to treat his Israelite servant in the way that he was allowed to treat his permanent heathen slaves.

But this distinction between freeman and slave does not explain why this case law required the owner to treat him as a hired servant. What was the distinguishing mark of the hired servant? Answer: he could walk away from the household of the man who hired him. To retain his services, the renter of his labor services had to pay him a wage.

---

3. The resident alien did not have to pay him a wage. This law did not apply to the resident alien, who was no brother. This gave the resident alien a competitive position in the market for Israelite servants. He could pay a higher price for the net value of expected stream of income, since the net was higher: no wage expense. This was not a civil law. Civil laws had to apply equally to all residents (Ex. 12:49).

Wages

This means that in order to obey this law, an Israelite master must have had to pay a wage to an Israelite bondservant. The master was to this extent not an owner but a renter of services. Yet the servant had been sold into servitude. We must examine the apparent discrepancy between these judicial conditions: owner vs. employer; bondservant vs. hired servant.

The wage was crucial to the servant. If saved, it was this money or goods that would serve as his source of re-capitalization in the year of jubilee. He did not have to be given anything at the time of his departure in the jubilee year, unlike the land-owning poor Israelite who had defaulted on a charitable loan (Deut. 15:14-15). He had to be paid a wage, also unlike the Deuteronomic (sabbatical) bondservant. The jubilee bondservant was under bondage for a much longer period than the Deuteronomic bondservant, except in the seventh cycle of sabbatical years that preceded the jubilee. He could amass more wealth through thrift because he had more years of bondservice in which to save.

This arrangement raises a significant question. If the buyer could go into the open market and hire an Israelite for a day, or a month, or a year, why would he buy a full-time hired servant? The latter had to be cared for in bad times, whereas a hired servant could be dismissed. The buyer's expected stream of net income had to reflect the costs of feeding, clothing, and housing the servant, in good times and bad, and also paying him a wage. Why would anyone bother to buy such a servant? Answer: the buyer was securing a permanent hired worker who could not legally depart in search of higher wages elsewhere or better working conditions elsewhere. What the buyer was securing was a hired servant who could not be bid away from the buyer's household. The servant could not leave at will. *He was placed within a legal boundary*: the household of the family that had purchased him. The buyer was buying a stream of labor services until the jubilee. The servant could not lawfully cut off this stream of service by walking away.

Did the Israelite owner-renter have to pay the bondservant a wage equal to that paid to a hired servant? The text is not explicit on this point. It says only that the Israelite must be treated as a hired servant. If a hired servant could leave at any time in response to a better offer, did the owner-renter have to match every offer? This seems unlikely, given the status of the bondservant as a member of the household until redemption. The bondservant gained security; this always comes at a price. The price of security is the loss of entrepreneurial opportunities – in this case, the future prospect of renting one's services to another employer. So, the wages paid would have been discounted to compensate the owner-renter for the "lifetime (jubilee) employment contract" costs of employing the servant.

The legal option of liberty was always open: buying one's way out of bondage. But would he do this? This decision depended heavily on the owner's treatment. If his wages were high enough, he might do this. I conclude that wages that would not have enabled a man to buy his way out of servitude before the jubilee should have been judged as too low by a church court. But there was another factor that limited his personal exodus. The jubilee Israelite bondservant had no land to return to. He probably would have preferred the security of servitude, given the fact that his wages could accumulate to serve as his capitalization in the year of jubilee.

The passive language indicates that the individual did not sell himself; he was *sold to* the buyer. Who would do this? A previous owner? No; the law stipulates that "he shall be with thee, and shall serve thee unto the year of jubile." He had to be taken care of. *He was not a commodity to be bought and sold at will.* He had been a local resident: "thy brother that dwelleth by thee." He did not expect to be sent away from the neighborhood.

An Exception to the Law: Criminal Trespass

The criminal did not go free in the jubilee year. Had he received such a release, a criminal, seeing the approach of the jubilee year, might think to himself: "If I get away with this crime, I will benefit. If I do not get away with it, I will not have to remain in another man's service for very long. The larger the value of what I steal, the better the risk-reward ratio is." The closer to the jubilee year, the better the risk-reward ratio for crimes against property. The criminal's victim could not expect anything like double restitution from the sale of a criminal if the jubilee year was near. The stream of expected labor services would be cut off by the jubilee. Thus, the sale price of the criminal would be low. If the criminal was to be liberated at the jubilee, this legal arrangement would not only subsidize theft, it would subsidize high-value thefts. The victims would be penalized because of the liberation aspect of the jubilee year.

My conclusion is that the year of jubilee did not apply to convicted criminals. Neither did the law mandating owners to treat Israelite bondservants as hired workers. Criminals were sold into slavery in order to repay their victims and meet God's judicial requirements. The most important issue was not the liberation of the criminal; rather, it was the maximization of the criminal's selling price, so that the victim would receive double restitution. The law of God does not discriminate against victims of crime in the name of liberation. The principle of victim's rights lies at the heart of the Bible's criminal justice system.[4] The criminal must have remained outside the protection of the jubilee, and therefore *outside the judicial status of citizen*, until he repaid his debt to his victim. He could regain his citizenship only when his debt was paid. His adult sons, however,

---

4. Gary North, *Tools of Dominion: The Case Laws of Exodus* (Tyler, Texas: Institute for Christian Economics, 1990), chaps. 7, 8, 11-14. See also Gary North, *Victim's Rights: The Biblical View of Civil Justice* (Tyler, Texas: Institute for Christian Economics, 1990).

could return to the family's land at the time of the jubilee. Their inheritance was not forfeited by their father's crime, for the sins of the father do not transfer to his children (Deut. 24:16). As redeemers, they might even have paid off his debt.

The biblical warrant for this interpretation is Israel's experience in the Babylonian captivity. God removed most of them from the land for 70 years. They had violated His sabbath year of release and the land's rest for 490 years (II Chron. 36:17, 21). God did not allow them to return to their individual patrimonies in the normal jubilee year. They were under criminal sanctions, repaying their victim: the land itself. They could not return to their patrimonies until the debt was repaid. They temporarily lost their judicial status as judges in the land.

The Price of Redemption

If my view is correct, then the closer the jubilee year, the larger the market for buying convicted criminals. As the legal term of service shortened for Israelite bondservants, and their market prices dropped accordingly, those in the market for long-term bondservants would have been forced increasingly to enter the market for heathen slaves and Israelite criminals.

Second, if I am correct about the unique inapplicability of the law governing the treatment of Israelite bondservants, the net return on an Israelite's investment in buying a convicted criminal would have equalled the return available to resident alien purchasers, who were not under the terms of this law. The price for criminals would have tended to be higher than the price of other Israelite bondservants, assuming that the criminal was not violent. The price-depressing aspects of buying a criminal would have been offset in whole or in part by the higher rate of return: no requirement to pay him a wage. This, too, was a benefit to the criminal's victim: a higher sale price was more likely to assure him of his double restitution payment.

The question arises: What was the proper redemption price? How long would he have to serve? Did he become a lifetime slave? If his kinsman-redeemer wanted to buy him out of bondage, how much did he owe the buyer? The prorated price of the jubilee year did not apply if he was not entitled to go out in the jubilee.

Let us consider modern business practice. If a man buys an interest-paying instrument at face value in order to receive a guaranteed income, and the company issuing the bond possesses the right of redemption, the company must repay the face value of the bond in order to cancel the debt. The buyer has received guaranteed income from the asset in the meantime.

The economic difference between a bond and a bondservant is that the buyer is not sure how much net income the bondservant will produce. The bond pays a guaranteed rate of return. It is purchased at a discount from its face value. The discount is based on the prevailing rate of interest. The face value – redemption price – of the bond and today's rate of interest are known in advance. The price and the rate of return can be calculated.

There is no guaranteed rate of return for a bondservant. The buyer must estimate the future net income from a bondservant. Then he must discount this by the prevailing rate of interest. The higher the estimated net income, the higher the market price. But how long will he retain control over the bondservant? Unlike a bond, there is no fixed time period. Unlike a bondservant under the protection of the jubilee, there is no fixed time period. There must be a way to reduce the number of variables, so that the victim gets paid. But how?

The higher the estimated value of the criminal's productivity as a servant, the higher the price he will bring. This means that a criminal with a good work ethic is less likely to be able to escape servitude; his redemption price will be too high. This is contrary to biblical law: a subsidy for evil. There must be a way around this anomaly. But what?

The solution solves both problems: 1) too many variables and 2) the subsidy for evil. His legal redemption price must be limited by the payment to the victim. The kinsman-redeemer must be allowed to buy him out of servitude for this payment. If a bidding war pushes the criminal's market price above this maximum restitution payment, who receives the extra money? Not the victim; he is not entitled to it. Not the State; it is not entitled to it. It must go to the criminal's account – money for his redemption. This puts a ceiling on the market price of criminals. A buyer is less likely to continue to bid if he knows that the criminal can use the money above the restitution payment to shorten his time of service. The extra money will make it less expensive for the man's kinsman-redeemer to put up the difference and buy him out of servitude. Conclusion: the purchase price of a convicted criminal on the competitive market for bondservants will not be significantly higher than the money owed to his victims. When this limit is reached, bidding will tend to cease as bidders drop out. This is as it should be: the punishment (servitude) should be proportional to the crime (damages produced).

But if he has no kinsman-redeemer who is willing to pay off his debt, he will remain in bondage forever. He cannot buy his way out. He has no assets and no way to earn any. The message is clear: an enslaved criminal needs a kinsman-redeemer who has both the assets and the willingness to sacrifice his own interests on behalf of his relative.

Holy War, Citizenship, and Liberty

A citizen is a person who has the authority to serve as a civil judge, declaring innocence or guilt. The Israelite bondservant's judicial status as a temporary slave removed his judicial status as a citizen. He could not serve as a civil judge during his period as a man bound to another man's household. He did remain an Israelite. He did possess post-jubilee title to his land. No text says the following, but my biblical law-immersed intuition tells me that for a man to become a bondservant was judicially the equivalent of having become a minor. An Israelite had become a slave in another man's house, under another's temporary authority. *Judicially, he had become a child.*

Citizenship in any holy commonwealth is the legal authority to declare or bring negative civil sanctions in God's name. The pre-eminent manifestation of this authority in Israel was service in the military: God's holy army. The army had the task of defending the boundaries of the land, i.e., keeping it holy, secure from foreign invaders. The army had to keep the land from being *profaned* by invaders: boundary violators. To be a member of the army required the payment of redemption blood money at the time of the numbering of the nation immediately prior to a holy war (Ex. 30:12-13).[5] Circumcised Israelite males became eligible to serve at age 20 (Ex. 30:14).

The Israelite slave had to treated as "as an hired servant," the text says. He had to be paid a wage by his Israelite master. He therefore had money to pay the redemption blood money to the priests. Did this give him the right to serve in the army? No; he was judicially a child even though he was over age 20. Only with his owner's permission could he serve in the army. He was not a free man; he was not a citizen.

Gentile Slaves

Was a gentile slave who paid his redemption blood money and also fought for Israel in a holy battle subsequently released from bondage? Abram had fighting men (Gen. 14:14), but they did not receive automatic freedom. However, this was before the Abrahamic covenant was established (Gen. 15). It may be that in Mosaic Israel, the willingness of a slave to risk his life in holy battle gained him his freedom, though not landed inheritance.[6] He became a citizen in a walled city. If nothing else,

---

5. North, *Tools of Dominion*, ch. 32: "Blood Money, Not Head Tax."

6. It is one of the most interesting facts about the American Civil War (1861-65) that in its final months, Southern leaders and generals began to discuss the possibility of granting freedom to any Negro slave who was willing to enlist in the Confederate

manumission might have been a bonus offered to him by his master. This view helps explain the considerable number of foreigners listed among David's 30 mighty men (I Chron. 12:3-6). It may also explain the presence in David's army of the most famous foreign officer of all, Uriah the Hittite.

What we do not know for sure is whether these gentile slaves would have been required by law to wait until the jubilee year in order to receive their freedom. They surely could not have remained citizens unless they continued to attend Passover, even though, as household slaves, they would automatically have been circumcised (Gen. 17:11-13). Circumcision was necessary but not sufficient to make an adult male a citizen. Attendance at Passover was mandatory. My view is that after the war was over, the bondservant would have returned to the household of his Israelite owner until the jubilee year, but because the servant had become an Israelite through military service, he would have been entitled to be treated as a hired servant, as the law governing Israelite "jubilee bondservants" required. In any case, his owner would have had to consent in the first place to his enrollment in God's holy army.

The same rule governed the Israelite bondservant, whether a bankrupt or a convicted criminal. His owner had to consent to his military service. The owner may have had to pay his blood money fee for him – certainly this was the case with a criminal. I do not think any bondservant could be called into service by the State unless his owner consented. He was not his own man. He was the lawful property of another man until his debt was paid.

---

army. But the South had gone to war to defend the region's right to slavery. With this public discussion, the war effort began to collapse. If the slaves could be trusted to defend the Confederacy, then the old myth of their innate status as children in need of supervision had been ludicrous. This called into question the legitimacy of the "peculiar institution" and the war to defend it. See Richard E. Berringer, *et al.*, *Why the South Lost the Civil War* (Athens: University of Georgia Press, 1986), ch. 15.

The Basis of Liberty

As New Covenant people, we have difficulty understanding the degree of importance associated with landed inheritance under the Mosaic economy. The connection between land and inheritance was extremely close. The question is: Was it unbreakable?

The section on the jubilee ends with these words: "For unto me the children of Israel are servants; they are my servants whom I brought forth out of the land of Egypt: I am the LORD your God" (Lev. 25:55). The legal status of later generations as *God's covenantal bondservants* rested on their ancestors' historical experience in the days of Moses: deliverance from bondage in Egypt. It also rested on the next generation's participation in the conquest of Canaan under Joshua. This participation was the legal foundation of landed inheritance in Mosaic Israel. From everything we find in this section of Leviticus, inheritance was the legal foundation of *every* aspect of the jubilee law. I see no exceptions. Even in the case of the enslavement of heathens (vv. 44-46), the judicial issue was perpetual inheritance, though not landed inheritance.

Freemanship

First, who was a free man under the Mosaic law? There were degrees of freedom. Every resident of Israel was free from arbitrary law. The same civil law code applied to all men: "One law shall be to him that is homeborn, and unto the stranger that sojourneth among you" (Ex. 12:49). But it is obvious that this principle of equality before the civil law did not apply to the jubilee law. The jubilee made a fundamental distinction between the resident who did not have an inalienable legal claim to landed inheritance and the resident who did. The resident who did have such a claim was identified by God as His servant, although God had other servants.

There was only one way that someone who had not participated in either the exodus or the conquest could become God's servant, so defined: by adoption. God adopted Abram and his covenantal heirs, but the promised inheritance was not secured until Joshua's day. That is, *God's promise to Abraham was not fulfilled until Joshua's day*. The fulfillment of this promise (Gen. 15:16) was God's proof in history of the reliability of His covenant and its promises. Adoption, promise, and inheritance were linked judicially in the Abrahamic covenant and the Mosaic Covenant.

Naturalization

Second, there were two forms of adoption: into a tribe (walled city) or into a family (rural land). The circumcised resident alien was offered the promise of citizenship for his heirs (Deut. 23:3-8): tribal adoption. The tenth-generation heir of a bastard Israelite was offered citizenship (Deut. 23:2): access into God's holy army. The supreme example was David, the ultimate holy warrior, the tenth-generation heir of Judah and Tamar (Ruth 4:18-22).[7]

Adoption for males was not automatic, except probably for those who volunteered for military service during a war. Presumably, three generations was the standard period of testing for most resident aliens (Deut. 23:8). This adoption must have been made in the name of the congregation, presumably by the local tribal congregation inside a walled city, but not by a specific family. Had citizenship been available only through adoption by a family, the naturalization laws would have forced a dilution of the landed inheritance of specific families. This would have been a mandatory program of economic disinheritance. No such program was mandated by the Mosaic law.

7. On gaps in this genealogy, see North, *Tools of Dominion*, pp. 149-51.

Criminals

Third, what about the criminal? The criminal lost his citizenship until the debt was repaid. He could not be numbered to fight in God's holy army until his debt was repaid; hence, he was not a citizen during this period. He was not a free man; hence, he was not a citizen. Having had civil judicial sanctions brought against him, he did not possess the right to participate as a civil judge, bringing the State's judicial sanctions on others. This restriction is not found any text, but it is inferred by the nature of citizenship: the lawful authority to bring God's civil sanctions against lawbreakers. Until the victim was repaid, or the buyer whose purchase had provided the funds was repaid, the judicial status of the criminal was that of non-citizen.

I argue that he also lost his claim to his family's land, and therefore lost his right to participate in the jubilee. That is, he did not automatically return to his land at the jubilee. This legal status did not apply to his adult male children. They could go back to the land at the jubilee if they broke with him publicly regarding his crime. They could then become his kinsman redeemers, which is another reason why they were allowed to return to the family plot. In this sense, *he could be adopted by his son or sons*. That is, he regained access to his forfeited inheritance through an act of redemption in his behalf.[8] Otherwise, the judicial status of the criminal as an heir in the jubilee was forfeited until his debt was repaid. Because he received no wage, his kinsman-redeemer had to buy him out of servitude.[9]

---

8. This is the judicial basis of the re-established inheritance of a portion of the sons of Adam. A son of Adam who was not under the negative sanction of forfeited citizenship had to break publicly with the crime of His earthly father, thereby reclaiming the inheritance on behalf of those whom He has chosen to redeem. This was the act of the supreme Kinsman-Redeemer, Jesus Christ, the last (second) Adam (I Cor. 15:45).

9. The New Covenant warns us: "The wages of sin is death" (Rom. 3:23). We are in need of grace from a kinsman-redeemer.

Possession or Confession?

Another problem case is the adopted immigrant. When an Israelite adopted an immigrant, he was conveying a kind of manumission to him: *manumission prior to enslavement*. The covenantally faithful adopted person and his heirs could not be lawfully enslaved permanently after the adoption except on the same basis that an Israelite could lose his citizenship and his inheritance, i.e., excommunication. This act of grace cost the adopting family something: the dilution of the sons' economic inheritance. It was a major step for a father with sons to adopt another son, at least in the period in which a few acres meant something economically to the heirs. This means that if God's covenantal blessings continued, and families grew large, the economic cost of adoption would decrease, since the economic cost of the dilution of acreage would have been minimal.

The circumcised immigrant could become a citizen, or his heirs eventually could, through adoption by a tribe, probably in a walled city, but he had no claim to land distributed at the conquest. Only adoption into an Israelite family could provide land. The jubilee year therefore offered no unique economic benefit for him. Did it confer any judicial benefit? Yes. The heathen slave law was part of the jubilee law. The heathen slave law expressly stated that all inheritable slaves had to be purchased from heathens (Lev. 25:44-46). This was the magna carta for the naturalized citizen. By breaking covenantally with heathendom, and by becoming a full citizen ready to serve as a holy warrior, the immigrant received a perpetual grant of manumission from inter-generational servitude. He could not be permanently enslaved inside Israel. The jubilee year therefore functioned as a year of release for every citizen, even those with no inheritable property.

The naturalized citizen could not hope to indebt himself by means of the collateral of an inheritable plot of land unless an Israelite family had adopted him. To this extent, he was less able to gain access to the market for loans. But with respect to his liberty, he could not lawfully be enslaved. Leviticus 25 does not say that the landless immigrant citizen would be released from debt bondage. The language is that of a return to the family's land. But because the slave law made it illegal to enslave an Israelite on an inter-generational basis, the jubilee year of release must have applied to the non-inheriting naturalized citizen. The trumpet announced release from bondage for every Israelite except the criminal.

Cross-Family Adoption

There were three ways out of slavery for gentiles. First, there was manumission, either as payment for physical brutality by his owner or through voluntary manumission by his owner, but this would not automatically have freed his family (Ex. 21:2-4).[10] Second, there was legal adoption by his owner. This would have freed his family from the threat of bondage forever. There was a third way out: *adoption by another Israelite family*. This act of grace would have transferred the right of inheritance to him. He and his family would then go out in the jubilee.

This aspect of the Mosaic law is never discussed by the commentators, yet it was fundamental to the redeeming work of Jesus Christ. *Adoption by one household head could liberate other men's slaves*. In fact, if one man had been willing to divide his sons' landed inheritance to the point of no economic return, he could have freed every slave in Israel. He would not even have been required to purchase the liberated slaves in order for them to receive their freedom at the jubilee. The moment he adopted them, they would have become *heirs of his estate*, meaning heirs of his judicial status. They would have become *citizens of Israel* at the next jubilee. No heir of the conquest could be legally kept in slavery beyond the jubilee year. This act of uni-

10. North, *Tools of Dominion*, ch. 5.

versal adoption would have made the liberator very unpopular, as we can easily imagine, but it was always a legal option under the Mosaic covenant. The most likely candidate to do this was a man with abolitionist sentiments and without biological heirs.

Would he have owed the slave owners anything? Only for the time remaining until the jubilee. This prorated payment would have become progressively smaller as the jubilee year approached. In the year of jubilee, he would have owed them nothing. There was only one exception to this rule: the criminal who had been sold into slavery to pay his victim. In this case, his owner had to be repaid fully before the slave could be released. The buyer had paid a price based on the amount of restitution the criminal owed to the victim, not the prorated value of his services until the jubilee. The criminal was not protected by the jubilee. God's law does not subsidize crime. So, in order for the redemption to be secured through adoption, the adopting redeemer would have had to pay to the owner whatever the owner had paid to the criminal's victim.

It is understandable why Israel may never have invoked the jubilee. *Had it been honored, almost every slave owner's investment would have been at risk.* All it would have taken to free all the gentile slaves in Israel was for one lawful heir to decide that the per capita economic value of his children's landed inheritance was worth forfeiting for the sake of a single mass adoption: the ultimate abolitionist.

The Ultimate Adoption

There was such a man. His name was Jesus. He publicly declared the judicial intent of His ministry by announcing the availability of liberation through adoption into His family (Luke 4:18-21). The result was predictable: the slave-owners and their accomplices killed Him. With the death of the Testator came the inheritance: judicial liberation.[11] But because of the jubilee

11. "For where a testament is, there must also of necessity be the death of the

law, this deliverance had to await the blowing of the trumpet at the next jubilee year: on the tenth day of the seventh month, the day of atonement (Lev. 25:9), *yom kippur*. I agree with James Jordan that this final jubilee year came three years after the crucifixion, in the same year as the inauguration of Paul's ministry to the gentiles.[12] On that historic *yom kippur*, God released from judicial bondage every gentile slave in Israel who had publicly professed faith in, and subordination to, the New Covenant's head of household. Because Old Covenant Israel refused to honor this adoption, having killed the adopter instead, God destroyed Old Covenant Israel.[13]

As I said, there was one exception to manumission through outside adoption: the criminal who had been sold into slavery to repay his victim. The adopter would have had to pay the owner's purchase price plus anything still owed to the victim. In the case of Jesus Christ, He made this supreme payment to the victim, God the Father, who had placed all of mankind into servitude because of man's rebellion in the garden.

This should end the debate over whether a man needs to profess the Lordship of Christ in order to be saved. A regenerate person has no choice but to profess Christ's comprehensive lordship. He cannot lawfully partake in the jubilee inheritance without this profession. But because of God's mercy, this oath can be taken for him representatively, either by his parents when they offer him for baptism as an infant or when he voluntarily consents to baptism after infancy. Whether the oath is verbally professed or not, it is an inescapable aspect of God's covenant. There is no lawful inheritance apart from this subordination to the head of the church.[14] There is therefore no

---

testator. For a testament is of force after men are dead: otherwise it is of no strength at all while the testator liveth" (Heb. 9:16-17).

12. James B. Jordan, "Jubilee, Part 3," *Biblical Chronology*, V (April 1993), p. 2.

13. David Chilton, *The Great Tribulation* (Ft. Worth, Texas: Dominion Press, 1987).

14. Some fundamentalists who have no doctrine of covenantal representation

liberation apart from such a confession.

To keep Christian slaves in bondage beyond that final jubilee year was a crime. Furthermore, all slaves who claimed Jesus' universal offer of adoption into His family after this jubilee year would have to be released at the next jubilee. But the fall of Jerusalem 37 years after this final jubilee year ended the temple's Passover system and the land inheritance system established by the Mosaic covenant. There would never again be a God-authorized jubilee. There could be no authorized blowing of the ram's horn. Thus, the fall of Jerusalem ended the legality of Mosaic slavery forever.

Conclusion

The jubilee law established protection for poor Israelites who were sold into servitude. This servitude was mild, requiring the masters to pay wages to their Israelite servants. It required them to treat these people as they would treat a hired servant who could leave an employer who was abusive.

The jubilee law established a legal distinction between a free man and a heathen slave. The heathen slave had no right to jubilee freedom, for he was not eligible for military service. He was outside the civil covenant. The legal basis of citizenship was adoption, either by a tribe or a family. A woman was adopted by marriage to an Israelite, e.g., Rahab and Ruth. This was adoption into a family. Citizenship was automatic with adoption.

Citizenship was possible for male gentile converts to the covenant. This judicial promise was carried out by tribes. This might take as long as ten generations (Deut. 23:2); it might take

---

keep arguing that a person can accept Jesus as Savior but not as Lord, yet still be saved. Zane Hodges is the most prominent theologian of my day who presents this argument. This is a theological rabbit trail. The convert may fail to confess Jesus publicly as Lord, but his oath-bound confession of the Lordship of Christ is nevertheless imputed to him at the time of his conversion. Lordship is inherent in the oath by which God consigns the convert to Himself.

as few as three (Deut. 23:7-8). Once they became citizens, they could not be permanently enslaved (Lev. 25:44-46). The heathen slave law served as a magna carta of liberty for the naturalized immigrant. He could achieve full legal status as a citizen despite the fact that he had no inheritance in the land. Citizenship was by confession, circumcision, and numbering in the holy army. But it was not granted overnight by a tribe, except during wartime.

Jesus Christ was the ultimate Heir, the promised Seed (Gal. 3:16), the One for whom the Mosaic system of tribal inheritance had been created. It was He who announced the jubilee year (Luke 4:18-21). It was He who offered men adoption into His family (John 1:12). It was He who paid the debts of the criminals He adopts into His family. Instead of a hole in the ear drilled by an awl at the doorway of an Israelite's household (Ex. 21:6), baptism is the new mark of adoption. The New Covenant's jubilee year of release was the final jubilee for Old Covenant Israel.

31

SLAVES AND FREEMEN

Both thy bondmen, and thy bondmaids, which thou shalt have, shall be of the heathen that are round about you; of them shall ye buy bondmen and bondmaids. Moreover of the children of the strangers that do sojourn among you, of them shall ye buy, and of their families that are with you, which they begat in your land: and they shall be your possession. And ye shall take them as an inheritance for your children after you, to inherit them for a possession; they shall be your bondmen for ever: but over your brethren the children of Israel, ye shall not rule one over another with rigour (Lev. 25:44-46).

The text must be taken literally. First, Israelites could buy slaves from other nations. These people were already slaves according to the laws of their own nations. The Israelites did not make them slaves; they merely changed the slaves' residence: new boundaries. Second, the Israelites could buy slaves from among strangers residing in the land. But there was no authorization to buy slaves from other Israelites. This means that slaves in one Israelite family could not be sold to another family. The laws of inheritance forbade such sales (v. 46). They became part of a family's permanent inheritance.

There is no question about it: Mosaic law legalized intergenerational slavery. If Leviticus 25:44-46 is still binding, then the enslavement of those who not part of the covenant by those who are is legal in God's eyes. Enslaved converts who make a profession of faith after their enslavement, or the descendants of slaves, would still remain permanently bound. But no Bible commentator today wants to conclude such things, unlike almost all commentators, Jews and Christians, up to the 1750's. The exegetical question facing every Bible commentator is this: Has this law been explicitly annulled by the New Covenant? If not, then on what explicitly biblical ethical basis is it no longer binding?

The theocentric principle undergirding this law is simple to state, but difficult for modern man to accept: God is the cosmic slavemaster, the holy one who employs the cosmic whip. Modern man rebels against this thought, just as he rebels against the thought of an eternal lake of fire: no exit from God's cosmic torture chamber. Even Christians are squeamish about this. They prefer not to think about its implications. They also do not like to think about the fact that God's Mosaic law authorized slavery, but it did. In fact, the decline of Western man's faith in the reality of eternal damnation loosely paralleled the decline of his faith in the moral legitimacy of slavery.

Prior to the 1750's, virtually the whole world believed in the moral legitimacy of slavery. The ideal of abolition came quite late to Western Civilization, in the era of the Enlightenment.[1] Yet it was not Enlightenment rationalists who proposed the idea. It was only with the decision of a handful of members of the Society of Friends (Quakers) that the ideal of abolition as morally obligatory began to be spread by an identifiable organized group. This began at the Philadelphia Yearly Meeting in 1758. The group agreed to cease doing business with members who bought or sold black slaves. In 1761, the London Yearly Meeting ruled that Quaker slave dealers should be disowned.[2]

---

1. In some cultures, most notably Islamic, the idea has yet to take deep root.

2. David Brion Davis, *Slavery and Human Progress* (New York: Oxford University Press, 1984), p. 107.

A little over a century later, slavery had been abolished in the West. This was one of the most remarkable theological, moral, and judicial transformations in history.[3]

In *Tools of Dominion*, I devoted over one hundred pages to a discussion of the biblical theology of slavery.[4] It would be unwise for me to reproduce that chapter here. It was appropriate to include such a discussion in a book dealing with the case laws of Exodus because the case laws begin with a consideration of the purchase of a slave (Ex. 21:2-6). Slaves on their way out of a generation of servitude and into freedom would have been interested in a law governing slavery. The economics of slavery was governed by the jubilee's laws of inheritance: the preservation of freemanship.[5] Without the jubilee law, slavery lost its legitimacy. This line of argument was never raised by abolitionists, whether Christians or Jews, nor is it acknowledged today by those few theologians who refuse to break with the principle of abolitionism.[6]

The Jubilee Context

It is my contention that the laws governing permanent heathen slaves were an unbreakable part of the jubilee laws. If I am correct, this means that the exegetical case in favor of the annulment of the heathen slave laws rests on the New Testament's annulment of all of the jubilee laws. It is also my conten-

---

3. *Ibid.*, p. 108.

4. Gary North, *Tools of Dominion: The Case Laws of Exodus* (Tyler, Texas: Institute for Christian Economics, 1990), ch. 4.

5. *Ibid.*, pp. 140-44, 166-68, 144-47. Reprinted with modifications in Gary North, *Boundaries and Dominion: The Economics of Leviticus* (computer edition; Tyler, Texas: Institute for Christian Economics, 1994), ch. 31, sections on "The Economics of Israelite Slavery," "Slavery and Hell," and "Jesus' Annulment of the Jubilee Land Laws."

6. Most notably in the Calvinist world, Professor John Murray of Westminster Seminary. Murray, *Principles of Conduct: Aspects of Biblical Ethics* (Grand Rapids, Michigan: Eerdmans, [1957] 1964), pp. 100-1. For a critique, see North, *Boundaries and Dominion*, ch. 31, section on "The Ethics of Slavery."

tion that if the heathen slave laws are not subsumed under the jubilee laws, then there is no New Testament case for the abolition of chattel slavery. On the contrary, abolitionism itself would be anti-biblical, since the Mosaic law clearly authorized slavery. Abolitionism's universal condemnation of slavery would then go against the Bible's authorization of a certain type of inter-generational chattel slavery. Abolitionism would then be sinful.

There are Christian social analysts today, on the right and the left, who call for the reintroduction of the jubilee laws. The conservatives want the jubilee's law regarding debt repudiation, while the liberationists want its laws of land redistribution, which they think should be applied to all forms of privately owned (but never State-owned) property. No one, however, is publicly calling for the restoration of inter-generational chattel slavery. This is a typical example of smorgasbord Christianity: "A little of this, a little of that, but not *that* over there, certainly; I never touch the stuff."

The Purpose of the Law

To understand the law of inter-generational heathen slavery, we first must understand the purposes of the jubilee law. Its overriding purpose was judicial: to create an inter-generational link between the families and tribes of the conquest with their heirs, culminating in the advent of the promised Seed.

Citizenship was by covenant: by circumcision and by participation in the national feasts, especially Passover. But this was not sufficient; household slaves also were circumcised (Gen. 17:12-13) and participated in the Passover (Ex. 12:44). *What identified a citizen in Israel was his eligibility for numbering in the army of Israel.* This made him a free man, or as citizens are often called, a freeman. Who was eligible? Adult circumcised men who were: 1) members in good standing in the church, and 2) eligible for the army. This would have included circumcised men who lived in walled cities, whether or not they owned real estate, and heirs of the original families that conquered Canaan. *An inheritance in rural land was a covenant-keeper's guaranteed legal status as a freeman.* He could permanently lose this civil status only through ecclesiastical excommunication.

The naturalized citizen was no less a citizen. He could not be enslaved even though he had no inheritance in the land. The inheritance proved that a man was a citizen, but it was not necessary that every citizen have an inheritance. The inheritance was proof of citizenship; it was not the only proof. Proof of adoption was equally valid.

What this points to is *the centrality of the doctrine of adoption in Israel's civil order*. The doctrine of adoption was placed by Ezekiel's revelation at the center of Israel's history. Israel had been adopted by God as His wife.

> Now when I passed by thee, and looked upon thee, behold, thy time was the time of love; and I spread my skirt over thee, and covered thy nakedness: yea, I sware unto thee, and entered into a covenant with thee, saith the Lord God, and thou becamest mine. Then washed I thee with water; yea, I throughly washed away thy blood from thee, and I anointed thee with oil. I clothed thee also with broidered work, and shod thee with badgers' skin, and I girded thee about with fine linen, and I covered thee with silk. I decked thee also with ornaments, and I put bracelets upon thy hands, and a chain on thy neck. And I put a jewel on thy forehead, and earrings in thine ears, and a beautiful crown upon thine head. Thus wast thou decked with gold and silver; and thy raiment was of fine linen, and silk, and broidered work; thou didst eat fine flour, and honey, and oil: and thou wast exceeding beautiful, and thou didst prosper into a kingdom. And thy renown went forth among the heathen for thy beauty: for it was perfect through my comeliness, which I had put upon thee, saith the Lord God (Ezek. 16:8-14).

For the convert to Judaism, adoption was the only way into guaranteed legal status as a free man. This could be family adoption. An Israelite family could adopt him and give him a portion of the family's inheritance. This is why the Jews were furious with Jesus' gospel of redemption: *it offered full legal status as free men to every any through adoption*. They understood exactly what He was doing legally. Paul wrote of his brethren in the flesh: "For I could wish that myself were accursed from Christ for my brethren, my kinsmen according to the flesh: Who are Israelites; to whom pertaineth the adoption, and the glory, and the covenants, and the giving of the law, and the service of God, and the promises; Whose are the fathers, and of whom as concerning the flesh Christ came, who is over all, God blessed for ever. Amen" (Rom. 9:3-5). The Jews had been the adopted ones, and now the gentiles would be, too. All of this liberating judicial inheritance would come to the gentiles through adoption by Christ.[7] He was offering them liberation through His redemption. *He was buying them out of slavery* – slavery to sin above all, but also slavery in the broadest sense.

Christians need to understand and frankly acknowledge this implication of the jubilee: *Jesus Christ was the ultimate abolitionist*. He paid the slaves' ultimate Owner the price required: the sacrifice even to death of a perfectly righteous man. But because those redeemed by Christ have been legally adopted, *they can never again fall into the ultimate judicial status of servitude: sin and eternal death*. "And we know that all things work together for good to them that love God, to them who are the called according to his purpose. For whom he did foreknow, he also did predestinate to be conformed to the image of his Son, that he might be the firstborn among many brethren" (Rom. 8:28-29). The issue is *judicial immunity*: "Who shall lay any thing to the charge of God's elect? It is God that justifieth. Who is he that condemneth? It is Christ that died, yea rather, that is risen again, who is even at the right hand of God, who also maketh intercession for us" (Rom. 8:33-34).

---

7. This is the mystery referred to in Ephesians 3:1-6. For a development of this, see Oswald T. Allis, *Prophecy and the Church* (Philadelphia: Presbyterian & Reformed, 1945), pp. 91-108.

Slavery as a Model of Sin

Heathen residents of Israel could be permanently enslaved to repay their debts. The presence of permanent slaves in Israelite households was a visible testimony of what it means to be outside the inheritance of God. Slave status was like a permanent sign in front of a person's eyes: "No Exit." This was the representative mark of eternal punishment. There is no exit for Adam's heirs apart from adoption into the family of God through Jesus Christ, the firstborn Son. The Seed – the culmination of the Abrahamic promise – lawfully inherited the land. Elect gentiles are heirs of this promise. But the focus of this promise is liberation from sin. Those who trust in the law for their inheritance are disinherited, replaced by those adopted by grace. This is why Jesus' message outraged the Jews. Paul spelled out the message in its judicial context: *promise, inheritance, and seed*. He began his discussion with the redeemed person's escape from the imputation of Adam's sin (Rom. 4:8-18).

It was Jesus Christ who sacrificed His lawful inheritance in the Promised Land in order to bring His brethren through adoption into the family of God. The son of David abandoned His lawful inheritance for the sake of His elect. In doing this – delivering to them the promised inheritance – He gave them their irrevocable judicial status as freemen.

It is worth noting that the judicial precedent for this act was Joseph's decision to forfeit his status as the namesake of a tribe of Israel for the sake of his Egyptian sons, Ephraim and Manasseh (Gen. 48). His father Jacob acquiesced to this transfer of inheritance: the name. Jacob thereby adopted into his household the foreign-born sons of an Egyptian mother: gentiles. Thus, even prior to the announcement regarding the promised Seed, Shiloh (Gen. 49:10), there had been an adoption by the patriarch which disinherited his son for the sake of this beloved son's gentile sons. Joseph, the kinsman-redeemer of Israel/Jacob, was the primary redemptive model in the Old Covenant for

Jesus, the Kinsman-Redeemer of the New Israel in the New Covenant.

Outraged Slave Owners

This had always been the threat to slave owners in Israel: a man might adopt another man's slave as his own son, thereby providing him with a lawful inheritance: citizenship. This legal status as an adopted son could not be taken away except through ecclesiastical excommunication – and even then, his sons would inherit.[8] At the sound of the trumpet in the jubilee year, the adopted slave would go free. It was the sound of the trumpet in the jubilee year that invoked every heir's legal status as a free man.

There was nothing that a slave owner could do to prevent this. If a lawful heir to the original conquest was willing to dilute his descendants' *economic* inheritance, he could share with anyone an undiluted *legal* inheritance. The point of the jubilee land law was not that it promised the heir a guarantee of some sort of economic future. Rather, it identified him and his descendants as free men. This was the ultimate form of civil liberation that any foreigner could hope for: to be an adopted son of a citizen of Israel. This grant of adoption could be offered to any slave. But there was no way that the slave could purchase this judicial grant of liberty. He had nothing of his own to give in exchange. His liberation was the result of an act of grace on the part of a head of an Israelite household.

The possibility of "formerly heathen" slave liberation always existed, but we have no record of anyone who reduced his sons' economic inheritance for the sake of liberating his own slaves or other men's slaves through adoption. This indicates that God's

8. To inherit, the sons of an excommunicated man would have had to renounce their father's act of rebellion. In the case of a man who became a eunuch while in slavery, the law is silent regarding his sons. It seems to me that their father's legal status at the time of their conception would have been legally determinative. They would have inherited at the jubilee.

covenant blessing of population growth was not granted for very long, and men clung to their few acres of land in the expectation that it was really worth more than the liberation of other men's slaves.

The slave, of course, could refuse this offer of liberation. He might prefer bondage to liberation, servitude to inheritance. If you regard this possibility of refusal as being so unlikely that it must be the speculation of a madman, consider the response of millions of sin-cursed slaves to the message of the gospel. They will not accept Christ's offer of liberation. They know that there are three conditions attached to this offer of freeman's status: acceptance of the adopting man's name; lifetime subordination to a priesthood; taking personal responsibility for one's actions. So it would have been in Mosaic Israel. First, the adopter would have a bad reputation among slave owners: the destroyer of the value of the lawful inheritance of slave-owning families. Second, the legal status of a freeman in Israel could be lost through excommunication. Third, his economic condition could sink quite low if he was incompetent.

But wouldn't a gentile slave have regarded these conditions as mild compared to lifetime servitude for himself and his heirs? Probably. Then what about an Israelite slave? But how could there have been any Israelite slaves? Didn't the jubilee law protect them from slavery? Not if they suffered excommunication and then fell into servitude through an economic crisis or some other negative sanction. This scenario is exactly what Jesus was threatening the Jews with if they rejected His offer of adoption: *excommunication, negative sanctions, and slavery*. He was the true High Priest who could lawfully excommunicate God's enemies, an authority that He demonstrated when He used a whip against the money changers in the temple. Did the Jews heed His warning? Not many did. Did they assent to being adopted by Him? Not many did. But gentiles did.

Biblical Law: Death and Resurrection

At this point, I ask myself: Could there be any Christian who has read this far and still not understand what the jubilee law was all about? Then I ask myself: Why do the commentators emphasize the jubilee law's economic inheritance and its supposed ramifications, applications, and implications? Why have expositors who are masters of Hebrew, with years of experience, failed to recognize what is so incredibly obvious that it screams at the reader? The moment anyone puts three obvious pieces together, he concludes that any predominantly economic interpretation of the jubilee is ridiculous. The three pieces are: 1) God's covenantal blessing of population growth; 2) a fixed supply of rural real estate; 3) an ever-shrinking economic inheritance in rural land under the conditions of covenantal blessing. I ask myself: Why has this not been obvious? Why (as far as I know) am I the first expositor who has seen all this?[9]

The most important factor in exegeting specific Old Testament laws is a presupposition: *the Mosaic law is a coherent system that culminates in the work of Jesus Christ*. Some Mosaic laws were buried with Him; others were resurrected with Him. Seed laws, food laws, and land laws stay buried. They are replaced, respectively, by the law of spiritual adoption, the Lord's Supper, and the worldwide kingdom of God. Once a person understands this simple preliminary set of hermeneutical rules, it takes only a little imagination and some attentive Bible reading to make sense of God's law. This is not to say that making the real-world applications is easy. This may take a lifetime of study in just one field. But the judicial principles are easy to understand, and not very difficult to become familiar with.[10]

9. If there have been others, their observations have not been picked up by the major commentators.

10. This is why God required that the Mosaic law be read to the assembled nation one year in seven (Deut. 31:10-13).

Conclusion

My conclusion in Chapter 4 of *Tools of Dominion* is my conclusion here, which I reprint below. I must add here an observation regarding freemanship. A freeman was eligible to serve in God's holy army. A slave was not a freeman. The jubilee law identified freemen: heirs of the original conquest. But they were not the only freemen in Israel. Circumcised resident aliens could be adopted by the tribes governing walled cities.

Economically, the jubilee inheritance law, if enforced, would have tended toward the manumission of heathen slaves. The net cost of owning slaves would have grown high as the size of inherited agricultural parcels shrank in response to a growing population. The same would also have been true in walled cities. Thus, we must regard the judicial aspect of the heathen slave law as more important than the economic: the Mosaic law's identification of freeman status for land-owning heirs of the conquest, so long as they remained members of the ecclesiastical covenant.

When Jesus annulled the jubilee laws, He annulled the heathen slave law. He removed the judicial basis for inter-generational slavery. In this sense, Jesus was an abolitionist. While it took the church over 17 centuries to begin to preach abolition, this legal and moral position was nevertheless implied by the abolition of the jubilee law. When covenantal freemanship no longer tied in any way to landed inheritance within the boundaries of Israel, but came exclusively through spiritual adoption into God's family, there was no longer any covenantal purpose for inter-generational heathen slavery. There was also no longer any covenantal purpose for geographical Israel.

As for the economics of the heathen slave law, the Conclusion in *Tools of Dominion* suffices.[11]

---

11. North, *Tools of Dominion*, pp. 203-6.

* * * * * * * * * * * * * * *

Servitude exists because sin exists and because God's judgments in history and eternity also exist. This was Augustine's argument a millennium and a half ago, an argument that was old when he offered it: *slavery is one of God's penal sanctions against sin.*[12] Richard Baxter warned slave owners in 1673: "If their sin have enslaved them to you, yet Nature made them your equals."[13]

Covenant theology teaches that slavery is an inescapable concept. Slavery's positive model is the indentured servant who buys his way out of poverty, or who is released in the sabbatical year or jubilee year. He learns the skills and worldview of dominion. He becomes self-governed under God, a free man. Slavery becomes a means of liberation when coupled with biblical ethics. The fundamental issue, as always, is ethical rather than economic. His ability to buy his way out is indicative of a change in his ethical behavior.

Slavery's negative model is God's judgment of covenant-breakers throughout eternity. He consigns them first to hell and then, at the resurrection, to the lake of fire (Rev. 20:14-15). God places people on the whipping block, and then He flogs them forever. Of course, what they actually experience for eternity is far more horrifying than the comparatively minor inconvenience of an eternal whip. I am only speaking figuratively of whips; the reality of eternal torment is far, far worse than mere lashes. Thus, the legal right of some people to enslave others under the limits imposed by God's revealed law is based on the ultimate legal right of God to impose eternal torment on covenant-breakers. Biblical servitude is a warning to sinners as well as a means of liberation.

---

12. Augustine, *City of God*, Book 19, Chap. 15. Cf. R. W. Carlyle and A. J. Carlyle, *A History of Mediaeval Political Theory in the West*, 6 vols. (2nd ed.; London: Blackwood, [1927] 1962), I, p. 113.

13. Richard Baxter, *A Christian Directory* (London: Robert White for Nevil Simmons, 1678), Part II, *Christian Oeconomicks*, p. 71. The first edition appeared in 1673.

What I am arguing is simple: *it is not chattel slavery as such that appalls most covenant-breakers and their Christian ideological accomplices; rather, it is the doctrine of eternal punishment.* The denial of the New Testament doctrine of eternal punishment, above all other denials, is the touchstone of modern humanism. It is this doctrine, above all others, that humanists reject. They stand, clenched fists waving in the air, and shout their defiance to God, "You have no authority over us!" But He does. They proclaim, "There is no hell!" But there is. And the lake of fire will be even worse.

For all his protests, modern man nevertheless still accepts the legitimacy of slavery. Humanists understand implicitly that the right to enslave others is an attribute of God's sovereignty. They declare the State as the true God of humanity, and then they proclaim the right of the State to enslave men.[14] They have created the modern penal system, with its heavy reliance on imprisonment, yet have rejected the criminal's obligation to make restitution to the victim. They allow murderers to go free after a few years of imprisonment or incarceration in a mental institution, to murder again, for humanists are unwilling to allow the State to turn the murderer's soul over to God as rapidly as possible, so that God may deal with him eternally. They regard man as the sovereign judge, not God. They have invented the slave-master institution of the modern prison, while they have steadily rejected the legitimacy of capital punishment. Better to let murderers go free, humanists assert, than to acknowledge covenantally and symbolically that the State has a heavenly judge above it, and that God requires human judges to turn murderers over to Him for His immediate judgment, once the earthly courts have declared them guilty as charged.

The humanist abolitionist tries to put God in the dock. He tries to put the State on the judgment throne of God. What he

---

14. Libertarian anarchists are exceptions to this rule, since they do not acknowledge the legitimacy of the State.

hates is the Bible, not slavery as such. The question is never slavery vs. no slavery. The question is: *Who will be the slave-master, and who will be the slave?* Autonomous man wants to put God and His law in bondage. On judgment day, this strategy will be exposed for the covenant-breaking revolution that it has always been. The abolitionists will then learn what full-time slavery is all about. It is a lesson that will be taught to them for eternity.

The spiritual heirs of Pharaoh's Hebrew agents (Ex. 5:20-21) are with us still. Christians are in spiritual and cultural bondage to the theology of the power religion, and therefore to the State. They must prepare for another exodus, meaning they should be prepared to experience at least a share of the preliminary plagues, just as the Israelites of Moses' day went through the first three out of 10. It is nevertheless time to leave Egypt, leeks and onions notwithstanding.

We must be prepared for numerous objections from Pharaoh's authorized and subsidized representatives inside the camp of the faithful. They owe their positions of influence to Pharaoh and his taskmasters, and they will not give up their authority without a confrontation. They will complain that their potential liberators are at fault for the increased burdens that Christians suffer (Ex. 5:20-21). They will continue to sing the praises of the welfare State. They will continue to sing the praises of tax-supported "neutral" education. They will tell the faithful that humanist slavery is freedom, and biblical freedom is barbaric. They will attract many followers within the camp, for there will always be camp followers close by any army. Choose this day whom you will serve.

32

MANDATORY REDEMPTION UPON PAYMENT

And if a sojourner or stranger wax rich by thee, and thy brother that dwelleth by him wax poor, and sell himself unto the stranger or sojourner by thee, or to the stock of the stranger's family: After that he is sold he may be redeemed again; one of his brethren may redeem him: Either his uncle, or his uncle's son, may redeem him, or any that is nigh of kin unto him of his family may redeem him; or if he be able, he may redeem himself. And he shall reckon with him that bought him from the year that he was sold to him unto the year of jubile: and the price of his sale shall be according unto the number of years, according to the time of an hired servant shall it be with him. If there be yet many years behind, according unto them he shall give again the price of his redemption out of the money that he was bought for. And if there remain but few years unto the year of jubile, then he shall count with him, and according unto his years shall he give him again the price of his redemption. And as a yearly hired servant shall he be with him: and the other shall not rule with rigour over him in thy sight. And if he be not redeemed in these years, then he shall go out in the year of jubile, both he, and his children with him. For unto me the children of Israel are servants; they are my servants whom I brought forth out of the land of Egypt: I am the LORD your God (Lev. 25:47-55).

The theocentric meaning of this passage is that deliverance out of bondage is an act of God's grace. The universal redemption of Israelite freemen out of bondage was to be automatic in the fiftieth year, the jubilee year. On the day of atonement in the jubilee year, the day on which the ram's horn sounded, no Israelite heir of the original conquest could lawfully be kept in bondage except for criminals and those who, through renunciation of the covenant or by excommunication, had lost their judicial status as freemen.

This law added another way of escape for the Israelite bondservant: *redemption by his kinsman-redeemer*. The first form of redemption – the jubilee – required no payment to the slave owner; the second did. The first was based on judicial inheritance; the second was based on personal grace by the nearest of kin.

Why would anyone have sold himself to a resident alien? Because he had finally run out of income. This raises another question: Had he already leased his land to another? I think he had. The sabbatical year system of morally mandatory interest-free charitable loans would have protected a person with a farm to return to. Defaulting on this kind of loan, he would have sold himself to another Israelite to repay it. His temporary owner then had to care for him and his family, although without paying him wages, and then was required to give him food and animals in the sabbatical year (Deut. 15:14-15). This implies that the man in year seven owned his own land to return to with his new flock. But the man in Leviticus 25 was in such desperate straits that he had to sell himself and his family into bondage until the next jubilee year. He would not be entitled to assets out of his master's capital at the end of his term of service. He had become a stranger in the land. This was only permitted by God until a kinsman-redeemer bought him back, or until he could buy his way out of bondage, or until the jubilee's trumpet sounded. But the foreigner was under no obligation to pay him a wage. This made the Israelite slave especially helpless.

God's Designated Agents

The kinsman-redeemer was God's designated agent of family redemption. He was the one who had the primary authority to buy back a close relative who had been forced to sell himself into bondservice.[1] That someone in his family had been reduced to such a desperate, humiliating act was a mark of family shame. It was such a shameful thing that a kinsman-redeemer would have felt some degree of moral obligation to make the purchase. But, as we shall see, there were also economic incentives involved.

An Israelite was supposed to serve God as God's designated agent in Old Covenant history. If an Israelite fell under the family authority of a resident alien, this would interfere with his service to God. A covenant-breaker would become an economic intermediary standing between God and the Israelite.

Then why was the resident alien allowed to buy an Israelite? Because he had been economically successful. Verse 47 identifies the nature of his success: "And if a sojourner or stranger wax rich by thee. . . ." His wealth not only enabled him to buy an Israelite; it authorized him to do so. The Mosaic law recognized that covenant-breakers sometimes possess skills that are more effective in meeting the demands of consumers than those possessed by covenant-keepers. These skills may be able to be imitated. By subordinating themselves to the authority of a rich resident alien, the poor Israelite and members of his family were placed in an educational relationship under an economically productive family. The Mosaic law acknowledged that it was better to be under the authority of an economically successful covenant-breaker than to live a life of economic failure, i.e., bankruptcy.

This indicates that God wants His people to be economically productive. He was willing to have covenant-keepers subordinate themselves to covenant-breakers as a means of educating

1. I use the word *slavery* to refer to the permanent enslavement of heathens.

covenant-keepers in the techniques of wealth accumulation. This education was a positive sanction of bondage.

Consumer Sovereignty

Nothing is said in this passage that would have prohibited another Israelite from buying the poor man. What is affirmed is that the resident alien could also enter the market. He was authorized by God's law to become a competitive bidder in the market's auction for the poor Israelite's labor services. This raised the market price of these services. Why did God allow this? First, in order to allocate scarce labor services according to the demand of consumers. Second, in order to enable the poor Israelite to become a more efficient economic agent of consumers. He had to become the subordinate agent of a covenant-keeper – a rich one. He would have to hew wood and draw water in a covenant-breaker's household until the day of his redemption. He would learn from the most aggressive bidder in the local market.

The covenant-breaker, acting as the *economic* agent of consumers, was allowed to purchase the capitalized labor services of covenant-keepers in order to meet the demands of consumers. The scarce economic resource of labor would then be channeled into goods and services that were demanded by consumers. What this means is that *preserving consumer sovereignty in Israel* was more fundamental in God's law than preserving freeman legal status of bankrupt Israelites, at least until redemption took place or the jubilee's trumpet sounded. In this case, that which served consumers most efficiently was authorized by God's law. A bankrupt Israelite's legal status as a freeman was not to defended, free of charge, at the expense of the consumer.

The kinsman-redeemer could lawfully buy back the servant's legal status as a freeman, but this involved a risk on his part. He would probably have had to take over the care of the man and his family, for they had no land to return to. Freemanship was not a free gift to a landless Israelite until the day of jubilee. Someone had to pay: the kinsman-redeemer.

The man in bondage retained the right to buy his own freedom: ". . . or if he be able, he may redeem himself." Where would he get the money to redeem himself? Probably from an inheritance. A relative died and left him the purchase price of his redemption.

A Stronger Competitor

The resident alien had no obligation to pay a wage to an Israelite who had been sold into bondage. In contrast, the Israelite who purchased another Israelite had to pay a wage (Lev. 25:39-40).[2] In both cases, the bondservant would go free in the jubilee year. Since the buyer was buying an expected stream of net income until the jubilee, which buyer could expect a larger stream of net income? Presumably, the resident alien. He did not have to pay a wage; the Israelite buyer did.

The resident alien was in a stronger bidding position than an Israelite buyer, but the Israelite might decide to outbid the alien in order to avoid the shame in Israel of the sale of an Israelite to a resident alien. Altruism and religious pride have limits, however; at some price, the Israelite bidders would have dropped out of the auction. This means that those Israelites who defaulted on the largest sums would have been most likely to serve in the households of resident aliens. The resident alien could better afford to bid a higher price for purchasing a debtor.[3] Also, in the jubilee year, the Israelite departed without capital from the household of a resident alien. Had he been under the authority of an Israelite, he could have saved his

2. See Chapter 30, above.

3. Once the auction price of the bondservant matched the debt he owed, any additional money raised by the bidding process went to the bondservant. This would have placed a loose cap on the bidding, since the additional money could be used by the bondservant to buy his way to freedom. The buyer was then subsidizing a reduced return on his investment: a shorter term of service.

wages. Conclusion: the more money a man owed, the more likely that only a resident alien could afford to buy him to discharge the man's debt. It was therefore better to owe less money than more money, in the hope that an Israelite would buy you in a crisis, out of charity. Charity has limits.

The greater the man's debt had been, the longer his years of servitude. This system of bondage was therefore a model of hell. Greater debts resulted in more burdensome servitude. "And that servant, which knew his lord's will, and prepared not himself, neither did according to his will, shall be beaten with many stripes. But he that knew not, and did commit things worthy of stripes, shall be beaten with few stripes. For unto whomsoever much is given, of him shall be much required: and to whom men have committed much, of him they will ask the more" (Luke 12:47-48). The difference was this: Israel had the jubilee year for those Israelites who were heirs of the conquest and who were still members of the ecclesiastical covenant. Hell has no jubilee year of release. There is no longer a jubilee year. Jesus Christ, the cosmic Kinsman-Redeemer, abolished it: definitively (Luke 4:18-21), progressively (through the adoption of gentiles: Paul's ministry), and finally (A.D. 70). Apart from His redemption, there is no escape from eternal servitude.

This means that the greater the debt, the more money the kinsman-redeemer would be required to pay to redeem his relative, or else the longer the man would have remained in bondage. The greater the debt, the greater the price of redemption; the greater the debt, the greater the grace of redemption.

A New Master

The Israelite who had been purchased from a resident alien was subsequently to be treated by his relative as a hired servant. He was to be paid a wage: "And as a yearly hired servant shall he be with him: and the other shall not rule with rigour over him in thy sight" (v. 53). This means that the kinsman-redeemer was leasing his relative's labor services, not simply liberating him. The poor man had no land to return to. Until the jubilee year came, he was tied to the kinsman-redeemer unless the latter voluntarily released him.

Then why buy him at all? First, to overcome the shame of the family: to liberate a brother from bondage in the household of a foreigner. Second, to keep the resident alien from profiting at the expense of an unpaid Israelite servant. If the price of labor had risen since the day that the stranger bought the man, the resident alien was reaping an entrepreneurial profit. The unexpected rise in the value of labor services was being pocketed by the foreigner. The jubilee law authorized the kinsman-redeemer to buy the future labor services of his relative, which would run out at the next jubilee. He paid the original purchase price minus the years already served. The value of these labor services was higher than when the alien purchased the Israelite, but the purchase price per year of servitude remaining was fixed by the jubilee law. The kinsman-redeemer was in a position to re-claim from the alien all remaining entrepreneurial profits, should they continue. The tithe on these profits would then revert to the Levites.

The kinsman-redeemer would have had to pay his kinsman a wage. This leads us to the third point: the presence of an economic return. What was the nature of this return? The kinsman-redeemer could always hire labor services on a piece-rate basis. Why, economically speaking, would he commit himself to buying an Israelite, who would be owed a wage? Answer: to reduce his risk. The kinsman-redeemer might buy his relative for the same reason that producers buy goods to put into an inventory. If a producer has very little time to get delivery of the particular resource input, he has to pay a higher price to buy it "off the shelf" – some seller's shelf. Instead, he puts it on his own shelf.[4] Keeping an inventory is a substitute for know-

4. Prior to widespread computerization of inventories in the 1980's, and prior to

ing the future perfectly, just as holding cash is. If we knew the future perfectly, we could time production and sales so well that we would need neither inventories nor cash in reserve.[5]

By purchasing his kinsman out of bondage, the kinsman-redeemer would have secured a permanent employee for himself until the jubilee year. The relative was still a bondservant who was not allowed to walk away. He was legally tied to the household of his redeemer until he could afford to redeem himself or the jubilee came. But he was at least out from under the authority of a resident alien. He would henceforth receive a wage. He was better off.

The kinsman-redeemer could buy his relative out of bondage at a price commensurate with the years remaining until the jubilee: a prorated price that dropped as the jubilee approached (v. 50). When the alien paid for the Israelite, the redemption price was locked in by civil law. The alien could not readily sell the capitalized services of the Israelite to the highest bidder, who probably would have been another resident alien. The price paid by the original purchaser established the maximum price that a kinsman had to pay to redeem his relative, and this price steadily dropped as the jubilee year approached. It is unlikely that any subsequent buyer would pay the original purchaser more than the redeemer's price, for he would have risked seeing the kinsman-redeemer buy the man out of bondage at a price based on the original owner's purchase price. It was legal for a resident alien to buy an Israelite servant, but the jubilee law placed limits on this market.

Federal Express and other overnight delivery private mail firms, inventories in American business were larger. The "just in time" techniques of computerized production did not exist, or existed only in a few firms.

5. If no one needed cash in reserve, there would be no cash; its value would fall to zero. Transactions would be by barter only. We cannot really imagine such a money-less world, for it is a world of man's omniscience, which is neither possible nor conceivable (Deut. 29:29). This is a major problem for economic theory, which assumes omniscience in the creation of such theoretical constructs as equilibrium.

Capitalized Value

The terms of redemption were the same for Israelite bondservants as for rural land (Lev. 25:14-16). It was a prorated redemption: the redeemer had to pay only for the time remaining before the jubilee. This means that the purchase price would be averaged on an annualized basis: from the time of purchase to the jubilee.

This means that the original buyer took a risk. If he "bought low," when the expected value of the land's output or the servant's output was low, on the assumption that prices for these services would rise, he could lose his entrepreneurial profit if a redeemer came to claim his right of purchase. The original buyer would be repaid whatever was owed to him based on the original purchase price, not on the new, higher value of the expected stream of services. On the other hand, if he "bought high," when the expected returns were high, and then the value of the services fell, the land or bondservant would be less likely to be redeemed, since the redeemer would have to pay a prorated price based on the original purchase price, which was high. This means that the original buyer was more likely to suffer losses than enjoy profits if the market value of the expected stream of services changed.

This was even more true of land redemptions. The kinsman-redeemer could re-purchase his kinsman's land from a buyer at a fixed price: whatever the buyer had paid prorated according to the years remaining till the jubilee. He had no wages to pay. When he bought a relative out of bondage, he had to pay him a wage. Not so with land.

What is clear is that the purchase of either rural land in Israel or an Israelite bondservant was a lease agreement. Because of the jubilee year's limits on both rural land transfers and Israelite servitude, this was not a purchase; it was a lease. It was a not a lease with an option to buy; it was a lease in which an outsider – the kinsman-redeemer – had the option to redeem the lease. The lease was a rental arrangement in which the redeemer could interrupt the long-term rental agreement by making a prorated payment to the lessor. God was the owner of the land and the Israelites; He set the terms of trade. This price system would have restricted the market for Israelite bondservants and rural land.

Leviticus on Rent: Anti-Populist

Rent is the economic return produced by some scarce resource over a specified time period. The resource may be land, but it could also be labor. What is the present value of this stream of income? We cannot know until we know the rate of interest: the time discount applied by economic actors to all streams of income. The origin of interest is human action: time preference. Rents will, through competition, tend to equal the rate of interest.[6]

In this world, there are defenders of a world without interest. Sometimes these people call themselves defenders of Christian economics: defenders of the Mosaic law's supposedly universal rejection of interest on loans. Sometimes they call themselves populists: defenders of the sovereign People. Because rent and interest tend to become equal under competition, the defender of a zero-interest economic system must, if he follows the logic of his system, also deny the moral legitimacy of all rental contracts. (There are very few populist analysts who have understood this implication of their system.)[7] But this section of Leviticus clearly affirms the legitimacy of such rental contracts. This poses an insolvable theoretical problem for those people who argue that, biblically speaking, rental contracts are illegitimate. They deal with this problem by ignoring it.[8]

---

6. See Chapter 26, above, subsection on "Interest and Rent."

7. S. C. Mooney, a defender of interest-free business loans, is one of the few populists who have understood this. He insists that "it is not lawful for one to sell the use of his property (rent)." S. C. Mooney, *Usury: Destroyer of Nations* (Warsaw, Ohio: Theopolis, 1988), p. 173.

8. Mooney refused to comment in his book on Leviticus 25:25-28 and 25:47-51.

Conclusion

The jubilee was the year of redemption in Israel. It reunited judicially the dispossessed Israelite and his landed inheritance. The maximum time limit placed by God's law on Israelite bondservice was therefore the same as the limit on the leasing of rural property: the next jubilee year.

The possibility of immediate redemption was available in both cases: land and labor. The kinsman-redeemer could buy his relative out of bondage by making a prorated payment to the buyer based on the original purchase price. This payment was based on the years remaining until the jubilee: the original purchase price divided by the number of years until the jubilee multiplied by the number of years remaining.

The presence of this law in the Mosaic law indicates how important the ideal of consumer sovereignty is in God's eyes. An Israelite who found himself in dire straits economically could lawfully sell himself to a resident alien. The economic success of the resident alien was legitimate. He had met the demands of consumers. The Israelite had failed to meet the demands of consumers. The resident alien was authorized to buy the Israelite until the next jubilee year. So important were the twin ideals of efficiency and profit that God was willing to see some of His people in temporary bondage to covenant-breakers within the boundaries of the Promised Land. Perhaps these less efficient Israelites would learn to become more efficient producers, thereby improving the options available to consumers.

Because the resident alien did not have to pay a wage to an Israelite bondservant, while Israelites were required to pay him a wage, this law gave a competitive advantage to the resident alien in the market for Israelite bondservants. It made it clear

---

For a critique of Mr. Mooney, see Gary North, *Tools of Dominion: The Case Laws of Exodus* (Tyler, Texas: Institute for Christian Economics, 1990), Appendix G: "Lots of Free Time: The Existentialist Utopia of S. C. Mooney."

what the consequence of bankruptcy was likely to be: long-term bondage to covenant-breakers.

What was illegal for an Israelite – the refusal to pay a wage to his Israelite bondservant – was not illegal for resident aliens. Why not? Because bondage to resident aliens was a model of hell: the wrath of God. It served as a reminder to the Israelites of their need for a kinsman-redeemer. They were all in debt to God. They could not afford to buy their way out of Adam's bondage. Only God's grace of the fulfilled jubilee offered the nation long-term hope, and only God's grace in the interim as their kinsman-redeemer offered short-term hope. God's designated Kinsman-Redeemer is Jesus Christ, who announced the fulfillment of the jubilee principle when He began his public prophetic ministry (Luke 4:18-21).

This law rested on a required wage payment, but there were no specifics regarding the amount of the wage. This made law enforcement difficult for the magistrates, and therefore also made legal predictability difficult for Israelite masters. I conclude that this law was enforced by the Levites, not the civil magistrate. They would have had more leeway in working out equitable arrangements with the masters. This law did not prohibit an evil act, i.e., the legitimate function of civil government. It mandated positive sanctions, and only for Israelite masters. It therefore discriminated economically against Israelite masters. But Mosaic civil law was to be equal for all (Ex. 12:49). So, this must have been an ecclesiastical law.

33

NATURE AS A SANCTIONING AGENT

If ye walk in my statutes, and keep my commandments, and do them; Then I will give you rain in due season, and the land shall yield her increase, and the trees of the field shall yield their fruit. And your threshing shall reach unto the vintage, and the vintage shall reach unto the sowing time: and ye shall eat your bread to the full, and dwell in your land safely. And I will give peace in the land, and ye shall lie down, and none shall make you afraid: and I will rid evil beasts out of the land, neither shall the sword go through your land (Lev. 26:3-6).

The theocentric message here is that God is the sovereign sustainer of the creation, who personally intervenes into the realm of nature in terms of His covenant. Because His covenant with Israel was judicial, the land was uniquely under His law's sanctions. This law was not impersonal-mathematical; it was ethical.

The covenantal blessings of Leviticus 26:3-6 were corporate. Rain in due season was promised by God for all the land within the boundaries of national Israel, not just for the land belonging to covenant-keeping individuals. The individual Israelite would receive these blessings only as a resident of a covenanted nation: inside the national covenant's geographical boundaries. These boundaries were primarily judicial and secondarily geographical. Only within these covenantal boundaries could the promised blessings be successfully invoked in God's name, generation after generation, and only if those living within these boundaries were actively conforming themselves to the ethical boundaries of God's revealed law. Only inside the land of promise – a covenanted nation – were there sufficient numbers of covenant-keepers and also publicly law-abiding covenant-breakers to call forth these promised blessings through the generations.[1] These were not cross-boundary laws.

As I shall argue later in this chapter, the covenantally predictable sanctions of rain and sunshine were exclusive to Mosaic Israel's economy. They were *land sanctions*, which are no longer God's means of imparting predictable blessings and curses. The New Covenant has transferred God's predictable sanctions from climate to society. What a society does in response to the terms of God's revealed law determines God's predictable blessings and cursings. Nature's climatic processes are no longer covenantally predictable, and hence are no longer covenantal sanctions. It is what society does in response to God's revealed law that will determine whether nature's covenantally unpredictable climatic processes become blessings or curses.

Does this mean that none of the Mosaic covenant's system of corporate sanctions applied outside of the boundaries? No, but it does mean that only inside Israel's boundaries was there any legitimate hope that positive blessings could be sustained long term. *The basis of God's blessings is always judicial: God's grace*. The

1. It is a theologically and psychologically disastrous misinterpretation of God's promises of wealth to place them within an exclusively personal or individual framework. The individualism of the "positive confession" charismatic movement is an example of just such a false interpretation of covenantal, corporate promises. God's blessings are not successfully invoked verbally; they are invoked corporately and ethically. Individual Christians are not supposed to "name it and claim it." Instead, we are to do the following: obey God personally by following His law; pray for the widespread movement of the Holy Spirit in what is called revival; work toward a corporate, constitutional, and civil affirmation of the absolute authority of the God of the Bible; and hope for the best until these covenantal requirements are met. Only after this can we be confident about predictable, sustainable corporate blessings.

nations outside the land could become the recipients of God's common grace, but only if they outwardly obeyed the terms of God's revealed law. But apart from special grace, common grace cannot be maintained long term. The covenant-breaking recipients of common grace will eventually revolt against God and His law. The blessings are not sufficient rewards to persuade them to remain outwardly faithful indefinitely. Large numbers of covenant-breakers must be converted to saving faith if they are not to rebel.[2]

The best example of this process of moral backsliding under the Mosaic Covenant economy is Nineveh, capital city of Assyria. The fact that God threatened Nineveh with destruction in 40 days indicates that the Levitical system of corporate sanctions was in operation outside the land of Israel – in this case, negative sanctions. These were not seed and land sanctions. Nineveh repented on a corporate but external basis in the face of Jonah's preaching of imminent negative sanctions. No one had to become circumcised, but the nation escaped external destruction because their flagrant sinning ended. Eventually Assyria revolted against God, invaded Israel, and carried off the residents of the Northern Kingdom. Then Babylon destroyed Assyria.

Common grace cannot be sustained apart from special grace. Covenant-breakers eventually return to their outward rebellion. God then gives them up to their lusts (Rom. 1:18-22). Apart from circumcision, there was no possibility of special grace under the Old Covenant after Abraham.[3] There could be no inheritance of covenantal blessings beyond the third and fourth generation of those who hated God (Ex. 20:5).

---

2. Gary North, *Dominion and Common Grace: The Biblical Basis of Progress* (Tyler, Texas: Institute for Christian Economics, 1987), ch. 6.

3. This is why Egypt was not brought to saving faith under Joseph. We know this because there was no covenantal succession; every Egyptian family suffered the death of the firstborn at the exodus. Egypt's faith was a common grace faith.

Sanctions and Representation

The blessings listed here are agricultural and social: bread, wine, and peace. These are positive sanctions.[4] Ten righteous representatives of Sodom would have kept God from bringing total negative sanctions against that city, but only because of Abraham's negotiation with God (Gen. 18:24-32). But what about positive sanctions in Israel? What had to be done in Israel in order to gain bread, wine, and peace? The people as a covenantal unit were told to obey God. The Bible never mentions a specific percentage of the population that must obey God in order for God's positive, visible sanctions to become predictable in history. This is why the absolute predictability of God's sanctions in history is an unobtainable ideal. But absolute *anything* in history is unobtainable by men, so this should not deter us in our quest to gain His positive sanctions. What the Bible teaches is that the number of active covenant-keepers must be large enough to represent the nation judicially. The society must be marked by widespread obedience to the civil laws set forth by God. Blessings apart from faithfulness are a prelude to negative sanctions on a comparable scale.

Covenantal Representation

God promised covenantal blessings to the residents of the nation of Israel in response to individuals' covenantal obedience. Obedience is always in part individual, for individuals are always held responsible by God for their actions. This responsibility is inescapable in history and at the day of final judgment.[5] Nevertheless, there is no doubt that God's promised historical responses to individual obedience were corporate

---

4. Peace might be considered the absence of war, but given the condition of mankind after Adam's rebellion, it takes God's active grace to bring peace to man. Peace is not normal even though it is normative. Peace is not passive. War and sin are the passive condition of covenant-breaking man (James 4:1).

5. The law's visible sanctions are more predictable at the final judgment.

sanctions. The question is: How many people in Israel had to obey God's law in order for the nation to receive these promised visible blessings? This is the question of covenantal representation.

In the bargaining process between Abraham and God over the fate of Sodom, Abraham persuaded God to drop the minimum-required number of righteous men to only 10 as the condition of avoiding total negative sanctions against the city (Gen. 18:24-32). These threatened corporate sanctions were both negative and total. There is nothing in the Mosaic law to indicate that a remnant of only 10 men would have preserved the nation of Israel from lesser negative sanctions, such as invasion or captivity. God told Elijah that He had kept 7,000 men from bowing the knee to Baal, but God did not on their account promise to spare Israel. On the contrary, He used Elijah as His agent to anoint Hazael the Syrian, who would then bring negative sanctions against Israel. This revelation from God came as a unit (I Ki. 19:15-18).

Abraham's bargaining was based on a theory of covenantal representation. Ten righteous men in Sodom could have served as representatives for the entire city, even though the city's population was perverse. This is an indication of the magnitude of God's grace. But His grace is not without ethical conditions. There did have to be 10 righteous men in Sodom in order for God to display His grace to all the other inhabitants. The 7,000 covenant-keepers of Elijah's day served as covenantal representatives who kept Israel from being totally destroyed, Sodom-like, but they did not protect the nation from lesser negative sanctions. God's grace sometimes temporarily offsets a widespread decline of faith, as it did in the days of Hezekiah (II Ki. 20:1-6), but if there is no widespread repentance during this period of grace, negative corporate sanctions will inevitably come. They are predictable in history.

Who was responsible for gaining these blessings? The text does not identify any single representative. Could a single agent represent the nation as a whole? In some cases, yes. God spared Judah for the sake of Hezekiah's repentance (II Ki. 20:1-6). The crucifixion of Jesus definitively proves the point.[6] By bringing Him under the negative sanction of public execution, Israel's representatives brought the whole nation under God's negative sanction of public execution in A.D. 70.[7] In Israel, covenantal representatives included the high priest, priests in general, Levites, civil rulers, prophets, and heads of households.[8] The people of Israel were to serve the world as a royal priesthood (Ex. 19:6). They represented other nations.[9] The Mosaic law did not single out civil officers as the nation's primary legal representatives. The office of high priest was far more important than the office of king. National Israel could and did exist without a king; it could not exist without a high priest. It is a sign of the modern world's perversity that the civil ruler is regarded as possessing the crucial form of sovereignty.[10] This same error governed pagan men's thinking in the ancient world.[11]

---

6. "And one of them, named Caiaphas, being the high priest that same year, said unto them, Ye know nothing at all, Nor consider that it is expedient for us, that one man should die for the people, and that the whole nation perish not. And this spake he not of himself: but being high priest that year, he prophesied that Jesus should die for that nation; And not for that nation only, but that also he should gather together in one the children of God that were scattered abroad" (John 11:49-52).

7. David Chilton, *The Days of Vengeance: An Exposition of the Book of Revelation* (Ft. Worth, Texas: Dominion Press, 1987).

8. In most cases, this would have been a circumcised male. In the case of widows and divorced women, they became the heads of their households, for they were required to fulfill their vows without initial approval by a male (Num. 30:9).

9. During the feast of tabernacles, Israel sacrificed a total of 70 bulls for the 70 nations (Jud. 1:7), plus one for Israel (Num. 29:13-36).

10. A representative discussion is Bertrand de Jouvenal, *Sovereignty: An Inquiry into the Political Good* (University of Chicago Press, 1957). The author was a conservative. This book was a sequel to his equally political study, *Power: The Natural History of Its Growth* (rev. ed.; London: Batchworth, [1945] 1952).

11. R. J. Rushdoony, *The One and the Many: Studies in the Philosophy of Order and Ultimacy* (Fairfax, Virginia: Thoburn Press, [1971] 1978), chaps. 3-5.

God's promises to a corporate entity do not mandate that there be a representative *political* agency to serve as His primary economic agent. This means that a central agricultural planning bureau should not be created by the State, nor should such an agency make the decisions about what to plant, where, and when. There must be no civil "Department of Bread and Wine." Neither it nor any another political agency should decide which crops to sell, at what price, and to whom, except during wartime, and then only because the State takes on a priestly function, when its corporate decisions are literally life-and-death representative decisions.[12] Nevertheless, the question remains: If God makes men responsible collectively, as His covenantal promises indicate that He does, then what kind of representative human authority should be established in order to monitor the arena – the boundaries – in which the sanctions are applied, both positive and negative?

Stipulations and Representation

God's covenantal promises in the Mosaic law were ethical, not magical or technical. They were governed by God's stipulations: the boundaries of legitimate behavior. Were these stipulations exclusively civil? No. Were they predominantly civil? No. The Mosaic laws matched the four covenants, i.e., the four biblically legitimate self-maledictory oaths: individual, familial, ecclesiastical, and civil. The problem in any covenanted society is to discover which agency has primary jurisdiction in any specific instance. No human agency has final, total authority. Only God possesses absolute authority, an authority that He

12. Even during wartime, politicians should strive to let the market allocate resources in most instances. Fiscal policy – taxing and spending – not monetary inflation coupled with a system of compulsory rationing, should be the primary control device. This enables producers to make rational decisions about what to produce. The profit system motivates producers to create the most efficient weapons. Ludwig von Mises, *Human Action: A Treatise on Economics* (New Haven, Connecticut: Yale University Press, 1949), ch. 34, sect. 2.

transfers in history only to His incarnate living Word, Jesus Christ,[13] to the Holy Spirit,[14] and to His incarnate written word, the Bible.[15]

The primary form of biblical government is always self-government. The primary agency of jurisdiction is the individual conscience. It has to be: only at this level does the individual law-enforcer have sufficiently accurate and detailed information regarding both his motivation and the results of his actions. Furthermore, only the individual can search his own heart, and even then, such knowledge is flawed. "The heart is deceitful above all things, and desperately wicked: who can know it? I the LORD search the heart, I try the reins, even to give every man according to his ways, and according to the fruit of his doings" (Jer. 17:9-10). This is why God threatens eternal sanctions, positive and negative, on individuals: to persuade them to focus their attention in history on the requirement of obedience.

Adam was given a positive injunction: to dress and guard the garden (Gen. 2:15). He was also given a negative injunction: to avoid eating the fruit of a specific tree (Gen. 2:17). The first was a task of personal dominion. The second was a warning against false worship: eating a forbidden meal. Both stipulations necessarily involved corporate responsibility: familial (dominion) and ecclesiastical (communion). *Corporate responsibility flows from*

---

13. "In the beginning was the Word, and the Word was with God, and the Word was God. The same was in the beginning with God. All things were made by him; and without him was not any thing made that was made" (John 1:1-3).

14. Jesus said: "But when the Comforter is come, whom I will send unto you from the Father, even the Spirit of truth, which proceedeth from the Father, he shall testify of me" (John 15:26). "Howbeit when he, the Spirit of truth, is come, he will guide you into all truth: for he shall not speak of himself; but whatsoever he shall hear, that shall he speak: and he will shew you things to come" (John 16:13).

15. Jesus said: "I have given them thy word; and the world hath hated them, because they are not of the world, even as I am not of the world" (John 17:14). "Sanctify them through thy truth: thy word is truth" (John 17:17). Paul wrote: "All scripture is given by inspiration of God, and is profitable for doctrine, for reproof, for correction, for instruction in righteousness" (II Tim. 3:16).

individual responsibility. The point is, responsibility does flow outward from the individual. There is more to biblical responsibility than personal responsibility because *personal responsibility in a covenantal order is necessarily representative*. The representative models of the principle of representation are Adam and Christ.

The Mosaic law reflects this judicial fact of life, especially in Leviticus, the premier book of stipulations. Leviticus begins with ecclesiastical stipulations: priestly laws governing the representative sacrifices and laws governing the enforcement of covenantal boundaries, i.e., excommunication from the congregation. The feasts and ritual sacrifices of the Mosaic Covenant are obvious examples of priestly laws.[16] Next in number and importance are the family-related statutes, mainly laws controlling sexual deviation (Lev. 18; 20), personal ethics and land management (Lev. 19), and inheritance (Lev. 25). Civil statutes and civil sanctions are a distant fourth in both number and importance.

The jubilee law defended the family. It was primarily concerned with a defense of legal rights – immunities from the State. It was concerned with defending freemanship, a civil legal status. The jubilee was not a law to transfer wealth from one economic class to another. It was a law to preserve the legal status of the citizens of Israel.[17]

Common Grace

The question arises: Did the covenantal promises of Leviticus 26 perish with the other land laws of Israel? The law promised predictable blessings: "If ye walk in my statutes, and keep my commandments, and do them; Then I will give you rain in due

16. In the New Covenant, the one feast is the Lord's Supper, which is the heir of the Passover and the other Mosaic Covenant feasts.

17. Gary North, *Boundaries and Dominion: The Economics of Leviticus* (computer edition; Tyler, Texas: Institute for Christian Economics, 1994), ch. 33, subsection on "Body and Head."

season, and the land shall yield her increase, and the trees of the field shall yield their fruit" (vv. 3-4). The New Testament seems to establish another principle, that of common grace: the rain falls on everyone indiscriminately, irrespective of covenantal status. The context of the New Testament teaching is individual behavior, but the sanctions are corporate:

> Ye have heard that it hath been said, Thou shalt love thy neighbor, and hate thine enemy. But I say unto you, Love your enemies, bless them that curse you, do good to them that hate you, and pray for them which despitefully use you, and persecute you; That ye may be the children of your Father which is in heaven: *for he maketh his sun to rise on the evil and on the good, and sendeth rain on the just and on the unjust.* For if ye love them which love you, what reward have ye? do not even the publicans the same? And if ye salute your brethren only, what do ye more than others? do not even the publicans so? Be ye therefore perfect, even as your Father which is in heaven is perfect (Matt. 5:43-48; emphasis added).

The context of this passage is the rule of law: *love thy neighbor*. Here is the biblical principle of love: "Love worketh no ill to his neighbor: therefore love is the fulfilling of the law" (Rom. 13:10). We are to treat friends and enemies lawfully. This is the personal application of the Mosaic law's principle of equality before the law: "One law shall be to him that is homeborn, and unto the stranger that sojourneth among you" (Ex. 12:49). Nature's patterns affect all men the same in New Covenant history, sending rain and sun on good men and evil men. We are therefore to treat all men justly. In this passage, *our righteous judgment is the equivalent of God's gift of rain and sun.*

The focus of Jesus' discussion of the rain and sun in the Sermon on the Mount is *God's unmerited gift of justice*: every man is to be the recipient of justice. Antinomian commentators shift the focus of this passage from our righteous treatment of other men to another topic: God's universal distribution of blessings in history. These blessings are indeed universal, *but they are also conditional*. They are as conditional as the positive sanctions of God's law. *The impartiality of God's justice mandates the conditionality of the blessings of justice*. Every decision on our part must be ethically conditional, even the positive sanction of charity.[18] The context of the passage is the mandatory distribution of our justice. It is not, as Meredith G. Kline would have it, the general unpredictability of God's corporate sanctions in New Covenant history.[19] Rather, the point that Jesus was making is that men must be utterly predictable in administering civil justice. All negative sanctions must match those mandated by God. They are ideally to be as predictable as the universality of both rain and sunshine. *These sanctions must be predictable because they are conditional*. Where does God prescribe these civil sanctions? Where else but in His revealed law? The promise of a peaceful and prosperous land has been universal in man's history.

But there is a problem: the question of the rain. There is no explicit indication that the Levitical promise of rain in due season – a unique positive sanction in the Mosaic law – continues into the New Covenant era. Kline has correctly recognized that this indicates a shift from the Old Covenant to the New Covenant. Kline then extrapolates from Jesus' announcement of the visible randomness (i.e., covenantal unpredictability) of the *rain* in the New Covenant to the visible randomness of *all* the promised sanctions in the Mosaic law. What Kline does is to assume that the rain, which was an aspect of the land laws, represents all the corporate sanctions in the New Testament. This assumption is incorrect. If it were correct, there could be

18. Ray R. Sutton, "Whose Conditions for Charity?" in Gary North (ed.), *Theonomy: An Informed Response* (Tyler, Texas: Institute for Christian Economics, 1991), ch. 9.

19. "And meanwhile it [the common grace order] must run its course within the uncertainties of the mutually conditioning principles of common grace and common curse, prosperity and adversity being experienced in a manner largely unpredictable because of the inscrutable sovereignty of the divine will that dispenses them in mysterious ways." Meredith G. Kline, "Comments on an Old-New Error," *Westminster Theological Journal*, XLI (Fall 1978), p. 184.

no uniquely biblical system of social theory.[20] This is why we must pay considerable attention to the positive covenantal sanction of rain in due season.

Rain in Due Season

The Levitical positive sanctions listed in the text are peace, wine, and bread. Rain in due season is a means of producing grain and grapes, meaning bread and wine. The rain is a blessing only insofar as it produces crops. Obviously, rain was no blessing in Noah's day. Too much rain ruins most crops. So, the promise was for rain *in due season*. It would be just the right quantity of rain to produce the positive economic sanction of agricultural productivity.

The New Testament's teaching is that rain and sunshine fall on all men. This is God's common grace. The New Testament's emphasis here is on a common blessing. As I have already argued, the twin blessings of sunshine and rain are representative of God's blessing of *righteous judgment*, which His covenant people are to emulate. But both rain and sunshine can become common curses: rain becomes flooding; sunshine becomes drought. The question we must get answered is this: Is nature under the New Covenant a means of God's *predictable* covenantal sanctions in history? It was in Moses' day, at least inside the boundaries of the Promised Land. The land had vomited out the Canaanites (Lev. 18:24-28).

But after the Promised Land ceased to be a kingdom boundary,[21] did nature still play this judgmental role? No. It is Jesus, not the land, who spews out His enemies. "So then because thou art lukewarm, and neither cold nor hot, I will spue thee

---

20. Gary North, *Millennialism and Social Theory* (Tyler, Texas: Institute for Christian Economics, 1990), chaps. 7, 8.

21. Jesus warned the Pharisees: "Therefore say I unto you, The kingdom of God shall be taken from you, and given to a nation bringing forth the fruits thereof" (Matt. 21:43).

out of my mouth" (Rev. 3:16). *Nature in the New Covenant has ceased to be a means of predictable covenantal judgment.* What determines the fruitfulness of the field today is adherence to God's laws, including his laws of ownership. Put another way, a Christian nation whose civil government imposes socialist ownership will not enjoy the large number of external blessings experienced by a pagan nation whose civil government defends free market ownership. Also, if the two nations were to reverse their systems of ownership, there would be no *predictable* long-term reversal of rainfall and sunshine patterns within their respective geographical boundaries. *The New Covenant moved from nature to society with respect to the locus of predictable sanctions.* More to the point, this shift culminated a shift that had begun at the time of the conquest of the land. The earlier shift in the locus of sanctions had been a far more radical shift: from *predictable manna* outside the Promised Land to *predictable inheritance* without manna inside the Promised Land. When the Israelites crossed the boundary from the wilderness into Canaan, the source of their bread ceased to be manna. "And the manna ceased on the morrow after they had eaten of the old corn of the land; neither had the children of Israel manna any more; but they did eat of the fruit of the land of Canaan that year" (Josh. 5:12).

The visible blessings are covenantally based, not environmentally based. The academic myth of late-nineteenth-century American Great Plains farming – that the rain follows the plow – was without evidence, as the dust bowl conditions of the 1930's proved. Equally unsupported was the political myth of the 1930's that the plow, apart from government regulation, destroys the environment.[22] The issue is the covenant: the conditionality of God's corporate blessings.[23] The tripartite eucharistic promise of the politics of salvation – peace, land,

---

22. North, *Boundaries and Dominion*, ch. 33, subsection on "The Plow and the Plains."

23. *Ibid.*, ch. 33, subsection on "Coals of Fire."

and bread – are God's gifts to man, not the State's.[24] It is God's system of economic freedom, based on private property, not State collectivism, that makes the land bloom. This is why, in the 1971-73 period, the average Soviet agricultural worker harvested four and a half tons of grain per year; meanwhile, the average U.S. agricultural worker harvested over 54 tons.[25] Poor land and a short growing season were not the main reasons for Soviet food shortages; collectivist tyranny was. The private owner, acting as God's agent to the consumers and the consumers' agent before God, best represents both parties. The State cannot be trusted in this matter.[26]

Conclusion

God's covenantal sanctions in history are corporate. Positive sanctions rest on the obedience of individuals: *representatives*. The boundaries of Mosaic Israel were primarily judicial and secondarily geographical. Within these boundaries, nature itself was bound to the stipulations of God's national covenant. The rain would fall in due season if the nation's representatives remained faithful. These representatives included the high priest, priests in general, Levites, civil rulers, and heads of households.

The positive sanctions listed in this passage are land and peace, bread and wine. The Levitical laws governing ownership prove that it was not the civil government which was the primary representative agent in Mosaic Israel. It was not the State which was to create national economic planning for agriculture. The success or failure of Israel's agriculture depended on the obedience of the people, manifested publicly in the behavior of

---

24. *Ibid.*, ch. 33, section on "Peace, Land, and Bread."

25. Mikhail Heller and Aleksandr Nekrich, *Utopia in Power: The History of the Soviet Union from 1917 to the Present* (New York: Summit, [1982] 1986), p. 633.

26. North, *Boundaries and Dominion*, ch. 33, section on "Two Forms of Representation."

their representatives, i.e., their leaders. The primary form of government is self-government, and the leaders had to begin with self-government, as did every other Israelite. Corporate responsibility flows from individual responsibility.

The promised sanction of rain in due season was unique to Mosaic Israel. In the New Covenant, the universality of common grace governs nature, just as it did outside of the place of residence of the Israelites under the Old Covenant. Rain and sunshine fall on covenant-breakers and covenant-keepers without distinction in the New Covenant. Nature is no longer God's agent of judicial sanctions. God's law governs man's legal relationships, and obedience to His law-order is what determines predictable corporate sanctions in New Covenant history. Societies can overcome the restraints (boundaries) of nature through obedience to God's law.

The doctrine of representation is inherent in any system of biblical authority. The judicial representatives of the land were the heirs of the conquest. The economic representatives of the consumers were those who were willing to buy their continued control over the land. Control over the land was to be maintained by those who used the land least wastefully in serving those who offered the high bids for the fruits of the land: consumers. It was the consumers' sovereignty over the land that Mosaic law defended in 49 years out of 50.

The covenantal promise of bread and wine has sacramental overtones. It points to the communion of God and man at a meal: the marriage supper of the lamb (Rev. 19:9). Israel was also promised land and peace. From an economic standpoint, land is not nearly so crucial as freedom in producing the largest possible quantities of bread and wine. The law of God provided freedom; the land was secondary. The law was given at Sinai before the generation of wandering. The stipulations would remain basic to continued prosperity in the land. Obedience was the foundation of the promised positive sanctions. Corporate prosperity is therefore ethically conditional.

34

LIMITS TO GROWTH

For I will have respect unto you, and make you fruitful, and multiply you, and establish my covenant with you. And ye shall eat old store, and bring forth the old because of the new (Lev. 26:9-10).

The theocentric meaning of this passage is easy to summarize: God, the author of life, establishes the covenantal laws governing life. The biological promise in verse 9 is two-fold: the multiplication of *obedient* covenant-keepers in history and the equal or greater multiplication of their crops. This two-fold promise is covenantal. It is therefore conditional. The dual positive sanctions of a growing population and growing food supplies are tied to the law of God. As in the case of every positive covenantal sanction, there is an unstated assumption: the threat of negative sanctions. In this case, the negative sanctions match the positive sanctions: 1) zero population growth or even population decline; 2) hunger. Corporate disobedience calls forth these negative sanctions.

Were these two sanctions part of what I have called seed and land laws? No. A seed law, in the sense that I am using it in this commentary, was tied to the promised Seed, the Messiah, the prophesied son of Judah. It had to do with maintaining the tribal divisions in Mosaic Israel until Shiloh came (Gen. 49:10).

The earlier promise given to Abraham regarding the multiplication of his heirs through the Seed, Jesus Christ (*seed*, in Paul's sense)[1] was not a seed law sanction in the sense that I am using the term, i.e., Jacob's later prophecy. Jacob's prophecy governed the promise up to the coming of the Seed: the end of the Old Covenant. God's promise to Abraham regarding the multiplication of his seed – heirs – applies to both Old and New Covenants: a cross-boundary covenant and promise (Gen. 15:5). Its mark in the Old Covenant was circumcision (Gen. 17:10). This was a covenantal stipulation in the sense of *confession* rather than geography: a visible boundary separation from covenant-breakers rather than geographical boundary separations among biological units (tribes). Leviticus 26:9 is an application of the Abrahamic covenant, not Jacob's tribal prophecy.

Broadly covenantal sanctions applied outside of the land of Israel. That is, these covenantal sanctions were *common grace sanctions*. Societies that obeyed the covenant's external laws would prosper; those that rebelled would not. The promise of high population growth in this passage was an implicit threat of reduced population for rebellion. The archetype of this threat was Noah's Flood: a pre-Abrahamic sanction. God will not again bring a flood to cut off all mankind, but He does reduce the populations of rebellious societies, primarily through the covenantally predictable effects of social organization in a particular natural environment.

The Curse of Hunger

Hunger is a major covenantal threat in God's law. "Because thou servedst not the LORD thy God with joyfulness, and with gladness of heart, for the abundance of all things; Therefore shalt thou serve thine enemies which the LORD shall send against thee, in hunger, and in thirst, and in nakedness, and in

---

1. "Now to Abraham and his seed were the promises made. He saith not, And to seeds, as of many; but as of one, And to thy seed, which is Christ" (Gal. 3:16).

want of all things: and he shall put a yoke of iron upon thy neck, until he have destroyed thee" (Deut. 28:47-48). Again, "They that be slain with the sword are better than they that be slain with hunger: for these pine away, stricken through for want of the fruits of the field" (Lam. 4:9).

Food is therefore a major covenantal blessing. This blessing is stated in Leviticus 25:10 in a way that is easily recognized by an agricultural people: "And ye shall eat old store, and bring forth the old because of the new." The time of greatest potential crisis for an agricultural society is the period immediately preceding the harvest. The old store is running low; the new store has not yet arrived. The word for "old" is used with regard to the stored produce in the year following the jubilee year. "And ye shall sow the eighth year, and eat yet of old fruit until the ninth year; until her fruits come in ye shall eat of the old store" (Lev. 25:22). God's promise is not slack. Israel need not fear famine; the stored crop will not be entirely consumed before the new crop is harvested.

This means that the covenantal blessing of "fruitfulness" was comprehensive, applying equally to the fertility of obedient covenant-keeping families and to their crops. The rate of human population growth inside the boundaries of Israel would be matched by the rate of population growth in the fields. In this way, God promised to confirm His covenant publicly. He promised a growing population in Israel: the application of Genesis 1:28 and Genesis 9:7 to His covenant people, the true heirs of the promise. This means that God's corporate, covenantal standard for the expansion of covenant-keeping families is above two children per family, the biological replacement rate.[2]

The modern world understands hunger as a threat to humanity – not a curse, which is personal, but a threat. Unlike the Bible, a majority of modern humanist intellectuals and their

2. Actually, 2.1 children, since some children do not marry and reproduce.

accomplices within Christianity have contrasted the blessing of food with population growth. They have argued since the mid-1960's that in order for the world's poorest people to attain sufficient food supplies, they must be willing to reduce the size of their families. These intellectuals have also frequently argued that the West, which has abundant quantities of food, must give away food to the world's poor. This means having Western governments give food away to the governments of Third World (aid-receiving) nations. Such political food transfers have been going on throughout the post-World War II era.

Anti-population growth proponents refuse to admit that there is no specter of famine haunting the vast majority of humanity, and where it does haunt a handful of small, backward nations, all located in Africa, this is the result of government policies, such as: 1) war, especially civil war; 2) a government monopoly on the purchase of food from farmers, with prices set far below market prices; or 3) government intervention into the local agricultural economy.[3] That is to say, people face food shortages because the free market is not allowed to function.[4]

Physical Limits to Growth

Boundaries are limits. In a finite world, there are limits to every promise of growth. These limits may be geographical or they may be economic, but there are limits to growth. This is the inescapable reality of finitude. The process of compound physical growth cannot go on forever in a finite world. Growth has temporal limits.[5]

---

3. An example: the decision by Western nations in the late 1960's to dig water wells in sub-Sahara Africa, which led the nomads to locate their herds close to the "free" water. This produced overgrazing and famine in the mid-1970's. See Claire Sterling, "The Making of the Sub-Saharan Wasteland," *Atlantic Monthly* (May 1974).

4. See Gary North, *Boundaries and Dominion: The Economics of Leviticus* (computer edition; Tyler, Texas: Institute for Christian Economics, 1994), Appendix I: "Malthusianism vs. Covenantalism."

5. Gary North, "The Theology of the Exponential Curve," *The Freeman* (May

God calls for population growth because He calls for covenantal obedience. He wants to see positive growth in covenant-keeping societies. *Long-term compound growth is a moral imperative in God's covenantal universe.* Long-term stagnation is a sign of God's curse. Yet there are unquestionably limits to growth. This is why God's call for population growth points to God's final judgment at the end of history and the transformation of mankind into a host like the angels: fixed numbers, either in the lake of fire (Rev. 20:14-15) or in the resurrected New Heaven and New Earth (Rev. 21:1-2).

Covenant-breakers who do not wish to think about the final judgment have become advocates of zero population growth: an exchange, either compulsory or voluntary, either natural or political, of a compounding human population for extra eons of time. The growing acceptance by intellectuals in the West of the zero-population growth movement[6] and the zero economic growth movement,[7] which became a unified cause and intellectual fad almost overnight in the mid-1960's, testifies to the presence of widespread covenant-breaking and philosophies to

1970); reprinted in North, *An Introduction to Christian Economics* (Nutley, New Jersey: Craig Press, 1973), ch. 8.

6. Lincoln H. and Alice Taylor Day, *Too Many Americans* (New York: Delta, [1963] 1965); William and Paul Paddock, *Famine – 1975! America's Decision: Who Will Survive?* (Boston: Little, Brown, 1967); Paul Ehrlich, *The Population Bomb* (New York: Ballantine, 1968); Gordon Rattray Taylor, *The Biological Time Bomb* (New York: World, 1968); *Population and the American Future*, the Report of the Commission on Population Growth and the American Future (New York: New American Library, 1972). For an economist's critique, see Jacqueline Kasun, *The War Against Population: The Economics and Ideology of World Population Control* (San Francisco: Ignatius, 1988).

7. Ezra J. Mishan, *The Costs of Economic Growth* (New York: Praeger, 1967); Mishan, *The Economic Growth Debate: An Assessment* (London: George Allen & Unwin, 1977); Donella Meadows, *et al.*, *The Limits to Growth* (New York: Universe Books, 1972); E. F. Schumacher, *Small Is Beautiful: Economics As If People Mattered* (New York: Harper & Row, 1973); Mancur Olson and Hans H. Landsberg (eds.), *The No-Growth Society* (New York: Norton, 1973); Leopold Kohr, *The Overdeveloped Nations: The Diseconomies of Scale* (New York: Schocken, 1977). For a critique, see E. Calvin Beisner, *Prospects for Growth: A Biblical View of Population, Resources, and the Future* (Westchester, Illinois: Crossway, 1990).

match. In 1970, the world's population could have been housed in American middle-class comfort in a city the size of Texas and New Mexico – 15 percent of U.S. land – with a population density no larger than what one-third of Americans experienced. If people had been content to live in a city as crowded as New York City, they could all have fit in the state of Montana.[8] Yet intellectuals became fearful of the "population bomb."

Living Space

At some point, even covenant-keepers will run out of living space if they continue to grow in number. They will reach environmental limits: boundaries beyond which man's dominion cannot extend. We need to consider three facts regarding man's limits to growth. *First*, any rate of growth, if compounded, eventually becomes exponential. The population of any multiplying species approaches infinity as a limit. But environmental finitude makes its presence felt long before population infinitude is reached. The environment places limits on growth. No species can maintain a positive growth rate indefinitely. *Second*, mankind, unlike the angels, is not a numerically fixed host in history. Yet mankind is ultimately limited by the environment. This fact points to the ultimate limit to growth: time. At some point, mankind will reach its maximum population. *Third*, and by far the most significant fact, this point in time of maximum population is reached when God returns in final judgment. What must be understood is that *this maximum population limit is covenantal more than environmental*. It comes because God runs out of mercy for covenant-breakers, not because mankind runs out of living space or food.

The limits of nature and the reality of compound growth indicate a point in history when mankind reaches a maximum.

8. Robert L. Sasone, *Handbook on Population* (Author, 1972), p. 98.

We do not know where this point is – it is in this sense indeterminate – but we know that the environment does impose limits. The economist's evidence for this is the rising price of some goods in relation to others. One thing cannot grow forever. It is governed by what the economist calls the law of diminishing returns.[9] But this "Newtonian" insight is significant only insofar as it warns rational covenant-breakers of the reality of finitude and the limits to growth. The reality of finitude is not nearly so significant a limit as the reality of covenantal rebellion. It is not mankind's fertility in general that presses our species toward its *biological limits*; it is rather covenant-breaking man's rebellion that reaches God's *judicial limits* in history. While the logic of finitude does warn scientific man of autonomous mankind's limits – the destruction of all meaning in the heat death of the universe[10] – this insight can be misinterpreted by covenant-breakers. They can (and have) proposed technical solutions to a covenantal problem. One such proposed solution is the zero-growth ideology.

Limits: Newtonian vs. Covenantal

According to a strictly Newtonian interpretation of the environmental limits to growth, the faster the rate of compound growth, the sooner growth will cease or time will run out. The greater the blessings of growth, the shorter the time remaining before time runs out or mankind ceases to grow. Man's limits are regarded as exclusively environmental.

The Bible speaks of other limits as more fundamental. God brings final judgment in response to a final rebellion of human covenant-breakers against human covenant-keepers (Rev. 20:7-10). The discussion of the limits to growth needs to be framed

---

9. Gary North, *The Dominion Covenant: Genesis* (2nd ed; Tyler, Texas: Institute for Christian Economics, 1987), ch. 21.

10. Gary North, *Is the World Running Down? Crisis in the Christian Worldview* (Tyler, Texas: Institute for Christian Economics, 1988), ch. 2.

in terms of the Bible's covenantal limits – moral, judicial, and eschatological – rather than in terms of Newtonian environmental limits: mathematical, physical, and biological.[11]

The growth of population points either to the limits of growth or the limits of time. Because the Bible affirms that the limits to covenant-keeping man's population growth are covenantal rather than biological, the Bible affirms that there will be a final judgment. The Bible's promise of growth in one segment of the human population – covenant-keepers – is a testimony to the end of history. Men are expected to obey God's law; if they do, God promises to extend to them the positive sanction of growth. Therefore, time will run out. But, the Bible also tells us, time will run out before mankind presses against unyielding environmental limits. The primary limit to growth in history is covenantal. The environmental limits to growth are merely theoretical – not hypothetical, but *determinate physical limits* that are *indeterminate in man's knowledge*.

---

11. There are some journalists and social thinkers who prefer to substitute quantum mechanics for Newtonian mechanics as a model for social theory. They want to escape the Newtonian world's determinate limits to growth by means of an appeal to the indeterminacy of the quantum world: physical indeterminacy, not merely conceptual. The two most prominent American authors who take this approach are George Gilder and Warren Brookes. At the time of his death in December of 1991, Brookes was working on a book developing this idea. He and I had spent hours on the phone discussing this issue. He had presented an early version of his thesis in *The Economy in Mind* (New York: Universe Books, 1982), ch. 1. He was a Christian Scientist and leaned toward accepting non-physical explanations of man's condition. Gilder outlines his thesis in *Microcosm* (New York: Simon & Schuster, 1989). Eloquent as Gilder is regarding the exponential increase in the power of computers, he cannot apply his thesis to population growth. Bodies cannot escape into the realm of the quantum in order to evade the limits to growth. Gilder invokes Moore's Law, which says that the number of transistors on commercial microchips doubles every 18 months. This law has held true since the late 1950's. The law seems to overcome certain physical limits. But Moore's Law does not overcome the limits on biological growth. Moore's Law was discovered by Gordon Moore, the co-founder of Intel, the largest American microchip producer. On Moore's Law and its commercial implications, see Robert X. Cringely (pseudonym), *Accidental Empires* (New York: Addison-Wesley, 1992), pp. 41, 144, 306-7.

Social Limits to Growth

The more fundamental limits to growth are social. This is the economic manifestation of the covenantal principle of hierarchy. Not everyone can attend the best universities, drive the finest automobiles, and wear the latest fashions. These goods are limited in supply. We cannot produce many more of them, so competition to use or own them is intense. Fred Hirsch uses the analogy of the person at a sporting event who wants to see the game more clearly. He stands up. But eventually, others also stand up. Then one person stands on tiptoe. Others do the same. Eventually, the tallest people with the strongest lower leg muscles get the best view. So, society informally agrees to sit down at sporting events and in concert halls, since this is less taxing on everyone's leg muscles, and in the long run, nobody can overcome his height limits. Hirsch's point: in this case – seeing over everyone's head – what a few people can do, not everyone can do *at the same time*. He calls such goods and services *positional goods*.[12] As economic growth continues, more and more people can afford to buy these goods, so more will be produced. When this happens, these goods lose their crucial character: providing the owners with status, i.e., position. Other goods and services, more fixed in number, are then sought by those seeking status. There will always be positional goods.

The rich gain access to such goods first. As the middle class becomes more wealthy, the competition for positional goods intensifies. The middle class outnumbers the rich and so can outbid them. Consider scarce land, such as ocean front property. To defend their claims, the rich call on the State to defend their nearly exclusive control, making it illegal for the middle class to buy up the land. This impulse lies behind much of the environmental legislation in the United States that protects the

---

12. Fred Hirsch, *The Social Limits to Growth* (London: Routledge & Kegan Paul, 1978), p. 11.

not-quite-virgin wilderness or coastal property, where the rich have already staked their claims.[13]

Angelic Hosts Are Fixed; Races Are Not

Living species multiply. Angels do not. The angels constitute a fixed host. In heaven and hell, the number of angels remains constant. This fact of life is rarely discussed by theologians and never by social theorists. It should be. It is fundamental to understanding the ultimate origin of the zero population growth ideology.

Satan rules representatively, just as God does. He rules hierarchically. But unlike God, Satan is neither omniscient nor omnipotent. His decree is that of a creature: under God's decree. This has organizational consequences for the way he exercises power. He is dependent on the supply of information flowing to him, whether from demonic beings or from other sources. This flow of information is limited. It contains "noise," just as it does for humans. God is omniscient; Satan is not. He gets confused. He has trouble monitoring the thoughts and activities of those under his covenant.

This flow of information is finite. So is his power to make decisions and enforce them. To the extent that his sources of information and power depend on the activities of those under his command, he faces a problem. The more people he needs to monitor, the greater the flow of accurate information necessary to his empire. The greater the number of people, the more strain this places on the resources at his disposal. In short, Satan's host is put under ever-greater pressure as the human population under their covenantal authority grows. This is even more true of the pressures brought by those under God's covenantal authority. The more covenant-keepers on earth, the

13. North, *Boundaries and Dominion*, ch. 34, subsection on "Legal Barriers to Entry."

more the breakdown of Satan's control. Like a juggler who has to keep a growing number of oranges in the air, so is Satan.

People are a threat to Satan. They multiply; his demonic host does not. Even covenant-breakers pose a problem: the coordination of Satan's plans becomes more difficult as mankind's numbers increase. Then there is the eschatological threat: a major move by the Holy Spirit could adopt large numbers of covenant-breakers into the family of God. When this happens, Satan's fixed host will have their hands full, to use a non-angelic expression. More than full: they will find control over events slipping through the equivalent of their fingers.

The increase of mankind's numbers poses no threat to the host of heaven, for God is absolutely sovereign. God is not dependent on His angels for information. God does not suffer from information overload. There is no noise in God's perception. The angels of heaven need not rely on their own mastery of history. They rely on God. Thus, for the angels, the multiplication of humanity poses no organizational threat. They outnumber Satan's host by two to one. Stars and angels are linked symbolically in Scripture. We read: "And there appeared another wonder in heaven; and behold a great red dragon, having seven heads and ten horns, and seven crowns upon his heads. And his tail drew the third part of the stars of heaven, and did cast them to the earth: and the dragon stood before the woman which was ready to be delivered, for to devour her child as soon as it was born" (Rev. 12:3-4).[14] Two-thirds were loyal.

A growing population creates problems for any creature who would seek to control history. The addition of more humans creates problems for Satan and his host. Men represent either God or Satan in history. Those who represent Satan are rebels, just as he is. They cannot be trusted, just as he cannot be trust-

14. The numbers of the judgments on earth described in Revelation 8 also indicate a two-to-one advantage.

ed. Thus, Satan benefits from a growing population only insofar as he can keep them under his covenant and entrap them in hell. The threat of their rejection of his covenant grows ever-greater over time: more humans to join God's forces, and more likelihood that God will send His promised days of blessing.[15] This is why the zero population growth movement, like the abortion movement, can be accurately described as satanic.

Israel's Limits

The question for Israel was this: When these limits to population growth were reached inside the nation's geographical boundaries, how did God expect the Israelites to overcome these population limits? There were either geographical limits or population limits. Walking to the feasts placed geographical limits on Israel, but without limits on Israel's population, Israel's geographical limits would be breached. Conclusion: God mandated another exodus beyond the borders of Israel when He established population expansion as His covenantal standard. The Israelites were expected to move outside of the geographical boundaries of Israel. This was the meaning of Christ's metaphor of new wine in old wineskins (Matt. 9:17): the fermenting new wine would burst its inflexible container. His people were always intended to inherit the earth, not just the land of Israel. "For evildoers shall be cut off: but those that wait upon the LORD, they shall inherit the earth" (Ps. 37:9). "But the meek shall inherit the earth; and shall delight themselves in the abundance of peace" (Ps. 37:11). "For such as be blessed of him shall inherit the earth; and they that be cursed of him shall be cut off" (Ps. 37:22).

Inheritance in Israel implied growth for obedient covenant-keepers: growth in the number of heirs and growth in the value of their individual inheritances. But geographical limits –

---

15. Kenneth L. Gentry, Jr., *He Shall Have Dominion: A Postmillennial Eschatology* (Tyler, Texas: Institute for Christian Economics, 1992).

family land, tribal land, national land – were judicially fixed by the terms of the conquest. A growing number of heirs necessitated a declining per capita landed inheritance within the Promised Land. This pointed to the eschatological nature of God's covenantal laws of inheritance: a transcending of Israel's geographical boundaries. The promised inheritance of covenant-keepers pointed to the breaking of the boundaries of the Promised Land. The limits to growth of *confessional Israel* would not be the boundaries of *geographical Israel*. The original conquest of Canaan would cease to be a limiting factor in the extension of God's covenantal boundaries.

Enemies of Growth

The covenant-breaker prefers not to think about final judgment. To escape the very thought of such an event, modern man has invented a theory of the heat death of the universe. The universe is supposedly being pushed by the second law of thermodynamics toward absolute zero and total randomness. Any thought that man's population growth will extend to a limit in history – ending history – is rejected out of hand. The limits to growth are seen as environmental rather than temporal. The Bible teaches otherwise. It teaches that God's blessings can continue until the end of time, and one of these blessing's is mankind's population growth. This points to the Second Coming, not the heat death of the universe in billions of years.[16] Mankind's limits are covenantal, not temporal.[17]

The advocates of zero-population growth (ZPG) are intellectual heirs of Rev. T. Robert Malthus, whose anonymous 1798 *Essay on Population* argued that man's growth is geometrical, while man's food supply grows merely arithmetically – a preposterous claim theoretically and refuted empirically by two centuries of rapidly growing food supplies. He dropped this

---

16. North, *Is the World Running Down?*

17. North, *Boundaries and Dominion*, ch. 34, section on "Entropy."

argument in later editions, but its outlook still dominates the ZPG advocates. His earlier outlook is hostile to the biblical idea of man's dominion over nature. Post-Adamic nature is neither autonomous nor permanent. This idea upsets modern Malthusians. They see nature as autonomous and man under nature rather than both man and nature under a Creator God.[18]

Conclusion

The fundamental economic issue is not population growth. It is not the increase of food per capita. It is not capital invested per person. The fundamental economic issue is ethical: *God's covenant*. Nevertheless, the language of Leviticus 26:9-10 is agricultural. Why? Because in an agricultural society, the mark of God's blessing is food. God promised to provide bread for all. He also promised to increase their numbers.

This does not mean that He promised nothing else to them. He promised an agricultural people access in history to the city of God, the New Jerusalem (Isa. 65:17-20). The city of God is the image of a regenerate society. The city is therefore not inherently evil. Urban life is not inherently depersonalizing. Covenant-breaking is evil and depersonalizing. Covenant-breaking is made less expensive in cities because of the higher costs of gathering information about individual actions, as well as the higher costs of imposing informal social sanctions. But covenant-breaking is not inherent to cities. It can be overcome through God's grace.

If this were not the case, then the promise of population growth would be a threat to the covenant. A covenantal blessing would inevitably become a covenantal curse. The grace of God would necessarily produce the wrath of God. This is the operational viewpoint of both premillennialism and amillennialism regarding church history, but it is a false view of history.[19]

18. *Ibid.*, ch. 34, section on "The Malthusians."

19. Gary North, *Millennialism and Social Theory* (Tyler, Texas: Institute for

While covenantal blessings can and have led to corporate covenant-breaking, just as God warns (Lev. 26; Deut. 8; 28), they do not inevitably lead to them. The covenant's blessings are conditional; they do not continue indefinitely irrespective of corporate obedience. God's negative corporate sanctions come in history, and then society is given another opportunity to repent and rebuild: "And they shall build the old wastes, they shall raise up the former desolations, and they shall repair the waste cities, the desolations of many generations" (Isa. 61:4).

The biblical view of history is growth-oriented. It not only proclaims the possibility of population expansion and increasing wealth per capita, it also establishes these as mandatory corporate goals in history. Until mankind becomes a fixed host at the end of history – covenant-breakers in the lake of fire eternally (Rev. 20:14-15), covenant-keepers developing the New Heaven and New Earth (Rev. 21; 22) – covenant-keeping mankind is expected by God to grow in numbers, wealth, and influence.

Christian Economics, 1990), chaps. 4, 5, 9.

35

GOD'S ESCALATING WRATH

I am the Lord *your God, which brought you forth out of the land of Egypt, that ye should not be their bondmen; and I have broken the bands of your yoke, and made you go upright. But if ye will not hearken unto me, and will not do all these commandments; And if ye shall despise my statutes, or if your soul abhor my judgments, so that ye will not do all my commandments, but that ye break my covenant: I also will do this unto you; I will even appoint over you terror, consumption, and the burning ague, that shall consume the eyes, and cause sorrow of heart: and ye shall sow your seed in vain, for your enemies shall eat it. And I will set my face against you, and ye shall be slain before your enemies: they that hate you shall reign over you; and ye shall flee when none pursueth you (Lev. 26:13-17).*

This passage introduces that section of Leviticus 26 which lists the types of negative corporate sanctions in history that Israel could expect if God's covenant people violated God's law. As is true of Deuteronomy 28, a parallel passage on corporate sanctions, the negative sanctions greatly outnumber the positive sanctions. The Israelites were to understand the theocentric basis of wisdom: "The fear of the Lord is the beginning of wisdom: and the knowledge of the holy is understanding" (Prov. 9:10).

This section on sanctions appears in the fifth section of the Book of Leviticus. The fifth point of the covenant deals with succession. Why does a section on sanctions appear here? Because sanctions are linked covenantally to succession. This is why eschatology cannot be separated covenantally from theonomy, i.e., God's law and its biblically mandated sanctions. Sanctions determine who will inherit what: inheritance and disinheritance. God identifies Himself as the God of the covenant: deliverer, law-giver, and sanctions-bringer. God's threat of temporal wrath is to redirect the attention of citizens of a holy commonwealth to the possibility of disinheritance in history: wrath as the prelude to corporate disinheritance.

The Fear of God

The passage begins with a reminder: the God who threatens these historical sanctions is the God of corporate grace in history. He led them out of bondage in Egypt. They had been bent under the yoke of slavery, but He had broken their yoke and made them walk upright. This upright physical walk was analogous to an upright ethical walk. The language of walking before God is the language of covenantal obedience, both individual and corporate.[1] The morally crooked walk is mirrored by the bent walk of the slave who is under a yoke.

---

1. "And when Abram was ninety years old and nine, the LORD appeared to Abram, and said unto him, I am the Almighty God; walk before me, and be thou perfect" (Gen. 17:1). "And ye shall not walk in the manners of the nation, which I cast out before you: for they committed all these things, and therefore I abhorred them" (Lev. 20:23). "In the ninth year of Hoshea the king of Assyria took Samaria, and carried Israel away into Assyria, and placed them in Halah and in Habor by the river of Gozan, and in the cities of the Medes. For so it was, that the children of Israel had sinned against the LORD their God, which had brought them up out of the land of Egypt, from under the hand of Pharaoh king of Egypt, and had feared other gods, And walked in the statutes of the heathen, whom the LORD cast out from before the children of Israel, and of the kings of Israel, which they had made" (II Ki. 17:6-8).

The temptation is always disobedience to God's standards (point three of the biblical covenant model). "But if ye will not hearken unto me, and will not do all these commandments; And if ye shall despise my statutes, or if your soul abhor my judgments, so that ye will not do all my commandments, but that ye break my covenant." This necessarily involves the threat of negative sanctions (point four). "I will even appoint over you terror, consumption, and the burning ague, that shall consume the eyes, and cause sorrow of heart." The essence of this sanction is disinheritance (point five). "And ye shall sow your seed in vain, for your enemies shall eat it." Invaders will inherit: "And I will set my face against you, and ye shall be slain before your enemies: they that hate you shall reign over you; and ye shall flee when none pursueth you." So fearful will God's people become that they will flee when none pursue.

The covenantal issue is the fear of God. When men refuse to fear God, He raises up others who will terrify them. Covenant-breakers will thereby learn to fear God's human agents of wrath, so that they might better learn to fear God. The point is this: God is worth fearing even more than military invaders. If the stipulations of the Creator are widely ignored, then military invaders will become increasingly difficult to ignore. In this regard, the covenant-breaking adult is as foolish as a child. A father spanks a child when the child runs into a busy street. The real threat to the child is the street's traffic, but the child is fearless before this external threat. He must learn to fear his father in order to learn the greater fearfulness of the street. He fears the lesser threat more than the greater threat. Similarly, the covenant-breaker loses his fear of the Father – the far greater threat – and must be reminded to fear God by a lesser external threat. The magnitude of God's wrath is manifested by the magnitude of the threat of military sanctions: God's wrath is more of a threat than a military defeat. The lesser threat is imposed by God in order to remind men of the greater threat.

Softening Their Resistance

The first negative sanction is both psychological and physical: terror and consumption. This will produce sorrow. This defensive mentality is the mentality of the slave and the prisoner. The second threatened negative sanction is military defeat. If this threat fails to persuade them to repent, the sanctions will escalate further. "And if ye will not yet for all this hearken unto me, then I will punish you seven times more for your sins" (Lev. 26:18). The stated punishment is drought. God's wrath is manifested by His destruction of a nation's food supply. This was a major threat to a pre-modern agricultural society. "And I will break the pride of your power; and I will make your heaven as iron, and your earth as brass: And your strength shall be spent in vain: for your land shall not yield her increase, neither shall the trees of the land yield their fruits" (Lev. 26:19-20). Drought was God's means of softening up the resistance of King Ahab against Elijah's message (I Ki. 17:1).

As in the case of Egypt, the next sanction involved the children: "And if ye walk contrary unto me, and will not hearken unto me; I will bring seven times more plagues upon you according to your sins. I will also send wild beasts among you, which shall rob you of your children, and destroy your cattle, and make you few in number; and your high ways shall be desolate" (Lev. 26:21-22). God sent beasts against those children who mocked the prophet Elisha: "And he went up from thence unto Bethel: and as he was going up by the way, there came forth little children out of the city, and mocked him, and said unto him, Go up, thou bald head; go up, thou bald head. And he turned back, and looked on them, and cursed them in the name of the LORD. And there came forth two she bears out of the wood, and tare [tore] forty and two children of them" (II Ki. 2:23-24).

The judgments are again military: "And if ye will not be reformed by me by these things, but will walk contrary unto me; Then will I also walk contrary unto you, and will punish you yet seven times for your sins. And I will bring a sword upon you, that shall avenge the quarrel of my covenant: and when ye are gathered together within your cities, I will send the pestilence among you; and ye shall be delivered into the hand of the enemy. And when I have broken the staff of your bread, ten women shall bake your bread in one oven, and they shall deliver you your bread again by weight: and ye shall eat, and not be satisfied" (Lev. 26:23-26). Enemies laying siege outside the gates, pestilence and hunger inside the gates: so shall covenant-breakers be reminded of the importance of God's law.

But even this may prove futile. "And if ye will not for all this hearken unto me, but walk contrary unto me; Then I will walk contrary unto you also in fury; and I, even I, will chastise you seven times for your sins. And ye shall eat the flesh of your sons, and the flesh of your daughters shall ye eat" (Lev. 26:27-29). This was fulfilled in the days of Elisha, during Ben-hadad's siege of Samaria:

> And it came to pass after this, that Ben-hadad king of Syria gathered all his host, and went up, and besieged Samaria. And there was a great famine in Samaria: and, behold, they besieged it, until an ass's head was sold for fourscore pieces of silver, and the fourth part of a cab of dove's dung for five pieces of silver. And as the king of Israel was passing by upon the wall, there cried a woman unto him, saying, Help, my lord, O king. And he said, If the LORD do not help thee, whence shall I help thee? out of the barnfloor, or out of the winepress? And the king said unto her, What aileth thee? And she answered, This woman said unto me, Give thy son, that we may eat him to day, and we will eat my son to morrow. So we boiled my son, and did eat him: and I said unto her on the next day, Give thy son, that we may eat him: and she hath hid her son. And it came to pass, when the king heard the words of the woman, that he rent his clothes; and he passed by upon the wall, and the people looked, and, behold, he had sackcloth within upon his flesh (II Ki. 6:24-30).

Captivity

Destruction would come upon all the land, rural and urban. If men refused to honor the sabbatical year of release, God promised to give the land its rest through the captivity of the nation. "And I will make your cities waste, and bring your sanctuaries unto desolation, and I will not smell the savour of your sweet odours. And I will bring the land into desolation: and your enemies which dwell therein shall be astonished at it. And I will scatter you among the heathen, and will draw out a sword after you: and your land shall be desolate, and your cities waste. Then shall the land enjoy her sabbaths, as long as it lieth desolate, and ye be in your enemies' land; even then shall the land rest, and enjoy her sabbaths. As long as it lieth desolate it shall rest; because it did not rest in your sabbaths, when ye dwelt upon it" (Lev. 26:31-35). The captivity of the people of Israel would be a negative sanction against the people and a positive sanction for the land: "The land also shall be left of them, and shall enjoy her sabbaths, while she lieth desolate without them: and they shall accept of the punishment of their iniquity: because, even because they despised my judgments, and because their soul abhorred my statutes" (Lev. 26:43). This judgment was imposed by God in the days of Jeremiah: "And they [the Chaldeans] burnt the house of God, and brake down the wall of Jerusalem, and burnt all the palaces thereof with fire, and destroyed all the goodly vessels thereof. And them that had escaped from the sword carried he away to Babylon; where they were servants to him and his sons until the reign of the kingdom of Persia: To fulfil the word of the LORD by the mouth of Jeremiah, until the land had enjoyed her sabbaths: for as long as she lay desolate she kept sabbath, to fulfil threescore and ten years" (II Chron. 36:19-21).

The people were to eat the fat of the land of promise. This was God's promised positive sanction. They would feed on the land. In contrast, the negative sanction of captivity was pictured as another kind of feast: the eating of the people by a foreign land. "And ye shall perish among the heathen, and the land of your enemies shall eat you up. And they that are left of you shall pine away in their iniquity in your enemies' lands; and also in the iniquities of their fathers shall they pine away with them" (Lev. 26:38-39).

Step by step, sanction by sanction, God would bring them face to face with the magnitude of their rebellion. The goal was their repentance: "If they shall confess their iniquity, and the iniquity of their fathers, with their trespass which they trespassed against me, and that also they have walked contrary unto me; And that I also have walked contrary unto them, and have brought them into the land of their enemies; if then their uncircumcised hearts be humbled, and they then accept of the punishment of their iniquity: Then will I remember my covenant with Jacob, and also my covenant with Isaac, and also my covenant with Abraham will I remember; and I will remember the land" (Lev. 26:40-42). Negative corporate sanctions in history are designed to restore covenantal faithfulness on the part of God's people. They are not judgments unto oblivion but judgments unto restoration.

Conclusion

God's escalating wrath in history serves as a means of restoring dominion by covenant. These negative sanctions are positive in intent: restoring faithfulness and, in the case of captivity, providing rest to the land itself. These sanctions were part of the covenantal law-order of Israel. This is why the section listing the sanctions ends with these words: "These are the statutes and judgments and laws, which the LORD made between him and the children of Israel in mount Sinai by the hand of Moses" (Lev. 26:46). There is no doubt that the sanctions were part of the stipulations. There was no way to obey God's law without imposing the required negative sanctions. If the authorities refused to impose the stipulated negative sanctions, God would impose His stipulated negative sanctions. These negative sanctions would become progressively more painful. God's negative sanctions were designed to persuade men of the integrity – the seamlessness – of God's revealed law. If the people refused to learn from one set of punishments, God threatened to impose worse punishments.

The principle underlying this escalation of negative sanctions is simple to state: "But he that knew not, and did commit things worthy of stripes, shall be beaten with few stripes. For unto whomsoever much is given, of him shall be much required: and to whom men have committed much, of him they will ask the more" (Luke 12:48). The escalating sanctions in Israel were a form of covenant-affirmation: establishing the social predictability of God's law. The reliability of God's law was visible in the escalation of God's corporate sanctions, both positive and negative.

Modern Christian theologians assume that the Mosaic Covenant's divine sanctions no longer operate in the New Covenant era.[2] From this idea (or at least paralleling it), they conclude that the Mosaic Covenant's civil sanctions are no longer valid. This is logical, given the incorrect presupposition. The divine sanctions undergirded the Bible-revealed familial, civil, and ecclesiastical stipulations; if the authorities refused to impose these mandatory sanctions, God would then impose His sanctions. If the threat of God's corporate sanctions are removed, then the sanctions undergirding the institutional sanctions are absent. Without sanctions, there is no law. *Biblical sanctions are inseparable from biblical stipulations: no sanctions = no law*. Remove God's corporate sanctions in history, and the legal order becomes judicially autonomous in history.

The autonomy of society from God's law is the agreed-upon agenda of an implicit alliance between the humanists and the pietists. The humanists assume that God's corporate sanctions

2. Gary North, *Millennialism and Social Theory* (Tyler, Texas: Institute for Christian Economics, 1990), ch. 7.

have always been mythological. Christian pietists assume that these sanctions have been annulled by the New Covenant. This pair of false assumptions serves as the judicial basis of the humanist-pietist alliance against the ideal of God's theocratic kingdom in history: Christendom.

If God's sanctions did not operate predictably in history, it would be impossible to produce a self-consciously biblical form of social theory. Christians would have to rely on some version of pagan natural law theory in order to construct their social theories. This is what they have done for almost two millennia. With the collapse of natural law theory after Darwin, Christian social theory has floundered. Darwin's target was William Paley's providential and teleological order; he hit his target.[3] Everyone standing behind this target has been epistemologically defenseless ever since.

3. Gary North, *The Dominion Covenant: Genesis* (2nd ed.; Tyler, Texas: Institute for Christian Economics, 1987), pp. 256-57.

36

THE PRIESTHOOD: BARRIERS TO ENTRY

Speak unto the children of Israel, and say unto them, When a man shall make a singular vow, the persons shall be for the L*ORD* *by thy estimation. And thy estimation shall be of the male from twenty years old even unto sixty years old, even thy estimation shall be fifty shekels of silver, after the shekel of the sanctuary. And if it be a female, then thy estimation shall be thirty shekels. And if it be from five years old even unto twenty years old, then thy estimation shall be of the male twenty shekels, and for the female ten shekels. And if it be from a month old even unto five years old, then thy estimation shall be of the male five shekels of silver, and for the female thy estimation shall be three shekels of silver. And if it be from sixty years old and above; if it be a male, then thy estimation shall be fifteen shekels, and for the female ten shekels. But if he be poorer than thy estimation, then he shall present himself before the priest, and the priest shall value him; according to his ability that vowed shall the priest value him (Lev. 27:2-8).*

The theocentric basis of this passage is that the God of the covenant does allow vows. The question is, what kind of vow is in view here? This is one of the most peculiar passages in the Mosaic law. The rabbinical commentators do not do a better job than the Christians in explaining it, and the Christians are universally perplexed. It is obvious that vows were involved. Money payments were also involved. We need to answer two questions: What was the nature of the vow? What was the function of the money payment?

Vows and Succession

Commentators argue about the possible reasons for the placement of this chapter at the end of Leviticus. Why should a section on vows appear at the end of a book on holiness? Gordon Wenham writes: "It is a puzzle why ch. 27, which deals with vows, should appear in its present position, since ch. 26 with its blessings and curses would have made a fitting conclusion to the book."[1] He offers two possible explanations, neither of them convincing.

I suggest the following explanation: the end of Leviticus marks a transition from a book that centers on point three of the biblical covenant model – holiness, boundaries – to a book that centers on point four: oaths, sanctions. But what about part five of the book, inheritance? Here is the central theme of this passage: the loss of inheritance in one tribe in exchange for inheritance in another tribe.

The previous chapter, Leviticus 26, deals with God's positive and negative corporate sanctions in history. The move from an emphasis on point four of the biblical covenant model – sanctions – in Chapter 26 to point five – succession – in Chapter 27 is quite appropriate.[2] Negative sanctions in the context of Chapter 26 have to do with disinheritance. Chapter 26 presents a catalogue of God's corporate covenantal sanctions; Chapter 27 begins with rules governing a particular type of personal vow. This in turn raises the issue of covenantal continuity. Jordan writes: "Payment of vows relates to the fifth commandment, as we give to our Divine parent and thereby honor Him, and to

---

1. Gordon J. Wenham, *The Book of Leviticus* (Grand Rapids, Michigan: Eerdmans, 1979), p. 336.

2. James B. Jordan, *Covenant Sequence in Leviticus and Deuteronomy* (Tyler, Texas: Institute for Christian Economics, 1989), p. 17.

the tenth commandment, since payment of vows and tithes is the opposite of covetousness. Thus, this final section of Leviticus has everything to do with continuity."[3] The passage is where it belongs: in part five. The vow relates to inheritance: family continuity over time.

Devoted to Temple Service: Irreversible

The text does not tell us what stipulations governed this type of vow. The text also does not provide a context. This is why the commentators get so confused. The old line about "text without context is pretext" is applicable. The law was addressed to priests: "the persons shall be for the LORD by thy estimation." Whose estimation? The priests. Anything dedicated to the Lord is assumed by commentators to have been dedicated to or through the priesthood. The text is silent about the nature of the dedication; it speaks only of pricing. A gift of individuals was in some way involved because specific prices are associated in the text with specific genders and ages. I argue that the terms of the vow were not symbolic, and the payment was not a substitute.

Devotion: Change in Legal Status

In the case of heathen slaves, Israelites possessed lawful title to the slave and the slave's heirs (Lev. 25:44-45). There is no reason to assume that an Israelite could not transfer ownership of his slave to an individual priest or to the temple. The tabernacle-temple already employed permanent pagan slaves: the Gibeonites (Josh. 9:23). They were permanently set apart – *devoted* – for temple service. This was the result of their deception in gaining the vow of peace from Joshua (Josh. 9). We conclude that there is nothing in the Mosaic Covenant to indicate that pagan slaves could not be assigned to temple service

3. *Ibid.*, p. 39.

even though they could not lawfully assist with the sacrifices. They were not allowed inside those temple boundaries that were lawfully accessible only to priests, but they still could work for the priests outside these boundaries. Thus, a symbolic transfer of ownership of a pagan slave to the priests is not the concern of this passage. The deciding issue contextually cannot be priestly ownership as such. The issue is also not the dedication or sanctification of household slaves. There was nothing special in Israel about the dedication of household slaves – nothing "singular." It has to be something more fundamental: *service within the normally sealed boundaries of the temple*.

Then who were the vow-governed individuals of Leviticus 27:2-8? *They were family members under the lawful authority of the vow-taker*. The vow was a specific kind of vow, a vow of devotion. Devotion here was not an emotional state; it was a change in judicial status.

Devotion vs. Sanctification

At this point, I have to introduce a crucial distinction of the Mosaic law: devotion vs. sanctification. A sanctified item was set apart for God's use, though not necessarily on a permanent basis. A devoted thing was set apart permanently for priestly service or sacrifice. This distinction is based on the law that appears later in this section of Leviticus: "Notwithstanding no devoted thing, that a man shall devote unto the LORD of all that he hath, both of man and beast, and of the field of his possession, shall be sold or redeemed: every devoted thing is most holy unto the LORD. None devoted, which shall be devoted of men, shall be redeemed; but shall surely be put to death" (Lev. 27:28-29).

Death here was not necessarily physical death; it was, however, necessarily *covenantal death*. This meant that the devoted item was placed within the irreversible boundaries of God's ban. This form of covenantal death meant that the item was *beyond human redemption*. The devoted object came under God's absolute control. In many passages in Scripture, the Hebrew word for "devoted" (*khayrem*) is translated as "accursed" or "cursed." Such a cursed item could not be used for anything other than sacrifice to God. If it was subsequently misused – violated or profaned, in other words – the person who violated God's boundary himself came under the ban: beyond human redemption. The ban applied to Jericho (Josh. 6:17-18), to Achan's family (Josh. 7:1), and later, to the spoils of the Amalekites (I Sam. 15:21).[4]

The devoted item could not be redeemed by the payment of a price. It had been permanently transferred covenantally to God as a sacrificial offering. This is the meaning of the singular vow. *The singular vow was a vow whose stipulations were irreversible*. The devoted item was placed within the confines of an absolutely holy boundary: beyond human redemption. The vow was voluntary; the resulting transfer was irreversible: a singular vow.

Devotion Through Adoption

Could an Israelite lawfully devote his child to priestly service? Yes; as we shall see, Jephthah's daughter was so devoted by her father. Once a person was adopted into the family of Aaron specifically or into the tribe of Levi, he could not reenter another Israelite tribe by a subsequent act of adoption. He had been devoted to the temple: beyond redemption. So had his covenantal heirs. If I am correct about this, then in the context of marriage – another form of legal adoption[5] – there

---

4. It is worth noting that this Hebrew word is the very last word that occurs in the Old Testament, in the passage that prophesies the coming of Elijah (John the Baptist), the man Jesus identified as the last man of the Old Covenant (Luke 16:16). "Behold, I will send you Elijah the prophet before the coming of the great and dreadful day of the LORD: And he shall turn the heart of the fathers to the children, and the heart of the children to their fathers, lest I come and smite the earth with a *curse*" (Mal. 4:5-6). This was God's threatened negative sanction: *covenantal disinheritance* – fathers vs. sons – that involved God's curse on Old Covenant Israel.

5. Gary North, *Tools of Dominion: The Case Laws of Exodus* (Tyler, Texas: Institute

was no option for an Israelite father to buy back his daughter from her priestly husband by returning the bride price to his son-in-law.[6] Similarly, there was no way for a man to buy back himself, his wife, or his children from formally devoted service to God. In short, there was no redemption price for this kind of vow. This is why the vow was *pawlaw*: "singular."

There is no indication that a man could place his adult male children into mandated priestly service. An adult son was not eligible for compulsory adoption. He was a lawful heir to the land and the legal status of his tribe and family. He could not be disinherited at his father's prerogative. The crucial legal issue for identifying adulthood for men was military numbering. An adult male was eligible to be numbered at age 20 to fight in a holy war: "This they shall give, every one that passeth among them that are numbered, half a shekel after the shekel of the sanctuary: (a shekel is twenty gerahs:) an half shekel shall be the offering of the LORD" (Ex. 30:13). At age 20, a man came under the threat of God's negative sanctions: going into battle without first having paid blood money to the temple.[7] Once he became judicially eligible for numbering as a member of his tribe, he became judicially responsible for his own vows. He became, as we say, "his own man." He became a member of God's holy army. A father could no longer act in the son's name.

A daughter could not legally be numbered for service in God's army. Thus, an unmarried daughter could be delivered into a priestly family, as we see in the case of Jephthah's daughter (Jud. 11:34-39).[8] Jephthah's vow to sacrifice the first thing to come out of his house could not legally be applied literally to

---

for Christian Economics, 1990), pp. 218-19.

6. The dowry remained with the wife in any case; it was her protection, her inheritance from her father.

7. *Ibid.*, ch. 32: "Blood Money, Not Head Tax."

8. I accept the standard interpretation of this story: she was not literally executed by her father.

a person. He could not lawfully burn a person, nor could the priests; therefore, any person who came under the terms of such a lawful vow had to be devoted to God in temple service.[9] Jephthah had made a singular vow. It was irreversible. This means that his daughter had to be disinherited.[10] She was beyond redemption. As his only child (Jud. 11:34), she was the lawful heir of his land and its accompanying legal status, but only so long as she did not marry outside his tribe (Num. 35:6-9). By being adopted into the tribe of Levi, she could not thereafter marry outside of the tribe of Levi. Thus, she had to forfeit her inheritance from Jephthah. She could not inherit her father's political kingdom as an adopted member of the tribe of Levi. But she was, as the phrase goes, "her daddy's girl": a dynasty-coveting power-seeker. When her virginity cost her the inheritance of her father's political dynasty, she bewailed her virginity. Her heart was not right with God. What was an enormous honor – adoption into the tribe of Levi, the spiritual counsellors of the nation – she saw as a thing to bewail in the mountains for two months (Jud. 11:37).[11]

Not a Redemption Price

In the section of Leviticus 27 that follows this one, we read of the redemption price of animals that are set apart (sanctified) to be offered as sacrifices (vv. 9-13). Then, in the section following that one, we read of the redemption price of a house sanctified to the priesthood (vv. 14-15). Finally, in the next section, the laws governing sanctified fields are listed (vv. 16-25). In the second and third cases, the term "sanctify" (*kawdash*, holy) is used.[12] In all three cases, the redemption price was the market

---

9. Jordan, *Judges*, pp. 204-13.

10. *Ibid.*, p. 205.

11. Gary North, *Boundaries and Dominion: The Economics of Leviticus* (computer edition; Tyler, Texas: Institute for Christian Economics, 1994), ch. 35, subsection on "The Disinheritance of Jephthah's Daughter."

12. In the first case, sacrificial animals, the cognate term for "sanctify" is used:

price at the time of the redemption plus 20 percent (vv. 13, 15, 19).

Then comes Leviticus 27:26: "Only the firstling of the beasts, which should be the LORD'S firstling, no man shall sanctify it; whether it be ox, or sheep: it is the LORD'S." This law specifically denies the legitimacy of sanctifying the animal. This means that no redemption of the animal was legal. It was a devoted animal, not a sanctified animal. *Sanctification* in this context meant "set apart until redeemed." This legal condition was less rigorous than devotion. *Devotion* meant that the legal boundary around the object was permanent. The same is true of the vow of Leviticus 27:2-8. In this passage, there is no mention of a supplemental payment of one-fifth. This is evidence that what is being considered in verses 2-8 is not a series of redemption prices. Then what does this section refer to?

Members of the tribe of Levi could not normally own rural land outside of 48 specified cities (Num. 35:7).[13] Thus, any person who was delivered by a vow and payment into temple service lost his or her claim on his or her ancestral land. A father alienated his family's inheritance forever from his heirs if his male children were under age 20 or his daughters were unmarried at the time he made his vow. This did not mean that they lost their legal status as freemen; Levites possessed freeman status. But the heirs did lose their former claim on the family's land. Could the priest annul the vow? Yes. There was no compulsion that he adopt someone into his family. The vow was analogous to the vow of a daughter or married woman: it could be annulled within 24 hours by the male head of the household (Num. 30:3-8). The priests, acting in God's name, as the heads of God's ecclesiastical household, could lawfully annul

kodesh, holy (vv. 9, 10).

13. There were two exceptions: 1) when a family dedicated a piece of land to the priesthood and then refused to redeem it before the next jubilee year; 2) when a family dedicated a piece of land to the priesthood but then leased the whole property to someone else (Lev. 27:16-21). See Chapter 37, below.

someone's vow of adoption into the tribe. But if the vow was accepted by a priest in authority, the vow-taker and any other members of his family covered by his vow were then adopted into the tribe of Levi if they could pay the entry fee. There was no way back into non-Levitical freemanship in Israel; the adopted family's original inheritance had been forfeited to the kinsman-redeemer, the closest relative in their original tribe (Num. 27:9-11). They could retain their status as freemen only as members of the tribe of Levi.

The Restrictive Function of Price

These prices were not market prices. They had nothing to do with comparative rates of economic productivity.[14] They were instead barriers to entry into the tribe of the priests. Primary judicial authority in Israel was supposed to be inside the tribe of Levi, for the Levites had unique access to the written law of God. They were the spiritual *and therefore the judicial* counsellors in Israel.[15] It was not easy to gain access to this position of honor and authority. Adoption into the tribe of Levi was legal, but it was not cheap.

The entry price for an adult male was set at 50 shekels of silver.[16] The price for an adult female was 30 shekels.[17] The male child's price was 20 shekels; the female child's was 10

14. I have summarized a possible explanation of these prices as redemption prices. See North, *Boundaries and Dominion*, ch. 36, subsection on "Explanation: Economic Productivity."

15. This is why Paul speaks of the double honor of those who labor in the word: "Let the elders that rule well be counted worthy of double honour, especially they who labour in the word and doctrine" (I Tim. 5:17).

16. This was the same as another judicial price: the formal bride price owed by a seducer of a virgin to her father. North, *Tools of Dominion*, pp. 649-57. It rests on an interpretation of the false accuser's penalty of Deuteronomy 22:19: "And they shall amerce him in an hundred shekels of silver, and give them unto the father of the damsel, because he hath brought up an evil name upon a virgin of Israel: and she shall be his wife; he may not put her away all his days." One hundred shekels was double restitution.

17. The same price that was owed to the owner of a gored slave (Ex. 21:32).

shekels. Very young children's prices were lower: 5 shekels (male) and 3 shekels (female). For the elderly, the prices were 15 shekels (male) and 10 shekels (female).

The formal prices of the sexes differed. Males were priced higher than females in every age group. Similarly, old people were priced higher than very young children, but less than children age 5 to 20. Why? Did this have something to do with market pricing? These were not cases of pure market pricing, but can the differences in formal prices be explained in terms of expected productivity, just as market prices can be explained? Yes, but such an explanation is misleading.[18]

Prices always serve as barriers. The question is: Were prices in this instance barriers to entry or barriers to escape; that is, were they entry prices or redemption prices? Were they based on the value of services to be redeemed or were they tests of authority to be honored?

Submission to Authority

Let us begin with an assumption: these prices were dowries, not redemption prices. Why was the highest entry price required of an adult male? Because the adult head of a household was a man who was used to exercising family authority and perhaps other kinds of civil authority. By placing a high entry price on his adoption into the tribe of Levi, God protected His priestly servants from invasion by two groups: 1) power-seekers seeking to extend their authority into the church; 2) poor people seeking a guaranteed income as members of the tithe-receiving tribe. The power-seekers first had to abandon all legal claim to their original inheritance and also had to provide a considerable entry fee. Married men also had to pay for their wives' and minor children's entry into the tribe of Levi. This further restricted entry into the priestly class.

---

18. North, *Boundaries and Dominion*, ch. 36, subsection on "Explanation: Economic Productivity."

God established an entry fee higher for aged people – age 60 and over (v. 7) – than for very young children: under age 5 (v. 6). Why? Because old people tend to be more set in their ways, more used to deference from younger people, even priests. They would be more trouble to govern than very young children. The very young child would grow up in the presence of the Levites and the priests. He would learn to respect authority. He would not be a major threat to the ecclesiastical hierarchy. There was less need for a monetary barrier to his entry into the household of the church.

God established lower prices for old men than for male children ages 5-19 (v. 5). The prices for females, young and old, were the same: 10 shekels. Why? The issue was authority: males had more authority than females did. Children of this age group reflected their parents' attitudes. The boys would have been more difficult to control than aged men. Young girls and old women were judged of equal difficulty.

So, the discrepancies in these dowry prices can be explained in terms of *expected resistance to ecclesiastical authority*. But what about the lower price for females in each age group? This is also consistent with the hypothesis that this law was imposed by God in order to reduce the Levite adoptees' resistance to ecclesiastical authority. Israelite women were accustomed to obey male heads of household. They were more likely to respect hierarchical authority. Thus, they were less of a threat to the established ecclesiastical order. The payment could be smaller because the need to establish a barrier to entry was less.

Sonship Is Judicial

It was an honor to be a member of the tribe of Levi. This tribe guarded the law of the covenant, a guardianship symbolized by the two tablets of the law inside the Ark of the Covenant (Deut. 31:26). The priests were in charge of guarding the Ark. That is, the priests policed the boundaries between the Ark and the world outside.

Adoption is always an aspect of God's law. This included adoption into the tribe of Levi, and even the family of Aaron. Sonship is judicial. Biblical sonship must always place covenantal faithfulness above biological relationships. When Eli elevated his sons to the priesthood, judicially ignoring the presence of faithful servant Samuel, God cut off Eli's inheritance by executing his sons. Eli had warned both of them what would happen, but they had refused to listen: "If one man sin against another, the judge shall judge him: but if a man sin against the LORD, who shall intreat for him? Notwithstanding they hearkened not unto the voice of their father, because the LORD would slay them" (I Sam. 2:25). Eli refused to impose the negative sanction of disinheritance through excommunication, so God disinherited them through execution. He did this by subjecting the whole nation to a military defeat by the Philistines. A man of God warned Eli of what was about to happen (I Sam. 2:27-36), but Eli refused to take effective steps to evade God's wrath. He could have adopted Samuel from the beginning, had his mother consented, which she was obviously ready to do, having dedicated him to God for life (I Sam. 1:11). At any time, Eli could have adopted Samuel in place of his sons, making him a priest at age 30.[19] Instead, he honored biological sonship above adoptive sonship. Adoption is fundamental in establishing covenant-keeping sonship; biology is not. Eli had decided to maintain a boundary between Samuel and the altar; God therefore placed a boundary between Eli and his inheritance. Samuel could have become Eli's heir; by honoring his sons, Eli chose to disinherit his family's name.

Eli's decision cost Israel dearly, as priestly rebellion always does. Because Eli had made his sons the priests of Israel, Samuel later became a prophet who brought God's covenant lawsuit against Saul (I Sam. 15). Samuel, not the high priest, anointed

19. Age 30 was the minimum age of service in the temple (Num. 4:3, 23, 30, 35, 39, 40, 43, 47).

David (I Sam. 16). Had Samuel been a priest, the priesthood would have retained more of its temporal authority. God honored Samuel more than He honored the civil authority of the priesthood.

The Kinsman-Redeemer

Leviticus 27:2-8 is the passage governing the conditions of adoption into the tribe of Levi. There had to be a payment – the equivalent of a dowry – to the temple.[20] In the case of a slave, his owner had to provide the funds. If the adoptee was the head of a household, he had to make the payment on his own behalf, or find someone to make it for him.

Who was the most likely person to make the payment for him if he could not afford to pay? Both judicially and economically, there is little doubt: the kinsman-redeemer. He would inherit title to the land left behind by a newly adopted family. The entry price was high; no one else was likely to have the same incentive to make so large a payment. This points to the work of Christ as the Kinsman-Redeemer of Israel and mankind. He has paid the fee for all those who are adopted into the New Covenant priesthood. No one else has either the incentive or the ability to pay this price. In His case, the incentive is not economic, for two reasons. First, Jesus Christ already is God the Father's lawful heir in history and eternity. He will inherit everything. Second, the entry price is too high – far beyond the very high price of 50 shekels in Old Covenant Israel. The price is the death of the Kinsman-Redeemer. His motivation was

---

20. I do not think the price was paid to Levite families. Had the money gone to individual families, there would have been a strong motivation for Levites to recruit new members of the tribe. The entry fee was to serve as a barrier to entry, not a motivation to recruit new members. If the money went directly to the temple, local Levites would have had far less incentive to recruit non-Levites into the tribe. Aaronic priests would have possessed a veto over adoption: the men with the greatest authority in Israel. Adoption in this case was tribal, not familial, analogous to circumcised resident aliens who were adopted into tribal cities if they were accepted to serve in God's holy army.

grace, not profit. Christians inherit as heirs of their Kinsmen-Redeemer, Jesus Christ. Everyone else is eternally disinherited.

Verse 8 reads: "But if he be poorer than thy estimation, then he shall present himself before the priest, and the priest shall value him; according to his ability that vowed shall the priest value him." The high priest, Jesus Christ, has paid the maximum price for each of His saints – those set apart by God judicially for priestly service. Entering with nothing of our own, we do not need to plead before a priest for a lower entry fee. The high priest has paid it all.

Conclusion

If this analysis is correct, then it should be obvious that this law has been annulled with the New Covenant's change in the priesthood. The passage's variations in price – young vs. old, male vs. female – have nothing to do with economic productivity. They are irrelevant for the economic analysis of labor markets. They were equally irrelevant for such analytical purposes under the Mosaic Covenant.

The prices listed in Leviticus 27:2-8 were not redemption prices; they were entry barrier prices. They were not based on the expected economic productivity of people who were then immediately redeemed out of God's ecclesiastical service. They were based on the need to screen power-seekers and security-seekers from access to ecclesiastical service. They were not market prices; they were judicial prices. They were not barriers to *escape from* ecclesiastical service; they were barriers to *entry into* ecclesiastical service. Thus, rather than applying economic analysis to the productivity of the groups specified in Leviticus 27:2-8, we should apply economic analysis to the question of the judicial boundary separating the tribe of Levi from the other tribes.

37

THE REDEMPTION-PRICE SYSTEM

And if it be a beast, whereof men bring an offering unto the LORD, *all that any man giveth of such unto the* LORD *shall be holy. He shall not alter it, nor change it, a good for a bad, or a bad for a good: and if he shall at all change beast for beast, then it and the exchange thereof shall be holy. And if it be any unclean beast, of which they do not offer a sacrifice unto the* LORD, *then he shall present the beast before the priest: And the priest shall value it, whether it be good or bad: as thou valuest it, who art the priest, so shall it be. But if he will at all redeem it, then he shall add a fifth part thereof unto thy estimation. And when a man shall sanctify his house to be holy unto the* LORD, *then the priest shall estimate it, whether it be good or bad: as the priest shall estimate it, so shall it stand. And if he that sanctified it will redeem his house, then he shall add the fifth part of the money of thy estimation unto it, and it shall be his* (Lev. 27:9-15).

The theocentric meaning of this passage is simple: God is to be honored by sacrifice. A person could give an animal or a piece of real estate to God through the priesthood. If he changes his mind later and decided to buy it back, he paid a redemption fee of one-fifth above the estimated value of the gift. The recipient, the priest, made this original estimation. God was willing to allow men to change their minds regarding previous sacrifices, but not at zero price. Once offered as a sacrifice, the property did change ownership: from the original owner to the priest. Whatever benefits the owner received from making the sacrifice – self-esteem, public acclaim, etc. – were purchased upon redemption: an additional payment of one-fifth.

This passage deals with the re-purchase of animals and houses that had been given to priests either for ritual sacrifice or for resale by the priests. Later in this chapter, I will consider the third redemption payment: fields. In each case, the cash redemption price required an additional 20 percent payment.[1] This was what distinguished a redemption price from the previous passage's payment structure, which was not a redemption price but rather an entry fee into the tribe designated by God for holy service. The visible difference between the two forms of voluntary payment to the priesthood – dedication and devotion – was the presence of a penalty payment. The dedicated item did not become *hormah*: God's whole burnt offering. With dedication there was a possibility of economic redemption: de-sanctification.

Let the reader be forewarned: this a long chapter in this drastically stripped-down commentary. Its importance to the Mosaic law was not comparable to other Levitical laws that I have commented on in chapters that are far shorter. Nevertheless, I was unable to cut it, except for the final summary section that appears at the end of each chapter of *Boundaries and Dominion*. The reason why I could not cut back this chapter is because of the highly technical nature of the text. For example, all of the English translators have been baffled, for good reason, by the sparseness of the attached section on pricing: Leviticus 27:16-19. Verse 16 has been universally mistranslated into English – and, I suspect, most other languages as well. I was unable to cut out anything from my original exposition and still explain the meaning of this passage. As far as I can discover,

1. There was an exception, as we shall see: a lessee paid a cash redemption price but no 20 penalty.

Leviticus 27:16-19 has no modern application, but I could not pass over it in silence; it clearly is an economic passage. It was also intimately related to the New Testament's transfer of God's kingdom from Old Covenant Israel to the church.

This law's specific application to fields placed under a dedicatory vow had this curious aspect: it was the only exception to one of the foundational laws undergirding the decentralized Mosaic social order, namely, the prohibition against the ownership of rural land by the priests. I offer an explanation for this exception. Few commentators do. My explanation may be controversial: the law of dedicated fields established a lawful way for members of other tribes *to bribe unrighteous priests* into announcing the jubilee year and enforcing its terms.

Pricing and Penalties

A beast was designated by its owner as a sacrifice. The owner brought it to the priest. The beast was then identified as having become holy (*kodesh*). To be holy is to be set apart judicially, i.e., sanctified (*kawdash*). But the degree of separation was less than in the case of an offering that was devoted to God: it did not come under the ban.

The priests were Israel's agents of formal sanctification. They possessed the authority to set apart certain beasts for sacrificial purposes. The individual could not sacrifice his animal on his own authority if he expected to establish it as a judicially valid offering; he had to bring it to the priests. This dependence on the priesthood to validate sacramental offerings to God reinforced the social and legal authority of the priesthood. This arrangement did not limit men's ability to make economically significant offerings to God, but such unsanctified offerings were not sacramental. Laymen could show good faith, but they did not have the power to invoke God's sanctions authoritatively.[2]

---

2. One of the fundamental institutional differences between magical religion and

Once it had been dedicated – sanctified – the beast's owner had the right to change his mind about sacrificing this particular beast. For whatever reason, he could choose to spare the life of this animal. The priest would then estimate the value of this beast according to its market price. An additional 20 percent had to be paid by the owner: a redemption (buy-back) price. This specific redemption price is not established in the text, in contrast to verses 2-8, where specific prices are stated. This is because *the prices for sacrificial animals were not judicial prices; they were market prices*. They varied according to market conditions. The redemption price of an animal was tied to its market price. This was also the case in the price of a house dedicated to the temple (vv. 14-15).

The priest had the authority to fix the redemption prices of dedicated items (vv. 12, 15, 19) other than fields. If he set a price too high, the owner would not redeem the item. The priest would then wind up owning an asset worth only what the free market determined, when he could have had a market price plus 20 percent. He would thereby have forfeited the opportunity to enjoy what speculators call a quick turnaround. He was allowed to obtain the market price for the animal by selling it back, keeping the extra 20 percent for himself. *The presence of the 20 percent payment kept the priest's pricing relatively honest*, i.e., in close approximation to market prices. So, in this instance, the extra payment imposed in the redemption of sanctified items was not a penalty payment. It was more of a "keep the priests' redemption price valuations honest" payment. We should probably think of it as a transaction fee. The

---

biblical religion is seen in this distinction between sanctified offerings and unsanctified offerings. The person who invokes magic believes that his formal incantations and rituals allow him to manipulate supernatural power directly and authoritatively. Biblical religion denies such authority to all those who have not been anointed, either by birth or adoption (Old Covenant priesthood or prophetic anointing) or by the laying on of hands (New Covenant ministry-priesthood). The priest in the New Covenant does not offer a sacrifice to God (Heb. 9); rather, he offers to church members the sacramental means of covenant renewal: the Lord's Supper.

giver proved his dedication to God by dedicating the beast to a priest and then paying a 20 percent transaction fee in order to redeem it.

Priests and Fields

The jubilee law applied to houses in the 48 cities of the Levites and to the common land surrounding them (Lev. 25:32-33; Num. 35:7). These homes could not be permanently alienated from the families of the Levites. "Notwithstanding the cities of the Levites, and the houses of the cities of their possession, may the Levites redeem at any time. And if a man purchase of the Levites, then the house that was sold, and the city of his possession, shall go out in the year of jubile: for the houses of the cities of the Levites are their possession among the children of Israel" (Lev. 25:32-33). The jubilee law of inheritance applied to the Levites' homes in Levitical cities and to rural land in Israel. The Levites could not lawfully be excluded from their inheritance, but they were excluded from the other tribes' inheritance. To maintain their own inheritance, they had to defend the inheritance of the other tribal families. They had to preach the jubilee law. God gave them an inheritance in their cities; this served as an economic incentive for them to declare the jubilee year.

Priests could not normally own rural land; it was not part of their inheritance at the time of the conquest of Canaan. When enforced, the jubilee law made it impossible for the priesthood to extend its political influence into the other tribes apart from the exposition and application of the Mosaic law. *The jubilee law was designed to keep a centralized ecclesiocracy from being formed*. The jubilee land law was primarily a law of citizenship. It was designed to provide a permanent judicial veto for the tribes. The tribal system, when reinforced by the jubilee law, decentralized political power in Israel.

Levites could lease rural properties, however. They could also receive rural properties as gifts until the next jubilee year.

They were not prohibited from subleasing these sanctified fields. These fields would have provided them with a stream of income. Within a predominantly rural economy, this stream of income might have been significant, depending on the size and productivity of the dedicated plots.

A Righteous Bribe to Unrighteous Priests

The jubilee law's restriction on Levitical ownership of rural land was not primarily economic. The jubilee law itself was not primarily economic; it was judicial: a mark of freeman status for the heirs of the conquest. But there were economic incentives tied to the preservation of political freedom. A small but relevant aspect of these incentives was the law of the unredeemed field. Priests could in rare instances become permanent owners of rural land when an owner or his heirs failed to redeem a reclaimed dedicated plot. But in order for this transfer of title to take place, the jubilee year first had to be declared publicly throughout the nation. "And if he will not redeem the field, or if he have sold the field to another man, it shall not be redeemed any more. But the field, when it goeth out in the jubile, shall be holy unto the LORD, as a field devoted; the possession thereof shall be the priest's" (Lev. 27:20-21).

The existence of a law that tied the jubilee year to a permanent transfer of rural land to priestly members of the tribe of Levi delivered an important tool of influence into the hands of covenant-keeping rural land owners. If covenant-keeping men suspected that the civil authorities and the priests had conspired to avoid proclaiming the approaching jubilee year, they had a way to encourage the ecclesiastical authorities to proclaim the jubilee year on time. All the land owners had to do was dedicate some fields to the priests and then reclaim the fields for themselves, refusing to redeem these fields with cash plus a 20 percent payment. To inherit these fields at the jubilee, the priests would have to proclaim the jubilee year. The Mosaic law therefore provided the other tribes with a legal way to bribe otherwise dishonest priests into covenant-keeping with respect to the proclamation of the jubilee year.[3] This was an expensive way to persuade priests to honor the jubilee year; effective bribes normally involve considerable losses. At least until the plots shrank in size and value through population growth, this transfer of land could be significant.

Establishing the Redemption Price

The law governing sanctified fields provides one of the few cases of a specified price in the Mosaic law. This law identified a single crop as the economic measure: barley. This law applied to a single case: a field voluntarily dedicated to a priest.

> And if a man shall sanctify unto the LORD some part of a field of his possession, then thy estimation shall be according to the seed thereof: an homer of barley seed shall be valued at fifty shekels of silver. If he sanctify his field from the year of jubile, according to thy estimation it shall stand. But if he sanctify his field after the jubile, then the priest shall reckon unto him the money according to the years that remain, even unto the year of the jubile, and it shall be abated from thy estimation. And if he that sanctified the field will in any wise redeem it, then he shall add the fifth part of the money of thy estimation unto it, and it shall be assured to him (Lev. 27:16-19).

What was the redemption price of a piece of land? If sanctified land had been treated as if it had been any other capital asset, the free market would have informed owners and priests of its value. But this unique case was not to be decided by an appeal to the free market. Instead, the calculation had to begin with an estimation of a quantity of barley seed. As we shall see,

---

3. On the moral legitimacy of bribing corrupt judges, see Gary North, "In Defense of Biblical Bribery," in R. J. Rushdoony, *The Institutes of Biblical Law* (Nutley, New Jersey: Craig Press, 1973), Appendix 5. "A gift is as a precious stone in the eyes of him that hath it: whithersoever it turneth, it prospereth" (Prov. 17:8). "A gift in secret pacifieth anger: and a reward in the bosom strong wrath" (Prov. 21:14).

the appropriate unit of measurement to define the limits of a dedicated field was the field's output: one homer of barley seed per year. Nevertheless, the grammar of the text does not specify whether "seed" in this case law refers to input (seeds planted) or output (seeds harvested).[4] Because of input-output ratios, I accept the "output" interpretation (see below). Also, because prices are established in terms of the *expected value* of a resource factor's *future output*, I accept the output view's interpretation of "seed."

This case law specifies a particular crop: barley seed. It also specifies a unit of volume: *homer* (pronounced "khomer"). It refers to a unit of money: a shekel of silver. It refers to a number: 50. We must now seek to make sense of the passage: the redemption value of the land.

A Perplexing Translation

From Leviticus 27:2-8, we know that 50 shekels of silver represented a great deal of money. It was sufficient to serve as a major barrier against an adult male's entry into the tribe of Levi (Lev. 27:3).[5] Fifty shekels of silver bought an adult male slave in the ancient Near East.[6] The average wage of a worker was one shekel of silver per month.[7] We must bear this in mind as we study verse 16.

The literal Hebrew text of the pricing clause of verse 16 is somewhat obscure – five nouns without a verb, plus a numerical adjective: *homer barley seed fifty shekels silver*. The standard inter-

---

4. Some commentators believe that this referred to the amount of seed the field would produce (output view). Others think it means the amount of seed that a field would absorb (input view). Wenham, who follows R. de Vaux (*Ancient Israel*): "seed" refers to the field's output of barley seed, not its input of barley seed. Gordon J. Wenham, *The Book of Leviticus* (Grand Rapids, Michigan: Eerdmans, 1979), p. 340n. I agree with this view.

5. See Chapter 36.

6. Wenham, p. 338, citing I. Mendelsohn, *Slavery In the Ancient Near East* (New York: Oxford University Press, 1949), pp. 117ff.

7. Wenham, *idem.*, citing Mendelsohn, *ibid.*, p. 118.

pretation of this clause links the price of a homer of barley to the jubilee year. The difficult question is this: To what does the phrase "fifty shekels silver" refer? There is a sharp division of opinion between translators and commentators. The translators link the 50 shekels to the unit of measurement: the price of one homer of barley seed. The commentators link the 50 shekels to the jubilee cycle: the combined prices of an annual homer of barley seed through the cycle.

I side with the commentators. Here is my reasoning. It has been estimated that in Mesopotamia, the familiar price of barley was one shekel of silver per homer.[8] Because the jubilee year occurred every 50 years, it is tempting to conclude that the text really means output (or perhaps input) per land unit of one homer of barley a year for 50 years. A homer is variously estimated at between 29 gallons and 59 gallons.[9] Wenham says that a field yielding (output) a homer of barley seed was valued at one shekel, or 50 shekels per jubilee period. Harrison takes the view that "seed" means input: "The land being vowed was valued by the priest in terms of the amount of seed required for sowing it annually, each *homer of barley* representing a price of fifty shekels for the forty-nine year period. This is comparable to Mesopotamian practices, where a homer of barley cost a shekel."[10] The comment by Rashi[11] is similar: ". . . an area requiring a Khor of barley seed . . . is redeemable by fifty shekels. . . ."[12] All agree: 50 shekels per jubilee cycle.

---

8. *Ibid.*, p. 340. Wenham cites R. P. Maloney, *Catholic Biblical Quarterly* (1974), pp. 4ff; P. Garelli and V. Nikiprowetsky, *Le Proche-Orient Asiatique: Les Empires mésopotamiens, Israel* (University of Paris, 1974), pp. 273-74, 285-86.

9. *Ibid.*, p. 339.

10. R. K. Harrison, *Leviticus: An Introduction and Commentary* (Downers Grove, Illinois: Inter-Varsity Press, 1980), p. 237.

11. Rabbi Solomon (Shlomo) Yizchaki (1040-1105).

12. *Chumash with Targum Onkelos, Haphtaroth and Rashi's Commentary*, A. M. Silbermann and M. Rosenbaum, translators, 5 vols. (Jerusalem: Silbermann Family, [1934] 1985 [Jewish year: 5745]), III, p. 131b.

There is one minor problem with this interpretation: the maximum legal planting period was not 50 years or 49 years but 42 years. The seven sabbatical years were supposed to be honored. In the year prior to the sabbatical year of the jubilee year there would be a triple crop (Lev. 25:21), so the total output was the equivalent of 44 years of crops. If we figure from seed inputs, then the total is less: 42 years. The presumption has to be that a particular plot of ground that *on average* either can sustain (input view) a homer of barley seed or else can produce (output view) a homer of barley seed each year is to be valued at the beginning of the 49-year period at 50 shekels of silver. This seems to be a reasonable interpretation of the 50-shekel requirement.[13]

Output or Input?

My interpretation of the passage is that it refers to the crop's output of seeds rather than input of seeds. I begin with contemporary units of measurement. There are 8 gallons to the bushel. If the biblical homer was 59 gallons – the high estimate – this was about 7.3 bushels of barley. With modern agricultural techniques, an acre of land can produce up to 50 bushels of barley, or 6.8 homers.[14] In the Old Testament era, the land's output would have been far lower. At one-quarter of today's productivity, this would have been under 13 bushels per acre, or slightly under two homers. Using the high estimate of what a homer of barley was, we conclude that the land required to grow one homer was about half an acre. Using the lower estimate of 29 gallons per homer, or slightly over three bushels,

---

13. *Reasonable* as in "more reasonable than the alternative." The fact is, paying 50 shekels of silver in cash at the beginning of the jubilee cycle for 44 years of output meant paying far too much. The buyer-redeemer was forfeiting the interest that could have been earned. The market value of the final harvested homer of barley 50 years later was a small fraction of the value of a homer of barley at the beginning.

14. I say this on the authority of the highly efficient farmer who leases the ICE's farm in Maryland.

this output would have required a quarter of an acre. For a small farm – say, 10 acres – this seems like a reasonably sized plot to dedicate to the priesthood.

If we are discussing seed inputs, a modern farmer can get almost a 20-to-one increase from seeds planted. This ratio of output to input would have been far less in ancient Israel, but still the amount of acreage necessary to seed (input) one homer of barley would have been quite small. It therefore seems more likely that the text refers to output rather than input: the land required to produce one homer of barley.

The Economics of the Translators' Version

Were the King James and other versions' translators correct? Does the reference to 50 shekels mean "50 shekels per homer" rather than "50 homers of barley per jubilee cycle," i.e., one shekel of silver times 50? If the translation is correct, this redemption price was astronomical: 50 times the average market price of a homer of barley, plus 20 percent. But this would have been only the beginning of the redemption burden. The field's potential output of barley per year was then multiplied by 44: the years of production remaining until the next jubilee year. So, the total number of homers of barley that a field could produce was multiplied by 44 years, and this gross output figure was then multiplied by 50 shekels. There was a prorated reduction in price in terms of the number of years remaining until the jubilee, but with these huge payments, such prorating would have been economically irrelevant to most Israelites.

What was the redemption payment all about? It covered the case of a person who had vowed to transfer a field or a field's output to a priest. At some point before the jubilee, the original owner decided to reclaim the field for himself. To do this lawfully, he had to pay a cash redemption price to the priest at the time of the reclaiming. If the formal redemption price was established at 50 shekels per homer of barley, as the familiar translations suggest, then the typical owner could afford to redeem his field only in the final sabbatical year before the jubilee, when the unseeded output of the field would be minimal, or in the jubilee year itself.[15] If he or his surviving heirs decided not to redeem it, his family lost the field forever. The translators' interpretation of the 50 shekels – applying to a homer of barley – would lead us to the conclusion that the details of the prorated redemption payment structure were merely symbolic, for almost no one could have afforded to redeem his field much before the jubilee year.

If the conventional translation is correct, we are led inexorably to this unpalatable conclusion: once the owner dedicated the field to the priesthood, he could not expect to redeem it until the jubilee year. The price would have been far too high. This seems to be too radical a requirement: a redemption price totally disconnected from the market price. Conclusion: the reference to 50 shekels of silver refers to the fixed judicial price of a field that would produce one homer of barley per season through the entire jubilee cycle. The closer to the jubilee year, the lower the field's remaining redemption price. In short, the redemption price of a field capable of producing one homer of barley per year was 50 shekels of silver at the beginning of the jubilee cycle, plus 20 percent.

My conclusion is that the commentators' conventional interpretation, not the translators' conventional translation, is correct: the prorated redemption price was one shekel of silver per year remaining until the jubilee year per homer-producing unit of land. This means that translators should abandon the familiar translation: "[a] homer [of] barley seed [shall be priced at] fifty shekels [of] silver." It should be translated as follows: "[A field producing a] homer [of] barley seed [per year shall be priced at] fifty shekels [of] silver [at the beginning of the jubilee

15. Legally, the crop could not be harvested. Probably this would have been interpreted as a crop of zero output. If the estimation was made in terms of barley seed used for planting, the price had to be zero, since it was illegal for anyone to plant in a sabbatical year or a jubilee year.

cycle]." The problem is, such a translation imports so much interpretive material into the text that translators probably will never accept this translation. They will try to stick with the sparse Hebrew text as closely as possible. But when they do this, they destroy the economic relevance of the prorated land-redemption system. They create a text that misinterprets the law.

Priestly Inheritance

We now return to the unique law governing the inheritance of rural land by priests: "And if he will not redeem the field, or if he have sold the field to another man, it shall not be redeemed any more. But the field, when it goeth out in the jubile, shall be holy unto the LORD, as a field devoted; the possession thereof shall be the priest's" (Lev. 27:20-21).

There were only two ways that a priest could acquire rural property in Israel. The first case is easy to understand: the land's owner had dedicated the field to the priesthood. He or his heirs then refused to pay the priest its output, year by year, and also refused to pay the redemption price. The priest's family automatically inherited it by default in the jubilee. On the other hand, if the priest took immediate control of the dedicated plot, working the land himself or leasing it out, the owner would automatically receive it back at the jubilee. Here was a risk for the owner. When the priests or their agents took immediate control over dedicated land, they had a short-term economic incentive not to declare the jubilee year. They might prefer to keep working these dedicated lands for themselves indefinitely. But they would incur a long-term economic penalty for such lawlessness: land owners would be unlikely in the future to dedicate land to the priesthood. The priesthood would also lose respect in the eyes of the nation.

The second case – leased land – is more difficult to understand. The passage is no longer clear to us grammatically. There are two ways of interpreting it. *First*, a man dedicated a field to a priest, but then he sold (leased long term) the field to another man. If we understand the economics of the dedicated field as a gift of the output of the field, with the owner of the field cultivating the land and giving the produce to the priest after each harvest, then the subsequent lease appears to be a case of a default on the original pledge. The defaulting individual had leased his pledged field to another man. This lease contract was honored by the priest, but in the year of the jubilee, the field reverted to the priest.

The *second* interpretation assumes that a man who had already leased out his land to another person then dedicated a plot of ground to the priest. The lessor's contract with the lessee was honored by the priest. The lessee was allowed to use the field during the years remaining until the jubilee, but then ownership was transferred permanently to the priest.

In both interpretations, the claim of the lessor (land owner) took immediate precedence over the claim of the priest, but the priest became a permanent beneficiary in the jubilee year. I think both interpretations are plausible, but the first one seems more plausible. The land owner indebted himself to the priest: an implicit promise to farm the property for the priest's benefit. He subsequently sought to escape this debt burden without paying the field's prorated redemption price (including the 20 percent penalty) before leasing the land to another person. The new penalty was the permanent forfeiture of the field. The original owner thereby disinherited his heirs of the value of this property. The heirs still owned the remaining (non-dedicated) fields, but the economic value of the judicially sanctified field had been permanently removed from them.

Disinherited Sons and Priestly Heirs

The claims of the original owner were primary until the jubilee. He could evict a priest or the priest's agent from previously dedicated land. In times of famine, for example, an owner might decide to evict the priest or stop paying the priest the output of the dedicated field. But if, by the time of the jubilee, he had refused to redeem the land by the payment of one shekel of silver for every year of the eviction, plus 20 percent, he lost ownership of the land.

The priests had the possibility of inheriting rural land if the vow-designated land was not redeemed by the vow-taker. In such cases, the potential beneficiaries obviously had an economic incentive to oppose the debasement of the shekel (Isa. 1:22). A shekel of falling value would have made it less expensive for those who faced the permanent loss of their land to redeem it prior to the jubilee.

Would the owner of rural land ever have dedicated all of its output to a priest? Not unless he was willing to risk disinheriting his sons. If he was subsequently forced by economic pressures to reclaim the land's output, and then he or his sons failed to redeem the land at the mandatory price, plus 20 percent, all of his land would go to the priest in the jubilee year. Thus, there was an economic restraint on the over-commitment of land to the priesthood. The heirs of the conquest were to this degree protected. The only person who would have committed most or all of his land's output to a priest would have been a very rich absentee landlord who made his money in commerce. But to dedicate all of one's land in a grand display of wealth was risky. This person might subsequently fall into economic distress and be compelled to lease his property to another. The heirs of this individual would then have lost ownership of all the dedicated land. If their father had pledged all of their land, they would have lost their guaranteed status as freemen. Thus, the high risks of default would have tended to reduce the number of such large-scale pledges to priests.

Nevertheless, the possibility of disinheritance did exist. If a father was so distressed by the ethical rebellion of all of his sons, he had the ability to disinherit them. He could not disinherit one son among many in this way, but he could disinherit all of them. He could do this by dedicating all of his landed inheritance to a priest. He would then do one of two things: lease this land to someone else, or reclaim the land's output for himself. If his sons refused to redeem the land before the jubilee, or could not afford to, they lost their inheritance forever. The priest could not transfer the land back to the original owner. To do so would have meant disinheriting the tribe of Levi. The Mosaic law made no provision for such repatriation to the original owner's family. Once a piece of rural land passed into the possession of a priest, it had to remain there until he died. Then it passed to his nearest of kin. Unredeemed dedicated land became devoted land at the jubilee. It could never again lawfully leave the jurisdiction of the priesthood.

We have no historical example of this in Old Testament, but we have the archetype example in the New Testament: the transfer of title of the kingdom of God from the Jews to the church. How was this accomplished? First, Jesus announced that God the Father had promised the kingdom's inheritance to His new priesthood, the church. "Therefore I say unto you, The kingdom of God shall be taken from you, and given to a nation bringing forth the fruits thereof" (Matt. 21:43). This was a formal announcement of God's dedication of the Promised Land. But such a transfer of ownership could be made only to a priest. Rural land could be lawfully transferred from the family of one tribe to the family of another tribe only in this unique case: the formal dedication of the land's output to a priest followed by a failure to deliver this output and a failure to redeem it.

The New Testament's Fulfillment

This New Testament transfer of ownership was not to be to a single family of the priesthood; rather, it was made to a new nation. That nation is the church, which constitutes a new priesthood: a kingdom of priests (I Pet. 2:9). The representative priest of this nation of priests was the High Priest. The High Priest is Jesus Christ (Heb. 9). This public dedication was legally secured for the church by the death of Jesus Christ, i.e., *the death of the Testator*. "For a testament is of force after men are dead: otherwise it is of no strength at all while the testator liveth" (Heb. 9:17). The publicly visible evidence of the transfer of the High Priest's inheritance to His heirs came when the Holy Spirit fell on the church at Pentecost (Acts 2).

Old Covenant Israel had refused to honor this dedication. They crucified the new High Priest. They did not redeem the land. Prior to the next jubilee, the output of the land was not delivered to the new priests, nor was the mandatory 20 percent redemption payment. That is, *the dedicated output of the land was not redeemed by the heirs whose legal title had been at risk*. The Jews not only did not pay the new priesthood the mandatory redemption price of 20 percent; they persecuted the church. *This secured the irrevocable transfer of the kingdom by the new priesthood*.

When was the next jubilee year after the dedication? When did the transfer of legal title to the heirs of the High Priest take place? James Jordan's study of New Testament chronology dates Jesus' death in A.D. 30 (Jewish year: 3960). Paul was converted shortly thereafter, after Pentecost. The next year, Jordan concludes from his study of the calendar after the exiles' return from Medo-Persia, was the seventh sabbath year in the final jubilee cycle.[16] The jubilee came in 3962, the year that Paul's ministry to the gentiles began.[17] This, I conclude, was the date of the transfer to the church of legal title to the kingdom of God: the fulfillment of Jesus' prophecy in Matthew 21:43.

---

16. If Jordan is correct that Jesus was sacrificed in the year prior to the seventh sabbath, this would have been the year scheduled by God for the miraculous triple harvest. This was the year of the largest Firstfruits offering, which was delivered to the priesthood at Pentecost.

17. Jordan, "Jubilee, Part 3," *Biblical Chronology*, V (April 1993), [p. 2]. See also, "Chronology of the Gospels," *ibid*, IV (Dec. 1993). Jordan's forthcoming book, *The Date of Creation*, will provide the evidence in an easily accessible source.

Old Covenant Israel's failure to redeem this dedicated land was God's means of disinheriting all of His rebellious Israelite sons. They could be legally disinherited only as a family unit; selective disinheritance by a father was not possible. So long as any of the family's land remained in the father's possession, all of his sons would have a piece of the inheritance. Disinheritance would not remove them from their tribe. Tribal membership secured their legal status as freemen. Thus, disinheritance was in this case economic, not judicial. The sons would have no lawful claim on any portion of the land. In A.D. 70, the self-disinherited sons of God were evicted by Rome from the temple. After Bar Kochba's rebellion of A.D. 133-35, they were evicted by Rome from the land. The diaspora began.

The idea so prevalent in modern fundamentalism that the modern State of Israel is in some way biblically entitled to God's original grant of land to Abraham, which was secured by Joshua during the conquest, is inescapably a denial of the authority and binding character of God's revealed law. The Old Covenant sons of God forfeited forever their legal title to the Promised Land and their guaranteed citizenship in the kingdom of God by their persecution of the New Covenant priests, the heirs of the dedication: the church. The covenantal heirs of these disinherited sons can reclaim their citizenship in the kingdom only as adopted sons, i.e., as members of God's New Covenant church. There can never be a repatriation of either the Promised Land or the kingdom of God to the Jews. Once a dedicated piece of land passed into the possession of a priest at the jubilee, there was only one way for it ever to be transferred back to the original owner. The original owner had to become a priest, and not merely a priest: the nearest of kin to the priest who had been given the land. *He had to be adopted by that priest.* Only through the death of this adopting kinsman-priest could the original owner legally regain possession of his former inheritance.

The Kinsman-High Priest made this offer of adoption to every Jew as well as to every gentile. "But as many as received him, to them gave he power to become the sons of God, even to them that believe on his name" (John 1:12). He still makes it. There is no other way to secure a piece of the now-devoted inheritance in history, which is mandatory in order to secure it in eternity.

This means that the land comprising the modern State of Israel is not the Promised Land of the Old Covenant. It also has no judicial connection to the kingdom of God or any prophecy regarding this kingdom. The kingdom of God had been connected to the land prior to Jesus' ministry and death, but the legal transfer of the kingdom took place at the time of the final jubilee, when the Jews redeemed neither land nor kingdom from the church. God transferred to the church, the new priesthood, lawful title to the kingdom at the resurrection of Jesus (Matt. 28:18-20), but He allowed the Jews to stay in control over both the land and the temple until A.D. 70. When they failed to redeem the land from the church prior to the next (and final) jubilee, title automatically transferred to the new priesthood. The land ceased to have any covenantal relevance in A.D. 70, when it came under God's vengeance.[18]

Lessees: Exempt from Earthly Negative Sanctions

It was not just the original land owner who had the option of rewarding the priests by a temporary donation of their land's net output. So could the person who had leased land from an original owner. But his situation was judicially unique: he was spared the 20 percent redemption penalty. "And if a man sanctify unto the LORD a field which he hath bought, which is not of the fields of his possession; Then the priest shall reckon unto him the worth of thy estimation, even unto the year of the

18. David Chilton, *The Days of Vengeance: An Exposition of the Book of Revelation* (Ft. Worth, Texas: Dominion Press, 1987).

jubile: and he shall give thine estimation in that day, as a holy thing unto the LORD" (Lev. 27:22-23). This law specified that the field would return to the original owner in the jubilee year (Lev. 27:24). The law protected the original land owner from the consequences of vow-breaking by the lessee.

To Protect the Priests

The lessee also escaped the penalty of disinheritance. A lessee who broke his vow of dedication and reclaimed the land was not threatened by the loss of the land in the jubilee. In fact, this law specifies no penalty at all. It does not state that the lessee must forfeit an equivalent quantity of his own land. This means that there was far greater likelihood that he would break his vow of dedication, compared to an original owner. The question arises: Why was the lessee exempt from the 20 percent penalty? If he was not subject to the threat of losing the dedicated land – it was not his land – then why wasn't the redemption penalty even greater than 20 percent? Why were no penalties imposed? The text does not say. We can only guess. Let us guess intelligently.

The lessee owed the original owner regular payments unless he had already paid the owner in advance. This placed him in a weaker economic position, other things being equal, than the original land owner. Either he bore greater contractual risk than an original owner would have borne or, if he had already paid the owner in advance, he had less cash available to redeem the land from the priest. Since the goal of a land-dedication vow was to reward the priests, excessive economic barriers to redemption would have been a disincentive for such vows. Thus, the priest bore greater risk of having his plans disrupted by a lessee than by an original owner. The lessee was more likely to reclaim the dedicated property than an original owner was.

If he paid no 20 percent penalty for breaking his vow to the priest, what would have protected the priests? *They were protected by the inescapable phenomenon of interest.* The present value of future goods is less than the present value of identical present goods. This discount is called the rate of interest.[19] The priest could lawfully demand an immediate cash payment of all the shekels remaining to be paid until the jubilee. But the present value of the money to be accrued in the future is less than the present value of the same number of monetary units paid today in cash. So, the lessee paid a penalty to the priest: the difference between the present value of the cash shekels and the present value of those shekels to come. This was not the 20 percent penalty, but it was nonetheless a penalty.[20]

The fact is, however, the law provided no explicit earthly negative sanctions for a priest to impose on a lessee who reclaimed previously dedicated land. The priest had to rely on the conscience of the lessee not to reclaim it. We see here that the long-term sanctity of the *land as inheritance* judicially outweighed the short-term sanctity of the *land in priestly dedication.* Only original owners could bring this unique sanction of disinheritance on their heirs.

A Judicial Price: Fixed by Law

Why not use a free market price in establishing the redemption price of dedicated land? Why did the text specify a specific price and a specific crop? Samson Raphael Hirsch, the early nineteenth-century Orthodox Jewish commentator, offered this explanation: this case "was the one unique case, standing quite by itself, where a field could be sold and the purchase ultimately become permanent. Hence for buying back, for the redemption of such a field which could eventually become a permanent

19. Ludwig von Mises, *Human Action: A Treatise on Economics* (New Haven, Connecticut: Yale University Press, 1949), ch. 19.

20. Those who deny the universal phenomenon of time-preference (interest) will have to seek for another explanation of how the priests were protected from disruptions in their plans: forfeited vows by lessees.

purchase there could be no market price ascertained, so that the fixing of a universal fixed value was a necessity."[21] I do not accept his explanation, but I do accept his identification of the uniqueness of this fixed price – a non-market price.

When a specific price is established by the Mosaic law, it becomes a judicial price, not a market price. Hirsch acknowledged that this was not a market price. What is not plausible is his argument that the market price in this case would have been difficult to ascertain. At the beginning of a jubilee cycle, it would have been somewhat lower than the lease price.

There was another reason for a judicial price in this instance. The underlying problem was *the threat of monopolistic exploitation by the priest* – the possible misuse of his authority to declare arbitrarily a redemption price. The judicial price of 50 shekels protected the original owner. It was the priest's responsibility in all the redemption cases to declare the price, to which a 20 percent payment was added. In this unique case, however, the priest was given an opportunity to take permanent possession of land belonging to a member of another tribe. The temptation to cheat would have been very high. If the priest deliberately set the price too high, the original owner or his heirs could not afford to redeem the field until the jubilee year or the sabbatical year immediately preceding it.[22] But economic conditions might change prior to the jubilee year. The head of the family might be tempted later to lease it out if he needed money. The family would then lose the property forever at the jubilee year. The terms of redemption were therefore specified by law so that there could be no doubt on the part of the field's

---

21. Samson Raphael Hirsch, *The Pentateuch: Leviticus* (part II), translated by Isaac Levy (Gateshead, England: Judaica Press, 1989), p. 825.

22. In those two years, the input of the land was zero – no seeding was legal – and the output was not legal for harvesting. Thus, even a supposed 50-shekel per homer price would not have been a barrier to redemption. The legal market price of the crop was still zero.

redeemer or the civil and ecclesiastical authorities exactly what was owed by the redeemer.

Restricting the Accumulation of Priest-Owned Land

In the European Middle Ages, deathbed transfers of land to the church were common. The church and especially its monastic orders accumulated huge tracts of land over the centuries as a result of these and other forms of land transfer.[23] In contrast, a deathbed legacy of land to the priesthood on a permanent basis was almost impossible to make in Israel. A dying man might dedicate a plot of land to a priest, but the man's heirs could redeem it early or else wait for the jubilee year. The only possible deathbed transfer that might permanently have alienated land was a deathbed legacy from an owner – probably debt-ridden – who had leased out his plot of land and who then dedicated it to a priest. This assumes that the second interpretation of the leased land default is correct, which I do not accept. But if that interpretation is correct, then economically incompetent men were the most likely sources of such permanent transfers of rural land in ancient Israel. But it was the wealthy medieval landowner, not the poor peasant, who was the source of deathbed legacies.

C. W. Previté-Orton has commented on the two-fold threat to the medieval church in the twelfth century: too many lax men joining the monastic orders and too much wealth donated to these orders. "The extraordinary growth of monasticism new and old in the century of Church reform undoubtedly brought too many into the cloister, whether as converts or oblates, who had no true or lasting vocation for the ascetic life; and the enormous landed wealth lavished on them by the laity, either in devotion or in fear of Judgment Day, proved a dangerous ally

23. Marc Bloch, *Feudal Society* (University of Chicago Press, [1940] 1961), pp. 208-9; R. W. Southern, *Western Society and the Church in the Middle Ages* (Grand Rapids, Michigan: Eerdmans, 1970), pp. 261-63.

of laxity and degeneration."[24] This was not true in Mosaic Israel. First, the entry price system of Leviticus 27:2-8 reduced the likelihood of the influx of poor people into the tribe of Levi. Second, the jubilee law, when coupled with the price of 50 shekels per barley-producing land unit at the beginning of the jubilee cycle (Lev. 27:16) and the permanent transfer law of Leviticus 27:20-21, reduced the likelihood of deathbed transfers of land. Such a transfer was a penalty, not a righteous gift.

Conclusion

The redemption price of dedicated rural land was a judicial price, not a market price. It was somewhat arbitrary, although not excessively so, given the conventional Mesopotamian price of one shekel of silver per homer of barley. It provided a rough means of estimating the redemption price of a piece of land.

The presence of a penalty payment of 20 percent identified as redemption prices three of the four prices in this passage: beasts, houses, and owner-dedicated fields.[25] These three penalty payments also served to keep the priests honest in making their estimation of the redemption price of any property. If the priests estimated the price above the market price, the potential redeemer would not buy it back, so the priest would forfeit the 20 percent bonus available to him.

The law governing the redemption of sanctified fields created a unique opportunity for the priests: the right to inherit rural land. If the sanctified plot was subsequently reclaimed by the owner but not redeemed, it became the inheritance of the priest in the jubilee year. This law served as the land owners' means of bribing a corrupt priesthood into announcing the

---

24. C. W. Previté-Orton, *The Shorter Cambridge Medieval History*, 2 vols. (Cambridge: At the University Press, [1952] 1966), I, p. 506.

25. The fourth, exceptional price was the field dedicated by a leaseholder. He had to pay in cash the fixed shekel payments remaining on the property until the jubilee year, a price not discounted by the rate of interest.

jubilee year. The priests could not inherit unredeemed sanctified land unless they proclaimed the jubilee year. Set apart once by vow, the land could not be reclaimed – de-sanctified – by the vow-taking owner except by a cash redemption payment plus a 20 penalty.

This law placed a major restriction on the ability of a land owner to leave land to a priest. His heirs had the right to redeem the land. Thus, deathbed transfers of rural land were highly unlikely. The land owner would have had to sanctify the land on his deathbed without his heirs' paying an ever-smaller redemption price as the jubilee year approached.

38

TITHING: THE BENEFIT OF THE DOUBT

And all the tithe of the land, whether of the seed of the land, or of the fruit of the tree, is the LORD'S: *it is holy unto the* LORD. *And if a man will at all redeem ought of his tithes, he shall add thereto the fifth part thereof. And concerning the tithe of the herd, or of the flock, even of whatsoever passeth under the rod, the tenth shall be holy unto the* LORD. *He shall not search whether it be good or bad, neither shall he change it: and if he change it at all, then both it and the change thereof shall be holy; it shall not be redeemed (Lev. 27:30-33).*

We come at long last to the final and shortest exposition in this commentary. The theocentric meaning of this passage is that God, as the owner of all things, deserves a tithe. The tithe is described here as being holy (*kodesh*). It was judicially set apart for God by the Levites. That is, the tithe was sanctified. The tithe was not under the ban (see below). We know this because the 20 percent redemption payment was present in this law. The Levites enjoyed the tithe as God's representatives.

In a purely monetary society, the redemption law of the tithe is irrelevant. No one is going to pay a 20 percent payment to buy back his monetary tithe. This law is relevant only in a society in which income in kind is common: income measured in something other than money. In such societies, goods are sometimes retained by their producers to be used or enjoyed for themselves, not sold into the market for money.

Why would someone pay a commission to redeem an object? Only if that object has special meaning or importance for him. If the quality of grain in a tithed sack is identical to the grain in the other nine sacks, the tithe-payer is not going to pay a commission to buy back the tithed sack unless economic conditions have changed in the meantime. The assumption behind this law is that the impersonal collecting of the tithe may produce a personally significant loss for the tithe-payer. In order to enable him to minimize this loss, the law allows him to pay a 20 percent commission to buy back the special item.

There is no indication that this law has been annulled by subsequent biblical revelation. It applies only to agriculture, as the text indicates – primarily to herds of animals.

A Tithe on the Net Increase

The text reads: "And concerning the tithe of the herd, or of the flock, even of whatsoever passeth under the rod, the tenth shall be holy unto the LORD. He shall not search whether it be good or bad, neither shall he change it: and if he change it at all, then both it and the change thereof shall be holy; it shall not be redeemed." The tithe was collected from the increase of the herd. This increase was a net increase. If one animal of the herd had died since the time of the most recent payment of the tithe, the herd owner was allowed to set aside a replacement from the animals born since the last payment.[1] Had this not been the case, then losses from a disease that killed half a man's herd could not be deducted when assessing the net annual increase. This would constitute a tax on capital.

1. This is the economic equivalent of allowing a farmer to set aside from this year's crop an amount equal to last year's seed. A person pays the tithe on net output only once. He does not keep paying on capital, i.e., replaced producer goods.

This law reveals that God gave the benefit of the doubt to the herd owner. An old beast that had died could lawfully be replaced by a young beast without the payment of a tithe. Presumably, this exchange would have benefited the owner, since the newborn animal would have had many years of productivity ahead of it. There would have been an increase of net productivity for the herd but not a net increase in the size of the herd. In some cases, however, the older beast would have been more valuable, especially a prize animal used for breeding or a trained work animal. God, as sovereign over life and death, imposes net losses or gains on a herd's productivity, irrespective of the number of beasts in the herd.

What was not tolerated by God was any attempt by the owner to pick and choose from among the newborns. The owner could not lawfully select the best of the newborns to replace the dead animals, using the less desirable newborns to pay his tithe, thereby cheating God. Presumably, the birth order of the newborns would govern the replacement of any dead beasts. The first newborn after the death of another member of the herd would have been segregated immediately from the other newborns as not being eligible for the tithe.

Under the Rod

Those newborn beasts that remained after the owner had replaced any dead animals constituted the net increase of the herd. In this case law, the herd owner lined up the newborns, probably in a pen, and drove them one by one past the Levite. Each beast passed under a rod. Every tenth beast was taken by the Levite. The herd owner was not allowed to walk the beasts under the rod in any pre-planned order. The same law that governed the voluntary sanctification of beasts governed the involuntary sanctification of beasts: "He shall not alter it, nor change it, a good for a bad, or a bad for a good: and if he shall at all change beast for beast, then it and the exchange thereof shall be holy" (Lev. 27:10). The owner was allowed to buy back any sanctified beast, but only by paying the redemption price commission.

The herd owner was given the benefit of the doubt at the end of the line. Only the tenth beast was holy. If as many as nine of the final group of beasts passed under the rod, the herd owner owed no tithe on those nine beasts. Where the product could not be divided without destroying the life or value of the item, the tithe applied only to discrete items. All those animals that passed under the rod after the final group of 10 had been counted escaped the sanctification process.

Because God gave the benefit of the doubt to the tithe-payer, it was especially evil for him to arrange in advance the collection of the tithe, with or without the collusion of the Levite. The assembling process was to be humanly random. Neither the tithe-payer nor the Levite was to manipulate the crop or the herd to his own advantage, or to the other's advantage. God owned the tenth; He alone was authorized to arrange the collection process. Any attempt by man to arrange the process was not only theft from God, it was an assertion of man's autonomy. It was an attempt to manipulate the created order in a way prohibited by God.

The Ban

What if a tithe-payer defied God and manipulated the tithe-collection process? The tithed items came under the ban: "if he change it at all, then both it and the change thereof shall be holy; it shall not be redeemed." The tithed item became *hormah*: devoted to God. This degree of sanctification was absolute; once within the boundaries of God's possession, it could not lawfully be removed.

Why would a person manipulate the outcome of the collection process? Because he was trying to cheat God. He was unwilling to risk paying the 20 percent commission that would be imposed if he subsequently wanted to buy back a specific item. What was the penalty for this act of theft? Permanent loss. The very process of altering the outcome made the tithe holy – not holy as in sanctification, but holy as in devoted. The right of redemption ended.

There is no ban today – no *hormah*. That is because the New Covenant has annulled the sacrifice of animals. This aspect of the law is also annulled.[2]

Conclusion

The tithe was paid on the net increase of the herd. The owner of the herd paid his tithe only out of the newborn animals that remained after he had set aside replacement beasts for the ones that had died during the year. He was required to run the remaining newborns under a rod. He could not lawfully order the line of newborns so that the outcome of the tithe could be known in advance. The tenth beast became the property of the Levite. As in all cases of redemption, he could buy back that beast for a payment of its market value plus an additional payment of one-fifth.

If the owner violated this law by arranging the order of the beasts as they lined up, he could not buy back any of the animals. They became devoted to God – beyond redemption.

There is no New Testament evidence that the economics of this law has been altered. The tithe on the increase of a herd should still be honored.

What about the rod? Was its use tied exclusively to the office of Levite? The association with Moses and the rod indicates that its use was in some way tied to the Mosaic covenant. Aaron's rod was in the Ark of the Covenant (Heb. 9:4), but the Ark has disappeared. My conclusion is that there need be no rod in the process, but there must be a random distribution of the herd during the tithing process. We are not allowed to cheat God. If a prize animal gets tagged for collection by the church, the

2. By extension, the law of the military annihilation of all enemy males is also annulled (Deut. 20:13): no hormah.

owner can pay its market price plus 20 percent. The presumption is, however, that prize animals of breeding age will be segregated in advance. The tithe on the net increase in prize animals must come from the segregated herd of prize animals. Such segregation was not lawful in Mosaic Israel (Lev. 19:19).[3]

If, after counting everything owed, there are up to nine beasts left over, no tithe is imposed. God still gives herd owners the benefit of the doubt.

What about the ban? Today, we do not sacrifice animals to God. Thus, to place an animal under the ban is to misinterpret this law. The owner can buy back the beast at a market price, but probably at public auction. Then he pays an additional 20 percent to the church. No cheating is allowed; whatever he pays for the animal, and however he obtains it, he pays 20 percent of what the purchase price had been at the time of the auction or its initial sale by the church.

3. See Chapter 17: "The Preservation of the Seed."

CONCLUSION

CONCLUSION

Thrice in the year shall all your men children [males] appear before the Lord God, the God of Israel. For I will cast out the nations before thee, and enlarge thy borders: neither shall any man desire thy land, when thou shalt go up to appear before the LORD thy God thrice in the year (Ex. 34:23-24).

This was God's ultimate visible evidence of His covenantally predictable defense of Israel. The very boundaries of the land would become sacrosanct – sacred and set apart by God – during the three mandated annual festivals. God promised that during the Israelites' numerous corporate journeys to Jerusalem, which was the only authorized place of sacrifice on earth, their enemies would not even want to invade the land. In their times of greatest military vulnerability, when the unarmed army of the Lord was marching to Jerusalem, the nation would be sheltered by the divine intervention of God. Potential invaders would not even want to take advantage of them in these seasons of formal worship. The nation was holy: set apart by God. This included the land itself. The sacrilege of military invasion during the mandatory feasts could not take place for as long as God maintained His covenant with Mosaic Israel. Israel would not be profaned. The sign of God's rejection of Israel would be a military invasion during a feast, especially Passover.

In A.D. 70, during Passover, the Roman legions surrounded the holy city and laid siege to it.[1] This event was that which had been forecast by Jesus (Luke 21:20-24): the Great Tribulation.[2] When the city fell, the Romans set fire to the temple. What would have been the ultimate boundary violation under the Mosaic Covenant – the ultimate sacrilege – was not only permitted by God, it had been prophesied by God. It was God's answer to a heavenly prayer:

> And I looked, and behold a pale horse: and his name that sat on him was Death, and Hell followed with him. And power was given unto them over the fourth part of the earth, to kill with sword, and with hunger, and with death, and with the beasts of the earth. And when he had opened the fifth seal, I saw under the altar the souls of them that were slain for the word of God, and for the testimony which they held: And they cried with a loud voice, saying, *How long, O Lord, holy and true, dost thou not judge and avenge our blood on them that dwell on the earth?* And white robes were given unto every one of them; and it was said unto them, that they should rest yet for a little season, until their fellowservants also and their brethren, that should be killed as they were, should be fulfilled. And I beheld when he had opened the sixth seal, and, lo, there was a great earthquake; and the sun became black as sackcloth of hair, and the moon became as blood; And the stars of heaven fell unto the earth, even as a fig tree casteth her untimely figs, when she is shaken of a mighty wind (Rev. 6:8-13; emphasis added).[3]

The fall of Jerusalem to the Romans was God's final sign that the Jews' rebellion had terminated the Mosaic Covenant. Israel's national boundary was definitively and permanently breached by Rome during the nation's final Passover. The temple's sacred boundaries were eliminated. The sacrifices ended. These boundaries ceased to have covenantal relevance

---

1. Josephus, *The Wars of the Jews*, VI:IX:3.

2. David Chilton, *The Great Tribulation* (Ft. Worth, Texas: Dominion Press, 1987).

3. See David Chilton, *The Days of Vengeance: An Exposition of the Book of Revelation* (Ft. Worth, Texas: Dominion Press, 1987), pp. 193-95.

because the Mosaic Covenant had ceased to have any authority. God's predictable, covenantal, negative corporate sanctions were thoroughly applied to that nation which had broken His covenant. Divine protection for the boundaries of the land would never again defend Israel's residents.

Government and Sanctions

This raises a major question of biblical interpretation: What about those aspects of the Mosaic law that applied to Israel's civil government? Were they all annulled with the annulment of Israel's geographical boundaries? Were any of those laws cross-boundary phenomena? That is, did any of them serve as binding judicial standards for foreign nations? Deuteronomy 4:4-8 indicates that at least some of them did. Does this mean that these have been extended by God into the New Covenant era? Are they still covenantally binding and therefore judicial ideals toward which all nations should strive, and in terms of which all nations are judged in history?

My answer is the answer which is sometimes said to be the ultimate summary of all sociological theory: *some are, some aren't.* This answer in turn requires an additional principle of interpretation, a theological means of separating: 1) the cross-boundary Mosaic Covenant civil standards that are still judicially binding on men and nations from 2) the temporally and geographically bounded Mosaic standards. In short, the correct answer requires a hermeneutic: a principle of interpretation. The Book of Leviticus forces serious Christians to search for this biblical hermeneutic. Without this hermeneutic, Leviticus becomes a snare that traps antinomians in their total dismissal of all of its laws, and traps legalists in their total acceptance.

By Oath Consigned

In order to apply the Bible judicially to the governmental realm – personal, church, State, and family – we require two things: *a principle of institutional exclusion* and the presence of *negative sanctions* to enforce this exclusion. Exclusion and inclusion are two sides of the same fence. Every boundary has an inside and an outside. So it is with membership in God's authorized covenantal institutions.

Let us begin with the initial requirement for membership: the oath. There can be no lawful covenantal participation apart from a binding self-maledictory oath under God. A covenant is established only by a binding oath under God. People are, in the words of Meredith Kline, by oath consigned.[4] They are consigned by God[5] to heaven or hell in terms of a personal oath[6] of allegiance[7] and also by their lifelong adherence – "the perseverance of the saints"[8] – to its judicial stipulations.[9]

Let us consider political theory. People are consigned by oath, either implicit or explicit, to membership in one State or another. The primary jurisdiction of the civil government is geographical. Everything within the boundaries of a particular State is under its jurisdiction, although this jurisdiction is always shared in certain ways with the other two covenantal institutions and usually shared also with regional civil governments within the jurisdiction of the larger civil government. But one civil government has final civil jurisdiction, short of lawful rebellion by lower levels of civil government – the Protestant Reformation's doctrine of interposition.[10]

---

4. Meredith G. Kline, *By Oath Consigned: A Reinterpretation of the Covenant Signs of Circumcision and Baptism* (Grand Rapids, Michigan: Eerdmans, 1968).

5. Point one of the biblical covenant model: sovereignty.

6. Point four of the biblical covenant model: sanctions.

7. Point two of the biblical covenant model: hierarchy.

8. Point five of the biblical covenant model: inheritance.

9. Point three of the biblical covenant model: law.

10. John Calvin, *Institutes of the Christian Religion* (1559), IV:XX:31. See also Michael R. Gilstrap, "John Calvin's Theology of Resistance," *Christianity and Civilization,* No. 4 (1983), pp. 180-217; Tom Rose, "On Reconstruction and the Federal Republic," *ibid.*, pp. 285-310.

In contrast to their automatic subordination by implicit oath of obedience to the State on the basis of geography or birth, people may or may not be consigned by implicit oath to a church or a family. Those people who refuse to accept as binding on them the ethical and judicial terms of the covenantal oath in question cannot lawfully be part of the covenantal institution in question. Those who refuse to take this oath are not allowed in, and those inside who break the terms of this oath must be expelled: negative sanctions. There cannot be lawful government apart from oath and negative sanctions. The person's oath may be implicit,[11] but if the institution's sanctions are exclusively implicit, then there is neither a covenant nor a government: *no sanctions, no government.*

The Adamic Covenant

Inclusion into God's special covenant of redemption is by adoption. But there is another covenant, a more general covenant: the post-Edenic Adamic covenant. It was marked eucharisically ("graciously") by God's provision of animal coverings for Adam and Eve (Gen. 3:21). This general Adamic covenant also has laws and sanctions. It brings men under condemnation in eternity. The covenantally disinherited sons of Adam are still under its laws in history. Therefore, in order to pursue a better world, covenant-breakers must conform themselves to God's general covenantal law-order. The entire pre-Flood world should have repented. Similarly, Sodom should have repented. Nineveh was also required to repent. There is no doubt that God through Jonah threatened Nineveh with negative corporate sanctions in history, just as He threatened Sodom through Abraham and the angelic visitors. *The threat of such sanctions against non-covenanted nations testifies to the existence of covenantally*

11. In the United States, a person born in the U.S. or born of one U.S. parent need not take a formal oath in order to vote as American citizen at age 18.

binding laws. That is, the sanctions testify to the existence of *general covenant laws* that nations break at their peril.

The Ten Commandments and many of the Mosaic Covenant's case laws applied to the entire ancient world: cross-boundary laws. This was a form of covenantal inclusion. It was not inclusion within God's unique covenant of redemption, but it was inclusion within the general post-Eden Adamic covenant of temporal preservation: common grace. This grace is not given for the sake of covenant-breakers but for the sake of covenant-keepers.[12]

The existence of these general covenantal laws is affirmed by Paul's words: "For when Gentiles who do not have the Law do instinctively the things of the Law, these, not having the Law, are a law to themselves, in that they show the work of the Law written in their hearts, their conscience bearing witness, and their thoughts alternately accusing or else defending them, on the day when, according to my gospel, God will judge the secrets of men through Jesus Christ" (Rom. 2:14-16; NASB). The work of the law is written on all men's hearts – not the law itself, which resides only in the hearts of Christians (Heb. 8:10), but the work of the law.[13] If this were not true, on what legal basis could God condemn all covenant-breakers on the day of judgment and still remain faithful to His covenant with Adam? The existence of the universal sanction of death testifies to the continuing authority the laws of the Adamic covenant (Rom. 5:12-14).

This does not mean that Spiritually unaided human reason can discover the laws of the Adamic covenant. There is no such thing as Spiritually unaided human reason. God aids all men's reason to some degree in history. God grants varying degrees of common grace to men so that they can sense some aspects of

12. Gary North, *Dominion and Common Grace: The Biblical Basis of Progress* (Tyler, Texas: Institute for Christian Economics, 1987).

13. On the difference between these two operations, see John Murray, *The Epistle to the Romans*, 2 vols. (Grand Rapids, Michigan: Eerdmans, 1959), I, pp. 72-76.

His general social laws. He restrains their moral and intellectual rebellion. But the mind of covenant-breaking man is in rebellion, so as men become more perverse – more consistent with their covenant-breaking presuppositions – they rebel against the knowledge they possesses by common grace. They suppresses the truth that God constantly reveals to them in nature (Rom. 1:18-22). Therefore, covenant-breaking man's logic cannot be trusted to persuade him of the truth. It can be trusted only to condemn him before God. His logic is as corrupt as his morals are. He has a flawed epistemology (theory of knowledge) because of his moral rebellion.[14] This is why all natural law theory rests on an illusion: the illusion of logically shared moral standards and sanctions among all mankind. Natural law theory is the creation of covenant-breaking men: Stoics of the late Classical period and Newtonians of the modern era.

Covenant-breaking man is by Adamic oath consigned to hell. He is from conception an oath-breaker in Adam, his legal representative before God (Rom. 5). He is a disinherited son: in time and eternity. He has been excluded from eternal life *in history*. "He that believeth on the Son hath everlasting life: and he that believeth not the Son shall not see life; but the wrath of God abideth on him" (John 3:36). To the extent that he and his fellow covenant-breakers live consistently in history with their broken oaths, they will become progressively more rebellious and progressively more threatened by God's predictable corporate negative sanctions in history.

Political pluralists emphatically deny this. They deny any legitimate New Covenant judicial relationship between God's righteous exclusion of covenant-breaking men in eternity and a civil government's righteous exclusion of them from citizenship in history. They affirm the civil legitimacy another stan-

14. Cornelius Van Til, *A Christian Theory of Knowledge* (Nutley, New Jersey: Presbyterian & Reformed, 1969).

dard and another oath. To which theonomists reply: By what other standard?[15] By what other oath?

Theocracy: Trinitarian vs. Non-Trinitarian

In the New Covenant, every civil oath must be Trinitarian, for the New Covenant reveals that the God of the covenant is a Trinitarian God. There is no other God whose oath is binding in history and eternity. The Great Commission requires that Christians work to see to it that all nations are baptized into Christ (Matt. 28:18-20).[16] God requires that every nation on earth be brought under His civil covenant's administration through corporate affirmation: a Trinitarian oath. Civil magistrates are all supposed to be Christians.

Because a civil oath invokes a monopolistic God's laws and sanctions in history, and because the State's jurisdiction is geographical and therefore comprehensive within its boundaries – no separate jurisdictions[17] – any attempt to renounce the requirement of a Trinitarian civil oath is necessarily an attempt to invoke another god's covenant. But there can be no covenantal neutrality in history. Thus, inclusion in and exclusion from civil citizenship are required by God to be based on public Trinitarian confession. Citizenship – the authority to render binding judgment in a civil court, which includes the ballot box – must be based on restricted church membership (ecclesiastical bound-

---

15. Greg L. Bahnsen, *No Other Standard: Theonomy and Its Critics* (Tyler, Texas: Institute for Christian Economics, 1991).

16. Kenneth L. Gentry, Jr., *The Greatness of the Great Commission: The Christian Enterprise in a Fallen World* (Tyler, Texas: Institute for Christian Economics, 1990), ch. 10.

17. The only exceptions to this rule are foreign embassies. Inside their boundaries their home nations' laws prevail. I argue that no such grant of judicial immunity to any non-Trinitarian nation's embassy is biblically valid within a Christian nation. Every non-Christian nation must come to God's nations "on bended knee," to this extent: it is not entitled to a separate jurisdiction within the boundaries of one of God's covenanted nations.

aries) and a restricted franchise (civil boundaries).[18] It is this assertion regarding the civil oath which distinguishes Trinitarian theocratic movements (few and far between) from the broad range of post-Newtonian Christianity, i.e., political pluralism.[19]

Second, there must be the imposition of negative institutional sanctions in history to defend the stipulations of this oath. These negative sanctions are specified in the Mosaic covenant: formal warning or excommunication (ecclesiastical) and either economic restitution, public whipping, loss of citizenship, or public execution (civil). Modern Christians do not readily accept these general exclusionary requirements as legitimate if done in the name of Jesus Christ. Modern churches rarely excommunicate members. Many churches celebrate the Lord's Supper so infrequently that there is hardly anything to be excommunicated from.[20] It should therefore come as no surprise that Christians who are unwilling to excommunicate theologically deviant members are also hostile to any concept of citizenship based on a public, Trinitarian oath of allegiance. In this crucial judicial sense, *modern Christians have become inclusivists*. They have become civil Unitarians – belief in any god as sufficient for civil oath – and even civil atheists: binding civil oaths without reference to God. That is, they have become pluralists.[21] This ecclesiastical and civil inclusivism has steadily been extended from modern politics – which is accompanied by a common civil religion[22] – into theology. Evangelical leaders

---

18. North, *Political Polytheism*, ch. 2: "Sanctuary and Suffrage."

19. The problem for the American churches today is this: the United States of America is officially covenanted constitutionally to the god of humanism, i.e., religious neutrality (Article VI, Section III). *Ibid.*, pp. 385-92.

20. The Church of Christ denomination, following Alexander Campbell's rejection of Presbyterianism's closed communion, holds the Lord's Supper weekly, but then it denies the Supper's covenantal relevance by refusing to exclude anyone from participating.

21. North, *Political Polytheism*, Part 3.

22. Russell E. Ritchey and Donald G. Jones (eds.), *American Civil Religion* (New York: Harper & Row, 1974); Robert V. Bellah, *The Broken Covenant: American Civil*

have begun to abandon the biblical doctrine of hell and then lake of fire: the ultimate place of exclusion.[23]

Natural Law Theory

While modern Christians accept in theory the legitimacy of formal excommunications, however rare excommunications may be in our day – surely not a testimony to widespread exemplary living by Christians in our day – they do not believe in civil excommunication from the civil franchise on the basis of creedal confession. Protestant Christians for over three centuries, and Anglo-American Roman Catholics for at least a century, have adopted political pluralism as their civil ideal. This has required the adoption of *a common-ground judicial confession*: natural law philosophy. Today, however, only Christians and a tiny handful of secular scholars still defend natural law theory.

Natural law theory is a defunct world-and-life view in modern humanism. Charles Darwin and his followers by 1880 had destroyed the epistemological foundations of natural law philosophy.[24] Darwinism has enshrined the doctrine of *environmental determinism*. Binding biological laws at any moment in history are explained as the result of the conflict for survival: individuals vs. individuals, species vs. species, and species vs. geological environment. Similarly, binding social laws at any moment are explained as the result of competitive social groups and their

---

Religion in Time of Trial (New York: Seabury Crossroad, 1975); Bellah and Frederick E. Greenspahn, *Uncivil Religion: Interreligious Hostility in America* (New York: Crossroad, 1987); Sidney E. Mead, *The Lively Experiment: The Shaping of Christianity in America* (New York: Harper & Row, 1963); Richard V. Pierard and Robert D. Linder, *Civil Religion and the Presidency* (Grand Rapids, Michigan: Zondervan Academie, 1988).

23. In 1989, at a conference of almost 400 evangelical American Protestant theologians, a majority refused to affirm the doctrine of hell. *World* (June 3, 1989), p. 9.

24. Rousas J. Rushdoony, *The Biblical Philosophy of History* (Nutley, New Jersey: Presbyterian and Reformed, 1969), pp. 6-7; Gary North, *The Dominion Covenant: Genesis* (2nd ed.; Tyler, Texas: Institute for Christian Economics, 1987), Appendix A: "From Cosmic Purposelessness to Humanistic Sovereignty."

physical and social environments. There are therefore no permanently binding social or moral laws in the worldview of Darwinism. The triumph of the Darwinian worldview has been almost universal, even among groups that do not accept Darwin's doctrine of exclusively biological evolution.

Faith in ancient Stoicism's theory of a shared common-ground philosophy that unites all rational men is now fading even among Christians – its last defenders. This has left modern Christianity *judicially mute*: judicial salt without savor, fit for being trampled underfoot politically. This is exactly where God's enemies want us.

What Christians need is an authoritative foundation for their knowledge. Without this, those who represent Jesus Christ in history will remain incapable of defending the judicially binding character His oath. They will remain impotent to bring God's covenant lawsuit against covenant-breakers in every area of life. In short, they will continue to refuse to invoke God's corporate sanctions in history.

The Laws of Leviticus

How does Leviticus fit into a program of covenantal sanctions? Can Christians confidently invoke the corporate sanctions of Leviticus (Lev. 26) as God's continuing corporate historical sanctions, both positive and negative?

This commentary focuses on the narrow topic of economics. I have surveyed the Levitical laws governing economics. I have also distinguished temporary Mosaic laws of the land from permanent covenantal laws that crossed Israel's geographical boundaries during the Mosaic era and then passed into the New Covenant. It is appropriate here to review these laws.

I. Land Laws and Seed Laws

Land laws and seed laws were laws associated with God's covenantal promises to Abraham regarding his offspring (Gen.

15-17). There was a chronological boundary subsequently placed on the seed laws: Jacob's prophecy and promise. "The sceptre shall not depart from Judah, nor a lawgiver from between his feet, until Shiloh come; and unto him shall the gathering of the people be" (Gen. 49:10). After Shiloh came, Jacob said, the scepter would depart from Judah. The unified concept of *scepter and lawgiver* pointed to the civil covenant: physical sanctions and law. Jacob prophesied that the lawful enforcement of the civil covenant would eventually pass to another ruler: Shiloh, the Messiah.

The Levitical land laws were tied covenantally to the Abrahamic promise regarding a place of residence for the Israelites (Gen. 15:13-16). These land laws were also tied to the Abrahamic promise of the seed. "In the same day the LORD made a covenant with Abram, saying, Unto thy seed have I given this land, from the river of Egypt unto the great river, the river Euphrates" (Gen. 15:18). The mark of those included under the boundaries of these seed laws was the covenantal sign of circumcision (Gen. 17:9-14). Circumcision established a personal covenantal boundary. There were also family and tribal boundaries tied to the laws of inheritance. The ultimate inheritance law was above all a land law: the jubilee law (Lev. 25).

The fall of Jerusalem and the abolition of the temple's sacrifices forever ended the Mosaic Passover. The five sacrifices of Leviticus 1-7 also ended forever. There can be no question about the annulment of the inheritance laws by A.D. 70. *But with this annulment of the inheritance laws also came the annulment of the seed laws*. Once the Messiah came, there was no further need to separate Judah from his brothers. Once the temple was destroyed, there was no further need to separate Levi from his brothers. There was also no further need to separate the sons of Aaron (priests) from the sons of Levi (Levites). Therefore, the most important Mosaic family distinction within a single tribe – the Aaronic priesthood – was annulled: the ultimate representative case. *The tribal and family boundaries of the Abra-*

hamic covenant ceased to operate after A.D. 70. This annulled the Mosaic law's applications of the Abrahamic covenant's land and seed laws. The land and seed laws were aspects of a single administration: the Mosaic Covenant. The New Covenant – based exclusively and forthrightly on the covenantal concept of adoption[25] – replaced the Mosaic Covenant.

Land Laws

Biblical quarantine (Lev. 13:45-46). This law dealt with a unique disease that came upon men as a judgment. Only when a priest crossed the household boundary of a diseased house did everything within its walls become unclean. This quarantine law ended when this judicial disease ended when the Mosaic priesthood ended.[26]

Promised land as a covenantal agent (Lev. 18:24-29). The land no longer functions as a covenantal agent. That temporary office was operational only after the Israelites crossed into Canaan. That office was tied to the presence of the sanctuary.[27]

The laws of clean and unclean beasts (Lev. 20:22-26). This was a land law, for it was associated with the land's office as the agent of sanctions. These laws marked off Israel as a separate nation. This is true of the dietary laws generally, which is why God annulled them in a vision to Peter just before he was told to visit the house of Cornelius (Acts 10).[28]

The national sabbatical year of rest for the land (Lev. 25:1-7). This was an aspect of the jubilee year. The law was part of

25. Infant baptism is not a confirmation of covenantal inheritance through biological inclusion but rather its opposite: the confirmation of covenantal inheritance through adoption, i.e., adoption into the family of God, His church. The one who baptizes is an agent of the church, not an agent of the family. This was true under the Abrahamic covenant, too: the male head of the household circumcised the males born into that household, but as an agent of the priesthood.

26. Chapter 9.

27. Chapter 10.

28. Chapter 21.

God's original grant of leaseholds at the time of the conquest. There is no agency of enforcement today. There has been no national grant of land.[29]

The jubilee law (Lev. 25:8-13). This law applied only to national Israel. It was a law uniquely associated with Israel's conquest of Canaan. It was in part a land law and in part a seed law: inheritance and citizenship. It was more judicial – citizenship – than economic. The annulment of the jubilee law was announced by Jesus at the beginning of his ministry (Luke 4:17-19). This prophecy was fulfilled at the final jubilee year of national Israel.[30] This probably took place in the year that Paul's ministry to the gentiles began, two years after the crucifixion.[31]

The jubilee law prohibiting oppression centered around the possibility that the priests and magistrates might not enforce the jubilee law (Lev. 25:14-17). Thus, those who trusted the courts when leasing land would be oppressed by those who knew the courts were corrupt.[32]

The jubilee year was to be preceded by a miraculous year bringing a triple crop (Lev. 25:18-22). This designates the jubilee year law as a land law with a blessing analogous to the manna. The manna had ceased when the nation crossed the Jordan River and entered Canaan.[33]

The prohibition against the permanent sale of rural land (Lev. 25:23-24). This was a land law. It was an aspect of the conquest of Canaan: the original land grant. This law did not apply in walled cities that were not Levitical cities.[34]

The law promising rain, crops, peace in the land, and no wild beasts in response to corporate faithfulness (Lev. 26:3-6). This was a land

29. Chapter 24.

30. Chapter 25.

31. James Jordan, "Jubille (3)," *Biblical Chronology*, V (April 1993), [p. 2].

32. Chapter 26.

33. Chapter 27.

34. Chapter 28.

law. Nature's predictable covenantal blessings were tied to the office of the holy land as the agency of sanctions.[35]

Seed Laws

Gleaning (Lev. 19:9-10). The gleaning law applied only to Mosaic Israel's farms. It was a means of establishing a major form of charity in tribe-dominated rural regions. This law promoted localism and decentralization in Mosaic Israel. The moral principle of gleaning extends into New Covenant times as a charity law, but not as a seed law. The principle is this: *recipients of charity who can work hard should*. This law is not supposed to be applied literally. There were no applications in civil law. This law was enforced by the priesthood, not by the State, for no corporate negative sanctions were threatened by God, nor would it have been possible for judges to identify precisely which poor people had been unlawfully excluded.[36] This principle of interpretation also applies to the re-statement of the gleaning law in Leviticus 23:22.[37]

The laws against allowing different breeds of cattle to interbreed (Lev. 19:19). This was a temporary seed law. It reflected the laws of tribal separation. So did the law against sewing a field with mixed seeds. Also annulled is the prohibition against wearing wool-linen garments.[38]

The law against harvesting the fruit of newly planted trees for three years and setting aside the fourth year's crop as holy (Lev. 19:23-25). This was a seed law. It was a curse on Israel because of the failure of the exodus generation to circumcise their sons during the wilderness wandering. It is no longer in force.[39]

---

35. Chapter 33.
36. Chapter 11.
37. Chapter 22.
38. Chapter 17.
39. Chapter 18.

The law governing the enslavement of fellow Israelites (Lev. 25:39-43). This was a seed law, although by being governed by the jubilee law, there was an aspect of land law associated with it. There is no longer any long-term indentured servitude bringing a family under the authority of another family for up to 49 years.[40]

The law governing the permanent enslavement of foreigners (Lev. 25:44-46). This must have been a seed law rather than a land law, for it opened the possibility of adoption, either by the family that owned the foreign slaves or by another Israelite family.[41]

The law governing the redemption of an Israelite out of a foreigner's household by the kinsman-redeemer (Lev. 25:47-55). This was a seed law.[42]

II. Priestly Laws

The laws of five sacrifices (Lev. 1-7). These were all priestly laws. They are no longer in force.[43]

The law prohibiting wine drinking by priests while inside the tabernacle or temple (Lev. 10:8-11). This law was exclusive to priests as mediatorial agents. The wine belonged to God; it had to be poured out before the altar. This law was tied to the holiness of the temple. It did not apply to Levites or priests outside of the temple's geographical boundaries.[44]

The law establishing the official prices of people who take vows (Lev. 27:2-8). This was a law governing access to the priesthood. These vows governed those who were devoted – irrevocably adopted – to priestly service.[45]

---

40. Chapter 30.
41. Chapter 31.
42. Chapter 32.
43. Chapters 1-7.
44. Chapter 8.
45. Chapter 36.

The law establishing vows to priests and the inheritance of rural land (Lev. 27:9-15). This law was primarily priestly but secondarily a seed law: an aspect of inheritance. This law placed the negative sanction of disinheritance on those who vowed to support a priest through the productivity of a dedicated plot of land and then refused to honor the vow. The land went from being dedicated to devoted: beyond redemption.[46]

III. Cross-Boundary Laws

Cross-boundary laws are still in force under the New Covenant. These are properly designated as Deuteronomy 4 laws: designed by God to bring men to repentance through the testimony of civil justice within a holy commonwealth.

Fraud and false dealing (Lev. 19:11-12). The laws against theft still prevail. They had no unique association with either the land or the promised seed.[47]

The law against robbing an employee by paying him later than the end of the working day (Lev. 19:13). This law protects the weakest parties from unfair competition: the ability to wait to be paid.

The law against tripping the blind man and cursing the deaf man (Lev. 19:14). Weaker parties are to be protected by civil law.[48]

The prohibition against enforcing laws that discriminate in terms of wealth or power (Lev. 19:15). This law had no unique association with Israel's land or seed laws. Its theological presupposition is that God is not a respecter of persons: a theological principle upheld in both covenants.[49]

The prohibition against personal vengeance (Lev. 19:18). This establishes the civil government as God's monopoly agency of violence.[50]

---

46. Chapter 37.
47. Chapter 12.
48. Chapter 13.
49. Chapter 14.
50. Chapter 16.

The law prohibiting judicial discrimination against strangers in the land (non-citizens) (Lev. 19:33-36). This law an aspect of the just weights law. Laws governing justice were not land-based or seed-based.[51]

The law against offering a child to Molech (Lev. 20:2-5). This was a law governed by the principle of false worship, although it appears to be a seed law (inheritance) or perhaps a land law (agricultural blessings). It had to do with identifying the source of *positive sanctions* in history: either God or a false god. God's name is holy: *sanctified*.[52] This will never change.

The jubilee law prohibiting taking interest from poor fellow believers or resident aliens (Lev. 25:35-38). This law was an extension of Exodus 22:25. It was included in the jubilee code, but it was not derived from that code. In non-covenanted, non-Trinitarian nations, however, Christians are the resident aliens. Thus, the resident alien aspect of the law is annulled until such time as nations formally covenant under God.[53]

The law promising fruitfulness and multiplication of seed (Lev. 26:9-10). This law was covenantal, not tied to the holy land or the tribal structure of inheritance. It was a confessional law, but because of its universal promise, it was a common grace law.[54]

Negative corporate sanctions (Lev. 26:13-17). These were promised to Israel, but they were not tied to either the holy land or the promised seed. The governing issue was the fear of God, which is still in force.[55]

The law of the tithe that applied to animals passing under a rod (Lev. 27:30-37). This law still applies, though it is no longer very important in a non-agricultural setting. God still prohibits

51. Chapter 19.

52. Chapter 20.

53. Chapter 29.

54. Chapter 34.

55. Chapter 35.

individuals from structuring tithes in kind (goods) from pre-collection rearrangements that favor the tither.[56]

The Principle of the Boundary

I have argued that Christians need a Bible-based hermeneutic in order to interpret correctly the applications of the laws of the Old Covenant in the New Covenant era. This is also Professor Poythress' argument.[57] By now the reader should understand what this biblical principle of judicial interpretation is: the principle of the boundary.

This is a very long commentary. (*Boundaries and Dominion* is much longer.) Most of it has been devoted to an explanation of laws that are no longer binding: seed laws, land laws, and priestly laws. Why devote so much time, money, and space to a study of things no longer relevant? Answer: in order to be confident about the laws that are still relevant.

A scholar spends most of his life examining records, experiments, books, and articles that do not apply to his immediate concerns. Scholarship is the process of sifting through what is, for a scholar, mostly irrelevant information. He sifts in terms of a principle – a hermeneutic – which leads to scientific and intellectual breakthroughs. So it is with the New Covenant student of the laws of Leviticus. Our problem today is that there is no agreement among Christians regarding the proper principle governing this judicial sifting process.

Theonomists have a general principle of judicial interpretation: unless an Old Covenant law is in principle or specifically annulled by the New Testament, it is still in force. Bahnsen writes: "The *methodological* point, then, is that we presume our

56. Chapter 38.

57. Vern Sheridan Poythress, "Effects of Interpretive Frameworks on the Application of Old Testament Law," in *Theonomy: A Reformed Critique,* edited by William S. Barker and W. Robert Godfrey (Grand Rapids, Michigan: Zondervan Academie, 1990), ch. 5.

obligation to obey any Old Testament commandment unless the New Testament indicates otherwise. We must assume continuity with the Old Testament rather than discontinuity."[58] That is, the theonomist announces with respect to all Old Covenant laws: "Innocent until proven guilty." An unchallenged Old Covenant law is said to have been granted citizenship automatically by the New Testament. No additional proof of citizenship is required by law. Unless its citizenship has been revoked by the New Testament, a Mosaic law automatically crosses the boundary between the two covenants. The law's adoption into the New Covenant kingdom of God is automatic. The representative rhetorical hard case for this principle of interpretation is the law's mandated stoning of rebellious sons (Deut. 21:18-21).[59]

All other schools of Christian biblical interpretation assert a rival judicial hermeneutic: any Old Covenant law not repeated in the New Testament is automatically annulled. The non-theonomist announces with respect to every Old Covenant law: "Guilty until proven innocent." An Old Covenant law is automatically turned back at the border of the New Covenant unless it has had citizenship papers issued by the New Testament. Its disinheritance is automatic unless it has been explicitly adopted into God's New Covenant kingdom. The representative rhetorical hard case for this hermeneutic is bestiality (Lev. 18:23; 20:15-16).[60]

A majority of the economic laws of Leviticus were turned back at the covenantal border. But this rejection was not auto-

---

58. Greg L. Bahnsen, *By This Standard: The Authority of God's Law Today* (Tyler, Texas: Institute for Christian Economics, 1985), p. 3.

59. By mandating the execution of rebellious adolescents and adult sons, this case law declared war against any criminal class. The enforcement of this case law means that a criminal class cannot easily come into existence. R. J. Rushdoony, *The Institutes of Biblical Law* (Nutley, New Jersey: Craig Press, 1973), pp. 185-91.

60. See my response to Dan G. McCartney: Gary North, *Westminster's Confession: The Abandonment of Van Til's Legacy* (Tyler, Texas: Institute for Christian Economics, 1991), pp. 211, 214.

matic. The geographical and tribal promises that went to Abraham's seeds (plural) were fulfilled with the coming of the prophesied Seed (singular: Gal. 3:16) – the Messiah, Shiloh, Jesus Christ, the incarnate Son of God – who announced His ministry's fulfillment of the judicial terms of the jubilee year (Luke 4:16-21). This fulfilment was confirmed through His death and resurrection – the ultimate physical liberation. Israel's permanent disinheritance was prophesied by Jesus: "Therefore say I unto you, The kingdom of God shall be taken from you, and given to a nation bringing forth the fruits thereof" (Matt. 21:43). This transfer of the kingdom's inheritance to this new nation took place at Pentecost (Acts 2). The visible manifestation of the permanent revocation of the Abrahamic inheritance to his biological heirs was the fall of Jerusalem in A.D. 70. Israel had failed to keep the terms of the covenant. The predictable negative corporate sanctions came in history.

Discontinuity and Continuity in the Levitical Sacrifices

The whole burnt offering was annulled by the New Covenant. There is no evidence that its underlying principle of sacrifice was annulled: unblemished animal, the best of the flock, but only one. This was a high-cost sacrifice, but it was nevertheless limited. Conclusion: *man cannot pay God all that he owes*. This judicial principle was illustrated by the whole burnt offering, but it was not limited to it.

The meal offering was annulled, but not its underlying principle of the hierarchical authority of the priesthood. The salt of this earthly sacrifice is no longer lawfully administered by any priest; the eternal salt of the covenant (Mark 9:47-49) is administered by the High Priest, Jesus Christ. The judicial principle of the meal offering still is in force: if you do not bring a satisfactory offering to be salted and consumed by the fire, then you will become that offering.

The peace offering is no longer eaten by the offerer at a meal held inside the boundaries of the temple. But the *economic* principle of the leaven – the best a man can offer God from his "field" – has not been removed from the New Covenant's voluntary offerings. Neither has the *cultural* principle of leaven: expansion over time.

The related principles of corporate responsibility and corporate representation are no longer manifested in the sin offering, i.e., purification offering. Nevertheless, they are clearly revealed in the Adamic covenant and the New Covenant. The biblical principle of the delegation of earthly authority – from God to the people to their representative – was illustrated in the purification offering, but it was not inaugurated by this offering. It therefore did not perish with this offering. Also, we no longer bring an animal to serve as our trespass or reparation offering for a sin of omission, but the principle of the sacrifice proportionate to one's wealth still applies, in church and State.

A thief's reparation offering is no longer made by presenting a ram without blemish. But there is no indication that an offering comparable in value to a ram in the Mosaic economy should not still be presented to a church by the self-confessed thief, nor should his victim be denied the return of the thing stolen plus a reparation payment of 20 percent. The judicial boundary between sacred and common still exists. A violation of such a boundary still constitutes a profane act.

The annulment of the Levitical sacrifices has not annulled the principles that underlay these sacrifices, any more than the annulment of the priesthood has somehow annulled the principle of sacrifice. The High Priest's office still exists, but only one man holds it: the resurrected Jesus Christ. The mediatorial role of the Old Covenant priest in offering a bloody sacrifice has been annulled by Christ's perfect, one-time sacrifice (Heb. 9). This does not mean that the ministerial, judicial, and educational role of the Levites has been annulled. The diaconate has replaced the Levites' social role. Melchizedek, the priestly king of Salem, offered Abraham bread and wine, and Abraham paid his tithe to him (Gen. 14:18-20). The annulment of the Mosaic priesthood did not annul this Melchizedekan ecclesiastical role.

There is both judicial continuity and discontinuity in the transition between Old Covenant and New Covenant. Both of these principles must be forthrightly proclaimed and defended exegetically. This commentary is long because Christians have too often only intuitively recognized which features of the Mosaic law have been annulled and which are still binding. They have not applied a consistent hermeneutic. It is long because it is exegetical. Most of all, it is long because we require casuistry to make sense of Leviticus: the application of general law to specific cases, and the investigation of specific case laws to discover the general legal principle governing any of them. Casuistry is a tiring, highly detailed process of discovery that must continue in every generation if God's kingdom is to be extended. John Frame insisted in 1990, "*all* the exegetical work remains to be done!"[61] Not all. A great deal, no doubt, but not all. It is also worth noting that the modern "school of the non-prophets," which asserts an absolute judicial discontinuity between the whole of Leviticus and the New Covenant, has a great deal of work ahead of it, too.

I have said my piece regarding Leviticus. It has been a long piece. It is now my critics' turn to say theirs. Then we shall see just how much discontinuity they can prove, and what the moral and cultural effects of these alleged discontinuities will be. I suggest that they begin with the Levitical case laws governing bestiality. One thing is sure: if they turn to pre-Kant natural law as their suggested alternative to the Mosaic law, they will have to show why Hume was wrong, Kant was wrong, Hegel was wrong, Darwin was wrong, and existentialism is wrong. If the only civil stipulation they leave us with is the death penalty in Genesis 9, they have not left us with much.[62] They have in

61. John Frame, "The One, the Many, and Theonomy," in *Theonomy: A Reformed Critique*, p. 97.

62. H. Wayne House and Thomas D. Ice, *Dominion Theology: Blessing or Curse*

fact left us judicially defenseless. If we cannot appeal to God's justice, as manifested in His Bible-revealed law, to what should Christians appeal? The dispensationalist answers, "the Rapture." The amillennialist answers, "the end of history." But what happens to us if either event is delayed?

I answer: if we cling to a hermeneutic of personal judicial discontinuity, *we should prepare for negative corporate sanctions.* "Salt is good: but if the salt have lost his savour, wherewith shall it be seasoned? It is neither fit for the land, nor yet for the dunghill; but men cast it out. He that hath ears to hear, let him hear" (Luke 14:34-35).

Conclusion

For two decades, the critics of theonomy have issued this challenge: "Prove your case exegetically." Rushdoony's first volume of *The Institutes of Biblical Law* (1973) was theonomy's frontal assault. He suggested hundreds of ways in which Mosaic case laws still apply. He used the Ten Commandments as his integrating principle. Bahnsen's *Theonomy in Christian Ethics* (1976) provided a technical apologetic defense of theonomy, written in the arcane language called "theologian." It has received more attention – most of it negative – from the theologians than Rushdoony's *Institutes* because Bahnsen writes fluently in their adopted tongue, which the rest of us have difficulty following without a dictionary and a grammar handbook. I showed in *Tools of Dominion* (1990) how the case laws of Exodus still apply to economics and civil justice. These books all emphasized continuity.

Our critics have not been satisfied. They have continued to complain: "You say that you have a hermeneutical principle of discontinuity. Let us see it in action." They have implied that

(Portland, Oregon: Multnomah Press, 1988), pp. 127, 130. For a reply, see Greg L. Bahnsen and Kenneth L. Gentry, Jr., *House Divided: The Break-Up of Dispensational Theology* (Tyler, Texas: Institute for Christian Economics, 1989), pp. 93-96.

theonomists possess no hermeneutic of discontinuity, other than the obvious annulment of the laws sacrifice by the Epistle to the Hebrews. If our critics are honest – a gigantic *if* – we should now begin to see a muting of this criticism, or at least a mutating. I am not counting on this, however.

The latest of these challenges appeared in the Spring, 1993, issue of the *Bulletin* of the Association of Christian Economists. Westmont College economics professor Edd S. Noell, in a well-balanced summary of the theonomic (i.e., my) approach to economic analysis, concluded with this challenge to theonomists (i.e., to me): "They must more carefully delineate the Old Testament laws that are abolished by the New Testament and the exegetical basis for their position in this regard. They must consider more extensively the issue of the context of the ancient agrarian economy of Israel in which the Mosaic law was given. There is more work to be done to convince fellow Christian economists of some of the specific exegetical conclusions they reach (in regard to monetary reform as well as other policy applications)."[63]

This commentary is part of my response to this criticism. I also include my previous four volumes of economic commentaries, my *Introduction to Christian Economics* (1973), and two of my books in the Biblical Blueprint Series: *Honest Money* (1986) and *Inherit the Earth* (1987). So is my critique of Social Credit economics, *Salvation Through Inflation* (1993). So is my chapter in the book edited by Robert Clouse, *Wealth and Poverty: Four Christian Views of Economics* (1985). I should also mention fifteen years of my newsletter, *Biblical Economics Today* – over 1,600 double-spaced manuscript pages. There is, of course, always more work to be done, more Bible passages to consider. There are always more typesetting and printing expenses to pay. I plan to do the work and pay the expenses. But I think it is fair

63. Edd S. Noell, "A Reformed Approach to Christian Economics: Christian Reconstruction," *Bulletin* (Spring 1993), p. 16.

for me to ask my critics in 1994: "Where have all the other Christian economists been for the last 20 years? Unlike me, they are being paid good salaries by colleges and universities to write books and articles. Where are all those explicitly Christian economics books and articles?"

The Association of Christian Economists has been around since the mid-1980's, but so far as I know, no other member has produced even one volume of an economic commentary on the Bible. I also have seen nothing like my book, *The Coase Theorem* (1992): an expressly Christian critique of a Nobel Prize-winning secular economist. Other than the ill-fated attempts by Keynesian Christian economist Douglas Vickers to refute my approach to the Bible and to economics,[64] no other Christian economist has challenged me exegetically on the issues I have been raising. No one has addressed the foundational epistemological questions that I raised as long ago as 1976.[65] Noell comes close to admitting as much: "Outside of the Reconstructionist literature, one searches in vain for more than a handful of thoughtful, Biblically-based critiques of non-Christian economic methodology."[66] Christian critics have made it clear that they do not like my approach to economics, but not one of them has offered a systematic, integrated methodological alternative that he is willing to defend exegetically. The critics face the old problem of practical politics: they cannot beat something with nothing.

---

64. Douglas Vickers, *Economics and Man: Prelude to a Christian Critique* (Nutley, New Jersey: Craig Press, 1976). This was followed by his brief book, *A Christian Approach to Economics and the Cultural Situation* (Smithtown, New York: Exposition Press, 1982), which in fact did not specify what this "Christian approach" is. For a response to Vickers, see Ian Hodge, *Baptized Inflation: A Critique of "Christian" Keynesianism* (Tyler, Texas: Institute for Christian Economics, 1986).

65. Gary North, "Economics: From Reason to Intuition," in North (ed.), *Foundations of Christian Scholarship: Essays in the Van Til Perspective* (Vallecito, California: Ross House Books, 1976), ch. 5.

66. Noell, p. 10.

In this commentary, I have shown how the twin Mosaic principles of land and seed – ultimately, laws of inheritance – were limited both by time and geography. From the beginning, there were boundaries placed by God around all those laws that were judicial applications of the Abrahamic and Mosaic laws governing land and seed. There were also priestly laws that perished with the New Covenant, taking parts of Leviticus with them.

Let me cite once again my comments in Chapter 17, "The Preservation of the Seed."

* * * * * * * *

It is therefore mandatory on me or on another defender of theonomy's hermeneutic to do what Poythress says must be done: 1) identify the primary function of an Old Covenant law; 2) discover whether it is universal in a redemptive (healing) sense or whether 3) it is conditioned by its redemptive-historical context (i.e., annulled by the New Covenant). In short: What did the law mean, how did it apply in ancient Israel, and how should it apply today? This task is not always easy, but it is mandatory.

The question Poythress raises is the hermeneutical problem of identifying covenantal continuity and covenantal discontinuity. First, in questions of covenantal continuity, we need to ask: What is the underlying ethical principle? God does not change ethically. The moral law is still binding, but its application may not be. Second, this raises the question of covenantal discontinuity. What has changed as a result of the New Testament era's fulfillment of Old Covenant prophecy and the inauguration of the New Covenant? A continuity – prophetic-judicial fulfillment – has in some cases produced a judicial discontinuity: the annulment of a case law's application. A very good example of this is Leviticus 19:19.

I begin any investigation of any suspected judicial discontinuity with the following questions. First, is the case law related to the priesthood, which has changed (Heb. 7:11-12)? Second, is it related to the sacraments, which have changed? Third, is it related to the jubilee land laws (e.g., inheritance), which Christ fulfilled (Luke 4:18-21)? Fourth, is it related to the tribes (e.g., the seed laws), which Christ fulfilled in His office as Shiloh, the promised Seed? Fifth, is it related to the "middle wall of partition" between Jew and gentile, which Jesus Christ's gospel has broken down (Gal. 3:28; Eph. 2:14-20)?[67] These five principles prove fruitful in analyzing Leviticus 19:19.[68]

Let us ask another question: Is a change in the priesthood also accompanied by a change in the laws governing the family covenant? Jesus tightened the laws of divorce (Matt. 5:31-32). The church has denied the legality of polygamy. Did other changes in the family accompany this change in the priesthood? Specifically, have changes in inheritance taken place? Have these changes resulted in the annulment of the jubilee land laws of the Mosaic economy? Finally, has an annulment of the jubilee land laws annulled the laws of tribal administration?

* * * * * * * *

I hope the reader recognizes by now that there are principles of interpretation that are applicable to the laws of the

---

67. This application is especially important in dealing with Rushdoony's theory of "hybridization." See Gary North, *Boundaries and Dominion: The Economics of Leviticus* (computer edition; Tyler, Texas: Institute for Christian Economics, 1994), Appendix H.

68. There are several other hermeneutical questions that we can ask that relate to covenantal discontinuity. Sixth, is it an aspect of the weakness of the Israelites, which Christ's ministry has overcome, thereby intensifying the rigors of an Old Covenant law (Matt. 5:21-48)? Seventh, is it an aspect of the Old Covenant's cursed six day-one day work week rather than the one day-six day pattern of the New Covenant's now-redeemed week (Heb. 4:1-11)? Eighth, is it part of legal order of the once ritually polluted earth, which has now been cleansed by Christ (Acts 10; I Cor. 8)?

Mosaic Covenant. *The ultimate hermeneutic principle in the question of the continuity of the Old Covenant legal order in the New Covenant era is the principle of the boundary*. Such a boundary does exist. There is discontinuity. But other boundary principles allow us to determine whether a law has been resurrected with Jesus Christ in the New Covenant. Those case laws that have been resurrected with Christ and adopted into the New Covenant law-order provide Christians with their tools of dominion.

Scripture Index

Index

For a word-by-word electronically indexed manuscript, order a copy of *Boundaries and Dominion*, the computerized version of the original full text of this commentary. See "Note to the Reader" for details. This index was compiled by the author, as all idea-based indexes should be.

ABOUT THE AUTHOR

Gary North received his Ph.D. in history from the University of California, Riverside, in 1972. He specialized in colonial U.S. history. He wrote his doctoral dissertation on Puritan New England's economic history and the history of economic thought. A simplified version of this dissertation has been published as *Puritan Economic Experiments* (Institute for Christian Economics, 1988).

He is the author of approximately 35 books in the fields of economics, history, and theology. His first book, *Marx's Religion of Revolution*, appeared in 1968. His *Introduction to Christian Economics* appeared in 1973, the year he began writing a multi-volume economic commentary on the Bible, which now covers Genesis, Exodus (three volumes), and Leviticus. He was the general editor of the Biblical Blueprints Series (1986-87), a 10-volume set, for which he wrote four of the books.

Beginning in 1965, his articles and reviews have appeared in over three dozen newspapers and periodicals, including the *Wall Street Journal*, *Modern Age*, *Journal of Political Economy*, *National Review*, and *The Freeman*.

He edited the first fifteen issues of *The Journal of Christian Reconstruction*, 1974-81. He edited a *festschrift* for Cornelius Van Til, *Foundations of Christian Scholarship* (1976). He edited two issues of *Christianity and Civilization* in 1983: *The Theology of Christian Resistance* and *Tactics of Christian Resistance*. He edited *Theonomy: An Informed Response* (1991).

He is the editor of the monthly financial newsletter, *Remnant Review*. He writes two bi-monthly Christian newsletters, *Biblical Economics Today* and *Christian Reconstruction*, published by the Institute for Christian Economics.

He lives in Tyler, Texas, with his wife and four children.

Does the Bible *Really* Have the Answers?

"The Bible has the answers to life." Well-meaning Christians say this to non-Christians. But do they really mean it?

It's one thing to tell people that the Bible has the answers to all of life's problems. It's another thing to be able to provide these answers, and also provide the biblical evidence.

It's risky to tell someone that the Bible has all the answers if you don't know where to look up the answers in the Bible. Someone may call your bluff.

Meanwhile, most Christian college professors tell us: "The Bible isn't a textbook on [my academic subject]." In other words, they deny that the Bible has answers to life's questions. They deny that the Bible tells them what they should believe in their areas of authority.

Economic Questions

What if someone asks a Christian this: "What's the Bible's answer to poverty? To inflation? To unemployment? To tax policy? To economic depression?" What should the Christian answer? He will probably not know what to say.

The Institute for Christian Economics was established in 1976 to provide biblical answers for economic questions like these. The ICE is dedicated to applying the Bible to economic theory and policy.

The ICE has been publishing detailed books on economic questions since 1982. Gary North, the founder of the ICE, has written five volumes of his Economic Commentary on the Bible: Genesis through Leviticus. He has also written dozens of other books relating to economics, history, and theology.

If you want answers, you can find them in these books, or in one of the ICE's newsletters: *Biblical Economics Today, Christian Reconstruction*, and *Biblical Chronology*, which are sent to ICE's supporters.

Humanism Is Bankrupt

For three centuries, Christians have lived on the scraps that have fallen from humanism's table. But humanism's table has always been filled with food stolen from the Bible.

Now the humanists' pantry is almost bare. As humanists have abandoned belief in an orderly universe, in fixed moral law, and moral cause and effect, they have begun to lose faith in science, technology, and the free market.

Humanists are afraid of pollution, afraid of economic growth, afraid of bogeymen such as the greenhouse effect (no evidence of worldwide warming), the growing hole in the ozone layer (no evidence that ozone holes keep growing or that aerosol sprays cause them), and other non-existent horrors.

The Way to Turn Things Around

Christians can't beat something with nothing. If humanism is wrong, then where are the uniquely biblical answers? If Christians cannot suggest any, why should the public pay attention to them? Christians need biblical answers.

To get answers, sign up for a free six-month subscription to the ICE newsletters. Send your request to ICE, Box 8000, Tyler, TX 75711. Just say, "Sign me up for my free subscription."